PSYCHOLOGY

APPLIED to LIFE and WORK

PSYCHOLOGY
APPLIED to LIFE and WORK

by

HARRY WALKER HEPNER

*Professor of Psychology, Colleges of Liberal Arts
and Business Administration, Syracuse University. Consultant in Public and Personnel Relations. Formerly in charge of personnel research
for the Goodyear Tire & Rubber Co., Akron, Ohio;
The Philadelphia Company, & Affiliated Corporations; and Kaufmann's Department Store,
Pittsburgh, Pa.*

NEW YORK

PRENTICE-HALL, INC.

First Printing ....September, 1941
Second Printing ....March, 1942
Third Printing ....May, 1942
Fourth Printing ....January, 1943
Fifth Printing ....June, 1944
Sixth Printing............February, 1945
Seventh Printing...........November, 1945
Eighth Printing................May, 1946
Ninth Printing.................July, 1946
Tenth Printing ....January, 1947
Eleventh Printing...............May, 1947
Twelfth Printing...........September, 1947
Thirteenth Printing. ....June, 1948
Fourteenth Printing.......September, 1948

Preface

EVERY PERSON often finds that his most perplexing problems are psychological in nature. Indeed, the problems of materials, machines, and systems are likely to be of secondary importance. The individual who earns his living frequently realizes this fact and recognizes his need for a knowledge of psychologists' recent findings and techniques. However, when he attempts to read the journals and books of the science, he is often disappointed. For him, the subject matter of many textbooks on psychology is too abstruse and too far removed from the everyday problems of the office, of the shop, of the market, of the home, and of his own mental activities. The gap between the classroom and the life situations has been so wide that he can seldom see any relation between the fields of study and those of work. Accordingly, I have approached the problems of life and work as an applied psychologist writing for the layman.

My aim is to give the reader those psychological facts and methods that meet his needs as a citizen, or as a professional worker or businessman. My purpose will be attained if the reader gains a better realization of sound methods of interpreting and influencing the behavior of his friends, his business or professional associates, and his employees.

The men and women whose photographs appear are a few of the authors whose works are mentioned in the text or in the bibliographies. These pictures are included not for the sake of publicity but better to acquaint the reader with some of the writers who have been leaders in the field of applied psychology.

Naturally, I am indebted to my many colleagues who are not mentioned in the footnotes, for their assistance in writing this book.

v

Professors Edwin M. Chamberlin of Boston University, Francis M. Dowd of Rider College, Douglas F. Parry of Syracuse University, William F. Madden of Middlebury College, and Arnold Thomsen of the Elmo Roper staff made many helpful criticisms and suggestions. Mr. Thomsen suggested especially useful materials for the discussion of propaganda in Chapter 21. A. B. Siewers, M.D., read and corrected the section dealing with the endocrines. My friend and colleague Joseph L. Speicher, of the Psycho-Educational Service of Syracuse University, read the entire manuscript and gave much constructive criticism. His intelligent aid has added greatly to the accuracy and clarity of the text. Dr. Ernst Thelin's administrative kindnesses enabled me to concentrate on the writing of the manuscript without the distractions which so often beset the university teacher.

H. W. Hepner

Contents

PART FIVE: PREDICTING THE BEHAVIOR
OF THE GROUP

PART SIX: INFLUENCING THE BEHAVIOR
OF THE GROUP

PART SEVEN: PRINCIPLES OF RESEARCH FOR THE
STUDENT OF APPLIED PSYCHOLOGY

APPENDIX

PART ONE

Introduction

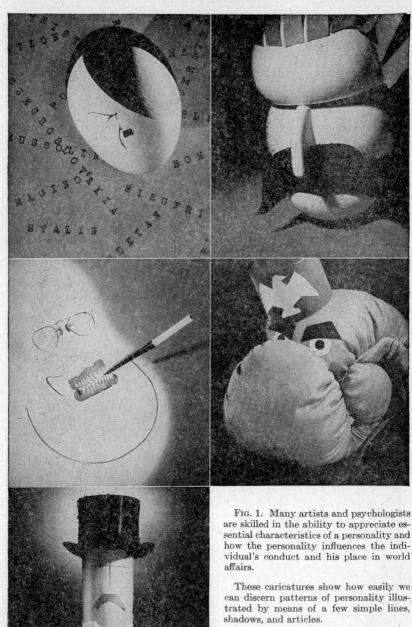

Fig. 1. Many artists and psychologists are skilled in the ability to appreciate essential characteristics of a personality and how the personality influences the individual's conduct and his place in world affairs.

These caricatures show how easily we can discern patterns of personality illustrated by means of a few simple lines, shadows, and articles.

One night in the Shigeta-Wright studios of Chicago, Harry K. Shigeta and Charles McKinney were discussing the state of the world. Mr. Shigeta utilized ordinary materials in the studio to produce these caricatures of important men of 1940 The fact that not all of these men have kept their places in world affairs makes these caricatures no less interesting. (*Reproduced by courtesy of Harry K. Shigeta.*)

1

Why We Study Psychology

People study psychology for various reasons. A few want to appreciate its influence in the big affairs of historical significance but most people study it as an aid in dealing with their own problems of life and work. This chapter reviews some of these personal problems and indicates how psychologists deal with them.

PSYCHOLOGY is surely among the most useful of all our sciences. Anyone who wonders whether psychological influences are important in world affairs need only study the mental characteristics of outstanding national leaders. He will see that internationally important policies often are the result of a leader's mental make-up rather than outgrowths of the nation's situation only. The people of a nation could often improve their national welfare if they would differentiate between the national policies promoted to satisfy the psychological needs of the leader and those which are promoted to meet the needs of the people themselves. Of course, the impulsions of the leader and the needs of the people are often complementary, but not always.

Recent events in world affairs have revealed to ordinary people some marked differences in the mental maturity and balance of leaders. The members of this generation are gradually learning about the close relation between the psychological characteristics of individual leaders and some effects those characteristics have on human affairs. Many people are beginning to realize that a leader may be so immature psychologically that he seeks to satisfy himself at the expense of his people, or may be so mature as to foster the satisfactions of the people for their personality development. Whenever we study the many historical influences in the shifting maps of the world, we note how, in some instances, millions of lives have been affected by the efforts of some mal-

3

adjusted dictator to satisfy his complexes and those of his blind followers. Psychology shows us how we, as well as our leaders, at times cling to immature and unintelligent patterns of behavior.

When a person trained in psychology listens to a politician, a preacher, or a reformer, he says to himself: "Has this man analyzed the conditions of which he speaks and come to a sound objective solution, or is he merely giving vent to the impulsions or perhaps even the venom of his own mind?" The dictators and the tyrants in all human affairs, whether of nation, corporation, school, or home, will continue to blight the lives of others until people learn enough applied psychology to recognize the personality differences between tyrants and statesmen, between bosses and leaders, between schoolmasters and educators, and between neurotic females and well-adjusted mothers.

Americans look out upon a sorely troubled world. The problems of international affairs are baffling, and the influences of leaders in international affairs are often discouraging. Furthermore, we can do little or nothing about many of the most discouraging problems beyond our own shores. Even with the best of psychological training, we could not cause the people of a foreign nation to choose or direct their leaders more intelligently. However, through the aid of psychological insight, we, in our own nation and niche in life, can often interpret the most hopeless of situations; and this ability to interpret the mental factors helps to lift us to a more intelligent plane of living.

The ability to recognize psychological currents in world affairs and to interpret them intelligently is a most desirable accomplishment. Sometimes it enables us to see more clearly the human problems in our own national affairs. The complexities of our industrial civilization call for a wisdom which the members of this generation have not as yet fully attained. The psychological problems around us, in this country and in our time, require the aid of all that psychological research can contribute. A listing of some of these problems may stimulate us to study the helpful findings of past psychological researches.

Outstanding problems that are partly of a psychological nature. One striking psychological problem arises from the fact that our magnificent industrial and technical development has not resulted in equally magnificent emotional satisfactions for many of our citizens. Engineers, scientists, and inventors have produced a technological age which is truly marvelous, but which has not always satisfied the hearts and minds of the men who operate its machines, or of the customers who benefit from its products. We are like children playing with powerful but somewhat dangerous toys. We cannot always keep our employable people busy making the things we should like to buy. In a recent year when we had need for both employment and the products of employment, 29.5 per cent of employable men and 34.4 per cent of employable women in a leading eastern city were wholly jobless. In addition to these, 10 per cent of the men and 16 per cent of the women employables of the industrial classifications were employed only part time.[1]

Economic insecurity, whether caused by political or other conditions, certainly has an important bearing on emotional insecurity. However, we must also recognize that economic security does not imply emotional security.[2] Many persons with high incomes feel insecure because of psychological problems that wealth does not solve. Furthermore, unemployment is not entirely an economic problem; many unemployed people have a psychological immaturity which would cause them to be unemployed in any economic system. If relatives or friends are not available to support these people, they are likely to attach themselves to charitable institutions or some form of government relief.

A recent survey in Chicago revealed that 47 per cent of the relief clients had been on the rolls four years or more, and that 43 per cent of these had been accepting charity since before 1932. Of course, they are the very ones who are most voluble in their advocacy of permanent relief. They are quite willing that the government should take over the role of bountiful and protective parent and consider their care one of its major obligations.[3]

The state of the mind is often more important than the state of the nation or the international situation. When a person no longer believes that individual ability determines individual success, he is apt to look to some stronger person or to some political system which promises to play the role of all-providing father.

[1] Gladys L. Palmer, *Employment and Unemployment in Philadelphia in 1936 and 1937*. Industrial Research Department, University of Pennsylvania, 1938.

[2] H. Meltzer, "Economic Security and Children's Attitudes to Parents," *American Journal of Orthopsychiatry*, 1936, Vol. 6, pp. 590-608.

[3] Robert N. McMurry, "The Unemployables," *The Atlantic Monthly*, July 1938.

According to a cross-sectional study of the young men and women of New York City, 80 per cent of the men and women from 15 to 34 years of age believed that ability does not offer assurance of success. Only 20 per cent believed that young men and women with ability are finding it no more difficult than at other times to get ahead. This survey also revealed that 80 per cent were guided less by religion than were their parents and that 87 per cent put less store by their parents' opinions on political, social, and economic matters than did their elders. In line with the same study, a survey of the national situation showed that 43 per cent of employed youth 16 to 25 years of age felt that they were in dead-end jobs.[4]

When people lose faith in themselves and their ability to cope with life's problems, they are likely to turn to an untried system of government or leadership; or to "escape" from the intolerable situation, as is exemplified by many of the 500,000 drug addicts in this country.[5] Or, certain mental ailments may develop, as found among the 653,000 persons resident in mental hospitals in a recent year.[6]

Personal problems reported by individuals. When we ask people about their own psychological problems, we find that less than 6 per cent[7] appear to be living without bothersome worries.

A study was made of the psychological problems of 1,000 people—500 men and 500 women. In this case, the introspections of the people were used, and an attempt was made to find out by questionnaire what they considered to be their greatest fears or worries, their most difficult tendencies, the things they lacked and needed most, the forms of their greatest inabilities, and their worst habits. The questionnaires were distributed through personal interviews, but were mailed unsigned by the answerers.

---

[4] Survey made by New York City Y.M.C.A. and reported in *The New York Times*, November 19, 1939.

[5] M. H. Seevers, "Drug Addiction Problems," *Sigma Xi Quarterly*, June 1939.

[6] Vital statistics reports showed that 499,879 patients were resident in the mental hospitals of the United States on January 1, 1938. Separations during the year were 139,145. An additional 153,124 were admitted during the year, so that a total of 653,003 were resident in mental hospitals at some time during 1938. See *Patients in Hospitals for Mental Disease: 1938*, Washington, D. C.: Bureau of the Census (*Vital Statistics—Special Reports*), May 27, 1940.

[7] *Science News Letter*, May 6, 1939.

The people studied were normal members of the general popu-lation, above average in education and income; not the unbal-anced types found in the psychiatric clinics.

Of course, the introspections of these 1,000 people are some-what unreliable. If a psychiatrist were to study each one of the persons, he would probably report problems of a nature somewhat different from those which the individuals themselves reported. However, Table I[8] presents the specific problems that had the highest and the lowest percentages under each of the five main classes of problems. The data indicate the psychological prob-lems which normal people believe' that they had. Problems in which the sexes differed widely are marked with an asterisk.

TABLE 1

THE PSYCHOLOGICAL PROBLEMS REPORTED BY 1,000 NORMAL PEOPLE

(500 Men and 500 Women)

My greatest fears or worries are:	Men	Women	Men and Women
(Highest)			
Criticisms by others	28%	31%	30%
Dental treatments	24	22	23
*Electrical storms	10	27	18
*Getting fat	8	27	17
(Lowest)			
*Going to Hell forever	7	3	5
Losing my job	6	3	5
Using the telephone	3	3	3
Stealing something	2	2	2
Ghosts	1	1	1
My most difficult tendencies are:			
(Highest)			
Being too self-conscious	29	35	32
Worrying about what others think of me	31	32	31
*Being too sensitive	22	32	27
*Having depressed moods	22	30	26
(Lowest)			
Being too curious about affairs of others	7	8	8
Being overemotional	7	9	8
*Being overfamiliar	8	3	6
Being quarrelsome	3	3	3

[8] More complete data regarding problems of individuals and of businessmen are published in Harry Walker Hepner, *Psychology in Modern Business*, Chap-ter I. Prentice-Hall, Inc., 1930.

I lack and need most:	Men	Women	Men and Women
(Highest)			
Confidence in my own ability............	29%	37%	33%
Concentration.........................	28	25	26
Initiative.............................	23	23	23
Sociability...........................	22	21	22
(Lowest)			
Sympathy for others...................	7	7	7
General education.....................	8	7	7
Interest in opposite sex................	7	6	7
Love for my own children..............	1	.4	1
My greatest inabilities are to:			
(Highest)			
Speak in public...............	38	36	37
Save money...........................	31	27	29
Spend money wisely....................	28	20	24
*Conduct an interesting conversation.......	30	19	24
(Lowest)			
*Control the sex instinct.................	15	3	9
Get along with relatives..................	6	7	7
Keep a secret.........................	5	8	6
Get along with teachers................	1	1	1
My worst habits are:			
(Highest)			
Worrying about opinions of others........	29	32	31
Daydreaming..........................	22	25	23
Procrastination........................	22	23	22
Sarcasm..............................	21	20	21
(Lowest)			
Biting my fingernails...................	9	9	9
Brusqueness...........................	8	7	8
Bad headaches........................	9	5	7
Stammering...........................	4	1	2

If the reader will note the personal problem under each heading which was reported by the highest percentages of men and women, he will recognize that the most outstanding problem seems to be related to the personal opinions of others toward him. "What do people think of me?" probably expresses the psychological problem reported most frequently.

If this is true, the situation may indicate that too many parents rear children using as an appeal to the child the parent's personal like or dislike for the child rather than an appeal based upon sound reasons why a childish act is right or wrong. For example, when a small child spills his glass of milk on the dinner table, the typical mother does not try to make the child understand why spilled milk is an undesirable happening: soiled napery, inconvenience to others, problem of correcting spoilage, etc. She simply has an emotional upset and shows the child she does not like him. She shows her dislike of him rather than of the act.

Furthermore, the fact that a parent dislikes a given childish act does not necessarily mean that the act is wrong. Several studies have shown that psychiatrists and parents differ markedly as to what is believed to be dangerous childish behavior. Parents, for example, do not consider introverted, withdrawing behavior as serious as do the child psychologists. Parents are often more concerned about rudeness and bad table manners than about the child's learning to deal confidently with his daily social problems.[9]

Most parents try very hard to rear their children well. No parent or psychologist, however skilled, could guarantee to rear every child perfectly. However, we can always study anew the sound psychological principles we seem to neglect. Parental failures in developing strong personalities in children later appear among the adults of the workaday world, as indicated by a study of the causes for discharge of approximately 4,000 office employees from 76 large business concerns. Table II reveals that only about 10 per cent of the employees discharged were fired because of lack of specific skills. Character and personality traits were the important factors in almost 90 per cent of the cases.

TABLE II

The Most Common Causes for Termination of Employment[10]

Lack of Specific Skills:

1.	Lack of ability in Shorthand	2.2%
2.	Lack of ability in Typewriting	1.6
3.	Lack of ability in English	1.6
4.	Lack of ability in Dictaphone work	1.3
5.	Lack of ability in Arithmetic	1.3
6.	Lack of ability in Machine Operation	.9
7.	Lack of ability in Bookkeeping	.6
8.	Lack of ability in Spelling	.6
9.	Lack of ability in Penmanship	.0
	Total—Lack of specific skills	10.1%

[9] Ralph M. Stogdill, "Parental Attitudes and Mental Hygiene Standards," *Mental Hygiene,* October 1931, pp. 813-827.

[10] H. Chandler Hunt, "Business Demands More Character Education," *The Pitmanite,* April 1937.

TABLE II (*Cont.*)

Lack of Character Traits:

1.	Carelessness	14.1%
2.	Non-co-operativeness	10.7
3.	Laziness	10.3
4.	Absences other than illness	8.5
5.	Dishonesty	8.1
6.	Attention to things other than office work during office hours	7.9
7.	Lack of initiative	7.6
8.	Lack of ambition	7.2
9.	Tardiness	6.7
10.	Lack of loyalty	3.5
11.	Lack of courtesy	2.2
12.	Insufficient care of or improper clothing	1.6
13.	Self-satisfaction	.9
14.	Irresponsibility	.3
15.	Unadaptability	.3

Total—Lack of character traits............ 89.9%

100.0%

When Alanson H. Edgerton had spent over twelve years in an extensive study of vocational education, he too found that personality and character traits are often more important than skill or intelligence for success in employment. He and his colleagues examined 144,279 actual jobs in 2,630 fields and followed 15,824 youths through ten years of school and work.

Successful employees, he reported, must be versatile. Three-fourths of the employers he questionnaired wanted youths skilled in at least two kinds of work (such as lawyers who also knew banking, or stenographers who could keep books).

But more important than skill or intelligence, he found, is personality. In one sub-survey, studies were made of 3,607 men and women who had lost their jobs. It turned out that 77 per cent had been fired for tactlessness, unfairness, irritability, bad manners, etc. Again, Dr. Edgerton rated a group of job holders for (1) intelligence and (2) personality. The most intelligent 33 per cent earned only $139.44 more per year than the least intelligent; but the highest 33 per cent in personality earned $842.73 more than the lowest.

Specifically, well-liked employees are co-operative, loyal, polite, tactful, friendly, patient, alert, daring, confident, and cheerful.[11]

Psychological problems of businessmen. The employees of business are not the only workers who have psychological problems, some of which result in discharge. Executives, too, have

---

[11] *Newsweek,* April 1, 1940, p. 39.

Fig. 2. Henry C. Link, Vice-President of the Psychological Corporation, New York. Anyone interested in further study on certain problems of personality development should refer to his book *The Rediscovery of Man* (The Macmillan Co., 1938).

their unique problems both as individuals and as executives. Approximately five hundred businessmen were asked to list the psychological problems which were most difficult for them. As a result of this survey, a list of 97 problems was tabulated. Later on, the list was submitted to several hundred other businessmen, and from 167 replies selected at random the percentage of businessmen who had each problem was found. The most frequently reported problems of the businessman as an individual and as an executive are shown in Table III.

A review of the three tables that have been presented indicates the universality of psychological problems. Indeed, if we ask a large number of persons to think of the most serious problems they have had in the previous year, problems that worried them a great deal, they report that about 85 per cent involved relationships with people. In short, we can truthfully say that the business of the world is mainly men and women.

People in business have no special psychology of their own. When we talk about businessmen and their psychological problems, we should recognize that the principles and problems of the mental life are common to the people of our civilized society. Business executives, employees, and customers have essentially the same emotions, feelings, and traits as individuals of other classifications. The psychological principles that apply to the

TABLE III

PSYCHOLOGICAL PROBLEMS REPORTED BY BUSINESSMEN

As an Individual		As an Executive	
Problem	Per Cent Having the Problem	Problem	Per cent Having the Problem
1. Remembering names and faces of people........	75.0	1. How to make employees enthusiastic and energetic.	72.6
2. Ability to forget business and enjoy yourself after working hours........	66.6	2. How to get employees to cooperate with others.....	62.4
3. How to turn down a salesman in such a way that he will respect your decision and call again, or not, as you wish.......	58.2	3. How and when to praise an employee.............	60.0
		4. Selecting suitable men for promotion............	58.8
4. How to get the most out of your time while at work.	55.2	5. When hiring, what questions should be asked....	58.8
5. How to make a good impression when entering a business office.........	54.0	6. How and when to reprimand an employee......	58.2
6. How to make a good impression when leaving a business office.........	51.0	7. Refusing an employee a raise in pay and at the same time keeping him working, unprejudiced and ambitious............	55.2
7. Selecting congenial business companions...........	43.2	8. How kindly to refuse a man a job................	53.4
8. How to be able to have faith in the business during a depression........	35.4	9. How to deal with an employee who constantly complains.............	52.2
9. How to ask for a raise or a promotion............	34.2	10. How to introduce new methods and systems to employees............	44.4
10. Developing a philosophy of business...........	31.2	11. How to create selling points for a product.........	39.6
11. How to keep relatives from expecting too much	30.6	12. Methods of displaying goods	39.0
12. How to deal with men who are always telling on the other fellow to put themselves in right.........	30.0	13. How to curb dissension when one or two employees start dissatisfying talk..	36.0
13. Acquiring a knowledge of trade journals.........	30.0	14. Selecting merchandise not to please yourself but to appeal to different types of customers..........	25.2
14. How to be popular in the social world as well as in business..............	28.8	15. Selection of a name for a new product..........	21.6
15. How to reduce fatigue.....	24.0		

person in the school and the home also apply to the same individual in the office and the factory. Basic principles are universal; only settings and techniques differ. As students of human behavior, we can be alert to the meanings in a person's behavior regardless of where he may be active.

When a man speaks to us he is always telling us two stories at once even though we commonly attend to but one of them. One is the tale he actually tells, and it may be about anything. The other is a story about himself—the story constituted by the fact that he, under the circumstances present, does tell us just that tale and tells it to us in just the way he does. The style and the matter of a man's speech or of his writings, it has been said, is a picture of what the man is—of his point of view, his character, his intellectual resources, his tastes, his temperament, et al. And all this is exhibited to us, if we but give it our attention, not only when a man expresses himself in language but equally where his mode of expression is of other sorts. How a man walks or sits, what sort of clothes he wears and how he wears them, what sort of house he builds, how he spends his leisure and his money, what he fights for and how he does it, the undertakings to which he devotes himself, the sort of gods he worships, which books he reads, the arts he cultivates and the sorts of products he makes them yield, the modes of conduct and the social institutions which he approves or disapproves—all these things provide us with a picture of the man and of his environment into which we can project ourselves in imagination as effectively as we can into the characters and situations represented in the stories he tells, the plays he acts, or the books he writes.[12]

The student who studies human behavior extensively wherever he finds it learns to see the patternful nature of the individual's activities, and how certain acts in behavior are related to other acts. The person's behavior becomes more meaningful as it fits into basic patterns that characterize the individual. For example, the executive who failed as a youth to learn how to compete in games with other boys is also apt to be unable to endure the presence of rivals in his business relations. Such an executive seldom hires subordinates or assistants who are as able as he. The department head who has ability but surrounds himself with weak personalities is harmful to the business concern and also is a problem to the college graduate who seeks to advance in that executive's department. The student, therefore, should seek to know psychological principles and patterns in behavior wherever he may find them in order that he may be able to use them when needed in business and other settings.

Very few corporations have hired psychologists to the extent to which they have hired, for example, engineers. Of the 2,306 members and associates of the American Psychological Association in 1937, only 47 were employed by business firms.[13] Most

[12] C. J. Ducasse, "Are the Humanities Worth Their Keep?" *American Scholar*, Vol. 6, No. 4, pp. 467-468.
[13] Paul S. Achilles, "The Role of the Psychological Corporation in Applied Psychology," *The American Journal of Psychology*, November 1937, p. 235.

psychologists are employed by universities, colleges, hospitals, and private schools, or are engaged in private clinical practice. Relatively few psychologists are employed by business firms, but an increasing number of psychologists' findings are used in business.

Accurate data are not available regarding the number of psychologists employed on a full-time basis in business. However, one study of the employment trends in applied psychology from 1916 to 1938 indicated that about one half of the total time of American psychologists is being devoted to applied psychology. In 1938, about 61 members and associates of the American Psychological Association were reported in the "industrial" group and engaged in industrial, commercial, and other similar private employment, including advertising, marketing, personnel work, and related fields of business. Other closely related groups were the 88 "guidance and personnel workers" and the 60 "consulting psychologists" members.[14]

In the light of these findings, it is obvious that very few college students will become *business psychologists*. Few psychology majors will ever wear the label, occupationally speaking, which they had as a major in their college studies. In this respect psychology is similar to mathematics. Very few students who major in mathematics ever have the occupational designation of *mathematician*, even though they use mathematics in their work. They are more likely to be called engineers, accountants, statisticians, or clerical workers; although they use mathematics constantly, they think of themselves, and their employers think of them as trained in some business field such as accounting, manufacturing, or selling. Similarly, students of psychology who go into business are likely to find many applications of their psychological knowledge even though they are not classified on a payroll as psychologists.

Knowledge of psychological principles and techniques is useful to students who go into business, as evidenced by the fact that businessmen frequently call on psychologists for assistance. Psychologists are invited with increasing frequency to give counsel on specific business problems. Also, psychologists do a

---

[14] F. H. Finch and M. E. Odoroff, "Employment Trends in Applied Psychology," *Journal of Consulting Psychology,* July-August 1939, pp. 118-122.

great deal of research on their own initiative regarding problems in business, as is shown by an examination of several issues of *The Journal of Applied Psychology*. Sometimes an entire issue[15] is devoted to psychological problems of business.

Examples of business problems which have been treated by psychologists.

1. "Please tell me which of these four pairs of stockings you like best" has been a request made of women by interviewers who, under the direction of a psychologist, were studying the effects of odor on preferences for clothing. In one study of odorized hosiery, three variously perfumed pairs of stockings and one unperfumed pair were used. All four pairs were of the same construction, style, color, and design, and the perfumed pairs were scented so faintly that only 6 of 250 women consciously noted the odor. The women were apparently examining the stockings for such qualities as texture, weave, weight, and wearing quality. When the data were finally analyzed, the women's selections as to the best of the four like pairs were as follows: The *narcissus* pair was preferred by 50 per cent of the women; the *fruity*, by 24 per cent; the *sachet*, by 18 per cent; and the *unperfumed*, by 8 per cent.[16]

This type of study has been used to increase sales not only of stockings but of many other articles, including bottled perfumes.

2. Laboratory studies of vision have shown that about 4 per cent of all males and two tenths of 1 per cent of all females are colorblind.[17] Some are unaware of their defect, as was discovered in a study of 375 salesmen who were selling colored goods in San Francisco department stores. The examination revealed that 27

[15] *The Journal of Applied Psychology*, February 1939 and December 1940, are devoted entirely to radio research.

[16] D. A. Laird, "How the Consumer Estimates Quality by Subconscious Sensory Impression," *The Journal of Applied Psychology*, 1932, Vol. 16, pp. 241-246.

[17] The disproportion of colorblindness between the sexes is usually explained as an inherited defect, "being transmitted by what is called *discontinuous heredity*, that is, remaining latent in the female and becoming manifest only in the male offspring." See *Pseudo-Isochromatic Plates for Testing Color Perception*, American Optical Company, copyright 1940 by The Beck Engraving Company, Inc.

The totally colorblind person sees only shades of gray. The most common type of color blindness is inability to discriminate between red and green. A more rare type is blue-yellow blindness. Each type may differ in its degree of blindness.

FIG. 3. Harry R. DeSilva, Director of Driver Research Center, Yale University. Those interested in further study on the problem of driver research should refer to his book *Why We Have Automobile Accidents* (John Wiley & Sons, 1942).

distinctly colorblind persons were actually selling colored materials.[18] Many of these men probably made mistakes which caused losses to their employers and customers.

3. In the 15-year period from 1920 to 1935, the number of persons in the United States killed by automobiles was 388,936. The number of yearly fatalities from automobile accidents is usually more than 30,000. The owners of bus lines, taxicab companies, and trucks, as well as the drivers of private cars, are constantly paying out money for these accidents. The persons injured and the families of the killed are paying a terrific and unnecessary emotional toll. Psychologists have studied drivers and have found that accident proneness may occur in all levels of intelligence and income. It may be related to defective vision, defective hearing, poor co-ordination, slow reaction time, daydreaming, attitude, or a combination of factors.[19]

4. Noise may not appear to affect the efficiency of employees,

---

[18] W. R. Miles and Homer Craig, Jr., "Color Blindness in Dry Goods Salesmen," *Personnel Journal*, 1931, Vol. 9, pp. 437-449.

[19] Albert P. Weiss and Alvhh R. Lauer, *Psychological Principles in Automotive Driving*, Ohio State University Studies, Graduate School Series, Contribution in Psychology No. 11, 1930.

but one carefully conducted study reproduced the noise conditions of 75 per cent of the light industrial establishments of the country. The findings indicated that noise, under certain conditions, cuts down production and costs money, and that the cost of noise varies directly with its volume.

> The noise equivalent to group conversation reduced production approximately 3 per cent. Unsteady and intermittent noises were most irritating. But the effect of the noise didn't stop with lower efficiency; it had definite results on the well-being of the workers. After periods of heavy noise, they complained of muscular stiffness—the direct result of tenseness caused by the clatter. The greater the noise, the more frequently they needed time-wasting rest periods. And buzzing noises lingered in the workers' ears for as long as three hours after the five o'clock whistle had blown.[20]

Other industrial psychologists have studied the proper distribution of rest pauses for workers, different degrees of illumination, and the selection of workers by means of psychological tests. Examples of their work are presented in succeeding chapters.

5. A leading industrial psychologist, Dr. R. S. Uhrbrock of a large manufacturing concern, has reported many examples of the application of psychology in business. His summary regarding the future of this work is of special interest to the college student:

> The industrial psychologist of the future probably will give as much attention to the discovery and development of important character traits as to the measurement of innate intelligence. Over a period of years at Purdue University, records have been maintained showing the intelligence and character traits of engineering students. A follow-up of graduates five years after leaving college indicated that the difference between the extremely bright students and those who had only enough intelligence to get through college made a difference in earning power of about $150 per year. Those with pleasing personalities, however, were earning nearly $1,000 per year more. Apparently industry is willing to pay for desirable personality traits. Tact, self-reliance, enthusiasm, accuracy, and aggressiveness are important characteristics that may be developed under proper industrial conditions. The problem offers a challenge to the industrial psychologist.[21]

6. Many of the most difficult psychological problems for businessmen and others occur in their dealings with the queer, maladjusted troublemakers who are found in industry as well as elsewhere. Clinically trained psychologists can recognize

---

[20] Donald A. Laird, "Noise Does Cut Production," *Forbes,* August 15, 1932.
[21] R. S. Uhrbrock, "The Importance of Psychology," *Industrial Medicine,* February 1934.

troublemakers and help them make better personality adjustments. Examples of psychiatric work in a business concern have been reported by Dr. V. V. Anderson, a psychiatrist formerly with R. H. Macy & Company, New York City. He said:

> Taking 1,200 employees as a fairly representative group indicating the "run-of-the-mine" of the store at large, we have found that 19 per cent of the sales people and 23 per cent of the non-sales force were problem individuals presenting conditions that caused their department heads to question their value as personnel risks to the store. Many of these individuals were actual liabilities. All of them were potential liabilities to the store.[22]

Recent psychological studies of business problems have given marked emphasis to the importance of attitudes of individuals. For example, when a National Research Council committee undertook an experiment on the effects of changes in factory illumination, it was found that factors of attitude, morale, and supervisory relationship were more potent than those of illumination, ventilation, rest periods, nutrition, wage incentives, or individual skills. Similarly, a motorman's susceptibility to accident could be effectively dealt with only when the supervisor's attitude was also considered.[23] The mental attitudes of workers have been found to be important factors in at least 85 per cent of industrial accidents.[24] Sometimes these attitudes are exceedingly difficult to recognize because they are very subtle. The individuals involved in dangerous behavior may not be able to give the real reasons for their own actions; only a psychologist experienced in analyzing subconscious impulses can explain them. Vague frustrations may be expressed in harmful forms of aggression, as exemplified in Dr. John P. Shea's study of people who start forest fires:

> Miles of forest fire running free in the South every year, destroying great treasures of woods and wildlife, are a burning signal of dangerous impoverishment in the lives of hundreds of thousands of American people.
> Nine out of ten of these great, hazardous forest fires of the Southland are set by human hands, most of them deliberately.
> The fire-setters would tell you that they burn the woods to kill snakes, to keep down the ticks, to destroy boll weevils. But the answer lies much

---

[22] V. V. Anderson, "The Problem Employee: His Study and Treatment," *Personnel Journal*, 1928, Vol. 7, pp. 203-225.

[23] Walter V. Bingham, "The Future of Industrial Psychology," *Journal of Consulting Psychology*, Vol. I, No. 1. Similar findings are presented in Chapter 16 of this book.

[24] E. R. Grannis, *Mental Hygiene*, July 1935, pp. 398-404.

deeper; it is revealed by a sociological-psychological study of the men and women in a typical forest-fire region just conducted for the U. S. Forest Service by Dr. John P. Shea.

The lives of these people are boresome. Families of as many as eleven persons live in three-room unpainted cabins, and their family income is about $12 a month. They go undernourished and poorly clothed.

Psychologically, they are just as impoverished. Their education is equivalent to only third or fourth grade. Exhaustion of game and fish deprived them of their two main recreations. Music, even fiddling, is conspicuous by its absence. Only a few do basket weaving.

They whittle. They talk. And they just "set."

Living constantly on the verge of dangerous frustration, they crave the excitement of fire with all the unusual activity of those who try to put it out.

Remedies urged by Dr. Shea in the current *American Forests* include: Secure the co-operation of a few "pappies" in a locality and make it possible for them to build a community center suitable for movies and dances. Supply it with soft pine sticks for whittling, also with cuspidors.

Provide simple games and contests such as horseshoe pitching and a shooting range. Organize 4-H clubs and local fish and game organizations. Let them feel that all these activities as well as any educational demonstrations are their own and not imposed on them by any external agency.

These Americans are willing to get their excitement in less destructive ways if they are available, and the forest fires may be looked upon as their unconscious signal for aid.[25]

These examples of applications of psychology to problems of life and work have been chosen not because of their simplicity but because they have been described in understandable terms. The problems were actually more complex than the necessarily brief quotations indicate. Many varieties of human behavior cannot be explained on a logical basis. To explain them we have to think in psychological terms which, at first, may appear to be quite illogical, as in the case of the woman who treats her friends shabbily because she seeks more friends. Whenever we can use the scientific method in the study of our chosen life and work problems, we shall do so. However, when the purely scientific method does not yield sufficient information to make worth while the treatment of an important psychological problem, the writer will add his own observations or include the observations of others, so that the reader may be given a unified and useful fund of information on the selected topics.

What psychology is not. In Greek mythology, Psyche was represented as a beautiful maiden having the wings of a butter-

---

[25] "Frustrated Forest Folk Set Fires for Excitement," *Science News Letter*, July 20, 1940.

fly. Psyche symbolized the soul. The butterfly symbolized human immortality. Originally psychology, from the root words *psyche,* soul, and *logy,* a suffix meaning a science—the science of the soul—was a branch of philosophy.

A generation ago psychology severed its formal relations with philosophy and became a science in itself. It no longer studies the soul, nor is it interested in such problems as communication with the dead. Psychology and psychical research are two different fields, and the psychologist does not have very much hope of successful discoveries in *psychic* realms. Psychology has lost its mystery. It is not interested in cults or in magical influences on people who happen to be about us. It does not take the place of the witch doctor.

Psychologists are not interested in character analysis from observation of superficial physical signs, except to report that such methods of analyzing people are largely fallacious. Many sales managers mistakenly think that they are psychologists when they try to predict a man's selling ability from the color of his hair or the shape of his chin. In a succeeding chapter (Chapter 10), we shall devote more space to this question and shall analyze established theories in regard to the relationship between physical and mental traits.

Psychologists are not interested in mind reading or in thought transference. They have not found that mental telepathy has sound foundations. Investigations of those incidents in the lives of their friends which indicated that mental telepathy might exist usually showed that such experiences were coincidences which occur in the life of everyone. When the psychologists have checked or examined phenomena of this sort, they have found that the apparently mystical should be treated in terms of natural laws.

Nor is psychology a short cut to success in business or in life. Many people who study psychology do so with the hope of finding an open sesame to success. It will not make a mentally strong and powerful individual out of a weakling. It is of assistance, of course, in bringing out the latent possibilities of people and in enabling them to adjust themselves to each other; but we should look upon psychology as a science.

Fig. 4. Willard L. Valentine, Northwestern University. If you wish to study further the scientific method in psychology, refer to his book *Experimental Foundations of General Psychology* (Farrar & Rinehart, 1941). This book presents the findings of many others in the study of representative psychological problems.

What psychology is. Psychology is method, not magic. The outstanding approach to the problems of our modern age is our highly developed technique for gaining insight into all aspects of our experiences—namely, the scientific method. Steps in the scientific method are: (a) observation of a chosen phenomenon; (b) collection of objective data; (c) analysis of the data; (d) drawing of conclusions from the data; and (e) verification of the findings by repetition of the observations made in the experiments. Delicate instruments have been invented to aid the observer in detecting and measuring variations of the phenomena under study. Involved statistical techniques have been developed for treatment of the data. The thousands of scientific studies being made by psychologists and other scientists are slowly modifying our daily work and living. They have already revealed possibilities for utilizing human and physical forces that were not dreamed of by our forefathers. The use of the scientific method for gaining insight has partially displaced unsound methods such as those of superstition and occultism.

The history of psychology indicates that we have given up the study of the soul, of the mind, and of consciousness, and we now define it as the "study of human behavior by scientific methods." *Behavior*, as used here, refers to more than conduct, deportment, or manner. It includes all normal and abnormal activities of the whole organism, even those of feeblemindedness and insanity. *The aims of applied psychology are the description, prediction, and control of human activities in order that we may understand and direct intelligently our own lives and influence the lives of others.*

Psychology is a most useful study because every man must live with himself and with others. Even though a person never studies it as a science, his every thought and act illustrate its principles. To live means to function, and behavior is the material of psychology. The unit of study is the individual.

Of course, a person may live a pleasant life and never study himself or his behavior. An angleworm and a cow are presumably content, but we have no evidence to indicate that they are intelligently happy. Happiness for the modern man demands more than mere organismic contentment. He wants to be physically comfortable, but he also wishes to know the laws of mental life, the principles of human behavior, so that he may utilize them for new satisfactions. Our present civilization rests upon the basis: "Let us study life and its conditions so that we may utilize our findings to rise to new and more intelligent levels of personal satisfactions and social relationships."

Every person is something of a psychologist. The roots of the subject are as old as the human species. However, modern scientific psychology is a relatively recent development. The first American laboratory was started in 1883 at Johns Hopkins University, and in 1889 the first title of "Professor of Psychology" was bestowed upon William James of Harvard University.[26] In 1940 the American Psychological Association, Inc., had 664 members and 2,075 associates.[27]

Now, gaining insight into any one field by scientific methods requires highly specialized training. Furthermore, some fields

---

[26] Emily S. Dexter and Katherine T. Omwake, *An Introduction to the Fields of Psychology*, p. 1. Prentice-Hall, Inc., 1938.
[27] *Yearbook 1940*, American Psychological Association, Inc.

lend themselves more readily to such studies than do others. Psychology differs from most other sciences in that the experimenter can ask his "subject" how he feels about the experiment. Psychologists use the introspective method to supplement the purely objective methods of study.

Psychology as taught today has certain limitations which should be recognized by students. Many laboratory experiments make use of scientific methods, but the laboratory situations do not always approximate actual life conditions. Hence we shall study human behavior in some of its everyday settings of life and work.

Another limitation is the kind of psychological training offered to our leaders by the academic psychologists. Pure psychology is analytical and does not offer programs for social or individual reform.

Anyone who deals with problem personalities soon learns that many possible solutions to a person's problems are not always feasible. A simple, everyday example is the employee who becomes maladjusted because his supervisor is maladjusted. The employee might be cured of his emotional difficulties if he could get rid of the major cause—his neurotic supervisor. However, this may not be a practicable solution under the circumstances. Objectively speaking, the employee's work situation may have to remain relatively fixed, but the employee's interpretation or emotional reaction to the work situation may be changed very markedly. Perhaps the psychologist can show the employee that his intense emotional response to the supervisor is merely the result of the strict way the employee was reared and that the supervisor symbolizes an earlier hateful experience.

Sometimes the only possible solution to a psychological problem is the clinical expert's help in gaining insight into and control over oneself in dealing with a trying situation. The many men who learn to rise above their problems in this intelligent manner are among the real heroes of modern life. They exemplify for us some very important principles of psychology. The mental lives of the very well balanced persons offer many valuable suggestions to the student of human nature. Helpful lessons may also be learned from contrasting personalities—namely, the poorly adjusted persons. We shall note how the mental habits of various types of persons have significant implications for us.

The scientists of one field are often unacquainted with the discoveries made by their fellow scientists in related fields. The layman—the average citizen—is often totally at sea regarding the interpretation of the masses of data and the volumes of reviews that are stored on near-by library shelves. In the business field, both the manager and the laborer are often unable to evaluate and interpret their own activities. They should seek the findings of the men who have devoted themselves to the scientific study of human behavior. Our present task is to see how psychologists' findings are related to our daily lives and work.

Outline of plan of treatment of these problems. Obviously it would be impossible to treat exhaustively all the problems listed in Tables I-III by businessmen and other individuals. Many of the problems are duplicates. Some problems cannot be answered, so far as we now know. However, we shall try to present certain contributions that psychology can make to the better understanding and treatment of these problems. We shall try to discuss them in the simplest possible terms and, when technical terms are used, they will be illustrated by examples from everyday life and business. For ease of discussion and to offer applications that are useful to many students, the following general outline will be followed:

I. Introduction—values and objectives.

II. Personality and its development.
1. Peculiar people.
2. The adjustment concept.
3. Organic factors in personality.
4. Methods of treating the maladjusted.
5. Developing your own personality.

III. *Predicting* the behavior of the *individual*.
1. Pseudo-scientific methods.
2. Hiring applicants for jobs.
3. Promoting the employee—rating people.
4. Choosing a vocation.

IV. *Influencing* the behavior of the *individual*.
1. Getting a job and gaining promotion.
2. Personal efficiency in study and work.
3. The executive and the individual employee.
4. The salesman and the prospect.

V. *Predicting* the behavior of the *group.*
   1. Marketing a product.
   2. Business cycles.
   3. Social evolution.

VI. *Influencing* the behavior of the *group.*
   1. Supervising employees.
   2. Advertising.

VII. Principles of psychological research.

While some of the immediate problems of the executive and employee will be discussed, a definite and more vital aim will be to prepare the student to become more than a technician in his occupational life. The technician does well only that which someone has taught him to do, whereas the leader develops the tasks for the technician and guides him in his work with everyday problems. The true leader looks upon his functions as far more than the mere making and delivering of commodities or services. He does more than perform today's job well. He devises better methods for the tasks of tomorrow and visualizes the challenges of new jobs of the day after tomorrow. Our dominant objectives are those which are consistent with leadership in a changing civilization.

References

Hildreth, G., "Psychology as a Career," *Journal of Consulting Psychology,* 1937, Vol. I, pp. 25-28.

Powers and others, *Psychology in Everyday Living,* Chapters I and II. D. C. Heath & Co., 1938.

Starch, Daniel, Hazel M. Stanton, and Wilhelmine Koerth, *Controlling Human Behavior,* Chapter I. The Macmillan Co., 1936.

Travis, Lee Edward, and Dorothy Walter Baruch, *Personal Problems of Everyday Life,* Part II. D. Appleton-Century Co., 1941.

Varnum, Walter C., *Psychology in Everyday Life,* Chapter I. McGraw-Hill Book Co., 1938.

Projects

1. No single textbook can possibly supply all the information now published in the field of applied psychology. Hence you should examine and note differences in the tables of contents of any of the following applied psychology textbooks that may be available in your library:

Crane, George W., *Psychology Applied.* Northwestern University Press, 1940.

Griffith, Coleman R., *An Introduction to Applied Psychology.* The Macmillan Co., 1936.

Husband, Richard W., *Applied Psychology*. Harper & Bros., 1934.

Jenkins, John G., *Psychology in Business and Industry*. John Wiley & Sons, 1935.

Moore, Herbert, *Psychology for Business and Industry*. McGraw-Hill Book Co., 1938.

Moss, Fred A., *Applications of Psychology*. Houghton Mifflin Co., 1929.

Poffenberger, A. T., *Applied Psychology*. D. Appleton-Century Co., 1927.

Strong, Edward K., Jr., *Psychological Aspects of Business*. McGraw-Hill Book Co., Inc., 1938.

2. Visit your library and examine the periodicals that might be of special value to the person who studies applied psychology. List the titles and content of several articles that appeal to you. Quote parts which you find interesting or of value to you. Be prepared to describe your findings to other students.

3. Do you know an adult who has been unemployed or irregularly employed for several years? Describe his psychological characteristics. Did unemployment cause his psychological problem, or did psychological problems cause his unemployment? Discuss.

4. Examine books and journals for descriptions of the work done by The Psychological Corporation. Perhaps you can read "The Role of The Psychological Corporation," by Paul S. Achilles, in *The American Journal of Psychology* (November 1937, pp. 229-247), or "Report of the Activities of the Psychological Corporation—1939," by Paul S. Achilles and Henry C. Link in the *Journal of Applied Psychology* (April 1940, pp. 109-121).

5. Examine biographies and autobiographies of famous contemporary leaders. Point out any relationships between the leader's psychological characteristics and his policies or achievements. Examine books such as E. S. Bogardus, *Leaders and Leadership*. D. Appleton-Century Co., 1934.

6. How does training to be a business technician differ from training to be a business leader?

2

A Major Objective in the Study of Psychology

For many people this is a hurly-burly world. They would like to feel more secure in it. There are those who try to attain security through wealth or knowledge. Others would revert back to the simple life of a pre-machine age. Is there a more intelligent objective, and what can psychology offer in its attainment?

SEVERAL years ago the writer called upon the energetic personnel director of a nationally known manufacturing concern. During the interview a middle-aged factory worker came into the office, and the personnel director at once rose to speak to him. They talked in low tones and in a manner that indicated a tenseness in feeling on the part of the worker and a sincere but helpless attitude on the part of the personnel man. In the course of the conversation, the employee was handed his pay envelope, which contained the much-feared blue discharge slip. The older man fingered it dazedly, and a few tears came into the corners of his eyes. Finally, with sagging shoulders and downcast gaze, the former employee left the building. The personnel man came back to his desk and sat down in order to continue the interrupted conversation, but his energetic manner had disappeared. He slumped in his chair, and a strained expression clouded his face. Suddenly he said:

"That was old Bill ——. He has been with this company for about 14 years. He has given us the best working years of his life. His wages have never been very high. He has a family and no reserve for this emergency. The firm had to let him go because the lack of orders is hitting us harder every week. If it gets much worse, I'll lose my job, too. Then I'll be on the street with Bill, looking for work."

One year after this conversation the personnel man was discharged as a result of a constantly decreasing labor force in the factory.

Three years after the conversation the entire factory had been closed and was for sale for taxes. Five years after this the factory building buzzed with production for national defense activities.

The American citizen, whether worker, executive, or employer, is a member of a vast economic system so complex and changing that everyone is apt to feel insecure. A great majority of the people cannot have the same feeling of self-reliance that we assume was present in the mind of the frontiersman who wandered through forest and plain knowing that he could always provide himself with sufficient food and shelter. The worker today has no suitable frontier land to which he can escape and which he can cultivate for himself. Even if settlers' lands were in abundance, he would be unable to meet the rigorous demands of frontier life because he has not been trained in that kind of self-reliance.

A generation ago, a man assumed that, if he learned a trade and saved his money for his old age, he would never be in need. Business depressions, technology, social changes, political realignments, and international disturbances have destroyed much of the average man's faith that his job is secure because he knows a trade. Skill does not insure employment; thrift does not spell old-age independence; home ownership does not guarantee permanent shelter; and honesty does not always bring its vaunted reward. Provisions such as unemployment compensation or social security programs for easing "industrial shocks," are still too few to meet the worker's daily needs. Though an employee performs tasks which are not subject to seasonal and other cyclical movements, he feels insecure because he knows that his fellow workers are constantly being shifted in their jobs. Furthermore, he is always somewhat at the mercy of a more or less whimsical supervisor.

Political, social, and other uncontrolled forces of evolution of this generation have toppled the educated and uneducated, the rich and the poor. Employees have discovered that their employers are, relatively, just as seriously affected by adversities as they are. They have seen wealthy factory owners who lost

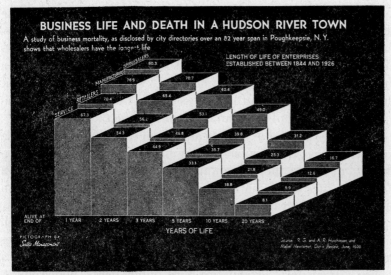

FIG. 5. Pictograph courtesy of *Sales Management*, July 15, 1939.

all their money and in their old age were compelled to take low-salaried jobs.   Intelligent persons have begun to realize that employer and employee, farmer and city man, college graduate and unschooled worker are likely to be pressed by the same socio-economic forces. All these uncertainties and complexities of life for the individual are simply modern examples of the old, old principles of evolution.

Examples of evolution in American living and thinking.   Everyone knows that times change.   The very businessmen whose buildings have gone to ruin repeated the same phrase, "Times change."   Yet they failed to grasp the significance of the phrase in time to adapt their businesses to the new requirements which slowly crept over and around them and shut them off from the successes of their competitors who anticipated and prepared for new demands on business. The businessman who is in the forefront in his prediction of the public's tastes in one season may, in the very next season, be out of step with the stride of that same public.

Change in itself is nothing new, but the speed with which change now takes place is the disconcerting element in this age. Let us review some of these changes in living and working that have taken place within the life span of people of today.

Periods of ten and twenty years often bring about complete obsolescence of an article that once was modern. For example, shaving soap, which was once hailed as up to date when it was made in the form of a small round cake to fit the bottom of a shaving mug, has since been made into shaving sticks, powder, tubes of soap-cream, and latherless creams; and now many men have discarded all of these and use the electric shaver.

The organ, which has disappeared from the mail-order catalog, was superseded by the piano. The piano was a sign of high social standing in the community. Later the ownership of a costly car had the same significance, and now possession of an airplane has taken its place.

Amusements a generation ago were simple and few. Children had little or no spending money. Sermons were long. Lectures and funerals were community diversions and subjects for a month's discussion. Today, we have public parks, playgrounds, moving pictures, community symphonies, motorcars, airplanes, radios, and television. Sport has been commercialized to such an extent that hundreds of millions of dollars are paid annually in admission fees.

Formerly, vacations were spent at resort hotels. Guests came by train, remained two or more weeks at the same hotel, and then took the train home. Now the vacationer often spends each night in a different town, and the tourist homes and gasoline stations have taken much of the vacation travel income from the railroads and hotels.

Decentralization has taken place in many of our cities. The stores and amusement places are no longer centered in the downtown sections, as they were when our larger communities first started. The motorcar, motion pictures, and chain stores have increased movement to the neighborhood business centers. Limited transportation facilities and insufficient parking space have contributed to ever-mounting percentages of purchases in the suburban centers. Certainly, merchants in downtown centers have to contend with much competition that has resulted from our transportation developments.

All these and many other changes have influenced business methods, and business itself has changed greatly and is continuing to change at an accelerated rate. When we note how machinery economizes human labor, we can understand why we have more leisure time than our grandparents.   One expert states:

In this country there is now expended about 13.5 horsepower hours per day per capita—the equivalent of a hundred human slaves for each of us; in England the figure is 6.7, in Germany 6.0, in France 4.5, in Japan 1.8, in Russia 0.9, in China 0.5.   In the last analysis, this use of power is why our most important social changes have come about.   This is why we no longer drive our ships with human slaves chained to the oars, as did the Romans and the Greeks.   This is why we no longer enslave whole peoples, as did the Pharaohs for building our public structures, and lash them to their tasks. This is why ten times as many boys and girls are in the high school today in the United States as were there in 1890—more than 5,000,000 now, half a million then.   This is why we have now an eight-hour day instead of, as then, a ten, a twelve—or sometimes a fourteen-hour day. • This is why we have on the average an automobile for every family in the country.   This is why the lowest class of male labor, i. e., unskilled labor, gets nearly twice as much in real wages in the United States as in England, three times as much as in Germany or France, and thirteen times as much as in Russia, and this is why the most abused class of labor in the world, domestic service, is even better off relatively in this country though completely unorganized, i. e., through the unhampered operation of economic laws, than is any other class of labor, skilled or unskilled.[1]

Some benefits from our recent technological changes.   In the past fifty years at least a million new jobs have been created in new industries such as motor vehicles, electrical machinery, rubber tires, gasoline, rayon, aluminum, typewriters, refrigerators, phonographs, motion pictures, and aircraft.[2]   Our standard of living has risen because we have learned how to use energy for man's advantage.   Goods and services have increased about in proportion to our ability to produce more goods and services through the aid of power machines.

Dr. Vergil D. Reed, assistant director of the Bureau of the Census, has reported some of the changes in the American way of life which have taken place during the past quarter-century:

Nowhere, perhaps, are these changes more dramatically evident than in the field of personal transportation.   In 1914, the country's production of carriages, sulkies, and buggies numbered 550,401.   In the same year only 543,881 passenger automobiles were manufactured in the United States.   In 1939, fewer than 1,000 carriages were built while the assembly lines ground out 4,362,000 autos.

Canned fruit and vegetable juices were not even mentioned in the Census

---

[1] R. A. Millikan in the New York *Herald Tribune*, April 21, 1939, p. 19.
[2] *Factory Management and Maintenance*, August 1936.

of 1914; today the combined value of citrus and other fruit, and tomato and other vegetable juices annually canned and bottled is about $50,000,000.

Another field in which large development has taken place . . . is that of the personal service industries, like beauty parlors and cleaning and pressing establishments. Today personal service businesses of this kind through the land number 321,000 and support more than 570,000 proprietors and employees. Such service establishments, according to recent census of business figures, reported receipts of $684,000,000 paying out wages amounting to $168,000,000.[3]

As a result of technology combined with intensive selling and attractive advertising, the modern consumer buys many more goods than did his parents or his grandparents.

American workers enjoy most of the privileges enjoyed by the wealthy. All attend the same public schools, motion pictures, churches, amusement parks, libraries, and athletic contests. They play golf on the same municipal or company-owned courses. In general the workmen's automobiles may be cheaper than those of the employers; but many members of the working classes own cars that are of the same price and appearance as those owned by members of the upper managerial ranks.

Many former lines of class distinction have been erased by persons of exceptional ability. A capable American laborer can rise above the environment and social status of the average laborer. If the worker has unusual ability, he can become a member of the managerial group and even of the employer class, socially and culturally. His lowly birth is not an insurmountable handicap to his wife's social ambitions or to his political aspirations. Actually, his early years in the slums or among laborers are likely to cause him to be admired by all classes. His humble origin is not a barrier to any intellectual privilege or luxury that his ability may earn, provided he also acquires the social amenities of the cultured.

The sciences that underlie our technologies have been beneficial to us not only in making us more comfortable but also in enabling us to increase the average length of life 12 years since 1900. The expectation of life at birth has increased about 26 years for females and 24 years for males in the period since the Revolutionary War. However, the rates have changed little for the older age groups. Improvements in health have resulted in

---

[3] Vergil D. Reed, "Results of the Census," *Science*, December 6, 1940.

keeping a larger proportion of the population alive until late adult life; but people who reach late adult life can expect to live very little, if any, longer than such persons did a century ago.[4]

Children have been benefited in many ways by this new era. We have accepted universal education as a function of the state and require it of each normal child. In 1920, only 28.3 per cent of youth between the ages of 14 and 17 attended high school. This percentage rose to 62.5 in 1936. In 1910 there were about 700,000 pupils in schools of the high school level. There are now almost 7 million. Our colleges and universities had less than 240,000 students in 1910. By 1938 the number had grown to 1,350,000.[5] Almost anyone who would really benefit from a college education may now obtain it.

Much of our thinking has changed. Women have been emancipated. They vote, smoke cigarettes, go into business, drive cars, and attend college in increasing numbers. And sex may be discussed in any public gathering, provided we phrase our conversation in Freudian terms. Most remarkable of all is the fact that the intimate accessories of women are advertised in our national magazines and no one objects, because the advertiser contributes to human welfare and phrases his statements with polite logic and an appeal to health and charm. Much of the old taboo regarding the mention of venereal diseases has disappeared as the press, radio, and moving picture have assisted in educational campaigns against disease.

---

[4] Conclusions by Harold F. Dorn, statistician of the United States Public Health Service. See *Public Health Reports*, Vol. 52, No. 49, December 3, 1937. The above figures, 26 and 24 for females and males, apply specifically to vital statistics for Massachusetts.

[5] Charles C. Fries, "Educating for Frustration," *School and Society*, November 30, 1940, presents the following data regarding the education of our citizens: "But of those who enter high school only 49.1 per cent finish. Of those who graduate from high school less than one fourth enter college. And of those who enter college as freshmen only 44.3 per cent are graduated."

In 1935 there were 75,215,000 adults in the United States. Of these, 48.4 per cent had not completed the 8th grade in school, 86 per cent had not completed high school, 4.88 per cent were completely illiterate, and only 2.9 per cent were college graduates.

"In other words, the American public that constitutes our present 'democracy' is made up of some 75 million adults of whom: (a) there are 50 per cent more illiterates than college graduates, (b) approximately half have less than an eighth-grade education, (c) only 14 per cent, or one in every seven, have a high-school education."

Fig. 6. One of the most important psychological changes which has taken place in recent generations is the displacement of negative directions by positive instruction. (*Photograph courtesy of General Foods.*)

Our attitude toward employees has also improved. The old master-servant relationship has tended to change in the direction of colleagueship. Managements no longer control the deportment of employees in the way they once did. For example, in 1879 the rules for the employees of Carson Pirie Scott & Company of Chicago were as follows:

Store must be open from 6 a.m. to 9 p.m. the year round.

Store must be swept; counters, base shelves, and showcases dusted. Lamps filled, trimmed and chimneys cleaned; pens made; doors and windows opened; a pail of water, also a bucket of coal brought in before breakfast (if there is time to do so) and attend to customers who call.

Store must not be opened on the Sabbath unless necessary, and then only for a few minutes.

The employee who is in the habit of smoking Spanish cigars, being shaved at the barber's, going to dances and other places of amusement will surely give his employer reason to be suspicious of his integrity and honesty.

Each employee must not pay less than $5 per year to the church and must attend Sunday school regularly.

Men employees are given one evening a week for courting and two if they go to prayer meeting.[6]

American workers do not look upon themselves as members of an inferior social class. Supervisors who give orders in a superior manner that implies inferiority on the part of the workers are likely to be displaced by men who can direct subordinates with a minimum of friction.

[6] *Sales Management*, August 15, 1939, p. 2.

Many enlightened and forward-looking managements are experimenting with employee-participation schemes, profit sharing, suggestion systems, group insurance, co-operative purchasing, stock ownership, and other devices aimed at the development of employee good will. Of course, some of these schemes are for the purpose of increasing profits for the employers, but many are also sincere efforts to effect a better understanding between employer and employees.

Further changes now on our horizon. New methods of management and new inventions are constantly affecting laborers in specific industries and the living of individual citizens. A few of the inventions that have come into recent use or are on the horizon are the mechanical cotton picker, artificial cotton and wool, plywoods stronger than steel, new plastics, quick-drying concrete, the photoelectric cell, prefabricated houses, television, gasoline from coal, glass-fiber clothing, substratosphere aircraft, synthetic rubber, synthetic vitamins, and tray agriculture.

Tray agriculture, for example, multiplies enormously plant productivity by controlled chemical feeding of roots. Eventually, many of our vegetables may be raised without any plowing, spading, hoeing, or pulling of weeds. Weather conditions will not affect the crop. Soilless or "hydroponic" farming has already produced potatoes at the rate of 2,506 bushels per acre. The average yield per acre under the old methods is only 116 bushels.

New fuels are appearing to compete with the established ones such as gasoline. Alcohol-gasoline[7] is an example of a blended motor fuel which has been used to some extent in this country. Further experimentation may result in millions of bushels of grain being made into alcohol for gasoline blends, and it may also seriously affect petroleum workers and motorists.

Some optimistic engineers even predict a foolproof car on foolproof roads. Motors will then receive their energy through ethereal waves, and photoelectric cells will control their speed and co-ordinate their movements.

These and many other possible influences of science, business, and society indicate that more, rather than fewer, adjustments

---

[7] The Chemical Foundation, 654 Madison Avenue, New York, has information available regarding the "Farm Chemurgic Movement," which directs researches in rayon, sweet-potato starch, soybeans, newsprint, and similar commodities.

will be necessary for the intelligent individual. Certainly some of the recent inventions have had beneficial effects on employment as well as on our standard of living.

For example, new products developed by the DuPont Company are giving employment to 19,000 of their 47,000 employees and account for 40 per cent of their sales. Of Armstrong Cork's sales, 24 per cent are from products developed within the past seven years. Of Johns-Manville's sales, 43 per cent are from new or improved products developed within the last ten years. Of General Electric Company's sales, 60 per cent are from products unknown ten years ago.[8]

When we criticize technology and science because we have acquired through them many psychological problems, we should also appreciate how they have helped us. For example, we now have one motorcar for every 4.3 persons. There are more automobiles than telephones. A pound of modern automobile costs less than a pound of butter. One out of every seven workers in this country is dependent directly or indirectly upon the automobile for his pay check.

On the whole, technological change, whether due to mechanization or to managerial improvement, tends to facilitate rising employment. Industries that have made the greatest technological advancements have also made the greatest employment increases. Certainly, many more persons are today employed in the automotive industries than the numbers formerly employed in building buggies and raising horses.

The social advantages resulting from new inventions and other elements of progress usually outweigh the disadvantages, such as periodic unemployment. We are going to continue to make these changes regardless of how the individual is affected, because man's very nature is evolutionary in tendency. He is a biological being.

Organic evolution as biologists describe it. Man's present tendencies to explore and advance are obedient to the same laws that have always governed all living things. Man is the product of evolutionary forces much older than the human race.

When evolution is mentioned to many a present-day news-

---

[8] *Notes and Quotes.* Connecticut General Life Insurance Company, October 1939.

FIG. 7. Microfilms illustrate one change that has already affected our methods of storing books and filing records. Microfilming consists in photographing records, checks, letters, books, and drawings. It saves space. Standard-size letters, 2,352 in number, can be filed in a space 4 by 4 by 1 inch. Hundreds of millions of Social Security and other documents and file cards have been microfilmed and stored in space which occupies less than 1 per cent of their former filing spaces.

paper reader, he suspects that it is a debatable theory and that it may be overthrown in another six months. This is not true. Evolution is here to stay. There is no more chance that it will be disproved or abandoned by the scientists than there is that some day we may believe the earth to be disc-shaped rather than spherical. The controversies among scientists which newspapers report merely bear upon minor parts of the theory.   The general theory is an accepted part of our education and culture; and, contrary to some, the basic principle of organic evolution is helpful in explaining certain phases of religion, for even modern theology is based upon evolution.

Millions of years were involved in the evolution to our present state.   The same laws and forces that we now see operating in changed international relations, changed living conditions, changed business conditions, and the changing demands of customers were operating through the long and tedious evolution of plants, animals, and man.   Many students and businessmen who have taken courses in geology or who have read books dealing with organic evolution fail to appreciate that the same forces which ruled the world during the evolution of man from the one-celled animal are forces that control man today.   The forces in the evolutionary process did not cease to operate several generations ago.   They are here with us now.

In the study of organic evolution, the biologist has collected a vast store of facts which he interprets in biological terms, and we should note a few of them.   One of the most important principles is that of *variation,* which means that the offspring are never exactly like their parents.   No two plants, animals, or human beings are ever precisely the same.   In nature's patterns there is perpetual variation.   Sometimes these variations are very small but an advantage in strength of 15 per cent may be important in the survival of animals.[9]

The biologist has also noted a second principle which is known to the businessman—the *struggle for existence.*   Every living creature does its best, its very best, to live and have young. Many species of animals lay thousands of eggs but have few offspring.   The struggle is too great for most of the young to survive.

In the struggle for existence, only the fittest survive.   The others perish.   A few have certain *adaptations* that enable them to survive.   In considering these adaptations of nature, we must bear in mind that the animals and plants do not consciously adapt

---

[9] A. R. Wallace, *Darwinism* (The Macmillan Co., 1912) offers examples of this principle.   The particular evolutionary concept presented in this chapter is Darwinian.   Other theories of evolution, such as the instability of the cell, confirm the principles of change which interest the student of applied psychology.

themselves to their environment. Adaptation in nature means that those species which, through the principle of variation, happen to have powers that fit into environment survive. Those whose muscles, legs, jaws, or wings are not strong enough to withstand the environment perish. This struggle for existence does not mean that nature is cruel or harsh. Nature is simply a name for the way things are.

Evolution does not guarantee progress; it guarantees only change. For us the change may be for better or for worse, depending upon how we deal with it. In comparison with the other creatures of the earth, man has one distinct advantage. He has intelligence. The biologists tell us that man has not changed in cranial capacity for twenty thousand years. Man did not have to change structurally in order to meet the rigors of his environment. He "used his head." Survival did not depend entirely upon the chance strength of muscle or length of arm, but also upon ability to cope with conditions by thinking. When man's environment does not fit, he changes it; if he does not, he perishes. When man found it cold and uncomfortable in the north, he did not migrate toward the equator but developed artificial means of heating his abode.

Most creatures have gained security by specializing in adjustment of structure and habit to particular environmental conditions, whereas man is a specialist in adjustability of structures and habits to a variety of environments. No other vertebrate can live as can he on Antarctic ice cap, in Amazonian jungle, beneath the surface of the sea, or high in the air.

Furthermore, man is the world's foremost specialist in transforming environments to bring them within the range of his powers. Far more efficient than the beaver or the mound-building ant, he drains the swamp, irrigates the desert, tunnels the mountain, bridges the river, digs the canal, conditions the air in home, factory, and office.[10]

The fact that man can adapt himself to changes in conditions which are not too great or too sudden is a most helpful factor in the situation of the individual who finds himself in cross-currents of rigorous conditions. .

However, one of the most mystifying aspects of the evolution of human beings is the difference among individuals in their use of

---

[10] Kirtley F. Mather, "The Future of Man as an Inhabitant of the Earth," *Sigma Xi Quarterly*, Vol. 28, No. 1, 1940, p. 7.

intelligence in dealing with the opportunities around them. For example, some people assimilate an education so that they use it to change their environments; others use it merely to obtain diplomas. Albert B. Crawford has presented the need for more than a diploma in one of his Yale University reports:

At the end of each year there are always a number of men in our files who remain unplaced. About 85 per cent of this group is composed of individuals who have just gone to college for four years and are being "graduated." They are not outstanding in any way; they have usually been students without much purpose or direction; they are still floundering at a time when employers and others expect them to have arrived at an intelligent decision as to the kind of career they want to follow, and to have done at least something to prepare themselves for it.

One of the basic characteristics of these individuals is their blind faith in the operation of some mechanistic or automatic principle leading them on infallibly and step by step towards some vague status of ultimate success. They live in the passive voice waiting to be acted upon rather than acting themselves, and apparently seeing no need for planning or thinking ahead in order that their conduct may be intelligently directed.

Instead of purposively seeking employment, these applicants merely file a registration with the Department and then wait to be informed of job openings. When this type of student is given the opportunity to interview a prospective employer, he often fails properly to prepare himself. When an interview ends, he waits for the employer to offer him a job; but the employer meanwhile has not been impressed and no job is forthcoming. The individual in this group has given little evidence of potential executive ability in his past performance, nor has he demonstrated any particular promise of leadership or qualities of imagination in his interview behavior. Yet administrative capacity is what employers are looking for; they are not interested in men merely because of their having attended college and received degrees.[11]

The truly educated man appreciates what is meant by the terms *struggle for existence, survival of the fittest,* and *adaptation.* He sees that more than change is taking place. He knows, if he is wise, that there is also a change in the rate of change. This *accelerated rate of change* is called the "new American tempo."

[11] Albert B. Crawford, "Report of the Director of the Department of Personnel Study and Bureau of Appointments for the Academic Year, 1938-1939, Yale University," pp. 6-7. Statement quoted from a special report on occupational guidance and placement activities, prepared by Stuart H. Clement and Ralph R. Wolf of the Department's Staff.

Fig. 8. Robert R. Updegraff, Scarsdale, N. Y., who originated the term "New American Tempo." Mr. Updegraff is not an academic psychologist, but he has written many articles that treat current economic problems by means of psychological approaches.

Causes of the new American tempo. Robert R. Updegraff,[12] who coined the term, attributed the change in the rate of change to five causes:

1. Invention.
2. Transportation.
3. Picturization.
4. World wars.
5. Availability.

We need only comment on the causes which he presented. The part which invention has played in modern life and business and will continue to play is obvious. Were it not for the engineer, we should still be cooking over fires of wood, pumping our water from a well in the back yard, sitting at home evenings and on Sundays, writing our letters in longhand, and taking months to cross the Atlantic. Transportation has helped to destroy provincialism in thinking and living. We seldom admire the old just because it is old. We see how strangers live and we adopt some of their thinking, just as the Renaissance was brought

[12] Robert R. Updegraff, "The New American Tempo," *Advertising and Selling*, May 5, 1926, p. 19.

about by the Crusaders who traveled in new lands and acquired new wants.

Picturization is exemplified by the moving picture. Time was when the faculty member of a university could always recognize the countrified freshman on the campus. It is more difficult to do so today because the rural boys and girls have learned, mostly through moving pictures, how to conduct themselves at a tea and what style of clothes to wear. Other examples of picturization are advertising and pictorial magazines.

Wars have a pronounced effect on the manufacturer; he learns how to change his factory from manufacturing typewriters to making war materials. Businessmen who have made the same product for years catch visions of new production programs when the government shows them the possibilities of new products and adaptations of old methods. During a war the people also learn to think in terms of the big, the stupendous, the unusual. Each day has a new thrill as the war news is read or as war actually reaches the civilian masses. The dowager and the spinster come out and mingle with the common people, and find that life has new meanings and new thrills.

The availability factor has been brought about by chain stores, large-scale production, departmentalized drug stores, motorized libraries, artistic window displays, and installment buying. If a resident of California wants an article which trains cannot bring quickly enough, the airplane cuts down the waiting time to a few hours.

To the factors suggested by Mr. Updegraff, we should add four others:

1. The developments of science.
2. Universal education.
3. The cumulative effects of changes.
4. A recognition of the biological principles of variation and adaptation.

The development of the scientific view of the universe and of human behavior has had more effect upon us than we realize. It is but a few generations ago that the great mass of mankind attributed many effects to supernatural rather than to natural causes. When a man could not find a logical explanation of his

experiences and surroundings, he invented superstitious interpretations. Because of the ready explanations of superstition
and their insistence on following trodden paths, men had little
need or desire to explore the new or the unknown.

Today scientists question all preconceived ideas. When a
scientist can substantiate his hypotheses with incontrovertible
data, he announces the discovery of a law. If his data do not
explain the variable studied, he presents only his results and per-
severes in the hope that he may further serve science. Pure
science has given us our basic concepts, and upon these basic concepts we are building further applications. Natives of the more
remote regions of this country still attempt to explain phenomena, indeed life itself, in terms of the magical and mysterious.
However, each scientific discovery destroys old superstitions and
paves the way for more intelligent living. Were it not for our
system of universal education, the public would seldom learn of
the scientist's discoveries.

When one attempts to put his finger on *the* causes of the new
American tempo, he tends to reason in circles. Change in the
rate of social and business change is furthered by the cumulative effect of previous changes. When advertising and engineering secured a sure footing, each branched out into new fields,
and some of these branches, in turn, gave rise to additional
branches. Indeed, it is impossible to point to any one cause or to
any definite group of unrelated causes for these changes. Some
say that the engineer and the advertising expert are the causes;
but they could not have progressed without the aid of many other
agencies. One change brings other changes. The old biological
principles of variation and adaptation are merely expressing
themselves less in man as an organism and more in man's intelligent control of his environment.

Paradoxically, the applications of scientific discoveries have
improved our standard of living at the same time that the length
of our working week has decreased; and we have cut the price of
electrical refrigerators in half in the course of ten years. However, we have made no such gain in the control of our social and
mental problems.

Psychology should contribute toward adjustment to change.
Certainly, we cannot stop change any more than we can stop

time. Almost every change which benefits some one person or industry brings new psychological problems to others. No one can prevent these changes which, in the long run, seem to spell progress. Nor would many care to turn back to the former modes of living, when life was simpler but everyone worked seventy hours a week and had to amuse himself by attending funerals and spelling bees. Every individual, stupid or intelligent, is jostled by the technological and social forces that surround him. What then can the intelligent individual do about it, if anything? What can he gain for this purpose from a study of psychology? A suggested major objective for the educated person of today is personal development in two important respects:

(a) To learn about the *modern techniques involved in dealing with people* such as the clinical method of analyzing personalities, tests in hiring applicants, rating scales in promoting employees, recent developments in supervising employees, predicting consumers' wants, influencing groups of people, using clarifying statistics, and other factual methods. These are examples of knowledge that may be learned through college classroom approaches.

(b) To gain something more important than knowledge only, namely, the mental quality which we term *adaptability on the part of the individual himself*. This means that he must catch the spirit of the age in which he lives and become an intelligent participant in the changes taking place about him.

Of course, no man can foresee all the great changes that will occur in the later years of his life, but he can adapt himself to the changes occurring in his own time and place. His guiding attitude should be that of expecting changes and preparing to meet them. A fundamental psychological purpose for the intelligent individual, regardless of sex, vocation, or environment, is that of adjusting himself to the accelerated rates of change taking place about him.

Adaptability is far more than knowledge. It is a mental habit that can be acquired by anyone who really seeks it. *Adaptability is the habit of finding and using opportunities in the environment and following not the lines of least resistance but those of greatest opportunity*. The habit of acquiring new points of view, new skills, new facts, and new habits can be learned. Everyone can to some extent travel, attend classes, read books, see moving pictures, listen to the radio, talk with others, and learn new ideas from various other available sources. However, more besides travel, education, and social contacts is necessary to bring about adaptability in one's self. Conscious recognition of one's mental habits or adjustments and intelligent direction of self-growth are most important. These principles will be treated in Chapters 3 to 9.

Once a person recognizes the importance of adaptability and then studies the principles of adjustment, he will discover how his psychological tendencies and habits can be modified in the direction of greater adaptability. The age-old laws of evolution are still with us. The struggle for existence is not new; only its form has changed. The machine has only accelerated the rate of change and accentuated the need for a certain kind of psychological development in order to capitalize the changes for individual benefit.

The individual who recognizes these rapidly changing conditions and their mental requirements may have two sustaining convictions. These are that the world still has many unsolved problems, and that determination to help solve an immediate problem always has been and always will be a worthwhile goal. Anyone can find self-expression in solving a near-by problem in his work through the three following channels of direct attack:

1. Improving the mechanical equipment.
2. Improving the methods of operating the equipment or of doing the work.
3. Improving the human relationships.

The fact that the worker in the past got much of his feeling of worthful participation from his craftsmanship does not mean that the present-day worker cannot achieve the same feeling. Anything now being done could be done better, more easily, more economically, or more pleasingly. For example, a stenographer cannot hope to improve the typewriter or office machines she uses, but she can always improve her methods of work. In times of depression when thousands of stenographers are walking the streets looking for jobs, certain employers are seeking more able stenographers.

The same situation applies to businessmen, teachers, and students. Many young people have not learned how to gain creative self-expression through the three general channels of improvement because the books they have read, the courses they have taken, and the diplomas which they have earned do not require development of adaptability. Some of their studies have taught them to criticize life as it is. Few have learned to recognize the rapidly changing conditions under which we live, to feel in control of themselves, to tackle systematically the problems of the immediate job, and to become adaptable. Every man with a job and a steady income should assume that he may some day lose the job and his income. Every girl who marries should assume that she may some day become a widow and have to earn her own living. No one can prevent catastrophe, but every intelligent person can prepare himself psychologically to deal with catastrophe.

Our ultimate dependence cannot be on systems of government or business, but on ourselves as individuals. Life and civilization always have been and always will be dangerous. Dangers change only their form. The entire history of civilization is one long series of crises. Some of the individuals who survived were only fortunate; others were intelligent. The spirited man is still master of his fate.

Some years ago when the *Titanic* sped across the Atlantic on her maiden voyage, she struck an iceberg and sank. One American newspaper cartoonist of unusual insight drew two contrasting illustrations of the tragedy. One drawing showed the ship broken and about to sink. Underneath that picture were the words: "The weakness of man—the supremacy of nature." The other drawing illustrated how a certain passenger stepped aside to give his place in the last lifeboat to a woman with a child. This picture had the words: "The weakness of nature—the supremacy of man."

Adaptability is far more than knowledge. It depends upon the ability to control one's habits and to change them intelligently. To do this, the individual needs the self-knowledge which psychology can often contribute. In the next few chapters we shall examine certain mental habits which inhibit and others that facilitate adaptability and thereby gain that insight which contributes to man's supremacy over himself as well as over nature.

References

Andrews, John N., and Carl A. Marsden, *Tomorrow in the Making*. Mc-Graw-Hill Book Co., 1939. This is a symposium in which twenty-six leaders of American thought discuss the most vital problems confronting America.

Ellis, Carleton, and Miller W. Swaney, *Soilless Growth of Plants*. Reinhold Publishing Corp., 1938.

Gericke, W. F., *The Complete Guide to Soilless Gardening*. Prentice-Hall, Inc., 1940.

Leonard, Jonathan N., *Tools of Tomorrow*. Viking Press, 1935.

Projects

1. Many scientists believe that human nature and the social sciences have not kept pace with the physical and chemical sciences. Some have suggested that we should retard certain sciences until human beings catch up with them. What arguments can you present for or against the suggestion? Should we choose the goal of improving human adaptability to keep pace with developments in all fields?

2. Culture has been defined as openness of mind, objectiveness of attitude, a sensitive appreciation of human values, an original point of view or philosophy of life, and a development of the potentialities of the human being. (a) Which courses in college have impressed you as being directed toward one or more of the five mentioned qualities? (b) Can you name any courses which are not directed toward one of these five qualities? (c) Can you name any work or recreation which could not be directed toward one or more of these five qualities if the individual so desired?

3. Theodore Roosevelt, in Chicago, April 10, 1899, said: "I wish to preach not the doctrine of ignoble ease but the doctrine of the strenuous life." Can you name any tendencies in recent American life, such as in legislation, where the doctrine seemed to be directed toward ignoble ease?

4. Does government regulation of business tend to stimulate adaptability or lack of adaptability on the part of the businessmen who are regulated?

5. Should employers encourage their employees to live on small plots of land which can be farmed for subsistence products, to enable employees to adapt themselves to periods of unemployment?

6. Per-capita meat consumption in the United States fell from 162 pounds in 1908 to 131 pounds in 1939. Our eating of meats has been lagging since 1920. Assume that you are a manufacturer of meat products. Would you try to increase the per-capita consumption of meat by advertising the desirability of eating more meat? Or, how would you try to increase your business?

7. Fill in the spaces to indicate some of the changes which have taken place during one generation in American life in the following fields:

	1910	Present year
Education		
Communication		
Transportation		
Woman's position . . .		
Employee's status . . .		
Medicine		

8. At present we are hearing much about the electric refrigerator. The manufacturers of ice refrigerators might assume that they must either make the iceless kind or go out of business; but that does not follow, because some 30 per cent of the American homes have no refrigerators at all. Besides, less than 20 per cent of farm dwellings have electricity. When a concern finds a market slipping away, it is necessary to adapt itself to the new conditions and to uncover the undeveloped markets.

If you are interested in a declining industry such as coal mining, study possible untapped markets of the chosen industry or business.

9. *The back-number employee.* William Johnson, 38 years old, has been working for his present employer for fifteen years. Several years ago his work changed, but he was not able to adapt himself to the changed conditions. The firm progressed but Mr. Johnson did not. The personnel manager has been unable to transfer him to a vacancy with the same rate of pay that he now has, and he refuses a demotion with a lower rate of pay. He is married, has several children, and his character and general record are excellent. The management is confronted with the problem of either forcing him to accept a demotion or allowing him to draw a higher rate of pay than his work really merits. Assume that you are the personnel manager. What would you do about Mr. Johnson's case?

PART TWO

Personality Development and the Adjustment Concept

3

Peculiar People—A Systematic Approach
Toward Understanding Them

Those forms of behavior which we are apt to classify as peculiar or abnormal really have important meanings. Abnormal or unusual behavior is not merely the effect of environment or the age in which a person lives. It always has purpose for the individual. It is part of his pattern of adjustment. Only when we recognize patterns of adjustment can we deal intelligently with the peculiar persons whom we meet in daily life and work.

HAVE YOU ever visited an institution for the mentally afflicted and observed the peculiar actions of the patients? If you have, you probably assumed that their ailments were caused by increased tensions from our mechanized life. Like most people, you wondered whether we are growing crazier because of the pace at which we work and amuse ourselves. If you yourself have been baffled by some of the problems resulting from the accelerated rate of change mentioned in the preceding chapter, you naturally inferred that the major cause of insanity was an inability to adapt ourselves to the "new American tempo."

Actually, careful analyses of the statistics of mental-hospital populations do not indicate that our so-called fast living has increased the problem of mental disease. H. F. Dorn,[1] for example, studied the number of first admissions to mental hospitals in Massachusetts, New York, and Illinois and found that the increases in mental diseases of recent years have not been caused by the stresses and strains of a complex urban environment. Much of the increase in admissions is attributed to the increase in the proportion of old people in our population, shown in Table IV.

[1] H. F. Dorn, "The Incidence and Future Expectancy of Mental Disease," *Public Health Report,* Washington, 1938, Vol. 53, pp. 1991-2004.

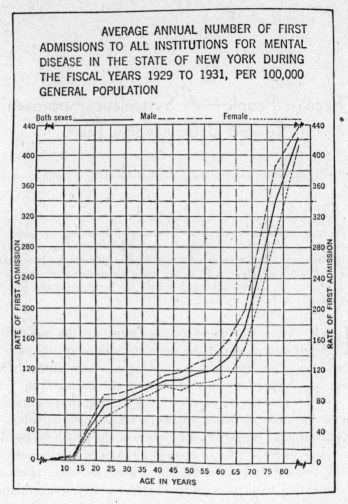

FIG. 9.   From B. Malzberg, "A Statistical Study of Age in Relation
to Mental Disease," *Mental Hygiene*, 1935, Vol. 19, pp. 449–476.

Similarly, Landis and Page[2] made an exhaustive study of the
incidence of mental disease in relation to a wide variety of factors
such as income, environment, and race.   They found that the
incidence of mental disorder did not increase during World
War I or during the depression period from 1929 to 1932.   The
highest incidence rates were not found among those in the adoles-

---

[2] Carney Landis and James D. Page, *Modern Society and Mental Disease*.
Farrar & Rinehart, 1938.

cent and adult years, the age-periods regarded as of greatest psychological stress, but among those over 60 years of age.

Mental diseases are found among American Indians, African Negroes, Europeans, and the Chinese, even though their cultures, environments, and methods of living differ greatly. The idea that the hustle and bustle of modern life are responsible for the occurrence of mental diseases is not convincing when many explorers report that natives of Africa and other primitive societies seem to suffer from the same mental diseases that are found among us.

In Russia, where the Soviet regime has wrought some major environmental changes, there is only one respect in which mental disease seems to differ from that of Czarist Russia. The devils persecuting hallucinated persons have been replaced by Stakhanovites, or "good workers." Formerly the voice of God accused the schizophrenic of sin. Later the voices of other workers accused such patients of not doing their duty toward the state. No real changes in mental disease had occurred.

The Soviet regime has brought about a change in the content of mental symptoms, but there is no evidence that it has either decreased the incidence of mental disease or altered the basic forms of mental disease.[3]

In summary, we may say that some variety of mental disease is present among 1.5 per cent of the adult population today and sooner or later mental disease will incapacitate, for a time, approximately ten per cent of the total population. No national, racial, regional or religious groups seem to be especially susceptible or resistant, and some of the differences that do appear are readily explicable. Finally, the available data contradict the popular belief that mental diseases are on the increase. The only major increase that has occurred during the past quarter century has resulted from the more extensive hospitalization of aged individuals.[4]

We are becoming a much older people. See Table IV. Increases in hospital admissions are also attributable in part to our improved facilities for discovering persons having mental ailments, the increased number of mental hospitals, and decreased social stigma attached to mental disease.

---

[3] James D. Page, "Mental Disease in Russia," *American Journal of Psychiatry*, 1938, Vol. 94, pp. 859-865.

[4] Carney Landis and James D. Page, "Magnitude of the Problem of Mental Disease," Publication No. 9 of The American Association for the Advancement of Science, *Mental Health*, pp. 149-155. Science Press, 1939.

The age distribution in the United States at successive epochs may be indicated in percentages as follows:

TABLE IV[5]

	1850	1920	1940	1950	1980
Under 20 years............	52.5	40.8	34.5	31.0	26.0
20 to 44 years.............	35.1	38.4	39.0	39.7	33.7
45 to 64 years.............	9.8	16.1	19.7	21.4	25.9
Over 65 years.............	2.6	4.7	6.8	7.9	14.4

FIG. 10. Carney Landis, Columbia University.

FIG. 11. James D. Page, University of Rochester.

Anyone interested in further study on the problem of mental disease should refer to a book on which Professors Landis and Page collaborated, *Modern Society and Mental Disease* (Farrar & Rinehart, 1938).

The prevalence of mental disease has been studied by scientists, and we know that among the people of certain states more than 5 per cent of the children born alive will spend some part of their lives in a mental hospital. The chances in 100 of eventually becoming a patient in a hospital for mental disease depends somewhat upon the age of the individual. At age twenty, 5.9 per cent of the male and 5.3 per cent of the female population are likely to be admitted to a mental hospital at some later date

[5] Louis I. Dublin, *Statistical and Social Implications in the Problem of Our Aging Population.* Metropolitan Life Insurance Company.

in their lives.[6] About one half of all hospital beds in the United States are allotted to patients suffering from nervous or mental diseases. Of course, most patients in mental hospitals are incapacitated for long periods of time whereas the average patient of a general hospital remains only about two weeks.

The many seriously maladjusted persons around us are an important subject of study for the purpose of preventing mental disease and also because we all meet peculiarly behaving people whom we would like to understand. Undoubtedly you have had some annoying experiences with fellow employees or students in college whom you consider queer, or sullen, overconscientious, oversuggestible, mentally twisted, disturbing, misfit, sexually perverted, and so on. How did their personalities become warped? What might be done, if anything, to help them?

If problem personalities are the result not merely of our complex civilization but of more deep-seated mental habits, how can we approach the study of the causes of their ailments? What facts and points of view are needed by executives and parents to facilitate the development of strong personalities in employees and children? How can you and I direct our own mental habits in order to have mental health? Perhaps we should begin our study of mental ailments by first noting their place among all human illnesses.

All human illnesses may be classified into the following groups:

A. *Organic.* The tissues have been impaired.
  1. Traumatic—Mechanical injuries or wounds, such as broken bones or cuts.
  2. Toxic—Poisons in the body, such as alcohol or drugs.
  3. Micro-organic, popularly called bacterial—Germ infections or such diseases as smallpox, typhoid fever, and colds.
  4. Glandular—Some of these are discussed in Chapter 7.
  5. Tissue changes—Cancer, tumor, arteriosclerosis, etc.
  6. Psychoses, organic—So far as insanity is concerned, approximately 42 per cent of the cases are caused by organic conditions. These diseases with their percentages of total admissions are mainly senile dementia (8%), cerebral arteriosclerosis (10%), general paresis (7%), and alcoholic psychoses (5%). In these disorders a definite physical or organic basis is known to be present. In business, these organically caused disorders are seen in the occa-

---

[6] "The Chances of Becoming Mentally Ill," *Statistical Bulletin,* Metropolitan Life Insurance Company, 1937, Vol. 18, No. 7, pp. 5-8.

sional cases of brain tumor, epilepsy, sleeping sickness, strokes, general paresis or syphilis of the central nervous system, hardening of the arteries, and senile dementia.

B. *Functional.* These ailments do not involve any measurable impairment of the tissues. About 58 per cent of all psychopathic or mentally ill cases appear to have a functional origin and cause.

1. Psychoses, functional—Pronounced mental disturbances, which unfit the individual for adjustment to his usual environment, principally dementia praecox (22%), manic-depressive psychoses (16%), involutional melancholia (2%), psychopathic personalities (1%), and others.[7] These ailments usually require institutional treatment.

2. Psychoneuroses—Mild mental disturbances or patterns of behavior which do not wholly unfit the individual for his usual environment. The most common examples are neurasthenia and psychasthenia. Often called "nervous cases" in business offices.

3. Common minor maladjustments—These are found among normal persons and are maladjustments only when the extremely inappropriate manifestations handicap the individual in life. Examples of terms used for some common maladjustments are:

    a. Compensatory mechanisms—"If I can't be a big businessman, I can be big in some side line."

    b. Oedipus complex—"If I can't succeed in business, mother will love me anyway."

    c. Identification—"Before I do anything, I always ask myself what my movie hero would want me to do."

    d. Regression—"If I can't be a big businessman, I can daydream of a former happy state."

    e. Fixed ideas—"You must do it my way."

    f. Negativism—"No, this is no good. No, you're wrong."

    g. Conquering hero mechanism—"Just watch me. I'm going to be a world beater."

    h. The suffering hero mechanism—"Just note the fact that I am superior to you because I have had more hard luck."

    i. Projection—"It's the other fellow's fault."

    j. Introjection—"I'm perfectly satisfied where I am."

    k. Phobias—"I'm afraid."

    l. Habit spasms—"People will notice my twitches."

---

[7] The percentages of total admissions, given in parentheses above, should be differentiated from vital statistics of this kind which usually show first admissions, readmissions, and resident population in state mental hospitals. The percentages in parentheses total only 73 per cent because of difficulty in classifying 27 per cent of all patients who are placed under headings such as "other psychoses." For more complete information on this topic, see latest annual report, *Patients in Hospitals for Mental Disease* (Bureau of the Census, Washington, D. C.). The percentages of total admissions given in parentheses are taken from Table I in Carney Landis and James D. Page, *Modern Society and Mental Disease* (Farrar & Rinehart, 1938). Their table is based upon data from *Patients in Hospitals for Mental Disease, 1933* (Bureau of the Census, U S. Government Printing Office, Washington, D. C., 1935).

m. Sexual anomalies, such as homosexuality, masturbation, sadism, masochism, and exhibitionism.

n. Invalidism—"I'm too sick to do much."

Most persons need not concern themselves about the organic psychoses—the severe breakdowns of the human machinery; nor with the functional psychoses—the extreme cases of mismanagement of one's self. The physician and psychiatrist must deal with these. In a brief survey of this kind, we must relegate cases which require hospital or institutional treatment to experts who specialize in those problems. Every person, particularly the executive, has frequent dealings with the psychoneuroses and minor maladjustments. At times every person exhibits symptoms of abnormality, in a mild degree, as 100 per cent management is not common to individuals any more than it is to businesses. "Qualitatively, we are all about the same; quantitatively, we differ widely." This old saying simply means that we all have the same general qualities or traits but we differ in the extent or degree to which we have them.

The human being operates in as natural a manner as do other parts of the physical world. Every human act could be understood if we knew all the pertinent facts. True, we do not know all the important facts needed to understand each person, but we believe that a person's behavior is no more mysterious than the operation of an automobile. To understand an individual we need a pattern for our thinking. Furthermore, we need a pattern for our thinking which is far more meaningful than a mere classification of the individual's behavior. Classifying a person's behavior does not help him; it usually merely annoys him.

A classification of human ailments such as the ones we have listed is somewhat convenient for discussion purposes and record, but we need a scheme of thinking that is more meaningful in handling people. A human being is a living, responding organism and can be understood only when we visualize him as an active, adjusting personality that evolves over a period of years. This means specifically that we can gain little help from statements such as "He has an inferiority complex," or "That's a defense mechanism." Such terms should be used mainly as points of departure for our thinking.

Nor is a knowledge of hereditary factors of much value to anyone who deals with problem persons. We may know, for example, that if one parent has a certain mental disease, the expectancy rate of mental disease for the offspring is 16 per cent, while, if both parents are so afflicted, the expectancy rate for the children is 68 per cent. This knowledge does not help us in practical situations, because we are always dealing with a specific individual. For example, if we know that both parents of a person have a particular mental ailment, is the subject of our analysis a member of the 68 per cent group who become afflicted or the 32 per cent group who never do become afflicted? Such statistics are of little aid to the educational advisor or the employment man. Often a knowledge of them does much harm, because the man who guides his human relations by means of statistics only is apt to be unfair to the many people to whom the figures do not apply.

Furthermore, many vital statistics have a kind of fatalistic effect on the individual to whom they seem to apply in part. He assumes that, his ancestry being what it is, there is little that he can do about or for himself through his own intelligent effort. This is a most unfortunate notion because everyone can direct his own psychological development to a surprisingly great extent.

A knowledge of environment has some value in dealing with people but only a very limited value when we deal with a person. The old arguments about heredity versus environment are usually beside the point because the individual is not a sum of the two. He is the *product* of the two in interaction. The individual is not a rubber stamp of his background. Rather, he is more like a live rubber ball. He not only rolls in the grooves of his environment but he also bounces away from parts of it. And, like those of a football, his "bounces" are often unpredictable, though a knowledge of the field or area where the "bounce" takes place often enables the experienced observer to predict the direction of some of the "bounces."

Sometimes a football bounces just as one would expect; at other times it veers off in a wholly unexpected direction. On some few occasions, too, it scarcely bounces at all but comes to rest very quickly. This football analogy is somewhat helpful whenever we study a person's environment. To understand any

FIG. 12. "I simply can't stand being cooped up here any longer!" Illustration
after Ralph Fuller. The environment is incidental; the way the individual adjusts
to the environment is most important. *Reproduced by special permission from the
artist and* The Saturday Evening Post (*November 25, 1933 issue*), *copyright 1933 by*
The Curtis Publishing Company.

individual in relation to his environment, we should ask three
general questions:

1. *To what influences of the environment did he learn to react
as expected?* That is, what influences has he adopted? Which
ones does he now follow habitually in his life? For example, if

he was reared on a farm, does he have a typical farmer's work habits and points of view? Or, if he was reared in the home of a Democrat, is he a Democrat? If he was reared in the slums, does he feel at home in the slums?

2. *To what influences of the environment did he learn to react in an unexpected or opposing manner?* For example, if he was reared on a farm, does he now despise farming and rural life? Similarly, does he dislike Democrats, and does he feel out of place in the slums?

3. *What influences of the environment might ordinarily be expected to affect the personality but have really had no effect?* Some people fail to react to certain influences in terms of acceptance or rejection; they react neither favorably nor unfavorably. Some farmers' sons grow up and neither like nor dislike the farm. The same principle can be noted when we study any person's background. His early environmental history may have had very little effect on many of his present habits.

These three concepts regarding the environment—*acceptance, rejection,* and *indifference*—compel us to seek for more than a knowledge of the peculiar person's environment.

The employment man who collects bulging files of data about his applicants should know how to organize and interpret the data. The college personnel man who has extensive card records of facts about each student needs a method of viewing the facts. The parent who learns the hundreds of incidents in the development of his children needs a pattern for his thinking in order to arrange the facts into psychological significance. Anyone who associates with people in business, in school, or in their homes should have a systematic approach to the interpretation of human personalities. The approach described here is known as the adjustment concept.

The adjustment concept. We can, if we wish, explain human behavior by many different systems of thinking, as shown by the several schools of thought in modern psychology. Each school makes its unique contributions by virtue of the fact that, when we study anything in terms of a given system of thinking, we often gain a new perspective of related matters. This particular system of thinking, the adjustment concept, is used by this writer because it is easily grasped and is most meaningful to persons who do not plan to become highly trained psychologists through years of graduate work in clinics and universities.

To understand a person, we may first think of him as in a state of activity. He is always active, whether he is sleeping, thinking, daydreaming, resting, playing, or working. Even dying is an activity. Some ongoing activities are always present, because the motive of life is to function. For us to think of a living individual who is totally inactive would be impossible, for he would be frozen, mummified, or calcified. Basic to our thinking of human beings is the point of view of interaction, the adjustment concept. To say that an individual is always active and that through his activity he develops may be trite, but to appreciate how a personality grows in the adjustment process is not always so simple as it sounds.

In his activities, the individual is always trying to achieve a satisfying state. In his functioning, his activity frequently is blocked or delayed by difficulties or barriers, and so he must learn how to overcome the difficulties or go around them.

A woodsman exploring in a forest exemplifies the adjustment idea. When he finds an obstruction in his path, he may use direct attack upon it, that is, remove it or go through it. Or he may go around it by means of a substitute or indirect route. Or he may decide to make a different kind of exploration, or even return to his home and do no more exploring at all.

Obviously, if the woodsman has once used a route, he will be apt to use it on the second and succeeding trips over the territory. He may use an old route even though he has found a better or easier one. An important part of the concept is that the woodsman does, at times, make new paths as a result of obstructions in his way. The barriers, often called frustrations, cause him to develop new mental habits and new urges to act.

Let us apply this barrier-adjustment idea to a few everyday situations. Assume that you are a student who is sitting comfortably in class and looking forward to a pleasant school experience. Suddenly the instructor announces an examination on some part of the course which you do not understand. You are annoyed by the barrier to your pleasant ongoing activity. You

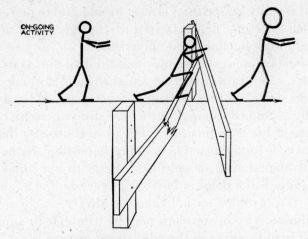

FIG. 13. *Adjustment by direct attack upon the barrier or problem.* The individual is in a state of ongoing activity, such as attending college. He finds that he must take a difficult examination. He studies diligently for the examination and overcomes the difficulty. If he fails in his first attempt, he persists until he succeeds.

The original goal is kept and the successful adjustment tends to build up the ego—the individual's feeling of self-worth. His personality is strengthened and he is, to that extent, better prepared to meet future problems that involve volitional effort.

must make an adjustment. The adjustment you make will be one or more of the four general varieties:

1. *Direct attack.* Examples:
    (a) Study for the examination.
    (b) Prepare for the examination by having someone quiz you on the accuracy of your present knowledge.
    (c) Outline the subject matter, recite to yourself all parts which you understand, and learn the important parts which are not clear to you.

2. *Substitute act.* Examples:
    (a) Change to another course.
    (b) Transfer to another school.
    (c) Decide to quit school and find a job in the business world.

3. *Evasion.* Examples:
    (a) Arrange to sit near a good student who will help you during the examination.
    (b) Prepare a "crib" for the examination.
    (c) Feign illness at the time of the examination and thus postpone or avoid taking it at the designated time.
    (d) Accuse the teacher of unfairness.
    (e) Berate or ridicule the students who study for the examination.

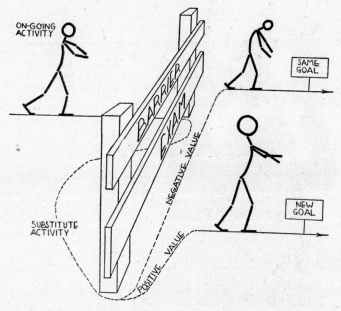

Fig. 14. *Adjustment by substitute activities, negative and positive.* In the lower part of the diagram, the positive substitute activity type is represented in terms of a new goal. Instead of taking the difficult examination, the student decides to quit college and go into business. His ego may or may not remain the same, depending upon the extent to which the original goal was associated with pleasant emotional patterns.

In the upper part of the diagram, the evasive substitute activity type is represented in terms of the original goal but achieved through subterfuge. This adjustment weakens the personality and lessens the feeling of self-worth. The reacting person's ability to meet similar problems has been decreased by the latter adjustment.

4. *Retreat.* Examples:
    (a) Imagine yourself the hero of fiction or motion picture adventures and ignore your problem.
    (b) Contemplate suicide.

Of course, the student who deals with the examination barrier by *direct attack* also prepares himself to deal more effectively with new or later examinations in the same and other courses. He builds up efficient study habits. His ego or feeling of self-worth is increased in a sound way. He achieves a more satisfying state. His personality is stronger than it was previous to his dealing with the barrier.

A *substitute act,* at times, may be a more logical adjustment than direct attack. Although the decision to choose a substitute act may result in a feeling of failure with regard to the barrier

Fig. 15. *Adjustment by retreat.* From a photograph of a state hospital patient whose emotional life has been turned wholly inward. He lives in a world of fantasy rather than of reality. His adjustment is of the retreat type.

ON-GOING ACTIVITY
SUCH AS ATTENDING COLLEGE

DAY DREAM

BARRIER
EXAM

RETREAT

thus avoided, it is likely to cause the individual to put extra energy into the substitute act. Not every student who fails in his school work and decides to go into business works harder in business than he did in school, but some do. A sense of failure in one field may stimulate the individual to put forth extra effort in another field.

The student who chooses to make an *evasive* adjustment weakens himself for the next problem. His ability has been lessened. The evasive experience has weakened his personality.

Retreat, of course, is an extreme degree of evasion and tends to develop weaknesses which may bring about a psychopathic personality. Habitual retreat eventually results in institutionalization.

Obviously, no person makes direct attack or intelligent substitute act adjustments in every situation. Everyone uses evasion and retreat at times, but the strong personality tends to use the first two habitually and the weak man ordinarily uses the latter two in dealing with life's problems.

If a given adjustment habit is once firmly established, it is easily repeated in dealing with the same or related barriers. Adjustments begin very early in life and are made every day until the end of life. Each time we deal with a problem, great or small, we contribute toward or detract from the effectiveness of our personalities. The employee who has worked in an unsatisfactory position for a year, a day, or even an hour is no longer quite the same employee that he was when he first began to work. In the course of his employment he has developed new mental habits or tendencies toward new habits. In his reacting he may have acquired either hatred or admiration for a department manager, or for certain kinds of work.

To repeat the adjustment concept, but to apply it to the worker who finds himself in an uncongenial job, the following outline elaborates the idea further:

1. *Direct attack.* Examples:
   - (a) Study the mechanical equipment used in the work, if any is used. Improve its design or invent new equipment.
   - (b) Study methods of doing the work. Practice the methods and improve them.
   - (c) Study the fellow workers and improve the human relationships. Influence the fellow employees and supervisors in order to have them like him as well as enjoy their work more fully.

2. *Substitute act.* Examples:
   - (a) Obtain or continue to seek a transfer to another job.
   - (b) Obtain or continue to seek employment elsewhere.
   - (c) Compensate for dissatisfaction through a hobby, athletics, church work, art, etc.

3. *Evasion.* Examples:
   - (a) Criticise the job, the boss, the fellow workers, or industry as a whole.
   - (b) Feign illness or, as a result of subconscious maladjustment, become too ill to work.

(c) Adopt an air of superiority toward the job.
(d) Feel inferior in the job and avoid thoughts of the work as much as possible.

4. *Retreat*. Examples:
(a) Daydream of his happy childhood.
(b) Imagine himself wealthy or famous or important.
(c) Immerse himself in some mystical cult or pseudo-science such as a Hindu philosophy, astrology, palmistry, etc.
(d) Isolate himself and avoid any possible failure by making no attempts to change his status.
(e) Long for death and release from all life's problems.

The worker who habitually deals by direct attack with the problems of his job increases his ability to deal with more difficult jobs. He may never attain any famed expertness, but he tends to feel in control of himself in relation to the problems around him. He earns his own self-respect. He finds that life offers him many opportunities for growth and genuine happiness. He is confident about the future. Furthermore, in the process of adjusting himself to the barriers in his job, he acquires new behavior patterns, such as a dislike for certain types of supervision or certain kinds of work that are associated with his annoying experiences. Through pleasant experiences he also develops satisfying associations.

Predisposing and precipitating influences. Every person has many *predisposing tendencies* when confronted by a new problem. He may be young in years but he is "old" psychologically. He is a member of a human race which is really millions of years of age in terms of biological influences. Furthermore, his bodily equipment—sex, size, glands, muscular and other structures—all contribute predisposing influences in behavior. *Conditionings* from (a) a single intense emotional experience such as a fright or (b) from repeated experiences of the same kind, such as customs, habits, beliefs, education, parental training, and the whole culture where he has lived, are additional predisposing influences. These have affected him over relatively long periods of time.

Precipitating factors are influences which act over a short period of time. These are likely to be emotional or exciting states such as a recent threat, thwarted habit, ridicule, failure, success, fatigue or disappointment. Obviously, the child who has just been scolded is likely to react to frustration somewhat differently from the way he would act at another time.

No one can unravel all the strands in the web of human personality. Life is too complex. We can, however, collect available facts about ourselves or others and try to see how the known facts arrange themselves into patternful relationships. A knowledge of psychology and the ability to use intelligently such concepts as adjustment often contribute to the art of dealing with people. It is especially useful to those who have counseling, guidance, or executive responsibilities. A starting point in this kind of analysis of a person is the sources of frustration or barriers.

Barriers. When we note the peculiar behavior of a maladjusted individual, we observe his peculiarity and then try to think of the way it originated. We try to think of the person's problems.

The sources of frustration in the lives of different individuals vary greatly, but we can mention typical barriers that necessitate adjustment. The problems or difficulties that stimulate the individual to seek adjustment may be a part of the external environment or within the personality. The particular nature of the barrier is not especially important. Any environmental situation or characteristic of a person may constitute a barrier. The important factor is the meaning of the situation or characteristic to the individual who is adjusting. A feeling of resentment, inadequacy, or inferiority toward the situation often indicates the presence of a barrier.

The two broad classes of barriers are (a) lack of capacity and (b) those which require abrupt changes in behavior. Obvious examples of capacity difficulties that demand adjustment are organic or physical conditions such as poor health or a crippled limb. Or there may be a chronic ailment or disability such as asthma, tuberculosis, heart murmur, epilepsy, color-blindness, or flat feet.

In the mental group may be found capacity problems such as phobias, low general intelligence, specific inaptitudes, emotional conflicts, bad habits, feelings of insecurity, lack of opportunity for training, and convictions of one's inferiority. Perhaps the most common personal difficulties are those which result from a lack of recognition for sincere efforts. This last type often occurs among children and students who think that they are doing well and then later find through comparisons with others that they appear to be inferior.

Bodily and mental punishment may accentuate the feelings of inadequacy. Many an adult introvert represents the effects of too many or too severe lashings of rod or tongue by the parent of the child. Any activity or situation may become a barrier if the individual is given punishment, neglect, or no approval in connection with it. Conversely, any activity may be satisfying if praise and prestige follow or accompany the activity.

Environmental barriers may be poverty, inhibiting customs or laws, and lack of opportunity for expression of the biological tendencies. However, the barrier objectively considered is not nearly so important as the interpretation that the person gives it. The same situation that is a barrier to one person may be a challenge or an opportunity to another. Among nations, a sterile soil and a harsh climate may result in the development of a virile nation, whereas a land of plentiful resources may have a race of fruitless people. Similarly, a poverty-stricken home may stimulate a child to achieve eminence while the son of the rich man on the hill becomes a weakling. It is significant that neither the poor boy nor the rich boy necessarily becomes strong or weak. The way each adjusts to his situation determines whether he will be strong or weak.

Nor can we hope to remove all difficulties from the life of anyone. To do so would only handicap him for life as it is. As Herbert Spencer said: "The ultimate result of shielding men from the effects of folly is to fill the world with fools."

Throughout infancy, childhood, youth, and adulthood, the individual is constantly bombarded by experiences in which he is shown his inferiorities and inadequacies. For many people, a few experiences of inadequacy cause them to develop habits, through their adjustments, which make ordinary activities such as the study of certain school subjects very difficult. Reasons for many inabilities and peculiarities can be traced to the early experiences of the child.

One girl could not be convinced that she was pretty enough to make a favorable impression on others. She had two sisters who were praised frequently for their beauty. One day a wealthy aunt visited the home and again praised the two sisters for their beauty. On one occasion, however, the aunt realized that she should make a favorable comment regarding the plain child and so she said to her: "And you, my dear, have a kind face." In spite of the fact that many people would rather have a kind face than mere beauty, this girl, who is now a woman, prefers work that isolates her from other people, especially those who are attractive in appearance. Any vocation that would require emphasis upon personal beauty or attractive attire is out of the question for her. She has given up all hope of making herself attractive to others.

Any situation may be a barrier to one person but a means of satisfaction to another. Personal appearance became a great barrier to the above-mentioned girl because her own appearance was associated with feelings of inferiority. However, to some women their personal appearance is an outstanding means of attaining satisfactions. Similarly, the study of music is a barrier to many children whose parents compel them to practice on the piano for hours. To other children, music is the one satisfying outlet for self-expression. Hundreds of school subjects, jobs, and activities are "meat for some and poison for others." The nature of the activity is incidental. What the activity means, represents, symbolizes, or is associated within the mind of the individual is the important factor.

Tasks that are easy to perform tend to be satisfying but are not necessarily so. Tasks that are difficult to perform tend to be annoying but are not necessarily so. Many students can learn certain school subjects far more easily than their classmates but prefer to study other subjects that are more difficult for them. Many housewives can do their housework with ease but they dislike it. Many employees can do the tasks in their jobs with ease but prefer to change their vocations. We should not assume that easily performed acts are always satisfying.

How executives contribute to the better adjustments of employees. Every executive can, and many do, facilitate the direct attack adjustments of individual employees. The executive may apply the adjustment concept when he finds that a salesman's volume has fallen off suddenly in a territory where the business activity of other companies has increased.

The manner of the failing salesman may indicate that something is bothering him. The astute manager tends to make inquiries regarding the failing salesman's habits, health, home conditions, and so on. If he finds that the salesman's wife has learned to consider her husband's job a socially inferior one since her nagging mother moved into the home, the manager can discuss the situation sympathetically and prove that the husband's job is important. A few special assignments that include a title may be all that is necessary to build up the salesman's self-respect and social prestige with the wife and mother-in-law.

Psychological insight and skill are applied in business whenever an executive feels with, thinks with, and works with employees who have disturbing emotional problems. The executive may not be able to give a technical psychological name to the employee's variety of maladjustment, but if he discovers the bothersome problem, notes the kind of evasive adjustment being made, and then instills confidence in the employee by showing him the possible direct-attack methods, the employee's behavior is likely to improve.

The adjustment concept causes us to recognize that we should not think of an employee as *being* this or that—as, for example, being conceited or sarcastic when dealing with difficult customers. The individual is not conceited or sarcastic, but he *uses* conceit or sarcasm when dealing with another personality. He has acquired the habit of using certain evasive methods, "personality tools," when dealing with other personalities.

Similarly, when an executive's stenographer becomes irritable, the psychologically minded executive tries to discover her problem. Perhaps her father has lost his job and makes little attempt to find another because he assumes that his employed daughter will support him. Or the girl's boy friend may have become interested in someone else. Or any one of thousands of other problems may have occurred, each of which might necessitate that the stenographer make an adjustment. During the process of adjustment, the insight and encouragement of the executive may be very helpful.

Of course, many men have attained the kind of growth characterized by the personality tools of direct attack and intelligent substitute acts even though they have never studied psychology. The psychologists have simply clarified the process of adjustment so that people who lack psychological insight may the more quickly acquire it.

We admire direct-attack adjustments. The human race has progressed because heroic individuals have used positive adjustments in the face of adverse situations. Most outstanding men have had difficult problems that required exceptional persistence in the use of direct attack. A remarkable example is Dan W. Boggs. While a young man, he was sentenced to life imprisonment at hard labor in the Ohio State Penitentiary. The first ten months he worked in the shirt shop. Then he managed to be transferred to the prison library, when an event occurred that made him determine to help his family. Let him tell the story:

Though I was getting along as nicely as could be expected, those near and dear to me were suffering. My father, who for some time had been failing in health and financially, suffered a stroke of paralysis. The doctors feared he would go completely blind. With Warden Thomas' permission, I spent a few hours at father's bedside.

All through the visit I could see that something was worrying him. Finally he explained that he feared for the welfare of my mother and sisters should anything serious happen to him. Not knowing how I was going to do it, I promised to look after them, if he were called to the Great Beyond. This promise eased his mind.

So I returned to the grim gray walls with a great deal more responsibility on my shoulders than I knew how to carry.

The next question was: How *could* I help? That was what worried me. Talk about being helpless! In prison for life—and penniless—that *is* a deuce of a fix. But when a fellow *has* to do a thing, generally there's a way, if he'll just try. . . .

Call it Luck, Chance, Fate—or what-have-you. Certainly it was a "lucky break" for me when a fellow-inmate showed me an article in *Postage,* telling how Louis Victor Eytinge, a prisoner in the Arizona penitentiary, had learned advertising and won fame by writing sales literature. Eytinge was called "The Man Who Came Back.". . .

Well, the next step was to get an advertising course and learn the business from the ground up. That's exactly what I did. But getting that course in advertising would have been *some job* for "yours truly" had it not been for the warden and the chaplain, for I was plumb broke, as flat as last year's tires. They arranged with the State Educational Department and the International Correspondence Schools to purchase courses on almost any beneficial subject desired. So I got mine in advertising.

That was the beginning of my career in the advertising business. But man. Oh, man! It didn't tell me a thing about all the hell I'd have to go through before I ever made a nickel out of the business. Nor did it reveal that I was going to spend month after month of worry, and endanger my health, by studying too much and working too hard under adverse circumstances. . . .

Anyone who likes to study can accomplish a lot, if everything is comfortable and quiet, where they can concentrate on the subject. But studying here is different! Generally, in the adjoining cell on the left, a jazz-king is playing Yankee Doodle on a squawking Victrola; in the right-hand apartment, a radio fiend is capturing all the beautiful static on the air; above, on the next range, perches a musical genius trying his best to pull sounds out of an old accordion; and three other fellows in the same cell are all trying to talk at once. A fine chance for a fellow who has to concentrate on studying and composing letters to tell a few thousand prospects why they should use a certain suction pump or get their shoes repaired at a certain cobbler's inn. Still, it *can* be done if you *want* to do it!

Because of this confusion, before the lights would go out at 9:15 each night, I could not study and get the most out of it, so I often stayed up until 12 or 1 o'clock to study after the other prisoners were in bed. This could be done by moving the book back and forth in the small shaft of light that filtered through the latticed steel bars. After a short siege of such study, I became thin and weak. Because of ill-health, I was transferred to the hospital as night nurse. There I could better care for myself by getting out into the fresh air evenings.

I kept on studying, harder than ever. Sometimes, instead of exercising, I went upstairs to delve deep into the realms of advertising at my desk of store-boxes.

Such persistence was bound to be rewarded. Finally I began making money. My prospects were convinced that I could write productive advertising literature. My one aim, above all, was to please. Often I wrote copy over and over again to get it just right. Thus far I have never had a dissatisfied customer. Most of them praise my advertising work and come back for more.

Here are a few illustrations:

My receipts have totaled more than $18,000. The most taken in during any one month was about $500. Since father died, about two years ago, I have supported my mother and several small sisters. An editor of a mail-order trade journal has hired me to write one advertising and business article a month for a year; another has hired me to conduct an Advertising Consultation Department in his magazine, a business trade journal; another magazine in the financial field has offered a position as Advertising Manager, which I was unable to accept, because of being unable to leave my present abode.[8]

During the eleven years Dan Boggs spent in prison, he managed to train himself and succeed in a vocation where competition is unusually keen. Many of his clients were surprised when they learned that he was a prisoner; but he is now a free man, the governor having pardoned him. At present he has two business offices, one in Columbus and another in Lancaster, Ohio.

Adjustments are more important than environment. From the standpoint of the incidence of mental disease, as discussed in

---

[8] Dan W. Boggs, "A 'Lifer' Borrowed $3 to Go into Business—and 'Broke' Jail," *Trained Men,* Spring, 1936.

the early part of this chapter, the adjustment concept means that the environment is often an incidental part in our important mental habits. The environment may be paced slowly or rapidly and be relatively simple or complex. The individual's adjustment to the pace, whatever it is, is what counts. In other words, it is just as easy to drive an automobile at fifty miles an hour as to drive a horse at twenty—once the driver has learned the art. The art of living is an individual matter and must be learned by the individual regardless of when or where he lives.

Whenever we compare the lives of those who succeeded in dealing with the conditions of life with those who have failed, we find that the strong persons developed good adjustment habits and the failures developed evasive and retreat habits. The same observation applies to the people of a nation. The strength of a nation does not wholly depend upon natural resources nor on geographical location but mainly upon the strength of personality of its people. We need only compare the resources and people of the various nations, as, for example, Switzerland versus Russia, to see ample evidence of this axiom. The leaders and citizens of the United States must recognize this basic truth or suffer through the lack of its application. If too many individuals learn to lean upon charity or other artificial aids rather than upon their own strong adjustment habits, this nation will become weaker and the eventual prey of the stronger. This means that everyone, regardless of race, culture, or age, can benefit from a thorough study of the adjustment process in order to guide his own adjustments intelligently.

One purpose of education in general and of psychology in particular is to assist the individual in learning those adjustment habits which are of the direct-attack and positive variety. You and I, as laymen in the field of mental hygiene, can do very little to assist the psychotic, but we can do a great deal toward the development of sound mental habits in ourselves and our associates.

Tables V and VI will enable the reader to see a general outline of the adjustment concept. This list of barriers and adjustments is not intended to be exhaustive, nor is any one item of behavior supposed to be fixed regarding its classification. As previously stated, any variety of behavior can be classified only in relation to its context or setting. However, a brief examination of these tables should help the reader in developing an alertness to the kinds of adjustment which he can observe in his everyday experiences.

TABLE V

EXAMPLES OF BARRIERS TO WHICH THE INDIVIDUAL ADJUSTS

I. "Capacity" barriers:

    A. *Insufficient capacity* to perform satisfactorily the activities that others expect the individual to perform or that he himself expects to perform:

        1. Organic or physical:
            a. Poor health.
            b. Atypical body shape or size.
            c. Endocrine imbalance.
            d. Lack of athletic ability.
            e. Defective sensory equipment, such as deafness.
            f. Defective motor equipment, such as stiff joints.
            g. Unattractive personal appearance, real or fancied.

        2. Intellectual:
            a. Intelligence too low; for example, inability to do satisfactory school work or to handle jobs requiring brain work.
            b. Ability evaluated too high; for example, individual's parent expects him to be an honor student or an accomplished musician.
            c. Specific inabilities, such as lack of ability in mathematics.

        3. Social:
            a. Lack of friends and inability to make friends.
            b. Lack of ability to maintain ego in the face of bullying, ridicule, snubs, nicknames, and so forth.
            c. Competing with superiors; for example, an average student rooms with a bragging superior student.

    B. *Capacity too great* for required or present activities:

        1. Rating of individual's capacity by parent, teacher, mental examiner, or supervisor much lower than it actually is.
        2. Constant association with inferiors in education, health, or social development.
        3. Environment unstimulating, as among children of foreigners and among fellow workers who set poor examples; working hours too long for normal development, and so forth.

II. Barriers arising from a *change* in activities:

    A. Barriers arising because the individual is compelled to change his activities *abruptly:*

        1. Birth of another child in a family in which the individual was an only child and a transfer of affection from the older child to the newborn.
        2. Adoption into a strange family.
        3. Death of a loved person.
        4. Sex experiences that occurred too early in life and could not be continued satisfactorily.
        5. Disappointment in love; betrayal of confidence.

    6. Conflicts in love that require immediate adjustment.
    7. Sudden change from a higher to a lower standard of living.
    8. Sudden change from a lower to a higher standard of living.
    9. Loss of a job; new job not satisfactory.

B. Barriers resulting from the individual's *lack of training or preparation* to meet his problems and his being thus compelled to accept new activities:
    1. Normal associations with other children forbidden by parents; consequently, child or adult now adapts himself to new environments or contacts with great difficulty.
    2. Puritanical, austere, or unsympathetic parents.
    3. Parents who have been too lenient and have not trained their child to solve adult problems, such as the wise spending of money, the acquisition of proper habits, freedom of choice, etc.
    4. Teachers who do not understand their pupils.
    5. Disinterest of parents in the child; broken home; mother who is employed or who is interested in other activities more than in the child's development.
    6. Compulsion to continue an unwanted education or to study subjects of no interest, such as music, languages, etc.
    7. Compulsion to take an unsatisfactory job.
    8. Association with superiors in studies or in work.
    9. Association with persons of greater wealth, refinement, ability, or charm, and a feeling of inferiority caused by the differences.
    10. Association with others of assumed superior race or nationality.

C. Barriers arising from the *continuance of activities* that should have been superseded by other activities:
    1. Remaining in a social environment too long for personal development.
    2. Remaining in a job too long.
    3. Continuation into adulthood of inefficient or childish habits, such as poor study habits, lisping, temper tantrums, sullenness.
    4. Continuation into adulthood of childhood emotional tendencies, such as parent fixations: *Oedipus complex, Electra complex.*
    5. Clinging to outmoded religious creeds that are not in harmony with new experiences—a condition found among some college students.

D. Frequent *interruptions* of ongoing activities:
    1. Frequent change of school.
    2. Frequent changes in the home.
    3. Frequent changes of home town.
    4. Frequent shiftings of tasks or of instructions in work.
    5. Reprimands by superiors.
    6. Naggings by mate.
    7. Frequent inhibition of desired acts that are not approved by society and the aroused energy of which is not directed into satisfying channels but accumulates from repeated thwartings.

TABLE VI

Examples of Adjustment Activities of the Individual

I. Adjustment by *direct attack* upon the problem:
A. As applied to any problem:
    1. Repeated attempts to solve the problem.
    2. Stoicism.

TABLE VI *(Cont.)*

    3. Enjoyment of difficulty.
    4. Refusal to accept defeat.
    5. Admission of the problem, recognition of its true nature, and treatment of it through intelligence and insight.

  B. As applied to an employee's situation when he wishes to grow through his work:
    1. Study and improve the equipment of the job.
    2. Study and improve the methods of work.
    3. Study the fellow workers and improve the human relationships.

II. *Positive substitute activities* that often enable the individual to go around a barrier or a problem:

  A. Activities in dealing with people:
    1. Doing favors for others.
    2. Taking positions of leadership.
    3. Being active in organizations, such as the church, a club, a lodge.
    4. Being socially popular.
    5. Speaking in public.
    6. Attending social functions.
    7. Debating.
    8. Making new acquaintances.
    9. "Playing politics."
    10. Playing games with people.
    11. Analyzing others.
    12. Supervising others.
    13. Associating with inferiors.
    14. Associating with superiors.
    15. Doing stunts or tricks.
    16. Persuading people.
    17. Selling things to people.
    18. Entertaining or amusing others.
    19. Improving or correcting others.
    20. Helping those who are weaker.
    21. Taking care of children.
    22. Impressing the opposite sex.
    23. Seeking the approval of others.
    24. Teaching others.
    25. Identification with another personality.

  B. Intellectual activities:
    1. Studying.
    2. Developing money-making schemes.
    3. Collecting stamps, books, and so forth.
    4. Creative writing.
    5. Creating mechanically.
    6. Inventing new systems, such as for production control.
    7. Studying and developing philosophies.

  C. Physical or manual activities:
    1. Mechanical work.
    2. Household work, such as sewing, cooking, etc.
    3. Physical labor.
    4. Outdoor work.
    5. Athletic activities.

  D. Emotional activities:
    1. Painting, or studying art.
    2. Studying music, vocal or instrumental.
    3. Writing or reading poetry.
    4. Religious activities.
    5. Impersonating others, acting.
    6. Symbolical behavior.

III. *Negative substitute* or *evasive* activities:

  A. Handicaps to the individual:
    1. Criticizing others.
    2. Annoying or teasing others.
    3. Rowdyism.
    4. Bullying.
    5. Air of superiority
    6. Bluffing, conceit.
    7. Cynicism.
    8. Sarcasm.
    9. Argumentative responses.
    10. Refusal to make decision.

B. Mere annoyance to others, or not positively developmental when carried to extreme degree:

1. Distinctive mannerisms.	10. Fictionizing.
2. "Show-off" behavior.	11. Overagreeableness.
3. Doing tricks or stunts.	12. Travel in order to get away
4. Joining organizations merely	from difficulties.
"to belong."	13. Exaggerated attempts to im-
5. Mimicry.	press the opposite sex.
6. Personal adornment.	14. Attending movies frequently.
7. Emphasis on clothing.	15. Excessive reading of fiction.
8. Talkativeness.	16. Ancestry worship.
9. Exaggeration.	

C. Serious evasive habits indicating minor maladjustments.

1. Excessive daydreaming.	5. Invalidism.
2. Regression.	6. Sulkiness.
3. Projection.	7. Introversion.
4. Introjection.	8. Alcoholism.

IV. *Retreat* adjustments:
   A. Solitude, stay-at-home habits to avoid ordinary problems.
   B. Mysticism.
   C. Living in another world—pronounced escape from reality.
   D. Death wish and suicidal tendencies.

References

Guthrie, E. R., *The Psychology of Human Conflict: the Clash of Motives Within the Individual.* Harper & Bros., 1938.

Hepner, H. W., *Human Relations in Changing Industry,* Chapters II and III. Prentice-Hall, Inc., 1934.

————, *Finding Yourself in Your Work,* Chapters I-III. D. Appleton-Century Co., 1937.

Landis, Carney, and James D. Page, *Modern Society and Mental Disease.* Farrar & Rinehart, 1938.

Malzberg, Benjamin, "A Statistical Study of Age in Relation to Mental Disease," *Mental Hygiene,* Vol. 19, 1935, pp. 449-476.

Shaffer, Laurance Frederic, *The Psychology of Adjustment,* Chapter V. Houghton Mifflin Co., 1936.

Spencer, Douglas, *Fulcra of Conflict.* World Book Co., 1939.

Projects

1. According to *Science News Letter,* May 7, 1938, a fatigue service for industrial employees has been established at the Neuro-Psychiatric Institute of the Hartford Retreat. Dr. C. Charles Burlingame, psychiatrist-in-chief of the institute, stated:

> These emotional difficulties are quite as incapacitating to the employee as a physical illness, and often more annoying to the industrial organization.
>
> Chronic fatigue, irritability, inability to get along with fellow-workers, feelings of persecution, a chronic state of "being agin' the government," crying for no good reason at all on the job or at home

may be outward evidence of a condition which may so affect the efficiency of the worker that much of his value to himself and to his employer is destroyed.

More progressive employers are beginning to realize the dollars and cents value of finding an answer. This interest is not of the welfare variety which implies a patronizing supplying of uplift facilities, recreational benefits, etc., but rather, an intelligent effort to get at the root of the individual mental disorders, just as industry is going at the problem of the employees' physical health.

(a) Why do you suppose that this service was called a "Fatigue Service"?
(b) If you were an employee of one of the companies in the vicinity of the Fatigue Service, would you be willing to avail yourself of it if you had the symptoms mentioned?
(c) Assume that you are an executive who has a maladjusted employee who should go to the Fatigue Service. What would you say to him in order to have him go there willingly?

2. Hendrik Willem Van Loon was reported as having said:

The purpose of education is to get a perspective of yourself so that you can understand yourself in relation to those around you. It enables you to have an active and pleasant life. It enables you to go through the world with the least amount of friction and a proper amount of understanding. That is all education is supposed to do. . . .

Let's look at our colleges and see what is going on. We find that they are doing little in the way of educating students. The colleges in the United States are simply big play pens where the incompetent can send their children for four years.

(a) Do you agree with Van Loon that colleges "are simply big play pens"?
(b) What evidence can you offer to refute his statement?

3. "Virginia Martin, 18, Salt Lake City, Utah, one-armed stenographer, turned in the only perfect copy during a recent typing contest."—*American Magazine*, February, 1935.
What term would you apply to her adjustment to her handicap?

4. Some sociologists and other students of human behavior believe that the environment alone deserves more recognition as a factor in mental disease than the content of this chapter would indicate. If you wish to investigate this question in order to reach your own conclusions or write a report on the topic, the following references will be useful:
(a) Elsworth Faris, in *The Nature of Human Nature* (McGraw-Hill Book Co.), has a chapter on "Culture and Personality Among the Forest Bantu" (of central Africa) partially summarized as follows:

The Forest Bantu are pre-individualistic. Unwritten mores in a constant and homogeneous stream of influence define the situations and their conduct. No one is forced to take a stand against popular opinion or to stand alone for the right. No one lives alone—and loneliness as modern men know it has not yet come to them. . . .
Inquiries were made at four large hospitals regarding the extent of

schizoid and manic-depressive psychoses. No records or memory of any such cases existed. Certain stereotyped forms of hysteria and manias due to infectious diseases were found, but no insanity. Social life appeared to be the answer. Apparently, sharp competition, feelings of inferiority, the mechanisms of projection and reference, and delusions of persecution belong to a society like ours where the swordfish alone can swim to security. The Bantu always has his friends.

(*b*) Robert E. L. Faris, "Some Observations on the Incidence of Schizophrenia in Primitive Societies," *Journal of Abnormal and Social Psychology,* Vol. 29, 1934, pp. 30-31.

(*c*) Robert E. L. Faris and H. Warren Dunham, *Mental Disorders in Urban Areas.* University of Chicago Press, 1939.

(*d*) G. Devereux, "A Sociological Theory of Schizophrenia," *Psychoanalytical Review,* July 1939.

4

Adjustment by Substitute Activities, Usually of Positive Value

Frustrations and feelings of inadequacy often result in adjustments such as compensation, radicalism, or identification. Certain adjustments, though rather unusual, give the individual the motivation which enables him to apply himself to a life program or vocation. If the object of the motivation becomes a program that serves others in the ways they wish to be served, the motivated person is likely to become successful or even famous.

EDGAR Rice Burroughs, author of the Tarzan stories, is one of the world's most successful writers. His books have been translated into fifty-six languages and dialects. Twenty-five million copies have been sold.

Alva Johnston has given us a psychological analysis of this world-famous writer from which the following paragraphs are taken:

Burroughs is clearly the man to tell the 130,000,000 Americans how to write. His life story ought to be the supreme textbook. The main rules for literary training that can be gathered from the experiences of Burroughs are:

1. Be a disappointed man.
2. Achieve no success at anything you touch.
3. Lead an unbearably drab and uninteresting life.
4. Hate civilization.
5. Learn no grammar.
6. Read little.
7. Write nothing.
8. Have an ordinary mind and commonplace tastes, approximating those of the great reading public.
9. Avoid subjects that you know about.

Burroughs had been an ill-paid employee and an unsuccessful small businessman for fifteen years before he wrote a word of fiction. The great difficulty in basing a college training on his rules is that of compressing into four years all the dullness, wretchedness, and futility which it took Burroughs fifteen years to assimilate.

Burroughs started at twenty as a cattle drover and then became an employee on a gold dredge in Oregon. For a time he was a railroad policeman in Salt Lake City. He put in stretches as an accountant, as a clerk and as a peddler. His most important position was that of head of the stenographic department of Sears-Roebuck, in Chicago. A docile employee, he was never fired. An inveterate reader of help-wanted ads, he was constantly obtaining new positions not quite equal to his old ones. Added to that, he was always ready to join his own pennilessness to the pennilessness of some other man, and to found a partnership on any naive dream of avarice. . . .

During his entire business career he never earned as much as his prep-school allowance. Twice he was compelled to pawn his family heirlooms in order to buy food for his wife and children. His failure as a businessman was so complete that he was reduced to earning a living by writing hints on how to become a successful businessman. . . .

He was too poverty-stricken to pay for any of the tired businessman's relaxations, but he hit upon a free method of making himself feel better. When he went to bed he would lie awake, telling himself stories. His dislike of civilization caused him frequently to pick localities in distant parts of the solar system. Every night he had his one crowded hour of glorious life. Creating noble characters and diabolical monsters, he made them fight in cockpits in the center of the earth or in distant astronomical regions. The duller the day at the office the weirder his nightly adventures. His waking nightmares became long-drawn-out action serials. . . .

Burroughs had given away serials to himself for five years or more before he learned that he could sell them. He had become a master of the slaughter-house branches of fiction.[1]

Obviously, many men have failed in business to the depth reached by Burroughs but they did not happen to adjust to failure in a way which pleased people. Burroughs' adjustment to his problems not only satisfied himself but also satisfied certain psychological needs of the millions of other people who became readers of his books. The important point for us to keep in mind is not that a man has problems or failures but how he adjusts to his barriers, and whether his adjustments have value for other people as well as satisfaction for himself.

Whenever we study the lives of famous men and women, we are likely to find that their chief psychological assets were their adjustments to severe handicaps. Beethoven was handicapped by deafness but wrote some of the world's best music. Byron's clubfoot and his poverty-stricken neurotic parents gave him a

---

[1] Alva Johnston, "How to Become a Great Writer," *The Saturday Evening Post*, July 29, 1939.

sense of inadequacy for which he compensated by writing poetry. Demosthenes and Moses were stutterers and yet both became famous leaders. Benjamin Disraeli suffered from ozena, a degenerative disease of the mucous membrane of the nose that produces a constant stench from the nostrils, but he became a prime minister of England. Arturo Toscanini, one-time conductor of the Metropolitan Opera Company and the New York Philharmonic-Symphony Orchestra, compensated for his near-sightedness by developing a remarkable memory. Steinmetz, though deformed in body, left an imprint on our civilization by means of his genius for pure research.

The great men of the world have had all kinds of personal problems—some severe, some minor. Many factors entered into their success—too many for us to unravel clearly and completely. The nature of their handicaps is less important than the intensity of effort which resulted from adjustment to the handicaps. Certain it is that many of life's biggest prizes go to those with physical[2] or mental handicaps, real or imaginary. Perhaps if the progress of the world depended upon only the purely normal people (if such exist!) we would all still be living in primitive fashion.

Compensatory mechanisms. Many people of no great importance illustrate the compensatory mechanisms as well as do the famous. For example, many sculptors, musicians, speed typists, experts in fine needlework, men who write name cards with flourishes, and others whose work demands delicateness of touch, developed their skills as the result of an effort to compensate for left-handedness. Many of these persons were potentially left-handed but were compelled to change to the right hand.[3] Of course, the right-handed person can achieve success in skilled movements just as readily as the left-hander, but the former

---

[2] Alfred Adler has stressed the idea and given many examples of compensation brought about by some organ inferiority. See "A Study of Organ Inferiority and Its Psychical Compensation," *Nervous and Mental Disease Monograph*, 1917, for his early writing in this field.

[3] The child's stuttering which occasionally accompanies the shift from the use of the left hand to the use of the right hand is not caused by the inability of the brain to make the change but by a sense of inferiority brought about by the parent's or teacher's harsh treatment of left-handedness. When a person loses the use of his writing hand through accident and changes to use of the other hand, no speech defect arises; he is not criticized for his awkwardness.

often lacks the urge. Every individual has some psychological handicaps regardless of bodily health or high intelligence. Barriers to adjustment may or may not be related to intelligence.[4]

The compensatory mechanism is easily recognized when we recall the example of anyone who, being little in stature or having physical defects, habitually assumes a haughty air, a cold gaze, a pompous manner, or a loud voice. Consider some of the military and political leaders of history who are known for their bombast as well as their short stature or physical defects.

Compensatory mechanisms are characterized by extra effort or aggressive conduct in order to defend the ego or feeling of self-worth. The individual's compensatory behavior enables him to reduce the tension caused by feelings of inadequacy. Confronted by a barrier to his ongoing activities, the individual naturally seeks to react in ways which appear to overcome the deficiency, decrease feelings of tension, and give increased feelings of self-worth.

Every person has some defects, and so we expect him to have the desire to feel superior in one or more respects. Each man wants to be worth while in his estimation of himself. If he is frustrated[5] in the attainment of his goals so that he cannot meet his obstacles in a positive manner, he will do so in an indirect manner. Inferiority cannot be endured. Superiority, or at least a sense of adequacy, must be achieved. A sense of failure, guilt, or shame is hard to accept. For example, the woman who feels inferior may ape the cultured or the rich and attend functions for which she does not care or lectures which she does not understand. Attendance at the opera may be imperative for her, because it puts her into the desired class of those who are admired.

When the individual is confronted with barriers to which he cannot make a direct adequate adjustment, he may seek satis-

---

[4] Agnes M. Conklin, *Failures of Highly Intelligent Pupils: A Study of Their Behavior by Means of the Control Group.* Teachers College Contributions to Education, 1940, No. 792. This study presents data concerning two groups of pupils of high intelligence; one group succeeded in school but the other failed.

[5] An excellent treatment of frustration with examples of adjustments is presented in *Frustration and Aggression,* by Dollard, Doob, Miller, Mowrer, Sears, et. al., published for The Institute of Human Relations, Yale University Press, 1939. See pages 12-17 for six good illustrations of the concept of frustration. Page 53 presents a summary of principles.

factions through substitute activities that have positive values. For example, pupils who cannot attain satisfaction in scholarship may do so on the athletic field. Girls who do not find their personal appearance attractive may become good students. High school students who find their studies very difficult are apt to quit school and seek jobs. The employee who feels disgraced because his father has been convicted as a criminal may achieve satisfaction by taking up art work, athletics, church work, stamp collecting, or by inventing new machinery.

When we study the lives of some labor leaders, we find that certain barriers confronted them in their earlier years of employment. They were not successful as workers themselves and so they dealt with their failure by helping the workers whom they believed to be as unhappy as themselves. Likewise, businessmen who cannot succeed in business often make an adjustment by entering another type of work, such as teaching. Teachers who cannot attain satisfactions in teaching may make an adjustment by going into business.

Compensations or substitute activities may be useless, even harmful, or they may be of great value to the individual and to society. The man who goes into the business world and finds that he is not a good businessman can substitute for that lack of attainment the satisfactions of church work and fraternal activities. Of course, the normal individual takes some interest in his community, his home, and other phases of good citizenship; but, if he remains in business and makes his outside activities a heavy sideline, he shows that he is not really well adjusted to his job. He is seeking compensation for some lack that he feels in his personality. It is usually well, therefore, that the general manager should frown upon outside activities of employees when those activities absorb very much time without bringing better adjustments to the man's job.

In this connection, we may ask whether every person goes into a chosen vocation in order to compensate for some inadequacy. Do not education and the examples of others have any influence in the choice of work? Of course they have some bearing with many individuals, as when a father tells his son about the money to be made in the legal profession and then has the son talk with some enthusiastic lawyer who convinces the lad that law is the most honorable and remunerative profession. Law, as a vocation, becomes associated with other desirable ideas of prestige, fame and wealth. However, it is also evident that many of the vocations we select are chosen as an avenue of expression for thwarted tendencies. If a boy is a poor athlete, he may take refuge in his books. If he cannot be worth while as a physical specimen, he may become a college professor, a scientist, a statistician, or an accountant.

Many positive or desirable substitute activities are compensations for inadequacies in social relations. They may also be thought of as *defense mechanisms* in relation to failures in social recognition. The individual who meets barriers that make him feel inadequate may learn to obtain personal satisfactions from being kind to others, public speaking, playing politics, doing tricks, taking care of children, or teaching others. All of these habits or tendencies are desirable and may be utilized vocationally. The understanding employer tries to give the employee the type of work that utilizes adjustment tendencies which are already well established.

The trained personnel man, vocational counselor, executive, and teacher are all interested in studying the individual in order that behavior tendencies may be utilized for greater self-expression. When a personnel man refuses to hire an applicant for a selling job and says to the applicant, "I will not hire you for the sales department because you really would not be happy there," the interviewer has recognized that the applicant's adjustments are not of the kind that would make him satisfied in sales work.

A man may be capable of selling and even have a good record in salesmanship work but still decide that he must do something else because his friends regard salesmanship as Babbitty and he feels inferior as a salesman. Hence, he wishes he were an artist or something respected by his friends. This principle is often important in labor problems.[6] Many dissatisfied employees are trying to find forms of self-expression whereby they may escape their feelings of social inferiority and appear superior in the es-

---

[6] Of course, a great deal of labor unrest comes from well-adjusted workers who believe they have a right to a larger share of the income from the business, better conditions of work, and so on. These desires may be no more evasive than those of a merchant who tries to get the highest possible price for his goods.

timation of their associates.   The job or experience that causes one man to feel socially superior may cause another to feel inferior.   A man's reactions to a job often depend upon how he is attempting to adjust his inner mental life rather than upon the job itself.

The Messiah complex.   Any person who finds himself in a predicament because his life is unsatisfying is likely to try to solve his own problem by attempting to alleviate the predicaments of others.   The student who plans to do college teaching and then later finds that he cannot do so may adjust himself by helping others who are in a difficulty similar to his.   This type of adjustment is, perhaps, one of the most common psychological origins of the professional adviser.   Teachers and executives who find their work unsatisfying or difficult often enter the advisory field as counselors, college deans, assistants to principals, welfare workers, or personnel men.   Such counselors become engrossed in their work and are likely to be sympathetic toward those who seek their advice.   This kind of adjustment is both psychologically sound and socially desirable.   When people make comments about a clinical psychologist to the effect that he is trying to help others make better adjustments because he really is trying to help himself make better adjustments, the comments are complimentary.   The adjustment is beneficial to both the advisees and the advisor.   Personality development should be reciprocal rather than one-sided.

If the person who has made such an adjustment in the direction of helping others has had an intensely unpleasant experience in connection with his problem, he may develop an extreme form of the Messiah complex—the radical reformer's tendency.   The radical wishes not only to help those toward whom he is sympathetic, but also to destroy all persons and features connected with the hated situation.   He wants a new educational system, or a new economic order, or a new religion, or even an entirely new civilization.   Back of every fanatic is an emotional history that explains his fanaticism.   Most malcontents have had very unhappy childhoods which have a direct relation to their radical ideas.

Rowdies and radicals.   The rowdy and the radical, who like to annoy or shock their associates, may have their desires to be noticed directed into worthy channels. Any skillful teacher knows that she can direct a rowdy pupil's impulsions into better channels by assigning to him the task of controlling the other rowdies in the room. Or she may give him recognition by appointing him traffic patrol leader. Or he may be induced to protect the girls instead of teasing them. His rowdiness may be an attempt to gain the limelight, and any personal recognition accompanied with an assignment of responsibility is likely to be more satisfying to him than a continuation of his annoying conduct.

Similarly, the college student who has radical tendencies toward the economic order is likely to moderate his extreme points of view if he is assigned the job of helping some of the chronic down-and-outers. Few experiences are so likely to change the young industrial radical into a conservative as the task of hiring some of the industrial misfits, supervising their work, and then paying their wages out of his own money. When he goes into business for himself and observes many a worker's carelessness, tardiness, and irresponsibility toward the employer's needs, he is apt to decide that his former panacea for economic disorders is impracticable.

The college student who realizes that he is considered a radical by his acquaintances often has difficulty in getting a job. Many employers shy away from him. He imagines that they deny him employment because of his "advanced" ideas which clash with their interests. Actually many intelligent employers have little fear of so-called advanced ideas but they realize that the radical employee is rarely a good team-worker. He is likely to be either a free lance or, if in a group, a disturber of the group. Most employers like to feel that their employees like each other and function smoothly as a "team." Hence many avoid the radical for his lack of group integration rather than because of his ideas as such.

Colleges are often accused of having nests of radicals among the student members. Some radicals can be found in any large group, but their numbers in the colleges are relatively small. For example, one study of 3,758 students of four state universities and fourteen church-affiliated colleges indicated that only 22 students made scores on a Conservatism-Radicalism "Opinionaire" that showed definite radicalism. The mean score of all students indicated, if anything, a slight tendency toward conservatism. There was a uniform tendency for seniors to be less conservative than freshmen. Women were uniformly more conservative than men. One college stood apart from the rest as definitely conservative.[7]

The small number of students who can be classified as radicals usually have problems in adjustment and are more in need of a clinical psychologist's services than a policeman's club.[8] Radicals reveal important personality changes in their histories, but the exact nature of the relationship between the changes and the radical political activity can be revealed only through analysis of each individual's adjustments.[9] Of course, many adjustments in the direction of helping others are expressed through mere misplaced sympathy. Merle Thorpe, Editor of *The Nation's Business*, told the following story:[10]

The governor of a Southern state said that an estimable woman of his state came to him recently with a petition several yards long.

"Governor," she said, "I have been working four months to get this petition around. It appeals to you to release from state's prison So-and-So."

"What!" exclaimed the governor. "You don't mean you want *him* set at liberty? Let me tell you something about him."

After ten minutes the woman threw up her hands and said, "Why, Governor, certainly we don't want him let loose. But, Governor," she added, "tell me something I *can* do."

Radicals, rowdies, and reformers need the same constructive treatment which we should accord to others who are maladjusted. The business executive who finds that he has hired radicals should think of them as stimulating critics and decide whether the benefits from their criticism outweigh the annoyances they cause him. If their actions become a burdensome task for the executive, he should recognize that the normal employees also deserve attention. When the normal employees are neglected so that maladjusted radicals may be given more time and thought, the

<hr />

[7] Erland Nelson, "Radicalism—Conservatism in Student Attitudes," *Psychological Monographs*, Vol. 50, No. 4. The Lentz Conservatism-Radicalism "Opinionaire," Form K, was used.

[8] Students of radicalism may wish to refer to Edward G. Benson, "Three Words," *Public Opinion Quarterly*, Vol. 2, pp. 130-134, and to E. S. Dexter, "Personality Traits Related to Conservatism and Radicalism," *Character & Personality*, Vol. 7, pp. 230-237.

[9] Solomon Diamond, "A Study of the Influences of Political Radicalism on Personality Development," *Archives of Psychology*, Vol. 29, No. 203, p. 53.

[10] *Nation's Business*, March 1925, p. 10.

executive should refer the maladjusted employees to the specialists of a clinic and devote his best efforts to the more ordinary members of his organization.

The Oedipus and "secretarial" complex. Occasionally we meet the boy of seventeen who marries a forty-year-old woman. Such a marriage does not necessarily indicate that the boy has a mercenary motive. The woman may be a widow or spinster who has no money. Sometimes the widow has several children older than the bridegroom. Why does a young man marry a "girl" of that type?

In the Greek myth, Oedipus was led to kill his own father and to marry his mother, Jocasta. Freud and his followers have presented some evidence to indicate that sons become attracted toward the mother and daughters toward the father. The former fixation is called the *Oedipus complex* and the latter is called the *Electra complex*. Clinical psychologists have found that the boy who fixates his emotional life in the mother image may be jealous of his father, who is a great barrier to his love for his mother. When the boy grows up he may become rebellious toward the schoolteacher or the executive, because they are symbolic of the authority of the father. Some of the greatest men of history never married until after their mothers died. Others married but respected their mothers more than they did their wives.

The attempt to duplicate the mother or father image takes form even in the frequent marriage of near relations by neurotics. From this new relation, they seek and often find the comfort denied them by a reality which insisted upon leading them away from the pleasure and security of infantile life.

Many creative artists have married and been "comforted" by wives older than themselves. Yet in their work they betray conflict and turmoil, stained with their neurotic symptoms, buried in the inner layers of their unconscious. Often the expedient does not succeed, and the artist hops from marriage to love affairs and then back to marriage, seeking relief from his psychic tension. The genius of Strindberg and Milton aches with the throb of unhappy sex lives; Shakespeare derides his Ann Hathaway in his "Taming of the Shrew." Dr. Samuel Johnson, a notorious sufferer from hypochondria, finds his plain, ignorant wife the apotheosis of all womanly virtues because she ministers to his neurosis and gives him the infantile comfort he still seeks. Even Socrates had his Xanthippe!

The failure to relieve the pressure of an Oedipus fixation upon his mother is the key to the life and literary creations of D. H. Lawrence. This artist, aware of the truth of psychoanalysis, tried and failed to dissolve the complex which marred his sex and love life. His books shriek with the sex motif; all his life was dedicated to a war against the censorship of sex in literature. His personal as well as creative life was marked by a species of exhibitionism; all this represented a conscious attempt to free himself of the invisible cord that bound him to his mother. But with all his efforts, he was impotent to escape from his prison: all his protests, his invectives hurled against a "sex-as-sin-conscious" society, his attempts to find sex happiness with many women, represent a whistling in the dark. He remained unhappy and unfulfilled because of an Oedipus complex that never was solved.[11]

When a mother hugs and kisses her small boy far more than she does her husband, she may be conditioning her child for bachelorhood or for a troublesome married life. It is often quite natural for mothers to direct their starved affections upon their children because the fathers are too busy in the office and the shop to be companionable to their wives. For a while after marriage, the husband may have given his young wife all the loving companionship that she craved; but, as time went by and the children came, father had to get his nose closer to the grindstone. Consequently, he delegated all the care of the children to the mother.

The "secretarial" complex in business is one result of the over-affectionate mother. Some executives have a child-like dependence upon their secretaries. The executive who claims that he has the perfect secretary would be surprised to know that she is really average in comparison with good secretaries. His admiration is often based upon the fact that he unconsciously associates his secretary with his mother. In such a situation the secretary represents the mother image to the executive; she may be the most powerful member in the organization. His subordinates soon learn that they must not antagonize her. The secretarial complex is not wholly disadvantageous in its mild form. To some men it is a logical and helpful means of emotional adjustment. It becomes questionable, however, when the employer happens to be married and divorces his wife in order to marry his secretary.

The ability to recognize the Oedipus complex is also of importance to the businessman when employees will not leave the home town of their parents, even though their parents do not need them at home. Sometimes the individual is in a state of

---

[11] Louis Berg, *The Human Personality*. Prentice-Hall, Inc., 1933.

mental conflict, because he is torn between the normal desire for a mate and the old love of his parent; or, if married, between the love of the mate and that of the affectionate mother. Emotional conflicts of this type are taking place in the minds of employees at times, and in this way may unfit them for a whole-hearted application to business and life.

Identification. The person who, when at the theater, identifies himself with the hero, fights his battles, endures his hardships, conquers the villain, and finally marries the heroine, is not, for the time being, a mere observer or onlooker, but is the character in the picture or the play, psychologically speaking. Such a person makes many incipient movements that give reality to his imaginary acting. In like manner, the loyal college student attending the football game of his alma mater gives the player who is carrying the ball many a vigorous "shove" from the grandstands. For the moment the spectator carries the ball. He has identified himself with the team and is mentally doing the same things that the team is trying to do.

Every sport fan knows that the successful football team is the one in which the members identify themselves with the team as a whole. Each player does not play an individual game but integrates his playing with that of the entire team.

Through the achievements of other persons, groups of persons, and institutions, the individual may reduce tensions arising from his own inadequacies. Identification may be made with social and political organizations or reform movements as a compensation. An individual may also identify himself with his material possessions, as exemplified by the housewife who cleans and protects her home so well that it becomes uncomfortable to others. Possessions such as the house, clothing, automobile, office desk, or factory machine may be used to gain many subconscious satisfactions as well as obvious prestige values.

Positive identification is one of human nature's most valuable means of making wholesome adjustment. It is present in the life of every well-balanced personality; it is absent from the mental lives of certain patients in hospitals for the mentally ill. In other patients, the identifications are carried to an extreme degree. They identify themselves so completely that they become "Napoleons," "Hitlers," "Messiahs," and so on. The well-balanced person of any age is the one who has learned the art of identifying himself intelligently with the people and the tasks of his daily contacts. The factors of his personality are integrated into an effective working unit. He feels at home with his associates, his supervisors, his family. Unlike the cynic, he finds the age in which he lives reasonably admirable because he has identified himself with its admirable movements.

Identification is the important fundamental of a happy married life. Ideally and typically, two people marry, not mainly for sexual gratification but for more complete identification of their personalities. In the course of history, society has developed many institutions in order to enable its members to identify themselves with satisfying personalities. In addition to marriage, we have the church, which aims to have the individual identify himself with the cosmic power.

The good citizen identifies himself with his community and his nation. The well-adjusted pupil identifies himself with his school and his teacher. The great teacher first acquires a strong personality and then enables his students to live partially within his personality in order that they may thus develop their own personalities.

Teachers and business executives should try to assist their pupils and employees in identifying themselves with the age in which they live, the institutions of which they are a part, the social groups in which they are nurtured, and the employers or others who give them employment. The true educator and builder of men instructs not by teaching subject matter only but by showing people their places in the scheme of things; by pointing out the trends of the past and the possible trends of the future; by discussing the problems of today that challenge us to excel our forefathers, and the beauties of the machines, of nature, and of man, in addition to their cruelties.

The skillful executive who enables employees to identify themselves with his personality must also help them to transfer their identifications to other tasks, persons, and institutions. He may direct them so well that they wish to become a boss "like him." Later, the employees may find they are really interested not in sic values of their tasks but in the person who happened vise them. The able executive who has insight into the processes of identification among his employees is careful to see that they clearly differentiate between interest in him and interest in their work.   Each worker should be led to find the intrinsic values of his work and to feel that he is a worth-while member of the institution to which he belongs.   The same admonition applies to the teacher in relations with his pupils.

Children who are maladjusted may be induced to reveal the nature of the barriers in their adjustments by means of analysis of their identifications.   Joseph C. Solomon, psychiatrist at the Baltimore Clinic of the Mental Hygiene Society of Baltimore, has reported how maladjusted children can be made to disclose "secrets that gnaw their minds."

The method consists in playing with dolls with the child.   "Active play," according to Dr. Solomon, is a new method in which the children play a game about themselves without disclosing their own identities.

"By active play therapy," he said, "the psychiatrist is able to secure first-hand information from the mouth of the child as to how he or she is reacting to his or her environment."

The young patient identifies himself with the doll, and in his play is prone to make the doll express his own feelings.

"The mere putting his thoughts into words plays an important role in the child's mental catharsis," Dr. Solomon said.   "It is generally accepted that the aeration of the child's mental conflicts has beneficial treatment value."

Children are also encouraged, he said, to express their animosities and to give physical expression to their hostilities, as well as to talk about them. After repeated demonstrations the patient no longer feels the need to express his hostility.

"It should be kept clearly in mind," Dr. Solomon warns, "that the method is partly a trick by which a child says things about himself that he ordinarily would not tell."

Resentment may result if the child feels he has been trapped.   During the treatment the physician participates actively, and from time to time, as a suitable occasion arises, makes suggestions to direct the child's future thinking.   Thus therapeutic suggestions are incorporated in the play.[12]

The alert executive recognizes adjustment tendencies and directs them into positive channels.   Some executives are very sensitive to the feeling tones in the lives of their employees; others are unaware of them.   The important action-channels of employees are not always those which are obvious to the observer. Such obvious emotions as the hysterical or angry expressions of the aroused worker are likely to be mere surface ripples.   The really significant emotions are hidden beneath the surface—

[12] *Science News Letter*, March 12, 1938, p. 167.

Fig. 16. Laurance F. Shaffer, Carnegie Institute of Technology. Those interested in further study of adjustment may read his book *The Psychology of Adjustment* (Houghton Mifflin Co., 1936).

they are undercurrents in the inner basins of the individual personality. People suffer in silence for years. They brood over injustices. Their resentments are cumulative. Their reservoirs of emotional energy are recognized only by the executive who is alert to human emotions and their meanings. Once these reservoirs are revealed to the capable analyst, he may be able to direct the energies of the employee into channels of activity that lead to a more satisfactory and constructive life.

The executive who is alert to the barriers and adjustments in the lives of his employees is also likely to be alert to their strong qualities. If he notices that an office employee is especially skillful in persuading others but also has some show-off tendencies, the executive can direct the employee into salesmanship and train him properly for the work.

Another employee may not have the knack of persuading people but likes to entertain them by clowning, being the "life of the party," and by telling stories. Such an employee is likely to be invited to many social affairs where he amuses others but fails to achieve anything valuable for the employer or for himself. Accordingly, the employer may counsel him regarding training for public relations work that will build goodwill in the community for the company. The entertaining ability can be focussed for a purpose which benefits both employer and employees.

The employee who is legally minded may be given the responsibility of keeping in touch with governmental rulings that affect the business.

The employee who is fussy, meticulous, and overly careful can usually be placed in work which requires those habits, such as handling cash or performing an operation requiring manual skill.

Most employees are somewhat adaptable. Their adjustment tendencies, whatever they are, can often be directed for the advantage of both employer and employee. But to do so means that the executive must be alert to the potentialities within the individual, his deep-seated emotional tendencies, his adjustment history. Furthermore, the executive should have the manner of a leader who can, through a definite vocational program, inspire men by showing them visions of their better selves.

References

Adler, Alfred, *The Pattern of Life,* pp. 3-63. Cosmopolitan Book Corporation, 1930.
Berg, Louis, *The Human Personality,* Chapters VI-VIII. Prentice-Hall, Inc., 1933.
Rivlin, Harry N., *Educating for Adjustment,* Chapter VII. D. Appleton-Century Co., 1936.
Shaffer, Laurance Frederic, *The Psychology of Adjustment,* Chapter VI. Houghton Mifflin Co., 1936.

Projects

1. Terms applied to the adjustments described in this chapter are mainly the following:

1. Substitute act having positive values.	4. Messiah complex.
2. Compensatory mechanism.	5. Oedipus complex.
3. Defense mechanism.	6. Electra complex.
	7. Identification.

How would you classify the adjustments present in the main characters described in the following paragraphs:

(*a*) Samuel is an office employee of a lumber company. He is intensely loyal to his employer, Mr. Brown. The town where they live is small, and Samuel and Mr. Brown have mutual acquaintances. Whenever Samuel can possibly do so, he praises his employer. Samuel's expressions of loyalty have become so extreme that Mr. Brown is often embarrassed.

(*b*)   John is a college student of intelligence but he has many unpleasant mannerisms such as sensitiveness to any comments about him. When he is not angry, he is likely to give the impression that he dares anyone to insult him.

(*c*)   William is the son of a well-to-do widow. He had never been away from home overnight until this fall when he entered college. He soon became homesick and returned to his home because he felt that his mother needed any money which he might be able to earn.

(*d*)   Marylee says that she won't marry until she finds a man as nice as her daddy.

(*e*)   Robert Burns resented the repressions of the Scotch and wrote literature to express his own revolt.

(*f*)   An injury resulting from a hemorrhage at birth left Earl Carlson with a permanent scar on his brain, an area the nerve currents could not bridge. Hence, if Earl wished to eat his soup, his brain would dispatch the message but the message would never arrive. Only a convulsive flood of energy with a series of haphazard muscular movements would result. The soup would never reach his mouth.

When Earl became an adult, he managed to go through college and became a physician. Today he is Director of the Department of Corrective Motor Education for the Birth-Injured and Allied Problems, the Neurological Institute, Columbia-Presbyterian Medical Center, New York, where he treats children with handicaps similar to his former handicap. (See Harry W. Hepner, *Finding Yourself in Your Work*, Chapter III. D. Appleton-Century Co., 1939.)

5

Adjustments by Evasion—Negative Substitute Activities

——

"Do you enjoy novel reading, Miss Prim?"
"Oh, very much. One can associate with people in fiction
that one wouldn't dare to speak to in real life."—*Speed.*

When happiness is difficult to attain and the individual lacks intelligent perspective of his barriers and adjustments, he is apt to
seek happiness through fictions, psychological returns to childhood,
blaming others for his situation; or to make some other form of
evasive adjustment. These habits of evasion tend to weaken the individual for dealing with future problems.

A SIMPLE example of adjustment by evasion is illustrated
by the cashier who steals money from the cash register.
Fundamentally, stealing is wrong; not because of the laws against
it, but because it weakens the personality for dealing with future
situations. This is the major criterion of an adjustment as to
whether the act has positive or negative values: Does it
strengthen or weaken the individual for dealing with future
problems?

Certain kinds of evasive adjustments are very common and
so have been given names, such as regression, projection, and
invalidism. Giving a type of adjustment a name has little
value except as a convenience for discussion. However, the
individual who knows the names of typical forms of evasion is
likely to be more alert in recognizing and dealing with them.

Evasive and retreat forms of behavior have meaning; they
indicate purpose and the use of poor habits in accomplishing
the purpose. A discussion of typical evasive habits should increase our ability to appreciate what the maladjusted individual
is trying to accomplish by means of his evasive behavior. Per-

haps we can suggest the substitution of good habits for poor ones. The following discussion of evasions should also help us increase our psychological alertness in recognizing typical evasions on our part and possibly suggest methods of improving our own mental habits.

Regression.[1]   We occasionally meet the man who acts and dresses in the manner of several decades ago.   We have also known the type of adult who talks of the "good old days when boys were gentlemanly and girls were virtuous."   Such expressions may mean that he is simply giving evidence of having partly outlived his age.   The problems of his present are too great for him to solve satisfactorily and he regresses mentally to a former happier state when life was more satisfying.

The employee who once had a good job but lost it may make an adjustment by living in that former happy state, or he may react to his present situation in an aggressive manner and look toward the future rather than the past.   Psychologically, old age sets in just as soon as the past appears to be more pleasant than the present and the future.   There is but one stage in the life of man when all his wants are satisfied just as soon as they occur, and that is when he is an embryo.   As soon as he is born he begins to have wants which are not always satisfied when they occur.   He must adjust himself to his world until death overtakes him and ends the process of adjustment.

The unmarried woman may regress to the days when she had a lover but lost him, or she may face the future with a zest for new loves and new adventures.   Barriers such as a broken engagement, failure in studies, bankruptcy in business, or discharge from a good job should cause no tears, but should motivate the individual for a stronger attack upon new ventures. Failure to do this is illustrated when an older employee has failed in a hard job or a business for himself, and the remark is made: "The experience took the heart right out of him."   In some forms of insanity, regression takes places to an extent that is almost unbelievable.   The patient goes back to childhood in talk and conduct.

---

[1] This tendency is also called retrogression by a few authors. See particularly Laurance Frederic Shaffer, *The Psychology of Adjustment,* p. 198. Houghton Mifflin Co., 1936.

Regression, of the kind which is a form of relaxation that leads to possible later attack on one's problems, is found in childish hobbies and games. Toy trains are an example.

The hobby of playing with toy trains now has more than 100,000 American men enthusiasts, who have invested at least $10,000,000 in their equipment and support three hundred local clubs, three magazines and a national association, which holds annual conventions. One millionaire even has one of these miniature railroads installed in a Wall Street building, where it occupies two entire floors.[2]

Many people who regress are unhappy because they are no longer children. The world has moved on but they are left behind. In trying to adjust themselves to modern problems they take refuge, through their imaginations, in the mental life experienced when they were happy, carefree children. They find it satisfying to regress at times:

> Backward, turn backward, O Time, in your flight!
> Make me a child again, just for to-night!

The girl who longs for the ignorance and the innocence of pre-adolescence finds adjustment difficult. It would be better for her to prepare for motherhood or, if unmarried, to sublimate her sex energies into socially acceptable channels. Also, the middle-aged married woman who has not developed a deep-seated interest in her own family or in a career is apt to take an excessive interest in young men, especially if she was attractive when young. The poor adjustment to her increasing age and declining beauty cause her to regress to her youth when boys admired her. Many middle-aged women grow bitter when they can neither achieve an acceptable relationship with young men nor develop another interest that is intrinsically sound. Well-adjusted women grow old gracefully.

Regression to childish mannerisms, *infantilism,* is exceedingly common. The average grown-up frequently shows his infantilism by his temper tantrums, pouting, dawdling, weeping, clowning to attract attention, making grimaces, or noisy nasal and throat habits. These childish mannerisms are so common and meaningful that we can often recognize what a maladjusted person is trying to do if we say to ourselves: "What would the

---

[2] Freling Foster, "Keep Up with the World," *Collier's,* November 9, 1940, p. 6.

person's behavior signify if it were performed by a four-year-old child?"

The college student who suffers from "homesickness" demonstrates that he has a barrier in the form of being too closely attached to the members of his family and that he must turn to them to shield him and make his decisions for him. In the new college environment, he finds barriers in the form of strangers among faculty and student body who pay little attention to him, and so he develops fears and anxieties which result in physiological imbalances that lead to such physical symptoms as headaches, indigestion, or loss of appetite. His physical symptoms now "prove" to himself and to others that he should return home at once!

Regression is a serious problem to the new executive who has been hired to put a money-losing company back into the profit-making column. Many of the old employees have fixed habits which once were sound but are now inefficient in comparison with modern methods. The old employees may be pursuing methods the very opposite of those pursued by the man who is in tune with the new American tempo. What should be the attitude of the new executive toward an organization that is antiquated in methods and attitude? Should he "clean house" and "fire" most of the old employees and executives, replacing them with new blood? Or should he try to revitalize the old members? We must remember that adjustment habits cannot be erased and new ones formed at a moment's notice. The behavior patterns that are in the nervous systems of the old employees were put there by many thousands of repetitions, and new ones are difficult to produce. Shock is the only quick method, but this also does much harm. To rebuild an old organization may require so much time and effort on the part of the key executives that the end does not justify the means. However, this does not imply that all the old timber of the structure is bad. Certain employees bearing the scars of battle may be better because of having withstood the onslaughts of competition. The better policy may be to save the good material and scrap the outworn.

Fixed ideas. Every businessman has met examples of the employee who was reprimanded for some slight infraction of the rules and who brooded over the reprimand for months—his feelings being wholly out of proportion to the seriousness of the affair; or the employee who had to be discharged and who returned again and again for a reconsideration of his case; or the old employee who demanded a pension even though the company has not given pensions to other employees and has never consciously given the impression that pensions were granted; or the executive who wants a decision in his favor, and, if it is not rendered wholly in his favor, reopens the case at each conference and insists upon discussing it, to the disgust of his fellows; or the person who loses a lawsuit and then carries the case to higher courts until the lawyers decide to neglect it or to postpone it indefinitely.

Why do these individuals persist in their fixed ideas? One reason may be that the ego of the complainant has been assailed. The case or adjustment in his favor is desired, not for its intrinsic worth, but, as he says, "It's the principle of the thing." He wants the decision in his favor because he needs it to make himself appear worth while in his own estimation. The complaint often indicates that the individual is adjusting to a barrier of a failure type and he resents that his desired success cannot be achieved through normal channels. The really big man is willing to make concessions to others and does not feel that he has compromised his own integrity or worth. It is the little fellow who cannot accept anything less than complete surrender from others. The person who has some great achievement to his credit is not likely to feel the need of small concessions. It is well, therefore, to try to make the complainant feel satisfied by showing him that you admire him for certain other qualities and that he really does not need what he desires—you like him as he is.

Most of the persons who develop these fixed ideas lead so routine or narrow a life that they lack practice in making the daily little adjustments which we learn to make when we associate with many people. The employee who operates a semi-automatic machine for six days of the week and then goes home to a lonely room where he sleeps until the next day is a fit victim for fixed ideas.

Sometimes managers wonder whether they do not supply too many side activities and forms of recreation for their employees.

Fig. 17. "American Gothic." How would you describe
the probable adjustments of these two characters so excellently
portrayed by Grant Wood? (*Courtesy of Grant Wood and the
Art Institute of Chicago.*)

The danger from these extra activities lies in the fact that they
are often patronized by one group or clique, and the backward
employees who need more contacts do not take an active part.
To prevent this, it is well to see to it that each employee does
take an active part in the company's recreational activities or
in some other activities not sponsored by the employer. Employees should appoint committees to look after the retiring
fellows who have no stimulating forms of recreations. Each
and every employee should be encouraged to attend some company recreational affairs.

Executives themselves may lead too narrow lives. Of all the
men whom the writer has ever met, the one most fixed in his
ideas is an executive who lives only for his business, which he
inherited. His two-year-old baby and his wife are merely inci-

dental parts of the home, like the furniture. His mental and emotional life is too circumscribed, and, when he attends a conference where he can talk, his associates become angry and disgusted with his harping upon non-essentials that were considered settled long ago. To be normally adjusted, everyone needs many varied intellectual, emotional, and physical exercises.

Negativism. One of the greatest problems of the executive is that of securing the co-operation of his associates and subordinates. Whenever any program of action is suggested that involves some absent member of the organization, the question arises as to how to handle the absent but important individual. The point is raised as to how to sell the idea to him. Some member of the group may suggest: "Let's ask him to do the opposite of what we want, and then he'll want to do it." A few employees always seem to carry a negative attitude toward any ideas that are proposed to them. How did they acquire such reaction patterns?

In many cases of negativism the habit pattern was established by the persons who reared the individual as a child. If we observe a mother rearing her child, we may find that she is constantly setting up barriers to the child by telling him what to do and what not to do. The commands flow in rapid succession: "Wash your face," "Say 'Thank you,'" "Give the toy to little brother," "Come here," "Stop that," and so on. Most of these demands from the adult come at times when the child is busily engaged in some absorbing activity, such as building a castle, flying an airship, or slaying a giant. Small wonder that he feels that adults are tyrants who spoil his fun and can be dealt with only by opposing them through breaking valuable articles or by other forms of naughtiness. Sometimes the repressions of childhood lead to later expressions of opposition to authority as in kleptomania or exhibitionism. These are simply adult varieties of "naughtiness" which the individual cannot explain as to why he does them.

Children who have the barrier of too much discipline from parents may withdraw into themselves and daydream rather than play active games, or they may voice their resistance in their dreams at night when they talk to themselves and say: "I don't have to," or "I won't do it." Boys who are reared by a mother and several older sisters who supervise every act of the child often acquire a negative attitude toward all women, and, if they marry, their wives are apt to say: "My husband loves me and I love him but he does just the opposite of anything I tell him to do." Small wonder that he is negatively set toward the requests of women, who have "lorded" it over him for years!

Adjustment by negativism may be expressed passively, as in doing nothing when something is expected, or it may be active negativism—doing the opposite of what is expected. In some forms of insanity the individual may be so negative as to refuse to obey the normal promptings of the bodily processes, such as swallowing the saliva.

In industry, negativism may find an outlet in joining labor organizations or in performing duties to the point ordered but no farther. The executive who finds that his employees are quarrelsome or do what is asked of them but no more may take stock of himself to learn whether he has hired a group of employees who were negative when hired or whether he has made them negative in attitude by the tone of his voice and the manner in which he gives orders. The dictatorial type of executive may get results by cowing his employees or by brilliant tactical strategy, but he seldom gets that teamwork which gives joy to the executive who knows that "the boys are with him to the utmost." The great leader of men has learned that it is best to explain the reasons for his requests in a straightforward but friendly tone and manner which convinces the employees that he believes in and likes them.

Fantasy, or daydreaming. The imaginary representation of satisfactions which the individual would like to attain but does not attain in everyday life is called *fantasy* or daydreaming. It is so easy an adjustment to make when a barrier arises that everyone daydreams to some extent.

In the *conquering hero* mechanism, the individual does not successfully face his situations in direct attacks, but pictures himself doing the deeds or possessing the things he desires. The boy who is thwarted in his attempts to do as he pleases at home can soar away in his imagination to wonderful lands of cannibals and kings, where he can conquer armies and achieve honor.

As he becomes older, he daydreams of financial success, with several large automobiles, a magnificent estate, a yacht, plenty of money, and then, to cap the climax, he will become a member of the board of education and fire all the teachers whom he does not like! On other days he may picture himself as a great prize fighter, a football player, a bandit, or a preacher. The girl daydreams of the social approval of others about her, where she is a great singer, a social worker, a missionary, or a Joan of Arc.

A certain amount of daydreaming is normal and natural for all persons; but when it becomes a substitute for reality, it eliminates the necessity of actual achievement and causes the individual to live in a world of fantasy. In hospitals for the mentally ill, we find patients who are satisfied to live within their imaginations. Some of them imagine they are great men and women, such as Napoleon or Queen Victoria. As Kipling said, if one can dream and not make dreams his master, he is a successful man.

G. H. Green [3] has suggested four types of fantasy which are varieties of the conquering hero daydream. In the *display* fantasy, the dreamer gains social recognition for some act of ability or daring. In the *saving* daydream, the dreamer pictures himself performing some brave deed under extreme difficulties and thereby gaining the affection of the person rescued. In the fantasy of *grandeur,* the individual imagines himself a great person such as a king or even a god. In the *homage* daydream, the dreamer imagines himself performing a service for someone whose love he desires. Many other kinds of daydreams are used by individuals as a means of adjusting themselves to problems, such as the *destruction* daydream in which enemies may be put to death, injured, or destroyed in the fantasy.

The *suffering hero* or *martyr* type of escape is also common, as in the small boy who, because he is reprimanded, decides that he will be a very wicked bandit, rob trains, be put in jail, and eventually be hanged. His body will be brought home and all his parents, relatives, friends, and teachers will be sorry that they mistreated him.

[3] G. H. Green, *Psychoanalysis in the Classroom,* Chapter II. G. P. Putnam's Sons, 1922.

This type of behavior is also expressed on a milder level by the stenographer who becomes peevish and sullen. Usually she can be stimulated in several different ways. Her supervisor may approach the issue in a direct frontal attack and tell her to "snap out of it" because she is making the day unpleasant for everyone around her, or he may give her so much work to do and demand it so soon that she simply will not have time to think about herself. However, a very sensitive girl may be paralyzed by a severe scolding. It is well, therefore, to treat each employee as an individual rather than as one of a class. One rule should govern the executive: The employees must be stimulated to deal with situations as they are rather than as they would prefer them to be.

Important questions for the executive are: "What are my employees really thinking? What kinds of daydreams are they having? Are their minds filled with pleasant imagery?" The employees may apparently be busy at their tasks, but their minds may be filled with unvoiced curses for the boss and wishes that they were a thousand miles away from him and his picayune job.

Factory workers who perform repetitive jobs usually overcome boredom by means of daydreams. Mind-wandering of the fantasy variety is a protection against monotony.[4] It compensates for the deficiencies of life in general, and many a poorly adjusted person has sought a repetitive job so that he might enjoy his fantasies without the interruptions of the alert thinking which would be a part of a more varied job. Many machine tenders are very happy while at work—their minds are roaming about in delightful worlds of fantasy.

All persons like to get away from monotony and routine in order to enjoy vicarious adventures. When we go to the moving picture show and throw ourselves into the emotionality of the plot, we not only escape from our humdrum world but also "experience" worlds which we can never hope to enjoy in actuality. One reason why we do not care to see moving pictures or plays that describe life in its daily routine is that we want to

---

[4] Morris S. Viteles, *Industrial Psychology*. W. W. Norton & Co., 1932. Chapter XXIV presents an excellent summary of specific influences in monotonous work.

escape our own realities and live in a new world rather than in the kind we have each day. Those of us who have routine jobs want to identify ourselves, for example, with the young man who was reared in the country but went to the city and there beat the captains of finance at their own game. We want to see beautiful women in the moving picture; women who are never troubled by boresome problems of taking care of crying babies and mending socks. We want the ideal pictured in the dramatizations to help us escape our problems. The happy ending is the only satisfying one, because we experience realistic living every day and do not find it sufficiently thrilling.

> . . . the movie . . . notoriously furnishes an antisocial "escape" that takes mere murder in its stride and delightfully threatens maid, matron, and debutante with the fate that is worse than death. All this in a theater darkened just enough to enjoy the moral support of one's beshadowed neighbors without actually suffering their active chaperonage. Motion pictures thus become, in a milder degree, a recognized mechanism for multiple defrustration, like mixed bathing and the country club drink-and-dance.[5]

Projection. Two automobile drivers collide with each other and telescope their fenders. What happens? Do the two drivers get out of their cars and apologize to each other? Is their first reaction that of arranging for an adjustment? Usually, the response indicates that each driver blames the other. It is often difficult for either driver to admit that he made a serious mistake.

Ask a drunkard the cause of his downfall and he will have some plausible explanation. It may have been his early companions, his mother-in-law, or his wife. This rationalization usually develops in some accidental manner, as when the intoxicated husband comes home and his mother-in-law meets him at the door and chases him away from home. He then broods over the affair and blames her rather than himself. Finally, he comes to use that explanation of his alcoholism as a satisfactory mechanism rather than admit frankly that he is unable to face his problems and must escape reality by the drink route.

Occasionally we hear unjustified rumors of immorality as a result of projection. A woman accuses some reputable and important member of the community of gross immoralities. Such

---

[5] Kenneth M. Goode, *What About Radio?* p. 30. Harper & Bros., 1937.

stories throw undeserved suspicion upon the accused individual. The suspicion should really be directed toward the accuser, for the accusing woman is merely projecting to someone else the impulses that she herself is trying so hard to combat. She could not bear to admit to herself her terrible impulses and so she built up pictures of others who did the things that shamed her self-respect. Many a reformer has retained the integrity of his selfhood by joining an organization to combat the same tendencies that he had to fight in his moral life.

Clever propagandists and demagogues often use the projective tendencies within the individuals of the masses. Some scapegoats are always available for popular condemnation. Propagandists know that it is easier for most people to blame their own troubles on some persons or institutions such as financiers, religionists, the educational system, foreign organizations, or any other popularly-accepted "devil." The political opportunist finds out who the unpopular "devils" are at the moment and speaks for the projectionists in demanding reforms.

Experiments show that frustration such as a ruined evening may bring anger toward far-away people.

This was revealed when two psychologists learned that a group of young men at a camp was to be given a series of tests which would be boring to them and which were so difficult that everyone was bound to fail miserably. The time taken to give the tests forced the men to miss what they considered the most interesting event of the week, Bank Night at the local theater. The men, it was anticipated, would be frustrated and made angry by this situation.

Before the men knew the nature of the tests and the fact that they would miss Bank Night, their attitude toward the people of a far-away nation was measured by means of rating-scales.

After they had taken the tests and realized that they could not enjoy the evening at the theater, they were once again asked to rate this nation. It was found that their attitudes after the frustrating tests were reliably more hostile toward the nation than before.

Similar groups who were not frustrated by the tests and who rated the same nation twice revealed no such change. . . .

The psychologists who turned the test evening into an experiment were Dr. Neal E. Miller, of Yale University, and Richard Bugelski, of the University of Toledo. They see in the results an expression of the tendency to blame someone else for an individual's own misfortunes, known to psychologists as the scapegoat device. . . .

"In ordinary social living," Dr. Miller points out, "men and women suffer frustrations especially when they are unemployed or are compelled to accept a reduction in pay. Their anger can spread to scapegoats in the same way

Fig. 18.   A stereotyped depiction of the reformer.   (*Copyright McCall's Magazine.*)   He likes to "do good" by depriving people of pleasure or by forcing them to accept his viewpoint.   The objective thinker realizes that the fanatical reformer's adjustments to his barriers have stimulated him to present only one side of a question—his side.   The balanced person who studies all sides of a question is seldom cocksure of its solution, nor does he try to have others accept only his views.   He seeks to present all available facts and allow the facts to speak for themselves.

that the anger of the men in the camp spread to the people of a foreign country. It is one of the functions of propaganda to induce people to use as scapegoats innocent foreigners who, even though not necessarily responsible for the frustration, are made to serve as targets for aggression."[6]

The fanatical reformer and chronic accuser are often unpopular among intelligent people, and the unpopularity is partly deserved. If one has a normal desire to improve the world, he will tend to do it in a quiet and tactful manner rather than by beating his chest and crying his aims from the housetops. The clinical psychologist who visits so-called liberal clubs is often amused by the large percentage of members who have not grown up emotionally and are projecting their own maladjustments upon a conjured monster, such as the economic or political system. Many of these club members are so maladjusted that they are unable to analyze modern problems objectively. Some prate glibly about co-operation and sharing with others when they themselves are rank individualists who emotionally could not co-operate even though they might intellectually wish to do so. We can rest assured that when our economic or political system does evolve into a better stage, its evolution will have been brought about by balanced personalities, and not by the self-styled projecting liberals. True, occasionally we all do some projecting because admission of our own deficiencies is painful, but we cannot solve our personal problems by "jumping on somebody's neck." The well-adjusted personality does not condemn his environment; he analyzes it objectively and utilizes it in new ways.

The student who has the barrier of failure in an examination often projects the cause to the unfairness of the teacher. The man who slips in his marital relations tends to cover up his digressions by accusing others of infidelity. The man who fails in business does not, as a rule, blame himself, but imputes his losses to the "powerful forces of Wall Street" or governmental interference. The production foreman who falls down on his schedule may have sound reasons for so doing; but it is to be expected that he will suggest that the blame should be placed on some other executive. Forceful executives often develop the

[6] This article is one of a series on the psychology of war and propaganda prepared by the Society for the Psychological Study of Social Issues especially for release through Science Service. *Science News Letter*. March 9, 1940, p. 157.

habit of asking their subordinates to perform certain jobs and of implying, when the orders are given, that excuses are not going to be even considered. This method has decided benefits, because it causes the subordinate executives to spend their mental efforts in working out schemes for the accomplishment of the desired end rather than in seeking excuses of the projectionist's kind. The executive who insists upon results and results only may develop the reputation of being hard-boiled, but his methods are sounder psychologically than those of the other man who accepts the excuses of poorly adjusted employees. Any organization that is made up of a large number of "projectors" is also a red ink organization.

The executive himself often projects his failures to factors other than himself. If the balance sheet figures are unsatisfactory, he can blame his employees, competitors, or government interferences; or he can calmly analyze the situation for the causes of failure and then busy himself on an improved plan of procedure for the next fiscal period. "Passing the buck" satisfies the "passer" but does not bring objective results.

Introjection. In projection, we shape the world to suit ourselves—to the satisfaction of the ego. In introjection, we do the opposite. The world shapes us in the images of itself. The introjectionist follows the surge of the crowd. In time of war, he believes all the propaganda that is put out by his side. In politics, he remains within the party lines and cheers without mental reservation for his candidate. He does not calmly analyze and then choose the better of two or more courses of action, but he adopts one course with all his emotional power. In business, he is the "carbon copy" man, the "yes" man. He tries to anticipate the slightest wishes and beliefs of his boss and then adopts those as his own. He likes to be dictated to and ordered about. He dwells within the shadow of his superior and scrapes and bows to the fiddling of those above him. His co-operation is as blind as it is devoted.

Many executives seem to prefer an organization of introjects. They are easy to handle. They satisfy the ego of the executive and he imagines that he is in full control of his employees, but his organization is one that neither thinks nor analyzes. It is too pliable. Too many companies are headed by men who like a pliable personnel. One business consultant claimed that he had one basic criterion for sizing up the strength or weakness of any business concern. His evaluation of the management was determined by comparing the top executive's ability with the ability of his associates. "If the top executive chooses associates, vice-presidents and department heads, who are as able as he, the whole organization is bound to be a strong one," according to this consultant.

The first grave charge against the one-man system (of business management) is that it created an organization with only one thinker. Eventually, the president who operates on the system will become the only thinker in his corporation. This does not mean that others in his organization will do no thinking about the business beyond their immediate concerns; but they will invalidate their constructive ideas by not freely expressing their thoughts. Either through fear or natural laziness, or a reluctance to feed another's vanity with the credit of their own ideas, they will lean more and more on the one-man head of the business for all decisions.

One of the greatest faults of the one-man system is that it stultifies creative desire, imagination, originality and ambition—all creators of ideas—by bringing together and training an organization of "yes" men. From my observation, we all have certain fundamental characteristics and we possess them from the cradle to the grave. Allow a child or a man to have his unopposed way long enough, and eventually he will be led to consider his own way as not only the best but the only way. His ego will encourage him to minimize or forget his mistakes and greatly exaggerate the importance of his successful decisions, and those around him who are dependent on him for their livelihood cannot be blamed for taking the easiest way and agreeing with their adversary quickly.

Throughout the plant and the office of a one-man business, men in high and low positions compete with each other, not on a basis of proved merit, but according to their standing with the "chief." And usually the most proficient "yesser" enjoys the highest standing. This is the greatest breeder of factory and office politics, of jealousy and ill-will. Disputes are not settled by the records or by other just means, but through front-office favoritism, and the organization is soon undermined by resentment and grosser emotions arising from the unfair competition.

In giving promotions and fixing wages and salaries, the system equally is at fault. Usually, advancement goes to the best factory or office politician. Loyalty and efficiency are seldom rewarded. That is why the morale of the personnel of any one-man business is often below par.

Throughout the last few years we have been surfeited with propaganda which exalts labor at the expense of capital. The purpose of the extreme radical always is to erect a vicious barrier between the two. Conflict is deliberately promoted where there must be complete understanding for an elimination of difficulties. Before the age-old problems of capital and labor can be solved, honest representatives of both classes must be convinced of the fact that neither is of any progressive value without the driving force of new ideas.[7]

What can the executive do when he finds that an otherwise good employee is too willing to imitate him? He can make at least one attempt to readjust him by explaining the situation very frankly and telling the "yes" man to agree less and to make more suggestions. The slavish employee may have been conditioned in· that way by some other executive who fired him for disagreeing with the boss. An executive cannot "jump" on employees for an honest questioning of his decisions and then expect them to be filled with helpful suggestions the next day. The fear of losing their jobs will give them introjective characteristics. Employees are not always to be blamed for "putty" minds. Certain executives have so strong an inferiority complex that they cannot endure the presence of subordinates who are their equals in ability.

Many introjectionists develop their introjective habits in their adjustments to cruel parents, stern teachers, or executives who resent suggestions. Through such experiences, the individual learns to cater to people at all times, rather than to cater to them some of the time and to oppose them when opposition is appropriate. An executive's study of the employee's past history will often reveal experiences which brought about the introjective behavior.

Compulsion neuroses and phobias. In the compulsion neurosis, the individual cannot explain why he feels that he must perform a given act, but he dreads failure to follow the ritual which he has set up in his own mind. In its mild forms, it is found among normal people and is generally treated as an idiosyncrasy or a superstition, as in the individuals who tap wood in order to avoid a calamity which they have escaped thus far. Such compulsive acts are trivial and do not affect emotional health.

The more serious compulsions are known as *manias* and are given specific names to indicate their type as *kleptomania,* the

---

[7] Charles P. McCormick, *Multiple Management,* pp. 50-52. Harper & Bros., 1938.

impulse to steal things that are not needed; *pyromania,* the impulse to set fire to things; *onomatomania,* the impulse to say a word again and again or to hunt for it in the memory; *dipsomania,* the periodic uncontrollable craving for alcoholic beverages; and *arithmomania,* the obsessive tendency to count everything, such as the stones in the sidewalk or the objects in a room. A mania is an exaggerated predilection toward a type of activity and is often contrasted with extreme dread of some specific type of situation as in a phobia.

A *phobia* is a persistent and irrational fear of a harmless object or situation. The individual may know quite well that he has no logical reason to fear the thing that he fears. Examples are *claustrophobia,* fear of closed places; *acrophobia,* fear of high places such as the tenth floor of an office building; *agoraphobia,* fear of open spaces, such as fields or wide streets; *pyrophobia,* fear of fire; *misophobia,* fear of dirt; and *aelurophobia,* the fear of cats, Napoleon's well-known fear. The phobia usually comes on very suddenly and overwhelms the patient, who is seized with trembling, sweating, pallor, and all the usual signs of extreme fear. All this, in spite of the fact that the patient knows quite well that his fears are merely morbid and under irrational control. Some persons having phobias are able to continue their daily work by avoiding the situations which stimulate the phobia responses. Others have phobias which unfit them for certain forms of economic life.

The woman who was afraid to look into a mirror for fear that she would find a hair on her face knew that the finding of a hair was no real cause for alarm; but still she became so fearful of seeing her reflection that she refused to handle silverware or to open her eyes in a room where there were windows. The executive who was seized with fear whenever he was in a building higher than the second floor knew that the building was perfectly safe; he simply could not go up to any height. The stenographer who spent most of her time washing her hands knew that her hands were reasonably clean, but still she feared they might be soiled. The bookkeeper who feared to make the figure five knew that figure was harmless, but still he feared it.

What are the barriers which give rise to such apparently irrational adjustments as manias and phobias?

Means[8] studied the fears of a thousand college women and found that only 38 per cent of them indicated any knowledge of the origin of their fears. About 70 per cent of the fears of known origin were due to some personal experience. The first five fears in their relative importance were: snakes, cancer, death of loved ones, death by burning, and bulls.

At least three of these fears are considered by psychoanalysts to be sexual in nature: snakes, burning, and bulls. If we accept the explanation of some psychoanalysts, we shall interpret these manifestations of abnormal fears and impulses as symbols of barriers which are inadmissible impulses. The woman who could not look into a mirror for fear she would see a hair on her face was unable to do so because hair symbolized some sexual wish that she refused consciously to admit to herself. The executive who could not go higher than the second floor of a building was fearful of a moral fall which might be brought about if he yielded to an immoral impulse. The stenographer's fear of contamination was caused by the fear of repressed desires to yield to an immoral impulse such as the sexual entreaties of her lover. The figure five represented the five fingers of the bookkeeper's hand which were used in a sex perversion. And so on for other impulsions, such as the oversolicitude for the health of a wealthy aunt which disguised the wish for her death.

In most analyses of phobias, psychiatrists find that the origin of the fear is closely coupled with a sense of guilt or shame. That is why Freud and his disciples can find many illustrations of his theory that the phobia masks a repressed sex desire. Sex, to most people, is something terrible and unmentionable rather than a perfectly normal impulse. As soon as the phobia-bound individual understands the origin of his fear and is allowed to express the repressed impulse that it symbolizes, the phobia is likely to disappear. Scolding the stenographer will not banish her fear, but uncovering the origin of it may. If the fear persists, the cause has not been found or the process of readjustment is incomplete. Of course, this process of readjustment is one for the attention of the clinical psychologist.

---

[8] M. H. Means, "Fears of One Thousand College Women," *Journal of Abnormal and Social Psychology*, 1936, Vol. 31, pp. 291-311.

We know that some fears are neither subconscious nor symbolical. The fear of failure in an examination may simply represent the recognition that it is deserved because of failure to do what should be done. Some phobias and manias are more easily and logically thought of in terms of conditioned responses or as associative linkages. It is certain that some of the maladjustments of the individual are brought about through simultaneous associations, as in the case of the man who, during a heart attack, collapses in an open section of the city. He may then have an agoraphobia for certain areas.

Parents can do much to prevent abnormal fears. The main form of instruction given to children by some parents seems to be "Shame on you"; "Nobody will like you if you are so naughty"; "You know that you are a naughty little boy, don't you?" and "God will punish little girls who tell lies." No wonder the children of oversolicitous parents often grow up to become fearful retiring nobodies while roughnecks of the slums develop into business and professional leaders. Fears do not dog the roughneck's every step. We must remember that the child fears in silence. Shame may be so strong that it is difficult to obtain admission. Cowardice may develop, and all because the father and mother and teacher have held up the bogey of shame. Every unnatural fear has a natural cause, and the attitude of the executive toward his employees and his children should be that of the analyst who sympathetically discovers the origin of the fear and aids the individual in gaining a better adjustment. A knowledge of what fears really mean is the first step in aiding the phobia-bound person.

Alcoholism. The late Dr. William A. White, who treated many sufferers from alcoholism when he was Superintendent of St. Elizabeth's Hospital, estimated that of ten people who develop a liking for alcoholic drink, seven will be able to take it or leave it and three will become addicted and unable to break the habit.[9] The total number of chronic alcoholics in the United States has been estimated as near 900,000 and the number of new cases as 56,000 annually. The incidence of alcoholism varies greatly with the distribution of urban and rural popula-

[9] *Science News Letter*, March 26, 1938, p. 200.

tion, with the sex ratio, age composition, and many other variables.[10]

The habitual use of alcohol is a result rather than a cause of maladjustment. When the victim of maladjustment is compelled to cease his drinking, the cessation of drinking does not solve his problems but only throws the personality disorders into bolder relief.[11] Persistent excessive drinking is a symptom rather than an illness in itself.

Statistically speaking, many drinkers have had overly solicitous mothers and harsh or cold fathers. In one sense, alcoholism is often a subconscious attempt to return to the earlier stage of mother dependence. At the same time there is also a compulsive striving for emancipation and complete manhood. Temporarily, the alcoholic excess offers an escape to the blissful state of infantilism. Usually the excessive drinker seeks oblivion rather than enjoyment. He is likely to be a solitary rather than a convivial drinker.

No particular factor is characteristic of all alcoholics, but statistical studies of alcoholics and non-alcoholics indicate that the former tend to have had a domineering but idealized mother and a stern, autocratic father who was feared by the child; strong feelings of insecurity, sin, and guilt; marked interest in the opposite sex, with many love affairs but poor marital adjustment; lack of self-consciousness with others; a keyed up emotional level, resulting in work done under high tension; and definitely expressed greater love for the mother than for the father.[12] The inner adjustments are far more important than the environmental variables.

The chronic alcoholic lacks organization of personality. In view of the lack of normal organization of personality, effective treatment is usually very difficult. The employer, wife, or friend of the alcoholic can seldom hope to overcome the victim's failures in adjustment. Psychiatric treatment is, however, far more likely to be effective than mere legislation. The business-

---

[10] Estimates by Dr. Norman Jolliffe of Bellevue Hospital and New York University, reported in *Science News Letter,* November 9, 1940.

[11] R. P. Knight, "The Psychodynamics of Chronic Alcoholism," *Journal of Mental Diseases,* 1937, Vol. 86, pp. 538-548.

[12] M. P. Wittman, "Developmental Characteristics and Personalities of Chronic Alcoholics," *Journal of Abnormal and Social Psychology,* 1939, Vol. 34, pp. 361-377.

Fig. 19. J. E. W. Wallin, Director of Special Education and Mental Hygiene for the State of Delaware and the Wilmington Schools. Anyone interested in adjustment problems of normal people should read his book *Minor Mental Maladjustments in Normal People* (Duke University Press, 1939).

man who finds that an employee or colleague is a chronic alcoholic must usually decide whether he shall sever their business relationships or get along with the victim in spite of his annoying derelictions. Some have qualities which compensate the employer for the alcoholic employee's recurring deficiencies; others can only be discharged, in the hope that they will find their way to an institution where positive treatment will be given them. Many will continue to drink until their adjustment problems have been removed and they have developed new mental habits.[13]

Habit spasms. Have you ever been in a railway station or some other public place and seen a woman stick out her tongue at intervals of every two minutes? Or have you seen the boy who recurrently pulls up one corner of his mouth until every passerby notices him and wonders, "What ails the kid?" Or the girl who rhythmically wrinkles her nose to the extent that she is called "Rabbit"? Have you heard of the man who was taken to the hospital because he would lie in bed, put his heels and the back of his head on the bed, and then give himself a toss up

---

[13] W. R. Miles, "Psychological Factors in Alcoholism," *Mental Hygiene*, 1937, Vol. 21, pp. 529-548.

toward the ceiling? Or have you seen cases of chorea or St. Vitus' dance? The term "tic" is usually given to those muscular twitches which involve only a few muscles. Movements that involve a large number of muscles or the whole body are called "choreic movements." Habit spasms are found most frequently in children, but adults of this type come into an employment office, and the employment man is apt to say, "Did you see that fellow with the 'heebie-jeebies'?"

Why do some people act in so peculiar a manner? The origin of some cases of chorea is in the brain-stem, but most of the "tics" in children develop from some simple irritation of the clothing, such as a tight sleeve, tickling of woolen underclothing, or a sore pimple. The child finds that the movement attracts attention to himself and continues to make the movement even after the cause has been removed. It acts as a sort of pacifier. The movement gives relief from the tension that comes with the urge to do an act when it is inhibited. The satisfaction gained is similar to that of the college girl who is anxious to be popular and, finding that the boys are not attracted to her in large numbers, then talks or acts in a loud manner; or an employee in business who has the ambition to be a big executive, but promotion is slow and he relieves the tension by adopting a distinctive mannerism. Recognition must be obtained in some manner, and it is natural for the habit spasm to continue after it has gained the ticquer much attention.

Does the tic indicate a dangerous adjustment so that the individual should not be hired? The answer is that he is no more dangerous than the individual who compensates in a less spectacular manner by taking up Sunday School teaching. Of course, if the individual attracts the attention of employees or customers to himself rather than to the work that the employees are to do or the goods that the customers should buy, then the ticquer is a nuisance. It is, however, inadvisable for the employment executive to hire the applicant having a tic with the thought that the habit spasm will soon pass away or that he can cure it. These habit movements are usually very resistant to curative treatment.

Sexual anomalies. The sex customs of modern civilization are the most remarkable illustration of the strength of the cortical control over the instinctive or animal nature of man. Bear in mind that throughout the millions of years of evolution of man's forbears, no males took part in that whole line of descent except those who had some sex impulse. Small wonder then that it is a strong force in the life of man. Freud and his followers have considerable evidence whereon to build their brand of psychology. With so strong a force, we need not wonder that perversions or anomalies take place in the sex lives of a small percentage of the people whom we meet. The occasions when it is necessary for the executive to deal with serious sex problems, such as perversions, are few in number. Many businessmen think that they can recognize a sex pervert when he applies for a job. This is not true. At least, no evidence has ever been obtained which indicates that it is possible to recognize the homosexual pervert. When someone meets a stranger and classifies him as a sex pervert merely on the basis of appearances, such as the gaze of the eyes, he is just guessing. The stranger may accidentally give him such an impression because of some characteristic of clothing or voice that unconsciously reminds him of a pervert whom he has met previously.

In terms of Freud, the tendencies of the child are *polymorphous,* or many-form. The sexual sense has not developed in the young child. Later, as it develops, it tends to center its aim in some special direction, usually toward the opposite sex and normal conduct in sex life. However, the child's sex tendencies may be developed in any direction according to the influences that take place in the educational and adjustment process.

The love life of the average individual passes through four stages: love of self, *babyhood;* love of parent, *childhood;* love of chum, *early youth;* and love of mate, *adolescence.* When the individual's love-object remains on the first level, self-love, he is an example of *narcissism;* when on the second level, attachment for a parent, the terms *Oedipus* or *Electra complex* are used; and when fixated on the third level, attraction for persons of the same sex, the general term *homosexuality* is used. The last term is often used in a broad general sense and is contrasted with *heterosexuality,* attraction toward individuals of the opposite sex, but neither of these last two terms necessarily implies perversion or a specific sex relation.

The best-adjusted persons also attain a fifth stage of love-life, *creative love*. They and their mates identify their personalities in absorbing tasks of rearing children, developing a happy home life, and pursuing successful vocational activities. Biologically, creative love is most commonly expressed in the rearing of children.

Nature has given man a strong sex impulse, but civilization has fenced in the impulse with dozens of taboos. It is only natural, therefore, that masturbation should be the most common perversion. A passing addiction to it in infancy is considered normal by many psychologists. Contrary to popular interpretation, masturbation is not to be considered as a cause of insanity but as a result or accompaniment of it. As stated by an eminent physician who has studied the subject:

Some young men go insane over their inability to abstain from masturbation. Warnings against masturbating may be well meant, but the pictured evils are vastly exaggerated, and the consequent harm done to young men and to girls is infinitely greater than any possible harm done from indulgence in the habit. Masturbation may occasionally do harm to a weak-minded subject, but the idiocy or nervous affections, 'loss of manhood,' etc., are less frequently the result of excessive masturbation than excessive masturbation is the result of idiocy; idiocy is not the *result* but the cause of masturbation.[14]

Pullias [15] made a study of the beliefs of seventy-five young men regarding masturbation and found that 87 per cent had heard of it as having a seriously damaging effect upon those who practice it. Huschka's [16] investigation disclosed that at least 128 of 320 problem children had been dealt with destructively concerning masturbation. Direct physical threats were employed and over half of these children had been threatened with actual genital injury, thus giving rise to what Freudians refer to as castration anxiety. Nearly all studies of masturbation have indicated that it is an important mental hygiene problem which often has serious effects on personality and should be handled by persons who have both intelligence and emotional balance regarding sex practices.

[14] O. A. Wall, *Sex and Sex Worship*, p. 166. C. V. Mosby Co., 1922.
[15] E. V. Pullias, "Masturbation as a Mental Hygiene Problem," *Journal of Abnormal & Social Psychology*, 1937, Vol. 32, pp. 216-222.
[16] M. Huschka, "The Incidence and Character of Masturbation Threats in a Group of Problem Children," *Psychoanalytic Quarterly*, 1938, Vol. 7, pp. 338-356.

Sadism (the *a* pronounced as in *say*) refers to some few individuals who do not express their sexual tendencies in a normal
direction but gratify sexual feelings by the infliction or sight of
pain. The pain may be real or it may be simulated, in which
case it is symbolic. This anomaly is found among men more
often than among women, as we would naturally expect. An
example is a famous American millionaire who raises rabbits
and then tears them to pieces with his own hands. In any large
organization, one is apt to find mild expressions of the sadistic
variety in the form of persons who like to pinch others or stick
pins into them.

Masochism is the opposite of sadism. The individual's sexual feelings are gratified when he suffers pain. The pain may
be real or simulated. The latter is symbolic. The masochistic
tendency is found among women more often than among men.

Exhibitionism is the gratification of sex by the exposure of
the body, especially erogenous parts. It is the showing-off
tendency in the extreme. Some analysts claim that the desire
of some leaders in business and public affairs to be the "whole
show" in the presence of others is merely substituting this type
of exhibitionism for a more perverted and unacceptable variety
of showing off.

Voyerism, a minor mental maladjustment which contrasts with
exhibitionism, is the tendency to derive sexual satisfaction from
looking at sexual objects and acts. The "Peeping Tom" [17] who
is occasionally caught by campus policemen is an extreme case
of voyerism. (The word comes from the French *voir*, to see.)

Less extreme are those people who show unusual interest in
case histories from medical books, who insist upon knowing the
intimate details of their friends' lives, and who are happy in
listening to a particular kind of gossip about movie stars and
other famous people. Some business concerns have "old maids"
who are forever curious about what their associates do after
working hours. These employees can make an office rather unpleasant for other workers.

This unusual type of adjustment is used largely by people

---

[17] "Night Club Patrons Cry 'Criminal' at 'Peeping Toms,'" *Science News
Letter*, November 27, 1937.

whose own lives are drab.   They are more or less unable to make
a satisfactory normal social adjustment, and so they devote
time to watching and hearing about others whose activities are
nearer normal.

Homosexuality, when used as signifying a perversion, is the
term given to the desire for sexual relations with persons of the
same sex.   In this connection we must bear in mind that no man
is wholly male, nor is any woman wholly female.   Sex-ness is
a relative trait.   We are mixtures of physical and mental traits.
Many women have the general bodily conformation and pilosity
which is characteristic of the male, and many men have some
typically female traits.   It is rather to be expected, then, that
some individuals would prefer members of their own sex.   An
exciting cause of homosexuality is that of isolation of the sexes
as in penitentiaries, on shipboard, and in one-sex boarding
schools.   "Crushes" are likely to develop where the sex impulse
has no normal outlets.   Coeducational colleges are more in harmony with the mental life of human beings than one-sex schools.
In the coeducational institutions the two sexes mingle with each
other in a normal manner.   The family type of social contacts is
present.   A boy is not some heroic sexless knight in armor to
the girl who sees him each day in the classroom and notes his
humanness when asked a question by the instructor.   Boys and
girls will continue to fall in love with each other until human
nature changes, and the best preventive of sexual anomalies is
to give the child and youth a sane and normal sex environment
where parents are not shocked by sexual digressions but are intelligent in redirecting them.

References

Louttit, C. M., *Clinical Psychology,* Chapter XII.   Harper & Bros., 1936.

Menninger, Karl A., *The Human Mind,* Chapter IV.   F. S. Crofts & Co.,
    1931.

Plant, J. S., *Personality and the Cultural Pattern.*   Commonwealth Fund,
    1937.

Shaffer, Laurance Frederic, *The Psychology of Adjustment,* Chapters VII and
    VIII.   Houghton Mifflin Co., 1936.

For an extensive bibliography on alcoholism, see Helen Marshall, "Alcohol:
    A Critical Review of the Literature, 1929-1940," *Psychological Bulletin,*
    Vol. 38, No. 4, April, 1941.

Projects

1. Study any tendencies you may have toward fantasy or daydreaming. Which of the following types seems to be dominant: Display fantasy; Saving daydream; Fantasy of grandeur; Homage daydream; Suffering hero daydream? Can you suggest possible causes for the direction the tendency takes?

2. Consider people whom you have known and list any examples of fixed ideas you may have noted. Can you discover rational relationships between the fixed ideas and their adjustment background?

3. Make a collection of newspaper clippings concerning persons whose peculiar behavior has gotten them mention in the newspapers. Compare any explanations given in the clippings with hypotheses of your own.

4. Read some recent articles on "Alcoholics Anonymous" such as the one by Jack Alexander in the March 1, 1941 issue of *The Saturday Evening Post*. Evaluate the benefits and limitations of the methods of this group.

5. Analyze for his compensatory behavior, an acquaintance of middle age who has never married. To what extent has such activity resulted in satisfactory adjustment?

6. Draw up a list of beneficial and possibly harmful adjustment influences in coeducational and non-coeducational schools. Check those which you can substantiate from your own or your friends' experiences.

6

Adjustment by Ailments

Patient: "Oh, doctor, I have the most awful pain somewhere in my shoulders."

Doctor: "And when did you first notice the pain, madam?"

Patient: "About two months ago, I think. Yes, it was two months ago. It was just about the time Mrs. Neighbor got her new fur coat; the snob."

A PSYCHIATRIST reported the case of a woman who claimed that she had stomach trouble because of a frog in her stomach. She "knew" she had swallowed a frog egg while on a picnic. Her physician ridiculed the idea but she was so insistent that he finally agreed to operate for the removal of the frog. Accordingly, he sent her to a hospital to be prepared for the operation and he, at the same time, hired a small boy to catch a frog for him. To give the woman the impression that she had really had an operation, an incision was made in her abdomen, and the doctor showed her the "frog," in a bottle of alcohol, which had presumably been removed from her stomach. The woman was delighted and at once recovered, but only temporarily. Three months after the psuedo-operation, she claimed that the first frog had laid some eggs and that she now had two frogs in her stomach!

This amusing example illustrates the uselessness of ordinary logical thinking in the consideration of the many ailments which are functional rather than organic.

When a surgeon is prevailed upon to operate for a functional disturbance, the operation does not, as a rule, result in permanent cure. A physician may occasionally give "placebos," pills which have no medicinal value, in order to satisfy a patient temporarily. However, physicians who treat the functionally ill realize that certain patients need an improved adjustment to their problems more than they need pills.

How illness often becomes a means of adjustment. Any form of invalidism is likely to be useful as a means of adjustment to problems. Almost every child learns that he can avoid unpleasant duties such as mowing the lawn, washing dishes, or studying his lessons, by feigning illness.

Jo is a boy of twelve who has been feeling very much out of the family picture. He is the youngest child. His sister is soon to be married and his brother has just started to work, but Jo is at an age when he is not particularly interesting to any member of the family. He has been doing only fairly well in his school work and he has definitely neglected his arithmetic.

One morning he went down to breakfast and ate rather heartily: he had oatmeal with cream, eggs, bacon, jam, and milk; and while he was eating he recalled that he was going to have an arithmetic test that morning. He had a queer, twitchy feeling of excitement in his stomach at the thought of the arithmetic test. He started walking slowly to school, thinking more about the test, and his stomach felt queerer and the oatmeal weighed very heavily on it. He had a vague feeling, which was hardly a thought, that if his breakfast were to come up he wouldn't have to go to school, and the arithmetic test came to mind again. Suddenly he found it hard to keep the breakfast down.

Shortly after his arrival at school, it did come up. He was sent home by the principal with a clear conscience to have a day in bed. The principal telephoned his mother, who immediately became concerned. She put Jo to bed in the guest room and made a fuss over him such as he had not experienced since he was quite a small boy. His sister came in and showed him her wedding presents; his brother stopped and had a talk with him before going out in the evening, an event which had not occurred for months; and his father spent the evening reading to him.

This upset stomach had a high value: no arithmetic test, and solicitude from all the people from whom he had been wishing attention for some time. The next time Jo was faced with a difficult situation and there was a queer feeling in his stomach, it was no longer necessary to go through all the preliminary steps. Now meals just come up without further consideration on his part.[1]

The child's convenient illness often brings about considerable sympathy and attention. Later the same child meets problems for which he lacks requisite skills or energies to solve. The poorly-adjusted individual cannot admit to himself his own lack of courage to make direct attack upon his problems or duties. That would lower his sense of self-worth. However, the old habits of evasion through ailment take place subcon-

---

[1] Caroline B. Zachry, *Emotion and Conduct in Adolescence*, pp. 69-70. D. Appleton-Century Co., 1940.

sciously because the pattern for that kind of adjustment has been used in the past. His ego is sustained because he himself is not aware of the true cause of his ailment. He believes that he is ill. In fact he is ill, but the origin of the illness has been forgotten. He repressed the recognition of his inabilities or deficiencies.

We must not confuse *Repression* with *Suppression*. The latter is a conscious process; we use it when we force an idea out of our minds by deliberately attending to something else. A person gets a letter containing bad news on the morning of an important examination; he forces himself to put it aside and go through with the examination. In other words, he suppresses his tendency to grief or anxiety for the time being. If it were *repressed*, he would forget that he had ever had the letter. Such repression does occur, especially in certain neurotic types of personalities, but not out of a clear sky; that is, the matter repressed is connected with earlier conflicts which underwent repression. A young woman stenographer lost her job because she forgot to transcribe an important letter, and when she maintained that she had not taken it she was thought to be lying. The letter was addressed to a man whose name was that of a former sweetheart who had jilted her. The normal adult, apparently, does not make much use of Repression; he handles his conflicts, his griefs and disappointments, in other ways.[2]

The executive whose office boy reports on the first day of the baseball season that he is too ill to work but at the same time winks knowingly to the boss, who himself enjoys baseball, has insight into the "illness." In contrast to the office boy, the stenographer, an introverted spinster, may have a splitting headache and find it necessary to go home and go to bed. She probably lacks insight into her adjustments because she fails to recognize that her illness is her subconscious method of avoiding a visit from a former classmate who always could capture more boy friends than she could.

Many ailments do have an organic basis, but some are wholly or partially functional. We must bear in mind that a pain is felt through the mechanisms of the brain rather than only at the point of injury. We say that the pain of the psychoneurotic is in his "head." Well, all pains are felt in the head. Surgeons tell us that, when they sever the foot of a soldier, the soldier can still "feel" the ache of his corns or the bedclothes pressing on his "foot." The war veteran who had had both feet cut off and

---

[2] Winifred V. Richmond, *Personality—Its Development and Hygiene*, p. 166. Farrar & Rinehart, 1937.

yet predicted the weather from the aches of his corns was not merely "joshing" his hearers. Stimuli passed over certain nerve tracts which formerly conveyed impulses from his corns, and the response in his brain was quite the same as it had been before he had had his feet cut off. A psychological pain, therefore, is just as painful as an organic pain. We do our friends an injustice when we tell them that they only imagine the pain and that, if they wanted to do so, they could forget it. They are not helped by scoldings. Rather, they become worse. But, on the other hand, we should not coddle the patient.

Some pains are conditioned responses, as we can readily see in many children. If father sits down to the table and tells mother that spinach gives him indigestion, the little members of the family tend to develop the same symptoms when required to eat their spinach. Mothers who suffer from painful menstruation condition their daughters to the same pains when they reach maturity. Epidemics of various sorts have been reported in schools, after one child had a real or a functional ailment that impressed the other children. For this reason, intelligent teachers and parents do not discuss their aches and pains in the presence of children.

One of the writer's colleagues in psychology specialized in certain phases of the subject, where he had frequent contacts with the surgeons of a large city hospital of New York State. He developed a close friendship with the two leading surgeons of the hospital staff. These two surgeons were good friends and worked together, but each smoked a different brand of cigar. Each surgeon claimed that the other's "rope" would make him ill if he should smoke one of that brand. One day the psychologist and the two surgeons were at work in the hospital laboratory and all of them were smoking their favorite cigars. The psychologist, unknown to the surgeons, changed the bands on the half-smoked cigars and allowed each to complete the smoking of his own cigar. He then called attention to the bands and said that each surgeon had smoked the other fellow's ·cigar. Each surgeon then claimed that he wondered why he had felt so peculiar and one of them actually became nauseated!

Medical students often develop the symptoms of the patients whom they study. When the writer arranges tours through state hospitals for the benefit of his students, he usually finds that one or two students develop enough symptoms to require some form of treatment. In some cases the student must be sent to a psychiatrist for mental treatment before he recovers. Suggestion, no doubt, plays an important part in many of our functional illnesses.

Functional illness enables the individual to evade barriers. In this discussion, we want to give emphasis to the part that illness plays as a means of escape from unpleasant problems. The classic case of the girl who was engaged to the man she loved and became totally deaf when she realized that he no longer loved her is illustrative of a definite attempt to escape reality through illness. She became deaf on the evening when her sweetheart called with the express purpose of telling her that he no longer loved her and wished to be released from the engagement. Deafness enabled her to evade the problem.

Illness may be an escape from an unpleasant situation even though such an adjustment will not be admitted or recognized by the patient. One businessman of unusual honesty borrowed money from his relatives and friends and earnestly expected to be able to pay it back from anticipated profits. Unfortunately, the business did not prosper and the money was lost. The debtor could not face his creditors; nor could he commit suicide because he loved his wife and child. Suddenly he became totally blind and has remained blind for several years. The examining physicians are convinced that the blindness has no organic cause. Strange as it may seem, his blindness is not a barrier to him but is an acceptable mode of adjustment to an otherwise unbearable situation.

Shell-shock is an excellent example of the way fear and anxiety play a part in bringing about illness. Dr. Sara Stinchfield-Hawk has expressed the nature of this adjustment in the following words:

We no longer speak of shell-shock, but of war-shock, and we find that the majority of nervous patients in our veterans' hospitals were, and still are, those who did not go overseas, were never subjected to bombardment, and never got beyond the officers' or regular training camps.[3]

---

[3] "Recovered Patient Re-lives Experience in Sanitarium," *Science News Letter*, September 14, 1940, p. 165.

FIG. 20. Fred A. Moss, Director of Tests, Association of American Medical Colleges. Those who are interested in the study of psychology and general medicine and mental disorders should refer to his book, *Applications of Psychology*, Chapters XIII and XIV (Houghton Mifflin Co., 1929).

Sickness not only keeps fearful men out of battle but also enables new employees to seek to evade failure on the new job, as reported by one executive:

In this connection I might say that it has been a continual source of amazement to me how frequently men stay home during the first few weeks on a new position. One would imagine that nothing short of serious illness would prevent prompt and regular attendance on the job until it was thoroughly mastered and a competent understudy was on hand to keep things properly moving. But such is not the case.[4]

Thousands of employees are uncertain regarding their abilities and, being unable to admit their limitations, they may make an adjustment by becoming sickly. Sickness is often an acceptable excuse for vocational mediocrity or failure. Many executives, too, realize that they cannot achieve outstanding business success, and so their desk drawers are filled with pills and medicine bottles. Sickness, conscious and subconscious in nature, is an acceptable excuse for our inability to achieve the eminence we desire. People who evade their barriers by means of illness feel that employers, teachers, parents, friends, and relatives have no right to expect the "sick" to accomplish very much when they are "too ill" to work. At the same time, they have the satisfac-

---

[4] Walter A. Lowen, *Advertising & Selling*, July 1940, p. 31.

tion of knowing that they do drag through the day's work when others tell them that they really ought to be home in bed!

Most members of our American culture are sympathetic toward persons who are organically sick and toward those who use illness as a means of evading problems. Almost everyone is practically encouraged to use illness as an excuse for failure. This situation should lead us to be suspicious of the real reason for any illness which is not obviously caused by some organic condition. Furthermore, a knowledge of common adjustment patterns which include illness should enable us to choose more intelligently the person with whom we work or live, such as the employee or the mate.

The young man or woman in love as well as the executive should be able to recognize the more common patterns for maladjustment such as neurasthenia. A neurasthenic wife, for example, is the kind of spouse who keeps her mate busy propping up a partner who insists upon being hard to live with. The neurasthenic mate is a true psychological "ball and chain." For the lover, the time to recognize the neurasthenic is before marriage; not after. For the executive, the best time to deal with psychoneurotic employees is before they are hired. Of course, if the prospective neurasthenic mate or employee has compensating qualities, the marriage or employment may be satisfactory, but the one who must bear the effects of their maladjustments should be aware of the extra load he will have to carry. The person who knows the *syndrome* (pattern of symptoms) of the more common psychoneurotic ailments has an important advantage in human relations.

The psychoneuroses. Some experts classify the psychoneuroses with the organic ailments. They do involve many physical symptoms, such as headache, backache, indigestion, constipation, and dysmenorrhea. The extent to which these bodily symptoms are cause or effect or mere accompaniments of maladjustments is unknown. However, we shall describe them for the benefit of the psychological neophyte so that he can recognize them when he finds himself, his friends, or his employees having the reaction patterns characteristic of the psychoneurotic.

Neurasthenia means literally *asthenia,* or exhaustion, of the nerves. It is often called nervous exhaustion or nervous breakdown.   However, it is really not so much an exhaustion of nerve energy as a case of misplaced energy.   It is more common among women than among men.   The main symptoms in the syndrome are (a) chronic bodily fatigue, (b) irritability (occasionally the patient exhibits pronounced exhilaration, but this is soon followed by fatigue and irritability), (c) inability to concentrate attention on any one task, (d) bad temper, (e) moodiness, and (f) self-analysis and self-pity; (g) *hypochondria,* or excessive attention to the functioning of the bodily organs, with continued functional pains, is a frequent accompaniment.   As soon as the doctor shows the neurasthenic that she cannot have that kind of pain where she has located it, she then claims that the pain has moved to some other part of the body.   The more attention the pain receives, the worse it becomes.   For this reason it is well to keep medical books in the physician's office and the public library. They should not be in most homes.   If the housewife is tempted to buy medical books, let her buy, instead, a book on how to operate a tourist home or how to rear her children.

What are the causes?   Some men attribute neurasthenia to heredity, but it is generally considered to be due very largely to an inability to face reality.   It is an evasional device.   As in most psychoneurotic ailments, the evading individual is likely to be in a state of conflict between his instinctive tendencies and his intelligent strivings.   A housewife, for example, has instinctive urges to meet and enjoy the company of handsome men whom she likes, but she also knows that she must obey the rules of conduct of our culture.   In her conflicts, physiological imbalances arise in her nervous system.   Freud [5] concluded that neurasthenia was nothing more nor less than the expression of suppressed sexual excitement.

Neurasthenia may be accentuated by bad habits such as late hours, sexual excesses, and alcoholism.   The endocrine glands may be a factor in the psychoneurosis, but that has not been demonstrated as yet.   The strenuous life of the present age is supposed to be responsible in many cases.   This is hardly correct.   The stress of modern life for many people lies in the fact that they do not have enough important things to do.   This ap-

---

[5] For an understandable discussion on this point of view, see John K. Winkler and Walter Bromberg, *Mind Explorers,* Chapter XV.   Reynal & Hitchcock, 1939.

plies particularly to the women of the middle and upper classes. Labor-saving devices have eliminated most of the hard but beneficial labor of the American home. In addition to finding themselves more or less useless, women have a kind of indefinable, unfulfilled longing to be something or to do something worth while. Many are out of the general scheme of things except as spectators or as they concoct something to do.

A commonly chosen device to help a woman to escape neurasthenia and to make herself a part of the scheme of things is to "take up a cause." She hears that certain factory workers are making only fifteen dollars a week and she starts a home for them; or she finds that some dogs do not have homes, so she starts a home for homeless dogs. Some of these "causes" are quite worthy and legitimate, but they are not a natural part of the lives of these women. As the term expresses it, "the cause is taken up."

Attaching one's self to a cause is better, however, than seeking relief in a continuous round of social pleasures. When a woman has a so-called nervous breakdown, because she has dashed from one meeting to the next meeting, then to a show, and then to a dance and supper at breakfast time, the breakdown is really caused by mental factors that caused her to dash around in circles. The rushing around to functions is merely the expression of a lack of adjustment to life, and the breakdown is just a nice name for a maladjustment. When effort is merely effort and not a part of a unified plan of living, then the effort becomes fatiguing and unsatisfying. The individual becomes irritable and moody. Life is futile.

What are the remedies? The usual method suggested by physicians is to take a rest cure at home or in a sanatorium. A rest cure of the right kind—a cure that builds up the mind as well as the body—is desirable. However, many cures are more harmful than beneficial for neurasthenics. If the patient merely goes to a new environment where she sits down and does nothing, she is not helped to build a new philosophy of life that will revitalize her. Temporarily the rest is helpful if it removes the patient to an environment which does not have some of her old problems, and in so far as the maladjustment may be accentuated by a rundown physical state.

If the attention is directed to the bodily organs or functions, harm is done. Sensations of pain and discomfort are soon established even though the organic state is perfect. Detailed attention to the diet often makes the indigestion worse. The physician's questions regarding symptoms are interpreted to mean that the symptoms are present and suggestibility runs wild.

Pains and aches should be minimized by friends and associates, and the patient should be given mental pictures of health and strength rather than pity and sympathy. Make her feel that she is missing fun by her illness. Social contacts should be with those of dynamic, positive personalities. The mental imagery should be of a very happy sort. Autosuggestion is of value if the patient can be trained to. apply it with complete belief. If she can do so with conviction, it is well for her to renew her interest in some religion and to acquire a philosophy of her own.

The real problem is that of getting the patient to live outside herself rather than within her own feelings. She should acquire absorbing and satisfying work that fits into some plausible scheme for her own philosophy of life. Work which necessity forces her to do is the main help. Mental re-education is the best route to attain this end of a healthy outlook; but the whole scheme of treatment is more easily applied on paper than to the patient. Most of these patients are not ill enough for scientists to spend much time and effort on them, and so they are neglected and allowed to grow worse. Neurasthenia is exceedingly difficult to relieve for any great length of time, and it is much harder to cure. One lesson that the neurasthenics indicate to the parent is that his son and daughter should be required to work at some steady occupation which is worth while to society and to the individual. From the standpoint of sound mental adjustment, we should have many women going into business or some other kind of work, unless they are, of course, needed in the home. If business will not accept them, then we must expect to have more neurasthenic wives and daughters and to supply institutions and "causes" to take care of them.

It is difficult to secure data to prove that women are more afflicted with neurasthenia than are men, but many physicians judge this to be true. If so, it may be partly caused by the fact that we are more solicitous of girls than of boys. When John-

nie, aged six, comes into the house, crying because of a skinned
nose, we tell him, "Be a man and stop crying." When his sister,
aged eight, comes into the house crying because of a skinned
knee we tell her, "Well now, that is too bad. Let's see that knee.
Maybe we can put something on it to make it feel better." We
still give women the impression that they are weaker than men
and, therefore, that we must defer to them because they are
women. Daughters should be required to work just as much as
sons. The work may be different, but they should sense the joy
of a positive productive life rather than the negative attitude
of attention through illness.

Psychasthenia[6] is classified by some medical men under the
heading of neurasthenia, but it has certain differences which
should be noted. Psychasthenia is characterized by (a) an exhaustion which follows mental work. The other symptoms are
(b) obsessions, (c) manias, (d) impulsions, and (e) phobias.
The individual may have a strong impulse to set fire to his home,
to steal money, or to injure someone. Some of the psychasthen-
ics wonder whether they are alive and whether they are really
themselves. They feel that they are not in control of themselves.
Sometimes the world seems to be closing in about them and
crushing them. They know that their fears and impulsions are
without any real basis, but still they continue to fight them.
We are not concerned here with the true or completely psychasthenic patient, but rather with the psychasthenic tendencies
that are found among the members of the office, the school, and
the home.

Worry is the most common tendency under this heading. In
general, we consider worry an unpleasant mental state, and yet,
like any other habit that is continued, it may become agreeable
in its own way. A worry may hide a symbolic wish, as does the
excessive worry regarding the health of a wealthy uncle whose
money we hope to inherit, but we never discuss the wish with
ourselves. A boy worries about the welfare of his mother when
she goes away from home. Inasmuch as she has kept him tied
to her apron string, he experiences a sense of relief and may

---

[6] Some psychologists do not use the term *psychasthenia* because they prefer
to treat phobias, obsessions, and compulsions as specific forms of adjustment
rather than the group term. However, the term is still useful as a designation
for certain patterns of symptoms, and it has been included here for that reason.

secretly hope that the train will be wrecked in order that he may be completely free. A mother sends her children out to play, and when they do not come home at the usual time, she worries; partly because of the fact that some neighbor's child was lost or killed, but also because she will have a greater thrill when the children do come back. In many cases the worry is a kind of thrill or a preparation for a thrill. It relieves the monotony of housework. Worry may also be a kind of mental random movement which can be made for the solution of a problem when physical attention is impossible.

Temporary worry is not so great a problem as the persistent apprehensive variety of worry regarding one's financial status, health, or studies. In many cases there is just cause for worry on these subjects, but the psychasthenic does nothing about it. If a student is failing in his studies, he should not worry about it but get to work. If a person worries about his health, the answer is to have a thorough physical examination and then, if the worry is unjustified, stop it. But here comes the difficulty. When the chronic worrier is told all about the fact that he has no real reason to worry, he still continues to worry. For this reason, it is well to ask the expert in worry whether he really wants to stop worrying. Even if he answers, "Of course I do," he should have the idea emphasized most strongly that he must really want to stop worrying before anything can be done for him. He must determine to picture in his mind positive, healthful, pleasant images rather than the expected unpleasant imagery. Furthermore, he must put into effect definite schedules of work and recreation which will help to develop new mental habits in dealing with his problems. He must use direct attack.

Stage fright is often a mild aspect of the psychasthenia syndrome. Why should anyone be fearful when he speaks before others? If he has nothing worth saying, he can simply say so and sit down; but, if he has a message of any importance, he ought to be glad to give it to his fellows. Of course, a talk in public puts one in a position where the ego is liable to be assailed. The speaker knows that some members of the audience may know more about the subject than he does, and he fears their disapproval. This can be overcome by the speaker's frank acknowledgment that he is presenting merely his own experiences or views and that he would like others there to tell him wherein he is wrong. This does not mean that the speaker who is called upon for a five-minute report or discussion should then spend a half-hour in making apologies. Nor need his talk begin with an apology. But his attitude should be that of the student and learner rather than that of the polished expert. In fact, very many of our psychological difficulties, particularly our self-conscious feelings and fears, would vanish if we could only get ourselves into the mental state of the true student. The true student seeks truth and the facts. Whatever his searches may uncover, it will not jeopardize his ego, because his ego is not involved. The true scientist is interested in finding the things that fail as well as the things that succeed, because he wants to know all aspects of the problem—not just those that give him prestige.

If the speaker makes up his mind that speaking in public is an opportunity for him to exchange ideas with his fellows and at the same time an opportunity to learn more than he can give, he is likely to have little trouble in speaking anywhere, unless he has had a serious shock while speaking in public. If he has had a decidedly unpleasant experience while speaking in public, then he will have to regain his ease of speaking by gradual steps. He should begin on small and sympathetic audiences. He should practice on people who know much less than he does of the subject he talks about. He should get away from the idea that he is competing with anyone. He is just going to tell what he knows as clearly and as well as he can, and thereby he hopes to learn more himself.

Abulia or the *abulic obsession* is also a common psychasthenic tendency. This term is applied to the inability to get started on the job that awaits our action. We have a report to prepare or a call to make. We often find ourselves postponing it and procrastinating until we are too embarrassed to do it. This is one reason why operating a business according to a definite schedule is better than trusting to the initiative of the employees. A large part of the executive's work consists of setting schedules for his associates and then seeing that the schedules are followed. Almost everyone often finds himself unable to do the things that he wants to do but somehow never gets done. The answer is to make a schedule for his annoying hang-over tasks. The student, for example, should set a definite date when an assignment is to be completed, and at once start a small part of the task. He should not plan to complete the whole job or a large part of it at one sitting, but should make the outline, and then he will find that he can continue for a reasonable length of time.

Another help is "whenpecking." By this is meant enlisting the co-operation of one's colleagues. The businessman can, for example, tell his wife or secretary that he wants to finish a task by a certain date and request her to jog his memory occasionally. Some evening when he may have made up his mind to go to a stag party, his wife will say: *"When* are you going to finish that fourth lesson in business management?" He may be more or less offended at the insinuation, but he will know that she is right and probably will get busy on the important task.

When definite and irrational psychasthenic tendencies are persistent, such as the handicapping phobia, compulsion neurosis, impulsions to say indecent words in public, and the desire to injure some person who is loved and admired, then it is well to consult the psychiatrist. These impulsions are symbolic of patterns which have been connected with the adjustment of the individual to some unrecognizable and inadmissible impulse, such as the sex impulse.

Hysteria is a word used in many different ways by the psychiatrists, but it is most frequently applied to certain unstable emotional states that come and go without apparent cause. An example is that of a housewife who, while busily engaged in her housework, such as sweeping the kitchen floor, suddenly breaks forth into a fit of intense weeping. She may cry bitterly for a few minutes and then pick up her broom and resume her work. When she is asked why she cried she says that she did not cry. She is unable to recall the incident because of her mental dissociation. In many cases the individual also acquires a paralysis of a limb or an area of anesthesia, or has tics and tremors, or may be in a state of mental stupor and have strong delusions.

Hysteria is a mental disorder which is characterized not by hysterical behavior such as crying but by mental dissociation. One famous case of hysteria had a history of five different personalities.[7]   Hysteria often includes pronounced disturbances in bodily and mental activity and may result in illnesses such as hysterical blindness, as in the case of the business man who became blind after he was unable to pay back money borrowed for his failing business, mentioned on page 129.[8]

In some cases of hysteria the patient seems to acquire his functional ailment as an accompaniment of an emotional outburst.   In the ordinary case of invalidism, the patient acquires the chronic ailing more slowly.   Invalidism is more common among intelligent persons.   Hysteria is more common among children and adults of low intelligence than among persons of high intelligence.   The hysteria patients have a tendency toward simulation and delusions.   Many of them have falsely accused those whom they love.   Children have caused their parents to be brought into court, because they claimed that their parents had locked them in the attic or the cellar and had given them no food for days at a time.

The chief suggestion for all of us is the fact that disease may be truly organic, functional, or a combination of the two.   If it is functional, it is just as serious as if it were organic, but it must be dealt with along psychological lines.

Malingering versus neurosis.   The executive who supervises large numbers of factory employees sooner or later has the problem of deciding whether an employee who claims compensation is suffering from an organic ailment or is merely malingering. True malingering places a premium on fraud.   Both malingering and neurosis may spring from maladjustments of personality, and differentiation between the two is very difficult.

An analysis of 1,000 consecutive disability insurance claims for psychoneurosis was made five years after disability had commenced.   Almost 30 per cent of the cases had been incorrectly diagnosed.   The mortality rate for these neurotics also showed that neurotics have a distinctly greater life expectancy than normal persons and that suicide is very rare among them.[9]

---

[7] Morton Prince, "Miss Beauchamp—The Theory and Psychogenesis of Multiple Personality," *Journal of Abnormal Psychology*, 1920, Vol. 15, pp. 82ff.

[8] Pierre Janet, *The Major Symptoms of Hysteria*, The Macmillan Co., 1920, presents some classic examples of hysteria.   A four-year case of functional blindness is described on page 168.

[9] P. G. Denker, "The Prognosis of Insured Neurotics," *New York State Journal of Medicine*, 1939, Vol. 39, pp. 238-247.

The fact that many neurotics, especially hysteria cases, do not have an organic ailment is often indicated by their ability to use muscles or limbs in certain situations but not when they are at work. One telegrapher, for example, could send messages perfectly when he knew that his key was connected to a testing machine, but he developed a cramp as soon as his key was attached to the main line. Many of these occupational neurotics can use their muscles very effectively at play but are unable to use them in work. The expert in diagnosis uses various tests to determine whether the claimant for compensation is malingering or neurotic. Important tests are willingness to take medicine regularly, to undergo surgical operations, to submit to repeated examinations, and the content of dreams and conversation.[10]

The occupational neurotic is usually very unhappy in his work or hates some part of it. Sometimes he merely associates some personal emotional problem with his work. Neuroses of this kind are more likely to occur when the worker is unable to quit his job because of his geographic isolation, requirements of a long-term contract, or enlistment in the army. An injury, fatigue of certain muscles, or an example of a fellow-worker may suggest the way in which the maladjustment can be made to disappear or how the patient's emotional problems can be corrected through systematic psychological treatment.

Allergies. *Allergy* may be defined as a special sensitivity to a substance that is harmless to most individuals. We all know persons who cannot eat certain foods without distress. Others cannot be in the presence of furry or hairy animals without developing asthma or skin eruptions. About 10 per cent of the people of the United States are allergic to a marked degree and another 40 per cent to a minor extent. Wheat foods, eggs, and milk are the most common causes of food allergies. The victims develop certain itches, aches, sneezes, and wheezes. In one community survey regarding allergies, it was found that 10 per cent of the people had hay fever, 3.6 per cent asthma, 2.9 per cent eczema, 3.7 per cent urticaria, and 3.3 per cent gastrointestinal allergy.[11]

---

[10] H. A. Davidson, "Neurosis and Malingering," *American Journal of Medical Jurisprudence,* 1939, Vol. 2, pp. 94-96.
[11] W. C. Service, *Journal of the American Medical Association,* May 1939.

Some allergies are undoubtedly of organic origin but many appear to be psychological. For example, one woman always suffered from asthma when she went to a certain railroad station. Someone told her that the station dust was of an unusual chemical nature and that she could be cured by having an injection of the dust. Her doctor injected her with a solution of common salt. After that the attacks of asthma ceased.[12]

When 50 adult patients with bronchial asthma were taken from an allergy clinic and studied psychiatrically, 37 patients appeared to have an emotional component in their asthmatic attacks, 20 patients reported that the first attack was emotionally precipitated, and 30 patients showed neurotic traits usually of a compulsive nature.[13]

Studies of patients having arthritis, colitis, and obesity indicate that many have deep-seated resentments or feelings of guilt. They are likely to have resentments toward employers, members of the family, or teachers. They are in prolonged states of anxiety. When primitive men were aroused to anger against an enemy, they could expend their aroused energies against the enemy. Civilized men have many arousals of their emotions, but the heightened bodily activities cannot be expressed promptly. When a man loses his job, he has the same fears experienced by his cave-man ancestors who needed food, but the stronger heartbeat and extra secretions are now superfluous. The biochemical changes which take place for increased action must be suppressed, but their suppression does not remove them. The aroused bodily resources find expression in protective and aggressive reactions of asthma, arthritis, colitis, allergies, and hundreds of other apparently unrelated manifestations.

To give these persons whose physiology of anxiety incapacitates them a label such as "psychoneurotic" or to accuse them of overworking their imagination does not help them. They merely drift from one doctor or faith healer to another. What each really needs is a reorganization of adjustment habits, to know the

---

[12] George W. Gray, "The Strange Ways of Allergy," *Harper's Magazine*, January 1939.

[13] M. T. McDermott and S. Cobb, "A Psychiatric Survey of Fifty Cases of Bronchial Asthma," *Psychosomatic Medicine*, 1939, Vol. 1, pp. 203-244.

A related study has been reported by J. L. Halliday, "Approach to Asthma," *British Journal of Medical Psychology*, 1937, Vol. 17, pp. 1-47.

"Darling, this is our last night together. Tomorrow my hay fever starts"

FIG. 21. *Courtesy of Crowell-Collier Publishing Co. From Collier's, July 22, 1939.*

true nature of his emotional problems, and to know how to develop new mental habits. For some, this may require the skills of the clinical psychologist. For other and milder cases, the friend or employer may be able to say to the psychoneurotic: "The problem that is really bothering you, young man, is the fact that you fear that the girl friend will tire of waiting for you and marry some other man. Face the issue. Talk it over with her. If you can't agree upon a practicable program of action, let her marry someone else and you do likewise. In the meantime, bear in mind that I'll give you my fellowship because I, too, once had the same problem."

An individual may make adjustments to his barriers quite differently from another because of differences in the weakness of certain organs, behavior habits, or constitution. As a result of frustration, one person may, for example, develop physiological imbalance which results in more colds. Another may have his repressed rages bring about physiological changes which result in high blood pressure or in doing more work. However, all persons need a recognition of the close relation between adjustment and health. For certain persons, poor health often means poor habits of thinking and of conduct. Almost any person who wants to feel faint can do so by saying to himself: "I am fainting. I want to faint." The neurotic achieves the same kind of end by subconscious wishes regarding his breathing, digestion, or circulation. An allergy, as well as other kinds of ailments, may simply be an evasion of some problem which he does not face consciously.

Remedies for invalidism. What should be done for those unfortunate psychoneurotics and others who try to make an adjustment to reality by the avenue of illness? Scolding will not help them; it only increases their problems. They need scientific analysis rather than censure.

An important remedy is that of never saying, "Use your will," but instead, "Understand the cause of your trouble." If the physician makes exhaustive tests and can find no just cause for the illness, then ask the patient to analyze himself or to have himself analyzed for problems which he is evading. Induce the patient to face the barrier which he dislikes to admit to himself. He must be convinced that the defect or the inability to accomplish his present aims should be used to achieve another end that is equally acceptable. The main remedy is the trite statement that the cause must be removed. To do this may require considerable assistance on the part of the psychiatrist or the clinical psychologist. Furthermore, in cases of serious maladjustment, the patient who is very intelligent and has read a number of books on abnormal psychology cannot analyze himself and make his readjustment alone. However, his special knowledge should make him more intelligently co-operative in developing better habits of adjustment.

Children are often told that they are "nervous" and should not study or work. This is a serious mistake. It is far better to allow them to learn the joys of strenuous work and play. If they are not reminded of illness, but are encouraged to face life by direct attack habits, they will seldom develop the maladjustments which fond mothers call "nervousness."

Adults are often told that they are "nervous" and should study or work less. This advice is usually a mistake. Work does not cause nervous breakdowns. Nervous breakdowns are the result of poor mental habits when adjustment problems, especially conflicts, appear. In the so-called mental breakdowns, the nature and the amount of work that the worker does is largely irrelevant; the emotional reaction of the worker toward the work is all-important. If the worker's adjustment habits have enabled him to gain satisfactions from the work, the amounts and hours of work are incidental.

Significant influences in some breakdowns are precipitating factors such as the boss's domineering manner toward the employee, the teacher's negligence of the pupil, the public's condemnation of a person, the husband's niggardliness, or the wife's nagging. When the poorly adjusted person is confronted by such barriers, his ongoing activities are blocked and a "breakdown" results. Such a person is not benefited by reminders of illness. He needs encouragement in performing his daily tasks and in becoming socially integrated.

Everyone should feel that he belongs in the social groups of his environment, but the maladjusted person has special need for being welcome in his groups. His associates should be friendly rather than critical toward him. Otherwise he will tend to withdraw into himself more than ever and will have more acute "pains." The attitude of the associates of the adult invalid should be one of encouragement to carry on his work more intelligently rather than mere sentimentality, condolence, or pampering.

As in practically all other maladjustments, the patient should be given work to do that requires complete attention. Of course, we should not ask others to work in order that they may be as wealthy or as important as someone else, but rather because, through work that is adapted to their capacities, they can achieve the adjustment that comes from doing well that which they are talented to do. If work is reasonably satisfying, it may be carried on at all hours and for any number of years so long as the body is given a normal amount of exercise and care. If the well-adjusted individual works very hard, he simply gets tired and takes a rest. The well-adjusted individual uses direct attack in dealing with his illnesses, especially those of a functional nature. An unusual example of direct attack regarding a functional illness may be found in the way one organically sick man dealt with his ailment.

In 1920 Dr. A. L. Muirhead, a professor of pharmacology in one of the leading medical schools, found himself stricken with Addison's disease. Realizing that his affliction would end in death in a short time and being not only a physician but also an expert in the science of drugs, he determined to devote the remainder of his life to find a cure. Instead of sitting back waiting for death in the Mayo Clinic, which he entered, he did all in his power to stave death off, chopped and dried adrenal gland substance which he put into capsules and took by mouth, and by rectum took preparations of the adrenal gland containing large quantities of adrenalin. In a short time he made a remarkable recovery, and for a while was apparently cured—the first instance in history of any such improvement in a sufferer from Addison's disease. The rejoicing, however, was premature, for Dr. Muirhead had not really been cured and had a relapse into his former condition. Although treatment was again instituted and although it did help a little, it did not prevent his death from this disease. But for several years the Muirhead treatment was the best that medicine could offer.[14]

References

Griffith, Coleman R., *An Introduction to Applied Psychology*, Chapters XIX and XX. The Macmillan Co., 1936.

Menninger, Karl A., *The Human Mind*, Chapter III. F. S. Crofts & Co., 1931.

Richmond, Winifred V., *Personality—Its Development and Hygiene*, Chapter XI. Farrar & Rinehart, 1937.

Shaffer, Laurance Frederic, *The Psychology of Adjustment*, Chapters IX and X. Houghton Mifflin Co., 1936.

References for the student of allergy and related adjustments:

Hochman, S., "Mental and Psychological Factors in Obesity," *Medical Record*, 1938, Vol. 148, pp. 108-111.

Montgomery, L., "Psychoanalysis of a Case of Acne Vulgaris," *The Psychoanalytic Review*, 1939, Vol. 26, pp. 155-177.

Murray, H. A., "Visceral Manifestations of Personality," *The Journal of Abnormal and Social Psychology*, 1937, Vol. 32, pp. 161-184.

Thorndike, R. L., "A Note on the Relationship of Allergy to Neurasthenic Traits," *Journal of General Psychology*, 1937, Vol. 17, pp. 153-155.

Projects

1. Listen to some personal-problem radio programs such as the "Court of Human Relations," and note the cases which seem to illustrate principles

[14] Edward Podolsky, M. D., "Gland Magic," *The American Scholar*, 1934, Vol. 3, p. 449.

set forth in this chapter. Analyze possible predisposing and precipitating factors. Compare your analyses with those of the radio adviser.

2. Examine available textbooks that deal with public speaking and note how stage fright is treated. Which methods seem to you to be the most helpful?

3. List some of the "worthy causes" of your community which are likely to appeal to neurasthenics.

4. Recall some of your own abulic tendencies, such as those in writing to friends, checking your finances, seeing your dentist, and so on. Outline a definite procedure in each case whereby the necessary action may be taken at the proper time.

5. Women of today do not faint as much as women of a generation or two ago. What possible reasons can you suggest for this change of behavior?

6. Make a list of some of the things you have worried about during the past year or two. Check and analyze those cases in which your apprehension was a distinct handicap to the solution of the problem. Did worrying contribute to the solution in other cases?

7. Consider an acquaintance who says that certain common foods make him ill. What physical and psychological factors might be involved? Set up a procedure by which you might test objectively which factors were predominant.

8. Construct a hypothetical case in which the subject reacts through sick headaches or other form of invalidism. Have several friends suggest possible treatment and compare these suggestions with your own ideas.

7

Glands and Nerves—Organic Factors in Adjustments

A certain six-year old girl who lives near the writer's home has the facial appearance of a forty-year old woman. The little girl matured long before she finished childhood. Which gland caused the physiological abnormality? We all know that the normal functioning of the glands and nerves is important.

We think especially of the nerves as forming that most magnificent phenomenon of the universe—the human brain. But its size is not especially important. Experiments show that large portions of the human brain can be removed without damage to the intelligence. How can we possibly explain the functioning of an organ so unusual?

THE HUMAN bodily and mental activities are interdependent and operate in a way that is similar to the interrelated activities of modern business. The glandular, circulatory, and nervous systems are similar to the transportation and communication systems of a vast country. Trains, trolleys, buses, automobiles, trucks, bicycles, telephones, and so on, are carrying messages and conveying materials to needy parts of the body. The living body acts as an integrated whole. Just as business would suffer if any part of the transportation system were to break down, so the individual is seriously affected if the bodily equilibrium is disturbed. The chemical balance and the maintenance of the human organism are carried on through the blood and such parts as the *duct glands*—salivary, gastric, sweat, and sex glands, and the liver, pancreas, lachrymals, and kidneys. The mental balance or the way in which the different adjustive factors are kept co-operating in a normal or sane manner, is partially a result of the functioning of the chemical agencies of the body. The maintenance of proper acid-alkaline balance, sup-

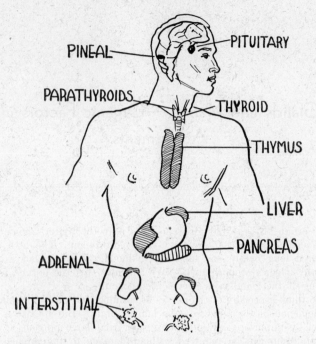

FIG. 22. Sketch to indicate the general locations of the principal endocrine glands. One of these glands does not usually appear in an adult as large, relatively, as shown here. Can you tell, from the text, which one?

plies of the different vitamins, certain amounts of iodine, calcium, and so on, are essential to the physiological and psychological equilibrium.

The Endocrine Glands

The functioning of the nervous system is greatly affected by the *ductless glands,* which are now being studied, and which give evidence of pronounced importance in human behavior. The ductless glands are also called the *endocrine glands* and the *glands of internal secretion.* These glands do not have ducts or channels for their secretions, but some glands with ducts as well as organs like the spleen and liver have endocrine functions. In typical endocrines the manufactured products are taken up directly by the blood and lymph streams as they pass through the gland structures. The manufactured products are called *hormones* or *autacoid substances.* The derivative meaning of the word "hormone" is "to set in motion." In a general way, this term illustrates their function, for they seem to act as controls for all other parts of the body. They accelerate or inhibit the vital organs and vital activities and have an important influence on mental life. All these glands are organized into a complicated interlocking system and the action of one modifies, and is modified by, others. To understand why people behave as they do, it is necessary for us to have an acquaintance with the functions of these glands. The main endocrines are:

1. The thyroid.
2. The parathyroids.
3. The thymus.
4. The pineal body.
5. The pituitary.
6. The adrenals.
7. The gonads.

The thyroid gland. In a certain valley in Switzerland, a large part of the population were found to be cretins because of serious deficiencies of thyroid secretion beginning at birth or in infancy. *Cretins* are decidedly stunted in height and have protruding abdomens. The skin is dry, scaly, and wrinkled. The hair is dry, coarse, and brittle. The tongue is thick. The head is short and broad. The facial expression is apathetic. The memory is weak, the thinking is slow, and intelligence is limited.

Almost every large colony for the feebleminded has numerous cretins.

A generation ago cretinism was regarded as incurable; but scientists have found that if the child is fed pellets of thyroid gland extract from sheep, or the synthetic product, it is possible for him to attain normal physical and mental development. The feeding, however, must be continued in adulthood to maintain the normal mental state. About 60 per cent of the thyroid secretion is iodine.

The thyroid gland consists of two masses of cells, one on each side of the windpipe and close to the larynx. The hormones of the thyroid act as a catalyst—a substance that accelerates chemical change without being chemically changed itself. Its function is important in the process of metabolism or the transformation of food into energy. If the thyroid is deficient in action, the body is soon clogged with waste products from kidneys, skin, and lungs. The activity of the thyroid can be indicated by the *basal metabolic rate*, which is found by measuring the amount of carbon dioxide in the expired air and comparing findings with norms for weight, height, and age.

In cases of adult underfunctioning of the thyroid, or *hypothyroidism*, the disease called *myxedema* develops. The gland may increase in size in order to increase the supply of thyroxin, a condition commonly termed "goiter." The largest goiter that the writer has ever seen was that of a woman who had given birth to twenty-two children. In this case the gland probably increased in size in order to supply the necessary amount of secretion for the embryos and the mother. In hypothyroidism the individual is slow, dull, indifferent, and clumsy. In the interior of the United States, where there is little iodine in air or water, some of the municipalities supply iodine in the water system to prevent goiters among children. The number of cases of goiter is much smaller near the seacoasts, where there is more iodine in the air and where people eat more sea foods. The best preventive of goiter in children is the taking of iodine by the pregnant mother, under the direction of a physician.

If the pregnant mother suffers from a serious lack of thyroid secretion, her baby is likely to be a misshapen creature of low vitality. If the baby's thyroid equipment is sufficiently defective, he will never attain normal growth or development unless the condition is corrected. In some cases of mental retardation of school children or the definitely feebleminded, the administration of thyroid has wrought dramatic changes in body and mind; but it has not been effective in every case which has been diagnosed as myxedema.

Some parents think that they can prevent goiter by the use of iodized salt in the cooking of foods. This method is questionable because some members of the family may already have too much iodine in their systems and they may develop *exophthalmic* goiters. Iodine should be administered to those individuals who need it, under the direction of a competent physician.

Marked *hyperthyroidism* or overdevelopment may give rise to exophthalmic goiter. Signs of this condition are protrusion of

FIG. 23.   Illustration of beneficial effects of thyroxin treatment.   The photograph at the left shows a child at the time thyroxin treatment was begun; at the right is the same child one year later.   Increase in height was six inches.   (*Reproduced by permission from E. C. Kendall*—The Harvey Lectures, 1919–20, *Figure 17, p. 46.*)

the eyeballs,[1] rapid heartbeat, high blood pressure, and a speeding-up of the whole organism.   The skin is flushed and the temperature is above normal.   The individual is high-strung, excitable, irritable, and unable to relax or to sleep.   Fear, anger, and hysterical joy are easily aroused, but the patient resents being thwarted or contradicted.   The individual is thin regardless of the amount of food that he eats.   The bodily reserves of energy

[1] Some studies indicate that exophthalmic goiter in which the eyeballs protrude is caused primarily by a pituitary hormone which causes the thyroid to swell and oversecrete, with a direct effect on the eyes.

are readily exhausted. In extreme cases the individual is filled with fear and apprehension. He may have hallucinations of hearing and vision. The voices usually say disagreeable things. When the patient reaches this stage the prognosis is bad. He usually dies.

Hyperthyroidism seems to be accentuated by mental stress. Cases have been reported of individuals who were too irritable to get along with their associates. An endocrinologist removed a part of the patient's thyroid gland or cut off some of its blood supply. The operation usually resulted in a more calm and normal emotional temperament and enabled the workman to perform his job efficiently. Of course, any degree of over- or under-functioning may exist. Perhaps some cases of "general poor health" and neurasthenia are accentuated by sluggishness from thyroid deficiency.

The parathyroids. These glands are four in number, about the size of peas, and located on the thyroids, although they have nothing to do with the thyroids. They seem to control the lime supply and calcium metabolism. For this reason they are important in maintaining the acid-base equilibrium and in healing bone fractures. It is certain that the lime supply is important, not only for the normal condition of blood and bones but also for the nervous system. When the parathyroids are removed, the organism becomes exceedingly excitable. Their underfunctioning causes marked muscle spasms. In some cases, when persons suffer from pronounced nervousness, insomnia, and tremors, the parathyroids are defective or diseased. When they are removed or diseased, the patient is likely to have seizures of rage and maniacal excitement. Scientists have now produced a synthetic secretion that aids the functioning of the parathyroids, although its use is still limited to the few specialists who have given emphasis to the study of the endocrines.

The thymus. This gland ("neck sweetbread" to the butcher) is located on the windpipe and is called the "gland of childhood," because it influences the early physical and mental development. It is relatively large in infancy and largest at puberty, after which it probably atrophies. Its action is believed to hold in check the development of the sex glands and those physical characteristics that go with the development of sex, such as hair on the body. It is probably very important in giantism and in those abnormal children who are sexually adult at five years of age. It is related to the gonads in function. It is so closely related to the lymphatic system that some scientists question whether it should be called an endocrine gland.

The pineal body. This gland lies in the medial plane and at the base of the brain. The pineal body has a glandular structure during childhood, but this is lost during puberty. It is considered important in the development of the nervous system and the sex organs.

The pituitary bodies. The pituitary gland (also called hypophysis) consists of two bodies or lobes—an anterior and a posterior lobe. The whole structure is about the size of a large pea and is located in a small pocket in the bony floor of the cranium, at the base of the brain in the center of the head. It is probably the best-protected functional unit of the body. It is structurally connected with the brain but does not take part in brain action. Until recently it was supposed to be vestigial. Its removal causes death within three days.

The anterior lobe has an important relationship to the nutritive condition of the body during growth, particularly the growth of the skeleton. If overactive in childhood, it causes *elephantism* or *giantism,* which is seen in the giants of the circus. If the overactivity takes place after childhood, the bones of the limbs and those of height do not become greater in length, but the facial characteristics change to those of the *acromegalic.* The nose and chin are prominent, the head is broad, the features are rugged, and the face has a gorilla-like appearance. The individual is mentally alert, and, as a result of his keen wit, has been pictured as the court jester. If the anterior lobe is underactive in childhood, the adult tends toward infantilism or babylike bodily proportions with a childlike, happy-go-lucky disposition.

The posterior lobe secretes a hormone that affects the tonus of the smooth muscles and the blood vessels. The heartbeat is decreased, the blood pressure is increased, and the contractions of the intestines and uterus are increased. That is why pituitrin is used for the uterine muscles during childbirth.

An extract, *pitressin,* from the posterior part of the pituitary, is sometimes used as an aid in anesthesia. It helps to relax abdominal walls for surgical operations, to maintain blood pressure and to prevent unpleasant after-effects from the anesthetic.

One of the hormones of the pituitary gland, *prolactin,* controls the secretion of milk.   When animals who are not parents have been administered a few doses of prolactin, their behavior changes toward mothering the young of their own species or even unrelated species.   They build nests and eagerly adopt any available "babies."   Mother love is partially a matter of hormone chemistry and the folk phrase, "the milk of human kindness," may have developed as a vague recognition of the functions of prolactin.   These findings regarding the pituitary should not, however, lead us to conclude that mother love is only a matter of prolactin.   Other chemical factors are important such as the amount of manganese and vitamin B_1 in the diet.   Furthermore, subtle psychological influences as well as chemical factors must be reckoned with for any ultimate understanding of mother love.

When the pituitary gland does not function normally, sex-hormone balance is upset.   A normal woman's sex-hormone supply includes 30 to 50 per cent of the male secretion, and 12 to 20 per cent of a man's supply consists of female sex-hormones. These percentages are maintained by the pituitary, which regulates the amount of sex-controlling substances that enter the blood stream.   Certain imbalances in the sex-hormone percentages[2] may cause an abnormal interest in persons of the same sex, but this is not the only reason for such abnormal attractions. Psychological factors are the causes in some cases.

In hyperpituitarism the individual is active, irritable, and suspicious of others.   In hypopituitarism he is slow and ambitionless.

The adrenals. Adrenals (suprarenals) are located on top of the kidneys, but have nothing to do with the kidneys in function.   They are called the "glands of war" because they are active in times of emotional stress, such as in fighting and fear. They are made up of two distinct parts—the medulla and the cortex, each having separate functions.

The adrenal cortex is called the "organ of masculinity" because

[2] C. A. Wright, "The Sex Offender's Endocrines," *Medical Record,* New York, 1939, Vol. 149, pp. 399-402, presents findings regarding 73 homosexuals and suggests treatment.

if it is deficient in a man, he tends to be effeminate, with the gestures, voice, and mode of walking of a woman. If it is hyperactive in a woman, she has masculine traits—hair on the lips and a deep voice. *Virilism* as seen in the bearded lady of the circus is the result of the overfunctioning of this gland.

The secretion of the outside portion of the adrenal glands, "cortin," is essential to life. In experimental animals, removal of the cortex causes death promptly. Pronounced deficiency in the secretion of cortin is the cause of *Addison's disease*, a condition of low blood pressure with death eventually resulting because of circulatory failure. It is possible that mild deficiencies of cortin may contribute toward the fatigability and depression of psychoneurotics.

The secretion of the medulla is "epinephrin." It can be made synthetically. Common trade names for it are "Suprarenalin" and "Adrenalin." When the medulla pours its secretion into the blood stream, the individual is prepared for combat. The digestive processes stop, the sweat glands open for action, the blood vessels are prepared for a larger flow of blood, the liver discharges a large amount of reserve blood and releases sugar for bodily combustion, the respiratory process is hastened, and the blood clots more readily. All these and other results have been studied by the scientists in their researches of the emotions of fear and anger. When the individual is thus stimulated, he can run faster and hit harder. That is why we are more likely to defer to the man whose anger is aroused than to the one who is in a quiescent state.

The gonads. The gonads (testicles and *interstitial cells* of male and ovaries and *corpus luteum* of female) are called sex glands; but this does not mean that they produce only the spermatozoa and the ova which take part in the process of fertilization. They are also important in the development of the secondary sex characteristics which distinguish male and female —differences in distribution of hair on the body, the coarseness of the beard, the mammary glands, and voice, height, and weight.

Some of the first known experimental work in the field of endocrinology was made by husbandmen who castrated domestic animals. We have all noted differences between the fiery stallion and his more placid brother the workhorse, between the pugnacious bull and the gentle ox, between the normal man and the eunuch, all of whose differences are influenced by the presence or absence of the sex glands.

Important changes in personality may occur when these glands remain in the body but do not function well. The woman who suffers from ovarian insufficiency is apt to lose the graciousness and charm which characterize the well-balanced feminine personality. The hypogonad character is egoistic, resentful of the world, full of self-pity, and very critical of others.

The gonads and sex glands have been given a great deal of publicity in the Sunday newspaper supplements because some scientists have performed experiments on the changing of the sex of birds by transplanting testes and ovaries from one sex to the other. Where this has been done in the laboratory, the results have been remarkable in that the fowl took the secondary sex characteristics of the sex to which the transplanted organ belonged. This does not suggest, however, that the sex of human beings can be controlled before or after birth. Nor can the fountain of youth be found by way of the gland route. As previously stated, the whole human being is an integrated mechanism, and it is not possible to have a new or rejuvenated machine by replacing one old part with a new part.

The endocrine glands of the body operate as a vast and complex system. They act as an integrated unit in conjunction with the blood stream and nerves. We can realize how their secretions may be carried to all parts of the body to unlock the organ for which the hormones have been adjusted when we recall the fact that the blood makes a complete trip around the body in the short period of from twenty to thirty seconds. This means that the blood stream makes about three thousand round trips in the course of each day. The hormones are thus carried to the specific organs which they stimulate or inhibit and thus maintain the equilibrium of body and mind. Small wonder, then, that disturbances of the endocrine system modify human behavior and tend to make us physically or mentally unbalanced. In the hospitals where certain forms of endocrine abnormality are treated, the specialists administer secretions of several glands rather than the secretion of only one gland.

Everyone, of course, has heard of *insulin,* the pancreatic hormone which regulates the sugar metabolism. Its deficiency causes the formerly hopeless disease, *diabetes mellitus*. The endocrine function of the pancreas is performed by the *islands of Langerhans* imbedded in it. Failure on the part of this gland has definite psychological effects, typically starting with depression and continuing to confusion.

Various types of subnormality and abnormality may be classified on the basis of the endocrines, but it is of little help to us to classify normal persons according to a glandular classification. Normal persons do not vary enough to enable us to be certain of our cataloging. However, we can make rough general classifications, such as hyperthyroid and hypothyroid, hyperpituitary and hypopituitary, overactivity or underactivity of the cortex of the adrenals. At any rate, we should know the physical bases of the mental balance in order that we may appreciate the valuable results from current study of the endocrines by the scientists.

Children with unusual glandular conditions are apt to develop characteristic adjustment mechanisms, as in the case of boys who have certain pituitary deficiencies; they become fat, weak, and sissy. Such boys are likely to be persecuted by their fellows, thus bringing about defense mechanisms. The endocrines certainly are important predisposing influences in many adjustments, especially those involving the energy supply, sexual behavior, and the general well-being of the individual.

Undoubtedly the endocrines occupy a place of importance in determining the mental soundness and personality of the individual, but their exact importance is still unknown. Glandular disorders are often found in seriously maladjusted persons, but some investigators believe that the emotional strains of mental disease throw the endocrine system out of balance. Our findings regarding cause and effect in the relations between endocrines and mental disease or mental deficiency are still very uncertain.[3]

---

[3] Until we have more definite evidence than at present which either proves or disproves the concept of a close relationship between the endocrines and mental disorders, it is premature to make vague generalizations regarding that relationship. Research is still being carried on to find the actual significance of the hormones in mental conditions, which may uncover data of very great importance to our knowledge of the human organism.—H. T. Carmichael, "The Role of the Endocrines in Mental Disorders," *Journal of Abnormal and Social Psychology,* 1938, Vol. 33, pp. 205-216.

The Nervous System

The various bodily mechanisms play so important a part in our conduct and personalities that a general acquaintance with both the glandular and nervous[4] systems is helpful. The operations of our nervous system are more complex and marvelous than those of any economic organization.

Our nervous system has billions of nerve cells, and, before we can do anything, certain changes must take place within it. The neurones or nerve cells are not rounded in shape, as are most tissue cells, but have many little branches. These branchlets may be greater in number and complexity at one end. The neurones do not grow together where they approach other neurones, but operate in continuity with other living substances. Each brain cell is a minute chemical factory and an electric battery. Each generates definite amounts of electric energy. Nerve currents are chemico-electrical impulses which travel, in some instances, at a rate of about 300 feet per second. The junction points where the neurones are near enough to each other for the nerve current to pass from one neurone to another are called "synapses" or "synaptic connections."

When a nerve current is rushing through a series of synapses in the cortex of an intelligent person, any one cell has less than 1/100,000 part of a second in which to transmit the impulse to the next cell. The exact nature of the nerve current is unknown. It appears to be neither wholly chemical nor wholly electrical. We do know, however, that it flows not as a steady stream but as a series of rapid impulses. The neural impulses that hold the extended hand in a steady tension are transmitted at the rate of about 40 per second. In old age, the speed of the pulsations may decrease, as shown in the quivering hand of the old man who cannot hold his teacup so steadily as he did in his youth. The flow of the current is somewhat similar to the alternating current in electricity. A common descriptive term of the neural excitation is not nerve current but "neural impulse." For sim-

---

[4] One of the terms used by laymen for some minor maladjusted persons is to refer to the person as having "nerves." These are more easily studied as adjustments and mental habits than as bodily disorders. Indeed, very few psychologists use the term "nerves" as a term for an ailment unless they wish to cater to a patient, but all study the nervous system and nerve cells.

plicity's sake, we use nerve current rather than the more technical term "recurrent neural impulses." The neurologists are convinced that each nerve cell has an individuality of its own and that it never grows fast to cells with which it is in contact. It is independent as a living unit. As a functional or reaction unit, it is a part of a series of other cells which act with it.

Let us compare the principle with that of electricity. If we place the ends of two wires near each other, the current will jump from one wire to the other. The closer the wires are to each other, the lower the resistance and the easier the transmission or passage of the current. If, instead of one wire, we place two or more wires near the charged wire, the current would jump to the one offering the least resistance rather than to the wire several feet away. However, when a nerve impulse passes over a neurone, the particular neurone to which it will next go is not necessarily the nearest one. Its direction depends upon the amount of resistance encountered at the synapse.

We can also illustrate the tendency of the nerve current to follow the pathways of least resistance by the analogy of the way in which a human being tends to follow pathways through a forest. Let us assume that a person is at the edge of a forest and wishes to get to the other side. He will tend to follow the footpath which has already been worn there by preceding travelers. Should there be few persons traveling that way, he will follow the pathways or places where he meets with the least resistance from obstructions, such as trees and rocks. And, should he travel that way again, he would tend to follow the pathway which he made on his first trip. Eventually, after many trips, he would travel over it far more quickly than he did on his initial trip.

The conduction of nerve currents is somewhat similar to our hypothetical traveler. Each pathway represents a *neural pattern* or mode of response which some nerve currents tend to traverse in making a behavior response. If a pathway has never before been made, a new path must be developed, and we have what is called *learning*. Forming new neural pathways in the nervous system appears to be part of the process of learning. Perhaps that is why learning is often difficult and requires real mental effort for most people. As we all know, learning is easier if we can relate the new subject to some well-known material.

In such a case, it appears that we are not making an entirely new pathway, but are utilizing some of the old pathways.

What is habit? Habit may be illustrated by the oft-traveled pathway through the forest. We know that we can travel with ease and without deliberation over an old route which we have traveled hundreds of times before. The habit is hard to break, because it is easier to travel the old pathway than to develop a new one. Should someone go with us through the forest and suggest that we take a path which is new to us, we would feel less comfortable and stumble more than we did over the old path.

In our analogy of forest pathways we did not illustrate the fact that the nervous system has many sets of pathways. The trapper may have a cabin centrally located, at the foot of each of seven adjoining hills. On each of these hills he may have a hundred pathways leading to a total of seven hundred traps. In the human brain and nervous system we have an incalculable number of pathways and extremely great possibilities for varied behavior.

A *neural pattern* or some series of connections between receivers of stimuli and organs of response underlies each of our behavior patterns. A *behavior pattern* is a sequence of actions which adjust the individual to some situation in his experience. Some behavior patterns are relatively simple such as sneezing or slapping a mosquito. Others are multiform. For example, the popular term "complex" usually refers to a group of emotionally-invested ideas which have unconscious influences, being partly or entirely repressed. The "inferiority complex" is the result of a number of humiliating experiences, more or less repressed, and it tends to influence the behavior in many situations where "humiliation" responses are not appropriate.

Through nerve currents and nerve patterns we think, talk, act, and do all those things which are a part of human behavior. The chief purpose in using the forest-path analogy, though inadequate, is to explain that nerve centers *appear* to follow the courses of least resistance; that nature provides some paths for us at birth, as in sucking; that new paths can be voluntarily made; and that it is easy for the current to traverse well-worn or established pathways. Also, any stimulus, such as a sound, which does not travel over a certain type of nerve pathway, does not enter consciousness and has no existence in the mind of the person who could have heard the sound but did not. We should, however, bear in mind that the nervous system also acts as a unit rather than in small parts only, as stated on page 171.

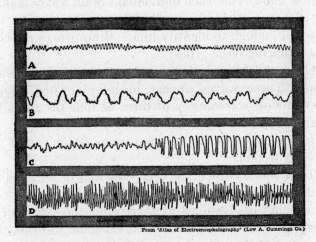

From 'Atlas of Electroencephalography' (Lew A. Cummings Co.)

FIG. 24. Examples of brain wave records. A, electroencephalogram or EEM of a waking normal person; B, deep sleep; C, "petit mal" form of epilepsy in which a person may become unconscious for a few seconds; and D, "grand mal" form of epilepsy characterized by thrashing fits, biting of tongue and long periods of unconsciousness. The use of EEM techniques of diagnosis enable the expert to locate brain tumors and injuries of the cortex with a high percentage of accuracy. (*Courtesy of Dr. Frederic A. Gibbs and Erna L. Gibbs.*)

The brain's electrical waves. Every living organism, plant or animal, has its voltage of electrical impulses. The electricity generated by the brain is infinitesimal. In a normal person the fluctuating potentials amount to one fifty-millionth of a volt. On this basis, it would require more than five times the combined electrical output of the brains of the world's population to light a fifty-watt lamp. However, scientists have taken advantage of this low voltage of the brain and developed the *electroencephalograph,* an instrument commonly known as the "brain wave recorder." This machine makes a record, called an *electroencephalogram* (abbreviated EEM), of the wave-like formations of electrical impulses emitted in brain-cell activity.

One way of making these measurements is to glue an electrode to the top of the forehead and attach other electrodes behind the ear and back of the head. Wires are run from the electrodes to an amplifier of the kind found in every radio set. The amplifier magnifies the electric effects several thousand times for transcription to the moving film record.

It is now known that each individual's brain waves make a pattern as characteristic of him as his fingerprints; not as uniform but constant enough to identify him. Brain waves are classified into the following basic types:

1. *Alpha rhythm,* which has a frequency of about ten waves a second. These waves appear in infants when about four months old with a frequency of three or four per second. The adult rate is reached when eight years old.[5]

2. *Beta rhythm,* which has an average frequency of twenty-five waves a second.

3. *Delta* waves, which are very slow and of longer duration, one-sixth of a second and more.

The fact that brain waves are taken from the skull and not directly from the brain surface has caused some to think that the waves are artifacts. This is not true, however, because the frequencies differ from those of muscle frequencies, although there is some evidence for differences due perhaps to different cell patterns in different regions of the skull.

At this writing, researchers have not been successful in finding patterns that characterize the various mental activities such as imagining and reasoning, but the various stages of sleep have characteristic wave patterns. Furthermore, different parts of the brain appear to go to sleep separately and to different degrees.[6] Several investigators have also found some evidence to indicate that the brain waves have a direct relationship with intelligence. In the feebleminded, brain waves seem to correspond more closely with mental age than with chronological age. Various types of epileptics and psychotics are also being studied, but we shall have to wait many years before we can use EEM's

---

[5] J. R. Smith, "The Electroencephalogram During Normal Infancy and Childhood," *Journal of Genetic Psychology,* 1938, Vol. 53, pp. 455-482. See also, D. B. Lindsley, "Electrical Potentials of the Brain in Children and Adults," *Journal of General Psychology,* 1938, Vol. 19, pp. 285-306.

[6] See H. Blake, "Brain Potentials and Depth of Sleep," *American Journal of Physiology,* 1937, Vol. 119, pp. 273-274, and other articles on same subject of the same issue of this journal. Also, Davis *et al.* in *Science,* 1937, Vol. 86, pp. 448-450.

as a basis for hiring employees or advising youth vocationally. In the meantime we should watch for reports on brain-wave studies as they are published by the hundreds of scientists who are now working in this field.

The brain and brain cortex.   The size of the brain mass has only a rough correlation with intelligence in normal human beings.   The brain of the sluggish Eskimo is above average in weight and that of the philosophical Hindu is below average. Nor do all geniuses have big brains.   For example, the brains of Napoleon and Walt Whitman were below average in weight.

It is not the mass of the brain as a whole that counts so much as the "bark" or cortex of gray matter that sheaths the convolutions of the cerebral hemispheres.   How intelligent we are depends on this cortex.   As we learn the design of the cortical gray matter, it becomes more complex.   So if we must study intelligence we must study cortices.   Listen to Professor C. Judson Herrick of the University of Chicago, authority on the brain, as he discourses on the subject:

"It has required upward of 20,000,000 years of evolutionary history to fabricate the architecture of this cortex out of the simpler nervous structures of the brain stem.   The larger outlines of this history can be read, yet we are still profoundly ignorant of how it performs the miracles of production that we know it does produce.   But these mysteries are not insoluble, and the last quarter century has contributed more toward the solution of the problem— how the brain thinks—than all the preceding centuries of scientific research yielded.   We have new instruments—oscillographs with radio tube amplifiers, and so forth—and new points of view that promise as great a revolution in the physiology of the nervous system as the invention of the microscope effected in the field of anatomy."

Even a good cortex is not enough.   If a man is to talk he must have the right kind of jaw, the right conformation of vocal organs, the right hands, the right eyes.   And all these must be properly co-ordinated with a brain of the right design. . . .

. . . Man is what he is not because his brain is bigger proportionately to the size and weight of his body but because skill in using his hands and his eyes accompanied his cerebral development.   Not one organ made us what we are but the correlation of many organs into a unifying organism.[7]

The cortex is the part of the brain from which we get our motions and our notions.   It is gray in color, because it is made up of the cell bodies and nerve endings of many millions of nerve cells, estimated to be about ten to fourteen billions in number. It is not more than a quarter of an inch thick at the deepest parts and about a tenth of an inch in the shallow parts.   It covers an

---

[7] Waldemar Kaempffert, "The Week in Science," *The New York Times,* October 11, 1936.

area about eighteen inches square. The nerve cells, obviously, are very small. If certain types of the cells were laid side by side, it would take 27,000 of them to make a lineal inch.

FROM WHERE I STAND

The telephone again. I wish—
I've got to study soon.
The trees are new and dusty;
A pink magnolia bloom.

I think of next September—
This summer will be long—
My desk is rather cluttered.
My cigarettes are gone.

My roommate's faithful. She says I—
Fresh strawberries for dinner.
I must get to the Castle now.
I think I'm getting thinner.

My mind is pledged to chaos.
These are the things I see:
The dandelions, a spider,
A pink magnolia tree.

You're wearing brown this morning,
It's warm enough for white;
The questions in the quiz were stiff;
The stars were sharp last night.

The ROTC's marching,
And Hitler's in the news,
I wonder what's important,
And where my money goes.
  —Dorothy Hedner, *Syracuse Daily*
  Orange, May 10, 1939.

One thought may lead to a great variety of other thoughts, as in the above examples of a college girl's cortical action.

These billions of nerve cells stand in close forest-like formation, in intimate contact with each other. These forests of cells are many layers deep and each twig, branch, and root is in contact with similar branches of surrounding cells. The cells in the cortex act in large groups, and nerve impulses spread from cell to cell in all directions. It is estimated that each of these millions of cells is potentially in anatomical and physiological relation with at least a hundred other cells, thus providing for an incalculable number of connections. This fact partially explains why a pianist can play classical music; performing the reading of notes, fingering, accidentals, pauses, pedaling, meter, and rhythm of pieces which require sixty mental operations a second.

The cortex is a kind of control executive of the brain and nervous system and it has several assistant executives, such as the cerebellum, the brain stem, and the nerve centers along the spinal cord. Responses which are old in the race, such as the conveyance of the impulse in reflexes, are handled by the "assistants," constituting the "old brain." An "assistant" is usually under the control of the cerebral cortex or "new brain," as when we carry a hot dish. The "assistant" may want to drop it, but the cortex compels us to hold on. Should the dish be unbearably hot, we would then have to drop it, because the old brain takes an emergency situation in hand, if the emergency is related to the survival of the individual.

The functioning of the neural patterns gives us our sensations, interprets these sensations, and does our thinking. For example, when a businessman sees his stenographer, he does not have one reaction pattern for the stenographer in entirety; but he has one reaction pattern for her hair color, another tells him that she is efficient, another that she is supporting her mother, another that she was tardy this morning, another that she is supposed to hand him a letter at this time, and so on. All these various pathways are connected by *association* neurones. When one kind of pathway is aroused, that in turn tends to arouse other related pathways. In other words, one thing reminds us of another. A very large part of the cerebrum is made up of millions of association neurones, which connect with each other in the cortex. The complexity of the neural system is staggering to the imagination. The student may be unable to understand how there can be any continuity or organization in the operations of these millions of nerve cells, pathways, and patterns. Fortunately the whole system is efficiently organized in the manner of a large business organization. The cortex is the general manager of our mental activities.

Association linkages. Neurologists have made studies of the nervous system in order to explain many important facts about its action which we shall have to omit here. We have, however, tried to explain in popular parlance how the nervous system operates in terms of neural pathways or patterns. So far as we know, any one neural pathway of the nervous system may become associated or connected with any other pathway. In our daily thinking, we know that we can think of one thing and then at once think of some apparently unrelated topic. In our dreams, for example, we have all sorts of combinations of ideas. It is probable that, if we thoroughly understood the workings of the nervous system, we would find that all its connections which give rise to ideas or muscular acts are connected in logical relationships.

We all know that events or experiences become associated with each other, and that these associations are often individual and specific. One employee may quake with fear whenever the boss calls him into the office, because the boss once gave him a severe reprimand which made a strong impression on him. The scolding "shocked" his nervous system. His neural patterns differ from those of the same boss's little daughter who shouts with joy when she sees her daddy. Her experiences with him have been of a more pleasant sort and her nervous system has not been stimulated as has that of the trembling employee. We use this method in training animals. The horse does not naturally stop when we yell "Whoa!" He has learned to stop because the two sets of neural pathways have become associated with each other—pain in the mouth and the particular sound made by the driver. The cat comes to us when we call "Kitty, kitty" because that sound has become associated with food and fondling. The hunting dog jumps with joy when he sees his master carrying a gun, because the gun has been associated or linked with pleasant hunting excursions.

Conditioning. By associations of neural pathways, any responses may be linked with any stimulus. A conditioned response is a variety of association linkage involving a rather fixed mechanism of response. The response takes place as a result of a simultaneous or near-simultaneous presentation of a particular stimulus. The process is mechanical because thinking or ideas are not necessary to have conditioning occur.

Pavlov, the Russian physiologist, showed that the salivary glands of a dog may be conditioned to secrete at the sound of a bell. Watson showed that certain children may be conditioned, after several trials, so as to cry with fright at the sight of a rabbit, simply by striking on an iron bar whenever the child sees and reaches for the rabbit. A child can also be "reconditioned" by having the rabbit visible, but at a distance, when the child is eating. Gradually, the rabbit is moved nearer and nearer to the child until the sight of the rabbit becomes associated with the pleasant response of eating.

The term "conditioning" is also used for a common type of behavior as in the case of a young man who labored for years under the impression that he was, by nature, a poor student of mathematics. In grammar school he thought that some children were naturally gifted in arithmetic, but that he happened to be born with a recalcitrant brain for arithmetic. This, however, was really not the situation. The cause of the weakness in arithmetic was an unfortunate series of conditionings with the subject, brought about by the fact that, in his first course in arithmetic in a lower grade, the teacher taught the subject by banging against the blackboard the heads of the children who presented incorrect answers to the problems assigned. In addition to banging their heads against the blackboard, she also scolded and shouted so that this man still has mental images of her angry face and rasping voice. In later years, when her influence wore away and a kind instructor made the subject interesting, the student found that he could do work in higher mathematics as well as the average college student.

Why is one woman very pleasing to one man and unnoticed by another man? Why will a girl "go wild" over a dissipated, worthless old reprobate when she knows a dozen kind and manly fellows who would make far better husbands than the hopeless wreck she admires? Is there some mysterious cosmic force that drives her on in spite of herself? So far as we know, the reason for her blind admiration lies in the fact that the "apple of her eye" happens to be to her a composite of a number of pleasant associations of her past life. His tone of voice, the twinkle of his eye, and his manner of greeting may merely be arousing the old pathways which were established in her childhood by the singing of a sweet old Sunday school teacher, a kind uncle who told her sea stories, and a southern gentleman whom she met in Memphis

It is probable that heredity explains some of the causes of differences in behavior patterns among human beings, but each year scientists seem to be losing interest in heredity as the cause of our human differences of behavior; and each year they become more convinced that our associations, conditionings, and adjustment habits are the major influences in forming psychological differences. It is quite probable that the successful businessmen are successful not because they were born with a forte for business but because they had certain experiences from which they formed associative linkages and adjustments that made business appear worth while and interesting. Had they made other adjustments, some of them might have become equally interested in art or science.

The importance of neural patterns in life and work. At first thought, the concept of neural patterns may appear to be an academic subject of interest only to scientists. The fact is that whether we are aware of it or not, we make use of the neural pattern concept in our business and social life. Our technological civilization is based upon division of labor. This simply means that a workman can do far more work when he uses the same *mental set,* that is, if he is allowed to perform the same operation continuously rather than to perform all the operations in a given process. We accept as axiomatic the fact that 100 shoemakers, each making a pair of shoes, from the cutting of the leather to the polishing of the finished shoe, cannot make nearly so many shoes as can 100 factory workers, where each man performs but one operation and then passes on the materials to the next worker. Each day we marvel at the small cost of some intricate product and wonder how it is possible to make it so cheaply. Imagine the cost of a modern automobile or an airplane if one or two men were to attempt to produce one of these individually under the old guild system. In modern business we arrange the work so as to have each employee use the same neural pattern repeatedly and thereby save an enormous amount of time and effort. Large-scale production has utilized this neurological principle through the specialization of activity for productive efficiency.

Objectively speaking, a fact is a fact, whether we recognize it or never hear of it. Psychologically, a fact becomes a fact only after it has been conducted over some pathway of the nervous system. Every salesman has talked to a prospect and failed to make the sale, and has said to himself, "Well, what I said to that fellow did not seem to register. I wonder why?" The reason why the salesman did not make an impression on the prospect was that the salesman failed to send his message over the established neural pathways of the prospect.

Ideas which give promise of success when analyzed in the office may be failures when used in the shop and retail stores because too few persons happen to have those neural patterns. Shows that interest playwrights and actors may be failures when presented on Broadway. Styles that enthrall the artists may never impress those on the outside of the studio, and so for hundreds of other situations. People can be influenced only when we find out the tendencies already present in their neural or behavior patterns and then connect a new proposal with the established tendencies.

No psychologist can re-make a maladjusted person; the psychologist can only connect his suggestions with the behavior tendencies established in the advisee's personality. No counselor can take a man and change him over into another person unless the advisee co-operates in making the change. We can recondition and redirect many behavior tendencies of our customers, employees, pupils, and children if we can first gain their co-operation in developing new convictions and attitudes. The individual's attitudes, his total orientations toward any idea or situation, are exceedingly important when we wish to modify his behavior, because the nervous system functions as an integrated unit.

The integrative action of the nervous system. Some years ago, in a farming section of Pennsylvania, a Dutch farmer and his wife went for a Sunday afternoon ride. An accident occurred and the wife's head was seriously injured. As a result of the accident, she was unable to walk and she lay in bed for two years. The farmer was forced to hire a housemaid to perform the work which would have been done by the wife had she been well. The first maid who was hired was rather old and unattractive. After a time the first maid left and a new one was hired. The new maid happened to be younger and more attractive. One day the wife, as she lay in bed, became worried and suspicious of her husband's relations with the maid.

She finally wrought herself up to so excited a state that she got out of bed, dressed herself, and walked downstairs to look for her husband. When he found her, she was walking almost as naturally as though she had never been in an accident. The neighbors often wondered whether the wife was malingering and had always been able to walk but had refused to do so. Some attributed the "cure" to the efficacy of prayer. It is probable, however, that the wife really was unable to walk after the accident; but, in the course of time, new "walking" neural patterns were formed, and under the stress of a strong emotional stimulus, she discovered that she could walk.

Instances have been recorded of cripples who appeared to be unable to walk for years but found that they ran when scared by imminent dangers, such as fire or murder. Each year many crippled and paralytic religious pilgrims visit shrines and receive "cures." Are these cures just as explainable as the recoveries of broken bones that can be adjusted and allowed to become as strong as ever?

Neurologists are certain that localization plays a considerable part in nervous action. However, Herrick[8] has shown that the human nervous system is somewhat similar to a complicated telephone system with local centers and exchanges. Two experimenters, Dr. S. I. Franz and Dr. Carl Spencer Lashley, have done much work in this field which indicates that human reactions are under the general supervision of the brain and that the nervous system acts as a unit rather than only in small parts. Doctor Franz taught animals to do certain tricks and then took out motor areas or parts of their brains. The animals were then unable to perform the tricks; but, when they were taught again, they recovered their ability. He also found that human beings who had lost the use of a limb through accident or disease could be trained to use the limb again.[9] Lashley

---

[8] C. J. Herrick, *Brains of Rats and Men.* University of Chicago Press, 1926.

[9] H. W. Newell, "The Effect of Head Injury on the Behavior and Personality of Children: A Study of Twenty Cases," *Medical Clinics of North America,* 1937, Vol. 21, p. 1335, reports a study of children with disturbances of behavior or personality following an injury to the head. There was little correlation between the changes in behavior and the severity of injury to the head. An important factor was the emotional attitude of the parents to the injury, especially when damage suits were threatened or pending. The most effective therapy was direct psychiatric treatment of the patient and advice to parents regarding methods of dealing with the child.

has shown that it is possible to remove various parts of the rat's brain cortex and yet leave the rat able to learn certain functions. If too large a part of the cortex is removed, the learning process is hindered. These experiments do not disprove the neural pathway principle, but they do show that the nervous system acts as a unit; that human reactions are under general supervision; and that, when one part of the nervous system is destroyed, some other part may conduct the nerve currents effectively.[10] The patterns of the neurones' actions are probably far more important than which particular neurones are involved in the actions. Perhaps the system is similar to that of our hypothetical trapper who has worn his pathways over the hills to his traps. If a flood removes a part of a path or a landslide covers it, he can still get to his traps by making a new pathway.

By integrative action we mean that the nervous system acts as a unit rather than as an innumerable number of small parts. The nerve currents tend to be united into a complex whole or unit. The body responds as a whole to any situation. For this reason, applied psychologists are keenly interested in learning about the total orientations of the individual as indicated by his adjustments, attitudes, and convictions.

A human personality is not a bundle of neural patterns but an integrated being who is so highly organized that many of his activities are still subject to further investigation; but his behavior can be predicted and controlled under certain conditions and within reasonable limits. Furthermore, he himself can direct his own mental life if he determines to do so and applies intelligence to this purpose. The mechanisms of his glands and nerves offer excellent possibilities for him to modify his behavior and that of his fellows, and adjustments and attitudes are especially important in the process of directed growth.

In the case just mentioned of the Pennsylvania Dutch farmer's wife, she regained the power to walk even though she herself did not at first realize that her nervous system had restored her walking ability. She regained the ability adventitiously and deserved no special credit for intelligent effort. The potentialities within her nervous system were unrealized by her. Her

---

[10] "Parts of Brain Removed, Intelligence Not Affected," *Science News Letter.* April 9, 1938, p. 230.

Fig. 25. Floyd C. Dockeray, Ohio State University. Further study on the foundations of behavior and levels of attainment will be found in his book *General Psychology*, Chapter XIV (Prentice-Hall, Inc., 1935).

case, therefore, should indicate to us that when our normal bodily mechanisms are consciously and intelligently directed by us, we can often attain remarkable results, as proved by other cases of injured persons who are told that they will never walk again. Those who develop convictions that they can and will walk again often accomplish results far beyond physicians' predictions. The mechanisms of glands and nerves, when intelligently utilized, can be made to contribute to healthful personality development; but adjustments, attitudes, convictions, and determinations are psychologically more important than the mechanisms alone.

References

Clegg, J. L., "Some Observations on Endocrines in the Emotional Psychoses," *Journal of Mental Science*, Vol. 83, pp. 52-60.

Dispensa, J., "Relationship of the Thyroid with Intelligence and Personality," *Journal of Psychology*, Vol. 6, pp. 181-186.

Jamieson, G. E., "Psychoses Associated with Hyperthyroidism," *Psychiatric Quarterly*, Vol. 10, pp. 464-479.

Marinus, C. J., "Psychological Patterns in School Children with Endocrine Disorders," *Journal of Exceptional Children*, Vol. 4, pp. 9-12.

Molitch, M., "Endocrine Disturbances in Behavior Problems," *American Journal of Psychiatry*, Vol. 93, pp. 1175-1180.

Shaffer, Laurance Frederic, *The Psychology of Adjustment*, Chapter XII. Houghton Mifflin Company, 1936.

The standard textbooks on elementary psychology offer helpful descriptions of both glands and nerves.

Projects

1. If your library has a number of books on the endocrines, examine the contents of the books to see which authors paint an optimistic picture regarding the control of personality and insanity through the use of glandular treatments. Also note which authors write in the vein of Dr. Hugh T. Carmichael, psychiatrist of the University of Chicago Medical School, who reported the following views:

> A recent survey showed that of a group of about 300 mental patients selected for endocrine diagnosis and treatment more than a third were so improved that they were able to leave the institution. But do not jump to the conclusion that it was gland treatment that saved them. Further analysis showed only 17 per cent of those selected for endocrine diagnosis actually had anything wrong with their glands and less than half of these had adequate gland treatment. In addition, many of those "cured" had had a type of mental disease that often disappears spontaneously.
>
> Mental disease and mental deficiencies are common. So also are glandular imbalances. That they are often found in the same individual could be simply a matter of chance.
>
> The role of the endocrines is still an unsolved problem and presents a fruitful field for future research.
>
> —*Science News Letter*, May 14, 1938.

2. Find examples, from newspapers or periodicals, of persons who have developed abnormal physiques because of glandular imbalance. Clip articles that have photographs and bring them to class for the benefit of other students and for class discussion. Note which glands are considered responsible in each case. How have any of the persons utilized their peculiarities vocationally?

3. Compare the physical and the mental or emotional results of glandular abnormality in several types of cases. Does there seem to be a relationship between these two aspects; if so, how are they interrelated?

4. Find from textbooks or other sources several theories or hypotheses concerning the functioning of the nervous system. Evaluate the theories on the bases of simplicity, logic, plausibility, and experimental evidence. Name the scientists associated with each of the theories.

5. Make a study of the neural organization of behavior. Refer to standard elementary texts such as John F. Dashiell's *Fundamentals of General Psychology*, Chapter X (Houghton Mifflin Company, 1937). Pay special attention to psychologists' theories regarding relation between mind and body. Do psychologists think of mind and body as separate entities that influence each other, or as aspects of the same organism?

8

Methods of Treating the Maladjusted

There are 75,000 new patients admitted to our mental institutions every year. Yet at least half of all mental illness could be prevented —if we acted in time. Furthermore, we could return to the community nearly 20 per cent more of those actually in hospitals—if we applied intensively the knowledge and techniques we have today. —C. M. Hincks, M. D., General Director, National Committee for Mental Hygiene, *Survey Graphic*, April 1938.

THE TREATMENT of the seriously maladjusted or insane requires years of special training in universities, hospitals, and clinics. This work is done by psychiatrists, that is, physicians who have specialized in the investigation and treatment of mental disorders. Obviously, only experts should treat psychotics, those persons who have a pathological mental condition which tends to constitute a disease-entity. In this chapter, therefore, we will differentiate between the serious and the minor maladjustments.

Treatment of the Major or Serious Maladjustments

The theories and methods that psychiatrists and clinical psychologists use are too complex for us to attempt a comprehensive discussion of them in this book. However, we can try to appreciate the importance of their work and to co-operate intelligently with them.

First, we should recognize our responsibility toward acquaintances who are suffering from serious mental ailments. One of the great lessons we have learned from our studies of the mentally ill is the need for realizing that a mentally sick person should be treated with the same consideration that we accord the physically ill. When a friend has a broken leg or a fever, we take him to a hospital, sympathize with him, send him

Fig. 26. Karl A. Menninger, M. D., Chief of Staff at the Menninger Clinic, Topeka, Kansas. If you are interested in examples of mental disorders, see his book *The Human Mind* (Alfred A. Knopf, 1937).

flowers, and visit him.   Similarly, when a friend is sent to a hospital for mental treatment we should treat him not as a "nut" but as a person who is sick, for that is what he is. We should not attach a social stigma to the person who has been in an institution for the insane any more than to a person who has been in a general hospital for an organic illness.   In many cases the former mental patient is not handicapped but to some people he is stigmatized. The stigma is based on unintelligent popular misconceptions regarding the possible permanence of insanity.   Many small employers still refuse to hire a former mental patient.[1]   One extensive study which covered a five-year period of investigation showed that at least 35 per cent of the mental patients were cured, 18 per cent were improved, 22 per cent died, and 25 per cent got worse or remained the same.[2]

Second, executives, parents, teachers, and personnel men should learn enough about the symptoms of mental disorders to know when it is advisable to refer employees, children, pupils, and acquaintances to experts for diagnosis. Psychiatrists and clinical psychologists are trained friends who may help increase

[1] A. A. Low, "Placement of the Former Mental Patient," *Employment Service News,* 1939, Vol. 6, No. 2, pp. 14-16.

[2] E. D. Bond and F. Y. Braceland, "Prognosis in Mental Disease," *American Journal of Psychiatry,* 1937, Vol. 94, pp. 263-274.

our happiness. They are not mere classifiers of mental ailments and custodians of asylums; they are counselors to whom we may go for occasional check-ups of our mental habits just as we may go to the family physician for an annual check-up of our bodily condition.

Third, we should learn some of the basic principles used in the treatment of the mentally ill so that we can co-operate intelligently with the psychotherapist. For example, some patients who voluntarily consult a psychiatrist report that they are not getting any help from the treatments. These statements are often made because the patient's treatment has progressed to the point where he must either live on a new basis or else continue to "enjoy" his old inadequate mental habits. At such times of doubt we should encourage the patient to continue the treatments until he learns to live more satisfyingly in terms of the new mental regimen.

Fourth, the investigations made by the specialists in mental disease have removed the fear of the direct inheritance of mental ills. Mental ills are not inherited like the color of eyes. Paradoxically, however, mental ills do run in families. Studies of sisters, brothers, uncles, aunts, parents, and grandparents of patients in mental hospitals have revealed no evidence of any exact theory of inheritance. There is no clear-cut case of Mendelian inheritance.[3] A mentally diseased parent cannot hand on this trait as he can hand on the color of his eyes.[4]

Mental disease does occur among the relatives of mental patients and among some racial groups[5] more often than it occurs in the general population. It is possible that a predisposition toward mental breakdown is inherited, but we are not certain be-

---

[3] T. A. Munro, "Consanguinity and Mental Disorder," *Journal of Mental Science,* 1938, Vol. 84, pp. 708-714, reports that 2.4 per cent of the 4,200 mental patients studied were of consanguineous parentage.

[4] "Mental Ills Not Inherited Like the Color of Eyes," *Science News Letter,* May 20, 1939, p. 313. This article is a summary of a study by Drs. Horatio M. Pollock, Benjamin Malzberg, and Raymond G. Fuller in a book *Hereditary and Environmental Factors in the Causation of Manic-Depressive Psychoses and Dementia Praecox.* State Hospitals Press, Utica, N. Y. 1939.

[5] J. Slawson and M. Moss, "Mental Illness Among Jews," *Jewish Social Service Quarterly,* June 1936, pp. 343-350. Comparative rates per 100,000 population of first admissions to 17 mental-hygiene clinics, New York City, 1934, pointed to a relatively greater prevalence of psychoneuroses and related disorders among Jews, and of committed insane among non-Jews.

Fig. 27. J. F. Brown, professor of psychology at the University of Kansas and Chief Psychologist at the Menninger Clinic, Topeka, Kansas. Those interested in further study on the problem of psychoanalysis should refer to his book *Psychodynamics of Abnormal Behavior* (McGraw-Hill Book Co., 1940).

cause the parents of the mentally diseased also bequeath to the children a particular sort of family circle in which to grow up. Mental habits have a close relationship with mental disease or health, and this fact offers us much hope in the intelligent control of our mental well-being. We can do a great deal toward the development of sound mental habits in ourselves regardless of who or what our parents were. The maladjusted person is not a poor helpless patient fatalistically sacrificed to his heredity or his environment. More powerful than the germ plasm or the parental pattern are courage and the desire to develop the adaptability necessary to deal adequately with one's barriers.

Fifth, we should appreciate the relation between bodily and mental health. A thorough physical examination should precede any psychotherapy, and the examination should be made by a physician who specializes in diagnosis rather than by an ordinary practitioner who is satisfied with taking the blood pressure and counting the pulse. An ailment such as arthritis is often treated as organic only. Yet family worry, grief, and other forms of emotional stress bear more than a chance relationship to the onset and flare-up of the chronic joint disease, rheumatoid arthritis, as indicated by a recent study of this ailment.[6]

---

[6] Stanley Cobb, Walter Bauer, and Isabel Whiting, *Journal of the American Medical Association,* August 19, 1939.

On the other hand, hallucinations may be erroneously treated as purely psychological; yet voices heard by the mentally ill may have a basis in ear infections. Almost one out of every five patients examined at the Boston Psychopathic Hospital was found to have a toxic type of deafness.[7] Certain patients who were free from toxic deafness also suffered from auditory hallucinations but described them differently. This study indicated that an examination of the physical condition is so important in understanding many mental conditions that the diagnoses should be made with the utmost care.

Physicians and psychiatrists are giving many different kinds of treatments to the body, particularly the nervous system, as an aid in curing patients who were considered hopelessly insane. Some of these newer treatments include electric shocks passed directly through the brain. Similar shock treatments are given by means of insulin[8] and metrazol. A non-shock treatment by means of nitrogen administration seems to offer hope of achieving the same effects as insulin and metrazol without their drastic shock effects.

No one knows what really happens as a result of these shock treatments. Perhaps some of the old nerve current pathways and synaptic junctions in the sick brains are so modified by the shock treatment that old neural patterns are lost.[9] Metabolic activity is changed. Chemical and physiological activities are modified, but only future research will possibly explain the reasons why shock and fever treatments are beneficial to some mental patients.

Many methods of treatment other than electrical and chemical are used. The therapeutic theatre is an example. Here patients are encouraged to go on a stage and blow off steam

[7] *Science News Letter,* November 26, 1938, p. 345. Findings reported by Dr. Elvin V. Semrad.

[8] E. Friedman, "The Irritative Therapy of Schizophrenia," *New York State Journal of Medicine,* 1937, Vol. 37, pp. 1813-1821.

Jane Stafford, "The Shock that Cures—Insulin Treatment Provides First Ray of Hope for 'Living Dead' Suffering from Dementia Praecox," *Science News Letter,* May 21, 1938. This article gives an understandable explanation of the method of treatment and quotes figures on the number of treated patients who were benefited.

[9] Marjorie Van De Water, "Electric Shock, A New Treatment," *Science News Letter,* July 20, 1940, p. 43.

through impromptu drama[10] while psychiatrists listen and offer guidance. Hypnosis and religion have also been used by certain psychotherapists with some success. So many different kinds of treatment are used that the layman is apt to wonder why chemical, physical and psychological approaches are at times used for patients who have the same or similar disorders.

If one asks how could psychological medicine possibly cure an organic condition, the answer is obvious. It could not possibly cure an organic condition. If at the same time one asks, "How could chemicals possibly cure an organic condition," the answer must be the same. It could not possibly. We then perceive that the questions have arisen out of a misconception of the mechanism by which cures are achieved. Processes which go on in the body are of necessity some expression of metabolism. The chemicals which we take when we feel diseased could hardly be said to repair the damaged condition of the organism. Rather their sole purpose is so to change conditions in the organism as to bring about those functional conditions which will enable the organism more readily to cure itself. The organism must always cure itself through its metabolic activities. It will be seen from this analysis that the effects of chemical medicines are purely functional. Viewed from this angle, the situation is somewhat clearer and the question is now as to whether or not the psychological medicine can be of value in bringing about the conditions which will enable the organism to cure itself.[11]

Unfortunately, the bringing about of conditions which will enable the organism to cure itself is often very difficult in psychopathic cases. However, one helpful point of view for the student is that many psychopathic persons develop their mental disorders because they are confronted by problems for which they have no satisfactory answers. Many are in states of conflict.

Conflicts. A humorist described a tardy man and woman standing on a pier watching an ocean liner disappear down the bay. The disappointed woman turned on her husband and said: "Don't just stand there—*do* something!" Obviously, the poor husband could do nothing about it, but the wife's senseless demand for action illustrates how conflicts are likely to arise when no action is possible.

[10] J. L. Moreno, "Psychodramatic Treatment of Marriage Problems," *Sociometry*, 1940, Vol. 3, No. 1, pp. 1-23.

R. Borden, "The Use of the Psychodrama in an Institution for Delinquent Girls," *Sociometry*, 1940, Vol. 3, No. 1, pp. 81-90.

[11] M. N. Chappell, "Psychology and the Organic Disorders," *The Psychological Exchange*, 1931-32.

Many experiments have shown the possible effects of conflicts on mental well-being. Pavlov was one of the first experimenters to prove that abnormalities of behavior can be produced in an animal when the animal has been trained to solve a problem by means of a specific act, and the conditions are changed so that the learned solution is no longer appropriate. Pavlov trained a dog by the conditioned-reflex method to discriminate between two visual patterns; the presentation of a circle of light was always followed by food, while the appearance of an ellipse whose axes had a ratio of 2:1 was not rewarded. The circle soon became a conditioned stimulus to salivation but the appearance of the ellipse inhibited salivation.

In the experiment, the conditions for the dog were changed. The ellipse was gradually changed to approach a circle and the dog continued to make perfect discriminations until the ratio of the axes had become 8:9, after which imperfect discriminations were made. Then the dog's behavior suddenly changed. He was unable to differentiate between the circle and the ellipse and became negative to all stimuli. As the training was continued, the formerly docile dog constantly struggled and howled. The dog had a "nervous breakdown." The confusion of the positive and negative stimuli was too much for him. The conflict could not be solved by any of his learned responses.[12]

Liddell,[13] Anderson, and other investigators have done considerable similar work with sheep. N. R. F. Maier[14] and his associates have studied experimentally produced neurotic behavior in the rat. Pigs, guinea pigs, and cats[15] have been used in similar experiments on the effects of frustration.

In Dr. Maier's experiments with rats, the rats were taught by reward and punishment to distinguish between two cards. Then, instead of being permitted a choice between a "reward" and a

---

[12] I. P. Pavlov, *Lectures on Conditioned Reflexes.* International Publishers, 1928.

[13] O. D. Anderson and H. S. Liddell, "Observations on Experimental Neurosis in Sheep," *Archives of Neurology and Psychiatry*, 1935, Vol. 34, pp. 330-354.

H. S. Liddell, "The Experimental Neurosis and the Problem of Mental Disorder," *American Journal of Psychiatry*, 1938, Vol. 94, pp. 1035-1043.

[14] N. R. F. Maier, *Studies of Abnormal Behavior in the Rat.* Harper & Bros., 1939. See also Maier, Glaser, and Klee in the *Journal of Experimental Psychology*, 1940, Vol. 26, pp. 521-546.

[15] "Studious Laboratory Cat Breaks Down Emotionally," *Science News Letter*, March 18, 1939.

Fig. 28. Norman R. F. Maier, University of Michigan. Those interested in abnormal behavior in animals should refer to his *Studies of Abnormal Behavior in the Rat* (Harper & Bros., 1939).

"punishment" card, an animal was shown only the "punishment" card while a blast of air was forcing him to jump. At the sight of the "punishment" card, the rat might resist action for as long as 15 minutes before he would jump. The rat was in a state of conflict. He did not have a suitable mode of response for the problem situation. Neurotic symptoms resulted in many rats. The "psychopathic" animal would tear out of the apparatus, run in circles on the floor, show intense tics, and then varying degrees of coma.

As a result of his experiments, Dr. Maier believes that the cure for frustrated neurotic human patients is to find a way for the person to act. Dr. Maier's cure for neurotic rats is to encourage them to find something to do even though it fails to solve the conflict that confronts them. He calls this "abortive behavior." To cure them, he taught them to make just a half-way jump toward solving their dilemma. Possible human applications[16] of this principle might be:

---

[16] Possible limitations of animal experiments as applied to frustrated human beings have been analyzed by L. S. Kubie in "The Experimental Induction of Neurotic Reactions in Man," *Yale Journal of Biology and Medicine,* 1939, Vol. 11, pp. 541-545.

A girl urged by her parents to marry might dislike both of two available suitors. Forced to marry, she would break down. If she engages herself to one but is cold to him, so that they drift apart, she is saved. A substitute activity, such as a career of nursing, would serve the same purpose.[17]

Pregnancy and the conflicts arising from sin contribute greatly to neurotic behavior by leaving no avenue for behavior and yet requiring that something be done. . . .

On the other hand, going to the electric chair, while it may produce tensions, does not produce neurosis because the individual knows just what he must do.[18]

These experiments with animals and the judgments of many specialists in mental disorders indicate that neurosis is often due to the fact that the individual patient is confronted by the conflicting character of difficulties imposed upon him, difficulties for which he has no direct attack or suitable substitute responses. The neurosis is a haven in his flight from reality.

The experiments with animals have suggested some valuable concepts for the treatment of psychopathics. However, the most interesting and frequently used concepts in the use of psychological approaches to the treatment of psychopaths may be obtained from a review of the principles and methods of psychoanalysis.

What is psychoanalysis? Sigmund Freud of Vienna was the originator of the technical method of psychoanalysis. He published his first investigations in 1895. Freud studied many cases of nervous disorders and was convinced that the main causes lay in repressed wishes or desires. The repressed desire or impulse was, he believed, of a sexual nature and had been repressed by the forces of education and social conventions. When the wish is repressed it remains alive and active in unconscious form. The theory, to many people, appears to be weird, while to others it holds a strong attraction for its interesting interpretations. Perhaps we should spend a moment reviewing the experiences which gave Freud his method of treating psychopathological maladies.

Before 1890, psychologists had already considered mental abnormalities. Hypnotism was known, and it was noted that, when patients were treated in certain ways, they developed multiple personalities. That is, they regarded themselves and acted as though they were different persons at different times.

---

[17] *Science News Letter*, January 13, 1940, p. 26.
[18] *Science News Letter*, December 31, 1938.

Sometimes one personality could not remember the other personality of the same individual. In other cases the various "personalities" might be more or less conscious of each other. This was then interpreted as indicating that nervous diseases were the result of a splitting-off of consciousness. One portion of the associations of the mental life broke off and formed a new or smaller "mind" of its own. Compulsions and obsessions were explained in this way, and the physicians of that time used hypnotism to reintegrate the dismembered personality or mind. In the hypnosis, the physician tried to suggest the split-off part of the mind back to the main body of the personality. Freud was a physician and treated his patients in this manner.

In the early years of his experimenting, Freud noted that some patients remembered things when they were hypnotized that they could not recall when in the normal state of consciousness. Then, when these forgotten facts of a painful nature were presented to the patient in his normal state he showed very strong emotions. He seemed to respond to these unpleasant and forgotten facts in the same manner as though he were actually experiencing the painful situation that had been buried·in the unconscious. In some cases the painful experience had occurred many years before and the patient had been unable to recall it. When, however, the painful experience was brought to the full attention of the patient and he reacted to the recalled situation with the same emotional responses that he should have had when the situation occurred years before, the patient became well. The conclusion was naturally reached that the abnormal mental states of the neurotics were caused by the fact that the neurotic had not made a complete and satisfying emotional response to some of his unpleasant impulsions and experiences. The bringing-about of a belated emotional response in order to clear up a neurosis was called the "method of catharsis" and the new or belated emotional response was called the "abreaction."

Freud found that some of his patients could not be hypnotized, but he also discovered that the patients could themselves recall their forgotten experiences when they were encouraged to talk freely and at random. In these experiments, Freud found that the dreams of his patients were often related to the unpleasant things that they were trying to recall or uncover. He made studies of thousands of dreams and learned that the dream is symbolic of some repressed or hidden wish, that it may relate to infantile experiences, and that the repressed wish is one which, ordinarily, we do not admit that we would even entertain. In some dreams, certain symbolisms occurred again and again, such as snakes, knives, seeds, mountains, and wild animals. Freud interpreted these symbolisms to represent repressed desires that

Did you ever have a dream like this?

MOST PEOPLE have had the dream of finding money scattered around, and picking it up hurriedly for fear some one would come along and take it away.

This dream, according to many psychologists, betrays a subconscious anxiety about the future, a fear of becoming suddenly poor. Is it

any wonder that the dream is so common?

But no such fears need haunt the man whose life and property are insured wisely and well. For he knows that both his own and his family's futures are provided for, by the simplest and safest means of protection known today.

You can achieve the same security, by con-

sulting a trained, experienced Travelers representative. Moral: Insure in The Travelers. All forms of insurance

• • •

The Travelers Insurance Company, The Travelers Indemnity Company, The Travelers Fire Insurance Company, Hartford, Connecticut.

FIG. 29.   An example of analysis of the unconscious as used in advertising.

we refuse to recognize or carry through emotionally, and so they are stored in the unconscious and are allowed to come forth only in the dream life of the patient or in some abnormal manner during his waking hours. Most of these desires were believed to be of a sexual nature, because sex is the one strong impulse that cannot be expressed freely in our civilization.[19]

The psychoanalyst considers the sex symbolisms as merely convenient means of reaching more certain conclusions, and he uses them in much the same manner that the mathematician uses the symbol x in algebra. The true psychoanalyst does not use these sex symbols as definite proof of the nature of the repression until he has further evidence from the past experiences of the patient. The faddist who dabbles in psychoanalysis is apt to jump to erroneous conclusions when he knows some of the sex symbols, but does not appreciate that the symbolisms[20] are merely working hypotheses until a verifiable conclusion is reached. Moreover, the psychoanalyst does not think of the sex impulse in quite the same way that the layman does. The former uses it in the genetic sense.

The "censor" (better, censorship) refers to the assumed group of influences which require the individual to repress his normal impulsions. These influences are the social standards of our times, the reproofs given in childhood, and the many repressive influences of modern life. The reason why the individual patient's dreams express the repressed impulses more readily than the acts of his waking life is that these repressive forces are not parts of his conscious or intellectual life. When we are asleep, the conscious controls are weaker, the censorship is relaxed, and the impulses come into the dream consciousness in symbolic form.

Psychoanalysis is a special method of psychological observation. All scientists find it necessary to set up special con-

---

[19] Many students of dreams of primitive peoples have indicated that the lack of sexual inhibition tends to reduce the number of disguised and symbolical sexual dreams. Among such savages, the most tormenting and easily remembered dreams are the nightmares of anxiety and hunger. See, for example, V. Elwin, "A Note on the Theory and Symbolism of Dreams Among the Baiga," *British Journal of Medical Psychology*, 1937, Vol. 16, pp. 237-254.

[20] E. A. Gutheil, *The Language of the Dream*. The Macmillan Co., 1939. This is a textbook of dream interpretation which presents dream symbols, analytical interpretations, and the uses of dream analysis in therapy.

cepts or formulas to explain the phenomena of their fields of study. Chemists have set up "atomic theories" to help them explain facts discovered by experiment. Astronomers, biologists, mathematicians, and others have deliberately set up theoretical constructs to give order to their data. Psychotherapists have found it helpful to follow the same procedure as indicated in the theoretical construct based on the "unconscious." *Psychoanalysis is a method of psychological observation in which dream analysis, free association, and study of transference of early attitudes toward the analyst are used to uncover the unconscious.*[21] It uses a unique set of theoretical constructs to give order to its data and to apply effective methods of psychotherapy.

Its theoretical constructs are a great deal more abstruse and difficult to understand than the barrier-adjustment concept used in this text. One explanation for the use of a more abstruse set of concepts by the psychonalysts is that the seriously maladjusted patient's behavior often requires a more involved system of thinking than is needed to explain the behavior of a normal or only slightly maladjusted person.

As previously stated, dream analysis is used. In addition to the study of the dream life of the patient, the psychoanalyst also uses "free association." In this method the psychoanalyst has the patient come to his office and makes him physically comfortable in an easy chair or on a couch. All possible distracting influences are removed. Perhaps monotonous noise is provided. The patient closes his eyes, and the psychoanalyst may ask him to think of some part of his personal history which the analyst wishes to investigate, and tells him to think aloud and to say everything that comes to his mind, no matter how trivial, how irrelevant, or how unpleasant it may seem to him. The object is to discover the repressed experience or submerged complex that had not been allowed full emotional expression when it occurred in the experience of the patient. The patient is asked to report his dreams and to express his thoughts freely. In this way the analyst tries to unravel the network of experiences that caused the disturbance.

The analyst may also use word associations. To do this he

[21] J. F. Brown, "The Position of Psychoanalysis in the Science of Psychology," *Journal of Abnormal and Social Psychology,* 1940, Vol. 35, pp. 29-44.

prepares a list of words that may have some relationship to the patient's history and asks the patient to give the first word that comes to mind when the words are spoken. The analyst records with a stop-watch the time required for each response to the stimulus word. After the list has been completed the patient is taken through the list again and differences in responses are noted. When a stimulus word touches upon the repressed experiences or complexes, certain disturbances are noted, such as the peculiarity of the kind of reaction, the increased length of time for the reaction, and the failure to repeat the former reaction. White[22] reported the associations of a patient who had made several attempts to commit suicide:

Stimulus Word	Reaction	Time	Reproduction
To harm......................	Self	6.6	Anyone
Stork........................	Large	4.4	Large
False........................	True	1.8	Not true

The average reaction time was about 1.6 seconds. In the above examples can be noted the lengthened time of reaction, inability to recall the reaction on repetition, and the irradiation of the disturbance to the next two reactions as shown by the lengthened time of the reaction. This patient had a brother who was arrested and brought into court, and she gave bond for him. She made the following responses: *Prison*—cell—4.2 seconds; *bond*—pay—4.2 seconds; and *judge*—to be judged—4 seconds.

In addition to the method of catharsis, the analyst may use *transference*. This is an attempt to relieve the emotional tension by having the patient project upon the analyst all the emotional tensions that are uncovered in the analysis. Emotionally, the analyst takes the place of parent, lover, or enemy. It is apparent that transference requires a great deal of skill on the part of the analyst and many specialists neglect to use it intelligently:

If psychoanalysis had never made but one contribution to our thinking, it would have been fully justified for what it has had to offer regarding the mechanism and nature of the process it designates as transference. One of the reasons I have in mind for advocating a further study of hypnotic phenomena is that here is an opportunity for the experimental study of this

[22] William A. White, *Outline of Psychiatry*, p. 338. Nervous and Mental Diseases Publishing Co., 1923.

process. My own feeling is that the transference is the most powerful tool which the physician has at his service for therapeutic purposes, and when we consider that in the vast majority of cases he has not the slightest idea of the existence of this process of which he himself is a part I have perhaps said enough to indicate the importance of its adequate understanding. All forms of therapy, no matter what—surgical, drug, dietary advice—all of them have their component, great or small, of psychotherapy, and the power and efficacy of psychotherapy are bound up in the mechanism of the transference. In addition to this the transference, because it represents a great force, is capable, when used ignorantly, of doing much damage. Under these circumstances it becomes of the utmost importance for the physician to acquaint himself with its meanings, significances, mechanisms, in order that he may make this force available at maximum efficiency for the welfare of his patient.[23]

To psychoanalyze a patient requires much time. Months and even years may be required to unearth the painful experiences and enable the patient to express the unpleasant emotions that were repressed years before. The personality of the psychoanalyst plays a very important part in the method. He offers not sympathy but understanding. The patient needs to realize that here is one person in the whole world who is able and willing to understand him. The psychoneurotic may have felt that he has been misunderstood and that he must hide his guilt and burden from his best friends. As proof of the fact that we are unwilling to express ourselves and tell all our emotional experiences, ask a group of persons to tell all the dreams that they can recall. Few indeed are the husbands who are willing to tell their wives all their dreams or the thoughts that have entered their minds. If maladjusted people could only realize that each and every impulse or idea that enters consciousness has a normal and natural cause, it would be easier for the mentally afflicted to deal with their own emotionally repressed impulses.

In the various studies of the maladjusted, it has been found that some have tried to overcome their unpleasant experiences and impulses by means of defense mechanisms. The boy who takes pride in being the worst roughneck of the neighborhood may be acting the part of the rowdy in order to make himself feel that he is virile. To tell him that he must be more gentle does not remove the cause of the rowdiness. The girl who takes refuge in invalidism to gain attention may not be helped by

---

[23] William A. White, *Twentieth Century Psychiatry*, pp. 50-51. W. W. Norton & Co., 1936.

punishment or advice to make up her mind to get well. The analyst tries to get at the cause of the maladjustment and then to enable the patient to *sublimate* the energies, that is, to direct them into substitute activities that are satisfying and socially acceptable. We can see examples of sublimation in daily life in the case of the man who loses his wife and then takes up golf and plays it strenuously, or the student who fails in his studies and then becomes a collector of stamps. It is probable that many of our strongest drives are attempts to sublimate energy and achieve a sense of worthwhileness because of failure to do so in some other activity.

Criticisms of psychoanalysis. Freud and his colleagues will go down in psychological history as pioneers and contributors in a field which needed them in their time. They opened new trails in the exploration of the human mind. Many of Freud's trails led to new discoveries of great value. Some, too, led into dead-end canyons or to insurmountable cliffs. Many of his earlier teachings have been modified by members of related schools of therapy, and they are now adding new contributions by their willingness to discard or correct some of the earlier concepts in his method:

1. A modification of the Freudian principles concerns the concept of the unconscious. Some critics claim that we are not motivated by suppressed wishes, but rather by a series of adjustments to our situations. These adjustments are not made by a part of the mind, but by the entire individual. The organism as a whole responds to the stimulus. By trial and accidental success we find that one kind of response results in failure and dissatisfaction whereas another response brings about success and satisfaction. The successful response is stamped into our neurological mechanisms and, therefore, is readily repeated. Repressed desires or suppressed wishes are not entities which have energy by themselves. They have no existence by themselves any more than my fingers have hidden peckings on a typewriter. It is only when I am stimulated as an integrated unit that my fingers peck on a typewriter. Therefore, it is often claimed, the "unconscious mind" is not subject to proof or observation but rather is an explanation of phenomena that can be interpreted more adequately by objective means.

2. Repressions, though inactive, may affect behavior, and so they cannot be ignored or belittled. Conflicts do take place between impulsions. A girl may react in a psychoneurotic manner because her love for a man may be in conflict with the wishes of her father who forbids her to see the man. A phobia may even arise, because of a desire which has been stimulated and not allowed expression, recognition, or admission. However, critics claim that normal stimuli may become associated through action of the nervous system rather than through a subconscious mind, with abnormal responses as in the case described by Bagby:

A man suffered from a phobia of being grasped from behind, the disturbance appearing early in childhood and persisting to his fifty-fifth year. When walking on the street he was under a compulsion to look back over his shoulder at intervals to see if he was closely followed. In social gatherings he arranged to have his chair against the wall. It was impossible for him to enter crowded places or to attend the theater. In his fifty-fifth year he returned to the town in which he had spent his childhood. After inspecting his old home, he went to the corner grocery and found that his old boyhood friend was still behind the counter. He introduced himself and they began to reminisce. Finally the grocer said this, "I want to tell you something that occurred when you were a boy: You used to go by this store on errands, and when you passed you often took a handful of peanuts from the stand in front. One day I saw you coming and hid behind a barrel. Just as you put your hand in the pile of peanuts, I jumped out and grabbed you from behind. You screamed and fell fainting on the sidewalk." The episode was remembered and the phobia, after a period of readjustment, disappeared.[24]

3. Dreams are not always wish-fulfillments. A dream of falling may be stimulated by a sagging bed spring rather than by the fear of a moral fall; or a dream of being choked may be brought about by the tightness of the bed covers. Mostly, dreams are the mere automatic and chance play of the cerebral associational mechanisms. One neural pathway happens to arouse another pathway and incongruous combinations of ideas result. Certainly many dreams are not related to the sex impulse. The child and the adult must suppress many impulses, such as those of self-assertion and gluttony. It is unfair to attribute all asocial impulsions to sex energies which are not allowed expressions by our form of civilization.

It is true that the body is full of energy—energy which must

---

[24] E. Bagby, "The Etiology of Phobias," *Journal of Abnormal and Social Psychology,* 1922, Vol. 17, p. 17.

be expressed in some form. The outlets for these energies may be socially acceptable or extremely harmful. One of the happiest men I ever met was a murderer who had shot and killed two of his enemies, and wounded two others. But he was an ignorant butcher who made his living killing cattle, cutting up meat, and grinding it for his customers. The court sent him to a hospital for the criminally insane.

4. The energy of the human organism may be thought of in many different ways. It may be called the *elan vital* or the *libido*, or we may accept it, as suggested by Jung, as a striving after larger experience. Adler considered this striving as an attempt to achieve safety and power. Or we may designate energy with reference to its objectives and call it tendencies or impulsions. It certainly may be analyzed without sex as a basis.

5. Conflicts between various impulsions do give rise to behavior which may be thought of as resulting in a *complex*. However, the complex should not be considered bad in all cases. Lee Wilson Dodd has written a book[25] wherein he shows that the complex is not a stain but an advantage; not a leaden drag but a golden spur. The lame foot of Byron stimulated him to become a master horseman, a good shot, and the best swimmer in England. The assurance thus gained enabled him to become a great lover, poet, and patriot.

The complex is a Freudian term, but the inferiority comes from Adler. Whether a handicap produces a sense of inferiority and induces a complex, or results in a heroic resolve to achieve despite it, seems to depend largely upon the type of nervous constitution and earlier adjustment habits of the individual who has the handicap.

Contributions of psychoanalysis.

1. Psychoanalysis has given us a method of treatment of the insane which has been of material help, even though the persons who use it sometimes do not believe all its published principles. In fact, some psychologists say that the bases of psychoanalysis are not true, but that it works. Since psychoanalysis has come into more or less common use in state hospitals, the percentage of cures, all factors considered, has probably increased. Whether these cures have been the result of psychoan-

[25] *The Golden Complex: A Defense of Inferiority*. John Day Co., 1927.

FIG. 30. *"Hush! Father mustn't be disturbed,"* and similar highly emotionalized admonitions to the small child may permanently influence the child regarding parental authority. Fortunately, some children are not permanently conditioned by such situations—they react by negative adaptation. (*Courtesy of General Foods Corporation.*)

alytical methods, chemical treatments, or both is still open to debate.

2. Psychoanalysis has given us some valuable points of view. It has shown the importance of the emotions, the strength of childhood influences, and the ways in which we deal with our

problems or evade them. It has shown us the dominating influence of the attitudes people have acquired about themselves, about others, and about their surroundings. Their adjustment habits have a great deal to do with their abilities, perhaps even their intelligence, or at least the ways in which intellectual capacity is expressed. We now have some evidence to show that psychoanalysis has even made substantial changes in the intelligence quotients of certain individuals.[26]

3. For the businessman, psychoanalysis has a pointed suggestion in dealing with problem employees—namely, the art of listening. The executive of the old order took a keen delight in dominating his men. He knew how to put the "fear of God" into his workers. The new executive, like the psychoanalyst, tries to find out why the employee acts as he does. He wants to know what the peculiar behavior of a problem employee means, that is, what are the individual's problems and his adjustments? Certainly, the studies of problem children have shown that the so-called problem child can be helped very much more easily if we think of him in terms of problem habits. Furthermore, the problem habits are likely to be the child's adjustments to "problem parents." In the business world, when an executive insists upon remaining hardboiled rather than analytical and skillfull in dealing with his employees, he must expect to have problem employees because he is a "problem executive."

The lazy employee, the embezzler, the liar, and other employees who have problem habits are examples of poor adjustments. Some of these can be improved by the specialists in mental disorders. The executive, too, should sit at the specialist's feet and learn to use intelligent methods in dealing with the problem employees in his organization.

4. Regardless of its theoretical defects, psychoanalysis has given us a point of view which enables us better to evaluate the statements of the successful businessman who grants interviews for articles of the "How to Succeed" variety. The captain of industry tells the youth of the land how he worked hard or used strategy to win in the big city. He thinks that he did it

[26] L. Chidester and K. A. Menninger, "The Application of Psychoanalytic Methods to the Study of Mental Retardation," *American Journal of Orthopsychiatry,* 1936, Vol. 6, pp. 616-625. This article reports an increase in IQ from 62 to 90

as an effort of will. As a matter of fact, he is likely to be quite unaware of the many influences in his own life. So far as ability to analyze the forces that have produced him is concerned, the big man in any field might better attribute his success to a lame foot, bad digestion, corpulent abdomen, disappointment in love, or a poor scholastic record than to his own unaided self.

Dealing with Minor Maladjustments

Everyone finds it necessary to deal with problem personalities, but we can deal with them more easily if we think of each problem person as a person with a problem. The maladjustments which we see in others or in ourselves mean that poor techniques or habits are being used.

In our ordinary associations with an employee or other acquaintance we collect many facts about him. These facts become useful in understanding him when we have a system such as the adjustment concept for our thinking.

Usually we begin our thinking with his childhood. We want to learn how he felt as a child. We want to learn how he reacted to the childhood situations and whether the childhood habits of adjustment still persist. We can, by direct and indirect questioning or by talking with his friends, learn about his childhood barriers and adjustments if we have in our own mind the typical barrier feelings and adjustments of Table VII.

To understand someone's problem personality, we can begin our collection of, facts with his childhood situations and think from them toward his present habits. The difficulty of doing this is often so great that we should think of our knowledge of him as an hypothesis for dealing with him rather than as a certain conclusion. However, we then have a working hypothesis and can use it experimentally. Furthermore, we must always use some assumptions in dealing with problem people in practical situations. The point is that our assumptions should not be mere random guesses but the results of intelligent thinking.

Anyone who will memorize the typical childhood barriers (column A of Table VII), adjustments in childhood (column B), and adult adjustments (column C) will have a valuable clinical tool for understanding the person with a problem. However,

TABLE VII

TYPICAL CHILDHOOD BARRIERS AND ADJUSTMENTS WHICH MAY LEAD TO PROBLEM
HABITS IN ADULTHOOD

A	B	C
As a child, did you feel that you were:	*Which method of adjustment did you use?*	*In adulthood, which method of adjustment do you now use?*
1. Small, helpless, of poor health, or defective in body?	1. Sickliness. "Nervousness" to prove need for special consideration.	1. Sickliness. "Nervousness." Pains that your family physician seems unable to cure.
2. The center of attention—a kind of toy or animated doll? Did games with others revolve mostly around you?	2. Unruliness in order to gain the limelight, sarcasm, bitter word-battles to deal with domineering parents.	2. Argumentativeness. Word-battles. Comedian knacks or witticisms to gain attention.
3. Disciplined severely, often punished for what you considered minor misdeeds? Suppressed?	3. Model behavior in order to deal with domineering parents, or hoping for affection by being a paragon of virtue. Self-righteousness.	3. Seek perfection for yourself. Self-righteousness. Consider yourself better than other people.
4. Extra "human freight," unwanted, and given little affection?	4. Keeping to yourself to avoid failure. Seclusiveness in games and comradeships. Shut-in personality.	4. Seclusiveness. You avoid games and social affairs. Have very few friends.
5. Denied your rights, to be seen rather than heard, forced to be quiet and courteous? Domineered? Discriminated against?	5. Belligerence. Spoiling the fun of others to avoid games where you might fail.	5. Radical tendencies. Cynicism. You believe you could remodel the world.
6. Laughed at, frequently ridiculed?	6. Fear lest you might be ridiculed. Not taking school or work seriously.	6. You laugh off your obligations. Change interests without any real reason for the change.

certain precautions are necessary. The child who had barrier number 2 may in adulthood make adjustment number 5. We cannot conclude that any one barrier always results in a corresponding adjustment tendency. We can recognize causal connections only when we have learned many pertinent facts about the individual and then see how the facts arrange themselves into a meaningful pattern. This fact makes necessary a wide knowledge of barriers and typical forms of adjustments. The lack of standard adjustments to specific barriers means that every individual must be given individual analysis in order to be understood. Clinical psychology is a complex study.

The person who wishes to learn the mode of thinking used by clinical psychologists may start to do so through the adjustment concept. The facts about a person's psychological development often arrange themselves in patternful relationships. Headings such as those of Table VIII are likely to occur in the clinician's thinking.

The psychological findings about a human being cannot be satisfactorily arranged in terms of some algebraic formula, but the facts can be thought of in patternful relationships as suggested by the Seven-Phase Outline of Table VIII. Such an arrangement of information about a problem person enables us to appreciate wherein he is a person with a problem and how his psychological background influences some of his conduct.

TABLE VIII

SEVEN-PHASE OUTLINE FOR STUDY OF PERSONS WITH ADJUSTMENT PROBLEMS

1. *The Barrier:* The problem or problems, ostensible or actual. See Table V, page 74, for a list of barriers.
2. *Predisposing Influences:* long term factors such as endocrine glands, bodily health, cultural environment, or personalities in the home. (See page 66.) These may be known or have to be assumed.
3. *Precipitating Influences:* relatively recent factors such as a failure, insult, or loss. (See page 66.) These may be known or have to be assumed.
4. *Direct Attack Adjustments* which the individual should have made, or might make in the future. (See Table VI—I.)
5. *Positive Substitute Activities:* These vary with the problem, the individual, the total situation, and so on. These adjustments tend to strengthen the personality for future problems but not usually for the problem involved in the adjustment under consideration. (See page 76.)
6. *Evasive or Retreat Adjustments:* These also vary with the situation but they tend to weaken the personality for dealing with the immediate and with future problems. (See Table VI, sections III and IV.)
7. *How Others Can Help Him:* Analyzing the adjustments of others has little value unless the analysis enables us to contribute to the positive adjustments and personality well-being of the person analyzed. Suggestions depend upon many factors, but especially upon the relation of the analyst to the person analyzed.

We should try to learn enough psychology to be able to see the significant adjustments which occur in the lives of those around us. Of course, if we have a professional responsibility for the mental health of others, we should read many books on psychology and attend clinics in order to become alert to the subtle influences in the lives of our maladjusted associates as well as in our own mental development. To attain such a working knowledge of psychology, the reading of biographies is helpful. Every person, famous, infamous, or ordinary, has some tendencies and purposes that have grown out of his own unique adjustments to his barriers rather than from intellectual reactions only to his environment. Every novel, for example, is both a narrative about imaginary characters and, to some degree, a treatise on its author's psychological experiences. We can never really appreciate a writer's novel, a philosopher's philosophy, a businessman's managerial systems, a politician's political program,[27] nor a parent's methods of child training until we know enough about the individual's personal history to see how his present convictions are tied up with his psychological background.

Facilitating the mental well-being of others means that the executive, parent, teacher, or counselor shall enable the individual to deal effectively and satisfyingly with the frustrating problems before him. Appropriate adjustments can be taught to most people. Efficiency in adjustment depends very greatly on the ability of an individual to continue varying his responses until success is achieved. The mentally ill person is one who has lost this ability.[28] Intelligent supervisors and counselors often show persons with adjustment problems how to vary their responses.

The main need of many people is ordinary friendly counsel and reassurance. Even animal experiments show the value of that. When dogs are purposely made neurotic by experiment,

---

[27] Some clinical psychologists believe that Thomas Jefferson and Alexander Hamilton differed in their ideas about government partially because of their different adjustment influences. Jefferson wanted a weak central government with a maximum of rights for the state and the individual. Jefferson had a dominant father who had oppressed him and so he believed in freedom for the individual and the state. Hamilton, on the other hand, wanted a strong central government with a minimum of rights for the individual and the state. Hamilton himself felt keenly his own fatherlessness. Many biographies and autobiographies point out similar relationships between early adjustments and later convictions. A good example of a book in this field is L. Pierce Clark's *Lincoln, A Psycho-biography*. Chas. Scribner's Sons, 1933.

[28] C. D. Norton, "The Psychology of Human Adjustment," *Mental Health Observer*, 1939, Vol. 6, pp. 1-6.

Fig. 31. Harry Walker Hepner, Syracuse University. Brief descriptions of typical employer-employee psychological problems will be found in his *Human Relations in Changing Industry* (Prentice-Hall, Inc., 1934).

the presence of a human being or a friendly dog in a room reassures the nervous animal so that he does not always have a neurotic attack. Similarly, people need assurance that what they are doing, they are doing well. They can often be given sympathetic intelligent friendship in learning suitable modes of action.

Practically, then, dealing **with the** minor maladjusted person means that the maladjusted person must learn to feel that his supervisors or counselors and associates like him and will encourage him while he learns effective habits which will displace the handicapping habits that we call evasion and retreat. The study of case problems, limited though such study must be, may be helpful to the student. The reader may gain some practice in the study of adjustments through reading and discussing the six case problems of the next pages. Discussion should lead to additional suggestions which may be written into the *other* spaces of the cases partially analyzed.

Employee refuses to accept an offer for advancement. Mr. Denison is one of your best and most intelligent workers. You find that you must promote a man to the position of foreman over thirty of Denison's fellow-workers, and Denison seems to be the logical man for the position. When you explain the work to Denison and offer him the foremanship, he says that he is not interested in becoming a foreman. He claims that he would be unable to direct the work of former associates because they know him too well. You, however, are convinced that he really would like to have the promotion.

1. *The Barrier:*
   a. Ostensibly, his lack of self-confidence.
   b. Actually, a fear of ridicule. (Assumed on analyst's part.)
   c. *Other assumption:*

2. *Predisposing Influences:*
   a. Has he developed a rut for himself in his present job?
   b. Has he failed in some previous position of leadership?
   c. *Other:*

3. *Precipitating Influences:*
   a. Has his wife recently discouraged him about his ability?
   b. Did any of his associates talk about his possible promotion?
   c. *Other:*

4. *Direct Attack Adjustments:*
   a. Take the job and try to develop self-confidence.
   b. Mingle more often with superiors.
   c. *Other:*

5. *Positive Substitute Activities:*
   a. Throw energy into lodge activities to gain satisfaction.
   b. Put energy into the present job, doing it exceptionally well.
   c. *Other:*

6. *Evasive or Retreat Adjustments:*
   a. Convince himself that his health would not stand more strain of responsibilities.
   b. Find satisfaction in solitude.
   c. *Other:*

7. *How Others Can Help Him:*
   a. Have him supervise only a few cooperative employees until confidence has been gained.
   b. *Other:*

The impractical dreamer. George is young and ambitious. He has been out of school for one year but has been unable to settle down to the routine position which he holds with a business firm. He is forever conceiving impracticable get-rich-quick schemes that would, he imagines, give him easy money quickly. His ideas are so impracticable, however, that he is missing opportunities to lay a foundation for his future in the firm where he is now employed.

1. *The Barrier:*

    a. Tendency to take short-cuts to an imagined success.
    b. Does not realize what success really is.
    c. *Other assumption:*

2. *Predisposing Influences:*

    a. Is he still in the adolescent age of daydreams?
    b. Does he feel insecure because his father and mother are incompatible?
    c. *Other:*

3. *Precipitating Influences:*

    a. Does he find his present work very boresome?
    b. Does he see better-educated workers pass him in advancement?
    c. *Other:*

4. *Direct Attack Adjustments:*

    a. Develop the possibilities in his own job.
    b. Enjoy small successes rather than dream of spectacular success.
    c. *Other:*

5. *Positive Substitute Activities:*

    a. Associate with inferiors whom he can impress.
    b. Develop a hobby of an unusual kind.
    c. *Other:*

6. *Evasive or Retreat Adjustments:*

    a. Adopt an air of superiority and tell others how clever he is.
    b. Picture himself in a comfortable "heaven."
    c. *Other:*

7. *How Others Can Help Him:*

    a. Explain to him the "romances" and "adventures" of his present job.
    b. *Other:*

Sex repressions. Richard is a young man who works in a large city office and is troubled with sordid thoughts, especially about girls. He comes from a small town and has never been away from home before. The apparent freedom in social relations between the young men and women in his office keeps him emotionally upset because he is too self-conscious to make satisfying acquaintances of the girls. He therefore thinks of girls in a strange, abnormal way.

1. *The Barrier:*

    a. Ostensibly, an unhealthy mental attitude.
    b. Actually, lack of normal associations.
    c. *Other assumption:*

2. *Predisposing Influences:*

    a. Was he ridiculed in childhood for associating with girls?
    b. Was he too closely supervised or pampered when young?
    c. *Other:*

3. *Precipitating Influences:*

    a. Has he been talking with maladjusted men about lewd aspects of sex?
    b. Is he still really living in the country?
    c. *Other:*

4. *Direct Attack Adjustments:*

    a. Associate with normal and well-balanced girls.
    b. Join a club and learn to dance.
    c. *Other:*

5. *Positive Substitute Activities:*

    a. Become intensely interested in his work and avoid women.
    b. Get a job in his home town.
    c. *Other:*

6. *Evasive or Retreat Adjustments:*

    a. Criticize the freedom in social relationships.
    b. Gain satisfaction through daydreaming.
    c. *Other:*

7. *How Others Can Help Him:*

    a. Invite him to attend a mixed social affair.
    b. *Other:*

Symbolic activity. Mr. Amulet is a middle-aged man of higher than average intelligence who suddenly realizes that he has become superstitious. He finds himself doing things for good luck or to ward off evil omens— superstitious acts which he would have scorned a few years ago. He tells himself that he must stop these foolish tendencies, but he claims that he cannot.

1. *The Barrier:*

    a. Ostensibly, a desire to avoid injury.
    b. Actually, an unadmitted fear of harm because of some act of which he is ashamed.
    c. *Other assumption:*

2. *Predisposing Influences:*

    a. Many emotional experiences have given him a sense of guilt.
    b. Have friends impressed him with the efficacy of their pet charms?
    c. *Other:*

3. *Precipitating Influences:*

    a. Does he believe he escaped an accident because he obeyed a "premonition"?
    b. Has he recently committed an immoral act that has caused him to fear disgrace?
    c. *Other:*

4. *Direct Attack Adjustments:*

    a. Study superstitions and how they may be ways to compensate for unadmitted mistakes.
    b. Visit a psychiatrist.
    c. *Other:*

5. *Positive Substitute Activities:*

    a. Take part in religious activities as a means to adjustment.
    b. *Other:*

6. *Evasive or Retreat Adjustments:*

    a. Immerse himself in the mystical.
    b. Become intoxicated in order to forget his superstitions.
    c. *Other:*

7. *How Others Can Help Him:*

    a. Explain to him how one of your fears symbolized feeling of guilt for a misdeed.
    b. *Other:*

The self-conscious employee. Perkins is thirty years old and is a mechanic in a garage. He is sensitive and becomes easily confused when the foreman, Graves, comes into the room where he is working. Graves knows that Perkins is a good worker, but when Graves stops to watch Perkins, the latter becomes flustered and cannot work efficiently.

1. *The Barrier:*

   a. Habit of dealing with people by thinking of himself.
   b. *Other assumption:*

2. *Predisposing Influences:*

   a. Was he reared by parents who criticized forwardness?
   b. Was he disciplined severely and made to think of himself as unwanted?
   c. *Other:*

3. *Precipitating Influences:*

   a. Has Graves ridiculed him about his work?
   b. Was he recently ignored when he tried to be friendly?
   c. *Other:*

4. *Direct Attack Adjustments:*

   a. Become active in an organization to develop his self-confidence.
   b. Entertain the boss socially.
   c. *Other:*

5. *Positive Substitute Activities:*

   a. Find another job.
   b. Boss his physical inferiors, such as children.
   c. *Other:*

6. *Evasive or Retreat Adjustments:*

   a. Criticize boss and firm.
   b. Daydream and picture himself a hero.
   c. *Other:*

7. *How Others Can Help Him:*

   a. Praise him for his "little" social successes.
   b. *Other:*

Behavior varies with the situation. Miss Palmer is considered a competent "complaint clerk" in the public utility office where she works. She is a pleasant and convincing talker. In the homes of her friends, however, she cannot carry on a conversation. She seems to have no opinion on any subject. When she is asked why she isn't more sociable, she says she just doesn't know what to say or talk about.

1. *The Barrier:*

    a. Early conditioning or a complex arising from an inferior social position.
    b. *Other assumption:*

2. *Predisposing Influences:*

    a. As a child, was she allowed to take part in family conversations?
    b. Were her parents socially inferior in the community?
    c. *Other:*

3. *Precipitating Influences:*

    a. Do her friends tell her that she is a wallflower?
    b. Has a confidence been betrayed by one of her "friends"?
    c. *Other:*

4. *Direct Attack Adjustments:*

    a. Tell her friends how she feels and ask them to help her gain confidence in herself.
    b. Take an interest in other people and talk to them about themselves.
    c. *Other:*

5. *Positive Substitute Activities:*

    a. Lead a group of younger girls who will respect her.
    b. Express herself in activities that do not require conversation.
    c. *Other:*

6. *Evasive or Retreat Adjustments:*

    a. Talk about and criticize the girls whom she knows.
    b. Adopt an air of silent superiority.
    c. *Other:*

7. *How Others Can Help Her:*

    a. Do not give her advice—just show by your manner that you like her as she is.
    b. *Other:*

References

Adamson, E. I., *So You're Going to a Psychiatrist.* Thomas Y. Crowell Co., 1936. A simply and popularly written account of modern psychiatric thought by a woman psychiatrist.

Jacobson, E., *Progressive Relaxation* (2nd ed.). University of Chicago Press, 1938. The author presents clinical, practical, and scientific discussion of the method of progressive relaxation whereby the subject is trained to reduce or to eliminate residual muscular tensions. With the consequent reduction of excitatory impulses there is a reduction in the irritability of nerve centers.

————, *You Can Sleep Well; the ABC's of Restful Sleep for the Average Person.* Whittlesey House, 1938. Instructions, written popularly in the second person, for applying the author's technique of relaxation to the therapy of insomnia.

Mikesell, William Henry, *Mental Hygiene.* Prentice-Hall, Inc., 1939. The author describes his ideas on how suggestion can be used by the individual to promote his efficiency and happiness.

Wallin, J. E. Wallace, *Minor Mental Maladjustments in Normal People.* Duke University Press, 1939.

Maier, Norman R. F., *Studies of Abnormal Behavior in the Rat.* University of Michigan, 1939.

Projects

1. Make a collection of your friends' automatic writings, often called "doodles." Compare their doodles with published statements of the symbolic significance of doodles. Suggested references are Russell M. Arundel, *Everybody's Pixillated* (Little, Brown & Co., 1937) and Winifred V. Richmond, *Personality—Its Development and Hygiene,* pp. 26 and 156 (Farrar & Rinehart, 1937). See *Tribune* ad, Chapter 25 of this book.

2. In Dr. G. V. Hamilton's study of *What Is Wrong with Marriage* (A. & C. Boni), he asked 200 normal, intelligent married men and women the question: "If by some miracle you could press a button and find that you had never been married, would you press the button?" Thirty-five per cent said "Yes" or hesitated.

Why do some married people fail to find reasonable happiness in marriage? List the psychological causes of incompatibility. Would companionate marriage be of real value? Prepare a set of rules for the young man or woman to use as a guide in choosing a life partner.

3. Some businessmen have a "check-book complex." What experiences may cause them to evaluate abnormally many personal acts and plans in terms of cost and profit rather than in terms of happiness?

4. The assistant head of a department was asked to give a talk on an academic subject over the radio. He gave it without consulting the department head. When the latter learned that he had been denied this opportunity for publicity, he discharged his assistant. Analyze the possible reasons for discharging the assistant.

5. Prepare a set of suggestions for parents which may be of value in preventing psychopathological conditions in children.

6. Analyze your behavior for evidence of inhibitions that are annoying and irrational. Can you think of experiences that caused them? Mention some things that your "censor" does not allow you to do.

7. To realize how energy may be dammed up, conduct this experiment. Have a person time you for ten trials of thirty seconds each. During each trial make the figure 5 as rapidly as you can in the usual manner of making a 5. Then make the figure 5 in an inverted manner as rapidly as possible for the same number of trials and the same number of seconds to each trial. Then make the 5 right side up as rapidly as you can for about five trials of the usual thirty seconds each. Do not allow more than ten seconds rest between any of the trials. Plot a curve of the number of 5's made in each of the 25 trials. Note the waves of efficiency and the release of the dammed-up energy.

9

Developing Your Own Personality

The mere reading of a book on personality will not make you popular nor skillful in handling people. It can only start you on the road to making yourself friendly and influential. It can suggest new ways to enjoy people and stimulate you to apply the methods that you already know but neglect to use. At times you may fail to achieve your ends. You may even be misunderstood. But failure should simply spur you on to improve your strategies.[1]

THE NUMBER of different definitions of personality is about the same as the number of persons who have defined it.[2] Most psychologists restrict the term *personality* to nonintellectual traits, applying it particularly to the traits which determine a person's social effectiveness and happiness in life. However, most definitions tend to fall into two general classes: (a) those that define personality as the unique pattern or organization of the individual's adjustment habits, that is, the fundamental organization of his mental life as developed through his capacities interacting with a complex social and physical world, and (b) definitions that give emphasis to the effect the individual has on other people with whom he comes in contact, his so-called social stimulus value.

Most people who wish to improve their personalities think of it in terms of their social stimulus value or effectiveness in dealing with people. They realize that they are not alert to the handling of social situations. They are likely to be self-conscious.

The very term "self-consciousness" expresses their basic problem—they are conscious of the wrong person. The socialized

---

[1] Harry Walker Hepner, *It's Nice to Know People Like You*, p. 9. D. Appleton-Century Co., 1939.
[2] Daniel Katz and Richard L. Schanck, *Social Psychology*, Chapters 12-15 (John Wiley & Sons, 1938), present a discussion of definitions of personality.

person is conscious of others rather than himself. Fortunately, the art of dealing with people can be acquired:

The habit of becoming more aware of others than of yourself can be learned. For example, certain introverted college students asked me to conduct classes in personality development. In these classes I taught one basic principle or rule: *Watch the other person and do whatever appears to be appropriate.*

When the classes were begun, the students were unknowingly given a standardized interview where the interviewer asked six questions. Two of the answers were written incorrectly by the interviewer. The interviewer then tried to erase the error, using a wooden pencil with the eraser worn down to the metal. (Each student had been given a pencil with a good eraser.) The test of the student's habituated use of the above rule was observed and recorded. The poorly socialized students failed to offer their erasers to the interviewer.

After this first test, the students were trained in the practical application of the basic principle. The students themselves suggested extensions and applications of the rule, but pencils and erasers were never mentioned. After eight hours of training, they were again given the same test. Most students made a definite improvement as shown by the moving pictures which were taken without their knowledge. They had learned to objectify some of their thinking; to lose their self-consciousness by becoming conscious of others. . . .

If you wish to have more friends or to be able to handle people happily, you, too, have to learn the art of forgetting yourself. You must lose self-consciousness by becoming more conscious of other people and by directing your thinking toward them. Personality, in this social sense, is not something that you have or are; *personality is what you do when you are with others. It is an activity, not a possession.* It is not a stagnant pool but a running brook.

This dynamic nature of personality is most fortunate. If you are seeking more friendships or wish to handle people more effectively, you can forget what you are. Simply concentrate upon others, and discover how to give them greater enjoyment. Think of each person as being a distinctive individual whom you try to understand and make a bit more happy. If you practise this fundamental principle, you will find, sooner or later, that you are popular and influential with others.

Your attainment of this social artistry is not so formidable a task as it may appear to be. You have already learned some knacks of handling people. If, on certain past occasions, you had not withdrawn into a shell of reserve when strangers or unkind persons were about, you would have learned more skills. Perhaps you were so wrapped up in your own feelings of doubt about your ability, imagined unattractiveness, or self-concern that you failed to watch the other person. Of course, if your thoughts and feelings were concentrated on yourself, you made a poor impression on him and you withdrew more quickly from contacts with the next stranger. . . .

Parents are at fault when they try to protect their children by isolating them from imperfect companions. Sooner or later the children may develop into first-class neurotics whose chief fault is the fact that in the game of life

FIG. 32. Robert G. Bernreuter, Pennsylvania State College. A test of introversion-extraversion and related personality traits appears in his *Personality Inventory* (Stanford University Press, 1935).

they "can't take it." Parents who constantly guard their children, not allowing them to play with other children for fear that they will learn the facts of life, are not fulfilling their parental responsibilities. Occasionally the children even run the risk of later becoming patients in hospitals for the mentally ill. The only way for a girl to learn how to handle men, or for a boy to learn how to get along with girls, is for both to go through a long practice period of training where each successful skill in getting along with people has been learned through hard experiences plus intelligent judgments. Socially speaking, every man is his own ancestor and his own heir—he makes his own future and he inherits his own past. What he does on a great occasion depends upon what he already is, and both depend upon the years of training acquired in the social arenas of life: the playground, the office, the shop, and the park bench on a moonlight night.[3]

The socialized personality and its resultant friendships must be earned.   Many persons who find it difficult to earn friendships would like to improve their personalities, but they have the habits of the *introvert* rather than those of the *extravert.*

Introversion-extraversion.   Introverts are characterized by their "shut-in" personality. They do not share their joys and sorrows with others, but keep them to themselves. They are largely self-sufficient for their emotional outlets. Anger, blushing, and laughter are examples of emotional outlets, and the introverts express them within themselves; that is, their emotions are introverted. Daydreaming is an example of an in-

[3] Harry Walker Hepner, *op. cit.,* pp. 5ff.

troverted emotional outlet. Introverts, in short, are vividly aware of their own inner lives.

Extraverts, in contrast, express their emotional outlets in action and in seeking the society of others. They do not sit alone with their thoughts, but depend upon others or upon activity for their happiness. Introverts are men of thought and extraverts are men of action. Scientists tend toward introversion and businessmen toward extraversion. Foremen and executives whose duties require the supervision of others are likely to be extraverts. The key executives of industry incline toward *ambiversion*, or a middle position on the scale of introversion-extraversion. Office workers, clerks, and stenographers incline toward introversion. Many accountants and research engineers are pronouncedly introverted.

It should not be assumed that all or most people are of either one type or the other. Rather, they tend to group themselves in the center of the scale. Each person has some qualities of each type, and his classification depends upon the degree to which he is introverted or extraverted rather than upon the absolute presence or absence of the characteristic traits. Laird[4] devised a scale for the measurement of introversion and extraversion. The personality signs he listed are:

1. The introvert blushes easily; the extravert rarely blushes.
2. The extravert laughs more readily than the introvert.
3. The introvert is usually outspoken; the extravert is usually careful not to hurt the feelings of others.
4. The extravert is a fluent talker; the introvert can prepare a report in writing more easily than he can tell it in conversation.
5. The extravert lends money and possessions more readily than the introvert.
6. The extravert moves faster than the introvert in the routine actions of the day, such as walking, dressing, talking, etc.
7. The extravert does not take particular care of his personal property, such as watches, clothes, etc.; the introvert is found continually oiling, polishing, and tinkering.
8. Introverts are usually reluctant about making friends among those of opposite sex, while extraverts are attracted by them.
9. Introverts are easily embarrassed by having to be in front of a crowd.
10. The extravert is a more natural public speaker.
11. The introvert likes to argue.

---

[4] Donald A. Laird, "How Personalities Are Found in Industry," *Industrial Psychology*, October 1926, pp. 1, 2.

12. The introvert is slow about making friends.

13. The introvert rewrites his letters, inserts interlineations, adds postscripts, and corrects every mistake of the typist.

Personality signs revealed in thinking and attitudes:

1. The introvert worries; the extravert has scarcely a care in the world.

2. The feelings of the introvert are easily hurt; the extravert is not bothered by what is said to him.

3. The introvert deliberates in great detail about everything—what to wear, where to eat, etc., and usually tells one why he decided to do what he did.

4. The introvert rebels when ordered to do a thing; the extravert accepts orders as a matter of course.

5. The introvert is urged to his best efforts by praise; the extravert is not affected by praise.

6. The introvert is suspicious of the motives of others.

7. The introvert is usually radical in religion and politics; the extravert—if he entertains any opinions—is usually conservative.

8. The introvert would rather struggle alone to solve a problem than to ask for help.

9. The introvert would rather work alone in a room than with others.

10. Extraverts follow athletics; introverts read books and "high brow" magazines.

11. The introvert is a poor loser.

12. The introvert daydreams a great deal.

13. The introvert prefers fine, delicate work (die making, accounting), while the extravert prefers work in which details do not bother.

14. The introvert is inclined to be moody at times.

15. The introvert is very conscientious.[5]

The study of personality traits or patterns of this kind has value to the supervisor, because those persons who are most introverted can be influenced by methods that are not successful with the extraverts. Praise, caution, and exactness appeal to introverts. Activity, speed, chance, and challenges appeal to the extraverts.

As salesmen are decidedly extraverted, it is hopeless to try to compel them to fill in and mail each day very detailed reports to the home office. Salesmen should have a minimum amount of clerical work to perform. Their paper work should be done by women, because women, as a group, are more introverted than men. Bank work usually attracts introverts. Bank workers who meet the public should be assisted by extraverted contact men and women in the lobby. Workmen who

---

[5] *Ibid.*

are to be promoted to supervisory positions should be extraverted rather than painstaking and retiring introverts.

In the forms of introversive adjustment which we call *retreat* the individual seeks solitude, prefers to stay at home, adopts cults of mysticism, studies his ancestry, or lives in a world of poetry, art, or fiction. Some religions have idealized this tendency by formalizing the retreat adjustment. Tibet, the center of religious fanaticism, has many old Buddhist monks who have kept themselves sealed up—except for small openings for food—in little huts since their early manhood. Some of them have not heard the voice, seen the face, nor touched the hand of a human being for more than forty years.

Many of our very studious college students are introverted, but college fraternities probably attract the extraverted and the introverted students in approximately equal numbers.[6] The differences between fraternities are likely to be greater than the differences between the fraternity and the non-fraternity groupings.

Some introverted students would like to become more extraverted but wonder whether it is possible to do so. The answer is a decided "Yes." On the other hand, many introverts say that they prefer to remain as they are because civilization needs introverts as well as extraverts. No one can argue with those who make this choice except in one important respect, namely, introverts are so very sensitive, their feelings are hurt so often, that they would be happier if they would learn greater skill in the social arts. Those who wish to acquire the social skills can do so by directing their thinking toward others and away from themselves.

Paradoxically, the socially skilled and interesting personality cannot be acquired if it is sought directly. It is a by-product, like happiness. "Happiness is a butterfly which, when pursued, is always just beyond your grasp, but which, if you will sit down quietly, may alight upon you." Or, as Hawthorne said: "Happiness in this world, when it comes, comes incidentally. Make it the object of pursuit, and it leads us a wild goose chase and is never attained."

---

[6] The 1939-40 scholastic averages of 2,081 independent and 911 fraternity men of one large eastern university revealed no significant difference.

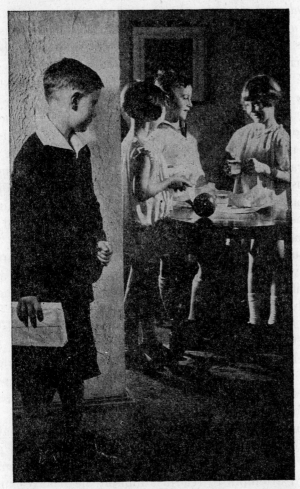

Fig. 33. "He didn't want to go to the party." The person
who tries to develop his own personality notices and tactfully
encourages children and adults who do not participate wholeheartedly in social activities. (*Photograph courtesy of The
Book House for Children, Chicago.*)

As previously stated, self-consciousness on the part of the
introvert means just what the term indicates—the individual
is more conscious of himself than of others. Self-pity and similar ego-centered tendencies can be changed by looking out—not
in. Extraversion can be attained by thinking more of external
and social values, particularly how to deal with and handle
people.

To socialize your personality, watch the other person and do whatever appears to be appropriate. In this social sense, personality is what you *do* with people; not something that you have.[7] Friendliness can be learned in the same way we learn arithmetic or French—by study and practice. The extent to which the college student, male or female, has learned commonly used information about social relations can be measured by the "Social Knowledge Test" in the Appendix of this book. The students who score high in the knowledge of the Lower Social Strata and low in the Upper Social Strata questions should consider the desirability of increasing their study of social information. The college man or woman who has limited his associations to either class may be somewhat handicapped in certain occupations.

The adjustments made in early childhood are very important in the development of effective social skills. Many a child finds it difficult to adapt himself to others because he feels emotionally insecure. He may feel insecure because, for instance, he took too seriously the ordinary family quarrels of his parents. The frictions between his parents may have caused him to feel that they, and his world as well, were not dependable. He became emotionally insecure because the most important persons of his experience, his parents, did not seem to merit his belief in their dependability.

If the emotionally insecure child is also nagged a great deal, he is apt to grow up to be impulsive, self-centered, and unable to identify himself with his associates. He feels left out and, in awkward attempts to readjust himself, he behaves in ways that cause others to avoid him, thus increasing his feeling of not belonging. However, if he later comes to realize how his insecurity came about, recognizes that many parents show their affection for each other by their bickering, and he secures some dependable person as a friend, he is likely to develop adjustment habits that result in a feeling of belongingness. Practically, this means that the individual should frequently participate in group activities appropriate to his age and social status: sports, team or group games, dancing, committee meetings, and so on. In

---

[7] The second person is often used in this chapter for the greater interest of readers who wish to develop the social stimulus values of their personalities.

FIG. 34.   The adjustment habits developed as a result of childhood experiences of this kind often have a profound influence on the later personality.   (*Courtesy of Warner Bros., Inc. A scene from "Penrod and Sam," a First National and Vitaphone Production.*)

this respect, chess and archery are likely to be less developmental than baseball or amateur theatricals.

The feeling of belongingness can be achieved by anyone who consciously practices the best methods of doing whatever seems to be appropriate in dealing with people.   This means that the intelligently socialized person not only accepts people but also thinks of them as sources of mutual enjoyment.   An important difference between the adjustment-minded person and the average layman is illustrated by the three ways in which we can deal with a problem person's annoying behavior: namely, (a) cumulative annoyance, (b) negative adaptation, and (c) insight-meaning.

Cumulative annoyance is exemplified by the employee who dislikes his boss and at the beginning of each day says to himself:

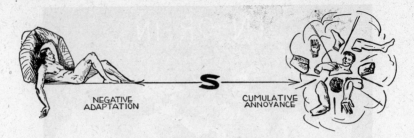

NEGATIVE
ADAPTATION

CUMULATIVE
ANNOYANCE

Fig. 35. *The adaptation-annoyance range.* When an individual is stimulated by the repetition of any given situation, he may, on the one hand, completely adapt himself to the situation, so that it no longer elicits any reaction except one of boredom and dullness.

On the other hand, each repetition of the stimulus may result in added annoyance. The effects of the stimulation are then summative. Each reaction adds to the accumulated annoyance of the previous sum.

The worker who responds to his job in the latter way soon develops feelings of strong resentment that result in rebellion. If he cannot escape from the summative effect of the annoyances of his job, he will have to "explode" or "break" under the strain. The "explosion" may be expressed through the channel of fighting the boss, or through bitter antagonism toward industry or toward anything that symbolizes the annoying situation. The "break" may be in the form of the so-called nervous breakdown. Contrast this with figure 36.

"Another day of that man! Every time I see him I hate him more. When can I get away from him?"   The individual who reacts to another person or situation in this manner soon develops intense feelings of resentment.   Eventually he rebels, perhaps violently. If circumstances, such as the need for a job in order to support a family, do not allow him to quit, he must "explode" or "break" under the strain.   He is the type of employee who is impelled to "tell the boss to go to Hell" and thereby lose the job he wanted to lose.   This type of worker, if he does not explode, is apt to become a bitter critic toward industry, modern business, or something else that happens to symbolize his baleful situation.   If he does not have an outlet for his pent-up emotions, he is likely to escape through the so-called "nervous breakdown."

Negative adaptation applies to many of our daily experiences with people. Some persons and situations are dealt with and forgotten. Examples of negative adaptation are the factory worker who has given up all hope of getting a better job and now does his work in a mechanical spiritless manner, the small child who does not react to his mother's constant scolding, or the husband who does not "hear" his wife's back-seat driving.

Insight-meaning is used by the worker who finds himself in an annoying situation, analyzes it, and discovers some interesting

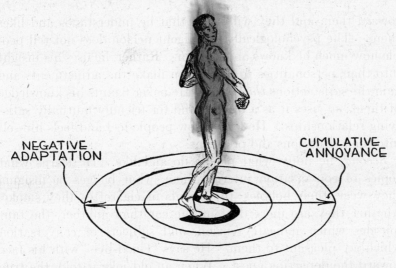

NEGATIVE
ADAPTATION

CUMULATIVE
ANNOYANCE

Fig. 36. *The insight-meaning response.* When an individual is stimulated by
the repetition of any given kind of situation, he need not adapt himself completely,
nor need he be cumulatively annoyed.   He may apply intelligence to the situation.
He may seek insight.
    When he seeks insight, he makes observations.   He notes annoying and satisfy-
ing factors.   He looks for causes and effects.   He discovers possible improvements.
He utilizes the situation for self-expression.   The situation acquires meanings for
him, and these meanings radiate in all directions from the situation and result in
the disappearance of feelings of dull acceptance or of resentment.
    The worker who reacts to his job in this manner becomes neither bored nor
carpingly critical.   He utilizes his job for creative self-expression.

aspects of it.   It is used by the boss who, when he is annoyed by
the mannerisms of an employee, learns that the employee has a
difficult home life and then tries to make the employee's life more
interesting by giving him extra attention while at work.   Insight-
meaning is always more satisfying than either dull acceptance
or cumulative annoyance.   It can be used every day with our
annoying associates such as the back-seat driver, the teacher who
scolds, the executive who threatens, the housewife who nags, the
girl-friend who insists on having repeated personal attentions,
and others.
    A first step in the insight-meaning relationship to people is
to become aware of their adjustments.   Anyone who learns to
apply the adjustment concept to the actions of people will soon
develop a feeling of kinship [8] toward them.   He will feel friendly

-----
    [8] "Empathy" is used by some psychologists to express the mental state wherein
one person identifies or feels himself into the state of mind of another person.
It is also used to mean mental projection of oneself into the elements of a work
of art or into a natural object.

toward them and they will sense that he understands and likes them. The psychologically intelligent person does not tell people how much he knows about them. Rather, he uses his insight into their personalities to help them make the adjustments and gain the satisfactions *they* seek. He never flaunts his knowledge of them but uses it as a background for friendly mutually satisfying relationships. He learns how people feel and feels himself into their situations and problems.

Second, he notes what people do and like. He learns what topics of conversation interest them, what badges or insignia they wear, their hobbies, the brands of cigarettes they smoke, whether they are more deaf in one ear than another, the taut muscles which indicate tension, and subjects of conversation which are pleasant to them. He says "Good-bye" with his face toward the departing guest. When an old joke is told, the true extravert does not show by his manner that he has heard it previously but laughs heartily. One of the tests of extraversion on the part of a listener is to look so interested when a story teller begins his story that the raconteur does not ask: "Or have you heard this before?"

This awareness of what people like does not mean that flattery can take the place of a sincere interest in others. Many misinformed persons fail to appreciate the importance of a genuine interest in work and people. They imagine that flattery is necessary to gain promotion, as indicated by the following typical case problem:

Should an employee use flattery in order to gain promotion if he believes that others are succeeding by this method? Mr. Edmunds is thirty-five years old, is married, and has been working for his present employer for ten years. He likes his work and, in general, he considers his employer fair. However, he believes that some of the younger men of the department who have been promoted gained their promotion through clever and tactful flattery toward his superior. Mr. Edmunds should:

1. Try to flatter his superior in order to gain promotion also.

2. Quit, and try to get a job where promotion depends upon ability rather than flattery.

3. Allow the others to do as they wish. He likes his work and he should be completely satisfied.

4. Discuss the situation as tactfully as possible with his superior.

5. Improve his ability by studying, taking an active part in technical associations, and contributing articles to trade journals. The future will take care of itself if he improves himself and builds a reputation for his ability.[9]

Third, The introvert who wishes to socialize himself should practice responding to others by means of his facial expressions. Typical introverts are surprised when they see moving pictures of themselves in conversation. They discover that they look as animated as the Statue of Liberty! If a person feels friendly, he should show it by lifting his eyebrows and smiling with his eyes as well as by grinning with his lips. Of course, friendliness is far more than facial expression. It is a sincere identification with others, but a sincere identification includes facial expressions which help to convey the feeling of friendship.

Fourth, the introvert should acquire the knack of asking questions in order to learn from others; not to argue with them. Usually, we can ask questions of a person about his occupation: what he does, who the leaders are in his field of work, changes since he has entered the field, and what successful experiences he himself has enjoyed.

Furthermore, the good conversationalist does not answer questions completely—he answers them only partially and then asks the questioner what he thinks about the unanswered aspect. He knows that when a person answers a question and then says, "Don't you think so, too?" the conversation is closed. The flow of conversation should not be shut off by requests for agreement but kept moving from topic to topic by requests for additional ideas.

Asking questions is an art which few introverts learn even though they argue frequently. They are so wrapped up in their own feelings about themselves that they cannot ask questions so as to enable the other person to expand. They are apt to ask questions to prove their own point, as found in this typical problem:

Who should take the initiative in correcting misunderstandings: the superior or the subordinate? A senior in a Liberal Arts College has had a reasonably good scholastic record. He is now in his last semester. In the first semester of his senior year, he failed a course under a certain pro-

[9] Harry W. Hepner, *Human Relations in Changing Industry,* p. 587. Prentice-Hall, Inc., 1934.

fessor, but continued the year course with this same professor. The student believes that he failed the first semester's work because he had a very heated argument with the professor. He also believes that he will fail this semester's work because he is sure that the professor does not like him. What should he do?

1. He should remain in the course, work hard, and say nothing to the professor.
2. He should request permission of his dean to change his course, explaining his reason.
3. He should discuss the matter with the professor and find out wherein he was wrong. He should then apologize, if necessary, and put himself on a friendly relationship with his professor.
4. He should tell the professor frankly what he thinks of his unfairness and demand that the professor treat him absolutely fairly.[10]

Fifth, the individual who seeks to make himself interesting to others usually finds it necessary to direct his thinking and working toward some definite end. He is apt to have a vocational program of some kind whereby he becomes a specialist or expert in some one field such as business, as exemplified by the mental habits of successful versus the non-successful businessmen. They have chosen vocations which are appropriate for their behavior patterns.

Psychologists have found that no one or two traits cause a man to be a successful businessman. All human beings possess the same traits, but they differ in the degree or amount of possession of each trait. That is, if we were to list all the traits or qualities of the one hundred greatest men of the world and then list the qualities of one hundred unimportant men, the two lists of traits would be the same. However, the two groups would differ widely in the degree or extent of possession of each trait on the list. For example, the second group of men would have less intelligence and initiative than the first group; but high intelligence alone does not enable the youth to become a leader, nor does a high degree of initiative. Success depends upon a proper combination of essential elements.

The skilled housewife's dough is a correct combination of the proper ingredients, and, when it is given the favorable environment of the oven, delicious cake results. Similarly, the great leaders in business are those who have the effective "personality ingredients" or patterns of behavior.

---

[10] *Ibid.,* p. 586.

Forty-one situations were described to 150 businessmen of five grades of income. Questions were asked and the answers were then treated quantitatively. The questions which gave differential values are shown in the "Executive Reaction Pattern" test in the Appendix. The results indicate that certain measurable differences do exist among the five classes. These differences have been statistically treated, and the questions can be used for employment purposes.

If the reader will check the appropriate items and then refer to the key in the Appendix of this book, he can score his answers and obtain an estimate of the financial rating of his own executive behavior pattern. The answers which have a plus value in the key are characteristic of the higher-salaried businessmen. The minus answers apply to the lower-salaried groups. The scorings of the answers to the 28 questions were not made during an "armchair" study, but were determined by a statistical analysis of differences in the behavior patterns. It would be difficult for a person to obtain the maximum rating by reasoning out the answers with the greatest plus values. For instance, in question 10, the highest plus value is given to the man who says that his family relations had a slight negative effect in stimulating him to do his best.

The student who wishes to develop the human relations skills of the executive must do far more than learn the correct answers to an executive reaction pattern test. Executive ability and skill in handling people are attained through daily practices in dealing with janitors, sales clerks, teachers, fellow employees, friends, and members of the family rather than through reading books. The following suggestions call attention to factors often neglected by those who wish to develop their personalities:

Ten Suggestions for Personality Development

1. *Be conscious of the other person and note what HE does.* Talk about the subjects that interest him and he will think of you as a person with an interesting personality. Forget yourself through an active interest in other people.

2. *Assume that people like you.* If you show that you want people to talk to you, they will respond warmly. On the other hand, if you act in a reserved, seclusive manner, people will as-

sume that you wish to be let alone.   If you show that you enjoy
your own company more than the company of others, they will
let you have yourself to yourself.

3. *When you greet a person, greet him emphatically.*   When
you say "Good morning," say: "GOOD MORNING"; don't say
"*good morning.*"   Also wave your hand and smile.   If you feel
that you are faking when you first attempt to be cordial, just
continue practicing cordiality until you do it naturally.

4. *Build up the other fellow's feelings of self-worth.*   Note
things about which he feels inferior.   Offer him sincere compliments which prove that he has better qualities than he thought
he had.   Do not talk about him but compliment him on his intelligent acts.   And remember that every woman likes to receive
feminine compliments regarding her beauty and personal attractiveness.   But phrase the compliment in an original way.

5. *Admit your own defects.*   You need not deliberately make
an ass of yourself but, when you have acted as one, let others
make humorous remarks at your expense.   It makes them feel
superior and keeps your personality more flexible.

6. *Practice use of the word YOU and avoid I.*   One measure
of your personality is the number of times you say *you, your, he,
his, she* and *her* rather than *I, me, my,* or *mine.*   The test of your
socialization is not the ideas that you give others but the number
of ideas that others give you.

7. *Admire your friends.*   Perhaps you have already done
many kindnesses for others which they repaid with meanness or
infidelity.   Perhaps you have lent money to some who never
paid it back and, moreover, do not care to pay it back.   These
lapses of loyalty, goodness, and integrity should not sour one for
the greater number of gifts received.   In the totality of human
relationships, human nature is remarkably good and fine.

8. *Love someone intensely.*   Man's normal state requires an
outlet for his affections.   If your wife is not of a lovable sort, love
your child.   If that is not feasible for you, assume responsibility
for someone's happiness.   A dog or a monkey may fill the gap,
but a normal person can better look himself in the face if he
gives his devotion to a human being instead of concentrating it
on a dumb animal.

9. *Change your environment occasionally.* Take a vacation when it is due. Go to a new part of the country. Meet some new people. Leave your wife and children at home when you take a vacation and allow them to take a vacation without you. Sell your house and buy another. Change your office furniture. Of course, you should have a den of your own, where you can litter the floor with cigarette butts or cigar bands; a place where you can put your feet on the desk and feel at home, but even a den becomes monotonous and a new surrounding is needed.

10. *Associate with people who are successful and happy.* Living within oneself alone is dangerous. We all need certain contacts to give us new points of view, new thoughts, and new hopes. Attend at least one social affair each week. Call on your neighbors. Meet the fellows at the club. Go to church. Compel yourself to play cards, or dance, or sing, or tell stories, or play golf. When you do associate with others, do not consider your associates as either inferiors or superiors. Let your motto be: "All men are my equals, but no man is my superior." Try to learn from those who are experts in other fields, but do not envy them their money or position. Happiness does not lie in wealth, fame, or personal beauty. It is achieved through intelligent adjustment to what we have and are.

Case Problems for Class Discussion

The case conference problems given below are taken from the author's *Human Relations in Changing Industry,* pages 605-618 (Prentice-Hall, Inc., 1934). As pointed out in Chapter XVI of that book, the answer chosen as a result of discussion is less important than the principles developed during the discussion. Psychological principles can be learned from all kinds of human relations. Problems in human relations can usually be classified under one of the four general headings:

1. *Adjustment*: exemplified by the executive who is a chronic alcoholic and projects his own emotional problems upon some member of his family.

2. *Information*: exemplified by the student who claimed in the interview for employment that he knew more accounting

than he actually knows and now has difficulty in keeping his supervisor from discovering his limited knowledge.

3. *Judgment*: exemplified by the employee who thinks that the boss is annoyed whenever the former asks questions about the work.

4. *Skill*: exemplified by the employee who hates to ask the boss for a raise, does ask only in desperation and then asks awkwardly.

Class discussion of these or similar cases may be of help to students who are interested in developing the social stimulus values of their personalities and in dealing with typical human relations problems.

How can the introvert sell himself to the management?   In college Mr. Abbe was a very brilliant student in engineering and attained a high scholastic average. Upon graduation, he went to work for the Blank Telephone Company. When working for or by himself he does excellent work, especially in the research line; he has devised many ways of saving money for the company. His great trouble is his inability to express himself. He is unable to explain his ideas to his superiors. He should:

1. Realize that he is an introvert and hope to achieve eminence in science, regardless of his personality.
2. Plan to attend more social affairs, especially those where he will come into contact with men in executive positions.
3. Take a course in public speaking.
4. Visit a psychoanalyst and take mental treatments.
5. Try to impress his superiors by giving them written reports of his work.
6. Write a memorandum to his superiors, explaining his inability to express himself and ask them to help him overcome his difficulty.

How much initiative should be shown by the new employee?   Harry Jones, in his freshman year in college, secured a position for the summer in the office of a manufacturing concern. He had high grades in school and felt that he had a good general idea about business. However, he found that school study carried no weight with his fellow employees, who at the beginning made him feel useless for a number of weeks. He hesitated to go ahead whenever a new problem arose, even though he was certain that he knew what to do. Harry Jones should have:

1. Asked a superior, if the matter seemed important enough, or else done what he thought was right.
2. Shifted the responsibility on one of his fellow employees by first asking the employee's advice.
3. Followed the policy of doing nothing unless he was certain that he knew what he should do.

4. Asked all the questions that he could, even though he became a nuisance to others by so doing.

When is superior education a psychological barrier in relations with fellow workers? Mary Margaret is a college girl working as a waitress at a summer resort. She has been promoted to a position in which she supervises extra girls who are called in for assistance when the work is unusually heavy. The extra girls resent her speaking to them about their work because they have been in the "racket" longer than she has. Also, they feel she is a college girl who "thinks she knows it all." What should Mary Margaret do?

1. She should give her "commands" to the extra girls in the form of suggestions regarding their work.
2. She should inform them that although she is only a young, inexperienced college girl, she is, nevertheless, their boss.
3. She should send the uncooperative trouble makers to the manager's office for discipline.
4. She should associate with them as much as possible and cultivate their friendship through social contacts.

What should be done with the fellow worker who gives ill-intentioned advice? Donald Adams works in a shoe factory, next to Mr. Green, an older man who has been there for years. Mr. Green shows Donald many signs of friendliness and persists in telling Donald that he works too hard and is cutting too many pairs of soles per hour. Donald observes, however, that Mr. Green seizes every opportunity to tell the foreman about the workers who do less work than he, Mr. Green, does. Donald should:

1. Disregard Mr. Green's advice and continue to do his best.
2. Tell Mr. Green frankly that he knows the real reason why Mr. Green is giving him such advice.
3. Tell the foreman that Mr. Green is interfering with his good work and ask to be moved away from him.
4. Pity Mr. Green, realizing that his age makes him less efficient and that he must use such tactics in order to keep his job.

Should an employee court the boss's daughter? Albert Jones works as a messenger in a bank. He is nineteen and is considered a bright boy with prospects for a good future. He has recently been introduced to the president's daughter, whom he likes and whose acquaintance he would like to cultivate, but he is afraid that her father would misunderstand his motive.

1. He should forget the girl and thus avoid all appearances that he is trying to gain advancement through her.
2. He should ask the girl for her opinion, explaining that he would not want anyone to misinterpret his actions.
3. He should see the girl occasionally, and by his work at the bank and his behavior with the girl try to dispel any suspicions.
4. He should watch for any signs of disapproval from the father and guide himself accordingly.
5. He should forget the girl's position and treat her as he would any other girl whom he admired, and let circumstances take their course.

Does inability in a sports activity affect an employer's estimate of an employee's ability? Clarence Buck is secretary to the president of a corporation. The president is an active, aggressive person who likes to help young men. He makes many speeches that inspire young men to work hard for success. In his dealings with employees he is rated a paternalist by labor unions but an autocrat by his immediate associates. He is an expert golf player, and he invites his secretary to play golf on a certain Saturday. Clarence is a poor golfer, but knows that he cannot refuse his employer. He should:

1. Go with his employer and play as well as he can.
2. Play with his employer and apologize frequently for his lack of skill while he is playing.
3. Take a few lessons from a "pro" before Saturday.
4. Ask the president to instruct him in the art of the game.
5. Play as well as he can without delaying the game and compliment the president whenever possible.

References

Allport, Gordon W., *Personality, A Psychological Interpretation*. Henry Holt & Co., 1937.

Dashiell, John F., *Fundamentals of General Psychology*, Chapter XX. Houghton Mifflin Co., 1937.

Hepner, Harry W., *It's Nice to Know People Like You*. D. Appleton-Century Co., 1939.

Lockhart, Earl G., *Improving Your Personality*. Walton Publishing Co., 1939.

Pressey, S. L., J. E. Janney, and R. G. Kuhlen, *Life: A Psychological Survey*, Chapters XI and XIV. Harper & Bros., 1939.

Shellow, S. M., *How To Develop Your Personality*. Harper & Bros., 1932.

Thorpe, Louis P., *Psychological Foundations of Personality*. McGraw-Hill Book Co., 1938.

White, Wendell, *The Psychology of Dealing With People*. The Macmillan Co., 1936.

Projects

1. Obtain and study a copy of the Bernreuter Personality Inventory, obtainable from Stanford University Press (Stanford University, California) —or some other personality test. Study the items in relation to the traits they are presumed to measure.

2. Read descriptive material dealing with a number of personality tests. Suggest some ways in which such tests may be helpful to the individual and some situations in which they should be used with caution or not at all.

3. Study a number of friends who have achieved considerable success in their fields, and compare them with others who seem to be "marking time." What psychological differences can you discover between individuals in the two groups?

4. Study the behavior of a child or an adult who is considered to be dishonest or unreliable. Does this trait appear in all his behavior or only in certain kinds of situations?

5. Make a point of complimenting several acquaintances on some good qualities they possess. Note the various reactions and analyze these effects.

6. Visit a department store, used-car dealer, or other retailer and inspect a large number of sales items. Criticize the items shown to you and ask to see more without showing any evidence of intent to buy. Study the sales person's reactions. If you were the sales person, what would you have done to prevent a waste of your time and still maintain the customer's good will?

7. A prospective borrower from a bank was advised by a friend to apply to the sour-mannered loan executive rather than to the jovial friendly one on the basis that the sour-mannered one could say "Yes" while the jovial executive was paid to say "No" charmingly. How would you evaluate this advice—what psychological principles are involved?

8. Study a number of illustrated advertisements and list the qualities shown or implied by the central attractive figure. Check those qualities which seem to be superficial and those which have more intrinsic worth. Upon which set does the advertisement depend for effectiveness?

PART THREE
Predicting the Behavior of the Individual

10

The Pseudo-Scientific Methods of Analyzing People

WANTED.—First-class man with experience, for permanent position on staff of Vice President to shape and direct the advertising policy of a trunk-line railroad. To save time and trouble for both applicant and employer, kindly send in photographs—1 full length, 1 exact profile view (bust), and 1 front view (bust), full face, holding hands close in front of body, one palm outward and other palm inward. Call for recommendation and personal interview will come later.—"Vice President," Box 16. . . .

THIS advertisement and others of a similar nature have appeared from time to time in business publications. Many businessmen think that it is possible to analyze a stranger according to his physical characteristics and to predict accurately whether the stranger is able to sell goods, pay his bills, understand music, work hard, and so on. For example, a business periodical that is the leading publication in its field recently published an article in which the writers praised as a shrewd prescription for the sizing up of a person the following criteria:

"Look into his eyes for honesty; around his mouth for weakness; at his chin for strength; at his hands for temperament; at his nails for cleanliness. His tongue will tell you his experience." [1]

Hundreds of executives who are competent in their own fields still think that psychology is largely a study of facial or other bodily features. Students in modern universities who take their first course in psychology are often disappointed when told that scientifically trained psychologists are unanimous in denouncing as fallacious the analysis of character from facial features.

Every large city has its physiognomists and phrenologists as

---

[1] *Banking*, March 1940, p. 27.

well as its mediums, astrologers, and fortune tellers, many of whom call themselves psychologists. Laws have been passed to protect a gullible public but the laws can often be evaded. Some mediums do so by claiming that they are members of religious organizations. Astrologists assert that they follow a "science" because they report only what the stars are supposed to indicate. In the city of New York, approximately 25,000 fortune tellers of various varieties collect an estimated annual total of $25,000,000. About one-half the fortune tellers are located in Harlem.[2]

Some newspaper editors are also sufficiently benighted or opportunistic to publish syndicated psychic columns. The following questions and answers are taken from the psychic columns of a newspaper:

Question.—The doctors advise an operation for me. My husband does not want me to have it. What shall I do?
Answer.—You will get well without the operation. I see an osteopathic treatment can cure your ailment. It is not dangerous.

Question.—Some money disappeared from my desk in my office. Was it lost or stolen? The staff is worried.
Answer.—It was not lost but was taken by a man.

Lonesome, oppressed, maladjusted readers seek easy comfort because they have not learned how to deal with their problems by direct attack. The pseudo-sciences offer "solutions" by evasion.

Some of the pseudo-psychologists are sincere in their efforts to help others. They believe that they can diagnose and prescribe for the ills of people. Most of them, however, consider their work a game and merely want to make money. However, the desire to make money through applications of psychology is not objectionable. The chief objection is the fact that such men are not scientifically trained for their work. The features or aspects of human beings which are used by these analysts are of several varieties. We shall call them the pseudo-psychological approaches:

1. Phrenology.
2. Character analysis (physiognomy).
3. Graphology.

---

[2] Rebecca Hourwich, "Forecasters of the Future Who Flourish in New York," *The New York Times*, September 6, 1931, p. XX 10.

4. Miscellaneous types: numerology, vibrations, astrology, palmistry, and others.

Phrenology. The discussion of behavior patterns and brain action may have given the reader the erroneous impression that the whole brain is divided into various areas and that each area controls one function or a group of functions, such as memory and attention. Such a theory was held for many years, but has been discarded. It is true that physiologists have found that definite parts of the brain do function in a few mental and motor acts, but the number of these known areas is far smaller and less important than phrenologists assumed.

In the latter part of the eighteenth century, the upper classes, particularly those of the court, were interested in anatomical dissections. Where a portion of the brain had been removed and the exposed surface stimulated, it was noted that certain muscular movements followed. The surgeons then mapped out parts of the brain surface and guessed at the remainder. Franz Joseph Gall and others concluded that each character trait, such as vice, love of mate, and mathematical ability, had its own area or pigeonhole on the brain surface. They also made a second erroneous assumption when they thought that increase in the use and ability of an activity, such as mathematical study, increases the size of the area. The third assumption was that these growths in function and area push out the skull and that the topography of the brain could be analyzed from the protuberances of the skull surface. Since then we have found that all these assumptions are wrong. The brain has only a very few areas that are known to control definite activities. Increased ability does not show in the enlargement of the nerve structure but is found in the complexity of nerve action. Synapses do not make the nerve fibers any larger. They might even tend to make them smaller. Large heads do not necessarily indicate large brains. The large head may mean that the individual has unusually thick layers of bone in his skull. The brain does not fit the skull closely, because it is enveloped in three membranes. In the space outside these membranes is a watery fluid. There is room, therefore, for the brain to move a little within the skull. If a man stands on his head, the brain moves toward the top of

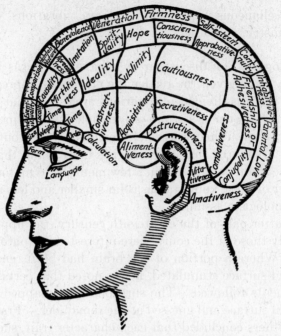

FIG. 37. This copy of an old chart of the topography of the
skull illustrates the teachings of the phrenologists, who thought
the brain had areas that controlled abstract traits. We now
know that this scheme of analyzing character is wholly false.

the skull; and, when he again stands upright, his brain slowly
sinks back to its usual position.

Daniel Webster was wont to point to the fact that the average
head size of women is smaller than the average head size of men.
He used this as a proof of the inferiority of women as compared
with men. Webster also used himself as an example of intelligence, because he had an unusually large head, but he did not
have an unusually large cranial capacity. His brain was examined after death and it was found that the brain was dispropor-
tionately small in comparison with the size of the skull.

The gross size of the brain does not correspond with intelligence
or ability. The average brain weight of men is approximately
48 ounces and of women 45 ounces. In Bischoff's tables of one
hundred fifty-nine brains, each weighing more than sixty-one
ounces, there was only one learned man, but thirteen criminals.
The two heaviest were the brains of a mechanic and a laborer.[3]

[3] According to Dr. Louis Casamajar as reported by Keene Sumner, "You Can't
Judge a Man's Mind by the Size of His Hat," *American Magazine*, 1923.

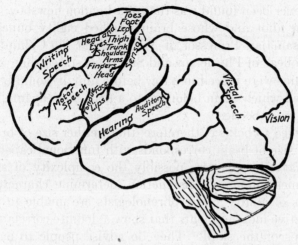

Fig. 38.   This diagram presents the more recent and accurate findings of modern brain studies.   The outer part of the brain has only a few known functional areas.   We know the specific functions of less than one third of the outer brain. The few known functional areas deal with sensory and motor experiences and not with personality traits, like self-esteem or amativeness.   The brain acts probably as a whole in most complex forms of behavior.

Dr. Sims tabulated the weights of a large number of brains of distinguished and other men.   Thackeray's brain weighed less than 58 ounces; those of Daniel Webster, Agassiz, and Napoleon ranged from 53.6 down to about 50 ounces.   The brains of the historian Grote, the scientist Bertillon, the great Frenchman Gambetta, and the scientist Liebig ranged from 49.9 down to only 40 ounces.   But Dr. Sims[4] furnished another list by way of contrast.   It included one hundred and twenty-five persons who were idiots, imbeciles, criminals, or persons of ordinary intelligence, yet all these brains were larger than those of the distinguished men in the above list.

For example:

	Ounces
Rustan, a workman	78.3
Dwarfed Indian squaw	73.5
Weak-minded illiterate	71.3
Congenital imbecile	70.5
Idiot	59.5

Many other cases have been found where the brains of idiots and imbeciles have weighed far more than the brains of great men such as Napoleon and Webster.   One of the largest brains

4 *Ibid.*

that has ever been found was that of a London newsboy who was almost an idiot and whose brain weighed eighty ounces. Dr. Louis Casamajar, Professor of Neurology at the Columbia University College of Physicians and Surgeons, stated that, if a half-dozen brains were placed in a row before him, it would be impossible to tell which brain belonged to a man of great intellect and which to an imbecile.

We are led to believe, therefore, that neither size of brain area nor gross size of brain corresponds with functional capacity, but rather that other factors, possibly the complexity of structure and chemical and molecular action, determine character traits and types of ability. The phrenologists are unable to point to any objective measurements that show a definite correlation with their maps of the skull. They do advise people to enter law, medicine, or art; and when asked to support their claims they simply point to the dogma of some other phrenologist or mention one or two cases of individuals whose heads *happen* to agree with their theory.

Character analysis from observation of physical features. The main features which the character analysts consider in the analysis of a stranger are color of the hair, color of the eyes, color of the skin, shape of the head, size of the head, profile, hardness of the muscles, shape of the body, texture of the skin, expression of the face, and condition of the clothing. The following sentences quoted from a book on the subject of character analysis indicate the type of teaching:

A forehead high in the crown shows benevolence, veneration, firmness, tenacity of purpose. Fullness in the middle third of the forehead indicates knowledge of human nature, keen comparative and reasoning power, a desire to connect cause with effect. Full upper forehead usually indicates a good talker of the flowery type, but not a close reasoner.

Hollow temples show an inclination toward pessimism.

Knotted brows indicate the abstract thinker.

Many books have been published which purport to explain reliable systems of character analysis and many executives have bought such books and believed them in spite of the findings of scientific studies conducted a generation ago. One of the leading character analysts stated:

The blond is found in large proportion among speculators, promoters, organizers, advertising men, traveling salesmen; while the more stable and constant brunet predominates among the plodders, the planners, the scientists, the administrators, and the conservators.

H. G. Kenagy asked each of about forty sales managers to select his four best salesmen. These executives then rated their men on the traits that are alleged to be associated with either blond or brunet. The final number of salesmen rated was 152. Of the 152 best salesmen, 82 were brunets and 70 were classed as blonds. Kenagy also found no significant difference between blonds and brunets in their possession of blond and brunet traits, as shown by the following table:[5]

TABLE IX

| | Per Cent Possessing Traits | |
Alleged Blond and Brunet Traits	Blonds	Brunets
Blond:		
Positive	95	90
Dynamic	68	64
Driving	64	66
Aggressive	87	88
Domineering	29	24
Impatient	40	41
Active	94	91
Quick	68	67
Hopeful	91	85
Speculative	39	37
Changeable	35	33
Variety-loving	48	47
Brunet:		
Negative	3	6
Static	13	13
Conservative	35	50
Imitative	39	40
Submissive	14	17
Cautious	43	49
Painstaking	74	63
Patient	57	50
Plodding	26	30
Slow	6	17
Deliberate	43	47
Serious	70	70
Thoughtful	77	80
Specializing	68	59

One character analyst claimed that the brunets are far more religious than the blonds and stated: "If you will go to any church in your community and count the number of blonds and

[5] H. G. Kenagy, "Do Blonds Make the Best Salesmen?" *Sales Management,* February 1923, pp. 325-326.

brunets, you will find that the brunets outnumber the blonds five to one. The brunets pay the bill for running the churches." To test the theory, a count was made by several investigators who stood at the doors of 69 churches in one city and classified the worshipers on the basis of hair color.

The principal conclusion of the observers was that, if the count was made in a Swedish Lutheran church, a predominance of blonds was found. If in a Catholic church in an Italian district of the city, the brunets predominated. Otherwise there was no preponderance of brunets when their number was compared with the percentage of brunets found in the general population of that city.

J. E. Walters and G. C. Brandenburg made a study of 100 seniors of the engineering school of a university to find the relationship between color of hair, color of skin, and profile with rated traits of leadership and initiative. They could find no constant relations.[6]

G. E. Cleeton and F. B. Knight made an intensive study of thirty persons wherein they studied thirty-six physical characteristics in relation to the following traits:

Sound judgment.	Frankness.
Intellectual capacity.	Will power.
Ability to make friends.	Originality.
Leadership.	Impulsiveness.

As a result of careful measurements and involved statistical evaluation of the data, they found that almost one-half the correlations were negative and the mean correlation was only 8 per cent better than chance.[7]

Many pages of data might be quoted from investigations that have been made in the study of the relation between physical and mental traits. No single study of the character analysis variety has resulted in evidence that predictions on the basis of bodily features are appreciably better than chance.

---

[6] G. C. Brandenburg, "Do Physical Traits Portray Character?" *Industrial Psychology*, September 1926, pp. 580ff.

[7] G. E. Cleeton and F. B. Knight, "Validity of Character Judgment Based on External Criteria," *Journal of Applied Psychology*, June 1924, pp. 215-231.

For a summary of studies on the relation between anatomical classifications and persistence, see David G. Ryans, "The Measurement of Persistence: An Historical Review," *Psychological Bulletin*, Vol. 36, p. 9, November 1939.

In spite of the scientific evidence against it, some men persist in their conviction that they, at least, can analyze people from their features. On several occasions, the writer has arranged for a special meeting of businessmen at which they attempted to analyze students for whom objective evidence of ability was available. The businessmen were told in advance that no character analyst analyzes people on the basis of physical features, such as color of eyes, shape of nose, prominence of chin, shape of mouth, distance between eyes; but rather according to the clothing and conversation of the person analyzed. The analysts were challenged to analyze strangers whose differences in clothing and conversation had been removed or disguised.

In one such demonstration, 88 members of the sales and advertising division of a chamber of commerce attempted to analyze a group of college students whose hair, clothing, and hands had been standardized. Only the faces were visible. The result was that the businessmen could not select the most intelligent or least intelligent member of the group, nor could they judge any other trait except with purely chance results. Some of the members of the judging group were sales managers who claimed that they could hire salesmen by the shape of the face and the forehead. The resultant data indicated that these "experts" could have done just as well if they had turned their backs to the persons whom they analyzed and then written down their rankings in random order. The students who took part in the experiment were not selected by the writer with any attempt to choose those who would be likely to be misjudged. All the students of an advanced course in psychology were asked to assist in the experiment and fourteen appeared at the appointed time.

Figure 39 shows photographs of the fourteen students who were rated by these businessmen. All the students had their clothing and hair covered with uniform covering so that their sex was not evident, and only three out of 88 businessmen judged correctly the sex of all the disguised students. The 88 businessmen were asked to designate the student who spent the greatest amount of time in study. Previous to the experiment, the 14 students had kept records for four weeks of the number of hours spent in study. The rankings of the businessmen correlated with the rankings of the students' records minus .29. The probable

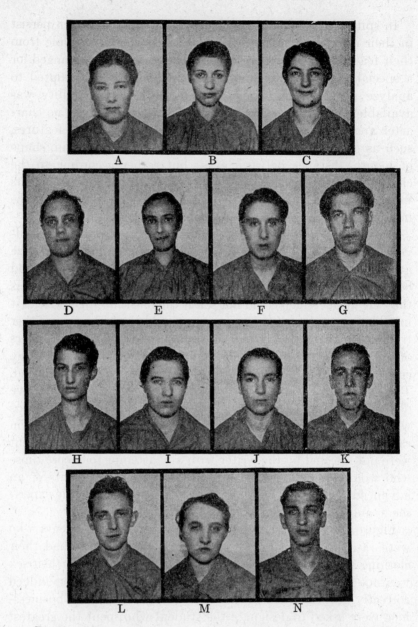

FIG. 39. Examine these pictures of college graduates who have been dressed in similar clothing. Classify each as to sex. Arrange them in order of merit according to what you think their scholastic record was while in college. Select the two least talkative of the group. Then refer to the Appendix for the correct answers.

error of the correlation was ±.16. This probable error is more than one-fourth the coefficient of correlation; hence the group estimate in this respect had no predictive value whatsoever.[8]

The businessmen were asked to make the following selections from the group: the student with the most beautiful profile; the student with the best leadership record; and the student with the highest intelligence. The girl who was selected as having the best profile was also selected as having the best leadership record and the highest intelligence, whereas she stood near the bottom of the group in intelligence and leadership. The one chosen as having the lowest intelligence of the group was actually fifth from the top. The two least talkative students were selected as the most talkative.

The photographs of the fourteen students of Figure 39 were taken without any head covering. If the ears of the boys had been pressed closer to their heads, the reader would have difficulty in discriminating between the boys and the girls. All the fourteen students photographed are college graduates and of above average ability. Two of them made outstandingly high scholastic records. One of these two has already demonstrated exceptional business ability. The reader is asked to:

1. Look at the photographs and select the two outstandingly good students.
2. Classify each of the fourteen as to sex.
3. Then arrange the fourteen in rank order according to their scholastic record while in college.

The Appendix will give the key to their records.

Can "experts" judge intelligence from photographs? One criticism of studies of analyses from photographs has been that the wide discrepancies of such studies might be due to the use of too few photographs and inexperienced judges. Accordingly, one investigator[9] used a large number of photographs and a group of judges who were accustomed to size up people on short notice.

---

[8] If the reader is unacquainted with the meaning of the coefficient of correlation, he can refer to Chapter 27 for an explanation.

[9] S. W. Cook, "The Judgment of Intelligence from Photographs," *Journal of Abnormal and Social Psychology*, 1939, Vol. 34, pp. 384-389.

Fig. 40. Stanley G. Estes, Northeastern University. Those interested in further study in regard to first-impression judgments of personality will wish to read his article "Judging Personality from Expressive Behavior," published in the *Journal of Abnormal and Social Psychology*, 1938, Vol. 33, pp. 217–236.

Photographs of the "passport" type were taken of 150 first-year male college students. All photographs of subjects were taken in the same position, at the same distance from the camera and facing it squarely. The intelligence of the subjects was estimated by the Thurstone Intelligence Test IV given by a person experienced in testing. The raw scores were found to range from 35 to 150.

Subsequently the photographs, numbered for identification purposes, were given to a group of ten experienced personnel managers and social workers with careful instructions to classify them according to the subject's intelligence into eight groups ranging from lowest to highest.

It was found that all the judges estimated intelligence with an approximately equal degree of inaccuracy, the pooled estimates of the judges had an equally low correlation with intelligence ($.07 \pm .055$), and the judges were no more accurate in estimating extremes of intelligence than they were in estimating average or near-average levels.

When psychologists have used photographs which portray emotional expressions, some slight consistency of judgments has appeared.[10]   However, the context of the situation in which an emotional expression occurs is likely to be more significant than the expression alone.   Our expressions of emotion are dictated by our culture.   For example, when a Chinese actor sticks out his tongue, he conveys surprise to his audience.   When he opens his eyes very wide, he is not surprised but angered.   When he claps his hands, he shows that he is worried.   When he says to the heroine that he "could eat her up," he expresses hatred; not love.   Only a very few physiological reactions indicate emotions which are understood in any culture.   These are when hairs stand on end, goose-pimples come out on the skin, cold perspiration breaks forth, inability to shriek because of fright, and the reddening of the face.[11]

Graphology and other pseudo-scientific methods of analysis. Graphology, like physiognomy, impresses the layman because most guesses are apt to be more or less true.   As previously stated, we all have the same traits but differ in the extent to which we have them.   This being true, the person whose handwriting is being analyzed thinks that he is learning something new when he is told that he has certain traits.   Any true analyst must do more than say that the subject has certain traits—he must show to what degree the traits are present.

Analyses of handwriting are based on analogies rather than on sound research.   If the reader will examine several books on graphology, he will find that the predictions are of the type quoted:

Two or more slopes of the letters indicate moodiness.
If the writing is shaded for effect, it indicates affectation.
If the endings of words ascend very high, the writer "lives in the clouds."

[10] S. G. Estes, "Judging Personality from Expressive Behavior," *Journal of Abnormal and Social Psychology*, 1938, Vol. 33, pp. 217-236.   This investigator used brief motion picture records of behavior and found some statistically significant results.   Some of his findings were the following: "The accuracy of the judgments is found to vary with the judge, the subject, and the aspects of the personality being judged.   Subjects who are introverted in the sense of having a liking and a capacity for contemplative observation tend to be least accurately judged.   Conspicuously well-judged traits are inhibition-impulsion, apathy-intensity, placidity-emotionality, and ascendance-submission.   Judges who have strong interests in either the graphic arts or dramatics are more successful than those whose dominant interests are in the sciences and philosophy."

[11] Studies by Otto Klineberg, reported in *Science News Letter*, April 16, 1938.   Some psychologists would prefer to think of these reactions as indicators of startle rather than emotion.

Square writing indicates mechanical ability.

If the cross of the "t" slopes upward, ambition is evident; if downward, pessimism and gloom.

Large letters indicate a spendthrift nature with optimism dominant.

Small letters indicate secretiveness.

If the first strokes of M, N, U, and W are very high, the writer possesses pride.

If the lines run below the basic line, the writer is easily discouraged and becomes despondent.

If the lines have an upward slope at the beginning and a downward slope at the end, such a person promises much but does not keep his promises or his appointments.

Several able scientists have made studies of the predictive potentialities of handwriting.[12] For example, 60 samples of handwriting were obtained from 30 men and 30 women, 15 of each sex being rated at each extreme of dominance on the basis of a social personality inventory and an interview. Ten judges were told to judge the writing as to the sex of the writer, asked to define the characteristics of the writing, and to judge the dominance of the writer. Sex judgments by the ten judges were 72 per cent correct. Major errors were made in judging the sex of non-dominant men and dominant women. However, the judgments of dominance from the handwriting were little better than chance expectation.[13]

Numerous attempts have been made to discover a link between handwriting and personality and character traits. The most classic of these is represented by the Downey Will-Temperament Test. . . . Results in this field, as in the case of anatomical judgments, have been consistently negative. Various claims made by the graphologists have associated persistence with such characteristics of handwriting as width of the downstrokes, connected letters, and the length of the crossbars on "t's." Miss L. E. Brown, working under the direction of Hull,[14] found ratings on persistence to correlate—0.05 with width of the downstrokes and—0.03 with disconnected writing. Hull and Montgomery[15] report a correlation coefficient of 0.00 between ratings on perseverance and length of the "t" bars. (When different sizes of writing were compensated for, the r was 0.16.)[16]

[12] Gordon Allport and Philip E. Vernon, *Studies in Expressive Movement*. The Macmillan Company, 1933.

[13] P. Eisenberg, "Judging Expressive Movements," *Journal of Applied Psychology*, 1938, Vol. 22, pp. 480-486.

[14] C. L. Hull, *Aptitude Testing*. World Book Co., 1928.

[15] C. L. Hull and R. B. Montgomery, "An Experimental Investigation of Certain Alleged Relations Between Character and Handwriting," *Psychological Review*, 1919, Vol. 26, pp. 63-75.

[16] David G. Ryans, "The Measurement of Persistence: an Historical Review." *Psychological Bulletin*, Vol. 36, p. 9, November 1939.

So far as now known, a person cannot be analyzed accurately on the basis of his p's and q's. Of course, several men have made excellent studies in identifying individual handwriting and in diagnosing mental disorders,[17] but such investigations are of little or no value in predicting ability, honesty, initiative, morals, and so on. We shall have to wait until valid graphological discoveries are made which will have predictive values, useful in practical situations.

Astrology. The widespread interest in this subject is indicated by the report that when a London newspaper omitted its usual horoscope one day, the editorial office received within twenty-four hours more than fifty thousand telegrams, telephone calls, and personal calls from complaining readers.[18]

Modern astronomers repudiate astrology because it is based on the absurdity of fixed constellations. Stars move even though it does take 25,800 years to make the heavenly circuit around the Zodiac. The horoscope chart is based on the twelve signs of the Zodiac, a belt of the heavens showing the positions of the sun and planets as the ancients knew them.

In spite of the obvious absurdity of the basis of this pseudoscience, psychologists have investigated the astrologers' predictions only to find that astrologers do not agree among themselves as to which zodiacal signs are supposed to be associated with the birth of individuals having specific characteristics.[19] For example, six standard books on astrology were scrutinized regarding the sign of musical capacity. It was found that for those books having the highest agreement, there is no correlation with the birth dates of 1,498 leading artists and musicians.[20] Also, predictions of vocational success and change of occupation for an army officer differed widely from one astrologer to another.[21]

Concerning palmistry, astrology, Hindu philosophies, numerology, vibrations, spiritualism, and others of their like, we must

[17] E. H. Alten, "The Psychology of Handwriting and Its Importance to the Physician," *Medical Record*, New York, 1939, Vol. 150, pp. 71-74.

[18] Freling Foster, "Keep Up with the World," *Collier's*, February 17, 1940.

[19] Henry F. Pringle, "What Do You Think of Astrology?" *Good Housekeeping*, November 1940.

[20] P. R. Farnsworth, "Aesthetic Behavior and Astrology," *Character & Personality*, 1938, Vol. 6, pp. 335-340.

[21] F. W. Parr, "How's Your Horoscope?" *Occupations*, 1937, Vol. 16, pp. 236-238.

allow the psychoneurotic and the uninformed to dabble in them. These cults seem to satisfy the inner cravings of the weak and maladjusted, who wander from one cult to the next only to find that they attain what they want for a short time and then must try some other "system." These cults and "philosophies" are a means of evasion of the difficulties of life. They offer a prompt and immediate answer to the poorly adjusted neurotic. If he would only realize that the facing of problems by matter-of-fact methods will bring the only lasting results, he would be vastly better off. All these last-named schemes for analyzing people or guiding them are considered unsound by the students of modern science.

Fire-walking. American newspapers frequently publish pictures which lead some readers to assume that certain individuals have mysterious gifts or abilities, such as fire-walking. Published demonstrations of this kind appear to be baffling simply because we have not examined the act.

Scientists have investigated fire-walking and found that they can duplicate the feats which appear phenomenal to the layman. In one experiment in England, for example, a fire-walker, Ahmed Hussain, weighing 126 pounds, took four steps without injury in 1.6 seconds over a trench 12 feet long, having a fire with a surface temperature of 800°C. A young Cambridge graduate, R. Adcock, weighting 160 pounds, walked the trench in 1.8 seconds, taking three steps without injury.[22]

It has been found that fire-walking is facilitated by factors such as the presence of ash, the coldness or wetness of the legs, contraction of the blood-vessels through self-hypnosis, the manner of firing the embers or stones, the chemicals on the feet, the manner of walking, the thickness of the soles, and the path taken.

Similarly, snake-handling religious cultists only appear to have supernatural powers. Sometimes the snakes are not as deadly as they appear, the devotees know how to handle the snakes without harm, or some individuals have developed an immunity which can be duplicated by scientists.[23]

Whenever we find that certain individuals appear to have

---

[22] H. Price, "Fire-Walking," *Nature,* London, 1937, Vol. 139, pp. 928-929. See also E. S. Thomas, "Fire-Walking," *Nature,* London, 1936, Vol. 137, pp. 213-215. See also issue of 1937, Vol. 139, pp. 660 of same journal.

[23] *Science News letter,* August 17, 1940, p. 103.

mysterious powers, it is well to seek the advice of a member of the Society of American Magicians who probably can duplicate or at least explain the feat. Modern magicians frankly use trickery, and they work as scientists work—by natural objective methods.

Extrasensory perception. An interesting example of the differences in methods of investigation used by pseudo-scientists and scientists is illustrated by the current work in extrasensory perception, ESP. The psychologists who are working in this borderline field between the questionable and the accepted sciences publish the results of their investigations and examine the criticisms made by other experts. Mathematical criteria are considered as well as personal opinions.

Extrasensory perception is a term coined by J. B. Rhine of Duke University to designate what is often called telepathy. Professor Rhine and his colleagues have conducted their experiments with decks of cards consisting of five suits. The cards in each suit have simple drawings: a circle, a star, a square, parallel wavy lines, or a cross. The cards are shuffled thoroughly, whereupon an "agent" draws a card, looks at it under proper safeguards, and a "percipient" calls it. This procedure has, of course, been varied as in experiments where the agent and percipient are in different rooms or separated by miles of distance.

Obviously, the chance of calling a card correctly is one in five. However, some percipients do very much better than the present known laws of probability would indicate. If our probability mathematics are correct, it would appear that either the experiments are improperly conducted or some kind of extrasensory perception exists.

Telepathy as an explanation is merely a name for an assumed phenomenon and not really an explanation. No one has demonstrated how the supposed communication between minds takes place. Telepathy is not "waves" of any physically demonstrated kind, and no claim is made as to how the communication takes place.

Many scientists are not willing to accept telepathy as a reality. Some critics claim that fraud may be involved, particularly on the part of percipients. Another explanation is that the phenomenon may be due to mathematical errors. Pure guessing would lead to consistent high scores occasionally, like a run of good cards in bridge. Perhaps undetected cues are involved as in the recorded cases of "talking horses" that could recognize minute sensory cues.

The whole controversy on which many volumes and articles[24] have been written and a scientific journal[25] published can be summed up by the admission that Rhine and his associates have made out what some believe to be a case for the possible occurrence of ESP. At present, a majority of psychologists prefer to withhold judgment on the claimed phenomenon but believe that a scientific investigation of ESP is legitimate.[26]

An experiment in "psychic waves." Many credit and other interviewers believe that their experiences in interviewing bring about a sort of intuitive ability to judge others by means of so-called psychic waves, expressed by one businessman as follows:

Not every man has a head for mathematics, and not every man has a sense of logic necessary for the practice of law. Just so, not every man has what I might call the "sixth sense" necessary to judge what I truly believe is a series of psychic waves which flows from one man to another when in conversation.[27]

Psychologists have been unable to find anything that would correspond to "psychic waves." Scientists are inclined to discard that theory. It is possible that the facial expressions, general bodily movements, bodily posture, and changes of pitch, in-

---

[24] Books dealing with extrasensory perception studies are:

J. B. Rhine, *New Frontiers of the Mind,* Farrar & Rinehart, 1937.

Pratt, Rhine, Smith, Stuart and Greenwood: *Extrasensory Perception After Sixty Years.* Henry Holt & Co., 1940.

Representative critical and summarizing articles are:

"Telepathy and Clairvoyance Being Boomed as a Science," *Science News Letter,* November 6, 1936, p. 298.

John L. Kennedy, "A Methodological Review of Extra-Sensory Perception," *Psychological Bulletin,* Vol. 36, No. 2, pp. 59-103.

Joseph Jastrow, "ESP, House of Cards," *American Scholar,* Vol. 8, No. 1, pp. 13-22.

W. S. Cox, "An Experiment on Extra-Sensory Perception," *Journal of Experimental Psychology,* 1936, Vol. 19, pp. 429-437.

L. D. Goodfellow, "The Effect of Patterns on Psychophysical Judgments," *Psychological Bulletin,* 1938, Vol. 35, pp. 627.

[25] *Journal of Parapsychology,* Duke University Press.

[26] L. Warner and C. C. Clark, "A Survey of Psychological Opinion on ESP," *Journal of Parapsychology,* 1938, Vol. 2, 296-301.

[27] J. H. Tregoe, "Can You Tell if a Customer Will Pay His Bills?" *Printers' Ink Weekly,* July 1, 1920, p. 141.

tensity, rapidity, and inflection in the voice are noted by those who have daily contacts with people and analyze their motives. Some executives have said that they tend to suspect the man who makes a statement and then leans back. Others have claimed that, when a lie is told, the speaker catches his breath. Salesmen say that they know when the prospect is sold by the fact that he leans toward the salesman. The writer decided to test the theory that experienced interviewers can detect false statements more accurately than inexperienced interviewers. Arrangements were made to have 11 experienced credit men and 14 experienced employment interviewers, 18 inexperienced men students and 7 inexperienced women students interview several hundred college students. These students who were to be interviewed were instructed to answer all the questions that any interviewer might ask, but to answer some truthfully and some falsely. The interviewers had the privilege of cross-examining the students.

The questions varied in nature, but were of the kind that would be answered in a definite manner, such as, "How old are you? How long have you been in college? How much money did you earn during your summer vacation? What were your grades in your college courses last semester?" Both the interviewer and the interviewed kept a written record of the questions and the answers, so that it was possible to record the interviewer's accuracy in judging the answers to each question. Records were tabulated of the interviewers' estimates of 3,205 questions. Analysis of the percentages of errors for the four classes of interviewers were as follows: the experienced credit men were wrong in 34 per cent of their judgments; the employment men in 42 per cent; the inexperienced men in 34 per cent; and the inexperienced women in 47.5 per cent.

Analysis of the judgments of each of the 25 experienced interviewers showed that some of the interviewers were better detectors of false statements than others. The experiment indicated the following points of note:

1. The experienced interviewers were unable to detect false statements when the "applicant" wanted to lie. His detection was largely a matter of chance. The results did not indicate

that experience in interviewing gives a person an extra power or "psychic wave" sense in judging the truthfulness of statements made by others.

2. An interviewer should depend upon records and objective information in evaluating statements of applicants rather than upon his "hunches" or "feel" or "atmosphere" or the movements of lips and hands. One interviewer claimed that he could detect false statements from the movements of the lips. The results showed that he was one of the poorest detectors in the group. Credit men should depend upon the records of the credit bureaus for guidance rather than upon the impressions made by the applicant's personality. Similarly, the employment man should depend upon the statements of former employers of the applicant.

3. The individual interviewers who made the best records in judging the statements of the students were those persons who had had previous experience in interviewing students and knew the general facts of student life. This indicates what one would expect: an interviewer should be acquainted with the facts of the type or class of people whom he interviews.

4. The individual interviewers who made the poorest records seemed to be the "fatherly" or trusting type of person who did not cross-examine the applicants. Conversely, the interviewers who made the best records were those who cross-examined the applicants, looked them in the eye, and pursued a policy of compelling the applicant to prove his statements.

5. The best of the interviewers made bad mistakes in their judgments of statements made by students who were adept in talking with strangers and who wished to baffle the interviewer. The experiment clearly demonstrated that, if a person wished to falsify his statements, the interviewer could not differentiate the false from the true unless he could check the statements objectively.

Apparently, when interviewers depend upon their impressions without reference to records of the applicants' past behavior, they succeed more often than they fail because most applicants want to tell the truth rather than to falsify. "Worked out from 7,000,000 cases, the law of averages tells the surety companies

TABLE X

Occupations	Credit Rating	Occupations	Credit Rating
Office employees.............	92.2	Auto mechanics...............	60.0
Retail grocers...............	89.6	Janitors....................	60.0
Chain store managers........	89.2	Farmers (tenants)............	59.2
Other retailers..............	89.0	Brickmasons................	59.0
School teachers..............	86.4	Firemen & Policemen........	58.2
Railroad trainmen...........	85.8	Railroad trackmen..........	57.8
Railroad shopmen............	85.2	Coal miners.................	57.6
Retail salespeople...........	83.2	College students.............	55.6
Dentists....................	82.2	Domestic servants...........	55.2
Doctors....................	80.4	Carpenters..................	52.6
Nurses.....................	71.2	Hotel employees.............	48.2
Farmers (owners)...........	70.8	Auto salesmen..............	47.0
Factory workers (men).......	70.0	Common laborers............	46.0
Traveling salesmen...........	68.8	Restaurant employees........	44.6
Filling station employees.....	63.0	Barbers....................	42.8
Factory workers (women).....	61.0	Truck & Bus drivers........	42.6
Lawyers....................	60.8	Painters & Decorators........	38.2

A large number of credit men supplied the data as to the relative credit worthiness of people of different occupations. The study was made by a group of University of Illinois students under the direction of Professor P. D. Converse. The original figures were put on a percentage basis so that 100 per cent represents the highest possible credit rating. Quoted from the *National Association of Finance Companies News.* March 1934.

that only one man in every hundred of those they bond . . . will go wrong, and, of each seventy that do get into trouble, only one will do so through deliberate criminal intent."[28] Most people are honest more often than dishonest, as indicated by our system of paying by checks. The large hotels of New York City, in cashing millions of dollars of checks annually for guests and patrons, average a loss of only one dollar out of every $2,600.[29]

The evidence of the experiment, as well as the judgments of experienced businessmen, indicates that we cannot, in some mysterious or intuitive manner, analyze or estimate the character traits of strangers. "Hunches" are less reliable than statistical studies. Hence modern credit men use little intuition and much arithmetic in predicting credit losses, as indicated in Table X, a credit rating of 24 occupational groups. Members of the National Association of Finance Companies furnished the data upon which the table is based.

The reader may believe in character analysis from observation

[28] Kenneth M. Goode and Harford Powel, Jr., *What About Advertising?* p. 156. Harper & Bros., 1928.
[29] Freling Foster, "Keep up with the World," *Collier's,* February 17, 1940, p. 6.

You can't tell the difference *between a new frock and a Persil-washed frock*

FIG. 41.   Example of an advertisement that seeks to gain attention through readers' interest in character analysis. In your judgment, "Which is the culprit?" (*Courtesy of Unilever, Ltd., Port Sunlight, England.*)

in spite of the statements presented here. He may have certain convictions which he has obtained in emotional situations, and it may be difficult for him to ignore his old neural patterns and to adopt a new set. The answer is that, if any one believes in character analysis and wishes to get at the truth of the situation, he must conduct some experiments in which he keeps accurate records and makes analyses of a large number of unselected individuals. Such an investigation would probably convince him. He should consult other psychologists associated with a university faculty and learn their opinions. It is important to mention that *psychologists* of the faculty should be consulted and not merely faculty members, because some college professors of chemistry, physics, languages, and other nonpsychological subjects do believe in character analysis. Let us now consider some of the factors that have erroneously convinced the general public of the value of character analysis.

Why people have accepted character analysis.

1.   Literature may give a person the impression that mental traits are indicated by the face.

Julius Cæsar, I, ii:
Yond Cassius has a lean and hungry look;
He thinks too much.
Midsummer Night's Dream, III, ii:
So should a murderer look, so dead, so grim, . . .
Yet you, the murderer, look as bright, as clear,
As yonder Venus;
All's Well, II, i:
A traitor you do look like.
All's Well, V, ii:
He looks like a poor, decayed, ingenious, foolish, rascally knave.

The moving-picture and the theater also suggest that certain physical or outward characteristics are associated with mental traits. We have a typical villain, hero, miser, banker, college boy, and so on. Many popular magazines publish articles on the pseudo-scientific methods of analyzing people which, to the uninformed, give the impression that such methods are sound.

2.   The character analysts are better advertisers than the psychologists. The academic psychologists are scientists who receive their pay from institutions of learning. It is not necessary for them to advertise their abilities. The pseudo-psychologists must obtain their incomes by appealing to the fringe of the public that is looking for something new and immediately helpful. The scientific training of the university develops cautiousness on the part of the student of truth. Truth is not suddenly or easily captured. It is easier to find the things that are not true than to find the things that are true. To the general public, the true psychologist appears to be negative. He often tells what is not sound, but does not always offer a better system to take the place of the colorful and alluring promises of the itinerant psychologist. This situation of the helplessness of the scientist, in that he cannot offer a panacea, much as he might like to do so, is annoying to the layman. But that is the price of sound progress in many situations.

3.   The systems of the pseudo-psychologist appear to be plausible. He goes into minute detail as to the various characteristics

that indicate certain traits. When a stranger listens to the lecturing analysts and reads their books, he is impressed with the detailed analyses which they appear to make. The only sad part of their analyses is the fact that they are not true. And the reader, who has not had training in conducting careful experiments to find out a few simple facts, assumes that the minutiæ of the itinerant lecturer are real evidence.

4. The systems of the pseudo-psychologists are easy to learn and to apply. The typical lecturer shows the audience a picture of George Washington and then says: "Now, ladies and gentlemen, we have here a man with a sloping forehead, who was also unusually aggressive and persistent. How many of you can think of some man who is unusually aggressive and has a sloping forehead?" A large part of the audience will raise their hands and think that they have learned something that they suspected but of which they were not sure.

5. Their predictions deal with generalities that apply to all members of the population. Scientists have demonstrated that as human beings we all have the same traits, but that we differ in the extent to which we have any one trait. Qualitatively, we are the same; quantitatively, we differ. Hence, when the analyst tells a stranger that he is ambitious but not so ambitious as he might be, he has merely stated a generality that applies to a very high percentage of the human race. If the analyses of character analysts are read with care, it will be noticed that the findings are of a generalized variety that applies to practically all people. The true psychologist measures the degree or extent to which the person has a trait instead of judging by the presence or absence of the trait.

Statistically considered, many of the statements of the analyst are certain to be true. One lecturing pseudo-psychologist claimed that he could teach prospective parents how to predetermine the sex of the unborn child. He charged a fee of $50 for the formula and guaranteed to pay the parents $55 if the child should be the opposite of the sex desired. This scheme was bound to make money for the schemer, in spite of the fact that his formula was the hocus-pocus of the primitive medicine man. Approximately one-half the babies are male and one-half female. Hence any scheme of predetermining sex will be correct in about

50 per cent of the cases.   If he sold his scheme to 100 parents, he received $5,000.   If he returned $55 for each of fifty failures, he still had a gross profit of $2,250.

6.   The systems of analysis are flexible.   The novice is told to apply the new system at once.   If he makes a serious mistake in a "reading," he is told that he failed to balance the variables properly.   Moreover, he can squirm out of an error if he is just slightly ingenious in suggesting another interpretation.

7.   The pseudo-analysts use fallacious reasoning.   They tell their audiences and readers of the great men who believe in character analysis and have been benefited by it.   Many of these famous characters may have been dead for a generation or two, but they are still offered as evidence of acceptance by great men. The general public does not realize that the discovery and knowledge of truth is a progressive and contemporary task, and that the testimonials and axioms of a generation ago may be questioned to-day.

Errors in logic are committed by reasoning reciprocally.   It is true that most mental defectives have poor teeth.   Deformities of the palate have been found in 82 per cent of mental defectives, in 76 per cent of epileptics, and in 80 per cent of the insane. But these findings do not allow us to reason reciprocally and say that, if a person has bad teeth or a deformity of the palate, therefore he is feeble-minded, epileptic, or insane.

They also present isolated cases to prove their theories.   The lecturer says that long fingers indicate artistic ability.   He presents the picture of an artist who happens to have long fingers and assumes that one or two cases prove a principle; but he never gives data which prove by actual measurement that the fingers of artists are longer than the fingers of those who have no artistic ability.   The true scientist must make painstaking measurements, tabulate the results, treat the data with adequate statistical formulas, and then probably look for more evidence before he feels safe in claiming more than a hypothesis.

References

Ellis, Robert S., *The Psychology of Individual Differences*, Chapters II and III.   D. Appleton-Century Co., 1928.

Gilliland, A. R. and E. L. Clark, *Psychology of Individual Differences*, Chapters IV-VII.   Prentice-Hall, Inc., 1939.

Paterson, Donald G., *Physique and Intellect*. D. Appleton-Century Co., 1930.

Wiggam, Albert E., *Sorry But You're Wrong About It*. Bobbs-Merrill Co., 1931.

Winkler, John K., and Walter Bromberg, *Mind Explorers*. Reynal & Hitchcock, 1939.

Projects

1. Ask several friends to rank in order of scholastic ability the fourteen college graduates whose photographs are presented in this chapter. Compare their rankings with yours. Ask the raters why they ranked them as they did.

2. Collect handwriting specimens of persons whom you know. Analyze the writing according to the system of analysis presented in a book on graphology. Estimate the value of the system.

3. Read an article by an astrologer and analyze the predictions for their generalities and worth.

4. Find pictures of several famous persons of whom you have heard but whose physical features you have not seen. In which cases were you disappointed by the pictures and in which were you pleased? Give possible reasons for your reaction in each case.

5. Collect published photographs of a famous person whom some people like and others dislike. Separate those poses which present him in a favorable light from those that show him to a disadvantage. List the differentiating elements betweeen the two sets. Suggest how propagandists might use each set of pictures.

6. Read material concerning lie detectors and evaluate their usefulness and limitations. List other methods you have heard of for telling when a person is lying.

7. Make a list of the nationalities often used in the drama or the movies to typify shrewdness, cunning, laziness, suavity, excitability, and other qualities. Suggest possible reasons for each stereotype.

8. Make this test for yourself at any time but demonstrate it to a friend who claims to see "ghosts" at night. Focus both eyes on any object in your range of vision and press your finger firmly against the lower part of one eyeball, keeping both open. If the object becomes "double" it is an actual object but has been interpreted wrongly, perhaps. If it remains single, it is a figment of imagination.

9. A professor of astronomy in a large university frequently receives letters asking for astrological advice, such as: "My son was born under the sign of Taurus. He is contemplating joining the navy. Will his life be safe?" Assume that you are the astronomer and compose a brief letter to the mother.

11

Hiring the Worker

The interview, as it is usually conducted, yields little information that is reliable, but it does allow employer and applicant to react to each other and decide whether they wish to work together in the same concern. A few employers are making studies of methods of predicting applicants' employment behavior. Tests and other techniques have proved to be of some value. However, the greatest limitation to the adoption of improved methods in hiring is the scarcity of businessmen who are willing to study and develop improved hiring techniques.

The unreliability of the usual interview. If 57 pieces of coal were handed to twelve mine foremen and they were asked to rank the pieces in order of the amount of carbon in each piece, and if some of the men claimed that one chunk was the best in the lot and others said that it was the poorest, we would question the ability of the men to judge coal. We would seek a better method of judging. Yet that is what happened when Hollingworth conducted an experiment in which twelve sales managers interviewed 57 applicants, each applicant to be given a rank from 1 to 57. A rank of 1 meant that the sales manager considered the applicant the most suitable for the position, and a rank of 57 meant that he considered the applicant the least suitable. Each interviewer was given a private room in which to do his interviewing, and he could ask any questions or do anything that he wished so long as he kept records of his judgments.

When the data were analyzed, it was found that one applicant had the following rankings: 1, 2, 6, 9, 10, 16, 20, 21, 26, 28, 53, and 57. Another applicant was ranked 2, 4, 9, 13, 16, 16, 19, 28, 32, 33, 46, and 55 by the managers. Much the same rankings

Fig. 42. Walter V. Bingham, director of
the Personnel Research Section, Adjutant
General's Office, War Department. Those
interested in the problem of occupational
fitness should refer to his book *Aptitudes
and Aptitude Testing* (Harper & Bros.,
1937).

were given the other applicants. Occasionally an applicant
tended toward low or toward high ratings.[1]

Several similar investigations of interviews have shown that
interviewers disagree among themselves regarding the same applicants, that some interviewers vary in the self-consistency of
their judgments, and that they vary in their abilities to judge
the applicants accurately. Many experienced employment men
realize that they cannot judge applicants with any great degree
of accuracy on the basis of the interview alone. They try to
obtain dependable information from former employers or to hire
the applicant for a probationary period. In spite of the unreliability of the interview, it will continue to play an important
part in modern hiring. Somehow human beings want to see each
other even though the meeting may not elicit valid information.
They want to find out whether they would like to work with each
other. Furthermore, studies of the interview—the conversation

---

[1] H. L. Hollingworth, *Judging Human Character*, pp. 62-66. D. Appleton-
Century Co., 1923.

with a purpose—prove that interviewing ability can be improved.[2]

Kinds of interviews. Interviews of applicants may be studied in terms of the techniques and emphases used:

1. The informal conversational talk.
2. Making it difficult for the applicant.
3. Systematic questioning.
4. The statistical interview.
5. The psychological test.
6. The adjustment analysis interview.

The informal conversational interview. This kind of interview is the most common in American industry and also the least reliable. It is the type that was used in the above experiment which gave such unreliable results. It usually consists of a series of random questions by which the interviewer tries to get the general history of the applicant. The typical questions asked are: Where did you work before? Are you married? How old are you? Why do you want to work for us? What education have you had? Do you go to church? How much money did you get on your last job? And so on. In some cases the interviewer tries to put the applicant at ease and have him talk about himself. In the meantime the interviewer decides whether he likes the applicant. He may be very favorably impressed or greatly annoyed, depending upon the associative linkages that happen to have been built in the interviewer by people whom the applicant resembles.

Prejudices are an important factor in this type of interview. If the employer has recently hired a man who once sold cash registers but failed on the job under consideration, he is apt to be prejudiced against all men who have sold cash registers. One executive claimed that all men who had mustaches failed with him. Even though only three men with mustaches, and dozens without mustaches, whom he had hired, had failed him, he still believed that a mustache was an indication of poor material for his organization. Some executives dislike applicants who have

---

[2] Walter Van Dyke Bingham and Bruce Victor Moore, *How to Interview* (Harper & Bros., 1934) offers a comprehensive treatise on interviewing.

red hair or bad teeth, or wear bow ties, green socks, derby hats, and so on. It is fortunate for the applicants that executives differ in their prejudices, because if one employer rejects them they can always go to some other employer who may like the very trait for which they were previously rejected.

Prejudices often affect interview findings which are supposed to be entirely objective. Rice[3] made an analysis of the findings of twelve trained interviewers as to the cause of the downfall of 2,000 vagrants who had applied for free lodging. The interviews were standardized, but different investigators obtained different results. One interviewer, a socialist, reported that 39 per cent of the men were down and out because of industrial conditions, and 22 per cent because of excessive use of alcohol. Another interviewer, an ardent prohibitionist, attributed but 7 per cent to industrial and economic conditions and 62 per cent to drink. Their prejudices are even more significant when we note that according to the socialist, the *vagrants themselves* gave as the cause of their downfall: industrial conditions, 60 per cent; drink, 11 per cent. According to the prohibitionist, the vagrants blamed industrial conditions in 42.5 per cent and drink in 34 per cent of the cases. Obviously, each interviewer influenced the interviewees to give answers in line with his own biases.

Occasionally a few objective criteria are developed by the interviewer who uses the informal interview. If he hires carpenters, he may observe the applicant's hands for calluses or his tools for their condition, or he may ask how many pine doors he can hang in a day. It is assumed that only a member of the trade can answer the last question. The chief purpose of the casual conversational interview is that of asking a few more or less relevant questions and then hiring the man who appears to be the most capable.

Some sales personnel men never hire a man who has worked for a competitor. They believe that the man who has been trained under one set of conditions will cling to those former beliefs and habits and refuse to become a teamworker in a new organization. Some managers will not hire salesmen who have had a systematic training course where they had to learn a stand-

---

[3] S. A. Rice, "Contagious Bias in the Interview," *American Journal of Sociology,* 1929, Vol. 35, pp. 420-423.

ardized sales talk. On the other hand, one life insurance company found that 20 per cent of the men who had had previous life insurance selling turned out successful.

Certain executives are greatly interested in the amount of money that an applicant owes to installment houses. They believe that a man hounded by bill collectors cannot do good work. If such a salesman is out in a territory away from home, he is apt to borrow money from customers, have worthless checks cashed, and ask for advances on his pay. If a salesman borrows money from a customer or gives a customer a worthless check, the employer must pay the loss or lose the customer.

Other executives do not hire recent college graduates because they believe that college men require three years in which to orient themselves. They are believed to want immediate promotions and to loathe doing any routine work. In college they studied international problems, the progress of civilization, the boundaries of the universe, great social forces, and historical movements; hence, small wonder that the college graduates are bored when they must spend hours checking detailed bills in a butter-and-egg firm. Once a college graduate finishes about three years of floundering, these executives will hire him without very much quizzing about his past failures. It is believed that he is then ready to fit himself into the business picture without demanding a front seat.

One executive claims that young single men succeed better than young married men. The young married men are either too greatly interested in their wives to study their jobs or they are ambitious to buy the wife expensive articles for her adornment.

Many executives insist that the applicant shall state the other concerns where application has been made. It is not unusual to hire a man, put him on the job for several weeks, and then have him quit because he has obtained a position with a firm where he had made previous application. Before hiring the new man, the executive should request him to write letters of withdrawal to all the firms where application has been made.

One executive may take applicants for important positions to dinner and gauge their ability by their table manners. Another may argue with the applicant to discover how he conducts himself toward an unruly stranger. The empirical rules for hiring vary with the executive. Most of these rules are merely the result of a few dramatic instances. Many are without sound statistical basis. If the number of jobs of any one classification is large enough to allow it, the executive in charge of interviews should make a statistical analysis of the factors that are relevant to success and failure of employees of his firm.

If such a statistical study is too much trouble, he can, at least, improve his technique by means of the following practices:

1. The interviewer should establish rapport and make the applicant feel at home by means of materials which interest applicants. Suitable materials are the mechanical equipment used on jobs, products made by the company and displayed in the interviewing room, magazines of the kind read by typical employees, and so on.

2. The interviewer should think of the hiring interview as having two divisions: (a) the sizing-up process or judging of the applicant and (b) the process of accepting the applicant and building goodwill. Unfortunately, many casual conversational interviewers mix these two divisions with the result that some applicants mistakenly assume that they are being hired. The interviewer should finish his analysis of the applicant's ability *before* anything is said to lead the applicant to think that he is being accepted.

3. The interviewer should note and compensate for his own prejudices such as likes or dislikes for applicants who have mustaches, use lipstick, reveal tobacco-stained fingers, or belong to certain racial classes. He should hire people who do good work rather than those who satisfy his own idiosyncrasies. Of course, if the interviewer is hiring applicants who are to be supervised by department heads, the interviewer must hire in accordance with the idiosyncrasies of each department head.

4. The interviewer should note the extent to which he suggests answers to his own questions, "How much education have you had?" is less suggestive of the answer expected than, "You graduated from high school, didn't you?" Nor should the interviewer nod his head or use inflections that guide the applicant's answers.

5. The interviewer should not describe the vacancies in the organization until after he has diagnosed the applicant's ability.

6. In the second or "accepted" division of the hiring interview, the interviewer should explain very clearly all facts of importance to the new employee. These include safety rules, wage rates, bonuses, peculiarities of supervisors, insurance privileges, shift hours, value of equipment or products with which the employee will work, costs of errors, how to ring the time clock, and so on.

Additional improvements in his techniques can be made by any interviewer who will ask friendly employment men from local industries to watch him in several interviews and tell him about his habits, good or bad, of which he may not be aware.

The interview that is made difficult for the applicant. The story of the way in which one sales manager accomplished this and then hired his applicants has become a classic in sales literature. This manager arranged his office so that he himself occupied the only chair. The hat rack and the nails on the wall had been removed. When an applicant stepped into the room, the manager said: "Hang up your hat and sit down." Then the manager continued to write at his desk. If the applicant simply stood and waited in an embarrassed manner while he hoped that the manager would look up and talk to him, the manager soon told him to leave as he did not want him. The manager was pleased, however, when he received an applicant who looked around the room for a chair and a place to hang his hat, and not finding any, came to the manager and said: "Well, brother, you'll have to show me how to do it." This manager assumed that the latter type of applicant had the requisite amount of initiative to be a good salesman.

This method, in milder form, is used by those employment managers who make it a rule not to hire any man on the first interview, but require him to fill in an application blank at home and mail it to the company. In some concerns, less than one fourth of the blanks given out are returned. This probably does eliminate the applicant who merely wants to "look" at jobs rather than actually to get one. Every employment man knows that some applicants drop in to see him by mere chance and many do not care whether they obtain a job with that particular concern. Some men have applications pending with several firms, and, in the meantime, apply at other places just to be on the safe side in case the expected job is not obtained. The more difficult the interview, the less effort will such applicants put forth to get a job, unless the hoped-for position does not materialize.

Managers of salesmen on a commission basis often adopt the difficult interview. They believe that painting the job as dark as possible eliminates the weak and the vacillating and has a better effect on the applicants than if they are told the brighter aspects of the work. No statistical evidence has been collected which proves or disproves the value of the difficult interview. It is certain, however, that some sales managers know that their best workers are those who snubbed the job when it was first offered them. If managers of insurance salesmen are questioned, it is probable that some of them will tell interesting stories of how they induced a man to take up the selling of insurance in spite of the fact that the admired individual at first disdained the job.

The systematic questioning type of interview. This is not a scientific interview, but it is the most practicable for most interviewers. The questions are asked not haphazardly but according to an organized procedure. The interviewer is guided by an interview blank and jots down answers as given, thus making a record of the results of the conversation with the applicant. He tries to ask questions that require factual answers rather than opinions. In some cases he adds some problems which are of a semi-trade nature. The questions in *The Interviewer's Guide,* opposite, were prepared by a group of employment men and executives who wished to have a list of definite questions to guide them. The thirteen suggested questions may be used in conjunction with the usual employment application blank. The questions may be phrased to suit the interviewer and the applicant, but it is essential that the interviewer ask each question and record the answer while he is conducting the interview. If he does not adhere to a definite procedure, he is apt to let the interview become a hit-or-miss conversation that will not give him complete information. Of course, the interview may be ended long before the last question if the applicant is obviously unfit.

THE INTERVIEWER'S GUIDE

Name.............................. Address...............................
Position wanted...................... Date............ Interviewer.........

1. Give me the names of your past employers. Begin with the last employer and go backward for the last five years.
2. Describe the work you did for each.
3. What did you do in your spare time: evenings, Saturdays, and Sundays? (Look for side lines and hobbies, reading of trade journals, clubs.)
4. What general education have you had?
5. What technical education have you had?
6. What is state of your health? How much time have you missed from your work because of sickness during the past two years?
7. For what other jobs have you applied with other concerns recently?
8. What is your financial condition: savings accounts, life insurance, investments, speculations, own home?
9. With what merchandise firms do you have credit accounts?
10. What are your plans for the future, vocationally?
11. What suggestions have you made regarding improvements in operations for your former employers?
12. Why do you want to work for us? Interviewer's deductions:

Be near friends....................	Just need a job....................
For home reasons.................	Seems restless.....................
Likes the community..............	Floater............................
Regularity of work...............	Family reasons....................
Self-expression...................	More pay..........................
More prestige....................	For opportunity...................
Union reasons....................	Other reason......................

13. What pay do you expect?
Overestimates his worth............
Underestimates his worth...........
Fair estimate.....................

DECISIONS FOR THE INTERVIEWER TO MAKE DURING THE INTERVIEW

14. Would his personality fit our organization? ....
15. Is applicant eager for the job? ....
16. Does the applicant fit the job that is open? ....

Too good for the vacancy..........	Undoubtedly satisfactory...........
Not suited to vacancy.............	Probably a safe man to hire........
Unable to do the work.............	Hire, if no better applies..........

17. Remarks: ....
....

The interviewer begins with this statement to himself: "This applicant will impress me according to my past experience with persons of whom he reminds me. I must keep a record of the facts and judge the applicant on the basis of the facts only. The applicant is a blank to me now."

The statistical interview. The interviewer, as stated above, acquires a number of preferences or rules of experience for the selection of employees.   When he uses personal experience rules, he soon finds that he must revise his rules, and then he wonders what a statistical study would reveal.   The executive who refuses to hire a married woman as his stenographer may be compelled, by force of circumstances, to allow one to work for him. To his surprise, she pleases him.   Exceptions soon arise in his hiring rules.   A statistical study of the relation between success on the job and the characteristics of the employees is, obviously, the only sound basis for hiring applicants.   The life insurance companies have led the procession in the statistical analyses of the human factors in their relation to success on the job.   See figures 43 and 44 and Tables XI and XII.

After a statistical analysis had been made of the characteristics of good and poor salesmen, a mathematical scoring was given to various degrees of each predictive factor.

The Phoenix Mutual Life Insurance Company and the Life Insurance Sales Research Bureau have conducted further extensive researches in the development of tests for prospective life insurance agents.   The *Rating Chart* used by the Phoenix Mutual Life Insurance Company predicts the applicant's success or failure on the basis of the personal history items shown in Table XI, the scoring weights assigned to each item being based on its ability to differentiate between those who succeeded and those who failed, in a group of 1,799 agents hired by that company.

A basically similar *Rating Chart* has been developed by the Life Insurance Sales Research Bureau on the basis of a statistical analysis of such personal history items as were available for 10,000 men hired by 11 different life insurance companies.   This *Rating Chart* has since become Part I of an *Aptitude Index*, which is being used by about 75 life insurance companies.

Fig. 43.   The Guardian Life Insurance Company has developed a chart system of salesman selection which in the case of 1,200 agents checks almost exactly with the sales achieved by these men.   It is based on a Man-Power Survey made in 1931 by the Life Insurance Sales Research Bureau in the course of which the records of some 21,000 agents were studied, and has resulted in appreciable savings in personnel efficiency since its inception in 1932. (A rating chart is shown on the opposite page.)

A maximum number of points is allotted to each of seven important qualifications, and a schedule of penalty points in each classification covers specific factors known to have an unfavorable bearing on an agent's probability of success.

During an interview with the prospective salesman, the manager fills in the chart and by subtracting penalty points from plus figures can speedily arrive at a net rating of the applicant. (*From "Chart System for Choosing Salesmen,"* Printers' Ink Monthly, *March 1939.*)

PERSONAL RATING CHART
Qualifications for Life Insurance Selling

Name....................

RATING SCALE

1 Factors	2 Qualifications for Standard Rating	3 Maximum Points	4 Penalties	5 Net Points
Age	25 to 40 Years, inclusive	3		
Education	College Graduate	3		
Marital Status	Married / Single, if under age 25	3		
Previous Experience	1 Year or more Outside Selling (see Penalty Table for exceptions) / Retail Store Proprietors / Executives / Insurance Clerks / Sales Promotion or Management	4		
FINANCIAL STATUS — Life Ins. Owned	Under Age 25—$1,000 or more / Ages 25-29—$3,000 or more / Ages 30 and over—$5,000 or more	1		
Savings (including Life Ins. C. V.)	Under Age 25—$250 or more / Ages 25-29—$500 or more / Ages 30 and over—$1,000 or more	1		
Years in Community	2 Years or more	3		
Employed	Employed	2		
	Total	20		

PENALTY POINT TABLE

6	7	8 Penalty Points
Age	Under age 25	2
	Ages 41-50 inclusive	2
	Over 50 years	3
Education	Less than College Graduate, but at least High School Graduate	1
	Less than High School Graduate, but at least 1 year High School	2
	Less than 1 Year High School	3
Marital Status	Single (Ages 25-40)	1
	Single (Ages 41 and over)	2
	Separated, Divorced, Widower	1
Previous Experience	Life or General Insurance Selling	1
	Two Years or more Financial Selling	2
	Less than 1 Year Outside Selling (less than 6 months—take prior occupation)	1
	Inside (Store) Selling	2
	Student, Teacher, Clergy, Social Service	1
	Clerical Workers (other than insurance)	2
	Bankers, Doctors, Lawyers, Scientists	3
	Non-Selling Occupations not Mentioned	3
FINANCIAL STATUS — Life Ins. Owned	Under age 25—less than $1,000 / Ages 25-29—less than $3,000 / Ages 30 and over—less than $5,000	1
Savings (including Life Ins. C. V.)	Under age 25—less than $250 / Ages 25-29—less than $500 / Ages 30 and over—less than $1,000	1
Years in Community	Less than 2 Years but more than 1 Year	1
	Less than 1 Year but more than 3 Months	2
	Less than 3 Months	3
Employed	Unemployed 3 to 6 Months	1
	Unemployed 6 Months or More	2

Pub. 326-37   THE GUARDIAN LIFE INSURANCE COMPANY OF AMERICA.

(Fig. 43.   See opposite page for acknowledgment.)

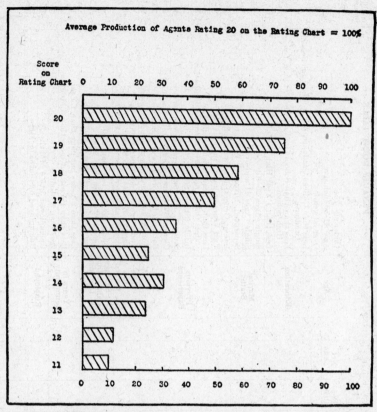

Average Production of Agents Rating 20 on the Rating Chart = 100%

FIG. 44. This graph shows the relation between scores on the rating chart and the average first-year sales of 1,190 full-time Guardian agents contracted between July 1, 1932, and June 30, 1936.

Experience with the chart has shown that the average first year's production of agents rating 16 points or better of a possible 20 is more than twice that of agents appointed with a rating less than 16. The company has also found that it does not pay to hire men whose rating is below 16.

The net result of the new selection and elimination used by Guardian Life is shown in the following facts:

(1) As of January 1, 1935, there were 813 regular agents.
(2) As of January 1, 1936, there were 559 regular agents.
(3) The total production from company agents in 1936 showed an increase over that for 1935 of 7½ per cent.
(4) The average production per agent in 1936 showed an increase of 54 per cent over the 1935 average.

(*See figure 43 for acknowledgment of source.*)

Part II of the *Aptitude Index* deals with personality charac-teristics such as self-confidence, emotional adjustment, and understanding of people. The statistical treatment and inter-pretation of Part II was originally based on studies of about 1,000 men, followed by a validation on a homogeneous group of

304 men.   Since then, a further validation of the entire *Aptitude Index* has been made on 1,385 men.*

Guides and keys for scoring applicants on the *Aptitude Index* are used by most of the companies who are members of the Life Insurance Sales Research Bureau.   These guides and keys are,

TABLE XI

PERSONAL HISTORY SCORE
Ages 30-39

Name............................. Agency.........................

Item	Applicant	Score
Marital Status........................		
Education............................		
Previous Income......................		
Insurance Owned......................		
Occupation...........................		
Selling Experience...................		
Living Expenses......................		
Length of Residence..................		
Present Organizations................		
Length of Negotiations...............		

Total Score.................

LOW	BORDERLINE	HIGH
0-45	46-57	58 & over

of course, not available for general publication and distribution. Albert K. Kurtz, who participated in the development of the *Aptitude Index*, has reported some results as follows:

This rating chart has proved surprisingly effective in forecasting the future success of prospective life insurance agents.   Those who score in the highest or *Excellent* group (approximately one fifth) and who also remain in the business for at least one year sell about three times as much as do those who score in the lowest or *Poor* group.   Since the survival rate of *Excellent* agents is nearly double that of *Poor* agents, it is thus necessary for a company to hire and to train about 50 agents with *Poor* ratings on the Rating Chart in order to get the same amount of business that would be obtained from 10 agents with *Excellent* ratings.

The *Aptitude Index* has been developed solely for life insurance agents, and the experimentation leading up to its development was confined to such agents.   Therefore, we seriously question the applicability of our results to salesmen in other fields and, as a result, we have to write out five or ten letters each month to persons in other lines of business who write in asking for this, without any realization of the possibility that it might not be applicable to them.

* Albert K. Kurtz. *How Well Does the Aptitude Index Work?*   Life Insurance Sales Research Bureau. Hartford, Connecticut, 1941, p. 74.

TABLE XII[4]

FIRST-YEAR PRODUCTION OF SURVIVORS AGE 26 AND OLDER

		Rating Chart Alone	Aptitude Index (Combination of Rating Chart and Personality Characteristics)
A.	(Excellent)	195%	206%
B.	(Very Good)	120	137
C.	(Good)	63	78
D.	(Fair)	76	39
E.	(Poor)	47	41
	Average for all groups combined	100%	100%

Data regarding the predictive value of the *Rating Chart* alone and the *Aptitude Index* are presented in Table XII.

A *Diagnostic Interviewer's Guide* (D.I.G.) or statistical evaluation of items on the interviewer's blank has been developed as part of the selection program of the Household Finance Corporation. Four pages of questions cover four general areas of the applicant's background and characteristics: (1) work history, (2) family history, (3) social history, and (4) personal history.

TABLE XIII[5]

PERCENTAGES OF INDIVIDUALS (1) STILL ON JOB, (2) RESIGNED, AND (3) DISMISSED IN VARIOUS CATEGORIES OF SCORES ON D. I. G.

Classification	Scores on D. I. G.				
	0-10	12-16	18-22	24-28	30-34
On job	38.9%	42.9%	47.2%	48.6%	59.2%
Resigned	22.2	25.7	29.2	29.4	34.7
Dismissed	38.9	31.4	23.6	22.0	6.1
Number	18	35	89	109	49

Answers to questions are scored plus or minus. The total score forms a basis for the rating of the applicant's qualifications. The relationships between ratings from a standardized interview procedure and success on the job for 300 individuals are shown in Table XIII.

---

[4] *Measuring Aptitude for Life Insurance Selling*, pp. 8, 11. Life Insurance Sales Research Bureau, Hartford, Conn., 1938.

[5] Carl Iver Hovland and E. F. Wonderlic, "Prediction of Industrial Success from a Standardized Interview," *Journal of Applied Psychology*, October 1939, Vol. 23, No. 5, p. 543.

When researches by a company enable the interviewers to establish a critical score for the characteristics of the applicant, the interviewer allows the scoring device to select the most acceptable applicants. After he has found those who are likely to succeed, he must then deal with the intangibles of the interview: the applicant's liking or distaste for the job, ability to finance himself, attitude toward the company, and so on. The statistical interview is scientifically the most sound, but it is limited by the need for a large number of employees before safe analyses of personal characteristics can be made. Each firm must make its own statistical analyses and establish its own critical scores. The scoring criteria of one firm may not fit the needs of another.

Psychological tests in hiring. Companies which conduct statistical researches of the various factors that enable them to predict the success of applicants often use psychological tests as one prediction variable. Tests alone are not sufficient for hiring or rejecting an applicant in most firms. They are merely one of the factors that must be evaluated, just as age or education must be weighed in the composite score. The tests may have greater predictive value than any other one variable, but in most firms the other variables must be considered in the total picture of the applicant. It is also necessary to point out that tests alone are not to be construed as a kind of interview, but, rather, as an important part of the statistical or other type of interview.

Psychological tests and intelligence tests are terms often used loosely by modern businessmen and even by scientists. In very many cases a businessman thinks he is using psychological or intelligence tests when actually he is merely asking a number of random questions. For example: a businessman may find that he needs a new secretary. Accordingly, he advertises in the usual manner and when he arrives at his office in the morning he may find an applicant there. He then opens the morning mail and chats with her while he is taking casual glances at the letters which await his attention. Then, deciding that it would be well for him to "test" the applicant, he picks up one of the letters which he must answer and dictates a reply. The applicant types the letter, gives it back to him, and he examines it for errors and appearance. He then dismisses the first applicant and awaits the coming of the second one, at which time he again answers

Fig. 45.   Herbert Moore, Business Research Corporation, Chicago. His book, *Experience with Employment Tests*, was published by The National Industrial Conference Board (247 Park Ave., New York, 1941. Studies in Personnel Policy No. 32).

another letter—an entirely different one. In this manner he "tests" five applicants, after which he makes his decision. He thinks he has given each one of the applicants a psychological or an intelligence test. As a matter of fact, he has not done so at all. If he were to give a psychological test, certain factors would have to be standardized for all applicants, namely:

1. *Materials.* The same letter and appliances must be used for each person.

2. *Instructions.* Each applicant must receive the same instructions regarding speed and accuracy. Instructions should be read.

3. *Technique.* The speed of dictation, enunciation, etc., must be kept the same.

4. *Conditions.* Distractions should vary as little as possible.

5. *Interpretation of score.* The score of each applicant must be compared with that of other stenographers of high, medium, and low ability.

Any test, to be of value, must fulfill three requirements: it must be *objective,* so that personal opinion does not enter into the scoring; it must be *valid,* that is, it must test the trait that it is supposed to test; and it must be *reliable,* that is, it must give the same results regardless of the particular individual who administers the test. Many of the tests that are published in magazines do not fulfill these three requirements. Such tests are still in the experimental state and may have promise of future results; but they should not be used as a basis for hiring until their predictive value has been statistically determined.

A psychological test is any problem or series of questions which has been tried out on persons of known ability; and it has been shown that the scores made by these persons correlate with their records in some other form of ability. Therefore, one of the chief requirements for preparing psychological tests is that of statistical training.

Many businessmen and scientists are using such tests, but the terminology is not very well standardized. The various terms used to describe them are: intelligence, aptitude, efficiency, mental alertness, information, specific ability, performance, mental, job, trade, and army tests.

Many past studies indicate that, in most individuals, intelligence is not greatly affected by education. For most children, the *intelligence quotient*

$$IQ = \frac{\text{Mental Age times } 100}{\text{Chronological Age}}$$

tends to remain about the same as the child becomes older. A child who has an IQ of 120 at eight years of age will tend to have the same IQ of 120 at fifteen years of age. This fact has caused some investigators to believe that intelligence is fixed by inheritance.[6]

However, we must bear in mind that almost all tests measure

---

[6] Certain investigators who believe that intelligence is inherited often dismiss the low-intelligence person whom they have tried to aid but could not with the remark: "He was gypped by the genes." The mechanisms of genes and chromosomes are blamed for the level of mental ability. However, if intelligence is wholly inherited, we still have much to learn about influences and factors in inheritance.

"Stoddard has cleverly observed that, while California state institutions over the past thirty years have sterilized 13,000 insane and feeble-minded persons, the follow-up, sixteen years later, of Terman's gifted children reveals that about 40 per cent of the parents of gifted children report mental abnormality among their near relatives. As Stoddard observed, 'Very likely a genius is himself safe in California, but it seems reasonable to say his near relatives had better watch out.'" See Addresses and Discussions Presenting the 39th Yearbook, NSSE, "Intelligence: Its Nature and Nurture," 1940, p. 49. Last paragraph quoted from John T. Wahlquist, "Is the IQ Controversy Philosophical?" *School and Society,* November 30, 1940.

FIG. 46. Beth Wellman, Professor, Iowa
Child Welfare Research Station, has written an article, "Iowa Studies on the Effects
of Schooling," published in 39th Yearbook
of the National Society for the Study of
Education, on "Intelligence: Its Nature
and Nurture, Part II."

results and not origins of capacities. This means that changes
may take place in intellectual and other capacities of many individuals. Many psychologists believe that the IQ is not fixed.
An individual may go through adjustment experiences which result in a raising or lowering of his intellectual capacity. In the
case of some children, favorable educational influences tend to
raise the IQ. The child who is encouraged to think independently, to use his intellectual curiosity, to have his ability challenged, and to gain satisfaction from his intellectual endeavors
may have an increase in his intelligence quotient.[7] The amount
of the increase or the exact conditions under which it does occur
is still largely a problem for future research.

In the field of education, tests have been useful in estimating
the learning capacities of pupils. For example, idiots (IQ under 25), imbeciles (IQ 25-49), and morons (IQ 50-69) have been
so limited in their learning abilities that special long-term in-

[7] Beth L. Wellman, "Our Changing Concept of Intelligence," *Journal of Con-
sulting Psychology,* July-August 1938, Vol. II. No. 4.
——— ———, "The IQ—A Reply," *Journal of Psychology,* 1939, Vol. 8, pp.
143-155.
——— ———, "The Fickle IQ," *Sigma Xi Quarterly,* Vol. 28, No. 2.
Benjamin R. Simpson, "The Wandering I.Q.: Is It Time for It to Settle
Down?" *Journal of Psychology,* 1939, Vol. 7, pp. 351-367.

struction is necessary to teach them the simplest habits. Idiots cannot learn to dress themselves or to say more than a few simple words. Imbeciles can learn to talk to a limited extent and even do simple manual labor under close supervision, but they cannot learn the value of money. Morons can learn to read and write and perform routine factory tasks, but they cannot be expected to go beyond the fifth grade in school.

Differences in levels of intelligence are often summarized as indicated in the following table:

TABLE XIV

	IQ	Percentage Population
Feebleminded:		
Idiot	below 25, M.A. 2 years or under ⎫	
Imbecile	25 - 49, M.A. 2-7 years ⎬	1
Moron	50 - 69, M.A. 7-11 years ⎭	
Borderline	70 - 79	5
Dull	80 - 89	14
Average	90 -109	60
Superior	110 -119	14
Very superior	120 -140 ⎫	6
Genius	above 140 ⎭	

Morons have normal impulses but they cannot foresee consequences of their own acts and so often get into trouble with the law. They buy goods on credit but forget to pay for them. Among the girls, the percentage of illegitimate motherhood is very high. Many of the boys are likely to become professional toughs or petty thieves, or transients. One study of 504 transients indicated that feeblemindedness was an important background factor in transiency. The transient group studied contained 12 times as many mental defectives as the population, relative to their numbers in both groups.[8]

Testing school children often reveals the gifted children. The records of gifted children have shown that, contrary to popular opinion, they do not become insane or die young. They do have some emotional problems but they tend to achieve happier and more successful lives than their less gifted brothers. Of the 1,400 gifted children selected as being the brightest among 250,000 Californians by Dr. Lewis M. Terman in 1922, one half of the

[8] D. Kaplun, "Feeblemindedness as a Factor in Transiency," *Mental Hygiene,* 1937, Vol. 21, pp. 96-100.

boys have entered the professions and a fourth are in semi-professional occupations or business.[9]

College students in general are of superior intelligence. However, when the scores on the American Council Psychological Examination were converted into equivalent IQ's by Arthur E. Traxler, using the recommended procedure, wide differences between colleges were found. The quartile and median IQ's at 323 colleges varied greatly, as shown by Table XV.[10] For admission to college, there is no unqualified answer to the question as to what intelligence quotient is necessary. The IQ needed depends upon the college considered.

TABLE XV

OTIS EQUATED IQ'S CORRESPONDING TO MEDIANS AND QUARTILES OR PERCENTILES OF TOTAL SCORES IN THE HIGHEST AND THE LOWEST OF 323 COLLEGES AND UNIVERSITIES ADMINISTERING THE 1937 EDITION OF THE AMERICAN COUNCIL ON EDUCATION PSYCHOLOGICAL EXAMINATION

Institution	Q_1 or P.R. 25	Md.	Q_3 or P.R. 75
Number 1	118	123	126
Number 323	87	94	102

Usually, we do not use the term IQ for adults. When children near the age of sixteen, it is difficult to compute the relation between mental development and chronological age. For adults, we prefer to specify the Percentile Rank (P.R.),[11] that is, the percentage of the population or group that ranks lower than the person tested. If a test shows that an applicant has a P. R. of 75, it means that 75 per cent of the population (or group) rank lower in the test than the applicant and 25 per cent rank higher.

---

[9] *Science News Letter,* March 11, 1939, p. 153.

[10] Arthur E. Traxler, "What Is a Satisfactory I. Q. for Admission to College?" *School and Society,* April 6, 1940.

[11] The term *centile* is also used by many authors. Whenever we use either *percentile* or *centile,* we should recognize the specific group to which the term applies. For example, a given college student's intelligence test score may place him below the 20th centile on a specific test administered to college students only. When the same or another intelligence test is administered to members of the general population, the same student may fall above the 70th centile for that group. On the other hand, centiles are a convenient device for showing a person's score on different kinds of tests such as intelligence, dominance, musical aptitude, and so on. Many psychographs or mental profiles are constructed on the basis of the centile concept.

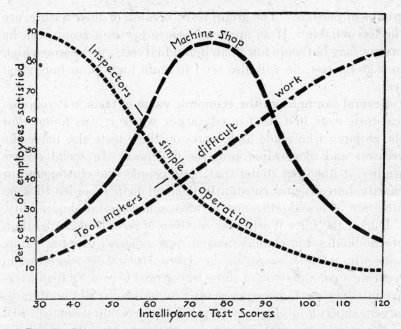

Fig. 47. Labor turnover and the intelligence of employees are closely related. Toolmaking is a grade of work that requires a high degree of intelligence. The toolmakers of high intelligence tend to be more satisfied than those of low intelligence. The inspectors in this particular company perform only simple operations. Hence the inspectors of low intelligence are more satisfied than those of high intelligence. The machine shop required an average grade of intelligence; consequently those of high and low intelligence were more dissatisfied than those of average intelligence.

Similarly, if he has a P. R. of 50, he is higher in that trait than 50 per cent of the population and lower than 50 per cent; hence he is average for that trait.

A psychological test does not evaluate all of the person's ability, but merely tests parts, samples, or symptoms of ability. The psychological test is very similar in nature to the tests made by the assayer of minerals. If a man were to purchase a vein of silver ore, he would first secure samples of it and have these analyzed by some competent chemist. On the basis of the samples, he would decide upon the value of the ore and the price he would be willing to pay for it. Obviously he could not test all the mineral in the vein of ore. Similarly, the psychologist tests samples of a person's abilities rather than all of them.

Some tests are designed to be given to individuals, others to groups of persons. The group tests, because of their nature, are the less reliable. If an applicant scores low in a group test, he may or may not score low in an individual test. If he scores high in a group test, he will also tend to score high in an individual test.

Several examples of the economic value of tests. Psychological tests were first used in education, where it was found that the children who made high scores on these tests also made the greatest and most rapid progress in school. In social service studies, it has been found that most people who clutter up our charity bureaus and constantly demand help in order to keep alive are of low intelligence, or have some mental abnormality.

During the First World War, analysis of records indicated that, of candidates for commissions in one officers' training camp, none who made E scores in the *Army Alpha Test* succeeded in securing a commission; of those who scored C plus, or high average intelligence, 45 per cent secured commissions; of the A grade, or very superior intelligence, 97 per cent were commissioned. All of the candidates were subjected to the same training course for three months.

In the Second World War, it was reported that the German army officer was given a series of psychological tests which lasted twenty-seven hours. The tests were supposed to place him in the field for which he was best suited, such as command of combat troops, supply service, mechanical supervision, or other duties. The tests revealed not just abilities but also character and personality traits. One series of ordeals was claimed to be 80 per cent in agreement with will power, the ability to go on in the face of extreme peril.[12]

In American industry, tests have been found economically valuable for the following purposes:

1. Weeding out the unfit applicants. For example, persons who have an intelligence quotient of less than 105 seldom succeed in clerical jobs of average difficulty. One personnel manager for a public utility firm reported that when tests were used in selecting applicants, less than 10 per cent of those hired failed on the

---

[12] "Psychology Test Picks Nazi Officer," *The New York Times*, May 11, 1941, Sec. 4, p. F5.

job. Without tests, the long-term record of failures in hiring approached 30 per cent.[13] At one time the Woodward Governor Co.
of Rockford, Illinois, found that they were hiring too many tramp
mechanics and other undesirables. Later the Psychological Corporation made a study of the company's personnel needs and
recommended the use of tests which, according to the general
manager of the company, succeeded in weeding out 85 per cent
of the untrainable men who applied for work.[14] Similarly, the
Lockheed Aircraft Corp. averaged six successful hirings out of ten
before testing. With testing, the average rose to nine and a half
out of ten.[15]

2. Tests enable the personnel manager to spot unsuspected
talent within the organization. For example, one third of the
line supervisors of the Pacific Lighting Companies first attracted
attention through results of their tests.[16] Several large concerns
use tests in selecting employees for apprentice, sales, or executive
training.

3. Several investigators have developed tests which reduce accidents in bus and truck driving through the selection of fewer
accident-prone drivers. In one study,[17] it was found that the
highest tenth of the drivers (according to composite profile
scores) had had 21.2 per cent less chargeable accidents than the
lowest tenth. A comparison of the average yearly accident rate
for the year following the tests and the three preceding years
showed an improvement with respect to chargeable accidents of
28.8 per cent. Another psychologist, C. A. Drake,[18] developed
a series of tests which reduced the average accident index rate 70
per cent for new employees during the first three months of
their work.

4. Psychological tests decrease favoritism in hiring and place
the securing of a job on an objective basis rather than on senti-

[13] Guy W. Wadsworth, Jr., "Hidden Abilities of Clerical Workers," *Office
Management Series 88,* American Management Association, 1939. Mr. Wadsworth
is Personnel Manager of Southern California Gas Company.

[14] "Testing for Talent," *Fortune,* January 1941, p. 96.

[15] *Ibid.*

[16] Guy W. Wadsworth, Jr., *op. cit.*

[17] H. R. DeSilva, R. G. Claflin, and W. J. Simon, "Making Safer Bus Drivers,"
Transit Journal, November 1938, pp. 1-3.

[18] Charles A. Drake, "Testing for Accident-Proneness," presented before the
American Association of Applied and Professional Psychology, University of
Minnesota, August 31, 1937.

ment.   Tests are a convenient device for avoiding pressure from
friends and politicians who may have some protégé who needs
a job.   Definite standards which every applicant must meet will
enable the executive to say to the man who has a nephew who
needs a position: "We shall be glad to have the young man apply
to us for a job, and if he meets the standards we have set up, we
will find a place for him."   However, the main value of tests is
in locating good applicants and employees.

TABLE XVI

INTELLIGENCE AND LENGTH OF SERVICE[19]

Test Score	Average Length of Service in Days
10 to 19	3
20 to 29	91
30 to 39	156
40 to 49	142
50 to 59	107
60 to 69	100
70 to 79	96
80 to 89	87
90 and above	35

Limitations of tests.   Psychological tests have demonstrated
their values in many phases of business, but are especially helpful
in reducing labor turnover.   When a critical score is once determined and an executive decides that no applicant shall be hired
unless he scores above that point, the executive is also apt to
go to the opposite extreme and try to hire only those who score
considerably above the critical point.   This may result in a high
turnover, for it is desirable to have a maximum score as well as a
minimum score or an *optimum range* (see Table XVI).   One
employment manager started to use tests for hiring and then
hired only persons with high intelligence for all his jobs.   His
method resulted in a high turnover, because few of the jobs
were worthy of a person of high intelligence.   The well-
manned corporation is like a well-manned army; it consists of
one general, a few high officers, many junior-grade officers, and
the great mass of the organization made up of people with average or low intelligence.   An elevator operator should have the
intelligence needed for that kind of work and not very much

[19] Harold E. Burtt, *Employment Psychology*, p. 289.   Houghton Mifflin Co.,
1926.

more.   If this country should suddenly embark upon a eugenical program and breed only people of very high intelligence, we might be worse off than we are now, because many jobs of a technological civilization require only average and below-average intelligence. Examples of such jobs are truck driving, elevator operating, factory machine tending, and so on.

When intelligence tests are used for selective purposes, it is well to know whether environmental conditions have been eliminating the unfit of the group to be tested.   The use of intelligence tests for the selection of students for admission to college does not result in very high correlations between scores in the tests and the scholastic records.   One reason for a low correlation is the selective process that has been operating through the school system.   The students of lowest intelligence find grammar school and high school work too difficult for them and tend to drop out according to the degrees of intelligence possessed. Hence, when a student is able to apply for admission to college, he has already survived a process of selection.   Only those above the average of intelligence are able to finish high school and apply for admission to college.

This process of selection by accomplishment requirements which is one of the causes of low relation between intelligence test scores and scholastic record in college is also at work in the selection of business executives.   Bingham and Davis measured the intelligence and business standing of 102 successful businessmen. The relation between intelligence test score and business standing was indicated by a zero coefficient.   Business competition had already set the dead line for entrance into the executive field by eliminating those of low or even of average intelligence. Those who had intelligence below the average of the population in general could not hope to become members of this executive group.

If an individual has a certain minimum of intelligence for a given occupation or job, his success depends upon other characteristics, such as temperament and personality.   The intelligence of the executive is merely one of several factors in his composite behavior pattern, as suggested in the chapters (3-9) on adjustment patterns.

Executives who decide to use psychological tests for hiring

often want to take the tests themselves. The experience of the writer has been that, if the executive interested in the tests happens to make the highest score of all the employees, he then believes that the tests are good. The executives who happened to score lower than one or two employees lost interest in the use of tests. Such an attitude is wholly unscientific and unsound. If the executive could only realize that the purpose of the tests is to hire employees of a behavior pattern type requiring qualities of a different nature from his own qualifications, he might not be so easily elated or offended over the results of the test procedure.

One of the most frequent criticisms of psychological tests is that they are unfair to the nervous applicants. It is claimed that a person may be in an unusual mood. His digestion may be bad or he may be in a state of worry and therefore not do justice to himself. Experience indicates that very few persons are emotionally disturbed while taking the tests administered by an experienced examiner. Tests may frighten employees and applicants when they are given without the necessary preliminary explanation of their limitations and values. However, when tests are properly handled, very few applicants object to taking them. A person of an especially timid or psychoneurotic nature may object, but such applicants are in a decided minority. In many situations it is not essential to tell the applicant that he is about to take a psychological test. It is better to ask him whether he objects to taking a short examination of his general fund of information or speed in figuring.

Employees who have been tested should not be given their scores. Such results should be kept in the personal file of the chief executive of the firm. As previously stated, if a person has a certain accomplishment level of intelligence, his success and advancement may depend upon factors which are not measured by the tests. When an employee or lower-rank executive is given his own test score and he knows how he compares with other members of the organization, he assumes that those employees who happen to be a few points above or below him are also above or below him in ability or chances for promotion. No tests are available that measure so fine a degree of differentiation. Their chief value is that of classifying individuals into broad or general groups.

Intelligence and other psychological tests have been used far more in the field of education than in industry. Almost every modern school uses some tests, but a survey made in 1936 by the National Industrial Conference Board showed that only 179 out of 2,452 reporting companies used tests.[20] An earlier survey of 195 leading concerns showed that 17 per cent used mental tests, 27 per cent used trade tests, and 45 per cent used clerical and stenographic tests.[21] These surveys dealt with the larger concerns, so that, when all employers are considered, only a very low percentage use tests for employment purposes.

High scores on scholastic records and intelligence tests are an indication of ability to do the kind of learning which requires some grasp of abstractions. However, ability to learn certain important business operations does not correlate with intelligence tests. The best example of this is stenographic ability. Many students of superior mental capacity make low marks in short-hand, and many who make high marks in shorthand have relatively low intelligence test scores.[22] This simply means that individual companies who use intelligence tests for hiring should use specific ability and skill tests as well as intelligence tests.

Character tests. Experiments are now being conducted with tests of character. Some people are high in intelligence but of abnormal character. In general, we do find that most socially desirable traits go together. People of high intelligence tend to be of good character, are better-looking, easier to get along with, and healthier. However, a high score in intelligence does not prove that a given individual is of good character. It merely indicates that the chances, statistically speaking, are greater that he is of good character than that he is not. Some of the first character tests dealt with school situations.

Children in school have been tested in deceit by giving them

---

[20] "What Employers Are Doing for Employees," National Industrial Conference Board, *Report No. 221*, March 1936, p. 24.

[21] S. B. Mathewson, "A Survey of Personnel Management in 195 Concerns," *Personnel Journal*, 1931-1932, Vol. 10, pp. 225-231.

[22] Raymond J. Worley, "Prognosis in Shorthand," *The Journal of Business Education*, September 1931.

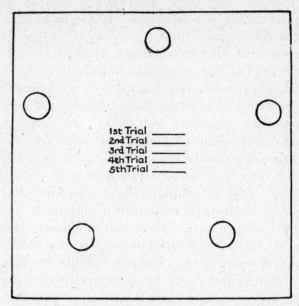

1st Trial _____
2nd Trial _____
3rd Trial _____
4th Trial _____
5th Trial _____

FIG. 48. *An example of a character test.* Close your eyes.
Move a pencil around the square three times without touch-
ing the paper. With eyes still closed, try to put a dot in each
circle. Do this for each of five trials. You must put a dot in
each of the five circles on each trial in order to have a plus
score for any one trial. Refer to the Appendix for the answer.
(*Adapted from V. M. Cady,* "*The Estimation of Juvenile Incor-
rigibility,*" Journal of Delinquency, *Monograph No. 2, April,*
1923.)

an examination, collecting the papers, making copies of each
child's answers, returning each child's papers to the child, giving
each a key to the correct answers, and asking each child to score
his own paper. The child's own scoring was then compared with
the office copies of the scores and definite discrepancies between
the two scorings were noted. It was found that some children
would correct their own papers while scoring them: some would
put dots over the letter "i" when it was a part of the test, others
would cross the letter "t," others would write in extra words,
and the worst offenders would erase writings in ink and write in
the correct answer in pencil. In most of these tests, the amount
of dishonesty varied with the degree of motivation. When children were impressed with the tremendous importance of making
a high score, they cheated far more than when they were allowed to think that a high score in the examination was of no
importance. This is in harmony with the businessman's em-

pirical experience. The executive who wishes to hire an employee for a position where, if he chooses, he can manipulate the company's finances for his own benefit does well when he selects a man who lives within his income and saves some money rather than a man who plays the stock market or happens to have a "social climber" for a wife. Our dishonesty tends to increase as the pressure for it increases.[23]

At present, tests are not available which tell the businessman whether an applicant is honest or dishonest. Honesty, like all character traits, is of a complex nature. It varies with the situation. A man may be scrupulously honest about paying his gambling debts and exceedingly lax about paying his room rent. One test will not measure any one character trait, because character traits are specific in their applications to situations. A "battery" or number of tests is needed to measure any one character trait, such as aggressiveness, although Moore and Gilliland got excellent results with an eye-control test. To use this test, select ten persons who are very aggressive and ten who are not aggressive. Let each applicant, while he adds simple numbers and gives the answers aloud, face the examiner and look him in the eye. For example: ask him to begin with 38, add 11 to it, and continue to add 11 to each sum, looking you in the eye meanwhile, until you tell him to stop. Have him do this for three trials of one minute each. Count the number of times he shifts his eyes from yours. In the Moore and Gilliland experiment, twenty-six persons were tested. Thirteen were known to be very aggressive, and thirteen to be lacking in aggressiveness. The average number of eye-movements for the aggressive persons was .5, the average number for the nonaggressive persons was 5.5.[24]

Tests of a similar sort have been used in selecting salesmen. The applicant for a selling job is seated at a table before the examiner. The examiner says to the applicant: "Here is a pencil. You are to write your name on this sheet of paper and continue to write, no matter what happens." After the applicant begins

---

[23] T. H. Howells, "Factors Influencing Honesty," *Journal of Social Psychology*, 1938, Vol. 9, pp. 97-102.

[24] H. T. Moore and A. R. Gilliland, "The Measurement of Aggressiveness," *Journal of Applied Psychology*, 1921, Vol. 5, pp. 97ff.

to write, the examiner takes his wallet and pushes against the writer's pencil. In one company it was found that the men who threw down the pencil and became angry were poorer salesmen than those who resisted the examiner's tactics. This test has not been standardized sufficiently to prove its predictive value; but it is suggestive of the type of test that will be improved and may become of value in testing character traits, such as persistence in the face of difficulty. This last-named test is difficult to score, and a test that must be scored by the subjective estimate of the examiner is less reliable than an objective test.

All tests are limited by the fact that they give a group prediction rather than a prediction for a specific individual. A test that has high positive predictive value means that anyone who scores high in the test tends to be high in the trait with which the test correlates. The high score means that, of one hundred persons who score high in the test, a certain percentage will also be high in the other trait.[25] If an employer hires a large number of employees for a specific job, as one does in life insurance selling or factory operations of large standard process shops, a set of psychological tests should be developed for the hiring of applicants; but most American business concerns do not have a large number of employees who do the same work. They have a few stenographers, several bookkeepers, a janitor, an office boy or two, and a larger number of miscellaneous machine operators. Unless the firm employs about fifty persons on the same kind of operation, it is difficult and expensive to develop reliable psychological tests. Even in the larger corporations, it is often arduous to invent profitable tests for more than one or two classes of employees.

Psychologists realize this limitation of tests and govern their decisions accordingly; but the novice who uses tests is apt to apply the prediction to specific individuals rather than to group relations. In general, no especially difficult technique is required to administer group psychological tests after they have been statistically treated; but to give them statistical interpreta-

---

[25] We shall not discuss the meaning of minus coefficients of correlation here, but leave that for the statistician who wishes to have a thorough knowledge of tests. However, the last chapter of this book presents some of the statistical methods of evaluating tests.

tion requires more technical application than most businessmen care to give. Executives should obtain the services of a trained tester if they wish to have any worthwhile results from psychological tests for hiring purposes. This is one reason why tests have been much discussed in business literature but have been little used.

The adjustment analysis interview. The statistical interview and psychological test are objective. The clinical and adjustment analysis interviews are decidedly subjective. Clinical psychologists and psychoanalysts have developed techniques which enable them to study the emotional life of the patient and discover or uncover the past experiences that influence the behavior of the individual. There is no doubt that the past experiences of a person do influence his impulses and interests. In most cases the person does not realize what experiences of his past are influencing his adult life. The man who wants to be in the forefront of the group and do the talking, as typified in the labor union lecturer or the preacher, has had certain adjustment experiences, perhaps in his youth, that cause him to obtain his ego-satisfactions by exhibiting himself before other people.

The psychiatrist and clinical psychologist can interview a person and note and classify forms of behavior that might escape the untrained interviewer. The person who has a desire to see blood may become a butcher if of low or average intelligence, whereas, if of high intelligence, he may become a surgeon. The "hand-fetishist" may take up glove-making, manicuring, or sculpturing. The person who has an abnormal sexual impulse and wishes to protect himself against it may become a reformer or a detective. The handicap of a physical defect may cause its owner to become an expert in chemistry or accounting. We all try to compensate for our subconscious feelings of inferiority, and the adjustment analyst can recognize the means whereby we attain our compensations.

At present, a few firms are hiring psychiatrists for the detection, prevention, and cure of emotional or personality defects. These men note delusions of persecution, tics, irritability, fluctuations in attention, complexes, and other psychopathological conditions. In the course of another decade or two they may become valuable in selecting employees who have impulses that fit them for specific occupations. In recent years, some progress has been made in the measurement of basic drives of the worker. The Humm-Wadsworth Temperament Scale is an attempt to measure potential work attitudes, social adjustment, and co-operative capacity.[26] The use of the test is restricted to those who have had some training in psychiatric principles. Much research must still be done in this kind of interviewing, but the interviewer should become acquainted with this field of human analysis. The chapters on adjustments (3 to 9) present a general background for this type of interview.

Letters of application. Our discussion of the interview would be incomplete without some mention of the letter of application. Carefully conducted investigations show that the letter of application cannot be judged with any great degree of accuracy. If thirteen experienced employment men are asked to rank several letters of application, the letter that stands at the head of the list of one interviewer is likely to be at the bottom of the list of another interviewer. See Table XVII. No executive has the right to assume that he can pick the wheat from the tares in letters of application. He can eliminate some of the decidedly unfit, but when he rates the remainder he is apt to commit serious errors. When a company advertises for applicants, no single executive should eliminate and rate the letters of application. A group of executives or other persons should select the letters whose writers are to be investigated further.

Eight letters of application were received in answer to the following advertisement:

"Required Secretary to Employment Manager of large Factory. Apply stating particulars to Box . . ."

These letters were ranked in order by thirteen experienced employment managers, none of whom knew any of the applicants personally. The results are shown in Table XVII.

It will be seen that half the applicants (four out of the eight) were ranked by different managers both top and bottom, that is, first and eighth.[27]

---

[26] Guy W. Wadsworth, Jr., "Hidden Abilities of Clerical Workers," *Office Management Series No. 88,* 1939, American Management Association; and Herbert Moore, "Experience with Employment Tests," *Studies in Personnel Policy,* No. 32, March 11, 1941, National Industrial Conference Board.

[27] *National Institute of Industrial Psychology News,* London, December 1938.

TABLE XVII

Applicants	J	K	L	M	N	O	P	Q	R	S	T	U	V
Miss A	3	7	8	1	7	7	6	6	4	5	6	5	4
Miss B	4	3	1	3	2	2	3	2	2	4	3	4	1
Miss C	5	6	7	6½	8	6	8	7	6	8	7	6	5
Miss D	8	5	6	5	3	4	7	8	7	6	8	8	6
Miss E	6	1	3	6½	4	1	1	5	5	2	1	3	2
Miss F	1	4	2	2	5	8	2	1	1	3	5	7	3
Miss G	7	2	4	8	6	3	5	3	7	1	4	1	8
Miss H	2	8	5	4	1	5	4	4	3	7	2	2	7

The header "Raters" spans columns J through V.

It is also important that the company advertising for help should give specific details in its advertisements. The following advertisement had been used by one executive who was seeking a combination type of service man and salesman:

MECHANIC wanted who can service electrical appliances. Must also be able to take orders occasionally from customers. He must have a neat appearance and a good personality.

When the advertisement was rewritten, better and fewer obviously unfit applicants applied to the company:

SERVICE MAN AND SALESMAN wanted who can make repairs on electrical appliances, as washing machines, refrigerators, ironers, and indoor wiring. He must also be able to:

1. Solicit orders from present users of our equipment. He will be paid an extra bonus for such orders.
2. Collect payment on unpaid accounts.
3. Drive a car.
4. Furnish bond, the cost of which is paid by the company.
5. Attend a training course one evening each week.

The persons who qualify will be paid a definite salary; but their ability to sell additional equipment will determine the main part of their income. Advancement to executive positions is possible.

Letters of recommendation. An instance of the questionable worth of letters of recommendation came to the attention of the writer when employed by a rubber company. An executive had hired a secretary who was exceptionally competent but was very temperamental. On several occasions he transferred her temporarily to other executives of the company who were friends of his, told them that she was difficult to handle, and asked them to discharge her. The other men refused to discharge her because they did not wish to withstand the fiery temper of the girl. Finally the executive who was responsible for her employment decided to have vengeance upon a friend, employed in another concern, who had beaten him in a poker game. The poker-playing friend happened to be an executive in his firm, so the girl was given an excellent letter of recommendation to him. When she applied for a position, her personality impressed him favorably and she was hired, largely because of the excellent letter of recommendation from her employer! This case is exceptional, but it illustrates the fact that many letters of recommendation and many references are given which do not tell the true story of the employee's past record.

A sales manager wrote to 100 sales managers and asked them: "In replying to a letter of inquiry from a prospective employer regarding the fitness of one of your former employees, do you tell only the good things you can say about the man?" Seventy-seven per cent said "Yes" and 23 per cent said "No." This indicates that about 8 out of 10 former employers will report only the pleasant qualities about a former employee rather than paint the complete picture. In this same investigation, to the question, "Do you always give the employee the benefits of any doubts?" · 85 per cent said "Yes." The third question: "Do you point out the man's failings and weaknesses as well as his strong points?" resulted in 39 per cent who said "Yes" and 61 per cent who said "No" or "Not usually." [28]

One sales manager who hires salesmen in all parts of the country telegraphs his requests for information from former employers who are given as references by applicants. He has found that he must demand about eight references and follow up each reference very carefully if he wishes to avoid hiring men with bad records. On one occasion he sent telegrams to eight references regarding an applicant whom he wished to hire. Two of the references did not reply at all, but telegrams from four were as follows:

"Glad to hear Walter K has applied to you for a position. I can recommend him highly as regards honesty and workmanship. He is 100%. Has worked for me 3 years."

"Walter K was with us for two months. Character and dependability very good. Would recommend."

"While Walter K was with us he was very satisfactory."

---

[28] By a New York Sales Manager, "To Whom It May Concern," *Sales Management*. October, 1923, pp. 9ff.

"I recommend Mr. K. very highly in every respect."

These telegrams from the references were quite satisfying to the employment man and he was about to hire the applicant when he received a long-distance telephone call from one of the former employers. The former employer described Walter's conduct with his firm and told how he had failed even to attempt to do the work for which he was hired, had led an immoral life, owed the company money, borrowed money from customers, and had been discharged for incompetency. A few hours later, another former employer telephoned the employment man and gave a similar report of gross misconduct. These executives refused to put their reports in writing, but used the telephone in an honest effort to save time and money for a prospective employer. This employment man frequently requests former employers to telephone him at his expense if they prefer to do so rather than write or telegraph him. He claims that he has saved his company thousands of dollars by asking for telephone answers, because former employers will give more honest reports in oral than in written form.

Most executives write a general letter to a person given as reference and the person answering usually gives a general reply, selecting those good points in the applicant's history that may be written without harming his chances for another job. A slightly better method is to use a special rating scale and ask the former employer to rate the applicant on a point scale as:

Rating	Points
Excellent	10
Very good	8
Good	6
Fair	4
Poor	2

General character traits such as initiative and honesty are listed and ratings are requested. Such a rating form for references is better than a general letter, but it is far more effective to ask for information on specific points, as:

1. Was the applicant discharged by you, let go because of decrease in work, or did he leave of his own accord?
2. Does he owe you any money now? *No.* *Yes.*
3. Would you rehire him if you needed a person for a vacancy that he had the ability to fill? *No.* *Yes.* *Possibly.*

4. How long did he work for you?
5. What date (month and year) did he leave your employ?
6. He states that his salary or income from you was .... per month.
Is this correct? *Yes.* *No.*
7. Did he use alcohol to any extent? *Yes.* *No.*
8. How do you rate his moral conduct? *Very Good.* *Satisfactory.*
Questionable.
9. Do you think that he possesses the ability to fill a job with us which
is .... *Yes.* *No.* *Don't know.*
10. How would you rate his record with your firm?
    a. Very satisfactory.
    b. Satisfactory.
    c. Fair.
    d. Questionable.
    e. Unsatisfactory.

The above questions should be made part of a two-page letter to the previous employer, the first page giving the name of the former employee and assuring the answerer that his report will be kept confidential. The questions and answers suggested may be varied, but they should deal with objective factors rather than ask for opinions. The possible answers should be suggested on the form so that the correct answer can be checked by the writer or written with a minimum of effort. This type of letter to a reference does not allow the previous employer to select the pleasant parts in the former employee's record and ignore the bad parts. Such forms have been used by a few progressive firms, but most employment men still accept a general letter of reply from persons given as references. They assume that, when an applicant has a bad record, the person answering will phrase his letter so that it is possible "to read between the lines" and grasp the real story. Such an expectation on the part of executives may be unfair to the applicant and it requires too much time on the part of the previous employers.

When letters are addressed to former employers of an applicant, they should be addressed to the "Employment Manager" rather than to individuals within the company. Some applicants who do not wish their real record to be revealed to prospective employers often give the name of a friend in the company as a reference. This friend is usually a person of no responsibility and his statement has no weight as a reference for a discharged employee.

Summary. The hiring of employees is still in the hands of the empiricists of business. The old rules of thumb and prejudice prevail. A few progressive concerns have made statistical studies of the factors which correlate with successful employment records. Some have used psychological tests in eliminating the unfit and reducing labor turnover, but such tests have several major limitations. They require a large number of employees, fifty or more, to be engaged on the same tasks, and their predictive value applies to groups rather than to individuals. However, any executive or employment manager who wishes to improve his hiring technique can do so by standardizing his procedure, keeping records of his findings, and then making careful statistical studies of his records. Such an attempt will yield results more valuable than the present haphazard treatment of the interview, letter of application, and letter of recommendation.

References

Bingham, Walter Van Dyke, *Aptitudes and Aptitude Testing.* Harper & Bros., 1937.

Buros, O. K., *The 1940 Mental Measurements Yearbook,* 32 Lincoln Ave., Highland Park, N. J.

Copeland, H. A , "Some Characteristics of Three Tests Used to Predict Clerical Success," *Journal of Applied Psychology,* 1936, Vol. 20, pp. 461-470.

Davidson, C. M., "Analysis of Clerical Tests," *Personnel Journal,* 1937, Vol. 16, pp. 95-98.

Drake, C. A., "Aptitude Tests Help You Hire," *Factory Management Maintenance,* 1937, Vol. 95, pp. 55-57.

————————, "Accident-Proneness: A Hypothesis," *Character and Personality,* 1940, Vol. 8, pp. 335-341.

Garrett, H. E., and Maximilian R. Schneck, *Psychological Tests, Methods and Results.* Harper & Bros., 1933.

Hildreth, G. H., *A Bibliography of Mental Tests and Rating Scales.* Psychological Corporation, 1939.

Hurt, J., "Evaluating Applicants by Dexterity Testing," *Employment Service News,* 1939, Vol. 6, No. 6, pp. 7-8.

Laird, D. A., *The Psychology of Selecting Employees.* McGraw-Hill Book Co., 1937.

Moore, Herbert, "Experience with Employment Tests," *Studies in Personnel Policy,* No. 32, 1941, National Industrial Conference Board.

Robinson, O. Preston, *Retail Personnel Relations,* Chapter VIII. Prentice-Hall, Inc., 1940.

South, E. B., *An Index of Periodical Literature on Testing.* Psychological Corporation, 1937.

Strang, R., "The Technique of the Interview," *Journal of Consulting Psychology,* 1939, Vol. 3, pp. 90-92.

Tiffin, J., and R. J. Greenly, "Employee Selection Tests for Electrical Fixture Assemblers and Radio Assemblers," *Journal of Applied Psychology*, 1939, Vol. 23, pp. 240-263.

"Testing for Talent," *Fortune*, January 1941, pp. 68ff.

Projects

1. Assume that all the employees of a large bank are to be given several psychological tests. Outline the complete plan of procedure for their administration and use.

2. A sales manager asks you to develop some psychological tests for hiring salesmen. Outline the main steps in the procedure you would follow in attempting to give him what he wants.

3. Try the Moore and Gilliland eye-control test on some friends and record the result. Evaluate the worth of the test for hiring purposes.

4. Collect some letters of application. Ask some friends or executives to rank them in the order of estimated desirability of the applicants. Discuss the differences in the rankings.

5. Read some of the recent literature on the stability of the IQ mentioned in the footnote on page 274. Prepare a list of all the possible factors which might result in the raising or lowering of an individual's IQ.

6. Intelligence test results are sometimes expressed in terms of IQ and sometimes in terms of percentiles. Which would you select in each of the following cases, and offer reasons for your choice. In the case of percentiles, define each group used as the base.

    a. For applicants for a night watchman's job.
    b. For admission to the graduate school of a university.
    c. For selecting soldiers for officers' training schools.
    d. For discovering mentally handicapped children.
    e. For rating stenographers in an office.

7. Construct a graph from the *Who's Who in America* column of Table XXVI. Show in the same graph how an entire class of 400 M.I.T. students would be distributed. Write below the graph a brief analysis of what the graph reveals to you.

8. The Tremco Manufacturing Co. of Cleveland sells paints and building maintenance materials. The company sells to the industrial and institutional markets exclusively. Applicants for selling positions have their characteristics scored by the sales manager, who uses the weightings of Table XVIII. Score yourself according to the following table and norms. The company found it doubtful whether anyone should be hired who scores less than 60 out of a possible 92 points. Of course, the data in this table are valid only for the Tremco Manufacturing Co. and should not be used for selection purposes elsewhere.

TABLE XVIII[29]

1. *Age*	*Score*
50	4
45-49	5
40-44	2
up-39	7

2. *Height*

72"-up	7
70"-71.9	5
69"-69.9	4
up-68.9	3

3. *Marital status*

Married	5
All others	3

4. *Number dependents*

4 or more	0
3	3
2	6
1	7
none	3

5. *Thousands of insurance*

10 or more	5
5 to 10	6
1 to 5	3
none	6

6. *Amount of debts*

None	4
Current	6
$500 or more	5

7. *Years of education*

Grades 1-8	6
9, 10, 11	3
12, College 1	6
College 2, 3	0
College 4, more	5

8. *Number of clubs*

None	6
One	4
Two	6
Three, more	3

9. *Years on last job*	*Score*
Less than 1	5
1 to 2 years	1
2	3
3	6
4-5	8
6-9	10
10 or more	5

10. *Experience in maintenance*

None	3
Any amount	6

11. *Average number years on all previous jobs*

1-2½	3
3-6	5
6½-10	8

12. *Average monthly earnings on last regular job*

Up to $150	5
$150-$199	4
200-249	8
250-349	1
350-399	5
400-up	6

13. *Reason for leaving last regular job*

Still employed	10
Job discontinued (depression) (company folded)	7
To better self (positive)	5
Negative reasons (friction)	2

[29] "Interviewing and Rating Men for Sales Jobs: A Soup-to-Nuts Plan," *Sales Management,* October 10, 1940, p. 9. See also O. A. Ohmann, "A Report of Research on the Selection of Salesmen at the Tremco Manufacturing Company," *Journal of Applied Psychology,* February 1941.

12

Rating and Promoting the Worker

The ambitious employee does not want managerial sermons or copybook maxims about how to become a big businessman. He needs definite and organized explanations regarding the actions he should take in order to deserve and achieve a feasible promotion. An inventory of personnel should be as important as a physical inventory.

THE WRITER once had the temerity to suggest to the general manager of a firm having three thousand employees that he ought to have a promotion and training system. His answer was: "Training and promotion? Bosh! Nothing doing. Why, do you know what I did several years ago? I arranged for several training courses to be given, hired the teachers, rented a special room in the center of town, and put a slip in the pay envelopes telling the employees that anyone taking the course would be directly in line for promotion and higher pay. The whole proposition was free. I almost begged some of them to take the training. About 50 per cent of our men are foreigners or too old to take any courses, but I estimated that about 1,200 could benefit by courses I had planned. Of the 1,200 possibilities, how many do you suppose took the courses? Well, you couldn't guess. I'll tell you. Eight started and two finished."

The experience of this manager is not exceptional. Many employees will not exercise the self-discipline necessary to merit important positions. Most employees do not seek responsibility. Some must be compelled to accept it. However, certain intelligent employees do desire promotion. When higher-grade applicants are hired, they often ask: "Where does this job lead to?" The most frequent answer is one of evasion, such as, "You do your work well and keep your eyes open and you'll be promoted when you really deserve it."

A more truthful statement to the applicant would be: "We have no well-planned system of promotion or advancement. We have never taken the trouble to study our employees and to explain how they can make themselves worth more to us. If you work for us and make good, it may be that in time we shall have an opening somewhere in the organization where we can use you. Of course, someone may have to die or leave before you can be promoted, but if you live long enough and work hard enough, you may get there. On the other hand, someone else may appeal more to us than you, and then the other fellow will get the promotion. We think we know who the good men in our company are, but we don't always know, so you must make a good impression on someone farther up. You must be able to sell us your ability as well as do good work."

The ambitious employee should recognize that salesmanship as well as ability is often essential to secure promotion. Some men are very able in their fields but are poor salesmen. Several experiments have proved that the employee who is liked by one executive may make no favorable impression on another executive. One executive may admire the enthusiastic type of employee and another may admire the quiet, steady variety. It is obvious that the executive's personality and personal likes and dislikes always will play a large part in promotions, but merit should be the chief consideration. It is also agreed that many executives do make an honest attempt to promote fairly and on a merit basis.

Executives who have tried to install an adequate system of rating employees have found that certain incompetent employees could not be displaced as easily as the management desired:

. . . whenever a system of rating is applied to a company force, some employees will be found holding better positions or drawing more pay than they or their jobs measure up to on any sound basis of man or job comparison. Favoritism, family relationships, luck, or just pure persistence have outweighed merit. Here, as elsewhere in personnel management, scientific theory runs up against the fact that "the squeaking wheel gets the grease."

However, in their job of greasing all the wheels, the promoters of new methods in the testing and adjustment of employees are making substantial progress. The list of concerns which are working on this program for smoother management is studded with big names. For years the telephone companies have been among the leaders and it is difficult to find a large insurance company, oil company or electric utility that does not now have a group of experts laboring at the problem. Likewise, many of the big steel companies are changing their methods to remove human error so far as possible from their placement and promotion policies.[1]

When a questionnaire regarding merit ratings was sent to 475 firms having a capitalization of $1,000,000 or over, 160 replies reported an interest in merit rating as follows:[2]

	Number	Per Cent
Using Merit Rating....................	43	26.8
Planning to Use it.	15	9.4
Not Using nor Planning to Use it......	102	64.8
Total........................	160	100

Merit ratings, to a large extent, must depend upon personal estimates because many important traits of employees cannot be measured by objective tests. Rating scales must be used. *A rating scale is a systematic method of estimating character or personality.*

The benefits of a rating scale. 1. Executives are prone to classify all employees into two large groups: the "good" and the "no-good." The executive may call the "no-good" group "passable," "tolerable," or "just satisfactory," depending upon the mood he is in at the time. Obviously, employees are neither wholly good nor wholly bad, but each has some traits to a high degree and others to a low degree. The use of a rating scale compels the executive to analyze his employees and to obtain a more accurate picture of each person under his supervision.

2. A rating scale also compels an executive to analyze his employees at regular intervals. Many an executive walks by some of his employees every working day for years and never thinks of their specific characteristics. If an employee commits a serious error or refuses to join a labor union, the executive may then hear of the matter and gauge the employee by a single dramatic incident. In most cases, the dramatic incident is an isolated defect of the employee's conduct, because his good qualities are taken for granted. Too many executives are negative-minded toward their employees. They can recite their weaknesses or failures, but are unable to list their positive points.

---

[1] "Rating the Job-Raters," *Business Week*, July 8, 1939.

[2] Asa A. Knowles, *Merit Rating in Industry*. Northeastern University. College of Business Administration, Bureau of Business Research, Boston, Mass.

3. The periodical use of a rating scale discovers the good men sooner and makes them available for the company. These men can be given special training, extra compensation, executive recognition, or opportunities for additional responsibilities or duties.

4. The executive can check or verify his own analyses of employees. If he should rate a man high one month and then rate him low six months later, the cause should be known. Perhaps a trivial incident has changed the estimate of the executive, or he may not really know the employee well enough to rate him. Having a record of his estimates of employees will enable the rater to ascertain his ability to analyze others. His ratings can be compared with those of other executives and his tendencies toward high or low ratings can be discovered. If an executive is a poor judge of human behavior, the rating scale will cause him to realize his peculiarity.

5. Just as the rating scale enables the executive to improve his ability to analyze the employee, so the employee also learns the particular qualities he should develop or eliminate. Few employees know their own strong and weak characteristics. They do not improve themselves, because the management does not tell them what to improve or how to do it. The "Success" books and pep lectures are too general or too inspirational to enable the employees to make direct and tangible applications to their own jobs.

6. The rating scale gives the soulless corporation a personality that is more tangible than the customary executive neglect. The employee is not a mere number on the payroll, nor a cog in the big scheme of industry, but a definite personality. A firm that has several hundred employees cannot depend upon chance to know them. A systematic effort must be made to give the workers the recognition that each human being deserves and desires. It is not necessary to depend upon friendship or chance meetings at clubs when ratings are made regularly. One ambitious employee had difficulty in gaining recognition in his job. Hence, when he learned that the president of the company was scheduled to make a long trip in a Pullman, he arranged to be on the same train, and to occupy a seat near that of the president. While on the train, the president took a liking to the

young man and later promoted him. So great an exhibition of diplomatic initiative should not have been necessary to become known to the man who controlled the progress of his employees.

Kinds of rating scales. The first-used and poorest form of rating scale is the "Yes"—"No" type, and some are still in use in supposedly progressive concerns. It consists of a set of questions which are to be answered "yes" or "no." The following questions are used to rate salesmen and are part of a list of fifty questions that are on the blank of a corporation having a nationally distributed sales force of several thousand men (X refers to the salesman who is to be rated):

1.	Is X a hard worker?	6.	Is X strong willed?
2.	Is X a deep thinker?	7.	Does X live in a big world?
3.	Is X popular?	8.	Is X spiritual?
4.	Is X tolerant?	9.	Is X self-conscious?
5.	Is X tactful?	10.	Is X loyal?

In spite of the fact that quantitative evaluations may be given the answers, such as 10 for perfect conduct or complete possession of a given trait, this rating form is dangerous. No man is either a hard worker or not a hard worker. The rater should not be asked to think in terms of the presence or absence of a generalized trait, but rather in the degrees of possession of the trait. If the general trait is applied to specific situations, then its presence or absence may be noted for those situations.

A more careful attempt to rate employees was the *man-to-man comparison* or *army officers' rating scale*. The officer performing the ratings was instructed to prepare a list of officers of all grades of ability. From this list, he selected persons of typical degrees of ability in a given trait. The names of the typical persons were then written on the "master scale" for that trait. Example of a master scale:

Physical qualities:

Consider physique, neatness, voice, energy, and endurance. Consider how he impresses his men in these respects:

Grade		Weight
Highest	Captain Hill	15
High	Captain Richards	12
Middle	Captain Dorn	9
Low	Captain Hopkins	6
Lowest	Captain Smith	3

After a rating officer had filled in a master scale for a quality, he could then use it for rating subordinates. The subordinate, Lieutenant Jones, was then compared with the various types of men on the master scale and given a numerical rating of from 3 to 15. After he was rated on all the qualities of the rating system, the various numbers for each quality were added together and a total rating recorded for the subordinate.[3]

One value of this kind of scale lies in its plan of getting away from the 100 per cent habit. Many raters have the old public school idea of rating a perfect pupil 100 and the poorest pupils about 70 or 80. To avoid the 100 per cent habit, numerical rating scales should have a maximum total considerably above or below 100.

The big defect in this kind of man-to-man comparison scheme is not in its intrinsic value but in the way it is used by the raters. Very few executives will take the trouble to construct a master scale for each quality to be rated. They will assign numerical grades to the subordinates without making the necessary careful comparisons between men. The scheme is too cumbersome for practical use and, moreover, is theoretically defective.

The graphic or adjective-checking scale, shown in figure 52, is the type of scale most popular among psychologists and businessmen. It is more definite than the army officer scale and takes less time than most other scales. However, it is decidedly deficient in certain important respects. Its chief defect is the fact that human qualities are not quite so general as such a scale implies. As previously stated, personality traits are specific. Initiative may be present under some conditions and in some

[3] Harold E. Burtt, in his *Principles of Employment Psychology,* pp. 333-334 (Houghton Mifflin Company, 1926), points out that "the master scale is a relatively permanent measuring device. One would not use a cotton yardstick for accurate physical measurements because it might shrink overnight. But one's notion of a '75 per cent man' or a 'B grade man' may shrink or stretch in similar fashion, depending on such causal things as the time of day, the digestive condition of the rater, or some compliment or insult that he has recently received. The master scale, however, should not shrink. Comparing the physical qualities of a group of officers with Smith, Jones, Brown, Doe, and Briggs (who ranged from highest to lowest) today and making similar comparisons next week should yield comparable results. For while a 'grouch' might lower one's opinion of the group that was being rated; it would also lower his opinion of Smith, Jones, Brown, Doe, and Briggs. The ratings would all be relative to Smith, Jones, etc., regardless of the mood of the rater."

situations, but almost absent in others.   Similarly, with self-confidence, honesty, industriousness, co-operativeness, and all other behavior qualities.   The riveter who is self-confident while walking along the beams of a thirty-story skyscraper may be a shrinking violet in the ballroom.   Each reader can analyze himself and list certain situations wherein he knows that he is self-confident and other situations where his confidence in himself is almost zero.

One of the most common causes of error in the use of the graphic rating scale is in the definition of each abstract quality. Each quality is defined and these definitions may involve so many different forms of behavior that aspects of the general quality are rated rather than the general quality itself.   An example of such a condition is taken from the "Rating Scale for Salesman Applicant," used by a large sales organization when hiring:

Personality and character.—Consider the applicant's (1) ability to express himself, (2) ability to use good grammar, (3) forcefulness of speech and pleasing voice, (4) ability to listen as well as to talk, (5) tact, (6) optimism, (7) general good fellowship, (8) freedom from bad habits, (9) loyalty to previous employers, (10) sincerity, (11) straightforwardness, (12) ability to win confidence, and (13) ability to hold confidence.

It is impossible for a single rater to keep in mind the thirteen aspects of one quality.   One rater will rate the applicant on one aspect and another will rate him on one or two of the thirteen aspects of the general quality.   Hence, by the mathematics of combinations, it is possible to have 4,096 different evaluations of the *Personality and Character* of the same applicant, and each of the evaluations might be made by the same rater!

Ratings of general traits do not give worthwhile predictions of the success of applicants.   One valuable experiment on the predictive value of such rating was reported by O. R. Johnson.[4] His company had one man who devoted nearly all his time to hiring salesmen and two men who conducted a training course where they became acquainted with the new men.   The two instructors taught the new men and had them give demonstrations of their sales canvasses.   They had an exceptional oppor-

---

[4] O. R. Johnson, "Is the Sales Manager's Opinion of That New Salesman Worth Anything?" *Printers' Ink Weekly,* August 28, 1924, p. 25 ff.

tunity to become acquainted with them and to estimate their ability. In the course of a six months' period, thirty-four salesmen were rated by the two instructors and the man who hired them. Each man made his ratings independently of the other two raters.

After each salesman had been in his territory for two months, a study was made of the predictive value of the rater's estimates according to the eight general qualities. The actual performance of the salesmen, measured in terms of sales, was correlated with the ratings, with the resultant low coefficients of correlation of Table XIX.[5]

TABLE XIX

Agreement between actual performance and A's ratings...	.27
Agreement between actual performance and B's ratings...	.21
Agreement between actual performance and C's ratings...	.16
Agreement between actual performance and the three ratings combined...	.16
Agreement between rater A and rater B...	.24
Agreement between rater A and rater C...	−.20
Agreement between rater B and rater C...	.26

The predictive values of these coefficients are so near chance that they are useless. The executive who attempts to hire applicants on the basis of ratings of general traits should not do so unless statistical investigations demonstrate the reliability of his method.

The above and other general quality rating scales deal with abstractions. The psychologists were compelled to discontinue the study of the mind, as such, and to confine their efforts to objective behavior traits. Executives who rate their employees must do the same thing. They should not think of their employees in terms of general abstract qualities, but rather in terms of the behavior of each employee in specific situations. To overcome the defects inherent in the general quality rating scale, the *specific behavior scale* has been designed for use in several corporations where the management wished to deal with definite characteristics of the employees.

The specific behavior scale consists of a list of the concrete situations or various limited forms of behavior that an employee

---

[5] *Ibid.*

should have or should not have.   This list is longer than that of
any other kind of scale, but it is answered just as readily and
just as easily.[6]

A scale having a specific list of items gives a more helpful picture of the person rated.   If an item has been checked by several
raters, it is a worthwhile indication that that item applies to the
person rated—or at least is sufficiently applicable to be used as
a basis for a conference between the executive and the employee.
See pages 323-326 for an example of this kind of scale.

The chief value of ratings which are made on specific characteristics rather than general qualities is that they enable the executive to give the employee definite suggestions as to what he
should or should not do.   To tell an employee that he should
improve his appearance is not so effective as to tell him that he
should shave more frequently or press his clothes regularly.   To
tell him that he should be more industrious is not so effective as
to ask him to do less "visiting" in the office or to come to work on
time.   When abstractions are rated and the supervisory executive wishes to have an intimate advisory talk with a subordinate,
he usually sermonizes to the employee.   However, if he discusses
definite items with the employee, the latter will know just exactly
what he should do to improve his chances for promotion.

General principles for using and making ratings.   Some of
the principles stated may appear to be dogmatic and academic;
but experience in the use of ratings and a desire to avoid technical
dissertations warrant the brevity of the statements.

1. *The purpose of ratings is constructive rather than critical*
so far as the employee is concerned. . Many executives who use
ratings for the first time give the employees the impression that
they are being spied upon.   Employees do not like to be analyzed merely for the benefit of the employer.   They resent being
catalogued.   They do not want to be analyzed and then labeled
and forgotten until the company needs a person of their classification.   Employees suspect that ratings are merely a device for
getting rid of those who are not up to the required standard of
efficiency.   Therefore, rating scales should not be applied in

[6] Harry Walker Hepner, "Better Judgments of Men," *Industrial Psychology*,
January 1926, p. 24.

any organization unless the employees have had an adequate explanation of the purposes of the ratings.   They should be told that the company wishes to help each employee to help himself, that sermons are not to be preached, but rather that the management wants to give the employees who desire it definite help and counsel in obtaining a promotion through merit.   If the executives can rate the employees without their knowledge, well and good.   However, very few companies can conduct systematic ratings without the knowledge of the employees, and, if it is not done openly, the employees will soon spread rumors of spies and detectives having been hired to catch them in any negligences or petty infractions of rules.   The better plan for the management is to put all the cards on the employees' table, explain the ratings, their constructive purpose, and then rate only those employees who wish to be rated.

2. *Have a joint committee develop the rating plan.*   Many companies that operate successful rating systems have developed the plan through a committee which uses the advice of executives, supervisors, and employees.   As reported in *Business Week:*

A cardinal feature of all plans, quoted again and again, is that "the employee must understand and approve of what is being done." And, in a growing number of such efforts, the labor unions are offering their help.

Summing up the results of such plans, administrators seem agreed that certain results are found in the following ways:

a.   Guesswork and doubt are removed in raising or reducing compensation.   If a man is refused a raise, there is a definite reason which can be proved to him.   And, if he is entitled to more money, he knows how to prove it.

b.   Careful judgment of each man's ability, habits, and adaptability often indicates a weak point which can be corrected.   Thus his right to advancement in position and pay can be more easily determined and gratified.

c.   The rate of "turnover" of misplaced workers is greatly lowered.

d.   Grievances resulting from unfair differentials are reduced, and the settlement of such complaints is greatly aided.

e.   The jobs of the foremen and supervisors are made easier, as they learn to interpret the evaluation and rating method to the employee.

f.   If an accurate and fair means of judging the higher-salaried employees can be worked out, the charges of some classes that "executives are paid too much" can be answered without guesswork.   Further, complaints from some salaried people about too loose a system of evaluation and payment can be ended.[7]

---

[7] "How to Rate Worker's Value," *Business Week,* February 25, 1939.

Rightly used, the development of a rating system[8] can be made the basis of an extensive company educational program. When employees do not participate in management's rating and educational plans, the employees do not respond wholeheartedly to management's well-meant efforts. The violation of this basic principle explains why the manager mentioned in the beginning of this chapter failed to get a worth-while response to his new training courses.

3. *Ratings should be used* once they are gathered. If the company records the ratings on the personnel records of the employees, some benefits can be derived. When a promotion is to be made, the executives do not have to make snap judgments. Ratings should be filed in advance of any emergencies. But their greatest worth may be obtained through a friendly discussion of the ratings with each employee. The executive should point out the strong points in the ratings, ignore those traits that are of no importance to the employer, and plan a definite program for the utilization of the positive qualities of each employee.

4. *Capitalize the strong qualities* of each employee. The negative-minded executive finds it easier to dwell upon the weaknesses of employees than to emphasize their good traits. Most human beings are too conscious of their defects. The tables of psychological problems in Chapter I of this book indicate that the opinions and criticisms of others are the outstanding worries of normal people. And yet human beings do not advance through consciousness of their defects, but rather through the use of their strong qualities. The counselor should try to show the employee how to make use of and capitalize his commendable qualities. The negative traits should be overlooked unless they have a direct bearing on the employee's value to the company.

---

[8] An example of the development of a rating system by co-operation between foremen and labor union workers is presented by C. S. Slocombe in "Psychology of Cooperation," *Personnel Journal*, 1938, vol. 16, pp. 325-332.

FIG. 49.   The card on the facing page is designed to conform to the procedure requiring that each company of the U. S. Steel Corporation shall establish and maintain an index for the purpose of (a) providing a record of eligible candidates for positions to be filled; (b) serving as a factual and statistical record of the operation and progress of the plan. The card is adapted to use in a sorting machine for the purpose of making statistical analyses of the personnel and for speed in finding the few employees, among many thousands, who have the specific qualifications desired to fill certain vacancies. (*From "Plan for Inventory and Appraisal of Executive Personnel," U. S. Steel Corporation, 1938, p. 6.*)

PLANT GENERAL SUPERINTENDENT

TITLE CODE	CODE NO.
2154	01-117-40521

No.	Field	Value
3	DATE OF BIRTH — MONTH	12
	DAY	13
	YEAR	04
4	PROMOTIONAL CLASSIFICATION	3
5	CONDENSED RATING	375
6	PRESENT SALARY PER ANNUM	12000
7	PREVIOUS SALARY PER ANNUM	10000
8	NO. OF SALARY CHANGES	111
9	NO. OF PROMOTIONS	111
10	NO. OF TRANSFERS	
11	NO. OF DEMOTIONS	
12	DISMISSED	
13	LAID OFF	
14	RETIRED	
15	TRAINING AND DEVELOPMENT PROGRAMS — ASSISTANCE-SUPERIOR	X
	GROUP	
	CO. SPECIALIST	
	"OUTSIDE" (Confer.)	
	POSITION ROTATION	
	SPECIAL TRAINING	
16	HEALTH — GOOD	X
	AVERAGE	
	POOR	
17	EDUCATION — HIGH SCHOOL GRAD.	
	COLLEGE GRADUATE	X
	SPECIAL TRAINING	X
18	OUTSTANDING QUALITIES — PERSONALITY	
	INTELLIGENCE	X
	EXECUTIVE ABILITY	X
	PERFORMANCE	
19	DEFICIENCIES — PERSONALITY	X
	INTELLIGENCE	
	EXECUTIVE ABILITY	
	PERFORMANCE	
20	EXPERIENCE — NO. OF YEARS PREVIOUS TO CORP.	10
	NO. OF YEARS WITH CORPORATION	5
21	NO. OF RELATIVES WITH CORP.	03
22	NATIONALITY CODE	13
23	AMERICAN CITIZEN (YES 1 NO 2)	13
24	MARITAL STATUS (MAR. 1 SINGLE 2)	
25	NO. CHILDREN AND OTHER DEPEND.	12
26	HOME (OWNED 1 RENTED 2)	
27	NO. LANGUAGES (EXCLUDING ENGLISH)	
28	GROUP INSURANCE (YES 1 NO 2)	1

Eligible for: (Specify titles of positions other than that currently occupied)

PUNCHING HEADINGS

1 2 3 4 5 6 7 8 9 10 11 12 13 14 15 16 17 18 19 20 21 22 23 24 25 26 27 28

1 2 3 4 5 6 7 8 9 10 11 12 13 14 15 16 17 18 19 20 21 22 23 24 25 26 27 28 29 30 31 32 33 34 35 36 37 38 39 40 41 42 43 44 45 46 47 48 49 50 51 52 53 54 55 56 57 58 59 60 61 62 63 64 65 66 67 68 69 70 71 72 73 74 75 76 77 78 79 80

It is well to remember that every great man had some defects, but that he became famous or successful because of his positive qualities, not because of his weaknesses.

5. *The qualities to be rated should be objective,* and should deal with reactions to tasks and impersonal situations. Investigations indicate that subjective traits and reactions to people cannot be rated with accuracy. However, such traits can often be expressed in objective or impersonal form. The following lists indicate objective and subjective traits:

Objective traits that can be rated	*Subjective traits and reactions to people that cannot be rated*
Talking about himself.	Egotism.
Moral conduct.	Moral attitude.
Output.	Loyalty.
Speed of work.	Personality.
Accuracy of work.	Intolerance.
Originality.	Fair-mindedness.
Carefulness.	Agreeableness.
Time spent in study.	Charm.
Talkativeness.	Power of will.
Leadership record.	Conceit.
Use of English.	Cheerfulness.
Punctuality.	Beauty.
Control of temper.	Sympathy.

6. *Ratings should be based upon past accomplishments rather than upon what the individual may be able to do in the future.* It is important to know what a person may be able to do, but we must judge the future by the past. When necessary to make predictions concerning the future possibilities of an employee, it is well to do it on the basis of all the known information of the employee—ratings, years of service, production, age, attitude toward the proposed new job, and so on. In large organizations it is also well to have rating scales adapted to the various kinds of workers. In most firms it is necessary to have four different rating forms—one for the factory workers, one for the executives, one for the salesmen, and one for the office workers.

7. *Only those who know the employee should rate him.* It may sound absurd to specify that strangers to the individual should not rate him, and yet, in many firms, it is difficult to find

FIG. 50. Harry L. Hollingworth of Co
lumbia University. Those interested in fur
ther study of ratings of people are referred
to his book *Judging Human Character* (D.
Appleton-Century Co., 1922). This is a
basic and classic text in the field of ratings.

persons in executive positions who know all the employees of
large departments.   If necessary, ratings may be made by supervisors or even by fellow employees.   In a department store, the
rating made by a floorman is apt to be more accurate than that
made by a buyer.   A buyer has so little direct contact with the
sales clerk that he does not know him from every angle.   Teachers are often asked to rate students or former students, but their
ratings should be limited to the classroom contacts and should
not include the many outside activities.   When a teacher has a
large class, he seldom becomes acquainted with the students.
Occasionally he does have direct associations with a student in
his home or on the athletic field, and then the classroom estimate
may be modified very decidedly.   The ratings made by ministers
and doctors have little value, because they know people under
limited conditions only.   Few of us conduct ourselves normally
when in the presence of preachers and physicians.

8. *Employees should be dealt with on the basis of more than
one person's ratings.*   No matter how impartial or intelligent the
rater may be, he is apt to commit serious errors, because of the
special conditions under which he deals with the ratee.   The
rater is also conditioned by his own childhood experiences and
has certain unconscious prejudices that will influence his ratings

in spite of his effort to be fair. To prevent unfair and erroneous estimates, it is necessary to have at least three persons rate each employee. If the specific behavior form of rating scale is used by three or more raters, then only those items checked or underlined by two or more raters should be recorded for the employee. If only one rater attributes a trait to an employee, that trait should be disregarded, as it is not indicative of the group estimate.

9. *Ratings do not tell the management what an employee actually is or does.* They show what the group thinks of the employee. However, in many situations, the attitude or estimate of the group is more important than what the person is or can do. If an applicant for a job gives people the impression that he is dishonest or incompetent, they will treat him according to their estimate of him rather than according to his actual qualities. When tests can be given the applicant or employee, it is better to do so than to use ratings, because ratings are a substitute for the measurement of qualities for which no tests now exist. In the course of time, scientific research may produce tests that will be more accurate and objective than our present recourse to group estimates.

10. *The "halo error" is common to all ratings.* The general impression of an individual markedly colors our evaluation of his specific traits. If a person impresses us favorably in a general way, or because of some specific quality that we know he possesses, or because of an outstanding experience with him, we then tend to invest his entire personality with a luster that causes us to overestimate his desirable traits and underestimate his undesirable characteristics. One executive was asked why he rated a certain employee so low in all traits. His answer was to the effect that he did not like people who have small mouths and the particular employee had a small mouth. Some previous experience caused small mouths to become associated with the undesirable kind of personality and this experience colored his estimates of people who had that incidental trait. As we all know, if we like a person, we are apt to attribute all good traits to him. Conversely, if we dislike him, we tend to assign to him all negative traits.

The halo influence on graphic rating scales can be overcome to some extent if the rater will fill in the rating blanks for all em-

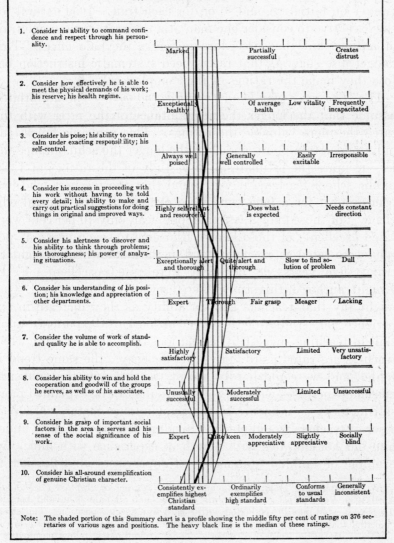

Profile Summary of
CONFIDENTIAL ACHIEVEMENT RATING
Published by the National Council Y. M. C. A.
347 Madison Avenue, New York City

1. Consider his ability to command confidence and respect through his personality.

Marked — Partially successful — Creates distrust

2. Consider how effectively he is able to meet the physical demands of his work; his reserve; his health regime.

Exceptionally healthy — Of average health — Low vitality — Frequently incapacitated

3. Consider his poise; his ability to remain calm under exacting responsibility; his self-control.

Always well poised — Generally well controlled — Easily excitable — Irresponsible

4. Consider his success in proceeding with his work without having to be told every detail; his ability to make and carry out practical suggestions for doing things in original and improved ways.

Highly self-reliant and resourceful — Does what is expected — Needs constant direction

5. Consider his alertness to discover and his ability to think through problems; his thoroughness; his power of analyzing situations.

Exceptionally alert and thorough — Quite alert and thorough — Slow to find solution of problem — Dull

6. Consider his understanding of his position; his knowledge and appreciation of other departments.

Expert — Thorough — Fair grasp — Meager — Lacking

7. Consider the volume of work of standard quality he is able to accomplish.

Highly satisfactory — Satisfactory — Limited — Very unsatisfactory

8. Consider his ability to win and hold the cooperation and goodwill of the groups he serves, as well as of his associates.

Unusually successful — Moderately successful — Limited — Unsuccessful

9. Consider his grasp of important social factors in the area he serves and his sense of the social significance of his work.

Expert — Quite keen — Moderately appreciative — Slightly appreciative — Socially blind

10. Consider his all-around exemplification of genuine Christian character.

Consistently exemplifies highest Christian standard — Ordinarily exemplifies high standard — Conforms to usual standards — Generally inconsistent

Note: The shaded portion of this Summary chart is a profile showing the middle fifty per cent of ratings on 376 secretaries of various ages and positions. The heavy black line is the median of these ratings.

FIG. 51. The shaded portion of this Summary Chart is a profile showing the middle 50 per cent of ratings on 376 secretaries of various ages and positions. The heavy black line is the median of these ratings. When this form is used, a red line represents the average of recent ratings secured on the person whose name appears at the top of this sheet. The chart illustrates the tendency for ratings to be bunched at the favorable end of the scale.

311

ployees by judging the employees on one trait at a time. For example, if twenty employees are to be rated on ten traits, the first trait on the scale being initiative, the judge should rate all twenty on initiative, and so on for each trait. It is natural for the executive to consider one man at a time rather than one trait at a time, but that procedure increases the halo effect. This danger also suggests that raters need systematic instruction before they make the ratings of their employees.[9]

11. *The rater may know the ratee too well.* The uninitiated assume that the longer the acquaintance of the rater with the ratee the more valuable the ratings. This principle holds true only to a certain point, and then the longer the acquaintance the less accurate the estimates. In a study of the ratings of 1,048 public school teachers, it was found that the teachers who had been known for a long time were overrated. In "general efficiency," of those known less than one year, only 10 per cent were rated excellent; of those known from one to seven years, 47 per cent were rated as excellent; and of those known from eight to twenty-five years, 68 per cent were rated excellent. F. B. Knight, author of this study, offered several explanations.[10] One might say that teachers gain in ability as they increase in experience, but studies of the effect of length of experience upon skill in teaching suggest little relationship. Furthermore, when teachers are rated as to "physical efficiency," the same trend is found, and we could hardly accept the principle that physical efficiency increases with age. The results can be explained more satisfactorily as influence of the acquaintance factor. ˑ A supervisor of teachers would not like to admit that the teachers under him did not improve with length of experience with him. An example of familiar statements of supervisors is: "Teacher A

---

[9] W. V. Bingham, "Halo, Invalid and Valid," *Journal of Applied Psychology,* April 1939, Vol. XXIII, No. 2, points out that not all halo is invalid because the person rated may be evaluated with regard to a specific position. This study indicated that "it is not the rater alone whose reactions to the candidate are in question. He is but typical of others—clients, subordinates, fellow employees—who will react to the subject not as a bundle of isolated traits but as a person with certain duties. The judgments and responses of all these people will unconsciously and inevitably manifest a halo effect which is, in part at least, valid."

[10] F. B. Knight, "The Effect of the Acquaintance Factor upon Personal Judgments," *Journal of Educational Psychology,* 1923, Vol. 14, pp. 129-142.

was pretty poor when I got her, but I have developed her into a first-class teacher."

Unconscious identification might also be accepted as an explanation of the older teachers being rated higher.

"One superintendent asked each principal to give the name of his best teacher and state why that teacher was best. Principal A gave as the reason for the superiority of his choice, 'He is a he-man.' Principal B gave as the reason for superiority of her choice, 'She holds up high ideals before her pupils.' Principal A is an ex-athletic director. Principal B is a vigorous Sunday school teacher. Identifying superiority in teachers with the judge's pet hobby seems to be operating here."

Knight also suggests the factor of negative adaptation. We all get used to people. Teachers who have annoying mannerisms soon cease to irritate us and become accepted, whereas the new teacher is more or less on trial. Trivial discrepancies in behavior on the part of new teachers, because they do not "know the ropes," may influence the supervisor's rating far more than efficiency or inefficiency in the classroom.

We might also suggest the tendency of the older teachers to adapt themselves to the idiosyncrasies of the supervisor. The new teacher may not know that the supervisor dislikes the teacher who smokes cigarettes and commits the error of doing so in his presence. The older teachers know the peculiarities of the supervisor and adjust their conduct accordingly. Graduate students in universities realize that they must adapt themselves to the whimsicalities of the major professor who happens to be the key man in determining whether the candidate shall receive the coveted advanced degree. Supervisory executives may pride themselves upon their fairness and impartiality toward subordinates; but it is highly probable that only a few would find ample reasons to promote an employee who openly disagreed with them in political, religious, and athletic interests. The older employee knows the hobbies and beliefs of the supervisor and agrees with them, or at least remains noncommittal on thorny differences.

When length of acquaintance is a matter of hours, days, and months, the longer acquaintances probably result in better ratings; but when it becomes a matter of years, the longer acquaintances are detrimental to accuracy of ratings. Another experiment indicated that we should not only ask the rater, "How long have you known the person to be rated?" but also, "How well do you know the person to be rated?"[11]

Job analyses for employment and promotion purposes.   To promote employees systematically requires several general steps:

1.   Know the employee: ratings, tests, past record, and so on.
2.   Know the jobs in the organization: the one the employee is now holding and the ones to which he might be promoted if he were qualified.
3.   Interview employees periodically, so that the manpower may be utilized for the benefit of employer and employee.

There are several kinds of job analyses, depending upon the purposes for which the analyses are made.   The most common variety is that of the industrial engineer who analyzes jobs for the improvement of working processes and methods.   He prepares, through time and motion studies, performance standards which show him how much work an employee should produce and the best way in which to produce it.   The job analyses of the psychologist or personnel man are for the human relation values in selecting new employees; in promoting, transferring, discharging, and training present employees; and in the establishment of health and equitable wage standards.   In this discussion we shall give emphasis to job analyses for the purpose of promotion.

Strictly speaking, a *job analysis* is simply an abstraction for a variety of operations made by the analyst.   It is the process of collecting information about the jobs in a company.   A *job* or *occupational specification* is a written statement of the facts obtained in the job analysis.   The job specification has two main parts—description of the job and description of the qualifications of the ideal person to fill the job.   The written report or estimate of the qualifications of the ideal person to fill the job should not be confused with the qualifications of the person who is actually on the job.   The person who now holds the job may or may not have the desired qualifications.

---

[11] E. Shen, "The Influence of Friendship upon Personal Ratings," *Journal of Applied Psychology*, September 1925, pp. 66-68.

TYPICAL WORK SHEET FILLED IN FOR A JOB SPECIFICATION
(R for required.   D for desired.   X for items that apply to job.)

GENERAL:
Name of Position—*In Charge of Suggestion Division.*   Symbol............
Dept.—*Better Letters Bureau.*   Div.—*Suggestion.*
No. in Position—*1.*   Number of Subordinates—*2.*
Immediate Superior—*Manager Better Letters Bureau.*
Time Required for Inexperienced Person to Learn Work—*3 years.*
Time Required for Experienced Person to Learn Details of Work Here—
18 months.

QUALIFICATIONS

R Male	D Married	Age Limits—*27 to 40*	Beginner
Female	Single		R Experienced
			Expert

EDUCATION: Common   High School   College
Required—None 6 7 8   I II III IV   A B C D   Desired   D
Courses Required—*Psychology, English.*
Courses Desired—*Salesmanship, Better Letters, Office Manager's Course, Factory Course.*

EXPERIENCE:
Required—*On Policy and Product.   1 year in Division as Assistant.*
Desired—*Office Manager, Salesman, Newspaper Work.*

Manual	Meets Public	x Desk	x Indoors
Clerical	xx Meets Employees	Standing	Outdoors
Correspondence		Stooping	
x Promotional	x Plans Broadly	x Walking	Travels Much
x Supervisory	x Attends Details		xx Travels Little
Technical		xx Varied	
Research	Major Responsibility	Routine	Artificial Light
Managerial	x Medium Responsibility	Automatic	x Natural Light
Executive	Minor Responsibility		

DESCRIPTION OF JOB:
1. State duties of supervision and responsibility.   2. Operations in work.
    3. Occasional duties.   4. Machines and appliances used.   5. Relationship to other jobs.
Works under supervision of Manager of Better Letters Bureau.   Is responsible to the Board of Control for making a preliminary survey of all suggestions submitted by employees of the General Offices, branches, and service stations; for tactfully informing employees of action taken in regard to their suggestions; and for the proper publicity of the suggestion system.
Eliminates only those suggestions which are obviously of no value; the others are investigated as to their worth and reviewed by the Suggestion Committee (a committee of three men, the man in charge of the Suggestion Division having an equal vote with the other two members).   All decisions are subject to review by Board of Control at any time.
Submits a detailed report every week to Board of Control showing in regard to suggestions: the number submitted, their value, the departments affected, reason for action taken, and a résumé of each.
When a suggestion is received, it is copied on a standard form and sent to qualified members of the organization, who report its worth.   Follows up these investigations to see that contents are made so that Suggestion Committee can make an intelligent and tactful reply to every person who submits a suggestion.

The job analysis procedure usually begins with the preparation of a work sheet wherewith the analyst can go into the shop or office and obtain the pertinent facts of the jobs in the organization. The analyst takes a supply of the work sheets to the department head or foreman and explains the purpose of the job analysis. By discussing the work and the kinds of jobs of the executive's department, the analyst obtains a general idea of the activities of the jobs and the relationships of the jobs which he is about to analyze. The employees on the several kinds of jobs are then interviewed and the work sheets are filled in in preparation for the typing of the complete job specification. When the data have been collected, written on the work sheets, and arranged in logical order, the revised work sheets or job specifications are then taken to the responsible department head for correction and approval. In most cases some corrections must be made. The data on the corrected work sheets are then typed on the final work sheet, which is now considered to be the job specification, as it includes the qualifications of the ideal person to fill the job. One specification is made for each kind of job in the organization.

The guide for classifying the jobs, or master job-classification chart. When the specifications have been completed for the various jobs in the organization, each job must be graded or zoned. The purpose of zoning or grading is to determine the relative value and importance of the jobs. The guide for classifying the jobs is a description of typical grades of jobs in the company. The classification chart is a kind of scale which enables the management to grade the jobs, determine the salary ranges for each zone, and prepare promotion charts for the development of each employee. Wage or salary studies can also be made of all the jobs in the company, as some employees who receive a Grade 4 salary may be doing Grade 5 work, or vice versa.

If the management wishes to succeed in increasing the efficiency of the individual employee, some responsible executive must know the nature and grade of the job of each employee. He should be able to evaluate correctly any job in relation to the other jobs in the organization and in relation to the jobs in other industrial concerns. It is very easy to overestimate the importance of low-grade jobs and to underestimate the higher-grade jobs.   Example: when an employee says that he is "Clerk on the Outgoing Requisitions of the Purchasing Department," it may mean that he is a little higher than the office boy or it may mean that he is an assistant purchasing agent.   By means of the guide for classifying jobs and the job specification, any job may be properly classified as to grade or zone of importance.   Such a guide or master job classification chart was made by the writer for the 1600 general office jobs of a large rubber concern and is shown in Table XX.

TABLE XX

GUIDE FOR CLASSIFYING JOBS

Grade 8.   DEPARTMENT MANAGER.   Salary range: $333 mo. and up.
  Is responsible for the efficient operation of a department:
    a.   Interprets and executes company policies relative to department.
    b.   Initiates and executes departmental policies.
    c.   Co-ordinates activities of divisions and actions of the department.
    d.   Co-ordinates activities of his own department with the activities of other departments.
    e.   Originates and puts into effect procedural changes in departmental activities.
    f.   Passes approval on all departmental expenditures.
Intelligence: Superior (A or B on Army Alpha).

Grade 7.   DIVISION HEAD.   Salary range: $250-350.
  Is responsible for the efficient operation of a recognized division:
    a.   Plans and carries out divisional activities.
    b.   Co-ordinates activities of sections and employees of the division.
    c.   Originates and, upon approval of department head, puts into effect procedural changes in activities of the division.
    d.   In division having specialized functions of a staff nature, is responsible for and assists in making investigations, preparing special reports on subjects such as sales, markets, industrial plants, etc.
    e.   In division having operating function, is responsible for the operation of the division—discipline of employees, planning and scheduling their work, preparing routine reports, etc.
Intelligence: Superior (A or B).

Grade 6.   SPECIALIST.   Salary range: $200 and up.
  Under supervision of a department or division head, investigates, analyzes, recommends, and prepares reports on subjects mostly of technical nature, such as markets, sales, finance, employment, inventions, company organizations, industrial plants, etc.
Intelligence: Superior (A or B).

Grade 5.   SENIOR CLERK OR CORRESPONDENT.   Salary range: $175-225.
  Performs varied clerical work requiring high intelligence, involving any or all of the following:
    a.   Directs other clerks doing work related to his own.
    b.   Prepares reports from complicated data which is unassembled and must be digested and analyzed.
    c.   Authorizes, under general supervision of supervisor, orders such as for shipment of advertising literature to dealers.

TABLE XX (*Continued*)

    d. Conducts correspondence which is incidental to clerical duties, such as answering inquiries and adjusting complaints from customers and branches.

    e. Uses mathematics and needs a thorough knowledge of use and principles of trade formulæ.

Intelligence: High average (C+).

Grade 4. GENERAL CLERK. Salary range: $140-175.

Performs varied clerical work, which requires average or above-average intelligence, involving any or all of the following:

    a. Gathers data without direct supervision for reports from files or from company employees. Reports are inspected and signed by a superior.

    b. Writes letters to branches over own signature on subjects of a routine nature or prepares letters involving company policies for signature of superior. Answers inquiries of a simple nature only.

    c. Investigates matters of clerical nature for superior.

    d. Uses arithmetic, such as percentages.

Intelligence: Average or High Average (C or C+).

Grade 3. UTILITY CLERK. Salary range: $110-140.

Performs clerical work of a semi-routine or repetitive nature, involving any or all of the following:

    a. Gathers data for reports from files under the direct supervision of higher-grade clerk or superior.

    b. Inspects card or other records for accuracy by comparing them with data which is not in same form as that of the record.

    c. Sorts data topically and prepares it for transcription.

    d. Answers telephone or personal inquiries which involve a knowledge of records and files.

    e. Sends form letters to branches requesting information.

    f. Uses simple arithmetic.

Intelligence: Average (C).

Grade 2. JUNIOR CLERK. Salary range: $65-110.

Performs such minor clerical work of a routine or automatic nature involving any or all of the following:

    a. Files correspondence or cards alphabetically.

    b. Transcribes data from temporary to permanent records.

    c. Sorts and assembles cards or papers in a numerical or alphabetical order.

    d. Posts noncomplicated data to proper cards or records.

    e. Checks lists with master lists.

    f. Answers telephone and refers to a superior all questions on phases of work except those of a very simple nature.

Intelligence: Average (C).

Grade 1. OFFICE BOY. Salary range: $52-65.

Runs errands, delivers messages, sorts and distributes papers, and does other miscellaneous work.

Intelligence: Low Average (C−).

One aid whereby employees can identify themselves with the company is to have a clear-cut promotion system which any employee can understand. Even though an employee may not be interested in becoming anything other than what he is, yet a concern which has a promotion system rates higher in the estimation of the employees than the firm where promotions are mysterious things that seem to be acquired by the "lucky fellows with a pull." Children go through school by doing the work of the specified grades. Promotion is systematic. Each child has a definite scholastic goal before him. The method of getting into the next grade is known to all pupils. In industry, the method of getting into a higher job is largely a mysterious thing about which nothing definite is understood. The promotion chart takes the mystery out of promotions. Most promotion charts of the past have been drawn up very elaborately and have shown how any employee must follow certain very definite lines of travel in going from the bottom to the top. The "railroad track" schemes of promotion do not work out under actual conditions, because human nature is adaptable. The employee adapts himself to the job and adjusts the job to his limitations.

The fact that a youth happens to be the office boy in the purchasing department does not mean that he must become a purchasing agent in order to use his native capacities. It is rather probable that he might become the head of the mail-order department or assistant to the traffic manager. In many large concerns one does not find that the general manager has had production, sales, finance, and other forms of business experience, but rather that he has come from some other field, and often an unrelated one. The reason why a lawyer can be a good general manager is not that law gives him the training he needs, but that the lawyer has high *general intelligence* and can adapt himself to managerial requirements. The same factor holds true with the rank and file of employees—the ones with high general intelligence, industry, initiative, and so on, could advance equally readily in any of several departments rather than in one particular department. The old idea that a man is fitted for only one particular occupation is not accepted by the psychologist. We find, rather, that each man is equally well fitted for several things and not perfectly fitted for any one of the several. Human beings are adaptable, and any scheme of promotion must recognize the factor of adaptability. Promotions should be interdepartmental as well as intradepartmental. Employees should be al-

lowed to see the promotion charts.   One large concern has found
it desirable to post the promotion chart for each department on
the wall of the office where the employees are working.

A promotion system connected with a training system.   Some
company managers try to follow a rigid policy that all promotions
should be made from within the organization.   Such a policy is
likely to result in an unhealthy inbreeding and an excess of deadwood in the supervisory force.

It has been our experience that promotion-from-within [without a training program] results in a very mediocre grade of supervision.   Occasionally
we were fortunate to get an outstanding man, but to most' of them supervision is only a higher degree of performance on their previous occupation.
They lack the breadth of viewpoint, and other inherent characteristics of
management usually apparent in men who are capable of assimilating good
educational background and experience.[12]

In view of the dangers mentioned above, some personnel managers have a definite policy to the effect that approximately 20
per cent of all promotions are made from the outside.   Employees
have the policy explained to them and the reasons for it.   Almost
every organization needs the stimulating effects of "new blood"
occasionally.   On the other hand, some companies believe that a
long history within the company is essential to the company's
welfare.

In the broad, the policy of our company throughout the years has been
one of promotion from within its own ranks as higher positions of responsibility have become vacant. A majority of our officers and principal employees have a long history with the company—many of them having come
in as students or apprentices at young years.   This is true not only of executives, but, in not a few cases, of men who are in high technical positions. . . .
There is, however, no question in our minds whatever but that our Works
Supervisors who come up from within the organization are those in whom
we can put the greatest dependence.[13]

It is apparent from the above and similar statements by industrial executives that developing effective supervisors and at
the same time using promotions to increase incentive among the
wage-earners is a continual process of careful selection for promotion from within, with sufficient infiltration of new employees

---

[12] Helen Baker, *Company Plans for Employee Promotions*, Industrial Relations
Section, Princeton University, 1939, Report No. 58.
[13] *Ibid.*

qualified for promotion into the supervisory level. More and more companies are making a special effort to employ and train college graduates for management jobs. When these better-educated employees are the only ones who are encouraged to prepare for advancement, there is usually some feeling of bitterness among other employees. When a plan of promotion from within applies to all employees and upgrading in all classes is according to acceptable technical requirements, then there seems to be little criticism against the special training program for college graduates.

The development program of every interested employee. In most modern concerns, many employees have already reached the limit of their capacity. Some employees recognize this and are contented. Others do not realize their limitations and picture themselves as sales managers or factory managers. The latter group must be handled very tactfully, and, inasmuch as they really are seeking some means of self-expression rather than responsible managerial jobs, the counselor of the personnel should explain these facts to the employee and help him to express his individuality in some manner which fits his capacity and circumstances.

A certain percentage of the employees, as shown by the ratings and job specifications, will be found capable of greater achievement. These are the employees most worthy of attention and are the ones which the company will need most in the future. The executive in charge of personnel should try to understand and appreciate these employees and outline a plan of development for each one of this group.

The number of executives in business who have interviews with their employees for the purpose of helping each employee to develop himself is small indeed. In fact, such executives are exceedingly rare. Moreover, when an executive does have a talk with an employee regarding his future development, the executive practically never clinches his counsel. The employee usually leaves with a vague or generalized set of platitudes which are of no practical value. The one thing which must be done to vitalize the interview is to help the employee to outline a definite development program so that he will know just what he should do in order to merit promotion.

EXAMPLE OF AN EMPLOYEE DEVELOPMENT PROGRAM

Employee's background:

Age 38. Married. College graduate. Present position that of assistant to the general manager. Has had 2 years of factory and 5 years of sales experience. Has been in supervisory and technical work in the offices for 6 years. Greatly interested in people. Good social poise. Jovial. A leader in the Boy Scout movement and one fraternal organization. Enjoys reading on all subjects. Subscribes for 8 business and semi-scientific magazines.

Goal:

Prepare for work of Personnel Counselor in an industrial concern having 2,000 factory workers and 250 office and sales employees.

Development program:

A. Read the following books:

1. Balderston, C. Canby, *Executive Guidance of Industrial Relations.* Univ. of Pennsylvania Press, 1935.

2. Baridon, F. E., and Loomis, E. H., *Personnel Problems, Methods of Analysis and Control.* McGraw-Hill Book Co., 1931.

3. Hepner, H. W., *Human Relations. in Changing Industry.* Prentice-Hall, Inc., 1934.

4. Hersey, Rexford B., *Workers' Emotions in Shop and Home.* Univ. of Pennsylvania Press, 1932.

5. Houser, J. David, *What People Want from Business.* McGraw-Hill Book Co., 1938.

6. Shepard, Jean L., *Human Nature at Work.* Harper & Bros., 1938.

7. Viteles, Morris S., *Industrial Psychology.* W. W. Norton & Co., 1932.

B. Practice of the analysis of men by analyzing several. Use psychological tests and other methods. Take the data to a university psychologist and let him criticize it.

C. Get into touch with several men in other concerns who have had experience in analyzing and handling men and find out what they do and how they do it.

D. Have dinner with key executives of our own company and discuss with them the individualizing of the relationship between employer and employee. Sell them on the idea.

E. Draw up a plan of employment office procedure for one year.

The program given above is for an unusual type of individual and job. In most cases the program would deal with the taking of correspondence or night school courses, the reading of certain books, the interviewing of certain men, and the correction of personality defects.

Very few executives have the time, the ability, or the inclination to interview their employees and plan a program of training for each ambitious employee. For this reason it is best to concentrate such individualized personnel work in the hands of one man, such as the personnel counselor, and then hold him responsible for results.

The executive in charge of promotions, training, or personnel should put his suggestions in writing. A duplicate copy of the program outlined for each employee should be kept in the files of the counselor, and, when the next interview is held with the employee, the counselor should find out what progress the employee has made. If changes in the program are desirable, they should be made, but the employee should be able to give a satisfactory explanation for the changes.

The chief value of such a personnel program lies in the fact that it individualizes the relation between the employer and the employee and puts the relationship on an economic rather than on a group philanthropic basis. Most writers who discuss personnel work hark back to a description of the guild system when each worker knew the master personally. This is supposed to be the ideal system, because the modern impersonal relation between the corporation and the employee was absent. The scheme set forth in this chapter is one means of individualizing the relation between the large corporation and the employee, in order that the relationship shall not be paternalistic but economically and psychologically sound.

Survey of Outstanding Traits

Name of Person to Be Analyzed ....

The purpose of this blank is constructive.

Very few people know the characteristics in which they are strong. Nor do they know the ones in which they are weak. This blank is to be filled in by three or more individuals who know the person mentioned above.

The person mentioned above has requested this survey in order to enable him to understand himself better. The data which you and his other raters give him will be summarized and then given to the person rated. He will not know what any one person has said of him, because all the data will be mixed into one summary. Therefore, you can feel free to be frank, because you will know that your statements will be confidential.

You need not fear that you may be prejudiced for or against the person rated, because any prejudices will probably be counter-balanced by the other persons who rate him.

As you will note, the points to be considered are divided into two lists: *Positive or Commendable Traits* and *Negative or Improvable Traits*. It is realized that no person in existence has all or even most of the commendable traits. Nor is it expected that any person should have all of them. We also realize that each person has some of the improvable traits. However, if the person rated knows what his good points are, he may then be able to utilize his good points to greater advantage. Likewise, if he knows the improvable traits, he can then improve or compensate for them.

Try to think of the outstanding characteristics of the person whose name is given above.

Check or underline the points which you believe to apply to him. You can check as many or as few items under any heading as you wish. If you want to make any additional comments on some items, write them in the margin.

POSITIVE OR COMMENDABLE TRAITS	NEGATIVE OR IMPROVABLE TRAITS

PHYSICAL CHARACTERISTICS

Has very good health.	Should improve his health.
	Bad breath.
Very calm in emergencies.	Certain muscles twitch.
	Bad odors about person.
Has lots of energy on the job.	Should show more energy and pep.
	Goes to pieces in emergencies.

APPEARANCE

	Should
Dresses very neatly.	Be more cleanly in person.
	Shave more frequently.
Good facial expression.	Improve facial expression.
	Use less cosmetics.
Always makes a good appearance.	Press clothes more frequently.

CONVERSATION

	Should
Uses very good grammar.	Improve grammar.
	Talk more.
Carries on conversation well.	Do less talking and more listening.
	Improve tone of voice.
Has very good sense of humor.	Be less solemn and more humorous.
	Be less sarcastic.
Is enthusiastic.	Be more enthusiastic.
	Argue less.
Speaks well of others.	Speak well of others more often.
	Talk less about own interests.
Retains company matters to self.	Keep company matters to self.
	Look people in eye while talking.
Can talk to all kinds of people.	Try to talk to all kinds of people.
	Listen more attentively.
Listens attentively.	Improve vocabulary.
	Omit pet phrases such as . . . .

POSITIVE OR COMMENDABLE TRAITS	NEGATIVE OR IMPROVABLE TRAITS

Manner Toward Others

Should

	Try to be more tactful.
Is very tactful.	Be less easily persuaded.
Understands human nature.	Learn more about human nature.
	Select better companions.
Mixes pleasure and work properly.	Attend more social affairs.
	Attend fewer social affairs.
Always greets people with a smile.	Smile more often.
	Not assume air of independence.
Shows right amount of appreciation.	Express appreciation more often.
	Be less familiar.
Can see the other fellow's views.	Try to see all sides of a question.
Never borrows money for trivialities.	Borrow less money.
Has very good manners.	Study social etiquette.

Mental Efficiency

Should

	Work more systematically.
Attacks work systematically.	Pay more attention to details.
Good memory for names of people.	Determine to remember names.
	Get more general knowledge.
Good memory for company facts.	Remember facts about work.
	Learn more about certain subjects
Always seeking new ideas.	such as ....

Attitude Toward Self

	Overestimates his worth.
Has proper respect for self.	Should
	Not look down on himself.
Controls temper well.	Control temper.
	Be less sensitive.
Troubles make little impression.	Think less about own troubles.
	Make less effort to be in limelight.
Stands up for what he believes right.	Stand up for own ideas.
	Be less self-conscious.
Accepts criticism in right spirit.	Realize that criticisms are to help and not to hurt.

Moral Traits

Believe him absolutely honest.	Doubt honesty under pressure.
	Should
Consider him very dependable.	Stop dissipating.
	Be more dependable.
Conversation is clean.	Control sex impulse.
	Use less profanity.

Conduct on the Job

(If you, the rater, have little knowledge of his work, check only those items that you know.)

	Is not loyal to his company.
	Should
Seldom loses time off job.	Take less time off the job.
Does more than just necessary.	

POSITIVE OR COMMENDABLE TRAITS	NEGATIVE OR IMPROVABLE TRAITS
	Should
Co-operates with superiors.	Do more than absolutely necessary.
Co-operates with everybody.	Co-operate with everybody.
Handles employees well.	Not fear the boss.
Popular with fellow-employees.	Try to please other employees.
Does not side-step blame.	Do less "visiting" at work.
Handles responsibilities well.	Accept blame when it is due.
Works without "crabbing."	Seek more responsibilities.
Works overtime without request.	Not "crab" about the work.
Gets work done on time.	Do his share of overtime.
Does work very accurately.	Try to get to work on time.
Turns out large quantities of work.	Improve accuracy.
Uses head on the job.	Turn out more work.
Makes many good suggestions.	Think more about *how* to do work.
Difficulties do not stop him.	Make some suggestions for work.
Very loyal to the company.	Not let difficulties stop him.
Gets to work on time.	Improve handwriting.
Concentrates well.	Waste less time on job.

Add any additional items which you think might be of value to the person rated. Explain any points which might be misunderstood.

....

....

For what kind of work do you think that this person is best fitted? Or how might he increase his chances for advancement?

....

....

NAME OF PERSON MAKING RATING...

PLEASE SEND THIS BLANK IN A SEALED ENVELOPE TO.........................

....

References

Bingham, W. V., "Halo, Invalid and Valid," *Journal of Applied Psychology*, April 1939, Vol. XXIII, No. 2, pp. 221-228.

Burtt, Harold E., *Principles of Employment Psychology*, Chapter XII. Houghton Mifflin Co., 1926.

Hay, Edward N., "Planning for Fair Salaries and Wages," *Personnel Journal*, October 1939.

Moore, Herbert, *Psychology for Business and Industry*, Chapter VIII. McGraw-Hill Book Co., 1939.

Riegel, John W., *Salary Determination*. Bureau of Industrial Relations, University of Michigan.

Strong, Edward K., Jr., *Psychological Aspects of Business*, Chapters XXIV and XXVI. McGraw-Hill Book Co., 1938.

Projects

1. Examine several graphic rating scales for general traits such as initiative, personality, etc. Select the traits that are objective in nature and those that are reactions to persons. Select several general traits and break them down into the specific forms of behavior to which they may apply.

2. Construct a "specific item" scale for the rating of employees of a firm whose personnel problems you know.

3. Construct a work sheet for the analysis of jobs within a company whose personnel problems you know. On it analyze and describe a particular job.

4. Describe the differences between a job analysis work sheet and a blank for the application of employment.

5. Grade the various jobs within a department or company and prepare a promotion chart for the employees who have the jobs. Suggest definite forms of training for the employee who wishes to be promoted to some definite job on the promotion chart.

6. Interview and study an employee and prepare a "Development Program" that seems to meet his situation and desires.

7. Discuss reasons why some students may disagree with an instructor regarding marks given in a course. Most students consider their marks satisfactory but a small percentage do not, as indicated by one study[14] of opinions of a group of college students concerning their marks. Students in education in the Eastern Illinois State Teachers College were asked to list courses taken in the winter quarter and to state (anonymously) whether they considered the marks too high or too low and why. Of 396 students, 80 per cent considered the marks satisfactory, 5 per cent too high, and 15 per cent too low. The percentage of satisfaction varied with the height of the mark. Slightly more men than women were dissatisfied. The reasons given for thinking the marks too high were: "Did too little work," "Received lower marks during the quarter," and "Knew too little about the course." The reasons given for thinking the marks too low were: "Received higher marks during the quarter," "Worked hard," and "Did as well as others."

8. Perhaps you think that a person can be judged more fairly by means of an anecdotal behavior journal, a cumulative record of characteristic behavior patterns, than by means of rating scales. If so, investigate the anecdotal behavior procedure. A good source with bibliography is J. A. Randall "The Anecdotal Behavior Journal," *Progressive Education,* January 1936.

9. If you were working in a company where employees on jobs of the same grade were paid inequitably, what would you do about the inequality? Consider, for example, the following situation:

Professor C. Canby Balderston of the Wharton School of Finance and Commerce of the University of Pennsylvania reported factual data resulting from job analyses applying to 12,000 employees of a single company where previously existing rates were set by a large number of department heads. The study showed that compensation varied as much as 460 per cent from minimum to maximum on one set of jobs graded for equal difficulty and as little as 25 per cent in another grade. The average spread of all jobs was 145 per cent. (Condensed from Ralph P. Worden, *Connecticut Industry,* March 1941.)

[14] E. Reinhardt, *School & Society,* 1937, Vol. 46, pp. 447-448.

RATING FORM FOR USE OF INTERVIEWERS

INSTRUCTIONS: Ask yourself how this applicant compares with those who are doing work of this kind. Consider whether his voice, appearance, etc., would be a liability or an asset in such a position. Rate him by making a check (√) at that point on each scale where, in your judgment, the applicant stands. Rate the following traits:

1. **VOICE AND SPEECH.** Is the applicant's voice irritating, or pleasant? Can you easily hear what he says? Does he mumble, or talk with an accent which offends or baffles the listener? Or is his speech clear and distinct, his voice so rich, resonant and well-modulated that it would be a valuable asset in this position?

2. **APPEARANCE.** What sort of first impression does he make? Does he look like a well-set-up, healthy, energetic person? Has he bodily or facial characteristics which might seriously hamper him? Is he well-groomed or slovenly? Erect or slouchy? Attractive or unattractive in appearance?

3. **ALERTNESS.** How readily does he grasp the meaning of a question? Is he slow to apprehend even the more obvious points, or does he understand quickly, even though the idea is new, involved or difficult?

4. **ABILITY TO PRESENT IDEAS.** Does he speak logically and convincingly? Or does he tend to be vague, confused or illogical?

5. **JUDGMENT.** Does he impress you as a person whose judgment would be dependable even under stress? Or is he hasty, erratic, biased, swayed by his feelings?

6. **EMOTIONAL STABILITY.** How well poised is he emotionally? Is he touchy, sensitive to criticism, easily upset? Is he irritated or impatient when things go wrong? Or does he keep an even keel?

7. **SELF-CONFIDENCE.** Does he seem to be uncertain of himself, hesitant, lacking in assurance, easily bluffed? Or is he wholesomely self-confident and assured?

8. **FRIENDLINESS.** Is he a likeable person? Will his fellow-workers and subordinates be drawn to him, or kept at a distance? Does he command personal loyalty and devotion?

9. **PERSONAL FITNESS FOR THE POSITION.** In the light of all the evidence regarding this person's characteristics (whether mentioned above or not) how do you rate his personal suitability for work such as he is considering? Recalling that it is not in his best interest to recommend him for such a position if he is better suited for something else, would you urge him to undertake this work? Do you endorse his application?

Fuller instructions and space for comments on applicant's behavior will be found on the back of this sheet (see pages 330 and 331).

Fig. 52. On the following four pages is a graphic or adjective-checking rating scale. Note that this form can be scored mechanically. This rating scale, prepared by W. V.

AND ORAL EXAMINERS — 2 — 1938

Applicant's Name or
Identification Number .... Date...............

Kind of work for which his
suitability is appraised ....

| Irritating or Indistinct | Understandable but rather unpleasant | Neither conspicuously pleasant nor unpleasant | Definitely pleasant and distinct | Exceptionally clear and pleasing |

| Unprepossessing or Unsuitable | Creates rather unfavorable impression | Suitable Acceptable | Creates distinctly favorable Impression | Impressive Commands admiration |

| Slow in grasping the obvious. Often misunderstands meaning of questions | Slow to understand subtle points. Requires explanation | Nearly always grasps intent of interviewer's questions | Rather quick in grasping questions and new ideas | Exceptionally keen and quick to understand |

| Confused and illogical | Tends to scatter or to become involved | Usually gets his ideas across well | Shows superior ability to express himself | Unusually logical clear and convincing |

| Notably lacking in balance and restraint | Shows some tendency to react impulsively and without restraint | Acts judiciously in ordinary circumstances Might be hasty in emergencies | Gives reassuring evidences of habit of considered judgment | Inspires unusual confidence in probable soundness of judgment |

| Over-sensitive Easily disconcerted | Occasionally impatient or irritated | Well poised most of the time | Superior self-command | Shows exceptional poise, calmness and good humor under stress |

| Timid. Hesitant Easily influenced | Appears to be over-self-conscious | Moderately confident of himself | Wholesomely self-confident | Shows superb self-assurance |

| Keeps people at a distance | Does not easily attract friends | Approachable Likeable | Draws many friends to him | An inspirer of personal devotion and loyalty |

| Unsuited for this work. Not endorsed | Might do well. Endorsed with hesitance | Endorsed | Endorsed with confidence | Endorsed with enthusiasm |

SIGNATURE OF RATER

This rating form prepared from suggestions furnished by W. V. Bingham.

Bingham, is explained by him in "Oral Examinations in Civil Service Recruitment,"
Pamphlet No. 13, February 1939, Civil Service Assembly, 1313 East 60th Street, Chicago.

329

Fig. 52 *(Cont.)*

INSTRUCTIONS TO INTERVIEWERS AND ORAL EXAMINERS

You are to rate the candidate on certain characteristics which have a bearing on the likelihood that he will be successful in the position for which he is an applicant but which are not measured by a rating of his experience and training, nor by his performance in a written examination, but which can be observed when you talk with him face to face.

Keeping in mind the kinds of duties the candidate will be called upon to perform, consider whether his personal characteristics, as they reveal themselves during the interview, will be an asset or a liability in filling such a position. Do not rate him on his technical knowledge or lack of knowledge of the job. Do not let your estimates of his personal qualities be colored by what he may tell you about his experience or lack of experience.

If his voice, for example, is so rasping or weak that it would give to those with whom he talks an unfavorable impression, you will rate him low in this trait, toward the left end of that scale. If it is neither noticeably pleasant nor unpleasant, you should rate him at or near the middle of the scale. If his speech is free from disturbing peculiarities of accent and his voice so clear and resonant that it would be a distinct asset in the work he will do, rate him somewhere on the right half of the scale.

Similarly, rate the candidate on each of the other traits, keeping in mind the definitions of these traits as given on the Rating Form. If a candidate has made no impression on you whatever, either favorable or unfavorable, so far as one of these traits is concerned, rate him at the midpoint of that particular scale. Record your tentative rating on each trait, by putting a check-mark (√) on the proper scale at the point where, in your judgment, the candidate belongs.

A rating need not fall exactly at one of the subdivisions of the scale. You may place it at either extreme, or anywhere between.

Base your estimates of the applicant's characteristics solely on evidences observed during the interview.

Be sure to record your rating of the applicant on each of the traits. Do not omit any.

When rating the last trait, "Personal Fitness," if—quite apart from any inexperience or lack of technical knowledge which he may have revealed—you consider him definitely unsuited for the position, rate him far to the left. If he barely qualifies, that is, if you are prepared to endorse him as personally suited for this work but can endorse him only with some hesitance, mark him midway between the lower end and the middle of the scale. If you can endorse him with confidence, or with enthusiasm, place your check mark well to the right of the middle.

After you have interviewed several candidates and discussed the evidences of their personal suitability with other examiners, you are at liberty to revise your ratings. This is done by putting your initials above each new check-mark you make.

You may use for comments the appropriate spaces to the right.

Fig. 52 *(Cont.)*

SPACE FOR COMMENT

1. VOICE AND SPEECH

2. APPEARANCE

3. ALERTNESS

4. ABILITY TO PRESENT IDEAS

5. JUDGMENT

6. EMOTIONAL STABILITY

7. SELF-CONFIDENCE

8. FRIENDLINESS

9. PERSONAL FITNESS FOR THE POSITION

SUGGESTIONS

13

Choosing a Vocation

Many people think of choosing a vocation as wholly a problem in prediction of the person's future vocational abilities, successes or failures. Psychologists, too, are interested in facilitating the individual's choice by means of valid prediction devices but they are even more interested in improving his adjustments to the possibilities within himself and his environment. The psychologically well-adjusted person is likely to be a vocationally happy person.

ONE OF the pioneers in the field of vocational guidance became interested in the work because he met a boy who worked in a bird store during the day and studied architectural drawing at night, but had an ambition to become a sea captain! We all know of similar persons who are heartily dissatisfied with their jobs, many others who accept their daily grind because they do not know what else to do, and a few who are really enthusiastic about their work.

The problem of vocational misfits. The editors of *Fortune* conducted a national survey on occupational contentment. The answers by age and sex to the question, "If you could go back to the age of eighteen and start life over again, would you choose a different career or occupation?" are given in Table XXI, by age and sex, as well as for the total response.

TABLE XXI[1]

	Total	Age		Sex	
		20 to 40	Over 40	Men	Women
Yes, a different career	41.0%	39.0%	43.0%	44.8%	37.0%
No	39.2	40.3	37.9	34.9	43.5
Depends on circumstances	15.2	15.9	14.6	15.9	14.6
Don't know	4.6	4.8	4.5	4.4	4.9

[1] Reprinted by permission of the editors of *Fortune,* Vol. XVII, No. 1, January 1938. This material is a part of the magazine's eleventh quarterly Survey of Public Opinion, based on "a controlled sampling of the public." Questions were

In comparison with the men, a slightly higher percentage of women were contented with their chosen lot. Of course, many of these were housewives rather than gainfully employed. The survey also indicated that 55.4 per cent of the prosperous were glad to cling to the careers by which they presumably became prosperous. Among the poor, only 30.2 per cent were reported as willing to repeat their choice of occupations. Professional status also appeared to be an important factor in satisfaction, as shown by a comparison of the professional and factory workers.

	Professional	Factory Labor
Yes, a different career.	29.0%	61.3%
No.	53.3	21.3

Daniel Starch made a national survey[2] which throws some light on the question of occupational contentment. A cross-section of average Americans were asked the question: "If you had your life to live over again, what three things would you do differently?"

Following are the most frequently mentioned things which people would do differently, ranked in the order of the percentages of all persons interviewed who mentioned each one:

Different occupation.	32.7
More education.	30.4
Save more money.	14.7

The Starch survey revealed that wholly satisfied individuals are to be found in all walks of life. The occupation as such is not so important as the individual's adjustment to it.

Educational institutions have in some instances recognized their responsibilities regarding the vocational adjustment of youth, but much more could be done. For example, in one study[3] of 400 college freshmen, 32 never had had any type of work ex-

---

put by personal interview to 5,000 people, "so selected as to age and sex, geographical distribution and density of population, and as to their economic level and relation to their communities, that they represent the U. S. faithfully in microcosm."

[2] Daniel Starch, "Most People Would Do Things Differently If They Could Make a Fresh Start," Syracuse (N. Y.) Post-Standard, November 8, 1936.

"Occupational Level and Job Satisfaction," of 273 men was studied by Donald E. Super and reported in the Journal of Applied Psychology, October 1939. Super found that slightly over 60 per cent of the group were satisfied with their jobs.

[3] G. A. Wallar, "Use of the Occupational Orientation Inquiry," Occupations, the Vocational Guidance Magazine, January 1939.

perience either full or part-time and 78 said that they had never had any useful contact with any opportunity in any type of work.

Henry C. Link has made a significant comment about our educational system and competent psychological guidance in the following words: "Our present educational system is better equipped to give eight years of the wrong kind of education to its pupils than eight hours of competent psychological guidance in the choice of the right type of education." He maintains that there are two critical periods in youth when such guidance is desirable. The first is before the choice of a type of high-school course— academic, commercial, or vocational. A second occurs among those who have to make the choice of a college—liberal arts, engineering, business, or other.[4]

In the case of college students, the statement is often made that they do much floundering around before they find permanent jobs. For example, in reviewing the history of the Harvard Class of 1911, John R. Tunis said that less than 5 per cent of those "who took jobs on leaving college have stuck to them."[5] However, job and vocation should not be synonymous in our thinking. Many college students do rather well in finding their vocational interests before or during college and in sticking to them.

At Oberlin College, College of Arts and Sciences, Hartson's study of five classes revealed that 97 per cent of the 1,600 freshmen had made (or thought they had made) a vocational choice. "The records show that in the case of seven men out of ten the later choices have been consistent with those expressed before entering Oberlin. The same is true of 57 per cent of the women." The question, of course, arose as to whether the choices persisted, which the investigator answered as follows:

An answer to this question, so far as it concerns Oberlin alumni, may be formulated, in part, from a study made of the nine classes, 1914 to 1922, which was made from data gathered in 1926. Examination of the case histories of this group of approximately 600 men and 1,000 women shows that they did remarkably little exploring before settling into the field of their final choice. Half of the men remained in the field of their first choice. For 27 per cent the final occupation was the second choice; 15 per cent experi-

[4] Henry C. Link, "Wheat and Chaff in Vocational Guidance," *Occupations*, October 1934.

[5] John R. Tunis, *Was College Worth While?* p. 17. George L. McLeod, 1936.

FIG. 53. Harry D. Kitson, Professor of Education, Teachers College, Columbia University, and Editor, *Occupations*, the Vocational Guidance Magazine. Those who are interested in choosing a vocation may wish to refer to his book *How to Find the Right Vocation* (rev. ed., Harper & Brothers, 1938.)

mented in two fields before finding one that satisfied them. In addition to the 50 per cent who remained in the field originally chosen, there were 14 per cent who returned to it after experimenting with another vocation. Moreover, many of the changes consisted of promotions within the business or educational fields. Adding the 11 per cent who belong in this group brings the proportion of men whose final occupation was either identical with or closely allied to their original choice to 75 per cent of the group.[6]

Studies of college students' abilities to make lasting vocational choices indicate that permanence of choice varies with the kind of professional training. Law and medical college students are more likely to enter and remain in their chosen professions than business students.

Some changes in occupations are probably beneficial and natural. A doctor who becomes interested in public health can make a logical and easy step to politics. The university teacher of chemistry may pass on to chemical research in a corporation. Our available evidence indicates that such shifting about in occupations does take place among the successful members of society. For example, a study of the persons listed in "Who's Who in

---

[6] L. D. Hartson, "Vocational Stability of Oberlin Alumni," *Personnel Journal*, 1928, Vol. VII, pp. 176-185. A 1941 study confirms above findings.

America" indicated that occupational changes were made after the age of 35 by one-third of these successful persons.[7]   Perhaps a great deal of the vocational shifting which constantly takes place is largely one of the ways in which individuals are making adjustments to the psychological problems within themselves as well as to the problems of making a living.

Many persons who have had to choose a way to make a living thought that the choice was determined by chance. But *chance* here, as elsewhere, is simply another name for the influence of a large number of unknown factors. Chance, in the determination of vocational choice, simply refers to the influences of many factors such as those of adjustment. These psychological influences are now being unraveled in some cases. However, chance will have to continue to play the major role for some generations to come, because science must make many discoveries before we can foretell the future of a youth. We shall probably never reach "that day when men's biographies can be written in advance." However, the man who is dissatisfied with his vocation, or who is at the threshold of his economic life and must choose an occupation, can be given some helpful suggestions.

Several important basic facts should first be fixed in the mind of the person who is seeking vocational guidance for himself or is trying to counsel others who are misfits. One of these basic facts is that "the square peg and the round hole" idea is an erroneous simile. This expression implies that the human being is vocationally fixed and unchangeable in his nature. It also implies that the occupation is rigid in its requirements. On the contrary, human beings are very adaptable. Consider the record of man's progress through the ages and note the many adaptations he has had to make. Few of us would choose the life of the cave man, and yet, if conditions demanded it, many men could meet the demands of primitive life in a highly successful manner. Few of us would choose the trade of the skilled artisan; but, if a sudden industrial upheaval demanded it, we could become blacksmiths and carpenters just as readily as we become salesmen, teachers, and lawyers. Each man who goes into any vocation

---

[7] Harry Dexter Kitson, *The Psychology of Vocational Adjustment*, p. 47.   J. B. Lippincott Co., 1925.

Fig. 54. (*Courtesy of the Oakland Motor Company.*) Many children change their vocational plans as they grow older. Many men, in childhood, had the ambition to become locomotive enginemen, firemen, or aviators. Later their interests became more stabilized. They learned to like certain definite activities and dislike others. The vocational interest test by Edward K. Strong, Jr., can be scored for maturity of interests.

must adapt himself to some extent; and he, in turn, also modifies the job to fit himself.

We are not fitted by nature for one occupation and one only. It is probable that most persons who are now successful in one field could also become equally successful in some other occupation. No one is perfectly fitted for any occupation. The choosing of a vocation means that we must choose the one that requires the least amount of adjustment and gives us the greatest amount of personal satisfaction. Very few individuals are "born" to any vocation. A person of high intelligence who has had a favorable previous environment could succeed in at least a dozen fields, unless one of those fields required some special organic quality, such as the ability to hear a wide range of musical notes or to distinguish sharply between shades of colors. However, limitations of the sense organs or motor equipment are exceptional in modern vocational adjustments.

So far as we now know, the brain does not at birth have certain neural patterns for specific vocational functions. Nor do such patterns develop in the brain except as the adjustments bring them about. Of course, we exclude such native endowments as exceptional qualities or limitations of the sensory apparatus. In so far as neural capacity is involved, a great majority of persons who are in doubt as to the vocation to be chosen could pick any one of several and succeed equally well in any of the several.

Vocational decisions must be made continuously. An individual cannot make a single decision that will settle his vocational future. Rather, he must make a series of decisions, not only as to the kind of work he shall do, but also as to the kind of training he shall acquire, the place of training, the job he shall seek, and the manner in which he shall advance in his chosen field. As he develops ability in a given occupation, he must choose the phase in which he shall specialize. And, later in life, he must decide upon the kind of activities that will give him the greatest amount of self-expression. Occasionally he must decide upon the factor that shall be construed as success or failure for him; whether his objective shall be happy associations with his children, opportunities to influence the lives of others, fame, or wealth. The selection of this objective cannot be made at the beginning of life but must be decided as time brings about new situations and conditions. Not only does the individual change, but society, business, and occupations change. The occupations which are important in one decade may be of little consequence in the next decade. The progress in aviation and the automobile industry could not be foreseen twenty-five years ago.

The writers of romance on the stage and in fiction have given people the impression that, if the youth does not happen to find the right mate, he will be destined to years of unhappiness with a shrew. And, later in his life, some kind providence will readjust the universe to satisfy the predestined scheme of things and allow him to live happily, though briefly, with the one mate that fate ordained that he should have. This kind of destiny-teaching is the opposite of the truth. It is true, rather, that any man could live as happily with any one of ten thousand women as with any of the other nine thousand nine hundred and ninety-nine. Likewise, no one is born for a particular occupation. Nor should we think that, if an individual fails to find his one niche in life, he will be doomed to a life of failure or mediocrity. No one should be continually looking for a "niche." If he is, it is quite probable that he never will find it, because each man must make his own.

Nor should we seek to follow the vocational pathways that some other successful individual traveled. Much as we admire Lincoln, none of us can be just like him or do what he did. We can hope only to make a place in life for ourselves which we can fill as well, proportionately, as he filled his. The man who hears of how some relative, classmate, neighbor, or friend has become wealthy or happy and then attempts to follow in the same footsteps is apt to find that his feet do not fit those footprints. We cannot take the personality and conditions of some other individual and superimpose them upon ourselves. Each man must establish his own career for himself and in his own way rather than by imitating a predecessor. He cannot even imitate, as a rule, his own father, unless the successful father gives the son so great a head start that it is difficult for the youth to fail. This rule also implies that the boy who goes to "dad's alma mater" just because his father happened to go there should realize that times have changed, and that his needs may not be the same as those of his father when he was young. The vocational advice of relatives and friends is likely to be defective in this and many other respects.

The vocational advice of parents and friends. Vocational guidance in the sense of predicting what a person should do is very difficult. It is very difficult for even the trained vocational psychologists. Most modern vocational psychologists do not try to study a youth in order to predict what he should do but to help him improve his adjustments to life by means of a vocation. Perhaps the psychologist also points out what the youth is likely to do. A boy may have certain adjustment tendencies which can be pointed out to him and suggestions may be given him for the utilization of his established tendencies. However, the boy's choice cannot be controlled.   The individual himself must make his own adjustments and his own choice.   Guidance cannot play the part of a benevolent parent who adjusts conditions for the child; guidance can only prepare the boy to meet his own difficulties.

Parents who attempt to influence the choice of vocation for their children often do so as a compensation for their own deficiencies.   The parent may say it is for the child's good.   Actually, it may be a form of display for the parent.   When parents find that they can no longer hope to become famous or to achieve their adolescent dreams, they project their hopes for glory into the brightest or favorite child of the family and compel the child to enter the profession which, in their opinion, offers the desired prestige or wealth.   When a boy fails in college and the personnel adviser suggests to the parent that his son should become a mechanic or a businessman rather than a surgeon, the parent is likely to answer disgustedly: "Why, that's no profession at all.   I want my son to amount to something."   Such an answer indicates that the parent is the one who really wants to amount to something.

The vocational guidance given by many teachers, employment managers, preachers, and lecturers is in the same class as the home remedy of the friend who never studied medicine or the human body.   The physician, with all his years of training and experience, makes many errors in diagnosing our bodily ills, but the untrained friend who tries to do so makes many more.

If a person is in need of vocational guidance and asks some of his friends for suggestions, he may be surprised to find that each person's advice differs from that of all the others.   Many friends can give only general and trivial suggestions which have but slight value.   For example, a case study was made of each of a number of adults who voluntarily sought vocational guidance. To assist in the analyses, each one of the subjects gave personality rating blanks to several persons, six or less, who knew him well.   These six friends were to check on the rating blank the items that applied to the person being rated and to offer any helpful vocational suggestions.   An analysis of the rating blanks for 36 ratees as filled in by the 191 raters resulted in the following table:

TABLE XXII

Traits	Percentage of 191 raters who listed the trait in their ratings
Learn to do things that you dislike...........	26
Control your temper......................	21
Be more patient..........................	17
Be less nervous..........................	17
Smile more often.........................	16
Be more tactful..........................	15
Think less about your own troubles.........	16
Do not sulk when things go wrong...........	16
Be more enthusiastic.....................	14
Improve your vocabulary..................	13
Learn to talk to all kinds of people...........	13
Be more aggressive.......................	13
Learn more about human nature.............	13
Be less sensitive.........................	13
Shave more frequently....................	9
Improve your table manners................	6
Don't tell shady stories...................	5
Prevent your halitosis....................	2

In addition to the above, many other characteristics were mentioned by the friends of the advisees; but this table will be sufficient to illustrate the nature of the suggestions of the friends who rated the individuals. Some helpful suggestions were given, and the ratings gave a composite picture of how the person rated appeared to the raters. The ratings were a group estimate of the individual, and, in some cases, suggested avenues for further psychological exploration. The main deficiency in the ratings of these persons who sought vocational guidance lay in the poverty of helpful suggestions regarding any specific occupations which the ratees should enter. Many of the traits listed are really suggestions for better adjustment habits.

The logical question arises: When the psychologist analyzes a person for the purpose of vocational guidance, how does his analysis differ from that of the acquaintances who know the individual? Chiefly, in two ways. First, the experienced psychologist who has had some clinical training knows much about adjustment patterns of individuals. He can recognize tendencies which can be utilized in a vocation in order to bring about better adjustment and more satisfying fruits from the advisee's efforts.

Second, the modern vocational psychologist supplements his clinical and other subjective estimates with objective tests. The

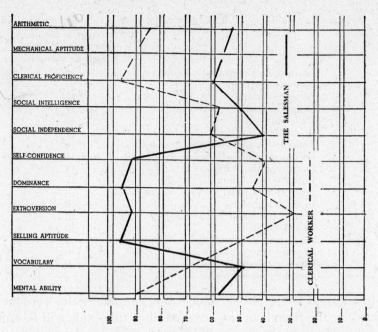

F<small>IG</small>. 55. These centile curves of test scores show the profile of the typical clerical worker and that of the typical salesman. These profiles are based on more than ten thousand records of men tested by The Personnel Institute, Inc., Chicago. A profile of the typical industrial worker and test profiles of workers of specific companies are published in *The Use of Ability and Aptitude Testing in Business*, The Personnel Institute, Inc., 1940.

tests which he uses have been standardized on thousands of individuals and are fairly accurate; so, if two psychologists test the same person, their findings tend to be the same. The psychologist also tries to find the specific channels through which the intelligence expresses itself, as in mathematics, music, mechanics, social contacts, and so forth.

An example of the value of the testing services of the psychologist may be shown in the case of a high school boy of a western New York high school who was sent to the commercial teacher by the principal. The principal told the teacher that the boy was of low intelligence and could not do good school work. The quality of the boy's work in all his courses was of such a low grade that the teachers had given up all hopes of teaching him. Because the other teachers were tired of the boy, he was sent to the new commercial teacher of the school. This teacher also found that the boy's reputation for poor work was correct so far as commercial subjects were concerned. He was the poorest student that this teacher had met in that school.

Fortunately, the commercial teacher had had courses in mental testing, and he gave the boy several intelligence tests just to find out whether his intelligence was as low as it appeared to be. To the teacher's surprise, the boy scored slightly above normal in all the tests. The teacher then gained the boy's confidence and found that he had a serious inferiority complex. One of his teachers whom he had had four years previously had convinced him that he was a "dub and a dumb-bell." After that he made no effort to do good work, but rather tried to live down to the kind of reputation he was given. The commercial teacher changed the boy's attitude and he then did good work in all his courses, because all his teachers knew that he could do good work and required him to do it.

In this example we see that the counselor used tests as an aid in his diagnosis of the boy, but he supplemented the test results with his own subjective insight into the boy's adjustment habits and helped the boy readjust himself to his barriers.

Methods of choosing a vocation. Some of the current methods whereby the individual can predict or tries to predict his own behavior for vocational adjustment have been mentioned, but we shall list the more common ones:

1. Pseudo-scientific schemes such as phrenology, character analysis, astrology, etc. These have no value and need not be discussed further.
2. Choose a problem to the solution of which you can devote your life.
3. Analyze yourself according to some systematic plan and make a decision.
4. Have yourself tested with the few valid psychological tests now available.
5. By means of a systematic analysis of your adjustments, recognize the conscious and unconscious drives in your own personality.
6. Allow yourself to be made a case study by a vocational psychologist.

One of the best ways for the intelligent person to choose a vocation is to select a problem that needs solution. The modern scientific student often does this and develops his interest in a problem into a new vocation. For example, a girl who was a student in a college of home economics found that the lowly mushroom had never been studied carefully. She then decided to make a study of mushrooms, and, when she was graduated, she was offered an excellent position where she utilized her interest in mushrooms.   Inventors often use this method.   So does the man who sees a need for some particular kind of business in his community and then starts a business to answer that need. Thousands of problems in all the professions and businesses are awaiting solution.   The man who determines to devote his efforts to answers to economic and social difficulties usually finds that he has found his vocation.   A few of many such problems are listed as suggestions and not as a complete list:

1.   Create a public sentiment whereby manual labor will be considered more honorable and desirable.

2.   Develop, through propagation, certain prolific weed plants into valuable food plants.

3.   Work out and install better systems of training and promotion for employees of large concerns.

4.   Much of the money now spent for advertising is wasted.   Someone should discover the laws of advertising, so that all money spent for advertising will be well spent and productive.

5.   Find out how to make public school work more interesting, more cultural, and more related to life.

6.   Many persons die or suffer unnecessarily because of lack of physical development and exercise.   Work out plans that will give the office workers more exercise.

7.   Develop better methods of settling difficulties between employers and workers.

8.   Work out methods for improving the personal efficiency of certain classes or kinds of persons.

9.   Teach and help people of this country to understand and appreciate art—the beautiful things of life as well as the practical.

10.   Discover the bases of personality and help others to improve their personalities.

11.   Study the problems of modern housekeeping.   Try to make it easier and less expensive.   Educate women in the best methods of housekeeping.

12.   At present our educational system is adapted to the average child. Some cities pay special attention to the backward or poor student.   Evolve a system that develops the exceptionally bright student to his utmost. Much of this latent ability is now being wasted.

13.   Religion is in a different environment from what it has been heretofore.   Some think that we must put religion on a basis that will appeal to the people of this age.

14.   Prevent or decrease crimes and learn how to re-educate criminals.

15.   Solve the parking problem in cities.

16.   Invent sidewalks which are less trying to our feet.

17.   Improve the lighting of rooms.

18.   Invent better children's games, especially games to be played by small children while riding in an automobile.

We Americans have hundreds of unsolved problems, and the solutions of certain problems would give employment to thousands of workers. To the well-adjusted intelligent worker, the pull of the future (toward the solution of a problem) should be more stimulating than the push from the past (his own adjustment tendencies). Unfortunately, however, most young people allow their own adjustment tendencies and the conventional occupational openings to determine the directions of their vocational efforts. Very few men devote themselves to the solution of some problem unless they first have had some profound emotional experience that pushes them in the direction of such devotion. For example, all of us recognize the need for greater safety in driving automobiles, but few among us will vigorously pursue safer driving as a life work unless we have had an intense emotional experience with bad driving, such as the death of a loved one in an unnecessary accident. Sometimes the vocational psychologist can recognize such adjustment tendencies, resulting from severe emotional problems, which can be utilized in solving a problem and giving the individual a well-motivated and satisfying career.

Self-analysis. Many of the first attempts at vocational guidance required the youth to answer a long series of questions regarding his vocational interests. He was asked not only to state whether he liked, disliked, or felt a neutral interest in listed occupations, but also to estimate himself in general traits as:

> Are you aggressive?
> Are you industrious?
> Do you have a pleasing personality?
> Are you neat in habits?
> Are you conceited?
> Do you co-operate with others?
> Do you look ahead?

Hollingworth and others have made studies of the reliability and accuracy of self-estimates of general traits. He conducted experiments wherein the individuals in a group rated the other members of the group and themselves in nine different traits. The results indicated that people cannot rate themselves with any great degree of accuracy. The natural expectation would be that we tend to overestimate ourselves in desirable traits and underestimate ourselves in undesirable traits. The following data[8] from his study of the estimates of fifty people show the presence of a factor of constant bias in self-estimation:

TABLE XXIII

SHOWING CONSTANT TENDENCIES OR BIAS IN SELF-ESTIMATION

Trait	Per Cent Overestimating Themselves	Per Cent Underestimating Themselves
Refinement	80	20
Humor	78	22
Intelligence	68	32
Sociability	68	32
Neatness	50	50
Beauty	50	50
Conceit	48	52
Snobbishness	36	64
Vulgarity	34	66

Hollingworth also found that the more admirable the trait the closer the relation between possession of the trait and the ability to judge it in others. His subjects who had reprehensible traits could not rate themselves very accurately in those traits. Of course, we must bear in mind that people cannot rate others accurately in generalized traits, and Hollingworth's experiment assumed that the group estimates of the raters were correct. The consensus of the acquaintances who did the rating was accepted as the true impression that an individual made on others. As pointed out in the chapter on interviewing, we found that close acquaintance with new salesmen did not enable the instructors to estimate their actual sales ability. It is also quite probable that, if objective measures had been available of Hollingworth's subjects in the nine traits he studied, they would not have agreed with the average ratings of the acquaintances.

The Allports'[9] experiment confirmed the principle that self-estimates in general traits are not accurate. Different people were asked to estimate their own intelligence by the rating scale method, and they were also given intelligence tests. Then their

[8] Adapted from H. L. Hollingworth, *Judging Human Behavior,* p. 52. D. Appleton-Century Co., New York, 1922.

[9] F. H. and G. W. Allport, *Journal of Abnormal and Social Psychology,* 1921, Vol. 16, pp. 6-40.

self-estimates and their scores in the tests were compared.   Those
who were high in intelligence tended to underestimate themselves and those who were low in intelligence tended to overestimate themselves.   The correlation between self-estimates of
ability and scores in the Otis Group Intelligence Test was —.67.
Self-estimates are not reliable,, unless they can be proved to be of
sound predictive value.   To prove their value requires careful statistical treatment, which has not yet been given for most
traits that are considered in vocational self-analyses.

Even though self-estimates are not reliable, they may have
some value in causing the individual to grade and recognize
his own inclinations, tendencies, and characteristics in relation
to an occupational choice.   In some cases, it may be well for
the individual to decide upon his personal likes and dislikes
and to try to avoid those occupations that require traits that
are definitely unpleasant or to seek occupations that require
traits that are pleasant to him.   For example, some persons
dislike to handle other people physically, which is necessary in
the work of the osteopath, the chiropodist, the barber, the nurse,
and the hairdresser.

When the individual's self-analyses are made by means of a
statistically treated list of occupational and other activities to
which the individual reacts in terms of liking for (L), indifference toward (I), or dislike for (D), the method of self-analysis
is called an *interest test*.

Vocational interest tests.   The most widely used interest test
is that of Edward K. Strong, Jr.   There are two forms of this test,
one for men and one for women.   Each form of the test is an
eight page leaflet listing some 400 items covering occupations,
school subjects, amusements, activities, peculiarities of people,
and self-estimates of personal abilities and characteristics.   The
average time needed by most persons to fill in the test is forty
minutes, though no time limit is set.

The scoring of the test is time-consuming and tedious, though
the scoring of the revised form for men has been facilitated by
a better arrangement of the items and a reduction in the score
weights.   Scoring is most easily done by means of a test scoring
machine.

Norms have been developed for some thirty-four occupations

for men and seventeen for women. Most of the occupations listed are on a professional level. This makes the administration of the test to a person of low intelligence or with no prospect of professional training, largely a waste of time. The test is best used with individuals of college and adult age levels, though it may be used to advantage with selected high school groups.

The interest test is not a measure of aptitude or ability, and so is used not to replace aptitude or ability tests but to supplement them. Results of the test do, however, suggest that the person whose pattern of interests is similar to that of the men or women in the criterion group has greater chances for satisfaction and success in that occupation than in one where his interests differ widely from successful persons in that field.

Scores on the Strong test may be translated as standard scores, percentile ranks, or letter ratings. The ratings A, B, and C are usually used to interpret the test results to the testee, since they are more easily understood. An A rating means that the testee has the interests characteristic of persons successfully engaged in the occupation specified; B has a similar implication, but there is less certainty; and C means that the testee does not have such interests. Any occupation in which the rating is an A or B+ may be suggested to the testee for serious consideration. An occupation in which the interest rating is C should be chosen only after careful consideration of other factors such as strong drives.

Strong made a follow-up study of Stanford University seniors and found that upperclass students, though ignorant of their test scores, tend to continue for at least two years with occupational plans in line with their tested interests. After a two-year period, 67 per cent were still planning to enter, or were engaged in, work in line with their first or second highest rating on the test.[10]

In at least one occupation, life insurance selling, Strong's interest test showed a high positive correlation between measured interests and success. See Table XXIV.

---

[10] Edward K. Strong, Jr., *Manual for Vocational Interest Blank* (Stanford University Press, 1937), and Walter VanDyke Bingham, *Aptitudes and Aptitude Testing* (Harper & Bros., 1937), present excellent information regarding this test.

TABLE XXIV[11]

PRODUCTIVENESS AND INTEREST RATINGS OF 181 LIFE INSURANCE AGENTS

Average Annual Production	Number	Percentage of Agents in Each Life Insurance Interest Rating Who Produced Indicated Amount of Paid-for Insurance				
		C	B−	B	B+	A
$0 to 49,000	19	31	20	17	21	2
50,000 to 99,000	37	44	20	33	26	13
100,000 to 149,000	29	12	20	17	8	18
150,000 to 199,000	40	6	20	28	16	26
200,000 up	56	0	20	5	29	41
Total	...	100	100	100	100	100
Number	181	16	5	17	38	105

Interest tests are a helpful device in confirming stated interests as well as in calling attention to occupational interests which the individual may have overlooked. The vocational psychologist is also concerned about certain aspects of interests other than the score on a test, especially about "absorbing interests" or intensive drives which may have developed in the adjustment history of the individual.

Other tests for vocational guidance. Many people who seek vocational guidance think that the psychologist can test the capacities of anyone so that the person tested will know just exactly what vocation he can and should follow. The psychologists also at one time thought that they might be able to develop predictive testing to that stage, but the recent researches indicate that they were too optimistic. Professor Seashore and his colleagues have spent some forty years in the analysis of musical talent. They have developed some tests with high predictive values, but the analysis of that one talent is not complete. If forty years of research in one field have not produced wholly satisfactory results, we should not expect too much from the use of other tests which have had far less attention than the musical aptitude tests. Certain schools of music now use musical aptitude tests and find them very helpful, but psychologists have probably made more progress in musical testing than in any other

---

[11] Edward K. Strong, Jr., "Manual for Vocational Interest Blank for Men," p. 12. Stanford University Press, 1937.

trait or capacity.   As stated in the previous discussion of tests, they do have some value, but they furnish a statistical prediction on the basis of what a group or number of individuals will do rather than what any single person can or will do.   In vocational guidance we want to know what a group can do, but we wish particularly to know what a specific individual can do.

Another difficulty in vocational guidance, based upon tests only, is the fact that a person who tests high in a given trait that could be capitalized vocationally may not care for that vocation.   Thousands of people are capable of becoming good undertakers, but most of them would object to it as a vocation because of emotional inhibitions.   Similarly, psychologists might make more statistical studies of the kinds of men and women that can marry each other with the greatest chances of a happy marriage, but such tests would have little value in decreasing matrimonial failures.   The persons whom scientific analyses would indicate as ideal mates might not care for each other at all and would refuse to go through with the ceremony.   Scientific marriages would not be nearly so inviting to the masses of people as the old-fashioned method of romance and chance.   Two individuals must be "drawn" to each other emotionally.   The individual must also be attracted to his vocation emotionally.

This statement of some of the limitations of tests should not be construed as making them valueless.   It is important to use tests as one factor to be considered when dealing with vocational problems.   Tests are particularly useful in pointing out certain vocations in which the individual would have small chance of success.   Certainly anyone who considers choosing music as a career should first have himself tested by someone who can administer the Seashore test or adaptations of it.

Other tests, helpful in certain problems of vocational analysis, can often be recommended by competent vocational psychologists and counselors.[12]   However, when the vocational counselor

---

[12] Herbert Moore, *Experience with Employment Tests,* Studies in Personnel Policy No. 32, March 11, 1941 (National Industrial Conference Board, Inc.) gives names and addresses of most leading test publishers. Tests are listed under five general headings as to kind: intelligence, clerical, mechanical, personality, and interest. An excellent comprehensive sourcebook regarding tests is Oscar Krisen Buros (Editor), *The 1940 Mental Measurements Yearbook* (Highland Park, N. J.).

attempts to find tests having unquestionable value in the vocational guidance of youth, he has difficulty in finding any that are
conclusive. He must resort to the use of general intelligence
tests. General intelligence has been defined in various ways,
but chiefly as the ability to adjust oneself to the problems of
one's environment, as the average of various abilities, as the
ability to learn, and as the ability to do school work. The last

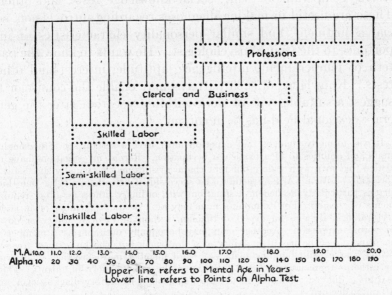

FIG. 56.   The range of intelligence scores of the middle 50 per cent of various
occupational groups, on the basis of the army examinations of 36,500 recruits.
Adapted from *Memoirs of the National Academy of Science*, Vol. 15, 1921, p. 829,
and H. L. Hollingworth, *Mental Growth and Decline*, p. 255.   D. Appleton-Century
Co., 1927.

definition appears to be the nearest to truth. Most studies
indicate a definite relationship between general intelligence or
mental ability and other desirable traits of vocational significance.

In cases of extremely high or low intelligence, we are safe in
making certain predictions. A person with an intelligence quotient of less than 100 could not do good work in most colleges.
Lack of intelligence can be compensated for, to some extent, by
an exceptionally great amount of effort, but even superior effort
would not enable a student of low intelligence to succeed in col-

lege.   The high school student who plans to enter college should try to select a college and a course that are in harmony with his intelligence level and high school marks.   See Table XV, page 276.

The vocational psychologist often supplements intelligence, interest, and special ability tests with personality inventories such as the Bernreuter Personality Inventory, the Humm-Wadsworth Temperament Scale, social knowledge tests, and others. These are useful in making diagnoses regarding introversion, social adjustment, and similar personality characteristics of importance to the trained psychologist.   He wants to know the pattern of temperament, intelligence, aptitude, interest and other tests.   Knowledge of such patterns may enable the counselor to suggest a suitable type of work within a vocation after the general vocational field has been chosen.

It was formerly thought that a person must have a certain set of personality traits and abilities to fit a particular occupation. Recent investigations have revealed that men with widely different characteristics may be equally successful in the same position. A man seems to be successful if he can supply the one thing that is particularly needed in a situation, with ordinary fitness for other requirements of the job. For example, a man may be a desirable member of an architectural firm if he is an expert draftsman, without any social ability or power of verbal expression. Another man may be equally desirable as a member of the same firm who has little ability as a draftsman but who knows how to meet people and explain building plans. A third member may specialize in drawing or esthetic appreciation. Legal firms have the same variety of talents. There is a great difference between a successful surgeon, a laboratory diagnostician, and a family doctor.[13]

We should recognize that vocational objectives and choices of college can be revised.   Educational and vocational growth are intertwined.   Civilizations and personalities are dynamic. Interests ripen.   The satisfactions derived from exercise of intelligence and aptitudes vary with the individual's adjustments to new barriers in his development.   This means that a study of adjustments, drives, and preferences should supplement any tests administered.

Adjustment analysis for choosing a vocation.   Some clinical psychologists believe that vocational counselors are simply meddlers and that the individual should be allowed to follow the directions of the "Unconscious."   They believe that all actions

---

[13] Paul P. Brainard and Frances G. Stewart, *Manual of Instructions for Specific Interest Inventories.*   Psychological Corporation, 1932.

are determined by unconscious motives that follow definite paths formed in the individual since childhood. A person's work or profession is a sublimating process in the service of hunger and love.[14]

The writer has attempted to assist several hundred persons in choosing a vocation. Some of these were students who were asked to have a vocational conference, but others, who heard of these conferences, requested guidance. Those who requested assistance in choosing a vocation certainly included an unusually high percentage of psychoneurotic and slightly psychopathological cases. Unfortunately it is not possible to present adequate statistics to prove that many adults who seek vocational guidance do so because of definite emotional maladjustments. An estimate, based upon experience in this field, suggests that at least one third of the adults who voluntarily seek vocational guidance are really seeking an adjustment to life in general rather than a vocation only. This estimate is probably too low.

Adjustment analysis is of assistance to many persons who are vocationally unsatisfied because it may indicate the manner in which the person with a feeling of inferiority might attempt to compensate for his sense of inadequacy. It is probably partially true that Napoleon became the conqueror of a large part of the civilized world through his adjustment to the taunts of his playmates in his childhood. Some of our poets achieved their eminence because of physical defects. In fact, Adler cited many cases of compensation brought about by some organic inferiority and concluded that some psychic reaction makes up for the deficiency of the physical organism.[15] This theory hardly explains every successful person. Many of us develop our feelings of inferiority as the result of comparing ourselves with others. A person who has average artistic ability when compared with other artists of the world may have a definite sense of inferiority because he knows that there are others considerably better than he. A person need not have any actual physical or mental inferiority in order to feel inferior. The odious comparisons of life may give him the impressions of inferiority. The business and profes-

---

[14] A. A. Brill, *Fundamental Conceptions of Psychoanalysis*, Chapter XIII. Harcourt, Brace & Co., 1921.

[15] Alfred Adler, "A Study of Organ Inferiority and Its Psychical Compensation." *Nervous and Mental Diseases Monograph*, 1917.

Fig. 57. "Bonaparte, a Novice in the School at Brienne," by Realier-Dumas. (*By permission of Gramstorff Bros., Inc., Malden, Mass.*) This painting is reproduced to illustrate the influence of subconscious drives in choosing a career. Napoleon may have become a conqueror as a compensation for a number of unhappy childhood experiences. An inferiority complex is often compensated for by a career that satisfies the ego's needs.

sional world has many examples of able individuals who attempt various methods of compensation because they realize that others are more successful or have higher salaries than they have. We can understand these people when we recall the typical adjustments discussed in Chapters 3-8.

The person who seeks a vocation that fits his personality should ask himself: What embarrassing or unpleasant experiences have I had for which I need compensation in my work? If he cannot answer the question himself, he might consult a vocational psychologist. Each year it is found that several college students who are barely able to do college work and just manage to graduate wish to take additional postgraduate work in another college which has a reputation for requiring unusually hard work. This desired prestige of having done graduate work in a famous institution is merely an attempt to compensate for the feeling of inferiority engendered by their inability to do college work of ordinary grade. In most cases it has been difficult to convince these poor students that they wish to do graduate work not be-

Fig. 58. "Young Raleigh," by John Everett Millais. (*By permission of Gramstorff Bros., Inc., Malden, Mass.*) This famous painting is reproduced to illustrate the fact that some individuals choose their vocation as the result of instructional influences. Not all careers are the result of subconscious drives—the following of directions of the "unconscious."

cause it is essential to their careers but because the contrast between themselves and other college students causes them to think that they are inferior. Actually they are fine young men who have developed an abnormal attitude toward the importance of college degrees and the college aura.

Adjustment by projection explains many of the dissatisfactions with occupational life. A bank clerk, for example, who is not especially ambitious or intelligent and who knows it, may suddenly develop a dislike for banking. Further analysis may show that his home relationships have become strained and that he would like to get married and set up a home of his own. His dissatisfaction has not been caused by the uninteresting nature of bank work, but he has blamed his work for the fact that he does not have the courage to set up a new home on the available income.

Sometimes a person highly trained and successful in a given

line of work suddenly tires of the vocation for which he has a high interest rating as measured by an interest test. His income and social prestige may also be excellent, but he refuses to continue in the work. In such cases, only an analysis of adjustment problems will reveal the true cause of his desire for a change.

Many a person has left a vocation and spent years in training himself for a new vocation because he thought that competition was far too keen, whereas he might have attained greater success by training himself more thoroughly in his original work. A typical example is a certain man who was a fairly successful printer. He blamed competition for his limited income, and decided to study dentistry. After six years of study and several years in developing his practice, he has become another average dentist. In the meantime, one or two printers in his city have become well-to-do. If he had devoted the same effort and capital to printing that he applied to learning dentistry, he might have become far more successful as a printer than he is as a dentist.

Whenever someone wishes to leave an occupation in which he is fairly well established, the counselor should look for the difficulty that the occupation symbolizes or represents to the person. The real reason for his eagerness to leave one job for another may be his irascible stepmother, a brighter sister, an unresponsive executive, or a fiancée who loves someone else.

In some cases a sudden interest in politics may be a protest against some injustice. A determination to travel may be an attempt to adjust to restraint or convention. A keen interest in the study of an obscure subject such as paleontology or Egyptology may be an attempt to prove to others that the individual is as bright as those whom he considers to be his rivals. By contrast with the knowledge of such unusual subjects on the part of most people, his meager fund of information gives him the intellectual recognition he unconsciously seeks.

The vocational psychologist frequently finds freakish interests on the part of persons who are dealing with a barrier, such as the crude man who wants to be an artist, the immoral person who wants to be a preacher, the homely girl who wants to be a beautician, and the failure who writes success books. Such attempts to gain adjustment through the vocation are not necessarily

wrong.   Many of the world's finest contributions have grown out
of such troubled personality strivings.   For example, Charlotte
Brontë wrote some very successful novels which resulted from an
overflow of emotions engendered by her father's unfortunate
influences.   The father was a hypochondriac, a dyspeptic, and
an ascetic.   He did not believe in marriage and was particularly
opposed to Charlotte's marrying.   He was fond and jealous of
her.   He was unable to get along with his associates and so became a tyrant in his home.   He tried to please her and showered
her with attention but he was moody and critical as well.   She
could not develop in a normal manner and was forced inward
emotionally.   She took refuge in books and fancies.   Her tragic
childhood was stamped deeply upon her personality, and the
books that she and her sisters wrote bear the effects of a maladjusted father upon motherless children.

The case method of vocational guidance.   The evidence presented in the preceding discussions suggests that while some
individuals do not need vocational guidance, many others do.
We must not assume that all wholly normal persons need no assistance in choosing a vocation.   The normal youth is not raw
material psychologically; he was raw material at birth, but
since birth he has developed many adjustments and conditionings.   He has certain likes and dislikes, some feelings of inferiority, self-confidence in certain situations and not in others, a
fairly definite level of intelligence, and accumulated experiences
of all degrees of importance, so that his psychological composite
in relation to his environment may not result in a happy vocational choice.   In many cases he finds that he has difficulty in
choosing a vocation.   Even though he thinks that he knows
what he wants to do, it may be well for him to attempt to obtain a bird's-eye view of himself and the world in which he lives.
He really knows only a few occupations, and those he does not
know comprehensively.   Such a case study involves the following
steps by a counselor:

I.   Analyze the individual.
   A.   History and general status.
      1.   Health record.
      2.   School record.
      3.   Financial status.
      4.   Leadership record.

    5. Hobbies and recreational activities.

    6. Psychological test scores.

B. Vocational likes and dislikes—self-analysis.

C. Estimates of associates and friends—ratings by others.

D. Peculiarities of personality.

E. Parental wishes.

II. Present the suggestions of the above to the advisee in a personal conference.

III. As a result of II, choose several occupations for the investigation of the advisee.

IV. After investigation of the several tentative occupations, choose one as a vocation.

V. Plan a program of training.

VI. Assist advisee to obtain a job or get started in the chosen field.

VII. Follow up advisee and revise his program as occasion demands.

Vocational guidance by use of the case method has the advantages and the defects of the physician's services. Its value is difficult to prove or to disprove. If the patient takes the doctor's prescriptions and gets well, it is often impossible to know whether the patient regained health because of the medicine or in spite of it. Similarly, investigations of the value of vocational guidance are not conclusive. No one knows what the advisee would have done if he had not followed the adviser's counsel. The writer made an intensive study of 58 individuals who sought vocational guidance. Two years later—each advisee was investigated regarding the number of suggestions that he had accepted and applied. The following table shows the results of their replies:

| | PERCENTAGE OF SUGGESTIONS ACCEPTED BY | |
Kinds of Suggestions Given	Students, under 20	Adults, over 20
For improvement of personality	58	48
Educational suggestions	86	57
Vocational suggestions	61	39

The table indicates what experience tells us: counseling should be along the lines of educational guidance and should begin with students under twenty years of age.

College education as a part of a vocational program. When a high school graduate wishes to enter business and plans his vocational program, he must decide whether he will go to college or enter a field of work without college training. When successful men in one field are compared with the unsuccessful, investiga-

tions show that many of the successful individuals in business
do not have a college education. We cannot say that a college
education is essential to business success. (See Table XXV.)
However, statistics of the value of college training based upon
men who graduated a generation ago are not entirely significant
for modern conditions. Going to college then required more
initiative and ability than it does today, when a college student
is no longer a community marvel as he was then.

TABLE XXV[16]

Is a College Degree Needed for Executive Success?

	Total No. Interviewed	College Trained
All executives	53,957	28%
Production executives	14,610	9
Engineering officials	13,247	46
Sales executives	14,720	38
Presidents	487	48

The main reason why college graduates make more money
than high school or common school graduates is superior intelligence and personality. A youth with high intelligence and
strong character traits is likely to go to college. He seeks the
college degree as part of his program of personal development.
College is the required or accepted education for many superior
individuals, and professional standards as well as many businessmen require college graduation for admission into many
occupations.

We can feel safe in saying that the percentage of college men
who succeed in business is higher than the percentage of the
group who do not go to college. There is also some evidence to
indicate that high scholastic standing in college is correlated
with future success in business. "E. K. Hall, who for two years
made a study of the relation between high scholarship in college
to success in the Bell Telephone system, found that the man who
during his course at a college stood among the first ten of his
class has one chance in two of standing in the first grade in
salary. On the other hand, he shows that the man in the lowest
third in scholarship in his class has, instead of one chance in two,
only one chance in five of standing in the highest grade in salary,

---

[16] From a study by General Motors Institute, and appearing in *Sales Management,* September 15, 1940.

and that there is nearly one chance in two that he will stand in the lowest grade."[17]

The student who attains high grades in college and then succeeds in business probably does so not because the college trained him to think or gave him technical training but because he has superior intellectual and character traits. We should not advise every high school student to go to college. If a student barely manages to get through high school and if his general intelligence in abstract subjects is low, it may be inadvisable to recommend college training. It is interesting to know that high school graduates of both low and high mental ability plan to attend college. The desire to attend college is not a reliable criterion of the ability to do college work. Thousands of college freshmen are dropped each year because they are unable to do the work. However, if a youth has the intelligence and personality that will enable him to benefit from a college education,

TABLE XXVI[18]

RELATION BETWEEN SCHOLASTIC STANDING IN COLLEGE AND LATER SUCCESS

Deciles	"Who's Who in America"		"Who's Who in Engineering"		"American Men of Science"		In all three volumes	
	No.*	%	No.	%	No.	%	No.	%
1	68	15.3	128	16.1	123	23.8	20	22.0
2	60	13.5	108	13.6	85	16.5	13	14.3
3	45	10.2	87	10.9	67	13.0	16	17.6
4	49	11.1	93	11.7	62	12.0	11	12.1
5	26	5.9	63	7.9	39	7.6	6	6.6
6	19	4.3	45	5.7	26	5.1	3	3.3
7	23	5.2	46	5.8	23	4.5	3	3.3
8	30	6.8	54	6.8	23	4.5	6	6.6
9	26	5.9	53	6.7	23	4.5	5	5.5
10	96	21.8	118	14.8	44	8.5	8	8.8
Totals	442	100.0	795	100.0	515	100.0	91	100.0

* The No. column indicates the Number of former M.I.T. students, from certain classes between 1868 and 1910, whose names appear in *Who's Who in America*. Thus 68 persons (or 15.3 per cent of the total) stood in the 1st decile or top tenth of their class; 60 persons (13.5 per cent) stood in the 2nd decile or second highest tenth—and so on for all ten deciles. The table can also be read as follows: "Of 442 former M.I.T. men listed in *Who's Who in America*, 96 or 21.8 per cent stood in the 10th or lowest decile, scholastically, of the members of their classes, etc."

[17] "Leaders or Just Scholars?" *Printers' Ink*, August 23, 1928, p. 65.
[18] F. Alexander Magoun, "Scholarship and Distinction," *The Technology Review*, Massachusetts Institute of Technology, Cambridge, Mass., May 1935, Vol. 37, No. 8.

Fig. 59. Richard W. Husband, Pennsylvania State College. Those interested in further study of vocational guidance should refer to his article "In Defense of Scientific Vocational Guidance," *Journal of Applied Psychology*, 1936, Vol. 20, pp. 586–590.

then he should by all means go to college, even though he may have to earn all his own funds for doing so.

The vocational program. The following conversation and appeal to a youth illustrates one kind of appeal that can be made when the counselor wishes the advisee to plan a definite program for training himself in his chosen vocation:

"Vocational success hinges partly upon not trusting your life to chance but knowing what you want and how to get it. The man of little ability who concentrates his efforts on one thing, in one direction, and on one goal is bound to succeed. He attains far greater height than the man of brilliant ability who lacks a goal.

After you have chosen a vocation or selected your vocational goal, you should do what successful business concerns do— schedule your plans. Decide upon what you want to accomplish each year for the next few years. Determine upon what you will do each year in order to attain your goal. Set up standards for yourself. Set a date when you will accomplish each step and keep that schedule before you. Look at it occasionally, especially when you are failing.

Whenever you find that your schedule needs revision, revise

TABLE XXVII

FACTORS TO BE CONSIDERED IN PLANNING MY VOCATION

Educational record:
High school graduate, college preparatory course.

Easy subjects:
English, history, languages.

Difficult subjects:
Math courses.

Grades:
Graduated in second quarter of class of 68 graduates. English grades highest.

Test results:
Otis S-A test of intelligence P.R. 90
Nelson-Denny Reading Test, P.R. 92
Iowa Placement, English Aptitude, P.R. 86
Introversion, P.R. 62.

Interest test results, rank order:
1. Copywriter
2. Advertising man
3. Journalist
4. Lawyer
5. Commercial teacher

Experience record:
Odd jobs in selling magazines, clerking in store.

Health record:
Children's diseases only.
Good health.

Financial resources:
Father will supply money for most expenses. Must earn money for personal expenses.

Parental wishes:
Parents have no vocational preferences but they expect me to make high grades.

Special opportunity:
Uncle is in textile industry but I as nephew could not expect any special opportunity from anyone.

Past difficulties that developed drives of vocational value, habits, conditionings, feelings of inferiority, resentment, etc.:
Oldest child in family of four boys, like to show off. Believe that my parents are more or less indifferent to me. A younger brother is praised for his very high grades. Feel inferior regarding my lack of athletic ability. Fear that I will be a failure. Resent close supervision. Resent "poverty" of family.

Reasons for suggesting this vocational program: likes, dislikes, aptitudes, etc.:
High record in English.
Practical minded rather than a student of English only.
Like to study people more than I care to influence them in personal contacts.

Advertising Copywriter

Nature of the Career I Wish to Attain: *Advertising Copywriter*

My Job Program

Sequence of jobs to reach the main occupation:

For this year:
Obtain part-time job in retail concern.

For next year:
Obtain part-time job on newspaper or magazine.

Later:
Write ads for local concerns even though the pay is small.

Possible employers:
Previous contacts may suggest possible employers.

Employment bureaus to be consulted:
Study trade journals for employment bureaus that specialize in my field of work.

Places of work:
Do a good advertising job in my own community and hope to get an agency job in a big city.

Vacation jobs:
Work in a summer resort patronized by businessmen.

My Training Program

that prepares for the vocation:

Schools to attend:
Enter a four-year college of business that offers cultural as well as business training.

Courses to take:
Major in advertising. Courses in commerce, art, psychology, sciences, sociology, philosophy.

Books to read:
Alden, James:
"Careers in Advertising"
The Macmillan Co., 1932

Trade journals:
Advertising & Selling
Printers' Ink
Sales Management

Persons to interview or know:
Call on advertising men and women of home town. Associate with all types of people.

Writing to do:
Some themes in college dealing with the characteristics of consumers.

My Personality Development Program.

List items, such as:

Friendships to make:
Establish friendship with business owners, advertising men, and salesmen.

Clubs to join:
Join local advertising or sales clubs. Later, join luncheon club.

Books to read:
Webb & Morgan:
Strategy in Handling People,
Garden City Pub. Co.

Tours to take:
Visit the advertising agencies of a large city.

Investment plans:
Save money when possible but spend in order to become acquainted with men and women in advertising and business. Attend trade conventions.

Health plans:
Analyze my personality once a year in order to keep a healthy mind.

The Undesirable Aspects

of this program which should be anticipated:

Opposition to expect from family, friends, or employers:
Parents who help me through college will expect me to get a well-paid job upon graduation. This is not likely.

Effect on plans for marriage or home:
Will prevent my getting married for next eight or ten years.

Unpleasant conditions of work:
Will have to do many menial jobs in order to get my education.

Difficulties in making advancements:
Department heads such as buyers of stores often blame advertising man for their own failures.

Income difficulties:
Will be out of work at times. Must shift employers frequently.

it. But follow a definite plan or you will drift, and drifting wood never reaches port. Table XXVII shows a sample vocational program which will illustrate how one can plan a career."

References

Clark, C. D., and Gist, N. P., "Intelligence as a Factor in Occupational Choice," *American Sociological Review*, 1938, Vol. 3, pp. 683-694.

Clark, H. F., and others, *Life Earnings in Selected Occupations in the United States*. Harper & Bros., 1937.

Husband, R. W., "In Defense of Scientific Vocational Guidance," *Journal of Applied Psychology*, 1936, Vol. 20, pp. 586-590.

Keller, F. J., and Viteles, M. S., *Vocational Guidance Throughout the World*. W. W. Norton & Co., 1937.

Maule, Frances, *Men Wanted; the New Opportunities and What They Demand*. Funk & Wagnalls, 1937.

O'Rourke, L. J., *Opportunities in Government Employment*. Garden City Publishing Co., 1940.

Stead, Wm. H., Shartle, C. L., Otis, J. L., et al., *Occupational Counseling Techniques*. American Book Co., 1940.

Projects

1. "Success in a vocation depends upon an adjustment to life in general rather than the fortunate selection of an occupation." Assume that this statement is true and prepare a list of mental habits that every person should acquire to be vocationally successful. Assume that the above statement is incomplete and add other forms of behavior that are essential.

2. "A rolling stone gathers no moss" and "A setting hen never gets fat." Which of these two epigrams is the more nearly correct? When should a man change his position?

3. Outline a program for obtaining valid occupational information that fits your needs.

4. Analyze yourself vocationally by means of the devices and suggestions presented in this chapter. Present the analysis in the form of a systematic report to your friends and ask them to criticize it. Then prepare a vocational program to fit your significant traits.

5. Outline a program for obtaining a position. Include an unsolicited letter of application, trade journal advertisement, list of firms where you might apply, and a written description of the facts about yourself that you would try to present to the prospective employers.

6. Prepare a graphic presentation of your past history. Use an outline map to show the places where you have worked in the past.

7. Compare the advantages and the disadvantages of going into business for yourself with those of working for an employer.

8. A *Fortune* survey (February 1939) asked this question in a nation-wide cross-section poll: "Which do you think has a better chance of earning a living today—a high school graduate who has had four years of experience, or a man just out of college?"

Results:

High school graduate.................................... 34.4%
College graduate....................................... 33.4
Depends on man and/or experience....................... 14.8
Experienced man better at first, college man better later..... 9.7
College man gets break regardless of merit.................. 2.8
Don't know... 4.9

List arguments that might be made to support each type of reply. Conduct a poll among your friends on the same question and analyze the results.

9. A *Fortune* survey (October 1939) of businessmen only included this question: "Do you think your son's opportunities for success are greater or less than those you had at his age?"

Results:

Greater.. 37.2%
Same.. 23.5
Same or greater for success, but less chance to make big money   2.0
Less.. 36.3
Don't know... 1.0

Present some of the reasons that might be given for each type of reply. Ask a number of businessmen's sons what their replies would be and compare the results with the above. List several factors that might be expected to cause a difference in the results.

10. Study the student employment opportunities in your college or one near by. List all the ways the students earn money to help support themselves. Check the jobs that contribute valuable vocational experience as well as financial reward.

11. List some occupations which may diminish in importance within the next 10 or 15 years. Suggest how workers in those occupations might utilize the change to their advantage rather than suffer because of it.

PART FOUR
Influencing the Behavior of the Individual

14

Getting a Job and Gaining Promotion

"How can I get a job when I haven't had any experience?" is the lament of many a young person when he leaves school or college. Actually, any normal individual who has a definite vocational goal, has seriously studied an industry, and developed a well-adjusted personality has excellent evidence of value to employers. But he must be able to present his worth in an effective manner.

EMPLOYERS do not expect factory workers or uneducated applicants to use clever job-getting methods. Employers assume that such applicants use the old haphazard methods of seeking employment through employment agencies, *Help-Wanted* advertisements, labor-union headquarters, and applications at personnel offices. However, the college-educated and other superior job seekers are expected to demonstrate their superiority to some extent by means of their applications. The people who need superior techniques of making application are the more highly trained workers such as engineers, accountants, statisticians, technical salesmen, and professional workers. These should know how to present their qualifications intelligently.

The intelligent candidate in the course of making his application should regard the following admonitions:

1. Know the kind of work you want and why you want it.
2. Study the employer's problems and interests.
3. Present a letter of application which proves your interest in the employer's problems and your qualifications for his needs.
4. Participate in an interview which reveals mutual interests.

Stating the kind of work desired. Many an ordinary applicant is so ego-centered when he needs a job that he can think only of his own needs. As a result of his concern about his own needs, he thinks and talks about himself. His argument for a job is similar to that of a candidate for a political office whose placard read: "I am the father of nine children and I need your support!"

The intelligent applicant's major thought is to understand his abilities, limitations, and vocational goals so well that he knows the kind of work he wants and why he believes he can do it. One employment man explained the deficiencies of applicants in this respect as follows:

> I interview hundreds of applicants, and when I ask them what they can do, a high percentage say "most anything." The answer is obviously false. I am not interested in the applicant who says that he can do anything, because that really means that he can do nothing well; nor does he know what he would like to do. But the applicant who says, "I have been studying motor transportation and I believe that I could be of help to your firm in cutting down your delivery costs," arouses a definite interest. Young people who leave school and college are especially weak in this respect. Many of them do not know whether they wish to work in a circus, a department store, a machine-shop, or a cheese factory. How can they expect to sell their services when they do not know what they have to sell?

The superior applicant, especially the one who has benefited from his college opportunities, knows the industry he wishes to enter and the kind of work he wants to learn to do. His textbook readings, classroom lectures, and personal contacts with men in the field of his choice have stimulated him to learn more about certain aspects of the work and to associate with those who are already actively engaged in his chosen field. Such an applicant has read trade journals and attended trade association meetings, and there he has learned the names and addresses of the leaders in his chosen industry. Because of his genuine interest and informed background, he can approach the professional leaders or heads of the best firms and talk with them in terms that he and they understand. The reactions of executives approached by such an applicant are likely to be: "This man knows what he wants and is going after it. He appears to be the kind of man we need in our organization. Let's try him out to discover whether he really means what he says."

Any college student who really wishes to use his college experiences in formulating definite vocational objectives can do so. Faculty members, friends in business, secretaries of trade associations, trade journals, psychological tests, and library books are usually available to him in his search to find himself in his work.[1]

Studying the employer's problems and interests. Whenever an applicant has decided what kind of work he would like to do, his knowledge will indicate which concerns would be logical employers for him. The advertisements and news articles in trade journals, listings in telephone directories, and suggestions from trade association secretaries will reveal names and addresses of many possible employers.

When he has collected such lists, he should select several preferred prospective employers and learn all he can about them. He should investigate the history of each company, study each company's product, interview their customers, and find out why people use the product. Why did they buy the product? Would they buy the same brand again? If not, why not? Of course, the purpose of this kind of investigating is not to impress the employer but to write an effective letter of application and to ask intelligent questions during the interview.

For example, a certain young man registered at an employment office. He had had experience in the retail gasoline and oil business, but had sought work unsuccessfully for some time. As he wanted to obtain employment with a certain retail gasoline company, the employment director suggested that he take definite steps to make himself valuable to this company. He was told that he should learn all he could about the business—if possible, find out if any of the company's local stations were not up to the usual company standards.

The young man found that a gas station belonging to the company where he had applied seemed to be getting less business than it should. To discover the reasons, he made a survey of all cars in the neighborhood to find whether their owners were buying gas from the station and, if not, whether there was any cause for dissatisfaction. When the survey was completed, the young man took it to the local manager of the gasoline company with a suggestion for increasing business at that station. The manager was impressed with the applicant's initiative and gave him

---

[1] *Finding Yourself in Your Work,* by H. W. Hepner (D. Appleton-Century Co., 1937), is one of many books available to college students who wish to refer to library books in setting up their vocational plans.

a position to prove his worth. The young man made good at that job and at several other difficult ones. His work was so satisfactory that in a short time he had risen to a responsible position in the local office of the company.[2]

Initiative and imagination in applying for a position are not limited to men; they can be used just as effectively by women.

Said the personnel manager of one of New York's largest department stores to me the other day: "Not one person in a hundred who comes before my desk has any ideas. Yet it's the girl with ideas who gets the job, the girl who has intelligence and interest enough to spend some time in the store looking around before she comes to me, who can suggest ways we may improve our service, who at least will be able to say: 'I watched the clerks and customers in the jewelry department yesterday and I believe I could sell in that line.' Most of them don't even do that."

But here is how one girl from the Middle West approached a New York department store. She had majored in art so she studied the art sections of all the rivals of the company. Then she wrote a letter of application in which she set forth some of the best ideas she had observed elsewhere. She got the job.

Your idea must be pertinent to the particular job you want. It should be specific and practical. Yet, even if your idea is valueless, you will nevertheless stand out above the crowd. . . . "Anyone with ideas," said the personnel director of one New York bank, "is a refreshing and potentially successful person."

"Ideas!" snorted the president of a publishing house when I brought up the question. "Ideas! Why most job hunters don't even know what the publishing business is. They all want to become editors; they aren't even aware of the existence of our other departments."

When scouting for ideas, first study the business that interests you. Read up on it, learn its problems. Then study particularly the concern with which you would like to be associated, and its competitors. Talk to their salesmen. Don't go near the firm until you know something about the business, and can demonstrate that you are the person who can be useful to it in some way. Getting a job is an examination in ideas, and you cannot afford to fail. . . .

Be sure of one thing. You cannot start too early in life to begin turning your imagination on the problem of how things can be done better. In school or in college, train yourself to observe people and their methods of doing business. You should be able by watching a worker in any occupation—a bus driver or a filling station attendant—to think of ways to make his particular job more efficient. The personnel manager of a world-wide corporation told me that not over 1 per cent of the thousands who passed before his desk as applicants ever dealt in ideas.

"How many of those who do have ideas land jobs?" I asked.

"Almost all," was the answer. It's so unusual to find a youngster with

---

[2] Charles H. Howard, "Help the Applicant to Help Himself," *Employment Service News,* December 1935.

ideas that we grab anyone who has them, even though his actual suggestions may have little value at the moment." [3]

The letter of application. Many college students can write letters which are grammatically correct but fail to reveal an interest in the employer or in doing his work. The employer is seldom a student of English nor does he care about the niceties of phrasing. He has work to be done, products to sell, payrolls to meet, taxes to pay, customers to please, and bills to collect. He does not care particularly whom he hires—he does want to get his work done quickly and economically.

This letter, written by a college graduate and published in *Postage Magazine*, is typical of letters of application constantly written by ego-centered applicants who have had no training in writing to employers:

Dear Mr. Publisher:

I am seeking editorial (or writing) work on a magazine staff.

My age is twenty-four. I am a graduate of Grinnell College (Grinnell, Iowa), and since graduation have done irregular work at Chicago and Columbia Universities. My chief aim has been to improve myself in the ability to write and in comparative study of literature. I have also specialized in history, psychology, sociology, philosophy, and advertising. Recently I completed a long novel, which is at present at Doran's, having received one favorable reading.

My college record was good. I am a Phi Beta Kappa and a Sigma Delta Chi member, having edited the last-named organization's comic weekly during my senior year in college. Before that I worked on the staffs of certain local newspapers. I also sold automobiles for a time and can use the trade language with some facility.

I have no present business connections. Since I was fifteen, I have incessantly aimed at journalism. My writing style perhaps tends to the search of the color-bearing word and the ironic, but within controllable limits. I read very rapidly (120 pages an hour) and analytically.

I am willing to start in any position which promises an opportunity for development and offers a reasonable wage.

Sincerely yours,

The comments of the recipient of this letter were:

This letter, written by a college graduate, contains eighteen "I's," "my's" and "myself's" but not a single "you." We can well imagine the publisher who wades through such a letter, searching for and finding the "ironic' word and using it without "controllable limit." Every year, millions of letters like this are written by young men looking for positions. We should like to recommend to every college in the land that a business course on "How

---

[3] Condensed from John R. Tunis, "Imagination Gets the Job," *Review of Reviews,* January 1935.

to Write a Letter" be delivered to its students, to cover the last six months of their term. Thousands of splendid positions are held by men who knew how to write a good letter and wrote it at the psychological time.

The following application letter, written by an alert college senior, was sent to the advertising managers of eighteen leading department stores and promptly resulted in offers of two jobs, one of which was accepted:

> 211 West 14th Street
> Meldon, Massachusetts
> July 5, 1939

Advertising Manager of (Name of Firm)
Street
City

Dear Sir:

Your advertising appeals to me. It suggests that you are following policies and procedures that would benefit the young advertising woman.

My ultimate goal is that of advertising manager of a retail store. To reach this point I realize that real experience is necessary.

I am anxious to have good supervision and direction in my training for this career and recognize the opportunities available in your store. Therefore, I am eager to attain any work in this line you can offer me.

As a beginner in your department, I offer the ability to take dictation and type. As your needs would demand, I could gradually make myself useful in writing copy or preparing advertisements. One of my sample advertisements for a local retail store is enclosed.

You will find further information and references on the attached personal data sheet. May I have your suggestions?

> Very truly yours,
> (Miss) Mary Doe

Personal Data Sheet (attached to above)

NAME AND ADDRESS:
    Mary Doe   211 West 14th Street, Meldon, Massachusetts

DATE AND PLACE OF BIRTH:
    February 7, 1918   Andover, New Hampshire

HEALTH RECORD:
    My general health has always been excellent. I have never had a serious illness.
    Height 5 feet, 6 inches   Weight: 120

EDUCATION:
    In June of this year, I graduated from ———— University with a B. S. degree, having majored in journalism and minored in advertising. My previous education was received in the public schools of Meldon.

ACTIVITIES:

President of Theta Sigma Phi, women's honorary and professional journalism fraternity. Member of Second Cabinet of University YWCA. Rifle Team. Reporter on college newspaper. My activities were few due to the fact that I partly worked my way through college.

EXPERIENCE:

I have written a series of ads for W. I. Addis Company, (exclusive women's shop) which appeared in the college daily. (A copy of the ad is attached to this letter.) Recently I won third place in an advertising contest conducted by the ———— Power Company.

RELIGION:

Protestant. For the past three years, I have been active in the young people's group and this year was chosen chairman of the discussion group.

REFERENCES:

(Names and addresses of four people listed)

This letter avoided the many "I's," "my's" and "myself's" through the use of a personal data sheet, an excellent device for most applicants. Furthermore, the applicant complimented the employer and indicated a genuine interest in learning *his* methods as an aid in her own development.

Many high school and college graduates claim that they cannot write a good letter of application because they cannot point to past experience as evidence of their ability. Some of these younger applicants visit employment offices where they are told that no jobs are open for inexperienced workers. These young applicants should recognize that the old answer: "Sorry, we have no opening now for persons without experience," often means that either the applicant did not appeal to the employment man or the applicant did not know how to present his qualifications effectively.

The intelligent inexperienced applicant who knows what kind of work he wants to learn and why, can, with reasonable persistence, find an interested employer. The youth has a most appealing argument whenever he applies to an employer with this type of approach:

"Mr. Employer, I have decided that I wish to learn the hardware business because I have worked in a hardware store during summer vacations and liked it. I know such simple details as the sizes of bolts and saws. I can drive a truck and check invoices. Besides my summer experience as evidence of interest, I read two trade journals in the hardware field. Three hardware dealers told me that if they were young again and wanted to learn the hardware business they would come to you. So here I am for your advice and, if I meet your requirements, for your employment."

Address
Date

Name of firm manager
Address

Dear Mr. Blank:

I wish to apply for a position as Junior Accountant in your firm, and am submitting for your convenience an analysis chart of myself. (See opposite.)

This chart will, in a brief way, I believe, present the information desired.

Very truly yours,

Dear Sir:

I have just read your advertisement.

You evidently want someone who understands what are the real duties of a secretary. He must

—transcribe your dictation accurately, promptly.
—"proofread" his letters for possible errors.
—receive your callers politely, civilly.
—separate the important ones from those who should wait or come again.
—open and assort your mail.
—make a list of your engagements, reminding you of them at the proper time.
—keep your personal accounts.
—keep your business to *himself.*

My experience covers eight years of stenographic and secretarial service, with knowledge of bookkeeping. Age, 25 years. Unmarried.

Let me come and see you. I feel confident of fulfilling your requirements. My telephone is Main 6000.

Yours truly,

This letter leaves no doubt that the writer understands what a secretary is expected to do. The advertisement was simply for a secretary. Instead of making his letter the usual hackneyed statement of qualifications and experience, he tabulates the duties of the post and thus modestly conveys the idea that he can perform them.

Any youth can present his qualifications and evidence of interest in a given vocation in an original manner. He can prepare a loose-leaf booklet or pamphlet of his background and characteristics. It can be illustrated with pictures from advertisements and include character references, copies of school report cards, Boy Scout badges, maps, school term papers, and so on.

Analysis Chart

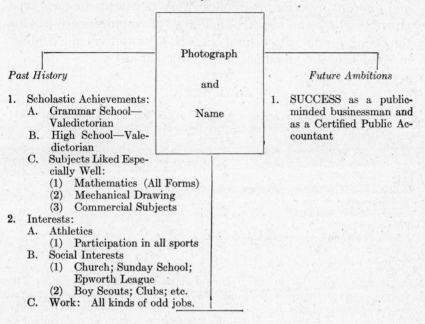

Photograph and Name

Past History

1. Scholastic Achievements:
   A. Grammar School— Valedictorian
   B. High School—Vale- dictorian
   C. Subjects Liked Espe- cially Well:
      (1) Mathematics (All Forms)
      (2) Mechanical Drawing
      (3) Commercial Subjects
2. Interests:
   A. Athletics
      (1) Participation in all sports
   B. Social Interests
      (1) Church; Sunday School; Epworth League
      (2) Boy Scouts; Clubs; etc.
   C. Work: All kinds of odd jobs.

Future Ambitions

1. SUCCESS as a public- minded businessman and as a Certified Public Ac- countant

Present Status

Graduate of

Syracuse University; College of Business Administration; Accounting

Scholastic Achievements

1. Winner of two Uni- versity Competitive Scholarships
2. Member of Beta Al- pha Psi (National honorary, Accounting Fraternity)
3. Member of Phi Kappa Phi (National schol- astic)
4. Scholarship Rating—B

Wholly Self-Supporting

1. College education was wholly self-financed by means of summer work, working six hours daily during school year, and schol- arships.

Activities

1. Athletics
   Wrestling — '30, '31, '32
      Intercollegiate Champion...'32
      Captain.......'32
      Soccer.......1931
2. Social Activities
3. Others: Scoutmaster

References

1. Name and address
2. Name and address
3. Name and address
4. Name and address

Personal Record

Birth—Jan. 30, 1910; Henderson, New York
Nationality—American
Religion—Methodist
Marital Status—Single
Height—5' 4"; Weight—135 lbs.
Health—Excellent; Defects—None.

Anyone's personal history offers many examples of good character and interest in performing honest work that leads to vocational growth and advancement. Thousands of employers are looking for young people who exhibit a spark of initiative and strategy in presenting their qualifications in original ways.

TABLE XXVIII[4]

THE APPLICANT SHOULD KNOW THE EMPLOYERS' PREFERRED SOURCES FOR OBTAINING EMPLOYEES IN THE FIELD HE WISHES TO ENTER

Sources of New Employees	Banks in New York (Figures are % of total Employed in 1938)			Banks in Other Cities		
	1	2	3	4	5	6
Recommended by officers and employees	30	12	} 30	42	51	33
By customers	13	8		7	5	8
Applied on own initiative	10	18	10	28	35	34
From agencies	46	55	60	8	6	17
From schools and business machine companies	1	7	—	15	3	8

The figures give the percentage from each source of the total number, 740, employed in one year. In the table, the New York banks have been grouped on one side and banks in Cleveland, Philadelphia, and Boston on the other. The principal difference is in the much larger proportion of new employees obtained by New York banks through employment agencies. The reason for this is due to the much larger size of the city of New York and the correspondingly larger number of eligible employers for any one applicant. The stenographer seeking a job, for example, would have a large number of employers to call on before getting a proper distribution of opportunity, whereas in smaller cities it is entirely possible for an applicant to call on most of the large employers.

The interview. The main purpose of a letter of application is to obtain an interview. The interview is an occasion where employer and applicant consider each other's mutual problems and interests. The applicant is not asking a favor nor is the employer granting a privilege. Each has something to give and each has needs which may or may not be of mutual advantage.

Many applicants are nervous because they think of themselves during the interview. They can often overcome or avoid nervousness by anticipating the questions that are likely to be asked in the interview. Typical questions which are asked many applicants are the following:

---

[4] Edward N. Hay, "Sources of Bank Personnel," *Banking,* December 1939, p. 24.

1. Tell me all about yourself.
2. Why do you want to work for us?
3. What can you do?
4. Why did you leave your last employer? (Why do you want to leave your present employer?)
5. Do you have any good ideas on how to do this work for which you are applying?
6. May I see some samples or proof of your ability?

The first question should not be answered by starting with the date of birth, early life, and leading up to the time of the interview. Rather, the question should be answered by reference to the present: "I completed college this spring and I majored in finance. While I was studying finance I became interested in banking. Perhaps my interest in banking was stimulated by the speakers whom I heard at the state bankers' convention held in Blankville two years ago. The problems discussed with regard to financing farmers' crops interested me so much that I would like to learn more about the problems involved in loans to farmers. I myself was raised on a farm in Spring Valley and my father often felt financially handicapped in his plans for modernizing his farm, etc."

One hundred college students and graduates who had applied for positions were asked to list the problems they had encoun-

THIS YOUNG MAN believing in the importance of a right start, is eager to go to work for an advertising agency at no salary until he has proved himself worthy of one. Twenty-two, college graduate, thorough training in advertising, background of retail sales experience, with character references of the best. Wrote for all college publications. Ambitious to do copy . . . start in anything leading up to it. Box 701, P. I.

ARE YOU PREJUDICED AGAINST A PHI BETA KAPPA KEY, University of Chicago? I confess I am—though I am a young woman who owns one.

I want to break into New York publishing or advertising or some similar employment—no matter how humble the starting place.

In extenuation, I offer:

1. One year's editorial experience on a Chicago publication.
2. Youth and enthusiasm—despite two years' public school teaching experience.
3. Some general business experience, including expert knowledge of typewriting.
4. A not unattractive, UNACADEMIC personality.

Will you grant me an interview? Box 432, Printers' Ink.

Advertisements for Positions

tered in their applications. The following list is made up of those problems most frequently reported by the interviewees. Each general problem listed below is followed by its frequency and examples of the problem.

Before the Interview

1. The question of experience (27 times). Examples:
   a. Should I admit that I have had no experience and face the possibility of not being hired? Or should I try to lie and take my chances on getting by if I do get the job?
   b. Is there any way in which I can compensate for the lack of experience?
   c. How can I be sure that I am qualified to apply?
2. The question whether or not to tell the truth (19 times). Examples:
   a. Religious affiliations—should I admit membership in my church if I know that my prospective employer is an adherent of another faith? (The laws of some states prohibit the asking of this question; if it is asked, it does not have to be answered.)
   b. Should I admit union membership if I am a member?
   c. Should I admit and discuss my political beliefs?
3. The interview itself (14 times). Examples:
   a. How can I best determine the type of approach to make?
   b. Should I emphasize my scholastic achievements?
   c. How should I sell myself?
   d. What type of references should I use?

During the Interview

1. The salary question (38 times). Examples:
   a. How can I answer, "What salary do you expect?"
   b. How am I to know that I will not ask too much? Or too little?
   c. Or should I ask for an approximate salary?
2. Reasons for choice of firm in making application (19 times). How can I answer, for example, the following:
   a. What can you do?
   b. Why did you choose this type of work?
   c. Why are you sure that you will like the work?
   d. Should I talk freely and frankly about what I consider my ability?
3. The job particulars (15 times). Examples:
   a. Should I ask questions about the job until I thoroughly understand all parts of it?
   b. Or should I wait until I get to the department to delve into the requisites of the job?
   c. Should I try to determine my chances for advancement, and its rapidity, while I am being interviewed?
   d. Should I ask questions about the firm during the interview? Or should I know many particulars concerning the firm before the interview?

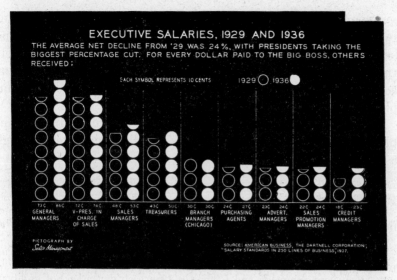

FIG. 60. The chart shows what the executives of various departments and with various responsibilities received in remuneration, relative to the amounts received by the presidents of the companies they worked for.

4. Nervousness (15 times). Examples:
   a. How can I overcome nervousness?
   b. How can I best conceal my nervousness?
   c. How can I break down the formal attitude of the interview?

After the Interview

1. The interview itself (25 times). Examples:
   a. How can I judge the success of the interview? ·
   b. How can I tell whether the questions were answered correctly?
   c. What kind of impression did I make?
2. The results (23 times). Examples:
   a. Should I return and keep after the interviewer until he hires? If so, how soon?
   b. Should I have influential friends intercede in my behalf?

No one can offer blanket answers to these and other questions which are asked of applicants and which they ask themselves. Neither questions nor answers can be standardized. The applicant can seek the counsel of some experienced person with regard to appropriate answers to questions such as these. A discussion of the questions and possible answers will be a considerable help to many applicants. However, if the employer's question, "Tell me all about yourself," can be answered in the foregoing suggested manner, many other questions can also be answered sincerely and intelligently. All the employer's questions can be answered naturally when the applicant has developed a genuine long-term interest in the work for which he is applying. Getting a job is merely one stage in a series of efforts to become acquainted with specific kinds of vocational problems, employers, and occupational opportunities.

Some arts of personal salesmanship are helpful and many applicants can improve their abilities to sell themselves through a consideration of the following suggestions:

1. Think and talk *work*, not yourself. Try to think of yourself as a profitable investment to the employer, not of what the job means to you.

2. Consider getting a job as an investment—not an expense. Spend some time and money in getting a job. If necessary, borrow money to get the job you want.

3. Develop confidence in yourself by first studying your prospective employer's product or service.

4. Plan your campaign and follow the plan each day. Do not go about it in a hit-or-miss manner. Know where you want to apply each day for the next month until you get a job.

5. Consider it a sales proposition. If your first and second prospects do not want you, keep on trying. The fiftieth prospect may be just the one who needs you.

6. When asked to fill an application blank, fill it completely and cheerfully. Put a check mark in the blank spaces not applying to you. Then the interviewer will know you did not overlook any items.

7. Convince the employer you did not stop studying when you left school or college. Show him you are studying your work by means of books, magazines, and night-school or correspondence courses.

8. No one can write a good letter of application for you—you must write it yourself. You must "feel" what you write, then your letter will carry conviction. Study good letters of application, but write your own. If you really feel you are good for something, your letter will show it.

9. Have several friends criticize your letter. You'll probably revise it at least five times before sending it.

10. Always give your complete record and full information when asked to do so. Do not omit your activities of certain months or years.

11. When sending a photograph, send a good one. If the job is worth applying for, it is worth having a special picture taken for it.

12. When discussing salary, state what you have been getting and what you believe yourself worth to the employer. Do not haggle over salary too much, but if the employer is one of the kind who wants to pay less than people are worth, refuse his offer. The fellow who wants something for nothing is not the kind of man you want to work for. Of course, he has a right to pay you a small salary until he knows what you are really worth to him. If you are a college graduate, your alumni secretary can probably give you some helpful figures on average or customary salaries of your fellow-alumni. See Table XXIX.

13. When you and the interviewer have discussed the vacant job to mutual satisfaction, the interviewer may hesitate to say, "Yes, you are the man we want." Many interviewers need subtle help in making decisions. If you feel that the interviewer really is willing to hire you but needs a "push" in your direction, you can help him by saying, "When would you want me to begin work if you decide to hire me?" The date of beginning work is a minor point but once the interviewer decides on the minor point he also usually hires you.

A survey made in 1940 of 1,608 Carnegie engineering graduates furnished the following information on salaries. The median earnings of the 1940 survey are compared with the median earnings reported in the survey of 1,449 Carnegie engineering graduates during 1929-30.

TABLE XXIX[5]

SALARY CHANGES AFTER GRADUATION

Year Since Graduation	Survey Made in 1929-30 Median Salary	Survey Made in 1940 Median Salary
1	$1,902	$1,569
2	2,328	1,691
3	2,586	1,918
4	2,894	2,071
5	3,054	2,290
6	3,350	2,243
7	3,591	2,444
8	3,909	2,529
9	3,958	2,522
10	4,365	2,865
11	4,292	3,525
12	4,083	3,510
13	5,367	3,667
14	4,775	4,032
15	5,000	3,887
16	5,600	3,866
17	5,125	4,300
18	4,688	5,082
19	5,167	4,917
20	6,500	4,666

Gaining promotion. The economic status and advancement of 46,000 college graduates, eight years after graduation, has been studied by federal government investigators. This study is summarized below so that college student readers may be able to use the progress records, made by college graduates of the past, as a basis of prediction for their own advancement.

---

[5] John D. Beatty, *Carnegie Alumnus*, June 1940. The table in the original article is somewhat more extended, including data for 22 years after graduation in the 1929-30 study and for 30 years after graduation in the 1940 study.

Economic Status of College Alumni[6]
A Study of 46,000 Graduates

Eight years after graduation the typical male college graduate finds himself in a job for which he specialized as an undergraduate, a job which he obtained on his own initiative; he never has been unemployed or on relief; at 30 years of age earns nearly $2,500 a year; is married but has no children; pays $38 per month for rent; lives and works in a city of 100,000 or more population.

These and many other facts of equal interest are uncovered in the published results of an exhaustive study of the records of 46,000 men and women graduates of 31 institutions of higher learning, classes of 1928 to 1935. . . .

The study on economic status is based on personal questionnaires received from 5 per cent of all living college graduates who received bachelor's degrees in the eight-year period 1928-35. "Large" (3,000 or more student enrollment) and "small" (fewer than 3,000 students) colleges were selected in each of four sections of the country: East, South, North, and West. The total return of usable questionnaires for all institutions was 48.3 per cent. Following is a summary of points of vocational interest contained in the published report:

Employment—Men tend to find work eventually that is in line with their specialization in college. Women find their work less in line with their major college study.

Undergraduate majors—Engineering and business administration are the most popular undergraduate majors for men. Women graduates majored most largely in education and English.

Self-help—Sixty-eight per cent of the men and 43 per cent of the women earned from one fourth to all of their college expenses.

Graduate study—One half of both men and women alumni in classes of 1928 through 1935 continued later with graduate study. . . .

First jobs—Personal initiative plus experience prior to graduation account for half the placement of college graduates in first jobs. Next in order are placement by college or faculty, and family influence or business. Least productive are alumni and fraternity contacts, and employment agencies, public and private.

Why chosen—Thirty-five per cent of the women and 27 per cent of the men reported choosing their first jobs because the work was the kind they wanted. Thirty per cent of the men and 19 per cent of the women were unable to find the work they wanted. .

Unemployment—Fifty-eight per cent of the men graduates and 61 per cent of the women graduates have never been idle at all since graduation. Graduates of the 1932 class were out of employment for the longest periods.

Relief—Ninety-eight per cent of the men alumni and 99 per cent of the women alumnae have never been on relief. . . .

Owners—After graduation 10 per cent of the men start out in a business or profession of their own. After eight years 31 per cent are independent of

[6] *Economic Status of College Alumni*, Bulletin 1937, No. 10, by Walter J. Greenleaf, Washington, D. C., U. S. Government Printing Office, Superintendent of Documents, 1939, pp. I-X and 207. Price 25 cents. Summaries taken from *Occupations*, June 1939.

Fig. 61. Walter James Greenleaf, Specialist in Occupational Information and Guidance, U. S. Office of Education. Those interested in the problem of the college graduate may refer to his book *Economic Status of College Alumni* (Government Printing Office, Washington, D. C., Bulletin 1937, No. 10).

employers. In the West 9.5 per cent of the women one year out of college own their own businesses. The proportion increases until after eight years 19 per cent are established as owners or part owners.

Employees—Fifty-three per cent of the college men found work after graduation as clerks or unskilled workers. Of the women graduates 52 per cent began with the clerical types of work.

Salaries—The salary scale of men alumni is higher than that of women alumnae, although older women receive more than younger men generally. The average college man out of school one year receives a typical salary of $1,314; the graduate out of school two years $1,455; three years, $1,551; four years, $1,684; five years $1,847; six years, $2,008; seven years, $2,138, and eight years, $2,383. Women graduates receive salaries ranging from $1,092 the first year out of college to $1,606 the eighth year.

Occupations—Nearly two thirds of the college alumni reported themselves in the professional group. Seventeen per cent of the men were teaching, 13 per cent were in engineering, 9 per cent in law, and 6 per cent in medicine. Forty-eight per cent of the women alumnae were following teaching careers, while 29 per cent reported general occupations, including 16 per cent in domestic work. . . .

Typical—In general a typical graduate will enter an occupation paying about $1,321 (median) for his first year. After eight years he will be receiving $2,416 (median). Eleven per cent of the alumni out of college eight years report earnings of from $4,000 to $5,000 or more while 11 per cent receive $1,500 or less.

For women—Nursing and teaching are the best-paid occupations for a woman during her first year out of college. The median salary for nursing is $1,692 and for teaching $1,236. A woman out of college one year receives typically $1,109 compared with $1,608 for the woman eight years out of college.

This study indicated that most college graduates become employees rather than employers, hence, we shall discuss methods of gaining promotion with employers.

1. One factor that will greatly aid an employee in obtaining advancement is to work for an executive who likes him. No one can study the personnel of modern business and claim that all men who deserve to hold good positions are actually holding them. Nor do all the executives who now hold important positions deserve them. Some have gained their high executive positions by inheritance, others have married strategically, and some have fallen into their positions by a chance combination of fortunate circumstances. Many men gain their promotions simply because they are moderately capable and the man above them happens to like them. Just as the choice of a wife or a husband is the result of unconscious influences rather than scientific analysis, so are many of the manager's selections of men for promotion the results of chance personal liking. The employee who wishes to be promoted should seek the goodwill and admiration of his superior or find a new superior who does like him.

Some readers may say: "If there is anything I hate it's a bootlicker, a yes-man, or the employee who sticks around the boss." Yet, we should not accuse the retailer of being a fawning flatterer because he dresses up his windows to attract those who are his logical buyers. The merchant merely utilizes some concrete advantages of his wares. Likewise the corporation employee should try to attract the prospective buyers of his services by appealing to his buyers in a way that can be understood.

2. The corporation clerical worker, salesman, or junior executive may be asking himself, "Why doesn't someone notice me?" If he is, he can answer his own question by asking himself, "What 'window dressing' have I done that will bring about recognition or a raise?" By this it is not implied that an employee should put every item of ability into the "showcase" and have no reserve in the "warehouse." It is well, however, to give emphasis to the need for concrete evidence of ability, presented in such form that one's colleagues, superiors, and subordinates may be able to judge one's worth.

We all tend to measure human ability and accomplishments in terms of the tangible—things that we can see, hear, smell, taste, or count in a definite manner. That is one reason why we find it easy to admire the wealthy man. We can say that he has accumulated $892,397.62 in the past forty years. Dollars are definite and concrete. Everyone understands what is meant by houses, automobiles, number of employees, talks or addresses made, and articles written. These things are far more easily grasped by the human mind than the abstract qualities of ability, capacity, judgment, effort, and initiative that made possible the dollars and automobiles. The ambitious corporation employee may have the abstract traits that deserve promotion, but he must put them into concrete form and display them to attract the right customers. The white-collar man must put concrete evidence into his "showcase." The employee should make charts or diagrams of the methods used in his work. It is possible but highly improbable that the supervisor knows how each employee does his work. The other men in the organization are so busy with their own problems that they do not have time to study what he is really doing. The daily efforts of the worker may seem childishly simple to himself, but they are mysteries to others. Therefore it is well to make some charts or diagrams that will tell those around and above the employee about the methods he is constantly using and the work he is doing. These charts should be so simple that anyone can understand them and the effects that the job is supposed to accomplish in the organization. If possible, the chart should show how the work was done years ago and how it is done now. Such a chart need not be a mere gesture to attract attention to one's self. It should enable the employee to locate some avenues which can be extended or improved.

3. A third possibility for the "showcase" is that of devising new systems or methods which will make more money or decrease costs for the employer. The alert employee who seeks methods of making money or cutting costs is often surprised to find some good ideas which others have overlooked or "kicked around." It is well to pick them up, polish them, try them out, and present them to superiors with a description of their values and limitations.

In some cases the general manager and the twenty-dollar clerk have the same grade of brains. But the clerk tends to think in twenty-dollar channels—of his own needs, grouches, enmities, and desires for luxuries. How can he expect to merit a raise when his brain cells are working overtime on personal matters, while those of the big men in the company are active on company problems of volume production, sales resistance, net profits, and lower costs? When the employee does find a good idea for his employer, he should collect some facts and figures to prove it. His suggestions should be shown to some of his trusted fellow employees, and, before they are presented to the "big boss," a sales talk of the values should be prepared in advance.

4. If an employee is holding a mediocre job and the general manager does not know him, then he should not jump over the heads of his superiors in trying to get recognition from the key man of the company. He must always remember that chances for promotion are determined by his supervisory executive, because the "big guns" of the company consult their department heads before raising the pay or the job of an employee. This means that it may be necessary at times to neglect one's own "showcase" and help to trim that of one's superior. This is merely a part of the game of business.

5. A fifth possible way of advertising one's ability is that of making special reports on existing conditions of the business or conditions which may affect the business. Some executives have a fetishlike admiration for reports that present column after column of figures. Sometimes reports of this sort are not read, but they usually create a favorable impression at the time. A consultant related an experience in a concern where he was to study certain conditions. At the end of his job he gave the manager a complete report of the situation. Several days later, the manager told him that he had read the report with much pleasure, but that it failed to show him what to do in the future. The writer took the report from his desk and turned to the thirty-six pages where the details which were thought to have been omitted were given. As a matter of fact, the manager had not read the report. He just glanced through it and judged it very largely on the basis of its external appearance—its size, typing, charts, and quality of paper. The standards which he used in evaluating hours of mental toil gave a shock and a lesson which indicated

that it is well to spend a large amount of time on the artistic aspects of reports. The colored charts may be unintelligible to a genius; but they should be beautiful enough to decorate the walls of an office carpeted with oriental rugs.

6. Another aspect of the report as a means of gaining recognition is that of the trade journal. Many office men think that it is necessary to be a professor of English or to use a Harvard accent to be able to write an article for a trade journal. Such is not the case. The trade journals are interested in shop talk, and any systems or ideas which have been of value to men in their field will be of interest to their readers. The good ideas should be described in as pleasing a manner as possible, but efforts should be concentrated on the ideas rather than the form. The editors will revise the article to fit the vernacular of the publication. Of course, one must be careful not to divulge information that should remain in the files of the employer. If in doubt on this matter, the manuscripts can be submitted to the proper authorities of the company before they are sent to the publisher. The average executive will probably be pleased to know that someone in his organization writes articles for his colleagues and competitors to read.

7. The head of a department can develop a training system for his employees. He can prepare a manual of instructions and conduct regular classes for them. Someone can act as secretary at the meetings, and the department head can present some information to the management that would not be uncovered without such a training group.

8. If possible to do so, it is well to attend some of the conventions of associations that influence the business. A good rule is never to attend a convention without making a report of valuable facts to the management. One may neglect to do this because the speeches will be printed and sent to the company later on. This fact should not deter one from making a report, because a delegate should study the undercurrents of the conferences and pick up valuable points that are not evident in the published reports. This is especially true of trends or tendencies of the times, which are seldom described in words but which the experienced technician uncovers when he meets ex-

perts in his own field. The management should be given the benefit of the meetings attended even though the employee has to pay his own expenses to the convention.

9. To gain promotion, it is important to associate with the men and women who have demonstrated their abilities. The old-timers in the business game can give valuable pointers. Membership in pertinent trade associations will stimulate the employee to work and give him valuable contacts.

10. A final suggestion for the employee's show window is illustrated in a recent occurrence. A certain department head operated his department with the same equipment bequeathed him some years before by his predecessor. The executive knew that his equipment and methods were slightly obsolete, but he thought that he was saving money for his employer by laboriously plugging along. He hated to ask his employer to spend money for needed machinery. The general manager finally decided that this department was too antiquated for the rest of the organization, fired the department head, and put a new man in charge.

The new man, realizing that he had to dress up the windows, at once spent all the money he could possibly get in making the department ultra modern. The new equipment could be seen and admired by his employer. It was tangible evidence of ability. Of course it cost a lot of money, but it was worth it. The new department head acquired the reputation of using progressive methods, and he was promoted again.

The advancement of any man in business depends upon his ability to please others. The owner of a business must please his customers. The employee of a corporation must please the man who is responsible for his efforts. His question should be, "What does this man want me to do?" not "What should I do for my best interests?" If the boss wants his men to come to work at seven o'clock in the morning, then seven o'clock is the proper time to start work. If he dislikes men who wear mustaches and part their hair in the middle, then the employee should go without a mustache and comb his hair in a satisfactory manner. If an employer is whimsical, it is vastly easier to please his whimsicalities than to try to change him. Boss management is almost as important as scientific management. If adjustment to a superior's peculiarities is too difficult or degrading, then a new employer should be sought.

Of course, every employer really wants results above all things else. If a special kind of bolt is needed for an emergency, it does little good to telephone all the local sources of bolt supplies and find that no one in the city can furnish the needed bolt. Excuses will not satisfy. The bolt must be obtained in another city or made to order. Most of the personal factors that produce results are not the work of genius but of habits of persistence and character in doing well the routine tasks of the job. However, an employee of a large corporation may be doing good work but the right executives may not realize it. Just as advertising is necessary in selling goods, so legitimate presentations of one's good works may be helpful to personal advancement in the large corporation.

References

Boynton, Paul W., *Six Ways to Get a Job.* Harper & Bros., 1940.

Edlund, S. W. and M. G., *Pick Your Job and Land It!* Prentice-Hall, Inc., 1938.

Fletcher, Wm. L., *How to Get the Job You Want.* William L. Fletcher, Inc., 1929.

Hepner, H. W., *Finding Yourself in Your Work.* D. Appleton-Century Co., 1937.

Kitson, Harry D., *How to Find the Right Vocation.* Harper & Bros., 1929.

——————, *I Find My Vocation.* McGraw-Hill Book Co., 1931.

Parker, Willard E., *Books About Jobs.* National Occupational Conference, 1936. A rich bibliographical source containing about 8,000 references listed under some 600 job classifications.

Ryder, Violet, and H. B. Doust, *Make Your Own Job.* H. W. Wilson Co., 1934.

Projects

1. Select a business or industry which interests you vocationally, and gather the following data about it:

    a. Names and location of the leading firms.

    b. Important individuals in the field.

    c. Names of trade associations related to the business or industry.

    d. Trade journals and associated periodicals.

    e. The closest local branches of the leading firms—the men in charge, and something about them personally.

2. From the list of questions on page 377 and any others you may care to add, select those that you have encountered most frequently yourself. Prepare a well-thought-out procedure for use in your next interview.

3. Listen to a radio employment program where applicants give their qualifications over the air. Take notes on each of several cases and suggest how the applicants could improve their cases.

4. Collect a number of unconvincing "situation wanted" ads from a newspaper or trade journal. Diagnose the difficulty in each case and rewrite the ad for effective results.

5. Name some specific "showcase" items that you can utilize in your present work or in a position with which you are familiar. Analyze the probable effect of each.

6. Write a letter of application for a position you would like to have. Include a personal data sheet and a list of specific skills, or things you could do at once for an employer while working toward the type of position you are aiming at. Use the following check list and add to it any items you think would be helpful.

Men	*Women*
Operate an engine.	Sew.
Repair automobiles.	Cook.
Do concrete-mixing.	Take care of children.
Do physical labor.	Do housework.
Collect bills.	Be a telephone operator.
Run errands.	Do filing.
Be a gas station attendant.	Take care of the sick.
Repair radios.	Design clothes.

Both Men and Women

Do typing.	Do statistical work.
Do bookkeeping.	Write legibly.
Do selling.	Be an information clerk.
Do clerical work.	Drive a car.
Be an office machine operator.	Sort mail.
Operate semi-automatic machines.	Be a cashier.
Do showcard writing.	Be a sales clerk.
Write a good letter.	Be a helper to a skilled worker.
Drawing, sketching.	Drive a car safely.
Do window dressing.	Persuade others.
Repair machinery.	Act as a group leader.
Say a pleasant "Good morning."	Make many friends.
Make a good first impression.	Supervise others.
Use strategy in buying.	Sell goods.
Know the rules of etiquette.	Use good English.
Talk interestingly.	Invent unusual phrases.
Speak several languages.	Write.
Speak in public.	Do research work.
Invent new devices.	Develop new services.
Invent new systems.	Manual dexterity.
Versed in current events.	

15

Personal Efficiency in Mental Work

A person's own convictions regarding his abilities are the most powerful factors in his mental efficiency. His convictions about himself can be changed and his methods of work improved, but his methods of work will not improve until such time as he himself determines to improve them and persists in learning the new and better habits.

The urge to achieve. A dynamic missionary was recently sent to a certain Indian reservation where he attempted to modernize the members of the tribe. He usually found a certain robust and intelligent brave sitting before his wigwam where he had spent many moons in peaceful daydreaming. The missionary decided that the Indian could improve himself by getting a job in a city near by, and the following conversation took place:

Missionary: Brother, why don't you go to the big city and get a job in a factory?

Indian: Suppose I get a job, what then?

M: If you get a job, you will get money and you can have many things.

I: What then?

M: Well, if you do your work well, you will be promoted, become a foreman, and have more money.

I: What then?

M: Oh, then you may become the superintendent of the factory if you work hard enough.

I: What then?

M: If you study all about the business and work harder, you may become the manager of the whole business.

I: Suppose I become the manager, how would that benefit me?

M: If you are an able manager, you can start a business of your own and have more money than ever.

I: Then what?

M: Oh, eventually, you will have so much money that you won't need to work at all.

I: That, paleface, is what I'm doing now. Why go to so much trouble to gain what I already have? The white man has the restless sea within his bosom, but the Indian dreams with the stars and looks on.

The achieving man has an urge, a drive, a "restless sea within" which demands constant activity. These drives are not placed within the individual by his own volition but result from inter-relations between his heredity, organic conditions, and adjustments. Psychological studies of intensive mental workers indicate that many have become studious because of an urge to compensate for a physical defect such as lameness or deafness. Others have developed drives through the sublimation of sex energies, the determination to avenge an insult, the attempt to adjust one's life to the nagging of a tormenting wife, or other barriers.

In Chapters 3 to 9 we saw how habits and attitudes growing out of adjustments tend to result in outstanding achievements. The drives developed in the processes of adjustment on the part of the individual are exceedingly important, not only in setting up and striving toward vocational and other goals, but also in the setting up of psychological resistances which handicap the individual in learning common school subjects. As pointed out in Chapter 7, the normal person's nervous system will perform the functions involved in learning one subject just as easily as in learning any other subject. Only the conditionings and habits growing out of adjustments result in inabilities to learn certain kinds of subject matter such as mathematics or languages. The individual's own definitions and convictions regarding himself are the potent factors in his talent and skills, or lack of them, as proved by the results from drills in spelling. Experiments show that when drills are given to a poor speller, he improves his spelling only when he himself really determines to improve it. Mere repetitious drill has almost no value—the individual's attitude toward the drill is all-important. Sometimes the individual's convictions regarding his inabilities are so deep-seated in his personality that a clinical approach is necessary to make the later exercises in spelling worth while.

The following statement by a psychologist who spoke at an annual meeting of the American College Personnel Association explains more fully the need for the clinical technique in dealing with certain inabilities:

The clinical technique which follows from the theoretical conception of the problem must therefore aim to bring about in the subject a re-examination of those ideas which block his development. Academic difficulties and social maladjustments are both conceived of as due to resistances arising from the subject's[1] idea of himself. Obviously, the method must rely upon inducing the subject to observe the system of contradictions in which he has become involved.

Let us take the case of an intelligent student who is deficient, let us say, in spelling. In almost every instance, poor spellers have been tutored and practiced in spelling over long periods without improvement. For some reason such a student has a special handicap in learning how to spell, though not in learning the other subjects which are usually considered more difficult. This deficiency is not due to a lack of ability, but rather to an active resistance which prevents him from learning how to spell in spite of the extra instruction. The resistance arises from the fact that at some time in the past the suggestion that he is a poor speller was accepted and incorporated into his definition of himself, and is now an integral part of his total personality. His difficulty is thus explained as a special instance of the general principle that a person can only be true to himself. If he defined himself as a poor speller, the misspelling of a certain proportion of the words which he uses becomes for him a moral issue. He misspells words for the same reason that he refuses to be a thief. That is, he must endeavor to behave in a manner consistent with his idea of himself.

In these cases, we find that this self-definition as a poor speller, and consequently the resistance to learning how to spell correctly, can usually be removed in from one to five interviews. The majority become average or better than average spellers within the space of two or three months.

A study of the spelling behavior of these students shows that each individual seems to have a definite standard of poor spelling which he unconsciously endeavors to maintain. If his spelling test is cut in two, it will be found that each half contains approximately the same number of misspelled words. If we study his letters or written theses, there is likewise a striking consistency in the number of misspelled words per page. Strange to say, the spelling of foreign languages seems to be impaired very little if at all, showing clearly that the difficulty cannot be attributed to eye movements, left-handedness, or other mechanical interferences. Evidently the conception of one's self as a poor speller usually has reference to one's native language only.

The clinical technique consists in first finding several strong values apparently unrelated to the value in question which can be used as levers, so to speak, and then demonstrating the inconsistency between these values and the one responsible for the deficiency. Almost every student considers himself independent and self-reliant, for example. On the other hand, it can readily be shown that the poor speller expects his defect to be condoned and treated sympathetically; that, in effect, he has his hand out begging for indulgence. If the contradiction can be demonstrated from his own viewpoint, a reorganization becomes compulsory. His definition of himself as a poor speller is vigorously rejected and a determined effort made to establish

---

[1] The reader will note that the word "subject" as used in this context refers to "the person experimented upon"; not to a course of study.

FIG. 62.   Prescott Lecky, Columbia University.   Those who wish to study further the problem of personal efficiency should refer to his article, "Preventing Failure by Removing Resistance," published in the *1938 Yearbook* of the New York Society for the Experimental Study of Education.

the opposite definition.   The result obtained is out of all proportion to the effort exerted to bring it about.   Spelling assumes such interest that it is studied at every opportunity, even from the advertisements on street cars and subway trains.   An elaborate analysis to convince the subject that his difficulty really is due to a fixed idea of himself does not seem to be necessary in the remedial treatment of spelling.   He should, however, be asked to recall when he first accepted the role of a poor speller, ceased to worry about it, and dismissed the question as closed.

It is significant that not only poor spellers, but stammerers and others with similar defects, freely admit as a rule that they accept themselves as they are and make no effort to change.   This is an excellent defense, of course, for they feel no inconsistency once the definition has been accepted.   And they often attempt to avoid the effort of maintaining a more useful definition by referring the defect to heredity or neuro-muscular maladjustment.

Our experience also shows that unless a person has an unusually optimistic view of the future he would not be likely to anticipate a lenient attitude on the part of others in regard to errors in spelling.   This optimism also appears in the fact that poor spellers seem almost universally to count on the services of stenographers who are good spellers, and many are able to quote the names of several people who became famous in spite of a deficiency in spelling.

Those who claim that they "do not have a mathematical mind" are likewise victims of their own resistance.   Such a student may have defined himself in childhood as the exact opposite of some unassimilable companion who had been held up as a shining example of mathematical proficiency.   In other cases, remarks by parents or teachers that the child was lacking in aptitude for mathematics seem to be the explanation.   The suggestion was accepted and is now a part of the student's conception of himself.   In one instance, a student who despised mathematics in high school, during his freshman year acquired a sudden attachment for the subject and is now a professional statistician. This boy's older brother was proficient in mathematics, and the two had been in conflict for years.[2]

The clinical technique is helpful in those cases where individuals have proved that they can learn many subjects but claim they are unable to learn one or two specific subjects. The individual is apt either to continue to assume that somehow he is incapable of learning the "difficult" subject or to use evasion such as searching for some magical or quick means of attaining his ends. He may, for example, read the biographies of great men, study success books, or books on "how to have power of will." Such epigrammatic books, articles, and lectures are inspiring; but, if adjustments to environment have already given him an urge, he can accomplish more by the practice of prosaic acts, such as outlining meaningful material, plotting graphic charts, and learning the cold facts of his courses and tasks.

The "will." Many psychologists no longer believe in the old concept of will. Most people think that the will is some mysterious force which one can, as it were, grab out of the universe, draw to himself, and have work within him like yeast in dough. This popular idea of will is questionable, for actually a strong will is largely a name for the habit of persistence and success, and a weak will is but a name for the habit of failure.

The Making and Breaking of Habits

One day through the primeval wood
A calf walked home as good calves should;
But made a trail all bent askew,
A crooked trail as all calves do.
Since then three hundred years have fled,
And I infer the calf is dead.

But still he left behind his trail,
And thereby hangs my moral tale.
The trail was taken up next day
By a lone dog that passed that way;
And then a wise bell-wether sheep
Pursued the trail o'er vale and steep,

---

[2] Prescott Lecky, "Personal Counseling; The Theory of Self-Consistency in Personnel Problems," Report of the Annual Meeting of the American College Personnel Association, 1935.

And drew the flock behind him, too,
As good bell-wethers always do.
And from that day, o'er hill and glade,
Through those old woods a path was made.

And many men wound in and out,
And dodged and turned and bent about,
And uttered words of righteous wrath
Because 'twas such a crooked path;
But still they followed—do not laugh—
The first migrations of that calf,
And through this winding woodway stalked
Because he wobbled when he walked.

The writer proceeds to tell us that the path became a lane, and that the lane became a road, where many a poor horse toiled on with his load beneath the burning sun and traveled some three miles to make one mile.

And men two centuries and a half
Trod in the footsteps of that calf.

For men are prone to go it blind
Along the calf-paths of the mind,
And work away from sun to sun,
To do what other men have done.[3]

The habits of success or failure are developed in childhood by the attitudes and disciplines of parents, teachers, and playmates. If the child is required to complete the little tasks he starts and is rewarded for the tasks successfully completed, effective habits will be developed. In later life he will not have the habits of failure, vacillation, or hesitancy.

The development of habits of persistence in the face of difficulties can be stated in the following simple rules:

1. If you wish to accomplish anything, outline a definite plan. If it is a simple program of study, outline it mentally. If a long program covering several months, outline it on paper and schedule the various stages by dates. Use the example of the modern business corporation which schedules the various stages in the construction of a building or production of parts.

---

[3] Sam Walter Foss, "The Calf Path," *Whiffs from Wild Meadows.* Lothrop, Lee & Shephard Co., 1895.

2.   Instead of saying to yourself, "I will do that," say, "I will do it in this particular way."   Put your mental efforts upon the *how* of the proposition.

3.   Plan to do, not to be.   Herein lies the cause of many failures in life and explains what we mean when we say that a man has a wishbone where his backbone ought to be.   Don't dream of what you will do once you become a millionaire.   Don't think of how you will look riding in a fancy limousine or playing golf on your country estate, or how you will build hospitals and orphanages, but think of what to do in order to make a million dollars.

4.   Be enthusiastic about your scheme, plan, or objective. Adopt it heartily as your own.   Discuss it with wife, sweetheart, or mother.   If in doubt about its practicability, discuss it with men who know more about it than you do and get their suggestions and enthusiasm.

5.   Measure your progress.   Occasionally you should stop and note how much you have accomplished.

6.   Don't try to complete the whole program at once but fix your attention upon one phase of the plan.   Do it by stages if it requires a long time.   Go step by step and the end will take care of itself.

7.   Make your motto "Do it now."

If you have often wished that you might be mentally efficient, apply these simple but practical rules and note their superior effectiveness as compared with studies of the so-called "power of will."

Suggestions for the Student

How to read.   The art of study is largely a matter of learning to read rapidly and thoroughly.   Anyone can train himself to give text material a rapid preliminary reading and then a more careful and thoughtful second reading.

The following rules or practices will help the student improve his reading methods:

1.   Prepare your mind before beginning to read.   Ask yourself how this book or article fits into your plan of development.   What questions should the author answer for you?   Recall other articles on the same subject and ask yourself how this article relates to your previous studies.

2. Make a preliminary survey. Note the exact title, the author's position and his other writings, the year the book was written, the publisher, and the preface. The intelligent student reads the preface to learn why the author wrote the book and the treatment or points of view which he believed to be of value to the reader.

After reading the preface, read the table of contents and page rapidly through the book to note other main headings and the illustrations. Get the outline of the book in your mind. Note the parts in italics or capital letters or ideas which the author wants to impress upon the reader. Reading a book twice may seem unnecessary and a waste of time—but it is not, because double reading aids the formation of stronger and more lasting pathways in the nervous system.

3. Read rapidly. Beware of "dozing" study. Don't think that you are studying when you merely hold a book in your hand and look at words. If you cannot throw yourself into your study and work at high pressure, stop entirely and stand before an open window, or take a few exercises.

Force yourself to read rapidly.[4] Urge yourself to speed up. Begin at once to read rapidly. At first this may interfere with the clarity of comprehension but if you persist, you will soon find that you can learn ten times as much by speeding up. Spending a lot of time in study is far less important than a small amount of time well spent at consistent intervals. Don't dawdle. Go to it full steam ahead. Whenever you find yourself gliding off into daydreams or irrelevant meditations, bring yourself back sharply. Let each digression act as a reminder to get back to the job at hand.

4. Vary the rate of your reading. Read the simple or already known parts rapidly, or skip them entirely. Concentrate upon the important and difficult parts. If you do not understand the meaning of a word, look it up in the dictionary. If you find it difficult to grasp a principle, try to draw a diagram illustrating it or make an outline of the author's own statements. Make it a rule never to do straightaway reading at a regular rate unless you read for entertainment.

5. Make marginal notes or underscore the main ideas. Try to summarize the author's ideas in your own words by writing a sentence in the margin. A good plan is to underscore important items or draw a vertical line in the margin for important paragraphs or sentences. Always read with a pencil or pen in your hand so that you can indicate important passages. A book well-read has many penciled passages.

6. Use "active self-recitation." Think while you read. Spend a large part of your study in thinking over what you have read. Do not accept the author's statements blindly. Consider his views in the light of your own ideas or those of others. Be open-minded and willing to learn, but do not accept without some analysis of statements. Ask yourself whether the author is stating the results of impartial investigations or merely his own opinions. Do his conclusions follow from his statements? Is he trying to sell you some pet idea?

---

[4] Luella W. Pressey, *A Manual of Reading Exercises for College Freshmen* (Ohio State University Press, 1928), presents some helpful exercises for students who read very slowly

Fig. 63. Coleman R. Griffith, University of Illinois. Those interested in further study of educational psychology may wish to refer to his book *Psychology Applied to Teaching and Learning* (Farrar & Rinehart, 1939).

Improving the memory. Many people dislike the idea of memorizing, because memory is thought of only as a mechanical process of "learning by heart." Thinking and memorizing are usually considered as alternatives. Actually they are a part of the same process and go together. Material which has been thought through is remembered without much effort. Memory is a by-product of study and the general principles of study apply to memorizing.

The main way to improve memory is to improve the methods of learning. However, the following rules may aid in improving the ability to remember:

1. Get the meaning of the material to be remembered. Be sure that you clearly understand the material you want to recall. Think of the new ideas from every angle and try to apply them to practical situations. Do this not only when you are reading but also when you are at leisure. When you are walking or riding to and from your home, do not waste the time in idle reverie. Utilize your spare time. Perhaps you may think it dangerous to keep active mentally so large a part of your time. Have no fear. No man ever went insane or had a breakdown from mental overwork, but a lot have gone insane or broken down from overworry or other inadequate mental habits. Most of the talk about breakdowns from mental overwork is rationalization. The idle and the ignorant are the ones who suffer most from neuroses; not those who are exceedingly busy.

2. Always study with the intent to remember. Herein lies the cause for much forgetfulness. Occasionally a teacher repeats certain outlines of lec-

tures to his students and asks them to memorize the outlines. Later on he finds that he himself cannot repeat the outline because he simply dictated the material from his lecture notes. Whenever you study, do so with a determination to remember the things studied, and you will be surprised how easy it is to recall your past mental efforts.

3. Stop frequently during your studying and check up what you have learned. Compel yourself to recall what you are learning. Spend about 40 per cent of your time reciting to yourself. If you cannot recall what you have read, turn back and read it again. By a little practice along this line you will treble your ability to remember what you have covered. Imagine you are teaching the material and see whether you know it so well that you can explain it clearly to someone else. If you are unable to explain the meaning to someone else, you do not understand or know it. Go over it again and study each sentence and paragraph until you are able to tell what it does mean.

4. Use repetition. Don't expect to recall everything that you study unless you repeat the difficult parts over and over. In the case of definitions of technical terms, formulas, dates, and outlines, where the material has few natural clues for recall, don't hesitate to commit to memory verbatim. Of course, parrotlike recitation is wasteful, but don't consider yourself above mechanical repetition of certain material.

5. In committing to memory it is better to read aloud than to read silently and it is better to read to someone else than to yourself. Attention is better sustained in this way, because an appeal it made to the ear as well as to the eye and some help is gotten from the "feel" of the words in the throat and mouth. The value of reading to another person is that it promotes accuracy of thinking and insures proper emphasis of the several ideas.

6. Attempt to remember only the important material. Confine your efforts to the essential and relegate the nonessential to references to the dictionary, encyclopedia, and textbooks. Some memory systems give elaborate suggestions for the remembering of numbers on box cars. Don't waste your time trying to remember box car numbers, football statistics, or stock quotations unless these things are important to your vocation or recreation.

7. Carry the learning of important items beyond the point necessary for immediate recall. Experiments show that we forget about 60 per cent of material barely learned within one day after learning. This means that information necessary in your life work must be studied more than is sufficient barely to recall it the next day. The fading of impressions must be met by overlearning. Superficial learning of the spelling of a word may satisfy the immediate need, but it will not satisfy the needs of correct spelling a year later.

8. Space your study. Experiments have shown that it is better to memorize a certain amount of material at intervals than to try to complete the job at one sitting. Don't try to do seven hours of studying in one evening of each week, but study one hour on seven evenings of each week. This allows the synaptic connections to "settle" before the mental energy is directed elsewhere.

9. If necessary, invent some artificial scheme for learning and recalling material which lacks rational associations. This is seldom necessary, but may be helpful in recalling material, such as the height of the volcano of

Fujiyama, which was reported as 12,365 feet. Simply remember that we have 12 months and 365 days in the year.

Or you can use acrostics. As one man said: "In my public school days we had a speaker give us a talk once a month. Of the fifty or more talks which I heard I recall the subject of but one. In that case the speaker's subject was 'Grow' and the method of growth which he suggested was 'Go right on working.' The first letter of each word forms the word 'Grow.'" Acrostics can be used to advantage in remembering lists of words or names.

For temporary recall, it may be very helpful to try to visualize facts or principles. Try to picture them in unusual lights, colors, positions, etc. However, it is best to depend upon logical connections by understanding the relationships of the material to be remembered.

Fig. 64. Albert T. Poffenberger, Columbia University. Anyone interested in further study on the problem of efficiency of the worker may read his article "The Effects of Continuous Mental Work" in *The American Journal of Psychology*, 1927, Vol. 39, pp. 283–296.

Techniques of creative thinking. Many persons who do original thinking seem to want the public to believe that they do their thinking with the efficiency of firmly disciplined methods. Actually, studies of creative thinkers indicate that they make many false starts, waste time in random and exploratory movements, have desultory periods, and waver between unmanageable fantasies and systematic attack.

Investigations indicate that some creative thinkers realize that they are driven by a kind of demon or creative urge. An investigator of creative thought has reported one man's consuming purpose and commented on such drives as follows:

Eden Phillpotts, the Devonshire novelist and dramatist, writes: "For my own part the creative urge is a demon that drives, and will doubtless continue to drive, while my intellect, such as it is, functions normally and does not begin to wither with age. As a boy at school there was a longing to make things. I was always drawing. Then I longed to be an actor and create character; then I found these mediums beyond my power and turned to writing."

Perhaps such a drive is instinctive, reaching down into the very foundations of the personality. Perhaps it is conditioned and due to education, perhaps to abundant and overflowing energy. There are a dozen theories to explain it. In some it is not always persistent. It may lie dormant for years and then, when aroused by an inexplicable circumstance, drive the mind with a lashing hand. Whatever its source, we are certain that the immediate occasion for creative activity is the adjustment to some inner and controlling purpose, the resolution of some dissatisfaction with the world as it is, the ambition to idealize reality.[5]

The several stages in the process of creative thinking have been designated by Graham Wallas[6] essentially as follows:

1. *Preparation.* This stage refers to the study of the problem, its essential aspects, and the consideration of similar problems and their solutions.

2. *Incubation.* When the thinker has made the first step, preparation, he often takes a walk, a drive, or carries on some other activities wholly unrelated to the main problem. During incubation, the unconscious mental activities may be applied to the problem while the individual is engaged in easy physical exercise or routine tasks. However, close attention to some other problem, or intense emotional reactions from thrilling motion pictures, seem to be less beneficial than the kind of mind wandering which we experience during a train ride or in easy reading for one's entertainment. Time spent in just "sitting still" is likely to facilitate incubation far more than vigorous continuous search for an answer. Idleness and relaxation are often more helpful than an attempt to stuff one's self with "good reading."

3. *Illumination.* This refers to the appearance of the "good idea," coming seemingly from nowhere. The thinker usually has an intimation of the coming of the sought answer. He is conscious of the "dawning" for which he has searched.

---

[5] Eliot D. Hutchinson, "The Technique of Creative Thought," *The American Scholar,* May 1932.

[6] Graham Wallas, *The Art of Thought.* Harcourt, Brace & Co., 1926.

FIG. 65. Eliot Dole Hutchinson, University of Rochester. Those who wish to study further the problem of creative thought should refer to his article "Varieties of Insight in Humans," published in *Psychiatry, Journal of the Biology and Pathology of Interpersonal Relations*, 1939, Vol. II, No. 3, pp. 323–332.

Sometimes the thinker may recognize that he has experienced a great discovery but decide to postpone its consideration. Later he may find that he cannot revive the great idea whose birth he throttled. Failure to record the "flash" or to follow through may result in tragic inability to do so later as reported regarding an artistic composition:

Berlioz struggled against the creative impulse and eventually killed it. He suffered from poverty while at the same time his wife's health was causing him anxiety. One night there came to him the inspiration for a symphony. It ran in his head, an allegro of two-four time in A-minor. He rose from his bed and began to write. But he thought: "If I begin this bit, I shall have to write the whole symphony. It will be a big thing and I shall have to spend three or four months over it. That means I shall write no more articles and earn no more money. And when the symphony is finished, I shall not be able to resist the temptation to have it copied (which will mean an expense of a thousand or twelve-hundred francs) and then of having it played. I shall have a concert, and the receipts will barely cover the cost. I shall lose what I have not got. The poor invalid will lack necesssities, and I shall be able to pay neither my personal expenses nor my son's fees when he goes on board ship. These thoughts made me shudder and I threw down my pen saying, 'Bah! Tomorrow I shall have forgotten the symphony.' But the next night I heard the allegro clearly and seemed to see it written down. I was filled with feverish agitation. I sang the theme. I was going to get up, but the reflections of the day before restrained me. I steeled myself against the temptation and clung to the thoughts of forgetting it. At last I went to sleep; the next day upon waking all remembrance of it had indeed gone forever."[7]

---

[7] Romain Rolland, *Musicians of Today*, translated by Mary Blaiklock. Henry Holt & Co., 1908.

What restless energy to create, disturbing even sleep! What fatal adjustment to inner reality! Such artistic immolation and the death of such an idea sears the mind. The blocking of a creative purpose either by circumstance or lack of technique not only smothers inspiration; it leaves the personality hobbled, unable longer to vault the fences to creative freedom. And it makes one shudder, but perhaps also admire an artist who was heroic enough—or was it mad enough?—to substitute duty for genius.[8]

Hutchinson investigated the frequency of "scientific hunch" as recognized by chemists, mathematicians, physicists, biologists, and men of similar standing. Answers to a questionnaire sent out by the Educational Department of the American Chemical Society yielded the report that 83 per cent of the 232 directors of research laboratories and "American Men of Science" replied affirmatively to the question: "Have you ever received assistance from the scientific revelation or 'hunch' in the solution of an important problem?"

Hutchinson has reported several examples of illuminations from the many sent him:

Bertrand Russell remarks, and in this his experience parallels that of a large number of scientists: "In all the creative work that I have done, what has come first is a problem, a puzzle, involving discomfort. Then comes concentrated voluntary application involving great effort. After this, a period without conscious thought; and finally a solution. This last stage is usually sudden."

Sir James Flinders Petrie, Egyptologist, illustrates the same points. "My work is mainly historical. I never try to settle a difficult problem off-hand. I first assemble the material, state the problem as definitely as possible, and then if no solution is evident, leave it alone. From time to time I look over it to refresh my memory, but never to force a solution. After waiting days or years I suddenly feel a wish to go over it again, and then everything runs smoothly and I can write without effort. . . ."

A physicist writes: "For two years I had been thinking about solid solutions or mixed crystals. There is a good bit known and some regularity has been discovered, summarized as Vegard's Law. (The law states that the crystal cell dimension is a linear function of the composition in molar percentages.) One morning on going to look up something in the *American Mineralogist,* I came across a paper which denied this law in regard to mixed crystals. Its denial was based on the measurement of crystal spacing and not on the cell dimension to which Vegard's Law is said to apply. This wrong application amazed and disgusted me. Being out of mood for further work, I went to meet a friend who was going to town and was vaguely glad of the relief. I returned to the laboratory for my hat and arrived at the

---

[8] Eliot D. Hutchinson, "The Technique of Creative Thought," *The American Scholar,* May 1932.

car before my friend. I was slightly annoyed at his delay. But suddenly, without warning, the idea flashed upon me that I could start with Vegard's Law and deduce a law for the variation in spacing which these men had measured, and could use all their measured data to check it."[9]

4. *Verification.* When the "good idea" or important solution has appeared to the thinker, he tests it in the light of known facts and reason. Perhaps he also explains it to colleagues in the same field of thought.

Creative thinking for most great thinkers has a pattern which may be described as drive, problem, conscious effort to solve it, passivity, repeated periods of conscious efforts and passivity, sudden illumination, and verification.[10]

The false doctrine of transfer of training. Years ago, particularly during the days of the phrenologists, people thought that our minds were divided into faculties. It was believed that the faculties or "departments of the mind" could be trained as we train individual muscles. The curricula of the day required students to study certain subjects for their so-called mental discipline. Indeed, many people still erroneously believe that dead languages, mathematics, logic, and sciences should be studied not because of any usefulness of the subjects themselves but because of the mental discipline which is supposed to be acquired for other subjects that are useful.

Numerous investigations of these old claims have been made and we now know that we do not have such general powers or faculties. For example, there is no power of memory, but many memories. One may have an excellent memory for certain kinds of facts such as baseball statistics and a very poor memory for historical dates. To him, the baseball statistics are important whereas the historical dates are needed only to pass an examina-

---

[9] *Ibid.*

[10] These stages in creative thinking have been studied in the work of artists. See the study by C. Patrick, "Creative Thought in Artists," *Journal of Psychology,* 1937, Vol. 4, pp. 35-73. The process of creative thought in sketching pictures was studied by having artists sketch pictures while expressing their thoughts aloud, and by having them answer questions concerning their usual practices. Fifty professional artists and 50 unpracticed sketchers served as subjects. The reports revealed the four stages of creative thought: namely preparation, incubation, illumination, and verification, already revealed in other studies of creation. The course of thought in artists and non-artists is similar. Non-artists draw more objects and more different kinds of objects than do artists.

tion. The learner's attitudes toward the materials to be learned are far more potent in his abilities to recall them than any previous drills in unrelated subjects such as history, geometry, or Latin. The recall of a past experience or bit of information is not at all like the playing over of a wax record which has been traced by study of unrelated subjects. Remembering is a creative process.[11]

A simple example of the need for creative remembering, and the transfer when training is rigid and extensive but not creative, has been aptly phrased by Thorndike: "Soldiers trained to unquestioning and immediate obedience to their superiors are not characterized by notable obedience to law, conscience, or the civil authorities." [12]

Transfer of training depends upon the conscious acceptance by the learner of methods, procedures, principles, sentiments, and ideals which are common to the past subject and present interest. We make transfers whenever and wherever we sense a later experience as being similar to a previous one. This sensing of similarities or relationships may be vague or it may reach the level of fully conscious understanding. The more clearly or fully the relationships are sensed or recognized, the greater is the likelihood of transfer.[13]

Of course, this fact does not mean that no one should ever study Latin, logic, geometry, or zoology. Good reasons for the study of such subjects may be found in direct needs for the subjects themselves or in the cultural backgrounds which they supply. A student should study these subjects when the subjects contribute something directly to the student's needs or interests.

Furthermore, almost any subject has so many intrinsic values and relationships to one's contacts with life that any subject, when well taught and thoroughly learned, can contribute to one's intellectual growth.

---

[11] Numerous experiments which indicate that remembering is a creative process are reported by F. C. Bartlett in *Remembering*. The Macmillan Co., 1932.

[12] E. L. Thorndike, "Human Nature and the Social Order," p. 307. The Macmillan Co., 1940.

[13] E. E. Bayles, "An Unemphasized Factor in Current Theories Regarding the Transfer of Training," *Journal of Educational Psychology*, 1936, Vol. 27, pp. 425-430. H. R. Hamley, "Formal Training: a Critical Survey of Experimental Work," *British Journal of Educational Psychology*, 1936, Vol. 6, pp. 233-249.

Suggestions for the Office and Professional Worker

Utilizing time efficiently.   It is obviously impossible to specify how much time any office or professional worker should spend on each operation in the day's work.   However, the places and occasions where one's time is wasted or misused are not in the performance of his regular duties but in the attention given to the bothersome trivialities adequately described by James Gordon Gilkey in his "Secrets of Effective Living":

> Once I read about a man who was tied down and the ants ate him.
> His fingers, his ears, his eyes, everything.
> At last they even devoured his brain,
> Emptying his skull bit by bit.
> I am tied down, too, and little things are eating me—
> The friend who calls me on the phone and talks and talks,
> The agent who is determined to sell me a new mop,
> The children who quarrel and will not do their lessons,
> The letters that must be answered before night somehow,
> The ice man's short weight, the butcher's carelessness,
> All these little things are devouring me alive. . . .

The time-consumers that "eat" us are social obligations, "being a good fellow," eating too much, and chasing ephemeral ideas that appear promising but end in rainbows without any pots of gold.

Our social obligations—receptions, playing bridge, golf, driving just for a drive, formal dinners, fraternal meetings, conventions, and community drives all appear essential to the development of a balanced personality and vocational advancement.   In many cases, wives insist upon them.   Some of these affairs do bring us in touch with people whom we ought to know.   Some do bring in business later, but it is a waste of time in the long run to cultivate people merely for the sake of getting business rather than as the result of a natural liking for them.   All these side lines become dangerous when they control us.   Selling tickets for charity affairs, putting up decorations, buying theater tickets, lending money, giving talks before Sunday schools, writing letters of introduction, and so on, all have their place, but they tend to devour time and effort and end nowhere.   It is seldom that people trust their fortunes or important problems to the accommodating man.   When we are seriously ill we go to the doctor who is so busy professionally that he has no time to give to little things. We prefer to deposit our money in the bank whose president is noted for his ability and stability rather than in the bank whose president is a public beast of burden.   To achieve things worthy of the respect of our fellows, we must respect the obligations of our own work to the extent that we fulfill them before we oblige others.

The ambitious individual need not confuse the performance of his own duties with an abrupt disregard for the needs and feelings of others.   To refuse to take time to be accommodating to others does not necessitate coldness of manner.   The daily acts of the worthwhile life can be invested with cordiality and friendliness.   Our social relations should be more than mechanically reciprocal.   They can be made delightfully pleasing.   If a person lends us a book, we can do more than just thank him. We can prove to him that we read and enjoyed it.   If we dine in a restaurant on a fifty-fifty basis, we should not forget the tips.   We need not say to a person, "I see you do not remember me," but can state our own name without reminding him of his failure.   When we win a big score in a bridge game, we need not go into a detailed recital of how it was done.   When we greet the stenographer and the elevator operator, we can make the greeting just as friendly as the one we bestow upon our best customers.   These little daily acts do not consume much time, but they do bring greater returns in human happiness and popularity than years of trifling services.

Memorizing names and faces.   Remembering the names of people whom we meet is not a mysterious gift that is given to politicians and denied to others.   The politician finds it necessary to know people's names when he meets them and he consciously practices learning them.   He seriously wants to know their names.   Students in laboratory courses in psychology have taken part in an experiment where they repeated the colors in a color-naming test.   The colors were only five in number and were irregularly arranged in one hundred bits, each of the five colors appearing twenty times.   After the colors had been named over as often as two hundred times by each student, not one student could repeat the colors from memory in correct sequential order. Their efforts had been concentrated upon naming the bits of color as seen and not in connecting them in a series that could be remembered.   Similarly, when we meet strangers, our attention is concentrated upon the impression that we make on the stranger and not upon knowing his name.   We are too conscious of ourselves to grasp the name of the stranger.   Our self-consciousness will tend to disappear if we determine to know and remember the names of those whom we meet.

Quite frequently, when we meet strangers and are formally introduced to them, we do not hear the name, or, if we do hear it, we get it incorrectly.   To insure clarity, we should spell the name and ask its owner whether it is correctly spelled and pronounced.   The chairmen at businessmen's luncheon clubs frequently ask each member to stand up and state his business affiliation.   After this ceremony is over, few, if any, have learned the names.   Most of the names are mumbled, and repeated too rapidly to make any neural impression.   If members of clubs wish to become acquainted, the leader should ask the secretary to write each name on a blackboard or have each person write his own name on the board.   Each of the other members should then write, on a piece of paper, the name of each stranger and try to connect the name and person in his own mind.   Before the meeting ends, each person should try to recall the name of each member and verify his recollection.

A similar method can be used at bridge parties, dances, and banquets.   Here the formal introduction must be hurried by the hosts and a request for enough time to write down each name and verify it would break into the smoothness of the occasion.   However, when the guests are seated or participating in the activities, then the names of strangers can be requested from a near-by associate.   Effort should be made to meet the strangers and learn something about their personalities.

Some memory-training systems advise the student to connect the name of the stranger in a grotesque or irrelevant way, as, Mr. Pitts might remind us of the fiery pit—Hell.   Or, Mr. Long may be very short and the contrast seems to enable us to associate the name with his height.   However, such irrational associations are not nearly so effective as a logical connection of facts regarding the personality of each stranger.   The time and effort expended in making such incongruous connections can be spent more profitably in making logical connections of correct facts about the person.

The feeling tone in names must also be recognized. Persons whom we like, we remember. The name of the girl at the dance who is most attractive to the youth will be remembered for years. He puts forth effort to learn her name, telephone number, and other items of information. Conversely, we tend to forget those whom we dislike or do not care for. If a number of older men are asked to state the number of times they were engaged to girls before they were married, one is apt to find that those who were engaged to three or more girls cannot recall their names. They cannot recall them simply because some unpleasant experiences are associated with their memories. The true politician likes people and his pleasant feeling toward them assists him in recalling their names.

When the name of the person is to be fixed so that it can be recalled, it should be repeated during the conversation as often as politeness permits. The average individual is able to recall about one-third more names when he has spoken the name once than when he has remained silent.[14] The salesman should get into the habit of prefacing many of his statements with "Mr. Prospect," and ending some of them with "Do you agree, Mr. Prospect?" After the stranger has left one's presence, it is well to think of him—not as "that fellow in the blue suit" but by name in one's thoughts of him. And he should be thought of in terms of a clear visual image.

Frequency of use and error. *Frequency of Use and Error* is a a principle worked out and successfully applied by Dr. John A. Stevenson, President of the Penn Mutual Life Insurance Co. This principle works, as proved by Mr. Stevenson himself, for he has had a remarkably successful career. He has been a salesman, a sales manager, and a college professor, and at the age of thirty-four he attained a high executive position in the business world.

This principle can be applied by anyone anywhere. It is so simple that one is likely to say that it has always been known in a general way. But, since it is simple, it can be applied with profit to many jobs. It can be applied to an employee's tasks as follows:

---

[14] Harold E. Burtt and A. C. Beck, "Remembering Names Connected with Faces," *Journal of Industrial Psychology,* January 1928, pp. 34-38.

Frequency of Use means that you:

1. Make a list of the things which you use or do in your daily work.
2. Find out how to improve these things which you use or do.
3. Perform your daily work according to the improved methods which you have discovered or found advisable.

Frequency of Error means that you:

1. Make a list of the mistakes which you often make in your daily work.
2. Find out how to eliminate these errors.
3. Eliminate the errors in your daily work.

Let me illustrate. Suppose you are a shoe salesman and are selling shoes of various kinds of leather and prices. Make a list of the things you do each day, such as meeting customers, finding out the kind of shoes they want, measuring their feet, finding shoes from stock which they might want, making sales, giving change, and so on. Then find out how to improve each of the things you constantly do and apply your improved methods.

Now make a list of the errors you make, such as saying the wrong things to customers, grammatical errors, misjudging the size of shoe needed, and so on. Learn how to correct these errors. Then eliminate them from your daily work.

It all sounds very trite, but it is more easily said than done. Just to find how interesting and practical it is, let the reader take two sheets of paper and on the one make a list of the "Frequencies of Use" and on the other "Frequencies of Error" of his own vocation. It is well for the individual to work out the principle for his particular work and try it. The results may be surprisingly effective.

References

Barlow, M. C., "Transfer of Training in Reasoning," *Journal of Educational Psychology*, 1937, Vol. 28, pp. 122-128.

Bird, Charles, *Effective Study Habits*. D. Appleton-Century Co., 1931.

Clark, E. L., *The Art of Thinking Straight*. D. Appleton-Century Co., 1934.

Kornhauser, A. W., *How to Study: Suggestions for High School and College Students*. University of Chicago Press, 1937.

Laird, Donald A., *Increasing Personal Efficiency*. Harper & Bros., 1936.

Mikesell, W. H., *Mental Hygiene*. Prentice-Hall, Inc., 1939.

Overstreet, H. A., *About Ourselves*. W. W. Norton & Co., 1927.

Schell, L. H., and M. Crawford, *Clear Thinking*. Harper & Bros., 1938.

Sorokin, P. A., and C. F. Berger, *Time-budgets of Human Behavior*. Harvard University Press, 1939.

Thouless, Robert H., *How to Think Straight*. Simon & Schuster, 1939.
Webster, D., *Can You Think?* D. Appleton-Century Co., 1939.
Young, James W., *A Technique for Producing Ideas*. Advertising Publications, Inc., 1940.

Projects

1. Investigate the subject of specific conscious intent and its correlates in performance. You may refer to articles such as Douglas Fryer's in the *British Journal of Psychology*, 1937, Vol. 27, pp. 364-393.

FIG. 66.   Douglas Fryer, New York University.

Intent determines the rate of performance with a high degree of exactness. Environmental changes, in the form of new instructions, may affect variability of performance through intentional acceptance or rejection of these changes as conscious stimuli, or through the development of various specific intents to control performance in the new situation. Changes in performance are closely related to these specific intents, which appear to be essential causative factors rather than the changes in the environment or increased general awareness of the situation.

2. Collect some examples which show that we do or do not have a will.

3. When an executive requests a subordinate to give him a report, the executive usually wants it as soon as possible. After the report has been submitted, the executive may neglect to read it for several days or weeks. What is the cause of this habit on the part of the executive? How can the subordinate adjust himself to such wishes of his superior?

4. To what extent does playing the stock market decrease the efficiency of businessmen who do it?   Should the ambitious businessman determine not to bother with speculation?

5.   Where can the businessman obtain his best ideas or do his most effective thinking—in the office, at home, in the club, on the golf course, or other places?

6.   Is a clean desk indicative of personal efficiency?   Make a study of this problem by preparing a list of the best executives whom you know and then observing the tops of their desks.

7.   What are the psychological reasons for the fact that some executives find it difficult to delegate routine tasks to subordinates?

8.   Experiments indicate that muscular tension and thinking go together. In one experiment, when the muscles of the arms were tensed, the learning time was reduced 13 per cent, and arithmetical problems were solved 10 per cent more rapidly and 6 per cent more accurately.   Should a man attempt to keep his muscles in a state of tension when he is on the job?

9.   One of the most common methods of judging the personality of a person is his conversation.   A number of individuals were asked what words, phrases, and questions they disliked to hear from other people.   The following list resulted.   (It is not to be considered complete.)

ain't	cuckoo	mess	runt	snob
brass	dumb-cluck	nut	shack	stink
bum	highbrow	piker	simp	stuff
Butch	huh?	pill	shorty	sucker
cake-eater	junk	prune	skinny	swell
crab	loafer	punk	slob	yeah
crumby	lousy	rotter	sloppy	yellow

Questions Disliked

D'ja eat?
How much did it cost?
Is that so?
What did I tell you?
What's it to you?
What's the big idea?
Why bring that up?
So what?

Haven't you finished yet?
How do you get that way?
How's every little thing?
Isn't that grand?
What did you do that for?
What makes you so sure?
What's on your mind?
What d'ya know?

Expressions Disliked

And how.
After me, you come first.
Bad egg.
Beautiful but dumb.
Believe me.
Cut it out.
Don't trouble yourself.
He means well.
Hello, old sock!
I done it.
I'll say so.

I'll tell the world.
Make it snappy.
Mind your own business.
No kiddin'!
None of your business.
Prove it to me.
Shut up.
That's just like you.
That's not true.
You flatter me.
You tell 'em.

CONVENIENT FORM FOR WEEKLY WORK SCHEDULE FOR STUDENT

		Sun-day	Mon-day	Tues-day	Wednes-day	Thurs-day	Fri-day	Satur-day
MORNING	8							
	9							
	10							
	11							
	12							
AFTERNOON	1							
	2							
	3							
	4							
	5							
EVENING	6							
	7							
	8							
	9							
	10							
	11							

Work Schedule of_____

a. Ask a number of your associates to check the items that they dislike to hear.

b. Check the items you use frequently. Then have a friend check those which he says you use. Compare the two lists.

c. Note the number of times you hear these terms used by low-salaried and by high-salaried businessmen. To what factors do you attribute any differences in their usage?

10. Analyze a definite job according to the principle of frequency of use and error.

16

Efficiency of the Worker

Factors in the efficiency of the worker are so numerous as to baffle the student investigator. Industrial engineers may show, for example, that output appears to be influenced by rest pauses, refreshments during working hours, length of working day, illumination, temperature, ventilation, rate of pay, and so on. The industrial psychologists find evidence to indicate that the worker's output is influenced by *knowledge* of rest pauses, *attitude* toward the way he is treated with regard to the working conditions arranged for him, and the *interpretations* he gives to the reactions of his fellow-workers toward him. We should study both classes of influences on efficiency but here more consideration is given to the psychological factors.

MOST investigators of the efficiency of the industrial worker have examined objective factors such as rest periods, illumination, noise, humidity, temperature, oxygen, alcohol, tobacco, caffeine, and food. These well-known objective influences on output have been studied by efficiency engineers and other researchers. Psychologists, however, have found that these physical and physiological influences on output are often of secondary importance. The really important factors in efficiency are the drives to activity, the *esprit de corps,* the incentives to action, attitudes, emotions, and the extent to which the worker "feels at home," or is emotionally well adjusted to his world. The latter influences on efficiency are subjective and therefore harder to measure than the more obvious objective factors, but the ability to sense the influences of the psychological factors is of primary concern to the alert executive. *The worker is a man of action far more than simply an organism of reaction.* His moods and work rhythms are largely "individual matters" and relatively independent of external factors.

Subjective Factors in Efficiency

The importance of the emotions and the worker's integration with his world have been ably illustrated by Henry B. Elkind in the following example from one of his investigations:

The case that I shall give is not an example of the psychiatric method in its *usual sense,* but is an example of the point of view and method of approach of the hygienist who is concerned with maintaining a high degree of health and efficiency on the part of the workers. This case deals with efforts made some time ago to find practical methods of discovering which workers in a group were out of adjustment. That is, we wanted to know how to pick out, quickly and cheaply, workers who were not doing well. To do this, we had in mind using production curves, so commonly employed in industry today. This experimental work was carried on in a factory of national prominence that employed the Bedeaux system of payment, in which production charts are used. The weekly average point-hours were plotted for all workers whose wages were computed by the Bedeaux system. . . .

We found many types of abnormal curves. These all showed great variations and great fluctuations. After we thought we knew how to distinguish an abnormal curve from a normal, we tried it out. We picked out the curve of a girl who had been working in a certain part of the factory. Her job was that of cementing uppers of rubber shoes, at which she had worked for about two and a half years. For about a year and a half she had been a high-point operator. Then she had dropped steadily down for the period of a year.

As we could not be sure whether or not the worker was to blame for the decline, or whether there was something about the job or the work that was to blame, we had to study all the variables in the whole situation. We secured for comparison the curve of another operator in the same room doing exactly the same work, who was declared by the forelady to be the best worker in the particular operation. Her work-curve was a consistently high-point curve, with, of course, minor fluctuations appearing rather frequently.

We watched both of these girls at work. The high-point worker apparently did not work at all. She was having a fine time at her job. When the other workers passed by, she talked with them; during most of the day she was heard singing or whistling; and whenever anyone talked with her, her conversation was cheerful.

But this other girl, who was now the inferior worker, we observed to be working very hard, straining every effort to do her day's work. Actually, however, she was earning less money, producing less goods, than the other girl. . . .

We examined the girl physically and found nothing especially wrong with her, except that she was somewhat undernourished and underweight. We discovered that she alone in her family was then employed. Her father had previously worked in that factory, but had been laid off and, when work was resumed, had not been rehired, because of high blood-pressure. She also had a younger brother who could not find a job. Thus it was very necessary for her to work. . . .

We made a number of interesting experiments in this particular case that showed that psychological or emotional factors do affect work. We arranged

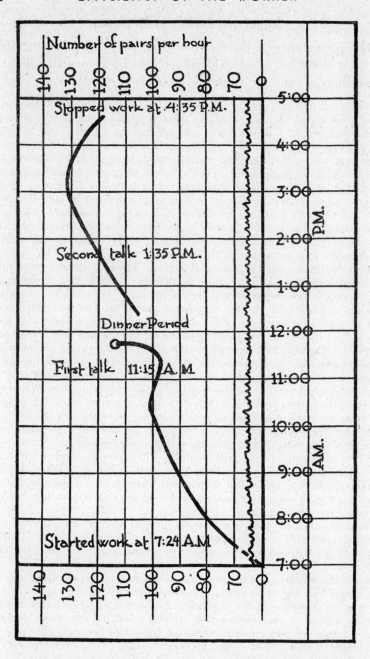

FIG. 67. Individual worker's production curve for one day, illustrating the "emotional release" theory. After Henry B. Elkind, *Preventive Management*, p. 113 (B. C. Forbes Publishing Co., 1931).

that one morning a time-study man should time the operations. The girl did not know it was to be done. At 11:15 I came into the room where she was working; the production had fallen off. It had begun to fall off shortly before the noon hour, which is usual. I told her that I would guarantee her base-rate and that she did not have to worry about wages. She would get her usual wages despite what the time-study man was doing. The production immediately went up. That same afternoon we continued the time-study. At about 1:35 p.m. I came to her again and told her that I had just secured a job for her young brother in the factory where she was working, and up went her production to a level much higher than had ever been reached in the morning.

Other experiments verify this result. Mayo's work is one instance. Remove the emotional blocks, and the resistances to efficiency are at least diminished, if not oftentimes eliminated. While I do not believe that by telling workers nice things we could always secure high rates of production, I do believe that production is strongly affected by emotional conditions.[1]

The Western Electric Company has conducted some of the most significant researches in industrial psychology. Important results and interpretations of these researches have been reported by Elton Mayo,[2] by F. J. Roethlisberger and W. J. Dickson,[3] and by T. North Whitehead.[4] These books are too voluminous to be summarized here. However, Whitehead has given helpful reports on the importance of social relationships in an industrial group studied in the Western Electric Company researches, and one report is summarized here for the student of industrial efficiency.

Social Relationships in a Factory: A Study of an Industrial Group.[5] In 1927, the Western Electric Company began a series of interrelated researches "having as their object the better understanding of the human factors in industry, with especial reference to employee satisfactions, as related to economic efficiency. These researches were broadly sociological in character, and were undertaken with the full consent and co-operation of the

---

[1] Henry B. Elkind, *Preventive Management,* pp. 106-114. B. C. Forbes Publishing Co., New York, 1931.

[2] Elton Mayo, *Human Problems of an Industrial Civilization.* The Macmillan Co., 1934.

[3] F. J. Roethlisberger and W. J. Dickson, *Management and the Worker.* Harvard University Press, 1939.

[4] T. North Whitehead, *The Industrial Worker* (2 vols.). Harvard University Press, 1939.

[5] This title was used by Whitehead for a paper read before Section J (Psychology) of a British Association meeting in Norwich, England, September 1935, and later published in *The Human Factor,* National Institute of Industrial Psychology, London, Vol. IX, No. 11.

employees themselves." One particular experiment has been described by Whitehead and is here summarized as follows:

In a special test room designed for the experiment, five girls assembled telephone relays at a work bench. Trays containing parts for assembly were opposite them. A sixth girl procured necessary parts for the assemblers and performed other routine duties. A male supervisor and one or two assistants sat facing the assemblers. The supervisor in charge obtained and kept numerous records relating to quality of output, reasons for temporary stops, length of time spent in bed by each girl every night, periodical medical reports of their physical condition, and other factors. Room temperatures and relative humidities were taken hourly. The supervisor and his assistants made extensive daily notes of conversation and of the relations developing between the workers. The workers were also occasionally interviewed in a separate room by an experienced interviewer. Furthermore, an automatic device recorded, to a fraction of a second, the instant at which each girl completed each assembled relay. Hence, a minute-to-minute record of output with supplementary information was available for each girl over a five-year period.

When the production of each worker was charted in graphic form, it was found that wave-like irregularities were exhibited by each graph. Some of the waves lasted for months; others only a week or two. The output figures also showed that similar irregularities occurred with durations of as little as a minute or two.

At first it was supposed that these variations in working speed might be related to the experimental changes deliberately introduced, or possibly to other changes in physical circumstance such as temperature or the worker's physical state. However, careful analysis of the data showed that irregularity in output failed to correlate with any known changes of physical circumstance.

When this negative conclusion was reached, the researchers next considered changes in the girls' social relationships. Study along these lines produced positive results. It was found that speed of work varied markedly with changes in the sentiments entertained by the workers toward each other, toward their supervisors, and toward the group. A social history of the test room from 1927 to 1932 offered an explanation of the major fluctuations found in the graphs.

Certain graphs showed an average increase in speed of about 30 per cent. The curves were not learning curves, because all the workers had had several years experience in the work before they came into the test room. The plateaus and spurts in output were decidedly suggestive, and analysis showed that:

> . . . It was the organization of human relations, rather than the organization of techniques, which accompanied spurts in these cases. This illustrates the futility of attending exclusively to the economic motivation of workers, or to their physical conditions of work. These things are of high importance; but no group of workers can be expected to remain satisfied, or co-operative, unless their social organization and sentiments are also protected at the working level.

As the experiment progressed, the girls developed common interests and loyalties. The girls took their discipline out of the hands of the supervisor and supervised themselves. For example, when a girl wished to have a half day's leave she had to obtain permission from the supervisor. However, the girls themselves developed a custom whereby no girl could ask for such leave unless the group approved the request.

In general, the output of individual workers was directly related to their sentiments toward each other. The feelings of *approval, antagonism,* and *indifference* toward each other influenced their individual variations in output.[6] One of Whitehead's final generalizations was the following:

> Perhaps the main conclusion to be chosen from this type of analysis is the vital importance of human relationship as a factor in the motivation of an industrial group, and in its ultimate stability. The logical motive in economic activity is financial; and endless ingenuity has been expended in devising schemes of payment, designed to secure a maximum of employee satisfaction and efficiency. But, in the last analysis, buying power is largely a means for satisfying social sentiments; and money incentives will never secure a full measure of activity and contentment until firms are organized with greater regard for the social stability of their own working groups, *at the working level.*[7]

---

[6] *Ibid.* The author's summary of this outstanding experiment in worker efficiency has of necessity omitted many important aspects. The reader should read the more complete and accurate reports listed in the preceding footnotes of this chapter.

[7] *Ibid.*

Objective Factors in Efficiency

Motion study. The subtle factors in efficiency—attitudes, feelings, adjustments, team spirit, and others—are potent influences and of special interest to the industrial psychologist. However, the psychotechnologist also realizes that a worker may be happy, admire his supervisor, like his work, and yet may perform his tasks inefficiently. We all know that workers left to their own devices seldom hit upon easy and economical methods of performing their work. The unguided worker is apt to make many unnecessary motions, waste time, and develop needless fatigue from his efforts. True time and motion study is not a mere speeding up of the worker but a systematic approach to *the one best method of work.* Motion study has been defined as "a common-sense method for analyzing operations performed by the left and right hands and for determining 'the one best way' of doing work, through elimination of all unnecessary motions and by rearranging all necessary motions into the most economical sequence." [8]

Motion study is not a newly discovered system of magic that will automatically reduce hand-operating costs 50 per cent. It is a modern method of practical analysis which has assisted the good judgment of thousands of executives in their search for better ways to produce standard-quality products with the least possible expenditure of time and energy for the worker. It has repeatedly produced savings from 10 to 70 per cent of production costs. Motion study has been extensively used in machine shops, foundries, and mechanical assembly work, and in a wide range of other industries.

The literature on modern scientific management began at the turn of the past century. The classic reference is Frederick Winslow Taylor's investigation of handling pig iron for the Bethlehem Steel Company. As an outgrowth of the Spanish American War, the company was confronted with the necessity of speeding up the loading of pig iron onto freight cars. Taylor was hired to make a study of the process of handling pig iron.

His analysis of the process, based upon his principles of scien-

[8] Frederick Winslow Taylor, *Principles of Scientific Management.* Harper & Bros., 1911. Presents a summary of many of Taylor's principles used in his pig-iron study.

Fig. 68. Lillian Moller Gilbreth, Consulting Engineer, Montclair, New Jersey, and Professor of Management at Purdue University. Those who are interested in the problem of applied motion study should refer to *Applied Motion Study*, by Frank B. and L. M. Gilbreth (Sturgis & Walton, 1917).

tific management,[9] suggested that a first-class worker should be able to carry 48 long tons a day. The men on the job were carrying only 12½ tons. Taylor experimented with several workers and, at the start, offered one man an appreciable increase in pay if he would agree to follow directions in carrying the pig iron and resting. As a result of experiments with this man, Taylor was able to raise his average daily output to 47½ tons. Ultimately, Taylor was able to train an entire group of workers to function according to a planned work-and-rest program which enabled them to maintain their output at Taylor's original estimate.

Taylor's major contributions to scientific management related to "time study" and the investigation of better tools to perform work. Later, Frank B. and Lillian M. Gilbreth originated what they called "Motion Study." Its purpose was to eliminate waste and to balance the development of the use of power, machines, and better methods with the development of the human element. This work is a combination of industrial psychology and industrial engineering. This is illustrated by its three divisions: *Fatigue study* is an endeavor to eliminate unnecessary fatigue

[9] *Ibid.*

and to provide for recovery from necessary fatigue. It includes investigations of the usefulness of rest periods, work and rest chairs, and a survey designed to determine sources of fatigue. *Motion study* has to do with utilizing the time and energy of the human being to produce most efficient, profitable, and satisfying work. It employs process charts for visualizing work problems; the micromotion method for making films recording work and analyzing them into the seventeen component elements of a work cycle which are then recorded on the simultaneous motion cycle chart from which standards are derived. *Skill study* considers the derivation, transfer, and increase of skill, which is defined as knowledge plus dexterity plus adaptability to meet changing situations. It utilizes the stereochronocyclegraph method to record skill and the motion model as a teaching device to facilitate its development and transfer. Through the work in these three areas the Gilbreths and those who are carrying on this work are endeavoring to teach people to be motion-minded and to improve their own techniques of work and of leisure.

One of the outstanding Gilbreth studies dealt with bricklaying, one of the oldest of all skilled trades. By changing the placing and handling of the materials, Frank Gilbreth brought the average number of bricks laid per hour from the traditional standard of 120 to 350 per man and reduced the number of movements in laying one brick from 18 to 4.

Gilbreth early recognized the importance of breaking down a total act into its components and the value of a shorthand method of designating the motions. As a result of his analysis of work movements, he analyzed all acts into 17 different component movements and devised an arbitrary shorthand symbol for each. These elements of movement were termed *therbligs*[10] (Gilbreth transposed). These symbols are still used by some investigators in recording their observations of a worker as he makes his movements in performing a task. Slow-motion picture cameras, split-second timers, and stereoscopic devices are

---

[10] The 17 therbligs are search, find, select, grasp, position, assemble, use, disassemble, inspect, transport empty, transport loaded, release load, prepare for next operation, plan, unavoidable delay, avoidable delay, and rest for overcoming fatigue. See F. B. Gilbreth, *Motion Study*. D. Van Nostrand, 1911.

also used to chart movements and discover "the one best way of work."

An understandable example of motion study technique as applied to hand packaging of drug products is given in figure 69. *A* and *B*, showing the "old method," are chiefly significant in showing that the right hand was idle during a large part of the packaging process. *C*, *D* and *E*, the "new method," indicate how a re-planning of the worker's movements resulted in a busy right hand. The actual savings brought about from this application of motion study to the hand packaging example, figure 69*F*, was a production increase from 120 boxes an hour to 215 boxes an hour, or a unit package cost decrease of 44 per cent.[11]

The use of time and motion study has resulted in some spectacular increases in output as well as marked decreases in fatigue of the workers. Improvements made in these studies have been along the lines of giving both hands useful work to do, pre-positioning tools and materials, arranging foot-pedals to relieve the hands, designing containers for materials whereby materials drop into the worker's hands, training the worker in making rhythmic movements of hands, and arranging for a suitable body position of the worker. All of these aids to the worker tend to reduce his fatigue as well as increase his production. Time and motion techniques have become a permanent part of our modern industrial economy. Obviously, the psychological factors must be considered in the use of such techniques with workers. Failure to obtain the co-operation of the workers when time and motion studies are made may bring about breakdowns of morale with resultant decreases in production. A classic example is that of the efficiency expert who proved to a group of laborers that they could shovel more sand when they shoveled *his* way. They admitted that he was right but when the expert left the workers, each worker cut an inch off his shovel blade just because they disliked the expert personally!

---

[11] Examples and illustrations reproduced by courtesy of Clifton H. Cox and *Modern Packaging* magazine under title "Motion Study Applied to Hand Packaging" and published in the issue of July 1939.

Illumination of work. Good lighting often helps the worker do more work with less effort. Furthermore, inadequate lighting is depressing to many people. Obviously, lighting should be adequate, constant, evenly distributed, and without glare. Contrary to popular opinion, direct sunlight does not always meet these four requirements, so that it must often be supplemented with artificial lighting.

Every kind of working situation is likely to have its unique lighting problems, and we cannot assume that what is good lighting for one worker and his work is also good lighting for the next worker and his work. However, many studies of lighting have indicated that better factory lighting tends to increase production. According to one report:

Research has shown that an average of 87 per cent of an industrial worker's motions are guided by his sight. Yet a survey of 3,000 plants in 22 states found the average of plant light intensity about 50 per cent below standard. In 38 plants where better lighting was installed, a 13 per cent increase in efficiency resulted.[12]

In eyesight surveys, 79.1 per cent of 618 employees in one concern had visual defects; correction resulted in an increase of 10 to 40 per cent in hourly earnings. By installing an "eye room" in one factory, $30,000 was saved in compensation cases in a 14-year period. Out of 612 employees in a watch-manufacturing concern, 212 had defective vision. The need for occasional surveys of visual conditions and constant check is apparent.[13]

Whenever results of illumination studies are reported, the reader should realize that marked increases in efficiency or lowering of costs are likely to be influenced by many factors other than illumination. For example, when the Detroit Edison Company checked the output of its draftsmen one summer, it was found that they were getting out 8,988 "work units" in 5,008 man-hours. The following summer the draftsmen were moved into a new windowless building, completely air-conditioned and illuminated electrically with 50 foot-candles of light at the drafting table. Under these improved conditions, the drafts-

---

[12] Victor Heiser, *Factory,* May 1939.
[13] M. A. Vogel, "Eyesight Surveys," *The Human Factor,* London, 1937, Vol. 11, pp. 394-398.

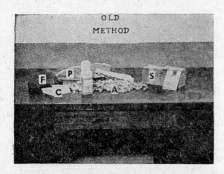

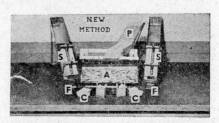

A. Table set-up of product and supplies under the old method of working. Letters identify the following: S—box sleeves, P—partition, A—ampules, F—files, C—circulars.

D. Contrast the new location of materials with that of A. Since the new method calls for assembly of two packages at once, some supplies are stacked in duplicate fixtures, gravity feeds being used for box sleeves.

B. How the operator performed the packaging operations under the old method. Note the random distribution of materials and the absence of fixtures which would hold these materials in the most convenient position for use.

E. Position of the operator's hands and arms in relation to the new material locations is clearly shown. Note how operator selects two box sleeves at the same time.

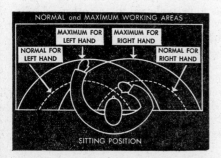

COMPARATIVE SUMMARY	OLD		NEW	
	L.H.	R.H.	L.H.	R.H.
Total number of transportations	13	2	15	13
Total number of operations	17	9	17	17
Total cycle time	.50 mins.		.56 mins.	
Number of pieces per cycle	1		2	
Cycle time per box	.50 mins.		.28 mins.	
SAVED—.22 mins. per box, or 44° of old method time.				

C. The chart shows normal and maximum working areas for operators working at assembly tables when properly seated. Supplies should all be available within the maximum area and performance of handling operations should, if possible, occur within the normal work area.

F. The comparative summary shows a saving of 44 per cent of old method time since the adoption of the new method. Note that while cycle time has increased fractionally, each new method cycle produces two finished packages.

Fig. 69. Diagrams A-E illustrate principles of motion study applied to hand packaging. Note the savings in time and motions as shown by the comparative summary table for old and new methods. From Clifton H. Cox, "Motion Study Applied to Hand Packaging," *Modern Packaging*, July 1939.

men required only 3,872 man-hours to do 10,474 work units; an increase in efficiency of 51.4 per cent.[14]

In this particular case, the management recognized that environmental conditions, other than illumination only, were improved. However, in many cases of reported improvements in efficiency as a result of better lighting, only the lighting is mentioned even though additional changes are made. Sometimes the most important factors are ignored. Furthermore, improvements in lighting, like any other marked improvement in conditions of work, result in increased efficiency. Such marked increases in efficiency are not always permanent because the "lift" in morale is likely to wear off after several months of work under the improved conditions.

Illumination standards for effective and comfortable vision. The surveys of lighting of homes, offices, factories, and schoolrooms have revealed many examples of inadequate and harmful illumination. The three aspects of lighting which are most often unhygienic are quality or color, brightness or intensity, and distribution or diffusion of illumination.

Tinker[15] has partly summarized certain studies regarding color as follows:

White light (sunlight), composed of rays from all parts of the spectrum, was superior to the yellow when the test object was black on a white background. In practice, however, yellow is to be preferred to any other color or combination of colors found in ordinary illuminants for discriminating fine details. Yellow light has the further advantage of being available (sodium-vapor lamps) at the brighter levels. It can find application in practical situations where fine visual discrimination is required, such as in industrial inspection work. Results indicate that no monochromatic color is superior to sunlight. There is ample evidence, however, that these findings have no bearing upon most supra-liminal tasks, such as ordinary reading, office work, and most factory operations. Thus with legible print and adequate intensity of light, there appears to be no appreciable disadvantage from chromatic aberration in reading with the common artificial illuminants. In general, one may employ whatever color he wishes for special effects and still maintain hygienic lighting, providing the factors of intensity and distribution are controlled.

Intensity of light. Intensity of light is measured in foot-candles. Foot-candle is a technical term which refers to "the

---

[14] News item in *Business Week*, September 16, 1939.

[15] Miles A. Tinker, "Illumination Standards for Effective and Comfortable Vision," Journal of Consulting Psychology, 1939, Vol. 3 (No. 1, January-February), pp. 12 ff. Quoted by permission of the author and the *Journal.*

amount of light illuminating a surface by a standard candle at a distance of one foot." Instruments for measuring brightness level, *light meters,* are available. Another instrument, the *visibility meter,* now makes it possible to specify the foot-candles necessary for various tasks so they may be performed with approximately the same degree of ease of seeing. Visibility can be roughly illustrated by holding a newspaper at arm's length. Most persons can read all the print regardless of the size of type but, the largest type is obviously of higher visibility than the smallest type.

The visibility meter makes it possible to reduce the visibility of any object or task by gradually reducing the contrast (and brightness) until you can barely see it. This threshold is a measurement which can readily be made. We can determine when the object or task is barely visible when it is viewed through this visibility meter. . . .

Thus there is now available a means for scientifically specifying the foot-candles necessary for various tasks to be performed with approximately the same degree of ease of seeing. . . .

It has been found that reading large print for prolonged periods is easiest when the level of illumination is more than 100 foot-candles. However, let us use as our very conservative standard the visibility of 8-point type (a type size slightly larger than that used in the average newspaper) when illuminated by only 10 foot-candles. The foot-candles necessary for various tasks to be of the same visibility are presented herewith.

FOOT-CANDLES NECESSARY FOR THESE TASKS TO BE OF
EQUAL VISIBILITY

Foot-candles

Reading 8-point type, well printed on white paper	10
Reading 6-point type, well printed on white paper	20
Reading average newspaper printed on newsprint	30
Reading handwriting with average pencil	50
Reading newspaper stock quotations	80
Distinguishing black thread on dark cloth	500

It is seen from the foregoing that the foot-candles required for making various tasks of the same visibility vary enormously. As the standard is raised, all the values are raised. For example, a black thread on dark cloth would have to be illuminated to a level of 4,000 foot-candles (approximately the average level of daylight outdoors) to make its visibility the same as that of 8-point type on white paper, and illuminated to a level of 100 foot-candles.[16]

Recommended Foot-candles

100 Foot-candles or more—For severe and prolonged tasks, such as fine needlework, fine engraving, fine penwork, fine assembly, sewing on dark goods and discrimination of fine details of low contrast, as in inspection.

---

[16] Matthew Luckiesh, *Seeing.* Lighting Research Laboratory, General Electric Company, Nela Park, Cleveland.

50 to 100 Foot-candles—For severe and prolonged tasks, such as proofreading, drafting, difficult reading, watch repairing, fine machine-work, average sewing and other needlework.

20 to 50 Foot-candles—For moderately critical and prolonged tasks, such as clerical work, ordinary reading, common benchwork, and average sewing and other needlework on light goods.

10 to 20 Foot-candles—For moderate and prolonged tasks of office and factory and, when not prolonged, ordinary reading and sewing on light goods.

5 to 10 Foot-candles—For visually controlled work in which seeing is important, but more or less interrupted or casual and does not involve discrimination of fine details or low contrasts.

0 to 5 Foot-candles—The danger zone for severe visual tasks, and for quick and certain seeing. Satisfactory for perceiving larger objects and for casual seeing.[17]

Researchers have used various criteria for the determination of the most desirable lighting conditions. One criterion frequently used has been the production or output of the worker under different conditions of lighting. However, studies of lighting based upon factors such as output, rate of performing useful work, and speed of reading must be supplemented with additional criteria. Psychological factors are often more difficult to measure than the relatively simple objective environmental factors.

One simple way to approach any problem of seeing or the influence of any controllable aid to seeing is to divide it into two parts: (1) the visibility of the object or task and (2) the comfort of the observer, or more broadly, ease of seeing. The visibility meter makes it possible to have all tasks of the same visibility by controlling various aids to seeing, including light and lighting. Through researches on physiological effects of seeing in which all the variables or aids to seeing were controlled, Lighting Research Laboratory workers have developed other criteria. The most promising of these is the rate of involuntary blinking. A number of major researches have been conducted using the rate of involuntary blinking as the criterion. This criterion has been found to be far more sensitive and meaningful than any other criterion heretofore used.[18]

---

[17] Ibid.

[18] Content of this paragraph provided by Matthew Luckiesh, Lighting Research Laboratory, General Electric Company, Nela Park, Cleveland. Extensive bibliographies and research reports in the science of seeing may be obtained from Lighting Research Laboratory.

Fig. 70. Miles A. Tinker, University of Minnesota. Lighting problems are discussed in his article, "Illumination Standards for Effective and Comfortable Vision," *Journal of Consulting Psychology*, 1939, Vol. 3, pp. 11–20.

Light distribution. Distribution of light is exceedingly important and can often be achieved with little effort. Unevenness of distribution is the most common error in lighting. Failure to maintain a proper diffusion of light produces eyestrain and decreases visual efficiency. Simple re-arrangements of work and changes in lighting fixtures often eliminate glare and the bright areas and shadows within the visual field. Tinker has summarized suggestions for certain improvements in distribution as follows:

The uncomfortable effects of bright spots of light above or off to the side of the line of vision while reading, doing other visual work, or even when no visual discrimination is involved, is common experience. Elimination of this disturbing peripheral illumination is necessary if hygienic vision is to be maintained. When these side lights become brighter or are moved closer to the line of direct vision, the immediate working surface, the fatiguing effects become greater. Furthermore, the greater the number of such peripheral light sources, the more detrimental is the effect upon vision.

Uncomfortable glare and loss of visual efficiency also result from highly polished or glazed objects within the field of vision. Examples are nickel-plated metal parts of a typewriter and glazed printing paper. Such glare is reduced by maintaining well-diffused illumination in the work room.

Visual fatigue and lessened efficiency are produced by brightness contrast within that portion of the visual field where critical vision is required and also within the immediate surroundings. When the eyes must shift back and forth from bright to dark areas or when there is a sharp division between dark and bright portions of the working area, the eyes must constantly re-adapt to the different degrees of brightness. Eyestrain soon results. Examples are (1) white paper on a dark desk, and (2) a dark under-surface of an opaque eye shade used in a brightly lighted room.

The following will aid in eliminating glare effects: (1) Avoid peripheral light sources, such as wall brackets and low-hanging fixtures which reach down into the field of vision. (2) Avoid as far as possible the use of glazed paper, polished metallic objects, and marked contrasts of brightness within the visual field. (3) Avoid strictly local lighting like that produced by most desk lamps with opaque shades. The latter produce a circle of bright light surrounded by dimly illuminated areas and shadows. (4) Maintain, in general, as equal a distribution of light as possible over the working surface.[19]

Noise. Work in almost every factory and office involves a certain amount of noise. Executives have recognized that noise is a distraction to many employees. Accordingly, some executives have attempted to overcome the problem by sound-proofing offices and other places of work.

Everyone knows, too, that the worker may become adapted to noise and that certain noises do not distract some workers. Experiments by psychologists indicate that the nature of the noise and the attitude of the individual toward the noise are of paramount importance regarding the distracting effects. A continuous noise may not have any harmful effects whereas an intermittent or unusual noise may. The steady noise such as that of a battery of typewriters is not likely to be as disturbing as irregular noises from automobile horns, strangers entering a room and banging a door, or persons talking more loudly than usual. Noise may even facilitate the individual worker's output if he has adopted a favorable attitude toward it.

Many workers accept a certain amount of noise, thinking of it as a necessary background for the work of the day. Several investigators have found that the significance of the noise for a particular individual rather than its intensity or nature determines its effects on the individual listener. Most of us have at some time been annoyed by a steam shovel or hoisting machine. However, it is probable that if the listener who is annoyed by the steam shovel were the inventor or manufacturer of the shovel, he would enjoy the noise rather than consider it a distraction.

---

[19] Tinker, *op. cit.*, pp. 17 f.

Various investigators of noise have pointed out that it should not be assumed, when a worker accepts noise as a background for his work, that his passive acceptance signifies an increase in efficiency. Furthermore, they have found that an increase in output is often accompanied by a considerable increase in the expenditure of energy involved. Several clever experiments of this kind have been conducted with keyboards. For example, the operator pressed appropriate keys similar to typewriter keys when he was given a designated stimulus. Careful measurements indicated that the operator exerted more pressure under distraction of noise than he did without the distraction.

Laird studied the air exhaled by typists and inferred from the greater consumption of oxygen during the noise periods that the typists expended more energy at a given task when conditions were noisy than when conditions were quiet. When typewriter keys were used to transcribe a code, J. J. B. Morgan found no difference in learning capacity when the room was noisy, but recorders attached to the keys indicated that more muscular pressure was then exerted by the operator. However, loudness and annoyance do not wholly go hand in hand. Loudness in relation to the background is often simply the dominating measurable feature of noise.

We can conclude, therefore, that when a noise really distracts the worker, a decrease in output or an increase in the expenditure of energy is likely to result. Also, when the noise is considered a background for the worker's activities, the sound which is noise for one observer may be a kind of pleasant environment for the person who has become adapted.

When noise of work cannot be reduced sufficiently to satisfy workers, the sufferers may gain some advantage by using ear defenders or plugs. Certain solid types of defenders are useful for relieving discomfort from intense noises and explosions. The wearer may still hear conversation. Complaints of traffic noise usually come from office workers in rooms facing the street, the sound usually being transmitted through windows or other openings. Closing the windows often keeps out the noise. Panes of heavy glass are helpful in further decreasing the noise. The best remedy is to use double windows and keep them closed, providing ventilation by quiet fans or vent ducts. When employees complain of noise from office appliances used by other members of the staff, annoyance can be reduced by the use of absorbent materials on the ceilings and walls. The absorbent materials may be tiles of a soft, porous nature or canvas, or perforated metals. Also, the machines can be insulated by means of bands of felt placed under them. An experienced sound engineer may discover many additional ways of reducing noise and making working conditions more comfortable.

Music. Hundreds of plant managers have used music to relax tensions and to stimulate production. Stevedores, cotton workers, and others know that music often helps to reduce fatigue.

Some years ago the Latz Advertising Service of New York was swamped with such an avalanche of orders that getting the work out on time seemed hopeless even with a force augmented to 500 girls. After several sleepless nights, the manager decided on two plans: a bonus for individual records, and —believe it or not—music. The girl typists, inserters, and letterers were to be treated to periodic doses of the heavenly muse throughout the work day. Results exceeded even sanguine expectations. Production was stepped up 20 per cent. When the mass of rush orders was completed, the bonus was withdrawn, but the music made such a hit it was retained. With music, production has been maintained from 7 to 10 per cent above normal.

British munitions works, auto plants, knitting mills, chocolate and cigarette factories are going for the idea. Cigar makers of Cuba, who formerly employed readers to mitigate the tedium of their tasks, now have music from loudspeakers. Factories in South America that do not employ musicians to play during the grind are outlawed—no music, no work. Longshoremen on Brooklyn docks are now kept healthier and happier as they load their ships. And where it has been possible to synchronize the work rhythm to music, unusual results have been noted.[20]

Managements of some department stores, banks, and other firms regularly devote a period of the working day to mass singing. Night clerks in some post offices handle mail to the music of the radio. We all know that many school children also study their lessons with an ear "glued" to the radio.

The few available studies of effects of music in relation to workers' production have been rather inconclusive. Investigators seem to agree that the rhythm of the music should not

---

[20] D. K. Antrim, "Music—for More Profits in Industry," *Connecticut Industry*, July 1939.

interfere with but facilitate the manual rhythm of the worker. Each individual tends to react to music in accordance with his personal preferences and conditionings. Consider, for example, the unpleasant emotional reactions of many cultured adults to the popular music enjoyed by members of the younger generation.

Fatigue factors. Certain biology teachers have likened man to a machine and tried to compute his efficiency in a manner similar to the ways of measuring the efficiency of motors. In terms of chemical energy consumed, the Diesel engine and the high-compression automobile engine surpass man's efficiency as a machine. In terms of chemical energy consumed as food and converted into external mechanical energy, man's efficiency usually ranges from 15 to 20 per cent.[21]

The term fatigue has various meanings. To the layman it simply means "feeling tired." Researchers usually call this *subjective fatigue* and it may be thought of with reference to certain muscles only, or it may be rather general and involve drowsiness. Laboratory experiments often show that subjective fatigue may be quite pronounced but the person having such feelings may actually be doing as much work as ever.

Subjective fatigue is often distinguished from *mental fatigue,* the tiredness that develops from work of a mental rather than a muscular nature. The fatigue that results from doing accounting or writing a book may be considered to be somewhat different from the subjective fatigue caused by the use of muscles. Perhaps the difference between the two is only one of degree or source. At any rate, mental workers often wish to change to some other activity, but the other activity at the time may simply have a greater appeal because of vague psychological influences and not because of physiological changes in the body.

In some fatigue experiments, the subject of the experiment may not feel tired but may do considerably less work. This decreased capacity for work because of exhaustion of energy-producing materials such as sugar products, especially glycogen, and the accumulation of waste products, mostly carbon dioxide and lactic acid, is called *objective fatigue.* Objective and subjective fatigue do not always correlate especially when the individ-

---

[21] J. D. Ratcliff, "What Makes You Tired," *Collier's*, December 21, 1940, p. 43

ual is offered a greatly desired reward for continued output. Of course, physiological conditions have pronounced bearings on the feelings of fatigue. For example, in hot industries workmen are given salt in tablet form or in drinking water in order to remedy the deficiency of body salt lost through perspiration. Glass making, baking, steel, and similar industries furnish salt to workers, especially during heat waves. Some football trainers feed salt, or bouillon, which is more palatable, to football players.

Caffeine is often used to overcome fatigue or to increase alertness. In general, caffeine, when administered as the raw alkaloid or as caffeine citrate, tends to reduce simple motor-sensory reaction time from 6 to 8 per cent, depending upon the individual.[22] Hollingworth has reported studies of differential effects of dosages and found that the speed of performance at typing was quickened by doses of one to three grains of caffeine but retarded by larger doses of four to six grains. Small doses seemed to decrease errors and increase speed in typing, but doses greater than six grains had opposite effects.[23]

In general, the effects of caffeine appear to be slight on the average, but they vary greatly with the type of work performed and the person involved.

Tobacco is used by many persons as an aid to efficiency in work. Numerous experimenters have tried to investigate its effects by setting up controlled conditions, using control subjects for comparisons, and attempting to eliminate influences of suggestion. Most of these studies have failed to exclude the influences of variables such as habit, attitude toward smoking, body weight, suggestion, and others. Accordingly, a few researchers have used rats as subjects for experiment. Nathan W. Shock has summarized the studies regarding many of our psychophysiological relations,[24] including certain experimental results on effects of tobacco:

[22] W. Shilling, "The Effect of Caffeine and Acetanilid on Simple Reaction Time," *Psychological Review,* 1921, Vol. 28, pp. 72-79.

[23] H. L. Hollingworth, "The Influence of Caffeine on the Speed and Quality of Performance in Typewriting," *Psychological Review,* 1912, Vol. 19, pp. 66-73.

[24] Nathan W. Shock, "Some Psychophysiological Relations," *Psychological Bulletin,* June 1939, Vol. 36, No. 6, pp. 447-476.

Pechstein and Reynolds[25] exposed rats to tobacco smoke over a period of 30 minutes to 3 hours daily for 30 to 60 days. The animals were exposed to smoke from 5 gr. of tobacco, so there is no indication whether the effects were produced by nicotine, carbon monoxide, pyridine, or some other combustion products of tobacco. After fuming, the animals were transferred to the maze, and learning curves were obtained. It was found that rats fumed with a limited amount of tobacco smoke excelled all normal and experimental groups in maze learning. Animals who were fumed over longer periods of time were less effective in learning, with greater variability in the female group. The authors concluded that tobacco smoke to a small degree acts as a stimulant and enhances learning, while excessive smoking depletes learning capacity to the point of inability by the fourth generation.

Professor Raymond Pearl, biologist at Johns Hopkins University, published several studies showing that tobacco smokers do not live as long as non-smokers:

This conclusion was based on life tables for the number, out of groups of 100,000 non-smoking men, 100,000 moderate smokers (men), and 100,000 heavy smokers (men), who were still alive at each age level after 30 years. At age 60, for example, 66,564 of the 100,000 non-smokers were still living; 61,911 of 100,000 moderate smokers were living; and 46,226 of 100,000 heavy smokers were still living.

The studies show that smoking is associated with a definite impairment of longevity. This impairment is proportional to the habitual amount of tobacco usage by smoking, being great for heavy smokers and less for moderate smokers, but even in the latter sufficient to be measurable and significant.

The effect of tobacco smoking on length of life is different from that of alcohol in that moderate as well as heavy smokers live less long than non-smokers, whereas moderate drinkers do not have appreciably shorter lives than total abstainers, although heavy drinkers do.

The effect of hard physical labor on length of life was also studied by statistical methods. Up to the age of about 40 years, hard labor either indoors or outdoors has no effect on life expectation, but after about age 40 such labor "definitely and considerably" shortens the length of life of the individuals.[26]

Summary

In general, we can say that fatigue and efficiency of the individual are influenced by many chemical and psychological influences. Furthermore, the individual can accommodate himself to almost any conditions. Man has permanent settlements

[25] L. A. Pechstein and W. R. Reynolds, "The Effect of Tobacco Smoke on the Growth and Learning Behavior of the Albino Rat and Its Progeny." *Journal of Comparative Psychology,* 1937, Vol. 24, pp. 459-469.

[26] "Smokers Less Long-Lived; Heavy Drinkers Die Earlier," *Science News Letter,* March 12, 1938.

Fig. 71. Gardner Murphy, College of the City of New York. Those interested in further study of problems in the conditions of work are referred to his book *General Psychology*, Chapter XXIV (Harper & Bros., 1933).

in towns that frequently have winter temperatures 50 degrees F. below zero and in deserts with sun temperatures of 150 degrees. Attitude is exceedingly important toward the adaptation. An experienced stevedore, for example, can toss freight all day without appreciable fatigue but will be worn out by several hours of simple effort while on a shopping trip with his wife who is looking for a hat!

In the case of industrial workers, Britain's Industrial Health Board has summarized recent researches on the effects of working hours and similar factors on output of workers.

It used to be thought that worker's and employer's interests were opposed —the worker wanting plenty of leisure and pay, the employer wanting the most work for the least expenditure. But now psychological researches into industry have shown that the best conditions of work for the greatest output are exactly the same as those that give health and a low accident rate to the worker.[27]

References

Burtt, H. E., *Psychology and Industrial Efficiency*. D. Appleton-Century Co., 1929.

Crane, George W., *Psychology Applied*, Chapter IX. Northwestern University Press, 1940.

[27] Marjorie Van De Water, *Science—Supplement*, Vol. 92, No. 2396, p. 12.

Griffith, C. R., *An Introduction to Applied Psychology*, Chapters XXVIII-XXX. The Macmillan Co., 1934.

Jenkins, John G., *Psychology in Business and Industry*, Chapters VII-X. John Wiley & Sons, 1935.

Moore, Herbert, *Psychology for Business and Industry*, Chapters VIII-XIII. McGraw-Hill Book Co., 1939.

Poffenberger, A. T., *Applied Psychology*, Chapters IX-XII, XVIII-XX. D. Appleton-Century Co., 1929.

Strong, Edward K., Jr., *Psychological Aspects of Business*, Chapters XXVIII-XXX. McGraw-Hill Book Co., 1938.

Noise

Davis, A. H., *Noise*. Ryerson Press, Toronto, 1937.

"Fewer Mistakes in Quiet Offices," *American Business*, Vol. 9, pp. 49-50, October 1939.

Harris, L. J., "What Kind of a Noise Annoys?" *Hygeia*, December 1938.

Laird, Donald A., "The Effects of Noise," *Journal of The Acoustical Society of America*, Vol. 1, p. 257, 1930.

Lindahl, R., "Noise; Effect on Workers," *Safety Engineering*, Vol. 78, p. 27, September 1939.

Morgan, J. J. B., "The Overcoming of Distraction and Other Resistances," *Archives of Psychology*, No. 35, 1916.

"Noise and Efficiency," *Safety Engineering*, Vol. 80, p. 41, August 1940.

Stone, N. D., "Less Noise, Fewer Errors," *Bankers Monthly*, Vol. 55, pp. 8-9, January 1941.

Music

Antrim, D. K., "Music for More Profits in Industry," *Management Review*, Vol. 28, pp. 293-294, September 1939.

Clark, K. S., *Music in Industry*. National Bureau for the Advancement of Music.

Deardorff, R., "Can Music Increase Production?" *American Business*. Vol. 10, p. 28, June 1940.

"Music in Factories?" *Management Review*, Vol. 28, pp. 265-266, August 1939,

Time and Motion Study

Barnes, R. M., *Motion and Time Study*. John Wiley & Sons, 1940.

Holmes, W. G., *Applied Time and Motion Study*. Ronald Press, 1938.

Mogensen, A. H., *Common Sense Applied to Time and Motion Study*. McGraw-Hill Book Co., 1932.

Shumard, F. W., *Primer of Time Study*. McGraw-Hill Book Co., 1940.

Viteles, M. S., *Industrial Psychology*. W. W. Norton & Co., 1932.

Tobacco

Dorsey, J. L., "Control of the Tobacco Habit," *Annals of Internal Medicine*, 1937, Vol. 10, pp. 628-631.

Fay, P. J., "The Effect of Cigarette Smoking on Simple and Choice Reaction Time to Colored Lights," *Journal of Experimental Psychology*, 1936, Vol. 19, pp. 592-603.

"Heart Disease More Frequent Among Tobacco Smokers," *Science News Letter*, November 2, 1940, p. 284.

Pearl, Raymond, "The Search for Longevity," *Science Monthly*, 1938, Vol. 46, pp. 462-483.

——————, "Tobacco Smoking and Longevity," *Science*, 1938, Vol. 87, pp. 216-217.

"Wager and Publicity Best Aids to Cutting Out Smoking," *Science News Letter*, May 20, 1939.

Fatigue

Dill, D. B., Bock, A. V., Edwards, H. T., and Kennedy, P. H., "Industrial Fatigue," *Journal of Industrial Hygiene*, 1937.

Miles, G. H., "Fatigue from the Industrial Point of View," *The Human Factor*, 1937, Vol. 11, pp. 8-15.

Taylor, H. C., "A Way to Reduce the Fatigue Allowance in Time Study," *Personnel Journal*, 1937, Vol. 13, pp. 83-93.

Taylor, J. H., "The Effect of Suggested Attitudes on Work Production and Feelings of Tiredness and Boredness," *Psychological Bulletin*, 1936, Vol. 33, pp. 815-816.

——————, "Tiredness," *Personnel Journal*, 1937, Vol. 13, pp. 102-109.

Tindall, G. M., "Rhythm for the Restless," *Personnel Journal*, 1937, Vol. 16, pp. 120-124.

Illumination

Ferree, C. E., and G. Rand, "Work and Its Illumination, I," *Personnel Journal*, 1940, Vol. 19, pp. 55-64.

Luckiesh, Matthew, and Frank K. Moss, *The Science of Seeing*. D. Van Nostrand Co., 1937.

The Magazine of Light, Lighting Research Laboratory, Nela Park, Cleveland, Ohio.

Tinker, M. A., "Facts Concerning Hygienic Illumination Intensities," *School & Society*, 1938, Vol. 47, pp. 120-121.

——————, "Illumination Standards for Effective and Comfortable Vision," *Journal of Consulting Psychology*, 1939, Vol. 3, pp. 11-19.

——————, "Illumination Standards for Efficient Work in the Home, School, Office, and Factory," *American Journal of Optometry*, 1938.

Vogel, M. A., "Eyesight Surveys," *The Human Factor*, London, 1937, Vol. 11, pp. 394-398.

Projects

1. Describe a number of comparatively recent changes in automobile design which have saved effort and waste motion for the driver and made for greater safety and better control.

2. If you were making a study of the subjective factors in efficiency of sales clerks in a large department store, what sort of information would you gather? List the items and explain what value each might have for your research.

3. Study carefully some work you do regularly such as washing dishes or folding letters and placing them in envelopes. Work out an improved pro-

cedure by applying some of the general principles of time and motion study. Evaluate the results in terms of both subjective and objective benefits.

4. Visit an industrial plant in your community and note evidences of the management's program for maintaining high morale among employees. Write a report suggesting additions to or improvements in the existing program.

5. Conduct a study among fellow students or associates regarding effects on efficiency of listening to the radio while reading or studying. Note the kind of music listened to, the loudness, and other pertinent factors.

6. Make a collection of advertisements for products claimed to promote restful sleep. Evaluate the possible benefits of each product and note any doubtful claims.

7. List a number of examples, other than those mentioned in the text, illustrating the importance of attitude in adaptation to unusual conditions.

17

The Executive and the Individual Employee

"Do you know the man who smiled at you?" asked the jealous suitor.
"Yes!" replied his girl. "He's a colleague of mine."
"What does he do?"
"He signs the letters I type."

MOST of the literature about psychological aspects of management is simply personal opinion stated by experienced businessmen who are too close to themselves and their situations to have a good perspective for their statements. However, we cannot afford to ignore entirely the viewpoints of those who have opened trails in our economic life. We must recognize that these non-scientific executives and their colleagues of the past, in their own time and in their own manner, helped to give us a great era of industrial and commercial development. Until such time as scientific evidence may become available, we shall limit ourselves to statements of certain principles which appear to be correct to leading students of psychology applied to our economic life.

Two major types of leaders. The executive of modern business is, or at least should be, a leader. Several students of leaders have found considerable evidence for classifying them into "master" and "educator" types. Of course, many executives fall into a mixed classification, but we can improve our own adjustments to economic life if we differentiate between these two types, also called the "autocratic" and "democratic."

The master type has the stronger desire for self-expression, is more interested in his personal ascendance over others, is more extraverted, and is likely to be in an older age range than his followers. He is likely to be characterized as egotistical.

In politics, this aggressive type strives to attract followers whose personalities he can exploit, even though he claims that what he does is for the benefit of those exploited. These autocratic leaders are likely to come from homes where discipline was strict or where the child resented an important aspect of the home environment.

The educator type is usually more interested in serving others —in helping his followers develop in the directions they wish to go—is himself introvertive, has a tendency toward self-doubt, and is characterized as sympathetic.[1]

The democratic or educator leader does not find it necessary to destroy other persons or their ideas because his drive is to lead others to go beyond the accepted conditions or ideas. He not only tolerates others but even encourages successors who will explore ahead and render his own work obsolete.[2]

In all fields of endeavor, leaders are needed, but most leaders of both types are self-appointed. Their rise usually grows out of the compelling demands of their adjustments rather than from any clamor on the part of the populace.

In the business world, a striking characteristic of most executives seems to be their humanness. They are not gods, as some of their underlings and a few of the executives themselves seem to think. Employees closely associated with key executives soon learn the whimsicalities, idiosyncrasies, and eccentricities of their superiors just as the small child soon recognizes the signs that indicate the pleasant and unpleasant future actions of the parent. When father comes down to breakfast and scowls at the cat, the small son knows that he had better wait until some other day to ask for a new bicycle. Just so with the executives. The employees soon learn the signs of danger and favor. Word is soon passed around that the big boss must not be approached in the morning until he has finished his first pipe of tobacco. A certain executive may discharge his subordinates rather recklessly, but they know that if they come to see him after he has paid his dinner check, they will be reinstated. Others must be ap-

---

[1] P. Pigors, "Types of Leaders in Group Work," *Sociological Social Research*, 1936, Vol. 21, pp. 3-17.

[2] "Leadership is Often Born of Resentment of Authority," *Science News Letter*, September 9, 1939, p. 169.

proached by means of flattery, a discussion of duck hunting, or a request for information about some new system that the boss is promulgating at that season. Executives who pride themselves on the impersonal nature of their methods are quite likely to be very human, and their humanness is often better-known by the employees than by themselves. Many a private secretary could tell her chief about his peculiarities that have been "worked" by his subordinates for years.

Family versus faction. The heads of some corporations who claim that all their employees are members of one big family may be unaware of the fact that the "family" is riddled with "politics." One of the most frequently met examples of company politics is that of the company that has been developed through years of effort by one strong man who heads the concern. When he becomes aged, he gradually passes on to others some of his responsibilities, and two factions then tend to develop. One faction is loyal to the "old man" and continues his policies and methods. The other faction develops among the leaders of the younger employees, and the two groups indulge in subtle little skirmishes. A new man who comes into the organization is soon lined up, often unconsciously, with one of these factions, and then the other faction awaits an opportunity to "knife" him. Consultants and others who pass in and out of many organizations soon learn the presence of such factions and guard against arousing antagonisms. It is for this reason that few experienced consultants care to do any work in a firm unless they are definitely and firmly backed up by some strongly intrenched executive of the company who has the unwavering confidence of his board of directors. Any new man who accepts a position of importance in a company should be on his guard for the possible machinations of politicians within the company. Company politics may be present in a concern even though the head of the company or the person who does the hiring boasts about the team spirit of the executives and employees.

Religion is a common cause of company politics. The president of one company stated that no attention is ever paid to the religion of his employees. No applicant is ever asked about his religion, and yet, when the seventeen leading executives and department heads of that company met at a dinner, sixteen of them

Fig. 72. Ordway Tead, Editor of Economic Books, Harper & Brothers, and Lecturer in Personnel Administration, Columbia University. Readers who are interested in the psychology of handling people may refer to his book *The Art of Leadership* (McGraw-Hill Book Co., 1935).

were members of the same type of church and twelve of them belonged to the same secret fraternal organization! Business analysts have found companies where a single department head gradually discharged the employees who were members of another religious denomination in order to hire adherents of his own faith. Some concerns find it necessary to ask for the religious affiliation of their employees and annually study the figures for each department so that factional differences in religion may be avoided.

Another factor that contributes to company politics is that of special discounts to certain big customers. The head of the company may ignore the sales manager and grant special discounts to customers who have been with the company for years or to men who are his personal friends. When irregular discounts are given some customers, factions are likely to arise. Some of the salesmen learn about the discounts and, when they wish to favor another customer, they will ignore the sales manager to get the discount. A barrier of feeling may then arise between the leading executives who promote the discounts and those who oppose them, and many of the employees will affiliate themselves with the executive or faction which appears to have the best chances of winning if an open struggle takes place.

The executive who happens to find himself in the subtle undercurrents of company politics and managerial lobbies sometimes cannot determine the best procedure for himself. He cannot go to the head of the company and explain his position, because he has no evidence to present, nor would he wish to do so if he had ample evidence. He cannot line up with one faction and take part in harassing the other side. He himself wishes to promote some ideas of his own and he may have to negotiate with a lobbyist in order to accomplish the things he wants done. Usually, his best procedure is to ignore the politics and endeavor to sell his plans to the management on the merits of the plans rather than through factional support. In most concerns such an aim is fairly easy to achieve. Most executives gain their ends by honest means. However, since human prejudices afflict all of us, we cannot wholly condemn the other person when he allows his prejudices to influence him. So long as human nature remains as it is, we shall have a certain amount of lobbying in business. Ambitious executives will explain their schemes to associates or others who have "logs to roll," and obtain their cooperation for ends that will benefit the company as well as the lobbyist. Such lobbying may be legitimate if it is done without an attempt at concealment and if the purpose of the maneuvering is that of profits for the company rather than for the person who manipulates the lobby.

Executive policies in dealing with the individual employee. Hundreds of articles have discussed the characteristics, policies, and attitudes of the responsible business executives, and one set of rules might be considered as good as another. However, a few of these rules or policies, which seem to be more fundamental than others, are given below:

1. *The employee prefers to be treated as an individual.* Successful executives seem to follow opposing policies with respect to the individuality of the employee. Some executives learn names, addresses, family life, and personal history of each of their employees and take a friendly interest in his welfare. Other executives spend little or no time in learning of the intimate lives of their employees but devote themselves to the development of a team spirit, playing the game of business, fighting competitors, and inventing new systems of production in order that

costs may be lowered. They prefer to study the accomplishments of groups of employees rather than of specific individuals. Each of these methods probably has its advantages and both must be used at times in every concern. However, the employee is an individual and has dreams for himself rather than visions for his group or the company. He has specific problems, such as paying his bills, rearing his children, and attaining worthwhileness. Executives who attempt to develop a family spirit in the organization by dealing with groups rather than individuals have chosen a difficult path to travel. In spite of our dependence upon the groups about us, we are all primarily interested in ourselves, and the executive who adopts a policy of knowing his employees as individuals, their family history, personal problems, and so on, probably will have a better team spirit than he who concentrates upon group methods, such as organized welfare work, house organ editorials, bulletin board notices, personnel record systems, company picnics, and annual banquets.

A personal interest in each employee does not necessitate a daily round among the employees to inquire about the babies' new teeth and the headaches of grandmothers, but it does mean that the executive will "back up" the employee who wishes to improve his position and worth. He must be willing to help a good employee get another job in another department or firm if the employee is ready for a better job. Comparatively few executives are willing to train men and then let them go to someone else, even though it may be better for the employee.

Sometimes a gentle prod from the supervisor might lift the employee into a better job and a new vocational life. A personal interest in the employee means that the executive will occasionally call into his office each of his capable employees and learn their hopes, clarify their ambitions, suggest courses of training, and outline definite vocational programs that will benefit the employee first, the company second, and the executive last. An honest effort of this kind seems to develop more *esprit de corps* than lectures on "family" spirit or schemes of profit sharing.

2. *The employee likes to know that his superior has confidence in him.* To have the employee realize that his superior has confidence in him requires a policy that does not produce the typical "yes-man." Many an executive is not very sure of himself and

his job, so he cannot admit any thoughts of incompetence or weakness on his own part. When he rails at the "dumbness" or lack of initiative of his subordinates, he is really telling his associates that he is not sure of himself. The employees know that, if they attempt to assert themselves or to plead for what they believe to be right, they are likely to be discharged and most of them cannot afford to be discharged. Many an employee is an introjectionist because he loves his family and must provide for them at the cost of his own individuality. Interestingly enough, when executives who have prided themselves on their impartiality and willingness to face facts have asked their employees to rate their executive conduct, they have received ratings which indicated that the employees considered them bulldozers and tyrants. Sometimes accusations of tyranny are unavoidable, and any executive is apt to have some disgruntled subordinates. If an executive wishes to learn the attitude of his employees, he can do so by means of a rating scale (see Chapter 12). The employees can be asked to rate the effectiveness of personnel policies and the treatment of employees by checking a form list of traits or terms and give the ratings to a third individual in whom the employees have confidence.

3. *Praise develops employees more readily than criticism.* One executive sat in his private office, waved his hand toward his employees, and said: "There isn't a man or woman out there who has any initiative. Not one of the seventy-two would be able to take my place if I were to leave. They are all afraid of their 'hides.' They're scared for fear they will lose their jobs." The natural reaction to such a statement is that the executive himself is responsible for such a condition. If he wishes to be a despot over his group and be undisturbed by those who disagree with his wishes, he can readily develop an organization of trembling vassals. .It is easier to develop a group of colorless employees than to build an organization of men and women who think and know that their ideas and personalities will be given appreciative recognition. If an irate employee were to come into the office of his superior and plainly and emphatically tell him that he was incompetent to manage a certain part of his own department, the average executive would usher the employee into the paymaster's office for his final pay. However, one of Ameri-

ca's leading executives had that happen to him and he promptly assigned the radical to the work he criticized. Later the employee became one of the best executives of the company.

When criticism must be given, it can be given so harshly that the person criticized will acquire a retiring and fearful personality, or it can cause the one at fault to boil over with wrath and quit, or it can be given so that he will be benefited and strengthened for the future. The executive who aims to get the first two results is merely indicating that his criticism has become a personal rather than a company matter. He is more interested in causing the failing subordinate to feel "small" than in improving him. If kindly directions and encouragement do not help the employee, then the company made a mistake in hiring him, or the executive does not know how to develop his erring employees. Criticisms should not involve mere personalities. They should be based upon the figures, conduct, or facts that are wrong. For example, if the manager of a sales district produces a 10 per cent increase in sales and the 10 per cent should have been accomplished three months before, it does much harm and little good to tell the manager that what he has done should have been accomplished months before. If he is shown the facts in the situation and that most of the other districts under the same conditions had previously turned in their increases, it will be more effective than a harsh belittling of the manager's ability. Criticisms can often be made most effective by asking the wrongdoer a number of searching questions that will reveal his conduct in a new light. Because department heads and district managers are apt to be sensitive, some general managers address their criticisms to the department or district at fault rather than to the responsible individual. This removes the sting and may be more effective than personal censure.

Some executives believe that an employee should not be praised. Their motto is, "The absence of criticism constitutes praise." Unfortunately for business leaders, no conclusive experiments are available which would prove or disprove such a personnel policy. We shall have to limit our analysis of this question to the suggestive psychological experiments on animals and school children that throw some light on such a policy. Animals definitely learn faster when rewarded for their trial efforts than when they are ignored or punished. Experiments with school children and college students indicate, in most cases, that praise is better than censure or the ignoring of the individual. Professor Thomas H. Briggs of Columbia University asked 370 graduate students to state whether they worked better, the same, or worse in high school under 21 different situations. These students had not been given any preparatory study or assignment relative to this subject. The reports indicated that reprimands, sarcasm, and ridicule, if they must be used, do less harm when rendered in private than in public. In general, praise and encouragement get the best results.

E. B. Hurlock conducted a laboratory experiment in which he used three kinds of incentives in stimulating school children of equivalent capacity. They were given a course of training in arithmetic for five days. The four groups of pupils and their respective scores are presented in Table XXX. The groups were:

a. *Control group.* These pupils were trained in a separate room and were free from the special influences of groups b, c, d.

b. *Praised group.* These pupils were praised for their work regardless of its quality.

c. *Reproved group.* These were reproved for their work regardless of its quality.

d. *Ignored group.* These pupils were able to hear the praise and reproval given groups b and c, but they themselves were ignored.

TABLE XXX

INFLUENCE OF VARIOUS INCENTIVES UPON OUTPUT

Groups	Day				
	1	2	3	4	5
Control.........	11.81	12.34	11.65	10.50	11.35
Praised..........	11.81	16.59	18.85	18.81	20.22
Reproved........	11.85	16.59	14.30	13.26	14.19
Ignored..........	11.84	14.19	13.30	12.92	12.38

The figures in the table are in terms of the score made in the work of the various days. Praise was the most effective incentive, when the output of the first and last days are compared, as the record of this group was approximately 75 per cent better than that of the control group, 60 per cent better than the ignored group, and 40 per cent better than the reproved group.[3] Certainly, the results indicated that the old adage, "The absence of criticism constitutes praise," was psychologically fallacious in this experiment. At first, reproof was as effective as praise, but its stimulating effects wore off. Experiments of psychological incentives suggest what skillful executives know: employees need constant attention, and the attention that inspires employees is more effective than that which depresses or frightens them.

4. *The use of humor with employees.* Some executives have acquired the art of correcting an employee by the use of humor. This kind of censure does not mean a jocular attitude toward grave errors, but a manner of criticizing humorously as well as effectively. We all know that many a truth is told in jest. No objective evidence is available to show that good executives have a greater sense of humor than poor executives, but a suggestive experiment was conducted with reference to teachers. Each of twenty-four college students was asked to interview twelve or more students of the university and to ask each of them to give ratings and answers to the following:

1. Think of some of the teachers you have had in high school and college. Include some of the best and some of the poorest.

2. Write the initials of the best teacher you have had.

3. Write the initials of the poorest teacher you have had. (No definition of a good teacher or a poor teacher was given. No explanation of the purpose of the experiment was given until after the initials of the two teachers had been recorded.)

4. Rate the best teacher on the following scale of humor in the classroom:

(5) Teacher usually tells several humorous stories or anecdotes each period. The class laughs rather frequently and heartily.

(4) Teacher occasionally tells humorous stories. Class averages one good laugh per period.

(3) Humor seldom expressed. Class has one good laugh in from 5 to 10 periods.

(2) Element of humor almost absent.

(1) Element of humor absent. Teacher takes his life and work so seriously that students would not think of laughing in his classes.

5. Now rate the poorest teacher on the same scale.

---

[3] E. B. Hurlock, "An Evaluation of Certain Incentives Used in School Work," *Journal of Educational Psychology*, 1925, Vol. 16, p. 145 ff.

The student experimenter then recorded the initials and ratings of the subject and went to the next student. When the various ratings were reported it was found that the best teachers, 284 in number, made an average of 3.95 on the above scale. The same number of poorest teachers had an average of 2.36 on the "humor scale."

It was also found that 86 of the so-called best teachers and 28 of the teachers considered the poorest had a rating of 5.

These data are presented to show, not that a high sense of humor makes a good teacher, but that a sense of humor in the classroom appears to be a trait of the good teacher more often than of the poor teacher.[4] It is not unlikely that good executives as well as good teachers have a better sense of humor than the poorer executives when dealing with employees.

5. *The executive should not generalize with the employee but deal with definite points.* Many executives give talks to the employees at meetings and to the individual employee in terms of generalized directions as, "Observe what is going on in the shop," and "Use your head." Sermonettes of this kind can be preached for years and yet the employees will not improve in their observation or mental ability. If the employee is to note certain activities in the shop, he should be told just what points to observe. If he does not know his job, he must be told the facts that he needs to know. They may be written on paper and handed to the employee. Then the executive should ask the employee to explain what he has been told. This procedure may not be necessary in well-known situations where directions are part of a regular routine; but specific directions are very helpful for new employees and for old employees in new situations. Some employees fail to carry out the directions of their executives because they are emotionally upset when in the presence of their superiors. Such an emotional state can make an employee incapable of remembering what he was told to do. Directions which are quite clear to the executive are not so clear to the employee who has a different set of mental associations and behavior patterns. Written directions will eliminate many misunderstand-

---

[4] Harry W. Hepner, "Good Teachers and the Sense of Humor," *School and Society*, September 25, 1926, pp. 395, 396.

FIG. 73.   (*Courtesy of Harry Newton Clarke, Counselor on Industrial Morale and Personnel Problems, Cleveland.*)

ings and enable the employee to know just exactly what he should do.

Executives are "salesmen" to their employees. Experienced salesmen soon learn that talking in generalities, such as "service," "wonderful value," and "fine stuff," does not sell the goods so quickly as definite statements of the merits of the product in terms like "This large rivet, one-half inch in diameter, prevents chatter and keeps the frame rigid when you drive your car over rough country roads." People do not see what they look at. They see what is pointed out to them. Consequently, the facts to be noted must be pointed out slowly enough for the employee to grasp and note each one. If more than three points or items are mentioned by the executive, they should be listed on paper, because the memory span of many employees is limited.

6. *Employees prefer an executive who has a positive manner.* The employee needs definite instructions, but he prefers them to be given in a manner that shows self-confidence and knowledge on the part of the executive.   If the executive hesitates and vacil-

lates in his instructions, they will not be effective.   Enthusiasm in the boss engenders enthusiasm and confidence in the employee. Such self-confidence cannot be a form of bluffing, for the employee will soon discover that it is bluff.   If the executive does not know the details of the employee's job, he should say so rather than attempt to hide his ignorance.   An executive who never admits that he is wrong or that he does not know all the minor details of an operation seldom keeps the confidence of his men.   Of course, self-confidence on the part of the executive toward his employees does not mean that he must use profanity or swagger.

To engender confidence in the employee, argument should be avoided.   Effective salesmanship may include a friendly give-and-take discussion.   The democratic executive does not lead debates, nor compel his subordinates to agree with him blindly. Rather, he is a teacher and a leader of men whom he admires and instructs.

The executive who has just cause for severely criticizing a subordinate often uses the old-fashioned method of threatening to discharge the man, because the threat of discharge appears to be the strongest emotional force that can be used with an employee.   However, the threat of discharge is not nearly so effective as some of the severe psychological methods that are used by executives who really have the art of handling men.   These experts in chastising men use dramatic settings, such as calling the errant employee into the boss's office and having him sit in the executive's chair.   Then the executive plays the part of the employee who is to be disciplined.   He makes a full confession, wherein he presents all the facts in the offense and asks the acting chief to make a decision and recommend the justified punishment or discipline.   Many of the men who occupy the boss's chair render a decision of discipline for themselves.

The motivation interview is often used in disciplinary problems.   Many of the foregoing principles are illustrated in the following sample problem situation and suggested treatment.[5]

Priscilla Parker, a college graduate, has been working for the Blank Company for the past three years.   She has never been tardy and has been absent

---

[5] The conversation presented in this example of the interview for motivation may sound unnatural to some readers.   However, as previously stated, each interviewer must use techniques that are spontaneous.   In real life, this example is not so unreal as it may sound.

only a few days. Her record, in general, is excellent. Some of her fellow employees have been tardy and absent more frequently than is necessary. The company decides to conduct a 'Be-On-Time-Campaign.' On the third morning of the campaign, Priscilla is caught in a traffic jam and is late. She records the correct time of her arrival. However, later in the day, she regrets her honesty and changes the record to show that she was on time. The timekeeper reports the falsification to her department manager, who calls her to his office for an interview.

The Department Manager's Thinking

"This girl has a good record and I must handle her in such a way that she will be strengthened by my treatment of her."

"I'll let her tell her side of the story."

"She ought to tell the whole story in her way."

"She must decide the significance of her act."

The Conversation

("D.M." is the department manager and "E." is the employee.)

D. M. "Good morning, Miss Parker. Won't you have a chair?"

E. "Thank you." (She drops into a chair, blushing and in an obvious state of nervousness.)

D. M. "The Timekeeping Department tells me that you ought to have a chat with me. Will you tell me your story?"

E. "Well, I left my home at the same time that I usually leave and I took the same trolley, but the car I was on had something wrong with it. It stopped several times and I realized that I might be late, so I decided to change to a Third Avenue car at Garden Street. I knew that I could walk the three blocks and make better time on the other line, but there was a fire at Garden Street and that detained me some more. When I finally got here I was late. I put down the right time when I came into the office. You know the rest, so there's no use my telling you."

D. M. "I know part of the remainder but I'd like you to tell me, and give me your reasons."

E. "Well, I thought of the punctuality campaign, and I was sorry my tardiness would help spoil our department's chances for winning the departmental cup for having the best record. I haven't been late for three years and I was anxious to keep my own record perfect. That's why I changed the time slip later in the morning. But I know it was against the rules to do that."

D. M. "Why do you suppose we have the rule that office employees must be honest in recording their comings and goings?"

E. "Because we're paid according to the record; but I had intended to work overtime to make up for the tardiness."

The Department Manager's Thinking	*The Conversation*

The Department Manager's Thinking

"She ought to realize how her conduct affects others."

The Conversation

D. M. "If you had worked overtime to compensate the company and no one had noticed your changing the record, would *you* have been satisfied with yourself? Would everything have been square for everybody?"

E. "The company would have been treated fairly, but I guess the people of the other departments would consider it unfair if our department should win the attendance prize. Wouldn't they?"

D. M. "Yes, they would consider it unfair and some might even assume that they would be justified in falsifying their records. How would that affect the Be-On-Time-Campaign?"

"Have the employee state the effects of her act on the company's efforts."

E. "Well, the campaign and the prizes wouldn't mean anything if we didn't play the game fairly."

D. M. "Exactly. Changing the record was unfair to the other employees. But do you think that the falsifying of the record also had any effect upon you?"

"Have employee see the effect of her act upon her personality."
"Find some redeeming feature in her act."

E. "Yes, I guess it did. I didn't feel very easy about it after it was done."

D. M. "I'm glad to know that you were not trying to bluff yourself into feeling proud of an unfair act. Perhaps your feeling of dishonesty and regret will help you to meet such problems in the future in a straightforward manner. You know that your record with us is very good, but if you were to cause us to lose confidence in you, we should feel that we had to watch you constantly, and that would be difficult for us."

E. "Yes, and it would be worse for me. I couldn't be happy if I worked in a place where people didn't trust me."

"Let the employee herself suggest the proper correction (punishment) of her mistake."

D. M. "Of course not. But that is where you stand now. Neither your department head nor the Timekeeping Department can trust you in the future unless you square yourself with them and convince them that your misjudgment has improved you. What do you think that you ought to do in order to square yourself and deserve our continued confidence?"

E. "I suppose I ought to explain the whole matter to the personnel manager and the chief timekeeper and tell them how the experience has affected me. I also want to apologize to you."

The Department Manager's Thinking

"Arrange for employee to close the incident in her thinking so that she has no 'emotional hang-over' to disturb her morale."

The Conversation

D.M. "Fine! You want to be square and we all want to forget about it. See the personnel man and the timekeeper. Convince them that you have benefited by this incident and I'm sure we can all forget about it. We want you to be happy here and have confidence in us and we want to have confidence in you."

E. "All right. I'll see them and come back and tell you about it. I'll be glad to get this off my mind. I want a clean slate."

"Allow the employee to think that she has solved her problem herself, but require a report of the completed correction."

D. M. "Good. Come back and tell me when you've cleaned the slate. Thank you for your honesty and willingness to correct the situation yourself. That will be all."[6]

Such a procedure requires an executive who tries to build employees by allowing them to build themselves. He must be normal in his adjustments, since the poorly adjusted executive will try to impress the errant employee with his authority—that is, he will make the employee feel inferior rather than a colleague of his. The educator type executive does not care to punish employees—he wants to enable them to use present situations to strengthen their personalities in order that they may be able to meet future problems more adequately. American businessmen are just beginning to study and practice skills in dealing with employees by methods that are more subtle than the older method of threat of discharge. Psychological approaches are more effective than force.

An example of counseling by an executive who uses the adjustment concept. The personnel man or executive who has the adjustment point of view regarding the problem employee thinks of him as an employee with a problem. The clinical-minded executive does not usually lecture employees on their adjustments. He does not, as a rule, use any psychological jargon in dealing with them. Occasionally, however, the trained executive may explain the adjustment idea to an exceptionally intelligent employee such as a dissatisfied college graduate who needs counseling. Some of the principles set forth in preceding chapters are

---

[6] Harry Walker Hepner, *Human Relations in Changing Industry*, pp. 378-381, Prentice-Hall, Inc., 1934.

illustrated in this typical example of the college-educated employee who has a problem in adjustment and is being counseled by a trained personnel man:[7]

John Milton graduated from college two years ago. After commencement he worked at several odd jobs for a year and then took a job as operator of a semi-automatic machine in the Burr Gear Company. He is the only college man in his department; most of the other men are illiterate. His production has been erratic, some months slightly above average, other months considerably below. He is paid on a piece-rate basis. He apparently dislikes his work, since he is absent frequently and seems to criticize the company and industry in the presence of his fellow employees. The foreman has recommended him for discharge but suggests that one of the higher executives talk to him in order to have him realize where he stands. An intelligent executive sends for him. The following conversation takes place:

Principles of Interviewing Stated and Illustrated in the Executive's Thinking

The Conversation

"I'll have to get at the trouble from his point of view."

Personnel Executive: "Mr. Milton, I have a report from your foreman which indicates that you are not very happy here. You appear to be dissatisfied with your job. Perhaps we should have had a chat before this but we didn't, and now is your chance to open up and tell me what you think of your work here. Let's be frank about it; we can make more headway than if either of us holds back his grievances. Besides, I want to assure you that you can be frank with me."

"He doesn't open up."

John Milton: "Why, I guess everything is all right. I don't think there is any need to be frank. I do my work and that seems to be all that is expected of me."

"I'll have to get his confidence."

P. E.: "No. According to the report I have, things are not all right. Your attendance and your production records indicate that you do not enjoy your work. Perhaps you are not satisfied with your job. Perhaps you expected something different when you finished college. I know that I did. It took me several years after I got out of college to get my feet on the first rung of the industrial ladder. As I look back now, I can see that I could have saved considerable time and made better progress if I had had a friend to talk to. Maybe you're in the same boat. Perhaps you are not well, or worry about some personal problem.

"I'll get him to express himself by suggesting the wrong causes for his dissatisfaction. If he corrects me, he will have to tell me the real nature of the difficulty."

---

[7] Harry Walker Hepner, *op. cit.,* pp. 407-412. Prentice-Hall, Inc., 1934.

*Principles of Interviewing Stated and
Illustrated in the Executive's Thinking*

The Conversation

"Most of these foreigners in that department are good physical specimens. Only a giant could do more work than they do."

"The old story—college man expects a promotion just because he's a college man. He hasn't grasped the competitive nature of life."
"I'll have to build up his ego before I can help him."

"Let him get rid of all the poison in his system."

"The perennial alibi—drag. Perhaps that is a good starting point for us to get together."

"Ignore the 'barbs' that are not important."

"Ask him some questions to which he answers yes."

J. M.: "No, my health is good. I'm not worried about anything in particular except the fact that I came here with big ambitions. In college, I was told that the world is waiting for hard-working, educated fellows, but I haven't found it so. I guess I was full of a lot of false enthusiasm. I'm working among a lot of dumb Bohunks who are stronger than I am. They work all day and don't mind it. When I work as fast as they do, I have to drag myself home at night. I used to think that if I got an education and worked hard I'd be promoted; but I haven't seen any promotion even when I did try for it. So far as I can see, a college education doesn't mean a thing on that kind of work."

P. E.: "Thanks, Milton. I'm glad you are frank. I'm beginning to see your point of view. If only everyone would be as honest as you are, we could avoid a lot of unhappiness. College, or something, has made you more willing to state facts as you see them. Now that you have told me about some of the difficulty, tell me more. How about your relations with the foreman? Has he treated you squarely?"

J. M.: "Oh, yes, he's okay. I feel sorry for him. He's been here for fifteen or sixteen years, and he's still a foreman. He doesn't seem to have any drag either."

P. E.: "No, he doesn't have any drag and he doesn't want any. Neither do you. You wouldn't feel so proud of yourself if you gained a better job through unfair influence as you would if you won it on ability, would you?"

J. M.: "No, I wouldn't, but even that might be better than competing with the physical giants in my department."

P. E.: "Only as an escape from an unbearable situation. Now let's see whether we can get straightened out on the value of your college training. You spent four years in college and you enjoyed it while you were there; or didn't you?"

J. M.: "I enjoyed it very much."

P. E.: "Did you learn some things you didn't know before?"

Principles of Interviewing Stated and
Illustrated in the Executive's Thinking

The Conversation

J. M.: "Sure, lots of them. In the classroom and outside."

P. E.: "Think of your freshman year. Did you have some difficulty in getting adjusted to college? Was it different from high school?"

J. M.: "Sure. It took me several months to like it."

"We have to get together on one point even though it is a minor one."

P. E.: "Would you agree that the step from college to industry is more difficult than the step from high school to college?"

J. M.: "You bet. Much harder for anyone."

P. E.: "It was for me, too. It took me a long time to realize that I had three choices: I could work *for* the company, I could '*work*' the company, or I could work *with* the company. Let me write them on this sheet of paper so that I can make them clear. (Writes them on paper.) In the past, you have been working for the company. You did what you had to do for the wages you received. You did not enjoy the work and you could not do so with your present point of view. To some extent, you worked the company when you held on to your job but did not work regularly. However, you might have tried to work us far more by catering to your foreman, tattling on the other fellows, or by restricting output through ostensible breakdowns of the machine you operate. You didn't do those things and I'm glad you are too much of a man to do them."

"Here's the crucial stage. I'll have to illustrate this so clearly that he will want to feel himself a part of the concern."

J. M.: "No, sir. I've played straight there."

"Ignore the fact that he tried to upset the morale of his fellow workers because he won't do that if I can enable him to express himself through his job."
"His objection is evidence of interest."

P. E.: "Fine. However, you failed to work *with* us. That is, you did not consistently and wholeheartedly work just as though you gained self-expression from your job."

J. M.: "How could I gain self-expression from a job I don't like?"

P. E.: "By recognizing the fact that the nature of any man's work is secondary to the meaning of the work to him. You will agree with me, I believe, when I say that almost any person would be glad to run the machine you operate if he believed that he was the only man in the world who could run it and if he were pointed out as the outstanding man in that work. Let me assure you that the

Principles of Interviewing Stated and Illustrated in the Executive's Thinking	The Conversation

Principles of Interviewing Stated and Illustrated in the Executive's Thinking

The Conversation

"He can realize that any job may be satisfying if it has pleasant associations."

nature of the work is incidental; the meaning of the work is most important. One can give his job meaning by one of three methods: First, he can do it better than anyone else. Second, he can improve the job by inventing a better machine or system to do the work. Third, he can improve the human relations in the job.

"Let's face the facts, pleasant or unpleasant."

"In your case, you cannot do the first because the other men are physically stronger than either one of us. You cannot do this second because you are not an engineer nor are you trained in production management. But you would do well to study the latter and see whether you could improve our production system.

"He has a real opportunity in his present situation, if he can utilize it."

"Your best chance is the third: namely, learn to understand how to influence the employees here. You may consider them Bohunks now, but the place and time to learn how to handle men is the place and time in which you happen to be. If you want to become an executive, you will have to conduct yourself in a manner which will cause those men to like and respect you."

J. M.: "That sounds all right. But how am I going to get them to admire me?"

"People learn to admire those who admire them."

P. E.: "By deserving their admiration. Study them and some of their customs. Realize their problems and you'll forget your own. Visit them in their humble homes. Let them give you some of their fine qualities. You, in turn, can give them some of your qualities."

J. M.: "What can I give them?"

P. E.: "Things you have that they do not have—your education. College should have given you some information in economics, psychology, sociology, and other fields. Find out what things interest them and contribute in simple language the things they want and need. Help them to learn to read and do simple arithmetic. Some of them came to America because they thought it the land of opportunity. Lose yourself in helping them and you will thereby find yourself in this company. There is the opportunity. Do you want to take it or to run away from it?"

"Every man has something to give other men if he can learn how to give it."

"Let him make the decision."

Principles of Interviewing Stated and
Illustrated in the Executive's Thinking

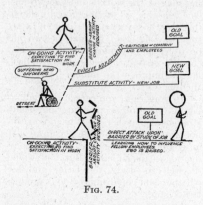

Fig. 74.

"Let him know that someone is following up his progress."

"Any problem in industry may be integrated for the advantage of all parties."

The Conversation

J. M.: "Can you explain the whole
situation in more detail?"

P. E.: "I'll try. Perhaps we can
both understand the problem and solution if we diagram it." (Draws the diagram in figure 74 and explains it
according to the principles presented in
Chapters 3-8. The evasive, substitute,
and retreat activities of J. M.'s behavior
are explained, and then direct attack is
offered as the one sound form of adjustment. The adviser also presents any
ideas that he believes to apply, such as
those expressed in Chapter 3.

J. M.: "Sounds pretty good. I never
thought of my job as having any opportunity in it. I'll try it."

P. E.: "Do it. I know you can if
you will. You have the intelligence.
All you need is the attitude and desire.
You'll find ways of doing it. Tell me
how you get along. Come to see me a
month from now. In the meantime, I'll
hear of your activities."

J. M.: "Thanks. I'll think it through
and see what I can do."

P. E.: "Do so. Remember that when
you help these other men, you also help
yourself and this company. All of us
will rise in ability as well as in satisfaction. Good-bye and good luck."

J. M.: "Good-bye."

A procedure such as this can be used successfully only by a
high-grade executive who can explain mental habits and adjustments in an intelligent and sincere manner. He must be able to
phrase his analyses in ways that the employee will understand
and respect.

One important objective to be kept in mind by the executive
is that his attempts to motivate the employee must be economically as well as psychologically sound. This means that the
executive's function is not that of apologizing for the economic
system, whatever it is, but to give the employee a sense of participation in the evolving economic scheme. Toward this end,
the executive may point out unsolved problems of industry
which the dissatisfied intelligent employee can help solve by his
own direct attack adjustments involved in his own job.

Employees who must be discharged. In spite of the best available methods of hiring, training courses, and the personal attention of supervisory executives, some employees must be discharged. However, a discharge is really an admission that the employee should not have been hired in the first place, or that the responsible executives were incapable of developing the employee. Being fired is a terrific psychological experience for most men and it often leaves a wound in the personality of the employee that years of satisfactory work do not heal. The executive who knows that some of his former employees have the right to say of him, "That man broke my spirit so that I have never been the same again," has less ability than he who can say, "Every man whom I kicked out fell forward and I honestly tried to help each to find himself."

It is probable that many of the men who have to be discharged from any department of business were never given adequate training. The fact that the new employee was given the personal attention of his superior for one hour every week, or that he worked with an experienced man, does not mean that the employee was trained. Rather, such haphazard methods of training are merely little talks that start nowhere and end in the same place. Systematic courses of training require months of effort to develop and experts to administer. Such courses have been found especially valuable in the training of office workers, foremen, and salesmen. Many reports of business training methods have been published, and executives seem to agree that systematic training is an aid in the reduction of labor turnover.

One particular executive who dislikes to discharge anyone finds that he must do so in a few cases. He has neither time nor the ability to develop some of the persons whom his company hires. To avoid actual discharge, he often helps the unsuccessful employees to get jobs with other concerns where he honestly believes that they will fit; he also has his secretary clip advertisements for "Help Wanted" from trade journals and newspapers and mail them to the weakest men on the force. Sometimes these advertisements are sent from another city in a plain envelope so that the employee thinks that another concern is anxious to take him away from his present employer.

The executive's contribution to morale. The morale of employees of any executive is partially determined by the policies of the company toward the employees in general. The group forms of treatment, such as welfare work, profit-sharing, vacations with pay, and wage rates, play a vital part in the morale of the employees. However, each executive has within his own power some important means of building or lowering the morale of his employees. If the executive is psychoneurotic and swaggers, discharges without just cause, insists upon truckling obeisance, or acts in other ways that indicate an abnormal personality, only the psychiatrist or chance can improve his methods. However, the normal executive can analyze his own contribution to the morale of his employees.

If he will compute the percentage of labor turnover for his own department and compare it with that of other departments and companies, he will obtain a rough measure of acute employee dissatisfaction. It is not unusual to find departments within the same company that have from three to ten times as much labor turnover as other departments. When such evidence is found, the causes may have a vital bearing upon morale. Apparently trivial incidents may have a significant bearing upon employee morale. If he finds that his employees assume a busy attitude as soon as he appears, it is probable that they wish to please him, but, at the same time, they fear him. Such spurts of industriousness may mean that his employees work *for* him rather than *with* him.

The manner in which the executive treats each employee is the main factor in establishing morale. If a foreman, department head, or other executive uses intelligent methods in hiring, discharging, training, and inspiring his men, the morale of his own department may be good even though the company may add little or nothing in the form of group methods for developing team spirit.

The manner in which orders are given may cause an employee to want to do the job or to want to quit. Voice and tact have been discussed so much by other writers that they need only be mentioned here. Moreover, the instructions to do a piece of work can be given to an employee with emphasis on the difficulties or on the pleasant parts of the job. If an employee is told only the difficult aspects of a job, he may decide that either he is a martyr or his superior has a great deal of confidence in his ability. When difficulties are pointed out to the employee, he should be told that he is given the work because his chief be-lieves in him. Quite often it is better to say nothing about the difficulties of the task, but to give the impression that the un-pleasant parts of the work are a natural part of the company's functions and need no special elaboration. Telling people how hard a job is does not, as a rule, make it easier for them.

Handling employees is not a science. It is an art. The great man who acquires the art does not know how he leads his men. He cannot impart to another that which is essentially a part of himself any more than the skillful artist can tell the bystander how to paint a great picture. However, if the by-stander has latent talents, he can learn much by studying the great artist's methods, and in time he himself may become a good artist.

The art of handling men cannot be acquired in a day, as illustrated by the experience of a certain college professor who decided that he wished to study labor psychology by working as a laborer. He obtained a job in a coal mine near Pittsburgh, where the only boarding place in the camp was a dirty shack so full of boarders that the professor had to accept a one-fourth share in a bed. The bed was occupied by two workers in the daytime and two others at night. It so happened that the pro-fessor's bed-fellow was a foreigner who was intoxicated most of the time. At the end of a week the professor decided that he had learned enough about labor psychology in that camp, and that he would go on to the next mine. When he prepared to leave, he paid his board to the landlady, but she was unable to give him the correct change. He then asked her to get the change while he finished packing his luggage. When he was ready to leave, he was unable to find the landlady, and he told her adult daughter about the matter, explaining the fact that her mother owed him a dollar. The daughter insisted that the mother did not owe him a dollar. The two argued the mat-ter for some time when the professor, filled with the emotions generated by his adjustments to a new and unpleasant environ-ment, decided that possibly he was using the wrong tactics.

He thought that perhaps he ought to talk to these people in the same language and terms that they used to each other, and use some profanity to show his disdain for the world as these workers seemed to do. Accordingly, he said to the woman, "Well, if you don't want to give me the dollar, you can go to Hell." When that remark was made, the woman was aroused to fighting passion with resentment and tried to seize the professor, who grabbed his bag and ran out of the house. As he turned to see what the "tigress" was doing, he was hit over the eye with a lump of coal. An excellent "shiner" adorned his face as he related the experience a few days later.

In analyzing this episode, we have several factors at work. The woman did not recognize the professor as an equal. She knew that he had more "learnin' " than she had. Nor did she recognize him as a leader, because he was not a genuine member of her group. When he spoke to her as she had been spoken to by members of her own group, her sense of self-worth-whileness was assaulted, and she reacted according to her primitive impulses.

The executive who feels that he is really not close to his employees and that he must "come down off his throne" and get acquainted with them is apt to do as the professor did. He cannot expect himself to live in one stratum of society for years and then suddenly become a true workingman. He may do the very same things that the laborers do, but they will note differences that betray his spuriousness. If the executive thinks that he is unnatural in his contacts with workingmen, he had better plan to spend a year with them, do the same things they do, and lead the life they lead. That is what the above-mentioned professor finally did, and he is now an international authority on labor relations. As most executives will not want to go to such extremes, they had better hire assistants who are natural leaders and associates of workingmen. Some of the most successful corporations have a diplomatic president and a forceful, driving general manager or superintendent. The dynamic factory superintendent may not be very tactful, but he may be able to supervise men successfully in a hard-boiled manner, because the men know that his manner is natural and not acquired from books or a brief contact with laborers.

References

Barnard, C. I., *The Functions of the Executive.* Harvard University Press, 1938.

Crane, George W., *Psychology Applied,* Chapters I and V. Northwestern University Press, 1940.

Dresser, H. W., *Knowing and Helping People.* The Beacon Press, Inc., 1933.

Elkind, H. B., and Kendall, H. P., *Preventive Management.* B. C. Forbes Publishing Co., 1931.

Husband, Richard W., *Applied Psychology,* Chapters X and XV. Harper & Bros., 1934.

Moore, Herbert, *Psychology for Business and Industry,* Chapter XIII. McGraw-Hill Book Co., 1939.

Shepard, J. L., *Human Nature at Work.* Harper & Bros., 1938.

Smith, E. D., *Psychology for Executives.* Harper & Bros., 1938.

Strong, Edward K., Jr., *Psychological Aspects of Business,* Chapter XXIX. McGraw-Hill Book Co., 1938.

Projects

1. To prevent politics in business, some managers hire employees of all kinds of religious and racial affiliations. What "mixtures" of religions, races, sexes, etc., would you consider to be most desirable to prevent company politics?

2. Construct a rating scale for the use of an executive who wishes to have his employees rate him on his executive characteristics and ability. Keep the tone and purpose of the rating scale constructive rather than critical in nature.

3. Tell how you would deal with the following kinds of employees who are in need of executive attention:

a. The employee who asks for a raise but does not deserve it.

b. The employee who thoughtlessly gives a company secret to a competitor.

c. The rank-and-file employee who masquerades as an important executive of the company.

d. The salaried employee who was absent because of intoxication.

e. The employee who pads his overtime card.

4. What rules should the supervisory executive follow, in order to be certain that his instructions to an employee are thoroughly understood by the employee?

5. What should be done by the executive who happens to appear unexpectedly among a group of workers on a day-wage basis of pay and finds that most of them are loafing on the job?

6. Tell how the autocratic type of executive might handle the cases listed in question 3. What would be some of the possible reactions of the employee in each case? How could an intelligent, well-adjusted employee handle himself in such circumstances?

7. Assume that you are a college professor and one of your students has been found cheating in an important examination. The student has been called to your office. Write a dialogue of your conversation along the lines of the two cases presented earlier in this chapter.

8. This chapter has presented certain differences between the methods of the autocratic and the democratic types of executives. Apply the same principles to the methods of present-day statesmen and rulers. Describe each of several statesmen and evaluate his methods from the point of view of the welfare of his nation.

9. Which of the following do you think the employees of an industrial plant would appreciate most, assuming that $5,000 were available for spending among 500 employees?

    a. Two days' vacation with pay.
    b. A well-equipped recreation center.
    c. A free educational program to aid workers better their positions.
    d. Improving the conditions of work, better equipment.
    e. A low-cost medical service for employees.
    f. A big all-day outing with free entertainment and food.
    g. Putting each employee's share in his pay envelope.

Ask several workers which they would choose and why. Note any significant reasons given which would throw light on the morale situation in the factory.

18

The Salesman and the Prospect

People do not buy what they really need merely because they need it. They must be sold. For example, in 1797, American farmers made their plows out of crooked tree-forks. The implement was so crude that it only scratched the soil and required a small herd of steers to drag it over the ground. In that year, Charles Newbold patented a metal plow that would turn the soil in neat, smooth furrows. The operation of the plow required only one man and two oxen. Newbold showed farmers fields of splendid grain for which his metal plows had turned the sod, but the farmers still believed that iron plows would poison the soil and produce only weeds. Years of salesmanship were necessary before farmers could be induced to use the better implement. People must be taught not only the psychological arts but also the use of available resources for material living.

MANY men claim that they cannot sell. Such a conviction is often unjustified. Some think they cannot sell because they have been *conditioned* against salesmanship. That often means that when they were children they heard mother scold the "bothersome peddlers" who thrust their feet into the doorway and sold her articles she did not want; or they heard father object to another installment payment on the piano; or, when they became older and associated with the girls, one girl might make a remark regarding an acquaintance such as, "Oh, he's *only* a salesman. I think Horace is doing much better; Horace works in a bank, you know." A man who has been conditioned in such a manner thinks that he cannot sell, or at least he does not want to sell, and consequently would be an ineffective member of a sales organization.

A second and more common reason why some people do not go into selling is found in their adjustment habits. When as children they met barriers of the kind described in Chapter 3, they made their adjustments in ways that did not lead to sales ability. The basis of success in salesmanship is skill in human relations. This skill usually originates in early childhood, and this explains why many sales managers think that good salesmen are born that way. The adjustments which lead to human-relations skills begin so early that observers imagine that the skill is hereditary or some accident of birth.

Potential sales ability on the part of some boys can be observed in many a typical American family at, let us say, the evening meal. Father comes home tired and eats in silence. Mother is busy serving the dinner. The children eat in silence or amuse themselves by picking on each other. But sometimes in such a family one boy cheerfully talks about the happenings of the day. He enjoys his sports. He likes to talk about his experiences and his friends. The others listen occasionally. Gradually he acquires skill in making others listen to him and respect his statements. In later adulthood, selling is a natural vocation for him, and his sales manager is likely to speak of him as a "born salesman."

The most common reason why college seniors do not go into selling is that they feel that there is a greater career for them in some other field of work—their adjustments have been of the non-selling variety. One thousand seniors of twelve colleges were interviewed regarding selling as a career and asked: "Would you like to take up some form of selling work after graduation?" "Yes" was the answer given by 31.3 per cent, and "Undecided, but lean toward selling" by 13.9 per cent. The chief reasons given for the choice of selling as a career were: "It is a good stepping stone to executive work," "Sales ability more than any other, is likely to be noticed by superiors," and, "Experience in selling is desirable even though later work is in other fields."[1]

Many college graduates drift into selling, especially those who find that their education has not trained them for any specific vocation. They drift into selling by force of circumstance rather than from a spontaneous or intelligent choice. Such men are almost certain to fail as salesmen unless they go through the

---

[1] Philip Salisbury, "How 1,000 College Seniors Rate Selling Work as a Career," *Sales Management,* February 1, 1940.

usual psychological steps which enable a person to enjoy selling. These steps are likely to involve one or more of the following:

1. An intellectual conviction that selling is a socially valuable vocation.

2. An emotional experience which makes selling an important vocation.

3. A series of adjustment habits which lead to satisfaction from dealing with people as exhibited by the typical extravert.

Social values of selling. An intelligent recognition of the importance of salesmanship may be brought about by an analysis of its value to people in general. Would society be better off with or without salesmen who annoy us and take our money away from us? The economist knows that salesmanship has been of immeasurable value in raising the standard of living and the magnificence of our civilization. Were it not for sales efforts of the past, few of our modern conveniences would now be among the necessities of life. Without salesmanship some of us might still be living in holes in the ground or in rude cabins, eating roots and dried meats. Through salesmanship we find it worth while to change raw materials into the luxuries of modern life.

Let us assume that a scientist, after spending several years experimenting on methods of child training, discovers a scheme of training which would give society a better generation. Which would be the better for society—to write an article or a book about it and get a fee or a royalty for it, or to put it into an attractive form and commercialize the system? Let us estimate the results to both author and society. If he were to write a complete description of it and sell it to a popular ten-cent magazine with a large circulation among mothers the author's compensation might be two thousand dollars. Two million mothers would then have access to the scheme. Perhaps 500,000 mothers might read the article. If very successful, 1 per cent, or 5,000 mothers, would apply the system and the children would be benefited by it.

Now let us suppose that the system were commercialized and a charge of ten dollars made for it. In the course of ten years, 200,000 copies of the scheme might be sold. Of these sold at the higher price, a far larger percentage of mothers would apply the system and more children would be benefited by it. We shall set this estimate at 25 per cent, or 50,000. Certainly society would be improved far more by a commercialization of the better system than if it were presented through noncommercial channels. This example is a hypothetical one, but it illustrates the fact that business is the great servant and helpmeet of society rather than its parasite. Hence the salesman, as the agent of the business enterpriser, is just as valuable to society as the preacher or the banker. Experience indicates that if 1,000 units can be sold at a price of one dollar without salesmanship, it is often possible with salesmanship to sell 10,000 units at a price of fifty cents. More people can have the article, more people have work to do, and more people have money to spend when salesmanship is applied to any useful article. Once a man grasps the economic importance of salesmanship, he may find it possible to lose his childhood prejudices against selling and become convinced of the respectability of the salesman's vocation.

However, a man cannot become a successful salesman just because he knows that salesmen are a necessary part of our economic system and modern civilization. Salesmanship must have a halo around it. If he sees someone selling poultry food to farmers, the job will not have any emotional approval; but if he recognizes the poultry food salesman as a man who shows farmers' wives how to get the hens to produce so that those wives may have better clothing, better health, better children, and better-educated sons and daughters, then the job of selling poultry food becomes just as socially valuable as the work of the nurse, the teacher, or the physician.

Placing a halo around the job of selling is not so effective in giving salesmanship an emotional tone as an overwhelming experience of an emotion-gripping type. One of the best salesmen in the country was unable to sell very many safety electric switch boxes until he had had such an overwhelming emotional experience. One day he called at a factory, tried to sell the manager some of his protective devices, and as usual failed to make the sale. On the way out of this factory he saw a worker pull an unprotected switch. The worker made a mistake, the current passed through his body, and the workman, a father with a wife and six children, suffered an early death, just because the thing the salesman failed to sell was not in use in that factory. After that the salesman could talk with an evangelistic zeal that aroused even the coldest prospects.

Training in selling is beneficial to all personality types. The need for careful selection and training of salesmen is indicated by the oft-repeated statement of sales managers that "the top quarter of the average sales force sells three-fourths of the total volume." The editors of *Sales Management*[2] asked several hundred subscribers regarding the truth of this statement and the answers were as follows:

In 8% of the companies, the top quarter sold 71 to 80% of total vol.
In 35% of the companies, the top quarter sold 51 to 70% of total vol.
In 29% of the companies, the top quarter sold 41 to 50% of total vol.
In 28% of the companies, the top quarter sold 30 to 40% of total vol.

Considerable statistical evidence is now available which indicates that sales results depend primarily on the selling methods used rather than on the personality type only. Field studies of the selling methods used by individual salesmen have been made by a number of organizations. C. Y. Belnap, of Trade-Ways, Inc., has furnished the following example of the close relation between selling methods and sales volume:

The salesmen in this case are food jobbers' men: driver salesmen operating in representative cities, towns, and rural areas throughout the United States.

After eliminating the factors of geographic differences, of city, town, and rural differences, and of store differences on the routes studied, there remained only two other factors which could account for the wide varations in sales as between the men. These two factors were variations either in the personalities of the salesmen themselves or in the methods they were using.

The experienced observers making the survey reported that as regards personality, the salesmen seemed to divide about equally into four groups:

1.   Men whose personalities appeared "negative, colorless, weak, drab."
2.   Men described as "quiet, serious, steady, plodding."
3.   Men described as "genial, cordial, familiar, easy-going, back-slapping."
4.   Men described as "aggressive, energetic, breezy, decisive, high pressurer."

As this type of sales operation is a routine daily grind, you'd suppose the men in the second group—the serious, steady, plodding type—would be the fellows who make the most sales. But they weren't. All four groups were getting just about the same average order per stop. But the individuals making up each group differed widely among themselves in volume of sales. So the methods which the men were using were checked against their orders

---

[2] "Marketing Pictograph," *Sales Management*, May 15, 1940.

to see whether it was differences *in what they did* which accounted for the differences in *how much they sold.*

Regardless of their personality rating, men who started their calls by making a physical count of the dealer's stock of the sixteen products in the line they handled, averaged orders two and one-half times as large as the orders obtained by the men who didn't make this their first step.

Again, the men who discussed the week's special offer with the dealer *before* trying for the regular order, averaged 27 per cent more per call than the men who wrote up the regular order first and then brought up the subject of the special.

Or take a third method. Only 15 per cent of the men suggested to the dealer what quantities of each item he should buy, but they averaged orders 300 per cent larger than the orders of the men who let the dealer himself suggest what he needed.

To be sure, this is only one sales operation. But it illustrates the point: that it's not so much the men themselves as it's the methods they use, which determine their sales volume.[3]

These and several other analyses of how salesmen spend their time and what they actually do in the presence of prospects have put a new emphasis on the development of effective methods regardless of the kind of personality that uses the methods. Studies of retail store complaints, exemplified in figure 75, indicate that selling methods can be improved. Also, observations of 4,000 cases in department stores throughout the country brought out the fact that in only 16 per cent of the cases observed was there any actual showing of merchandise by the sales people; 53 per cent did not use suggestive selling with regard to merchandise in their own departments, and only 2 per cent suggested merchandise in other departments.[4]

Formulas for selling. Most of the formulas for selling deal with mental states.[5] E. St. Elmo Lewis in 1898 formulated the slogan, "Attract attention, maintain interest, create desire." Later he added a fourth point, "Get action." Numerous additions and substitutions have been made to this theory of selling, such as "Gain confidence" and "Give satisfaction."

Strong[6] has formulated a theory of selling in terms of "Want,

---

[3] Corning White, "The Mathematics of Salesmanship," *Printers' Ink Monthly,* August 1940, p. 34.

[4] *Retailing,* April 30, 1934. See also *Domestic Commerce,* June 10, 1934, p. 158.

[5] Edward K. Strong, Jr., "Theories of Selling," *Journal of Applied Psychology,* March 1925, Vol. 9, No. 1, pp. 75-86. This article gives an excellent summary of various theories of selling.

[6] Edward K. Strong, Jr., *Psychology of Selling and Advertising,* Chapter XXII. McGraw-Hill Book Co., 1925.

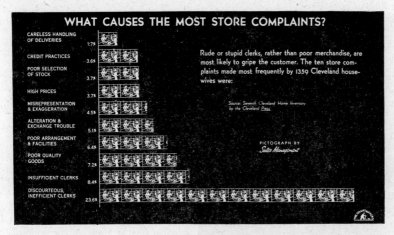

WHAT CAUSES THE MOST STORE COMPLAINTS?

CARELESS HANDLING OF DELIVERIES 1.7%

CREDIT PRACTICES 3.6%

POOR SELECTION OF STOCK 3.7%

HIGH PRICES 3.7%

MISREPRESENTATION & EXAGGERATION 4.5%

ALTERATION & EXCHANGE TROUBLE 5.1%

POOR ARRANGEMENT & FACILITIES 6.4%

POOR QUALITY GOODS 7.2%

INSUFFICIENT CLERKS 8.4%

DISCOURTEOUS, INEFFICIENT CLERKS 23.6%

Rude or stupid clerks, rather than poor merchandise, are most likely to gripe the customer. The ten store complaints made most frequently by 1359 Cleveland housewives were:

Source: Seventh Cleveland Home Inventory by the Cleveland Press

PICTOGRAPH BY Sales Management

Fig. 75.   (*Courtesy of* Sales Management, *May 15, 1940.*)

solution, action, and satisfaction." This formula, like its predecessors, also deals largely with mental states; it directs the attention and efforts toward what goes on in the prospect's mind. Some sales managers who have trained salesmen claim that it is very difficult and decidedly confusing for a salesman to focus attention upon what the prospect is thinking. An easier and more effective method is to train the salesman to think of what he himself does rather than what may be happening in the mind of his prospect. The mental states of the prospect cannot be ignored, but *the emphasis should be upon what the salesman does and the objective factors of the selling act.* The salesman should think in terms of:

1. *The prospect as an individual*—his education, health, business affiliations, and so on.

2. *The situation of the prospect*—his problems, financial status, and other objective characteristics relevant to the purchase of the salesman's product.

3. *The methods or acts in the sales canvas*—the time of day he calls, the methods of demonstrating, the words he speaks, the number of calls, the method of closing the sales talk, and other controllable acts on the part of the salesman.

Directing the sales talk toward the prospect's problem. The dominant attitude of the true salesman is that of the man who wishes to render service. Many men do not want to sell a pros-

Fig. 76.   Edward K. Strong, Jr., Stanford University.   Readers who are interested in further study on the problems of psychology applied to business may wish to refer to his book *Psychological Aspects of Business* (McGraw-Hill Book Co., 1938). Chapters I to XX deal with selling.

pect unless that prospect really needs the article under consideration.   Some concerns are even changing the title of salesman to "serviceman," or, in the case of those who sell to dealers, "merchandise counselors."   This attitude toward the prospect is expressed in the frequent mention of the " 'You' viewpoint," "Prospect analysis," or the "Objective attitude."   Selling has become a matter of "combing" the prospect's situation and then capitalizing that part of the situation which can be made more satisfying.

One salesman for a large paint manufacturer found it difficult to sell the first dealer he called upon in a certain city because of a pronounced business depression.   To the next dealer he called upon in that city, he presented the suggestion, "Now is the ideal time to advertise and push paint.   Men here are temporarily out of work and they can use their spare time to good advantage by painting at home and for others."   The argument was accepted by the dealers.   They advertised paint, and manufacturers, dealers, and the community benefited, because a salesman was able to capitalize the situation.

The best salesmen study the prospect, capitalize the immediate situation, and then arouse in the mind of the prospect a feeling of want.   The prospect must be made to feel that his present

situation could be better or more profitable. A man may wear
the same suit for a year, but he may not have any sense of want
for a new suit until his wife mentions his shabbiness so often
that he wants a new suit. The *need* may be present; but, until
that need is transformed into a *want,* it might as well not exist
so far as the salesman is concerned. The salesman must induce
in the prospect a feeling of inadequacy, a *felt need.* This feeling
of a need or a conscious want takes place as soon as the salesman
demonstrates his article in such a way that it fits into the prospect's problems. The suggested purchase becomes an answer or
a solution to a want. In a few cases the salesman finds it an
easy matter to fit his product or service into the wants of the
prospect, as in the case of the fire insurance salesman who finds
that his prospects want fire insurance right after a big fire in
the community. At such times, they have a felt need or a conscious want. However, it is usually necessary for the salesman
to arouse the want or to connect his product with some present
want.

The salesman who sells books for school children does not create a new want on the part of the mother, but he associates his
books with the "want" for her child's success. The automobile
salesman does not create new wants, but associates the new big
car with the prospect's present want of social prestige. He
shows the prospect how he can have his want satisfied *now.* The
skillful salesman is adept in the art of presenting means to *immediate* satisfactions.

To do this, the salesman does not emphasize the product itself
but describes the product as an *end.* The product is not even the
means to the desired end. It is rather a vivid description of the
prospect, who is pictured as enjoying those delights which the
product gives. The automobile salesman does not say: "When
you have this car, it will give your wife a lot of pleasure," but,
"When you have this big car, your wife and your friends will
realize that it is worthy of a man of your caliber."

It often happens that the inventor of a machine is unable to
sell it. The technical expert knows so much about it that he describes the machine. The salesman describes not only the things
that the machine does but also the satisfactions and pleasures
that it gives. He describes not just the means to the end but the

end in its most pleasant aspects. The dealer is given attractive descriptions of the profits to be made from handling the product rather than a description of the product itself.

Some salesmen who sell to dealers think that they are giving the dealer service when they arrange his stock for him, sweep the store, wait on customers, or wash the windows. These acts are not rendering a service based on the goods the salesman sells. They are merely a method of approach to put the dealer in a receptive state regarding the salesman's commodities. The approach may be made from any one of several angles.

The approach. Tricky approaches are popular with a few salesmen. They refuse to discuss their proposition with anyone except the "big boss," because they are calling on a "personal matter." The "personal matter" approach is an exceedingly weak and stereotyped start for an interview. It is a deceitful method of getting into an office, because any official can be made to leave a meeting of his board of directors if his secretary tells him that a man wants to see him about the "accident" his son just had.

The dramatic approach which was used by an insurance salesman demanded the prospects' attention, even though it may have irritated some of them. His method was to come into a prospect's office, stand in front of his desk, and say not a word for a full minute, but gaze steadily into the eyes of the prospect until he became embarrassed or angry, and then bring his fist down on the prospect's desk with a thunderous bang, and say: "I came in here, Mr. Man, to sell you some life insurance." The usual answer to the salesman was, "Is that so?" But the salesman stood his ground and plunged into an immediate attack. The method of approach was unique, but the salesman had an excellent record. (Perhaps his sales were good in spite of his approach rather than because of it.)

One firm whose canvassers found it difficult to gain admission to the homes of wealthy women instructed them to wear spats and carry a cane and light-colored kid gloves. The maids and butlers then assumed that the canvasser was making a social call and readily admitted him. Another woman who sold books hired a big car and a liveried chauffeur. Thereafter she had no difficulty in gaining admission to the homes of the well-to-do. Of course, simpler schemes are used, such as leaving a certificate for a small gift one day and presenting the gift the next day. This has been worked successfully, but it is of doubtful value in the long run, unless the companies promoting it can train their salesmen to use it skillfully.

Elmer Wheeler has conducted many researches regarding ten-second sales messages or "Tested Selling Sentences." He adapted his technique to Johns-Manville salesmen's needs in making an effective approach to arousing interest in home improvements on the part of housewives:

> Johns-Manville realized the importance of the first ten seconds. In a study of the psychological factors surrounding the sale of home improvements and to introduce the new Housing Guild plan, we watched J-M salesmen approach doors. We studied their opening words and their approaching techniques. Our observations again proved that what was said and done during the first ten seconds either got them past the door, or failed.
>
> One salesman would approach the door and say: "I'm from Johns-Manville. Would you be interested in knowing about the new Housing Guild plan of improving your home at a cost similar to the down payments made for your radio and refrigerator?"
>
> The answer was usually "No." Desire had not been aroused. Curiosity not piqued. Several different and shorter approaches were tested. Finally, this "Tested Selling Sentence" and the "Tested Technique" were evolved:
>
> The salesman approached the door. He rang the bell, stepped back slightly, and when the woman came to the door he held a booklet toward her and said:
>
> "This is *your free* copy of *101 Ways to Improve Your Home.*"
>
> As she unhooked the screen door, or opened the door wider, to reach out and receive the booklet, the salesman would quickly open the booklet to a page and say:
>
> "Here is a kitchen *before* remodeling, and here is one *afterwards.*"
>
> The woman was, naturally, interested in seeing how other women were remodeling their kitchens. Her interest was aroused in ten short seconds.[7]

Even so simple a device as putting mysterious-looking initials after the name of the salesman help to gain admittance:

MR. WILLIAM B. BAKER, S. M. CU.

---

[7] Elmer Wheeler, "The First Ten Seconds: The Crucial Turning Point of the Sales Talk," *Sales Management,* November 15, 1937, p. 49.

When this specialty salesman was asked what the S. M. Cu. meant, he answered, " 'Saving money for customers,' and that is what I want to talk to you about."

Many of the better salesmen do not use cards at all. The standard card which states the firm name, the address, and the name of the representative is far too trite to be effective. If deemed necessary to use a card, the firm and the salesman should show some originality by using a card of distinctive color, shape, or information. In most cases a card should not be used, and, when the secretary of a buyer insists upon a card, the salesman should write an interesting bit of news or information on a scratch pad for the secretary to hand to the buyer. Such notes may be similar to the information given in advance letters which are sent to prospects. Example: "When the Booneville Emporium placed two of our Beautybilt washers on the floor, they sold ten machines during the first week and made a profit of $473.87. May I explain the interesting plan they used?" The item of profit or saving made by a firm mentioned in the note should be one regarding an out-of-town firm in a similar business, or of a firm that has great business prestige, such as Marshall Field & Company.

The advance letter announcing the salesman's intended call should not attempt to sell the prospect. It should merely arouse his curiosity. The telephone is especially valuable in arranging convenient hours for the interview, but it is likely to be misused by the salesman who is too lazy to call. Every sales manager whose men use the telephone for appointments should check up on them to ascertain whether they are trying to do their selling by telephone. Order taking may be done by telephone, but not selling, except in a few exceptional cases.

If a salesman does not wish to use reprints of the company's advertising or an original card, he can make his approach through the use of unusually interesting photographs that show the value of his product or service, but have so much human interest that anyone will enjoy seeing them. One life insurance salesman found it easy to talk to his prospects when he went to the county poorhouse and took pictures of twenty old men who once had had money but who did not keep up their life insurance payments. On the bottom of each card he typed a short human-interest story of each inmate. Similarly, any product or service will lend itself to some sort of human-interest photography.

Sometimes an approach is made through an introduction arranged by some respected person in the community. One salesman of farm machinery obtained a letter of introduction from the local banker and then hired a retired farmer to accompany him on his calls among the farmers. His official introducer paved the way for his sales talk and made his sales efforts far more profitable than they would have been without the prepared introduction.

Salesmen often try to find out a prospect's hobby before they call. This kind of interest in a prospect's affairs is legitimate if the salesman does not try to bluff. His interest in the prospect's hobby should be that of a learner. He can have a genuine desire to learn something about the hobby, but if he exhibits an artificial interest merely to make a sale, he is likely to make himself ridiculous. The salesman should mention the hobbies of the prospect in such a way that the prospect is pleased with himself because the salesman is willing to listen to his exploits. Sincerity is always important for the salesman, but it is especially important when hobbies are discussed.

Furthermore, the prospect approached by the salesman should be a live prospect at the time of the call. Studies of automobile selling, for example, indicate that typical motorists who buy new cars gather information and think about cars for about two months before they purchase. During the last two weeks of the two months, they are "hot" prospects. If salesmen approach them during the last two weeks of their interest, the prospects are very likely to buy.

The demonstration and sales talk. When the salesman enters the presence of the prospect, he is apt to say: "I am Mr. So-and-so and I represent the Blank Company. I would like to show you one of our new grommets." This kind of opening is stereotyped and bores the prospect unless he happens to be in a receptive mood.

Some of the best salesmen omit introductory remarks and plunge at once into the demonstration. The various types of demonstration may be classified as follows:

1. *Sample in the salesman's hand.* In this common type of demonstration, the salesman shows the device to the prospect. He shows what it does and how it operates. The prospect looks on and shows interest, asks questions, or gives evidence of boredom.

2. *Sample in the prospect's hand.* The salesman hands the device immediately to the prospect. It is so placed that the prospect is compelled to touch, taste, smell, hear, see, or manipulate the article. If the article is novel in appearance, the prospect may be eager to observe or to try it. This method has been used with success in selling pianos and washing machines. The salesman delivers the article to the home, and the prospect accustoms herself to the use of it.

3. *This-is-what-you-are-losing method.* The salesman tries to show the prospect what a man in his position is actually losing in convenience or in dollars and cents. He takes out a pencil and a pad and asks the prospect just enough simple and generally known facts about his business to enable the salesman to compute the prospect's daily, monthly, or yearly loss. Some salesmen actually use a five-dollar gold piece or a hundred-dollar bill to dramatize the loss. One salesman had a printer make some blank checks with the name of the bank as "The Bank of Lost Money." To the prospect he handed a check for the amount that was being lost annually through failure to use his product.

4. *This device will enable you to do more or be more.* The salesman does not dwell on the old situation or the present situation, but proceeds at once to the future situation—the prospect's. He shows how much money the dealer can make if he stocks these goods.

5. *The comparison method.* This method combines 3 and 4. The salesman does not emphasize the commodity itself but shows the prospect his present situation and then shows him how much better the new or other device would be for his needs. This does not mean that the salesman should knock his competitor's product or give the prospect the impression that he must be a "boob" because he is not using his article. If tactfully done, even the correspondence school salesman can make the prospect feel, without embarrassment, that he could be using his evenings to better advantage and obtain more money and prestige if he were to

FIG. 77.   The use of the portable moving picture machine is increasing in sales-manship.   It is an effective method of demonstration.   (*Courtesy of The Jam Handy Organization, Detroit.*)

change his present status.   The salesman should always be care-ful to avoid statements that might make the prospect feel that the salesman considers him unfortunate or ignorant just because they have never met before.

6.   *The moving picture and graphic chart methods.*   It is often difficult for the salesman to demonstrate the service or article with the service or article itself, so he must depend upon some graphic means to enable the prospect to realize his present situa-tion and to visualize the best possible situation.   The film method of demonstration is one of the very best methods, because the prospect can really see the benefits claimed for the product instead of attempting to visualize them.   The moving picture machine is a means of demonstration that should be used more frequently.   The chief objection to most of the films seems to be that they deal with the manufacturer's problems rather than with the customer's problems.

7.   *The stunt method.*   The stunt is the favorite form of dem-onstration to the beginner in selling.   It has its place in the sales interview, but it often directs the prospect's attention to the

stunt as a stunt rather than to the article as a solution of the prospect's problems. Any dealer can crowd the sidewalk with people by putting a stunt in the window, but the store management does not want everybody to stop. Only the worth-while prospects should be attracted to the window. The circus side-show barker wants to attract everyone to his entertainment, and the stunt is legitimate advertising for him; but the salesman cannot depend upon a stunt to do his selling. The stunt may be made an attention-getter, but it should be relevant to one strong talking point.

The sales talk. The first rule of the successful sales talk is that it must deal with the prospect's situation and be directed toward a more satisfied, more contented, or more effective prospect-situation. The talk that starts nowhere and gets nowhere seldom leads to a sale. Even though a salesman dislikes the "canned" sales talk, he should have certain definite goals in each talk. Far more sales have been lost through lack of a planned sales talk than because of having the talk too highly standardized.

One "quota-beating" salesman who sells a specialty tells his prospect that he has planned his sales talk so that he, the prospect, will be able to see clearly what his machine can do and that the prospect can judge for himself as to whether the machine will make money for him. Then he hands the prospect a small printed card, saying: "This card has listed on it the six most common questions which my prospects ask or want to ask while I demonstrate this machine. If I do not make myself clear on some point, check that question. Of course, if you think of a point not on the card, be sure to ask that." A significant part of this scheme is the fact that the salesman has omitted from the card the most common question asked by the prospects and which every prospect is almost sure to ask. When the prospect raises that question, the salesman acts as though the prospect has thought of something no one ever before thought of. He scratches his head, then answers the point, and compliments the prospect's ingenuity; but at the same time the acceptance of that point practically commits the prospect to the purchase of the machine. The above method can be adapted to almost any product or service sold today.

A major fault of some salesmen is to talk in abstract terms. They discuss *quality* in a general way. The word "quality" and similar terms should never be used. Quality should be described by actual examples of what a user did with this machine under certain trying conditions. The salesmen of a paper company, selling paper towels, do not talk about superior absorbency. They take two inkwells having the same amount of ink in them and stick their own towel into one inkwell and a towel of another brand into the other inkwell. After a few seconds, the difference in their absorbent qualities can be seen by the prospect.

Advertisers long ago learned that people do not read advertisements that are full of abstract ideas. They want pictures that illustrate a concrete and definite situation. All abstractions such as *best, strongest, newest, value, service,* and *most economical* should be avoided; the talking point should be stated in terms of the concrete with actual instances of how that characteristic has been proved by other users.

More annoying than the talking of abstractions is the use of meaningless slangy expressions such as, "This is a world-beater," and, "I tell you what, you ain't never seen anything as good as this." Equally bad are the crudities: "Now listen to me," "You know what I mean," "And so on and so forth," and "D'ya get me?" The last two expressions seem to be very common in certain parts of the country and are used by people to cover embarrassment or to avoid thinking. Definite descriptive terms are far more effective than popular slang or meaningless verbiage.

The use of definite terms in the sales talk does not necessitate boresome technical descriptions of how the product is made, the kind of raw materials used, or the way it is sold. When technicalities are used, they should be related to the prospect's problems. The reason for a detailed description of a gear in a machine should be stated to the prospect to convince him that, while a specific part has been giving trouble in some machines of other makes, it cannot cause difficulties in this brand. The prospect wants definite facts that he can grasp.

The sales talk should be definite in its mental imagery, but it should also have human interest. Cold, intellectual appeals are not so stimulating to action as are the warmer emotions. The prospect wants to hear a story. He likes to have a lump in his throat and a tear in his eye.   He wants to hear about people and things that make him smile, that cause him to love more devotedly, to sacrifice a little, and to dream new dreams.   The prospect wants to take sides with what he believes to be right.   It is necessary to invest the sales talk with an emotional tone.   As the old banker said to a young salesman: "If you are trying to sell the services of a bank, show the prospect the pictures of your officers. Describe the little human-interest aspects of their work.   Tell how one of those officers helped a man to pull out of a bad situation and achieve business success.   Don't talk the usual talk about the financial strength of the bank."

Answering objections.   The true salesman hopes that the prospect will raise objections before he buys.   The objection offers the salesman an opportunity to demonstrate his product. One of the best salesman in the country always has a pang of regret when the prospect indicates that he is sold and wants to sign on the dotted line.   This salesman enjoys selling: the meeting of minds, the fencing-like encounter, the parries, the thrusts, and losing or gaining a new friend.   He sells because he loves the game of selling.

Objections are a natural part of the game of selling.   The prospect seldom welcomes the salesman with open arms.   Can we blame the prospect?   If we try to analyze the various ideas in the prospect's mind, we can understand why he does not, as a rule, want to see another salesman.   The reason is that the salesman interrupts the prospect's *ongoing activity*.   Even a newborn baby objects to having its activity thwarted or retarded.   Hold a baby with his arms tight against his body and he will soon show his anger in no uncertain manner.   When the salesman comes to see a prospect, he interrupts the flow of ideas and activities of the prospect.   The worth-while prospect is always busy doing something else, mentally or physically.   The most natural response of the prospect to the salesman is that he does not need or does not want what the salesman has to offer.   The salesman must, first of all, get the prospect into a new line of thought, and, if the salesman has planned his demonstration and sales talk in the right manner, the sale should follow as a matter of course.   The live prospect will make some objections in order to clarify his ideas and to ascertain whether he really understands what the salesman has just told him.

When the prospect says, "I am not interested," the salesman can say: "I know that you are not interested, Mr. Prospect. That's why I called.   You have never used this device and Mr. Blake of the Samson Company thought I ought to show it to you."   The salesman who can smile and accept the objection with nonchalance will be able to go ahead with the demonstration.   The objections of most dealers to buying because conditions are bad can be answered with definite, prepared figures to show the dealer that business will continue regardless of conditions.   Certain professional and other people who are not affected by the current conditions are always buying.   The bank clearings of the city may show that they are greater than last year in that town.   Ask the dealer to look out on the street and see the cars that are going up and down.   People are still wearing clothes and eating.

To answer objections, the salesman should be able to show facts and figures that have been collected by a disinterested person.   If the buyer does not believe that the salesman's shirts do not fade, the salesman should show the results of tests conducted under conditions that will satisfy the prospect.   The shirt that went through the tests should be handed to the prospect for inspection.   The salesman often depends upon his wits and bullying to answer objections, when the objections could be answered far more easily by just a tested sample, a page of charts, or a testimonial letter.

"The price is too high" is one of the arguments which should be answered in a straightforward manner rather than by evasion or humor.   If the price objection is evaded, the customer may not mention it again but may refuse to buy.   After all, the customer should know why the price asked is fair.   A direct answer to the price objection is the dramatized form of answer.   A salesman of washing machines capitalizes the high price of his machine by demonstrating the machine with money in his hand.   Every time he points out a strong feature of his machine, he places a dollar bill or a quarter on that part of the machine.   When he gets through he adds up the amount of money and shows the prospect that the price asked is fair in comparison to the value.

If the prospect has been sold during the sales talk, neither price nor any other objection will prevent the sale. The prospect may raise the question of price, but he may do it because he really desires to have ample justification for the price. The salesman who is unduly price-conscious has never been convinced that the product is worth the price asked. If his standard of living has been on a scale below that of the price level of the article he is selling, it will be necessary for the sales manager to re-educate the salesman.

When the prospect wants a handy excuse for not buying, he objects to the price. Only one other excuse is more common: *"I'll see you next time."* If the dealer presents this excuse, it simply means that the salesman has not done a good job of convincing the prospect that he can make money with the line. The salesman can answer: "Of course, I'll see you next time, but that will not be for three months. In the meantime, according to my quota, 4,600 people are going to buy this article in this county. They will pay the dealers who sell them a gross profit of $2,300. You will want to be one of the dealers to have your share in the profits."

The salesman should not have the impression that it is well to "annihilate" the prospect when he makes an objection. To knock the prospect's objection too hard causes him to lose his self-respect. When an objection is stated, the salesman should restate the objection briefly and fairly; then the prospect knows that his objection is appreciated. Pay the prospect a compliment when he raises a threadbare objection—act as if it were an unheard-of objection and answer it—not too quickly but satisfactorily to the prospect's sense of worthwhileness.

The answering of objections should never degenerate into an argument. The salesman may be able to win the argument; but, if he does, he loses his sale. As soon as the discussion between salesman and prospect tends toward the argumentative type, the salesman should use humor. In fact, since most salesmen do not take the trouble to prepare evidence that will meet objections, they should at least collect a set of anecdotes that will answer the most frequent objections.

The art of getting the order on the order book. The psychological moment to close has received much attention in sales discussions. As a matter of fact, there are few true psychological moments when the prospect wishes to order and the salesman catches the prospect off his guard for the order. Orders that must be "caught on the fly" are often countermanded. The salesman should not pounce upon the prospect for the order. If the salesman has studied the needs of the prospect and is anxious to render a real service, the order will follow of its own accord.

It is true, however, that some prospects find it difficult to make a decision and the salesman must help them to decide. A few salesmen claim that they can recognize the moment when the prospect is ready to decide. They note whether the prospect leans forward, toward the salesman, and toys with the sample. One salesman even claimed that a prospect once told him that he did not want the article under discussion but the salesman said: "Your lips tell me that you do not want the article and yet your body tells me that you do, because you leaned toward me when you said that you could not buy it now." The prospect admitted that he wanted the article, but that he had an inhibiting objection which he hesitated to mention. When the objection was stated and answered, the prospect bought. In the best sales canvasses, the salesman and the prospect get into the same mood or attitude, into a mental state of mutuality of interest, so that the salesman does not view the prospect as a mere plaything but as a fellow businessman whose interests are complementary to his own.

The salesman may help the prospect to make a decision by arranging the situation so that he need decide only a minor point. The experienced life insurance salesman does not, as a rule, ask the prospect whether he does or does not want his policy. Rather, he asks him: "Will it be convenient for you to have our medical examiner call at your home on Tuesday evening and give you the health examination?" If the prospect indicates that that time is satisfactory, he has also indicated incidentally that he will take the insurance. The jobber salesman often does the same when he asks about the method of shipment or the date of delivery, the salesman naming a plan that he knows will be satisfactory to the customer.

Some salesmen apply this "minor-decision" method too frequently, when they get into the habit of asking for a trial order. The trial order of a half-dozen lot is easily asked for and easily given. But a trial order simply means that the sale was not completed. The customer still has many mental reservations, or he would give a worth-while order. Of course, the trial order may be used as a starting point and the amount can be stepped up to a profitable figure.

The prospect will find it easier to buy if the salesman has succeeded in getting him to say "Yes" several times during the interview. The prospect who is in a hostile or negative attitude is hard to persuade, whereas the agreeing prospect is in a mood for further action. The unskillful salesman who tries to have his prospects "Yes" themselves into an order is likely to lose his grip on the situation. This method can be used only by those who are unusually adept at controlling the sales situation. The salesman can concentrate on the one point which appeared to appeal most to the prospect. Automobile salesmen know that the points about a car that appeal to those who know cars are not the points that appeal to prospects. The car salesmen tend to be interested in the mechanical qualities of the car, whereas many prospects are interested in the accessories, such as the cigar lighter and the vanity case. The real estate salesmen know that building construction does not interest the modern housewife nearly so much as the design of the fireplace and the arrangement of the cupboards in the kitchen. It is legitimate, therefore, to emphasize those factors that appeal most to the prospect in hand.

Each prospect varies in his susceptibility to assistance in making the decision to buy. Some prospects sell themselves. Others must be pushed and tugged at. Still others need a simple sales technique to do the thing they want to do but cannot, because the habit of turning down all salesmen is too strong to allow them to lift themselves out of the channels of indecision.

Aggressive selling produces more orders than easy-going salesmanship. The man who has lived among farmers knows the pleasure they get from chatting with strangers. It is often assumed that a sort of easy-going, chatty sales canvass is necessary when selling to farmers. A sales manager who traveled with a sales crew that sold a five-dollar product to farmers found that the salesmen who used the most aggressive and shortest canvass had the biggest sales records. The salesmen who spent not more than ten minutes with any farmer made the greatest number of sales. Action begets action. The most common methods of stimulating prospects to act are:

1. An aggressive, definite sales canvass.
2. The use of a minor decision, which makes it easy to buy without a big decision.
3. Getting the prospect into an agreeable and agreeing mood.
4. Showing the prospect that he can purchase with ease right now.
5. Showing him the danger of delay, such as "A coming change in price," "Temporary trial offer," "Only one to a customer," "You are now losing $50 per month by not having it," or "The continued inconvenience should be ended now."
6. Appealing to his emotions: "Prove that you are a man of decision," "Sign now and surprise the children," "This is worthy of a businessman of your prestige."

Failure to get the order. Salesmen are often asked how many calls they are willing to make on a prospect before dropping him. The correct answer may be one or a dozen. Some of the largest accounts that business firms have are the result of ten or more calls. One thousand retailers kept accurate check for six months to learn how many calls salesmen made on them before giving up the job as hopeless. Here is the surprising result of that check-up:

> 48.2 per cent made 1 call and quit.
> 24.4 per cent made 2 calls and quit.
> 14.7 per cent made 3 calls and quit.
> 12.7 per cent made 4 calls and quit.

Yet it was discovered that 60 per cent of their merchandise was bought by these dealers at the fifth call or after.[8]

Only careful research can reveal the extent to which persistence in selling is profitable. Trade-Ways, Inc., has published results of one study on "What Price Persistence?"

---

[8] *Sales Management*, January 1, 1938, p. 18.

Persistence is a virtue—but sometimes it's costly in selling. Here are some striking facts from a recent study of the work of a force of industrial salesmen.

	% of Time		% of Sales Volume	
Calls on active customers..............	19		80	
1st and 2nd calls on *new* prospects.....	25		17	
Follow-up calls on *old* prospects........	37	} 44%	2	} 3%
Calls on former customers.............	7		1	

Forty-four per cent of the actual selling time, to get 3% of the business.[9]

Persistence is just as essential in selling today as it ever was. But mere persistence may be only boresome to the prospect and fatiguing to the salesman. Persistence means more than footwork. It means headwork as well. Selling hard requires more than merely trying hard to sell. When the salesman finds that he cannot get an order, he should close his sample case without insisting upon an order, but he should prepare the way for his next call by saying: "I am sorry that I don't have a sample of our Palate brand of food with me. I shall ask the house to mail you a sample for your wife and when I call again in four weeks, you can tell me how you like it." Before the salesman makes his next call, he should write a friendly letter to the prospect and explain the profit or value of his article.

The salesman should, during the interview, have learned one subject that interests the prospect. He can bring the prospect a newspaper clipping, a photograph, a book, or any other article or idea that will interest him. Each call means that the salesman must present something new and worthy of the prospect's consideration. The turn-down should not actually take place. The good salesman does not allow it. No interview, when it ends, should give the salesman a sense of relief. It should simply pave the way for another interview when new ideas may be presented in a new way with more attractive applications.

Getting rid of high-pressure salesmen. Salesmen who can render a real service should always receive a courteous and prompt interview. They have a right to continue to call time after time in some industries and for some prospects. However, many persons find a large amount of their time wasted in listening to insistent salesmen who cannot possibly render them any

---

[9] From *Profit-Makers,* issued by Trade-Ways, Inc., New York. Also reported in *Printers' Ink,* April 19, 1940, p. 92.

service.   They should be given a prompt and emphatic "No."
To let them continue to talk or visit merely wastes their time
which should be spent with a logical prospect.

Several methods have been offered by buyers; these are stated
in the second person:

First and easiest, *watch the salesman's technique*.   Study his
method of selling.   Analyze his sales canvass for its reported
stages—the approach, arousing desire, establishing confidence,
and inducing action.   Just as the hypnotist cannot hypnotize a
subject so long as the subject studies the hypnotist, so the salesman cannot sell the prospect who studies his technique and does
not wish to buy.

Second, *heckle the salesman*.   Interrupt him on the slightest
pretext and argue.   If the salesman refuses to argue at first, just
keep after him with more criticisms and get him irritated.   Eventually, he will have to let go his self-control and argue, too.   Try
to make him so angry that he will say: "Mr. Prospect, you are
so gol-darn cantankerous, I wouldn't sell you if I could."

Third, *use the agreeable method*.   Interrupt him only to agree
with him.   Keep on telling him: "You certainly have a wonderful proposition"; "Say, you're an unusually good salesman";
and so on.   Let the salesman think he is "hooking" you and then
when he presents the order book, say: "You're a fine fellow and
I like you but I simply can't buy right now.   Perhaps some other
time, when I'm not so busy, I can do something for you.   Good-
bye."

Fourth, *keep the salesman where he will be at a disadvantage*.
Refuse to seat yourself even though it would be easy to do so.
Do not handle samples he offers.   Be inattentive when he persists.   Talk to him through an open window or over a counter
or in a corridor.   If possible, continue to walk to the door and,
when you get him there, shake hands with him and bid him
good-bye.

Hundreds of books have been written which give the salesman
suggestions on how to sell the prospect, but no books have been
published which show the beleaguered prospect how to deal with
the salesman.   After all, if salesmanship is really a game, as many
salesmen think of it, both sides in the game should have some
coaching.

References

Bennett, Charles, *Scientific Salesmanship*. American Efficiency Bureau, 1933.

Canfield, Bertrand R., *Salesmanship: Practice and Problems*. McGraw-Hill Book Co., 1940.

Crane, George W., *Psychology Applied*, Chapter VII. Northwestern University Press, 1940.

Haas, Harold M., *A Short Course in Salesmanship*. Prentice-Hall, Inc., 1939.

Moore, Herbert, *Psychology for Business and Industry*, Chapter XV. McGraw-Hill Book Co., 1939.

Spencer, George B., *How to be a Top-Flight Salesman*. D. Appleton-Century Co., 1940.

Strong, Edward K., Jr., *Psychological Aspects of Business*, Chapters XVII-XX. McGraw-Hill Book Co., 1938.

Wheeler, Elmer, *Sizzlemanship: New Tested Selling Sentences*. Prentice-Hall, Inc., 1940.

Projects

1. Have a friend co-operate with you in practicing dealer sales situations. He is the prospective buyer and you are attempting to sell him certain articles. Have your friend include the following objections as well as others he may think of:

    a. I want the exclusive agency.
    b. I never had a call for it.
    c. I'm all stocked up now. Got too much of your stuff on the shelf.
    d. I'm too busy to talk to you now.
    e. I'm satisfied with the house I buy from now.
    f. You come to see me only when you can't sell Jones, up on the corner.

After you have met your friend's objections, discuss with him the best methods of answering them.

2. List some of the expressions, methods, or mannerisms that irritate you when used by a salesman. Find out from others whether these are personal prejudices of your own or are general. Work out specific corrections for each item you have noted.

3. List the kinds of information a salesman should gather concerning a prospect before calling on him. Give possible sources where the information might be obtained.

4. Salesmen frequently carry a sample or some related object to show to the prospect while making the sales talk. Think of interesting and original related objects that might be used in selling the following:

    a. Lawnmowers.
    b. Office furniture.
    c. Home insulation.

   d. Fire insurance.
   e. Coal.
   f. Advertising space in a local paper.
   g. Safety equipment for a factory.
   h. Vacation trip by airplane.

Tell how and when you would use the related object in your sales talk.

5. Clip several magazine advertisements of articles you believe you could sell quite successfully. Analyze all the reasons for your choice. Do the same for an article you think you could not sell. Analyze your reasons from the standpoint of your own likes and dislikes, your personality, the qualities of the article, the nature of the market, and other possible factors. Which factors seem to be the most important?

6. Outline a program whereby a salesman might utilize to the fullest extent the manufacturer's advertising of his product over the radio, in periodicals and newspapers, and on outdoor posters. Illustrate specifically how each of these aids could be tied into the sales talk for a product such as a vacuum sweeper.

7. Read in trade papers about concerns that have done outstanding work in sales-training schools. Analyze the ideas gathered and present them in a letter of application to one of the companies, explaining to the company addressed why you chose the company as your preferred employer.

8. Outline a program for selecting inexperienced salesmen for a chosen product. If tests are used, specify which ones. Construct a report form or "profile" which would show at a glance the applicant's strong and weak points.

PART FIVE

Predicting the Behavior of the Group

19

Predictions in Marketing

A wise old merchandiser once summarized his experience in several maxims. One of them was that "in any campaign to 'educate' the public, most of the pupils will flunk." Another was that "millions of men have made hundreds of dollars by forcing some article on the public. But hundreds of men have made millions of dollars by letting public demand be their guide."[1]

On the other hand, a very successful editor and merchandiser has said, "Come down to the level which the public sets and it will leave you the moment you do it. It always expects of its leaders that they should keep a notch above or a step ahead. The American public always wants something a little better than it asks for, and the successful man, in catering to it, is he who follows this golden rule."[2]

Perhaps this means that marketing executives should find out what people want, learn the current trends in choice of economic satisfactions, and then offer them something a bit better than they thought they wanted.

A DIRECT-MAIL advertising man reported the following personal experience in making predictions of the behavior of certain groups of individuals:

I was associated with a Coney Island concessionaire who had a penny arcade on the boardwalk in which there were the usual amusement contrivances which required one cent for operation.

In the first place, I found that a number of people would drop a dime into a machine instead of using a copper and in sorting out the money each Saturday night, we could tell almost to the dollar the amount of total receipts merely by counting the dimes—for, strange to relate, the dimes invariably amounted to one per cent—$7.50 in dimes meant about $750 in pennies!

And here's another one. We had two rows of penny phonograph machines—about twenty in each row. At the end of each row there were two old, decrepit phonograph machines that each required a nickel for operation.

[1] Abbott Kimball, Inc., *Advertising & Selling*, August 4, 1932, pp. 42-43.
[2] Edward W. Bok, *The Americanization of Edward Bok*, p. 164. Chas. Scribner's Sons, 1920.

And every Saturday, all summer long, we regularly took 35 cents out of each machine! The penny machines took from $2 to $4 each.

Isn't this something to ponder over for those who study crowds and mass movements?[3]

Managers of modern restaurants must be able to predict the orders of their customers. Many of them know how much of each of the staple foods to order. A tabulation of the breakfast orders in the dining cars of a large railroad from March 1 to March 15 showed these interesting figures:[4]

Item	Orders	Per Cent of Total Orders
Apples	2,413	8.4
Figs	224	.8
Grapefruit	7,836	27.4
Lemons	3	.01
Oranges	6,009	21.1
Pineapple	165	.5
Prunes	1,588	5.5
Strawberries	139	.4
Total fruit orders	18,337	64.11
Orders without fruit	10,135	
Total breakfast orders	28,512	

The man who orders the supplies of food for these dining cars can be fairly certain that approximately 35 per cent of the breakfast orders will not include fruit and 65 per cent will include fruits in the percentages indicated. Furthermore, out of every 100 dining-car patrons who order coffee or tea, 85 want coffee and 15 order tea.[5]

The man who operates a New York hotel having 500 or more rooms can expect the following monthly losses per 100 rooms: 13 sheets, 17 pillowcases, 1 bedspread, 1 blanket, 29 bath towels, 105 smaller towels, and 4 bath mats.[6]

One of the leading businesses of America—the insurance business—is based upon predictions of the behavior of the group. The actuarial experts have calculated the death rate of all types of people and the members of all occupational groups. They

---

[3] Charles S. Wise, "For Those Who Study Mass Psychology," *Printers' Ink,* September 26, 1929, p. 212.

[4] Don Francisco, "How Advertising Is Helping to Solve the Farm Problem," *Printers' Ink,* September 6, 1928, p. 76.

[5] *Business Week,* October 31, 1936, p. 1.

[6] *Business Week,* September 16, 1939, p. 4. Figures furnished by Horwath & Horwath, hotel accountants.

know that fishermen, jewelers, farmers, clergymen, and black-smiths have a low mortality rate, and that stone cutters, miners, and locomotive firemen have a high rate.

Forecasting fads. One of the most difficult kinds of marketing predictions is for the sales of an article which is recognized as likely to have a short but intensive sale. Toys and games fall into this class. Most manufacturers of such articles realize that advertising and merchandising themselves do not create a fad. The life of such a craze may be prolonged by means of effective advertising, but the psychological basis for big sales is likely to be difficult to trace.

Most successful manufacturers of games and similar articles follow the policy of making several staple bread-and-butter games such as table tennis and dart games. When a new craze develops, they participate in its popularity but assume that the life of the new game will be relatively short.

Manufacturers recognize the difficulty of predicting the duration of a fad or cycle of popularity, but a fairly safe rule is that "the duration of interest is inversely proportional to its intensity and rate of acceptance." [7] This means that if a toy, for example, develops a great popularity within a very short time, its popularity is likely to be short-lived, though it may become popular again years later.

A second indication of the probable period of popularity of an article is the extent of its popularity in an off season. Indoor games as a rule are most popular during the winter months. If, therefore, an indoor game develops a good sale during the summer months, it is likely to be a better seller during the winter months and to continue to sell well for about two years.

A third criterion of probable popularity is whether the game is simply a revival of a once popular game.

There are recurrences of game crazes as there are of dress styles. For example, back in the 1840's there was a craze for "real life" games started off by one called "Mansion of Happiness" which illustrated how to be happily married. In the '80's and '90's there was a vogue for games based on business deals, the most famous being Pit, which was inspired by the Chicago wheat pit operations. Both of these game trends have been repeated in the last four years. A landslide craze for real estate trading brought a large

---

[7] James L. Fri, "Toy Fads," *Advertising & Selling,* December 1938, p. 33.

crop of games based on real life situations covering everything from stock market speculation to crime detection and social climbing.

At the turn of the century there was a whirl of public interest in games which scrambled the principles of standard checkers. This year there is a large crop of "Chinese Checker" games which are said to be an interpretation of the same idea.

A famous game favorite of the Victorian age was anagrams and this year there is a big vogue for streamline variations of the anagram technique. The "real life" situation games are still popular, too. So the game manufacturer looking for trends has plenty of signs to ponder over.

Table tennis and dart games have been steadily popular for the past 15 years, but in the decade before that they fell out of favor. For a while contract bridge cut into parlor games sales; but now the trend seems to be the other way. Five-suit bridge had the benefit of considerable advertising and a great deal of publicity; but game manufacturers had no fear of its stealing their craze market when summer sales failed to boom.

The old-line game manufacturers are great believers in test campaigns. They usually introduce a new game to a small social group and then, without benefit of advertising, see if stock will move in local department stores. If it does, advertising and demonstrations are scheduled. But the experienced game advertiser feels his way from week to week. He believes that he can accelerate a trend by advertising but he must be sure it is a real "trend" and not wishful thinking.[8]

Jigsaw puzzles have been popular at various times in the nation's history; usually during the early stages of a depression.

In addition to the three above-mentioned criteria of likely popularity, the manufacturer also studies trends such as what educators are teaching. If educators stress "Learn by doing," the manufacturers are likely to offer more games of the kinds recommended by the educators. The wise manufacturer, however, is apt to promote the recommended type of article only as public demand justifies his offerings. He cannot assume the role of the educator because he is a servant of his customers rather than a reformer of their tastes.

Predicting fashions. Many people think that fashions in dress develop as the results of the whims of a few former Parisians or Hollywood actresses only. Fashions do come up occasionally through the chance selection of some notable, but in most cases they arise through a rather complex system.

A distinction should be made between style and fashion. Manufacturers, couturiers, and tailors create styles. *Style* is a distinctive feature of any article. *Fashion* is an accepted style.

---

[8] *Ibid.*, p. 34.

All fashions are style, but not all styles are fashion. Style does not change, but fashion does. Nor do the fashion writers and stylists invent fashion. They simply observe and report the choices of fashionable persons all over the world. Fashion can be predicted, and the businessman who deals with fashion products must make successful predictions.

Time was when a manufacturer of women's clothing told his designers what to plan, the factory what to make, the salesmen what to sell, and the dealer what to buy. The dealer then told the public what to wear. In this way his mills could run on the same pattern for several months and his problems were far simpler than at present, when he must hire stylists and other experts to forecast what the public will buy. If his guess is correct, all is well; but, if it happens to be too far astray, profits are endangered. The manufacturer never suffers from overproduction of the fashionable patterns. The overproduction and losses come from poor patterns and "drops." One company that manufactures fashion products found that of thirty-six patterns the ten best-selling ones constituted 60 per cent of their total sales, whereas the remaining twenty-six patterns gave but 40 per cent of the volume. It is not unusual to find a few patterns that outsell scores of others in the same line.

In general, it appears that fashion is more powerful than sales promotion. Some advertising and publicity men believe that advertising will cause a style to become a fashion, but actually few important trends in fashion have ever been greatly influenced by advertising or sales promotion methods. Advertising may give impetus to widespread acceptance of a style, but it must ride with the tide rather than attempt to change the current. A definite help is to get valid information about fashion movements and how they develop.

The magazines that sell millions of paper patterns for women's clothing estimate the life of a pattern or a style as two years from the time of introduction to the final discard. The high spot in sales occurs between the sixth and the twelfth months after its first presentation. A single pattern appears to require six months for introduction, six months for its popularity duration, and twelve months for its gradual disappearance. Styles are created by a few experts, selected by a few socially prominent customers, and finally used by a still larger group of consumers. Most of the patterns do not meet with acceptance and are never heard of again. *Creation* by designers, *selection* by a few leaders, and *acceptance* by the masses are the three main principles of fashion development.

Designs in fashion products are changed gradually. The great prosperity of the American people and the new American tempo have made us fashion-conscious to a greater degree than at any other time in our history. The businessman cannot hope to control fashion, but he must predict it. When he decides to change the design of his wallpaper, cigar lighter, floor covering, automobile, and so on, he must know what the public wants. Some firms have gone ahead on the assumption that the public is art-conscious and wants the best designs that the minds of expert artists can originate. Such an assumption is dangerous, because the public taste changes gradually. The manufacturers of low-priced automobiles should not copy the design of the ultra-smart cars, but should gradually step up the design each year in accordance with the wishes of the general class of buyers who are one price-step higher.

One silk manufacturer has developed a three-phase system of prediction. Approximately 30 per cent of each year's production is devoted to novelties and new ideas; 40 per cent of the production is an improvement and development of the previous year's successful novelties and staples; the remaining 30 per cent transforms and adapts the preceding year's outstanding style successes in kindred industries. A floor covering concern plans 30 per cent of its production on new styles of each season and 70 per cent in staples, in the ratio of each pattern's sales of the previous season. Style experts seem to be agreed in pointing out the danger of a radical change in pattern, but proceed on the basis of keeping a part of the production in line with the acceptance of the previous season and a smaller part to constitute the bid for the new.

To assist manufacturers and distributors of style merchandise, a number of consulting organizations have been developed which render their clients a service similar to that of the established business forecasting services. Certain periodicals of the retail field also publish forecasts for their subscribers.[9] A few of the largest manufacturers also have style experts who co-operate with their dealers and keep in close touch with the movements of various styles and sizes. These organizations have proved that it is possible to predict style changes just as easily and accurately as general and specific industrial conditions.

Predicting the market for a new product. A new product is often the brain-child of an inventor or executive who has excellent ideas regarding the values of such an article, yet the public may not care for it. The public may need it, but it may be totally out of line with the wants of the people who are supposed to buy it. The writer was given a forcible lesson in this respect several years ago when he became interested in the psychological values of toys. Most of the toys which are now being sold for small children do not fit the mental make-up or needs of the child. On a trip to New York City, he visited one of the world's largest toy-distributing firms. This company also employed a very able man who invented new toys. The inventor spent several hours in showing the various toys from all parts of the world which were being shipped to dealers. However, very few of the toys were psychologically sound. This fact was pointed out to the inventor, who went to a table of toys and said: "These are the toys that I have invented and they were all commercially successful. We have made a lot of money on them, but I don't give them to my own children. Toys are made to sell to dealers and parents, and not for children. The small child wants any new and colorful object, but that does not mean that he ought to have it. If we were to make toys to fit children, we could not sell them. As soon as parents are educated to the right kind of toys, we shall sell that kind. Years of education will be necessary before toys can be sold that fit the mental needs of children."

What the public needs is one thing; what it demands is often something entirely different. The chief means of measuring the wants of consumers is to study their reactions. Sometimes the needs and wants are discovered by accident, as in the case of

[9] *Women's Wear Daily* is the best-known fashion-forecasting periodical in the retail field. Fashion-forecasting services are provided by Tobé, Felix Lilienthal & Co., Inc., and Meyer Both Co., all of New York.

Pyrex. The Corning Glass Works had been making glassware for semaphores and lanterns for years. This glass would stand a great deal of heat. One day the wife of a man who worked in the plant visited him and recalled that she needed a pudding-dish for her kitchen. She noticed one of the articles of glassware and decided to take it home and try it for cooking purposes. The glass proved to be an excellent baking utensil, and from this experience an old company developed a new and big business. Accidental discoveries of this sort do occasionally uncover a want of the consumer, but accident and guess are less reliable than scientifically conducted investigations of the market's possibilities. *Consumer analysis* refers to the study of the consumer's wants. *Product analysis* refers to the analysis of the product in order that it may be modified to fit the consumer's wishes.

Sales analysis refers to a study of past sales as a basis for a picture of the present status of the business and as a guide for further distribution efforts. *Market analysis* refers to the study of past sales, the product, and the consumer in relation to each other, in order that all factors may be effectively co-ordinated in future activities. A comprehensive market analysis offers the management a scientific measuring rod of the past efforts of the business and of the potentialities and channels for future business. Regardless of past successes of the business, the future must be forecast by frequent studies of the consumer and the distribution channels. The new American tempo, the accelerated rate of change in our living and working, requires it.

Methods of Obtaining Consumer Research Data

Several methods of securing consumer research data are in common use. The method varies with the need. A problem may demand a special type of laboratory, test campaign, questionnaire, analysis of company records, or field survey. Applied psychologists are interested particularly in the questionnaire and field survey. We shall discuss briefly the mailed questionnaire and the method of securing data through field investigators or interviewers.

The mailed questionnaire. The most common device in consumer research which involves psychological factors is the questionnaire.   It has been used to the extent that some people are annoyed as soon as they receive a letter with a questionnaire attached.   One reason for this attitude is that people like to answer their mail intelligently.   Many questionnaires in the past have been phrased in such general and vague terms that the person answering them may, while he is answering the questions, feel that his answers are going to be useless, because he is not sure that he understands the questions in the same way that others understand them.   Frequently, too, the answering of a questionnaire has involved a great deal of time and expense.   In spite of the fact that some persons dislike the questionnaire, it is still widely used and will continue to be used.   Fortunately, the phrasers of questionnaires are learning how to make them attractive, inviting, and reliable.   The chief psychological factors in securing a high percentage of replies to mailed questionnaires are:

1.   The questionnaire should have an attractive physical appearance.

2.   The recipient should be made to feel that the questionnaire is worth while.

3.   Compensate the answerer for his trouble.

4.   For some studies the identity of the real sender should be hidden.

5.   The questionnaire should be given a preliminary test on a small group before it is tried on the larger group.

6.   Make the questions easy and, if possible, interesting to answer.

1.   *The physical appearance of the questionnaire.*—A concern which sells by direct mail would not think of sending out a letter set in solid, monotonous type.   The direct-mail expert makes careful tests of returns with regard to copy, color of paper, quality of paper, postage, day of week mailed, and other pertinent factors.   It is necessary, therefore, to prepare the physical appearance of the questionnaire with consideration of the same factors used in direct mail.   The questionnaire can be illustrated with human-interest pictures that explain its purpose and enable the answerer to state his experience or wants with pleasure as well as ease.   Pictures on mailed questionnaires increase the returns greatly.   Color illustrations and attractive appearance are

essential to large returns in direct mail. They are just as essential to returns in questionnaires.

2. *The addressee should be made to feel that the questionnaire is worth while.*—The person who is asked to answer a questionnaire usually feels that he would be doing the sender a great favor by taking the time to answer the questions. In order to obtain answers, therefore, it is well to make the answerer feel that he is doing himself a favor. Most questionnaires introduce the request for answering as this one did: "We are compiling some data giving us statistics on our business and we would like you to fill in the inclosed questionnaire and return it to us in the inclosed stamped envelope."

Contrast that with this concern, which was trying to get the attitude of their 3,000 dealers toward them as jobbers:

Did you ever get mad at us?!! Perhaps we were at fault in some of your dealings with us. We are doing some housecleaning of our own minds and methods of doing business. Our friends and our enemies can help us improve our service to them by being frank with us. Please check over the following list and make any comments that you wish. We'll appreciate it and thank you in advance.

One jobber received 500 replies from 3,000 dealers by use of a similar request. The replies were followed up by the management through the salesmen.

The appeals which succeed in direct-mail advertising often succeed in questionnaires. One concern phrased its questionnaire to give the impression that a very charming woman was asking a very small favor. The letter gave the reader the impression that her employer had made a wager that the readers would not answer her questionnaire and she was trying to convince him that the recipients were really interested in helping those who wish to improve their methods of work.

When the questionnaire is sent to a specific group, such as kindergarten teachers, accountants, or shoe merchants, it is often possible to appeal to them by offering them a copy of the data when it has been compiled. In that case it is well to specify the date when the report will be completed and available. A request card for the report should be attached to the questionnaire to enable the person who answers the questionnaire to realize that he may have a free copy of the report.

If the copy of the report has no appeal, it is possible to increase the answers by offering a small gift for answering the questionnaire and returning it by a definite date.

3. *Better results may be obtained if the true identity of the sender is hidden.*—Magazine publishers occasionally wish to make an impartial investigation of their readers' preferences. In some cases the candid answers of the person who fills in the questionnaire may reflect against the publisher who sent the questionnaire. In cases where honest answers might offend the sender, it is well to give the recipient the impression that the investigation is being conducted by an accounting firm or by a statistical concern.

Much depends upon the purpose of the questionnaire. If it is to learn about the complaints of the customers, for example, the true identity must be stated.

4. *Decide upon the type or class of people that you wish to reach.*—In certain situations, it is easy to limit the sending of the questionnaire to the desired group. When a company wishes to get customers' reactions and the company has a complete list of customers, the problem of finding the right group is answered. When the reactions of the general public are desired, it is well to find out which segment of the public is to be reached.

When it is important to know what types of people answer the questionnaire, it is well to insert questions that will enable the investigators to tabulate the answers according to groups, such as occupation, education, sex, or age.

5. *Give the proposed questionnaire a preliminary trial on a test group.*—Again the principles of direct mail should be used with the questionnaire. The direct-mail specialist does not use a letter on a large group of prospects until he has tested it on a small group. He finds that he must do this even though he is absolutely certain that he has a good letter. Experience has taught him that it is dangerous to spend large sums of money until he has determined the percentage and quality of returns.

Questions which are quite clear to the researcher may be ambiguous, vague, impertinent, or unnecessary to a large number of strangers. Only a trial survey can determine the probable value of the mailing. In making the trial survey, it is well to have interviewers present the questionnaire to individuals in person and then note their remarks and questions as a guide to revision.

6. *Make the questions easy to answer.*—No one enjoys attempting to answer a question that he does not understand. The more certain the reader is that he understands the question, the more willingly he will answer it. For this reason, questions of opinion rather than concrete facts are inhibiting to the answerer of a questionnaire. Questions such as, "Why did you buy a Blank auto?" "What is your opinion regarding our powdered milk?" or "How would you advise us to change our displays?" are not clear and definite to the consumer, and he cannot answer them correctly. This type of question, however, may give a copy writer a great many suggestions for new copy in advertisements.

To achieve certainty of understanding, it is well to have the questions relate to matters of fact rather than opinion and then give all the possible types of answers after each question. Checking the correct answer will then be easy and will clear up any vagueness in the phrasing.

Questions should be stated positively rather than negatively. For example, it is better to say "Have you bought any Blank soap this week? Yes ——, No ——," than to say "Have you not bought any Blank soap this week? Yes ——, No ——."

Questions which involve the prestige or personal integrity of the person answering them, such as, "How much did you pay for your last hat?" "Do you do your own washing?" "Why don't you pay your bills promptly?" "How often do you take a bath?" do not elicit accurate results. When it is necessary to ask questions which involve the personal intimacies of the individual, the questionnaire must come from a third disinterested party or from someone who is able to assure the person that the answers will be kept confidential and used in a legitimate manner.

One concern made its mailed questionnaire attractive to housewives by writing an interesting short story, in pamphlet form, which described the problems of a housewife. The story also set forth the methods of work of the housewife. The reader was asked to check the method that she herself used under those conditions and in this way the manufacturer learned the conditions and methods under which housewives used his product.

The personal interview as a source of research data. Sometimes the questionnaire does not elicit the desired data when mailed. It may then be necessary to obtain the information by means of interviewers. If a study were to be made of the reactions of vegetable hucksters, factory workers, or shoe shiners, the results of a mailed questionnaire would be inadequate. When necessary to secure answers to a large number of questions, the interview may be the best method of getting representative answers. Sometimes the same people who will not answer a list of questions by mail will do so when called upon personally.

For research problems that cannot be studied through mailed questionnaires, personal interviews must be obtained. An example of this is the advertiser who wishes to find out which of three proposed headlines, illustrations, or layouts is the best. If the researcher were to hand copies of the three advertisements, identical in every respect except the factor under investigation, to fifty buyers, and ask each buyer of the commodity to state which of the three advertisements was the best, many of the fifty persons would cease to be consumers of the product advertised and become advertising critics. Their reactions would be artificial. By means of interviews, it is possible to plan a technique which will lessen the artificiality of the judgments.

If a study is to be made of three different kinds of copy, three advertisements can be prepared which are identical in all respects except for the copy. Ten other advertisements of different products can be mounted on cardboard. When the investigator calls on typical buyers of the product to obtain their reactions, he may fumble in his brief case for the ten advertisements and "accidentally" pull out the three advertisements and hand them to the prospect with a passing remark such as, "Do you care to look at these while I prepare my ten advertisements for your opinion?" In a few seconds he arranges the ten advertisements and the prospect lays aside the three important advertisements. After a five-minute discussion of the ten advertisements, the interviewer replaces in his brief case the ten advertisements, and then, *incidentally*, asks the prospect about the copy of the three layouts he saw in the early part of the interview. The reactions of the prospect will then approximate those which he would have if he saw the advertisements in a periodical where they would have to compete with many other interests.[10]

If the interview is used, it is essential to choose and standardize the questions just as carefully as for a mailed form. The interviewers must also be instructed as to how they are to present the questions. They must be trained so that they do not put the answers into the mouths of the informants. When persons are interviewed who are not accustomed to supplying information to oral questions, the interviewer should be trained not to write the answers in the presence of the informants. They may dislike the idea of having someone write their statements as they make them. In some cases the investigator can be taught to memorize the questions and then informally write the answers on the margin of a newspaper and copy them later.

The research interviewer should have some qualities of salesmanship. However, salesmen are not, as a rule, competent to do field work of a research nature. Salesmen are trained to influence the answers of the person interviewed. They are apt to see only those factors of the situation that agree with their own prejudices. They are promoters rather than analysts.

Experienced researchers find that a major problem in dealing with responsible directing executives is the lack of calm analysis of situations and reports by the examining executives. A manager who initiates and authorizes a costly research may be influenced more greatly by one or two dramatic personal experiences than by the reported reactions of a thousand strangers who use his product. His emotions blind his intellect. Many of the basic principles of valid research are common knowledge, but training in certain techniques such as sampling is essential.

Controlled sampling of consumers. In order that the mail questionnaire or the field survey may produce reliable and therefore usable results, it is necessary that the market researcher apply them in conformity with the principles of scientific sampling. The general theory of sampling may be illustrated in this way:

If an interviewer should stand on a busy street corner and ask 500 passers-by, "What is your favorite brand of cigarette?" and then should ask a second 500 persons the same question, the

---

[10] D. E. Robinson, "How to Use the Laboratory Method of Testing Advertisements," *Printers' Ink*, November 29, 1928.

results in each case would be remarkably similar. Furthermore, the replies of 10,000 additional persons would not deviate appreciably from those of the first 500. Thus it would be necessary to ask only 500 persons in order to get a reasonably accurate measure of the cigarette preferences of the many thousands in that locality. This same principle has long been employed by scientists in the field of physical research, by tradesmen who want to know the quality of the material they buy, and by the housewife who tests specimens of a basket of fruit, taking specimens from several parts of the basket before buying.

Such a procedure, however, is based upon the possibility of obtaining a completely random sampling of the larger classification one wishes to study, and for many reasons this is very difficult, especially when dealing with people rather than commodities. In its place, market researchers have developed the technique of the "controlled sample" as a more reliable method. By means of the controlled sample it is possible, within reasonable limits, to select a comparatively small group of people who will represent in correct proportions the significant qualities of the larger market to be studied. It is, in effect, a miniature of the larger population from which it is drawn.

The term "cross-section sample" is often heard these days, but the term means little unless there is a definition of the population that is sampled. It may be a cross-section of college students, of physicians, of a particular community, or perhaps of all adults. There has rarely, if ever, been a cross-sectional study based on all the people of the nation because very few issues, if any, involve us all. Even the public opinion polls at election time sample only qualified voters; not all of them. Market researches are usually even more limited in scope. They attempt to sample only those segments of the population that are relevant to the purposes of the particular problem at hand.

In order to obtain a truly proportional representation in the sample, certain control factors must be carefully worked out in advance and applied in the process of selection. Some of the more commonly used factors of control are:

1. *Geographic distribution.* The sample should be distributed over the area under study in the same manner as is the total population included within the scope of the survey, whether

it be nation-wide or limited to a single community. For example, if we were attempting to find out what the average American believes to be a decent living wage, it would make a great deal of difference whether we consulted only people living in New York state or only those living in the South. We would have to include each of these areas, as well as others, in proportion to their populations if our conclusions were to be representative of the nation.

2. *Economic status.* Persons in various income levels frequently have different likes and dislikes, different opinions, and favor different brands of products. Any market survey that is based on sampling must consider this aspect carefully. A company seeking potential buyers for high-priced automobiles might be completely misled if its survey ignored the financial position of the interviewees. A random sampling of the population would produce replies chiefly from those who are financially unable to buy the product. A controlled sample must contain the correct proportion of persons from each economic group covered by the survey. Furthermore, it is not always sufficient merely to consider income. A man living in New York City with an income of $3,000 may have considerably less purchasing power than a $3,000 man living in Centerville, Indiana, and possibly different tastes and purchasing habits. Marriage status, size of family, and other considerations are often relevant variables to be considered.

3. *Age classification.* Many public opinion polls break down their results on certain issues in terms of age classifications of the respondents, because old people do not always have the same opinions as youth. Old people also tend to buy different products, or different styles of a product. If a survey is to present a sensitive picture of a market, it should include proper controls for the age factor. A house-to-house interviewing campaign, especially on holidays or in the evenings, may obtain far more replies from stay-at-home old people than justified unless definite quotas for each age group have been set up.

4. *Sex.* If a questionnaire or field survey is intended to apply to both sexes, care must be taken to see that the correct proportions of men and women are included. There are many situations in which men and women have different opinions, prefer-

ences, and even methods of stating facts. A random sampling during the morning hours might very well include many more women than men, because women shoppers or housewives may be more available than men, many of whom are in offices or factories at that time. Frequently a survey is limited to the members of one sex, but where the study concerns both, correct quotas must be made out for men and women.

5. *Size of the sample.* The number of persons to be given questionnaires or to be interviewed must be large enough to be statistically reliable. In some cases 500 may be sufficient, in others several thousand might be needed. The Gallup and the Fortune public opinion polls as a rule use about 3,000 and 5,000 cases, respectively, except for special studies. Tables have been worked out which indicate the number of persons needed for a "reliable" sample under various conditions and within stated degrees of accuracy, but such tables can serve only as a rough preliminary guide.

One practical method of determining the necessary size of the sample is through the "cumulative frequency" method. A chart is kept of the replies of a survey as they come in, each new batch being added to those already received, and a line is plotted indicating the responses of the interviewees. At first the line on the chart may fluctuate rather wildly, owing to the small number of cases received, but as more replies come in and are added to the cumulative total, the line begins to "settle down" and fluctuate within narrower and narrower limits. Finally a point will be reached when the line reaches relative stability and further incoming replies do not change its direction perceptibly. At this point it may be assumed that a sufficiently large sample has been obtained.

A number of other useful methods for estimating the size necessary for a sample to be statistically significant have been devised, but an adequate sample alone is not sufficient to guarantee valid results. All proper control factors, such as those mentioned above, and possibly others such as urban-rural distributions, occupations, educational background, and such special controls as the specific problem calls for, must be applied with exactness and intelligence. Accurate information upon which these control factors are to be based should be obtained from reliable sources and must be up-to-date, if the sample is to be representative.

Neither an adequate sample nor one that is a true miniature of the larger population can insure trustworthy results. The time factor, the nature of the questions, the length of the questionnaire, the skill and objectivity of those conducting the survey, the co-operation of the respondents, and other considerations, many of them difficult to measure or analyze, are all vital to the ultimate success of the investigation. Complex as its problems may be, modern sampling techniques furnish us with one of the most useful tools available in the field of consumer study.

Important factors to be included in reports of market investigations. One of the most common channels for making suggestive market investigations is the advertising agency. Many executives hesitate to authorize investigations by such organizations because some agencies prefer to give emphasis to those findings that require the expenditure of money in advertising that will benefit the agency. However, many of the reports of advertising agencies are unbiased, and not all of them recommend an extensive program of national advertising. Researches can also be made by professional research organizations which submit their findings without recommendations of advertising campaigns. The chief factor to be considered in market research is that of freedom from prejudicial influences either without or within the company. All the facts must be obtained and presented, regardless of any evidence that may appear to reflect upon the ability of important officials of the company.

The research man's investigations must include the facts of the production of the product as well as its sale. All trails must be followed no matter where they lead. When this is done, the analyst is likely to find that a strongly intrenched officer of the company is at fault. Facts that are already known to be basic in the problem of high sales cost and low sales volume are brought into the open and faced courageously, even though the favorite department of the company's president may be put into an unfavorable light. In one company the chief obstacle was the attitude of the president, who believed that his product was of such unusual quality that it would sell itself, and yet his sales curve did not rise in line with that of the entire industry.

The salesmen of a company that made a style product found that dealers made so many objections to the styles that the salesmen spent most of their time arguing with the dealers and vindicating the policy of the house. When they reported the complaints to the management, the sales manager passed them on to the vice-president who was in charge of styles. This official resented any reflections on his ability as a stylist. The sales manager was told to get more orders and fewer complaints. The salesmen then shifted their criticisms to other aspects of the line which were given to the vice-president in charge of production. This official accepted criticisms with less grace than the style man. A serious danger to the future of the business was averted only by a market analyst who was brave enough to present the facts to the board of directors. It was only after an independent style man was hired and a working arrangement made with the production manager that the company was able to regain its prestige.

The executive in charge of production whose costs are too high may insist that his costs are right, but that the competitor does not know how to figure costs and must sooner or later go out of business. This kind of argument is usually an alibi, because the competitors do not often go out of business. When the highest official of a company blames the incompetence of a competitor, it is well to dig underneath his claims, find the actual costs, and locate the leaks. Little slips here and there in many different departments may disclose an aggregate of costs that absorb the profits. Blaming competitors does not solve the problem of marketing at a loss or at a small profit.

Too often the number of pages in a market report is accepted as evidence of great value. The competent market analyst does more than tabulate the consumers' wishes; he also presents known facts in their proper relation to the executives of the company. The human side of research reports may be more significant than the thousands of statistical tabulations that are colorfully graphed. The human side of a market analysis is not limited to the executives of the company. Quite often the crucial human factor in unsatisfactory sales lies within a class of individuals in the chain of distribution, as with mechanics who dislike to install an article, or with labor unions, sales clerks, or transportation company employees.

The market research man should do more than ask executives for their opinions as to what customers want and think. He must study the company's records as well. Bausch & Lomb Optical Company analyzed its sales in terms of *whom to sell, what to sell, when to sell,* and *where to sell.* It classified its goods into 24 major groups and 428 subgroups, the prospects into 8 major groups and 204 detail groups. This showed what to sell and to whom to sell it. The company was under the impression that the market of one product was limited to 600 outlets; the research revealed more than 6,000. Each classification has its own advertising budget, and any direct-mail expenditures can be checked and modified for the best results. Waste is reduced to a minimum. It was found that 8,000 pieces of direct mail per month had been saved by eliminating duplications and dead prospects. In some cases, the company had been sending out five catalogues to one man, and each catalogue cost about one dollar! At the same time many good prospects were not getting catalogues. Also, each salesman's territory was analyzed for him, so that he knew where his prospects were located and how to reach them. This plan of analysis was first tried out in one territory and was found so profitable that it was applied to the whole country.[11]

In testing the salability of a new product, some established companies have given their dealers a stock of the new article and then allowed the article to sell itself. They assume that, if the article will sell on its own merits without the producer's assistance, it will therefore sell much better with extra effort. Pursuit of such a policy is dangerous, because many new articles, though meritorious, need some educational efforts to supplement their intrinsic worth. The better method is to plan a definite trial or test campaign in selected and typical trading areas or with typical classes of customers.

[11] Benjamin J. Ramaker, and G. R. Salisbury, "Bausch & Lomb Apply the Four W's to Sales," *Sales Management and Advertisers' Weekly,* October 27, 1928, p. 230 ff.

The Consumer Movement

A major trend to be recognized in marketing is the consumer movement. The consumer movement in various forms has extended over more than one hundred years of our history. However, it began to have a significant influence in our distribution of goods in the 1930's when the depression of that period stimulated a desire for more complete information in buying, better values for the consumer's dollars, truth in advertising, and good taste in the presentation of the advertiser's message.[12] The purposes on the part of the consumers are mainly the following:

1. More and better information that will enable customers to spend their money more effectively.

2. More intelligent consideration of sellers for the preferences and interests of buyers.

3. Better protection against intentional fraud on the part of unethical sellers.

The articulate leaders in the consumer movement have been a relatively small number of individual consumers. A few of them have been so vehement in their reform activities as to appear to need clinical attention. The few fanatical leaders have given some observers the impression that the consumer movement has been, at times, a subversive movement. This is a wrong interpretation of its meaning in America. George H. Tichenor has defined its true nature as follows:

The majority of consumers have no consciousness of belonging to a "movement." The East Side mother trying to get graded meat and cheaper milk through a depot; the intelligent buyer who would like grade labeling of canned goods and other products; the subscribing member of a consumer testing agency; the member of a women's club working for an effective food-and-drug law; and many an average citizen with a small share of idealism and a large antipathy for being gypped, who finds succor in his co-op store—all these are members of the consumer movement. It is in large part a rather bemazed section of humanity and, significantly, it appears terrifying to the consciences of some, who hear it just beginning to speak. It is not Red-led. It is moved chiefly by millions of housewives who are beginning to look to various agencies for the information they need to find their way about in an economic system increasingly complex and bewildering.[13]

---

[12] For definitions of the consumer movement, see Werner K. Gabler, *Labeling the Consumer Movement*, p. 14 (American Retail Federation, 1939), and A. T. Falk, *What Is the Consumer Movement* (Advertising Federation of America, 1941).

[13] George H. Tichenor, "War on Consumers." *The Forum*, January 1940, pp. 28-29.

PREDICTIONS IN MARKETING

The average woman who has wanted to be an intelligent purchasing agent for the home has been often annoyed by the bombastic advertising claims coming to her by radio, magazine, newspaper, and direct mail. Fears have been emphasized—fear of body odors, of bad breath, of loss of husband, of infections, and so on. Additional abuses were pseudo-scientific claims: "Doctors recommend," "Laboratory tests reveal," and so forth. Some statements were definitely false; others were partially so or gave a false impression because important facts were omitted. Many advertising men recognized these exaggerations and injustices. Some even recommended regulatory legislation.[14]

In addition to the efforts of the more enlightened leaders, both within and without business, effective legislation in the interest of the consumers was passed March 22, 1938. In 1940, two years after the Wheeler-Lea amendment added "unfair and deceptive acts and practices" to Section 15 of the Federal Trade Commission Act of 1914, a comprehensive analysis of the effects of the amendment was reported in one of the journals of advertising. The commission's activities in the interest of consumers is shown by one division of the commission which regularly reviewed 533 magazines and 432 newspapers. In the fiscal year, ending June 30, 1939, the commission examined 220,760 advertisements which had appeared in magazines and newspapers and noted 26,176 which seemed to warrant further investigation. In addition, many mail-order catalogs, circulars, and almanacs were examined. In one year the Radio and Periodical Division read and evaluated in terms of the law an average of 4,539 pages of radio script each working day.[15]

---

[14] Examples of attempts by advertisers and other businessmen to bring about reforms in marketing and for the consumers' benefits are reported in the following:

John Benson, "Trends in Consumer Advertising," an address delivered before the American Marketing Association, Washington, D. C., May 1938, and reported in *The Journal of Marketing,* July 1938, pp. 25-26.

Printers' Ink, May 31, 1940, reports: "Forty-two states now have on their books the *Printers' Ink* Model Statute or a modification of it, or some statute designed to accomplish many, if not all, of the purposes of the Model Statute."

[15] PGad Bryan Morehouse, "After Two Years of Wheeler-Lea," *Advertising & Selling,* May 1940. This article by the director of the Radio and Periodical Division of the Federal Trade Commission presents an excellent summary of the effects of the act on advertising.

A complete description of how the F.T.C. does its work is published in *Printers' Ink,* March 1, 1940, pp. 21-24.

The work of the Commission has been highly constructive in the correction of certain advertising abuses;[16] and, in line with this trend of giving the consumer more accurate information, some advertisers are developing informative and grade labeling. For example, informative labels for cloth give specific, understandable facts, such as color fastness, fiber content, thread count, and safe methods of cleaning. Many food manufacturers are also beginning to appreciate that the consumer does not know what is meant when eggs are graded as *Special A, A, B,* or *C,* or when olives are graded as *Medium, Large, Extra Large, Mammoth, Giant, Jumbo, Colossal,* or *Super Colossal.*

Many products are difficult to grade. Flavor in food products is a psychological matter, and no adequate system of grading it has yet been developed. Any grading system is likely to be deficient in some respects. In the purchase of cloth, style or color may be more important to certain buyers than durability. Furthermore, some people do not care to read labels and do not try to learn how to buy intelligently.

Several consumer service organizations have been organized for the purpose of grading products or otherwise informing consumers regarding the values of commodities. One or two of the highly self-advertised consumer service organizations have had a dubious history of ethical practices; but, in the main, most have attempted to furnish reliable information to their subscribers. Some of them have had to spend a large part of their income from subscriptions in obtaining new subscribers and thus have had relatively insufficient amounts of money to conduct complete and adequate tests of products. Few or none of these rating organizations have done what scientists have found necessary when they publish results of laboratory tests: namely, furnish readers with the name of each tester, a description of his experimental equipment, a statement of his exact procedures, and the complete results of the tests made. The need for better testing and the difficulties in measuring psychological reactions to products, such as taste of foods, should stimulate both the consumer service or-

---

[16] "Verboten Sign Looms Large in Toiletry Field," *Advertising Age,* March 11, 1940. See also "Check List of F.T.C. Taboos," *Advertising & Selling,* March 1940.

ganizations and the marketers to render increasingly better services to consumers.[17]

The modern marketing executive recognizes that the consumer deserves accurate and complete information. He also realizes that the "policing" of his practices by commercialized consumer service organizations or by governmental bureaus should be made unnecessary through the spontaneous offer of better advertising and information than laws demand. He has an inherent responsibility for the education of consumers. Marketers, consumers, and educators can contribute to the interests of everyone if they believe that they have joint responsibilities in making improvements in serving consumers. The interests of all are mutual; not antagonistic. Some few consumers, some advertising men, and some critics of business will always be of the kind who practice unethical methods. Regulation by governmental or other bureaus will always be necessary to combat their influences. But the really worth-while contribution to the solutions of the problems highlighted by the modern consumer movement will take place through the joint educational efforts of consumers, advertisers, and constructive critics. Certainly the present trend toward the seeking and giving of complete information about commercial products and services will continue to grow.

Probable Changes in Marketing Management

Market studies and consumer analyses are so common that they have been used as burlesque material in popular magazines. But these researches have just begun.

The signposts of the present indicate that traveling salesmen of the future may decrease in number and local salesmen may increase. The former will be displaced by cheaper and quicker methods of selling. In many cases the men will have to be of a higher type than the salesmen of today, for often they will have

---

[17] Louis Bader and J. P. Wernette, "Consumer Movements and Business," *The Journal of Marketing,* July 1938, Vol. III, No. 1, p. 8.

R. I. Elliott, "The Consumer Movement Today," *Advertising & Selling,* November 18, 1937.

"Grade Labels 30% Wrong, 14-City Analysis Proves Labels Found Unreliable and Co-op Prices Higher than Others," study by St. Louis Better Business Bureau and reported in *Advertising Age,* June 9, 1941

SALES GO UP AND PRICES GO DOWN

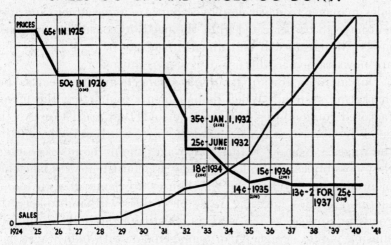

PRICES

65¢ IN 1925

50¢ IN 1926
(230)

35¢ JAN. 1, 1932
(240)

25¢ JUNE 1932
(180)

18¢ 1934
(240)

15¢ 1936
(200)

14¢ 1935
(200)

13¢-2 FOR 25¢
1937 (200)

SALES

0

1924 '25 '26 '27 '28 '29 '30 '31 '32 '33 '34 '35 '36 '37 '38 '39 '40 '41

The fallacy that advertising raises prices is definitely refuted in this simple chart, showing how a rising sales curve has resulted in a constantly declining price curve.

FIG. 78. (*Courtesy of the manufacturers of Kleenex.*) From a booklet on the history of Kleenex, "Today Is My 17th Birthday," International Cellucotton Products Co. See also *Advertising Age*, May 12, 1941.

to act as service or merchandise men, and, consequently, must be men who understand management and merchandising methods. They will have to become counselors of merchandise methods and assist the local distributor rather than merely take his order or persuade him to buy.

The sales manager also will change. He will no longer be a kind of god who calls salesmen on the carpet and bawls them out or bullies them into courageous attacks on the quota. He will not be a kind of mental lasher of the stragglers on the force; instead, he will be a keen analyst of human nature who has sat at the feet of the clinical psychologist and learned how to modify the behavior of the cub salesman so that he will have the behavior patterns of the veteran.

In selecting the raw human materials for the sales force, the employment man will use psychological tests more than he has in the past. These tests have been much discussed but little used. Many of them had little predictive value and few of the executives understood how to use those that did have value. Eventually, competition and governmental influences will compel the sales manager to select employees with more accuracy, and tests will have to be perfected to fit the needs of consumers and business. Managers will be trained in the use of tests just as they are now trained in the use of cost accounting.

Our attitude toward labor has changed and is affecting our marketing system. When managements found that the manufactured commodities could not be sold, they tried to move the goods by lowering the price, and the price was lowered by cutting the wages. Now we realize that wages should be just as high as they possibly can be so long as they are consistent with efficiency in production. When the warehouses are jammed with manufactured articles, lowering wages of workers will tend to keep the goods in storage, as the workers constitute the bulk of the purchasing public. Sagacity in management, with high wages, will tend to move the goods out of the warehouse into the consumers' hands.

The open sesame to all these and many other changes which we cannot yet anticipate is *research*. Government data and laboratories will be of greater usefulness each year. The government researchers now can furnish any company with data on consumer purchasing capacity for every county of the country, but only a very few companies are using it for their sales territories. This information will be gathered and will be put into form which will enable the businessman to understand and use it.

To utilize the possibilities of research and prepare for the coming changes, it will be necessary that the boards of directors of corporations be chosen for their ability to analyze and establish corporate policies rather than for their holdings of stock, or because of the personal friendship of the president.

In spite of the important part that will be played by scientific analyses of the objective facts, the surviving concerns will be the ones who can combine the scientific with the human factors in business. Business will never become wholly mechanized. Some humans will still have to operate it, and human beings are going to remain very human. The psychologically sound principles are the ones that will have the greatest effect and will make the most important contributions to business and social advancements.

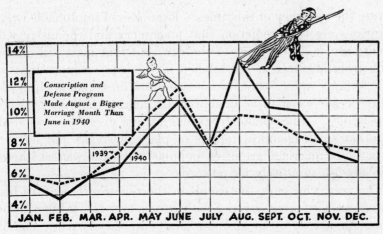

FIG. 79. Human behavior which involves thousands of individuals, such as marriages, can usually be predicted with considerable accuracy. However, exceptional conditions may influence the predictions to a marked extent. (*Courtesy of the* Jewelers' Circular-Keystone, *February 1941, 100 E. 42nd St., New York.*)

Dangers of predicting group behavior. It is difficult to predict the social life, the business methods, and the consumer purchases of the distant future. Even immediate conditions cannot always be correctly prophesied. During the First World War, when skirts were long, the fashion experts predicted that skirts would become shorter. The shoe manufacturers misjudged the effect for, as one said, "Dame Fashion has come to the assistance of the shoe dealer by announcing that the new fall skirts will be shorter. Shorter skirts mean higher shoes." Actually, skirts became shorter but high shoes did not become fashionable during all the later years.

When prohibition was repealed, some business prophets predicted that the sales and profits of soft-drink businesses would decline. Yet a leading soft-drink company for which dire effects were predicted has increased its earnings tremendously. New and unappreciated influences increased sales of soft drinks regardless of the status of alcoholic beverages.

At present, we can find many prophets among our contemporary writers. Some of the world's best writers and scientists have produced whole volumes on probable changes in social life, industry, education, art, women, youth, religion, and many other subjects. Most of these writers study the present and then exaggerate the tendency of the times. Examples of improbable exaggerations are the prediction that machinery and chemistry will eventually take the place of the cow and that man will obtain milk from a faucet in the kitchen in the same manner that he now obtains water. Since women tend to dress like men, in another decade we shall be unable to distinguish them by outward appearance. Since chemistry is making new discoveries, we shall soon eat small chemical tablets in place of steaks and lettuce. Attacks on marriage are often popular and some writers, therefore, abolish it entirely for posterity.

The men who built the canals in the nineteenth century had visions of a country covered with canals and all transportation being carried on by means of inland waterways. They merely exaggerated their present. Their guesses now seem childish to us. We cannot assume that the tendencies of the present will continue uninterruptedly. New and unknown factors will bear upon the forces in social and economic life, and the highly successful methods and definite tendencies of the present may, in the distant future, be relegated to the curiosity shop. In the meantime, we shall limit our predictions about consumers' wants to the near-future effects of established recognizable trends.

The fact that women wear their hair shorter than they did years ago does not mean, obviously, that they will shave their heads another season. Long-range prediction by extension of the present is dangerous; sometimes it gives ludicrous results. Even though forecasts of the remote future are difficult, predictions of changes in the immediate future can be and often must be made.

References

Agnew, H. E., and Dale Houghton, *Marketing Policies*, Chapters III and IV. McGraw-Hill Book Co., 1941.

Brown, Lyndon O., *Market Research and Analysis*. Ronald Press, 1937.

Coutant, F. R., and J. R. Doubman, *Simplified Market Research*. Walther Printing House, 1935.

Hepner, H. W., *Effective Advertising*, Chapters VIII-XII. McGraw-Hill Book Co., 1941.

Jenkins, John G., *Psychology in Business and Industry*, Chapters XIV, XV, and XVI. John Wiley & Sons, 1935.

Kornhauser, A. W., and P. F. Lazarsfeld, *Techniques of Market Research from Standpoint of the Psychologist*. American Management Association, 1935.

Strong, Edward K., Jr., *Psychological Aspects of Business,* Chapters XI, XXI-XXVII. McGraw-Hill Book Co., 1938.

Wheeler, Ferdinand C., et al., *The Technique of Marketing Research.* Mc-Graw-Hill Book Co., 1937.

Projects

1. Alexander Hamilton Institute ran advertisements with the following headings:

   a. "Those Who Shy at Unpleasant Facts Should Not Read This Page."

   b. "Men Who Are Satisfied to Wait Ten Years for Success Will Find Nothing Interesting on This Page."

   c. "Afraid to Face the Facts—then Don't Read This Page."

   d. "Men Who Know It All Are Not Invited to Read This Page."

   One of these pulled marvelous results. Select the one that pulled best (*Printers' Ink,* November 8, 1928, p. 132). See Appendix for answer.

2. Obtain a mail-order catalog of a number of years ago and list articles that are no longer on the market or which have been radically changed. Check those which were fads and suggest reasons why the others have disappeared or have been greatly altered.

3. Select a number of articles in popular use today but which you think may no longer be on the market 10 years from now. Present reasons for your selection and indicate what type of article may replace them. How could the manufacturers of the products adjust themselves to the change?

4. Look up the ratings of a number of products in both Consumers Union and Consumers' Research reports in your library. To what extent do the ratings of the two organizations agree?

5. Test the "cumulative frequency" method of determining the proper size of a sample by the following experiment: Toss ten coins into the air and note the number that come up heads. Plot the number of heads on a graph. Repeat the coin tossing, each time adding the number of heads to the cumulative total—and plot each succeeding total on the graph. At what point did the curve become relatively stable? How many coins need to be tossed to arrive at an adequate sample?

6. Obtain a copy of a mail questionnaire and analyze it from the viewpoint of the principles discussed in this chapter. Rewrite it if you believe it can be made more effective.

7. Outline the steps you would take in conducting a field survey to determine the potential market for a new type of electric toaster.

20

Business Cycles

There is a dream of human progress which makes it to consist in a gradual *easing* of the lot of man, in the gradual lightening of his task, until the last straw of difficulty has been lifted out of his path, the last peril extinguished, the last lee shore weathered and all smooth sailing for ever afterward. May it never come true! . . . But the alleviation of misery which is good with few qualifications, must not be confused with the *removal of difficulty*, which is not good without many qualifications.[1]

The cycles of business. Everyone, whether employer, employee, or consumer, must try to foresee and make adjustments to the recurrent periods of business depression and prosperity. The student of psychology is especially concerned about the ebb and flow of "hard times" and "good times" that appear in our era because unemployment in hard times often makes stern demands on individual and family life.

The psychological ravages of unemployment visible in the disintegration of stable family life and the warped personalities of children and young people were recounted in a study by the University of Newark.

The study made at the university's Research Center by Dr. Phillip Eisenberg is a "survey of surveys," a compendium of conclusions reached by psychologists and sociologists throughout the world of what happens to an individual's personality when he is without a job. More than 100 such papers were analyzed and their opinions synthesized.

The crushing psychological impact of unemployment and low economic status is felt more deeply by children and youth because the disaster occurs during "the most impressionable years in the life of man," asserts Dr. Eisenberg.

Loss of prestige with their fellows whose parents are employed, deterioration of school work, emotional conflicts because of diminution of "the support of authority which resided in the parent before unemployment" are visible among such children.

Even more complex are the problems of adolescents. If parents are em-

---

[1] L. P. Jacks, *The Challenge of Life.* Harper & Bros., 1924.

ployed and young people unemployed, there is the "resentment at being dependent on their parents when they desire to be independent."

Referring to numerous surveys, the Newark study indicates that children tend to become "emotionally unstable in somewhat the same way as their parents do," and one of the manifestations of the effects of unemployment on personality is shown in the marked effects on school work.

The causes for lowering of school grades are ascribed to two main factors: reduction in health and emotional disturbances at home. As subsidiary hypotheses, he suggests that the unemployed parent "may not be giving the child as much help with his school work as before unemployment" and, secondly, "the younger children suffer more than the older probably because they are more dependent on their parents and have had less opportunity to build up resistance to catastrophic situations."

Among youth between 14 and 20 years of age, the studies stress loss of ambition, a feeling of "superfluousness" in society, desertion of the parental home, and increase in criminality.

According to the Newark report, all writers describing the course of unemployment agree on the following points:

"First, there is fear, rage, or shame followed by a hopeful active hunt for a job during which the individual is still optimistic and unresigned. He still has an unbroken attitude.

"Secondly, when all efforts fail, the individual becomes pessimistic and anxious, and he suffers active distress; this is the most crucial state of all. And thirdly, the individual becomes fatalistic and adapts himself to his new state but with a narrower scope. He now has a broken attitude."

Relief, Dr. Eisenberg found, is no solution for a jobseeker "because his ego is not satisfied. He must have a job, especially a job that he values, in order for him to recover." [2]

The student of unemployment, industrial relations, international conflicts, world affairs, and similar aspects of civilized life may be carrying on his study during a period of prosperity or depression. It makes little difference when he studies business cycles. Cycles and fluctuations in economic activity have provoked many psychological problems for countless generations and apparently will continue to do so for individuals of future generations.

The business cycle must be distinguished from some of the other fluctuations in business activity.

By *business cycle* is usually meant the rhythmic movement of business depression and prosperity. It is a constant recurrence of irregularly separated booms and slumps; it has received so much attention that universities offer courses in its study and professional experts prepare periodic reports on the

[2] *The New York Times,* February 13, 1938, p. D7.

rise and fall of the business activity curves. Some experts believe that the cycle has definite predictable fluctuations and that it passes through five phases:

1. Depression.
2. Revival.
3. Prosperity.
4. Financial strain.
5. Collapse.[3]

In plotting the indices of the movements of business, note is taken of the *seasonal variation* or movements of goods within the year. Just as the temperature changes within the year, so business activities rise and fall systematically year after year. This seasonal variation is important in certain kinds of business and the aggressive sales manager tries to level the seasonal variation curves for the employees of his own firm.

The *secular trend* refers to the regular increase or decrease over a number of years. In most cases, it is a growth or decline element that depends upon population or the conditions of industry. The secular trend is usually portrayed as a straight line, the slope of which measures the growth of the industry or business in its general trend toward greater or less volume or value.

Business depressions are old in the history of civilized group life. In the following quotation and comment, George I. Cochran[4] called attention to one of the earliest depressions:

"The laws are cast out and men walk upon them in public. The lawbreaker is lord of wealth, the rich man has lost all. Scanty is gold; craftsmen are without work; the reaper of the harvests gets nothing, while he who plowed not profits. The land is depleted. I show thee a land turned upside down."

That was published in the Egyptian city of Memphis, on papyrus, 5,000 years ago. So you see that gang rule and business depression were rampant in the land of the Pharaohs more than 3,000 years ago, before the birth of the Christian era. But history reveals that the calamitous period thus pictured was followed by one of unexampled prosperity.

---

[3] A writer for the Chicago *Tribune* designates each current phase of the business cycle—in the opinion of many people—in one of the following terms: "Betterment starts, optimism growing, expanding faster, whoopee, curtailment starts, pessimism growing, curtailment overdone, Ouch!"

[4] B. C. Forbes, New York *American,* May 10, 1932.

Fig. 80. In times past, prophets have predicted the end of civilization. History has shown that many of the periods of maladjustment ushered in new advancements. (*Drawing by Orr; copyrighted by the Chicago* Tribune, *1931.*)

The business cycle is evident in the history of the Pharaohs of Egypt. Biblical students are acquainted with the succeeding periods of fat and lean years of the Old Testament and the story of how Joseph saw the need for foresight and induced the people to prepare for the "depression." In 594 B. C., a depression spread over what was then known as the whole of the civilized world. In 33 A. D. the Roman Empire was in the grip of a pronounced economic crisis brought about to a great extent by a large, unprofitable investment incurred in connection with a huge army and navy. Unemployment became so

serious a problem that free distribution of grain—the dole of
that day—was necessary. A migration of races in the fourth
century contributed toward another depression. A century and
a half later a ravaging plague caused economic disturbances
in Europe. In the tenth century, distress throughout Europe
was so great that one historian wrote, "Not to be killed and to
have a good sheepskin coat in winter, for many people, is the
height of felicity."

An exhibition called "Depressions the World Has Lived
Through" was shown in Schermerhorn Hall, Columbia University. The years of publication and titles of a few of the
books were:

1700 "A letter to a Member of Parliament Occasioned by the Growing
Poverty of the Nation, from the Want and Decay of Trade and Wrong
Management; With Some Overtures for Increasing and Promoting the One
and Rectifying the Other."
1816 "A Review of the Present Ruined Conditions of the Landed and
Agricultural Interests."
1842 "Not Over-Production, but Deficient Consumption, the Source of
Our Sufferings."
1873 "The Terrible Financial Panic of 1873."
1884 "Excessive Saving, A Cause of Commercial Distress: Being a Series
of Assaults Upon Accepted Principles of Political Economy."

Miss Dorthula Wilcox,[5] who arranged the exhibition, told re-
porters:

We have about one hundred and fifty volumes in our collection on depressions since the seventeenth century and they are practically all the same.
Every one of them declares theirs is the worst depression that ever happened; they all say it should teach the world something; they all offer the
same panaceas; and they all blame it on the same causes. They always blame
the tariff and poor laws, or what we now call the dole, and since the industrial
revolution they all blame technological unemployment.

In the United States, the end of the Revolutionary War
marked the beginning of a great land boom that resulted in the
unjustifiable establishment of many towns and the purchase of
large areas of land on credit. The crash came in 1819 when
land values declined as much as 70 per cent, merchants were
ruined, and unemployment spread rapidly.

The economic cycle after the Revolutionary War traced the
same general curve and illustrated the same conditions that we

---

[5] *The New York Times*, February 29, 1932, p. N2.

experienced after the First World War: namely, about two
years of hectic prosperity, two years of primary post-war depression, and then several years of wild speculation followed by a
secondary post-war crash. Furthermore, this crash came when
we had no steam power, electricity, modern banking, or mass
production.

When the hard times of 1819 were forgotten, people became
enthusiastic about the building of roads and canals. Speculation started again. Prices rose. The circulation of money increased abnormally and bank loans jumped from $137,000,000
to $510,000,000. At the peak of this boom, people began to
realize that steamboats and the growing railroad industry might
disturb their investments; an abnormal number tried to sell
their securities in order to avoid losses, and thus brought on the
severe panic of 1837.

The panics of 1837, 1893, 1907, 1921, and 1929 have been
largely repetitions of the same old story. The previous depression gradually lost its severity and a period of expansion developed. Industrial concerns overbuilt, speculation became rampant, budgets of cities and the Federal government rose to new
top-heavy heights, business as well as political scandals became
numerous. Fears about the future arose, and the collapse of
the optimistic trends ended the orgy. As a result, factories
closed, breadlines grew, the tramp evil and lawlessness became
a menace to life and property while governments struggled to
supply a quick remedy. Each panic has retarded the progress
of the too-rapidly flowing currents in our economic stream,
halted social advancements, forced realignments in our political
life, and moved us forward into new forms of social change,
prosperity and depression.

The following popular explanations of depressions are questionable or inadequate: technological unemployment, wasteful
manufacture and distribution, general overproduction, speculation, installment buying, wars and breakdowns of international
trade and credit. Each of these factors has been present in
many of our economic collapses, but none has been of sufficient
importance in itself to create a breakdown.[6]

---

[6] "Engineers to Seek National Program," *The New York Times*, September 25,
1932, p. F9.

Un-co-ordinated changes bring about our economic maladjustments. Civilized life has many influences working upon the individuals of any generation. All these influences are changing; some rapidly, others slowly. Some, such as war, bring numerous other pressures to bear upon our conditions of life. Physical sciences, for example, develop more rapidly than the social sciences, and so maladjustments occur in our rates of change. The more one studies political, socio-economic, and other movements, the more likely he is to see that progressions take place in un-co-ordinated lines of advancement. Furthermore, we shall have to expect such changes to continue to take place in uneven trends because life cannot be sufficiently mechanized to bring about the co-ordinations necessary for the elimination of the business cycle.

Some of the general influences which are part of the very essence of life, and that cannot be nicely controlled by any power or person, are the following:

1. *Individual differences.* These are an outstanding finding in the study of psychology. Children may have the same parents and the same general external environment, but they certainly do not have exactly the same patterns of human traits. Differences in adjustment and other aspects of personality result in differences in abilities, living habits, and ambitions.

Some people, for example, have individual differences in abilities and ambitions which make them unusually greedy. They and their interest groups exert so much pressure on prices that a collapse or decline must eventually take place. Prices in one industry do not rise or recede as rapidly as in another. For example, building rose sharply during the building-boom days of the 1920's. The costs of building were out of line with the price levels of other industries.[7]

2. *Environmental pressures.* These include such differences as found in religious convictions, traditions, customs, international relations, natural resources, and climatic conditions. No one, no matter how powerful he may be politically, can control these influences in and on our life. We are not mechanisms

---

[7] "What About Building Costs?" *Business Week,* December 14, 1940, presents data concerning price levels of various industries in comparison with those of building costs.

whose cultural heritages can be promptly modified to fit some planner's plan for co-ordinating changes.

3. *Interest groups.* These are present in every society. Certain people perceive that certain other people have like interests and so they combine, for purposes of benefit to themselves. Examples of interest groups in the United States are the American Federation of Labor, the National Grange, the Chamber of Commerce of the United States, the Methodist Board of Temperance, Prohibition and Public Morals, the National Catholic Welfare Council, numerous veterans' groups, and thousands of other organizations which may have either self-interest or public-interest ambitions and legislative programs. These interest groups and the factors which bring about their existence tend indirectly to influence the economic cycle. Consider, for example, the effects on business conditions of the pressures exerted by our veterans' organizations who believe they have special rights in making demands upon the public treasury. Of course, such pressure groups should not be considered as "plunderbunds" only. They are always present in a dynamic civilization. They will continue to be with us, but they often have pronounced influence on the maladjustments growing out of uneven rates of change.

Among the important factors that cause un-co-ordinated changes in our economic life are price differences, epidemics, migrations, crop failures, elections, taxations, tariffs, inventions, and mismanagement. While business is good, employment at its height, and prosperity active, the many relatively minor disruptions due to slacks and lags are less noticeable, since they are more or less absorbed in the gainful activities. Ordinarily these maladjustments do not cause dissatisfaction, except among minorities, until they converge into one big impasse. At the time of the impasse, a depression is precipitated.

We cannot look at our economic life as static, in connection with the possibility of its maintaining an exact equilibrium in the balance between the human and non-human influences in its production, consumption, and facilities for sustenance. We must take the broad view that modifications in material culture, brought about by inventions, technological change, wars, tariffs, fashions, and other influences, are not promptly co-ordinated by adaptations in usage, legislation, and international relations.[8] Hence adjustment is bound to be upset, and the resultant maladjustment affects every individual whether employer or worker.

Strong economic forces undoubtedly do operate in causing the rises and falls in the curves of business activity. Still the causes of these fluctuations are often the result of men's mental states rather than non-human physical or economic laws, as illustrated in this incident:

There was once a successful French artist. It was his custom to eat dinner every evening in a small but select restaurant near his studio, and, being of discriminating tastes, it was his practice to have one small bottle of rare wine with his meal.

One evening he entered the restaurant, and, while waiting for his order to be taken, picked up a copy of a newspaper which was lying on the table where some earlier diner apparently had left it. In the section devoted to financial news of the day he read an article which said that there were evidences of depression throughout France.

His waiter appearing, the artist ordered his meal and purposely neglected to ask for his bottle of fine wine.

When the waiter expostulated, the artist explained that he would dine without wine as times were hard.

This brought the proprietor to his table with concern written plainly on his usually placid face. Again explaining that he was going without his wine because times were bad, the artist finished his dinner and left the café.

The next day the proprietor of the restaurant visited his tailor and said: "Times are hard and you need not make up that new dinner jacket I ordered."

The day following the tailor countermanded an order he had put in for a new automobile and gave as his reason "hard times."

That night the automobile man met the artist at a social gathering and said: "Business is terrible and I think I shall withdraw that commission for my wife's portrait."

So the artist returned to his studio and, as he sat bemoaning his ill luck, his eyes fell upon the paper in which he had read the account of financial depression. To his astonishment, he found that it was dated a full three years before.

The following night he ordered rare wine with his evening repast.

The next day the restaurateur ordered a new suit.

The tailor bought a new car and the artist painted the portrait of the automobile man's wife.

Beats statistics, doesn't it?[9]

---

[8] Alvin H. Hansen, *Economic Stabilization in an Unbalanced World.* Harcourt, Brace & Co., 1932. Part One presents a thorough treatment of international causes of instability.

[9] *The Magazine of Wall Street,* July 16, 1927, p. 485.

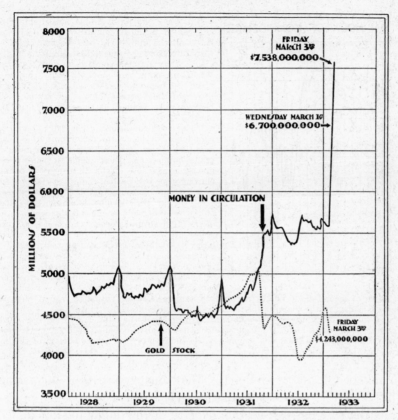

FIG. 81. A dramatic example of the importance of public confidence was experienced during the marked decrease in gold reserves and increased money in circulation, March 1933. It is doubtful whether business depressions can be controlled through any form of centralized planning so long as public confidence cannot be controlled. (*Chart from* Business Week, *March 15, 1933, p. 30.*)

As the artist, proprietor, tailor, and automobile man were affected by the attitude of each other in this simple cycle, so people often contribute to the fluctuations in the business cycle by their attitude toward each other.

The economic cycle is greatly influenced by psychological factors. It has often been said that "if a period of prosperity could be expressed in a single word, that word would be 'confidence' and conversely, if a period of adversity could be expressed in a single word, that word would be 'distrust.' " [10]

[10] Leonard P. Ayres, "This Business Relapse," *The Atlantic Monthly*, February 1938.

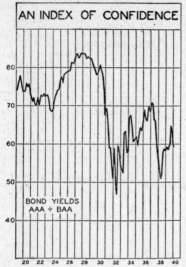

Fig. 82. The most simple measurement of changes in business confidence is one that is based on the differences between the yields of corporate bonds of the highest quality and the yields of corporation bonds of medium quality. When investors are optimistically confident about the general business outlook, they begin to regard the prospects of weaker companies as being almost as good as those of the stronger ones.

Under such conditions of generally prevailing confidence in the prospects for profitable business, the investors bid up the prices of second-grade bonds until their yields are not much greater than those of the highest-grade bonds. On the other hand, when the prospects for business become discouraging, the investors seek safety rather than income, and then the prices of the second-grade bonds fall far below those of the highest-grade issues, and as a result the yields of the less secure bonds become much larger than those of the well-secured ones.

These recurring changes in the attitudes of investors make it possible to construct an index of business confidence by computing the percentages that the yields of high-grade bonds are of those of second-grade bonds from month to month over a period of years. Such an index is shown in the diagram for the period of 22 years from 1919 into 1940.

The index reflects the strong confidence of business in the New Era period from 1923 through 1927, and a moderate decline before the climax of speculation in 1929. It indicates that the lowest level was reached in the summer of 1932 at the bottom of the depression. (*From the Cleveland Trust Company* Business Bulletin, *April 15, 1940.*)

When people have confidence, they buy goods, thus increasing the turnover or velocity of the dollar. In a period of depression, distrust has caused the velocity of the dollar to slow down. For example, in 1929 when people had confidence, the dollar turned over about thirty times within the year. In 1936 when we had not yet regained confidence, the dollar turned over only fifteen times.[11] This speed with which the dollar changes hands is largely a psychological factor. Fortunately, a famous political economist has described psychological aspects of the business cycle.

First, as to the business cycle. For nearly forty years I have been, at times or continuously, a banker, a historian, a student of economics, and an investor not only for myself but for trust funds in my care. As a result of both study and experience, I have come to the conclusion that what we call the economic cycle is in reality a psychological cycle.

[11] H. B. Elliston, "Blaming the Money Managers," *The Atlantic Monthly,* July 1938. A discussion of bank deposits in relation to the velocity of circulation of money and credit may be found in the *Business Bulletin,* Cleveland Trust Company, April 15, 1941.

It is no less real on that account, but it is a by-product of the workings of human nature and not of the non-human forces of the universe. The stresses and strains that eventually produce an earthquake are wholly independent of man, but the stresses and strains that produce panic and depression are wholly dependent on man. . . .

But the inevitability of an economic law is different from the inevitability of a law of what we call the natural world. It comes from the nature of man and not from the nature of the universe, if we can differentiate between the two. If there were no such thing as man, two atoms of hydrogen gas combining with one atom of oxygen would still make what we call water, and we cannot imagine a universe in which such natural laws would not remain constant.

Economic laws, on the contrary, are dependent on human nature, and are constant only as human nature does not change. They are, so to say, the shadow pictures on the screen of the workings of the human mind. In so far as those workings remain constant, and they seem to, the succession of shadow pictures remains constant and we talk of economic "laws."

Let us translate the "economic cycle"—the shadow picture—into the reality of the "psychological cycle." What actually happens? At the bottom of a depression everybody, as we say, has "lost his shirt." People are loaded with debt which they contracted in the boom period, and many have lost their jobs. Now they cut expenses to the bone and try to work themselves out of the holes they have found themselves in. They reduce their scale of living.

Gradually, after some years, one and another begin to get their heads above water and feel a little easier. They have denied themselves not only luxuries but the essentials of life. Replacements of clothing and other things have to be made, and an increasing number of people reach the point where they feel they can afford to make them. A modest buying movement starts.

That means increased profits for some lines of business and increased employment, both of which, in turn, enlarge buying power. Business "picks up." A spirit of optimism and mild confidence replaces the bleak pessimism of the depression. This enlarges the buying movement. The sun of prosperity shines once more. Prices go up.

To take advantage of that, speculation begins again. People gradually forget the hard times, expand their scale of living, and borrow for all sorts of enterprises or speculative undertakings. Unwarranted debt again begins to accumulate, and when the unstable structure thus built up reaches a certain stage of instability another crash occurs and we fall again to the point from which we started.

That seems to be the way the human mind works regardless of external conditions. . . .

Man is essentially an optimistic animal. If he were not, and if he did not feel an urge to better himself, he would never have risen from the stage of the ape-man. But it would seem that the very urge which has carried him so far is the root of the "business cycle." [12]

[12] James Truslow Adams, "Parties and Panics—What Link? A Historian Holds the Cycle of Depressions Unrolls Unmindful of Who Is in Power," *The New York Times Magazine*, September 20, 1936.

Economic planning to control the business cycle. In recent years many people have sought means of controlling, wholly or partly, the business cycle. The theorists having this purpose have been called the *equilibrium school* of economic thinkers. A great deal of the political planning involved in the New Deal legislation of the 1930's was done by members of this school of thought. Many college students also find it difficult to think of themselves as helpless victims of our economic cycles and hope that some new road to economic stability may be found. Let us, however, consider a few of the difficulties involved in economic planning.

1. Many influences of economic cycles are beyond the control of any planning agency. Consider shifting international relations and the many other factors beyond our direct control, such as those listed as environmental pressures. So long as a farmer cannot tell whether he will get five or fifty bushels from an acre of land, there must necessarily be some room for overproduction or underproduction.

2. The rationing of production is much easier in some industries than in others; each industry's output affects other industries. Coal cannot be stabilized without considering oil, natural gas, and electricity. Railways must be considered in relation to highways. An invention may at any time modify the demand for the products of any industry. In a recent year, when the secretary of agriculture was trying to control the production of wheat, the real difficulty in wheat tied into corn and cotton. More than three million acres of cotton land were in wheat because of cotton quotas, and more than nine million acres of corn land were in wheat because of corn quotas in Southern states. Obviously the secretary could not raise quotas of cotton and corn to relieve the wheat situation, because cotton and corn situations were just as bad as wheat.[13]

The same difficulty of control applies to labor. When jobs are scarce, laborers become more industrious and thereby decrease the number of available jobs. When jobs are plentiful, labor becomes less efficient and thereby helps to raise production costs.

---

[13] *Business Week,* August 20, 1938.

3. The recommendations of a planning agency face the continuous possibility of defeat at the hands of popular prejudice, ignorance, and misunderstanding. What chance, for instance, would the warning of such an agency, to stop the speculative mania, have had in 1929 when it held so many millions of Americans in its grip?

4. The record of economic planners of the past is not at all impressive. At the time when the Southern cotton planter first had his acreage restricted in order to hold up the price, the price was 18 cents. Nine years later the world supply of cotton was greater than ever and the price was less than nine cents a pound. Certainly, the depression of the 1930's was not solved in the United States by any astute economic planning—it was displaced by preparation for war. Similarly, when Great Britain planned about rubber, rubber prices fell. When Cuba planned about sugar, sugar prices fell. When Brazil planned about coffee, $30,000,000 worth of coffee had to be dumped into the ocean or otherwise destroyed. Japan planned about silk prices and silk prices continued to go downward. Italy planned about sulphur, Chile about nitrates, and copper producers of the world planned about copper with the usual record of failure in such planning. The people of these countries forgot about their economic planning, after it had failed, because their thinking and efforts were concentrated on their own wars or on the effects upon them of other nations' wars.

5. One of the major causes of failure in planning is the problem of timing. Price control and similar economic programs must be timed to fit into international relations as well as the existent trends within the nation. Any governmental expansion program which is started too late in a depression may not be at all effective in arresting the course of the business decline but may even destroy the recovery after it has begun.

6. James Truslow Adams has summarized some of the important aspects of attempts to control the business cycle as follows:

Overproduction, accumulation of unbearable debts, and other economic phenomena are the reflections of a state of mind at a particular stage of the psychological cycle as indubitably, I think, as is, say, the appearance of a rose on its bush at a certain stage of its growth. By pruning, fertilizing, and

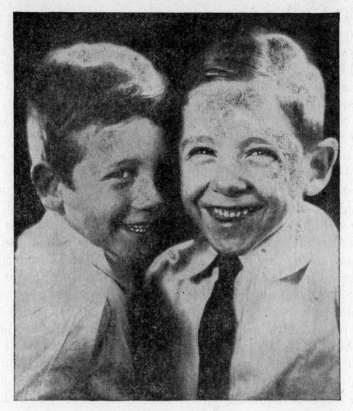

Fig. 83. An important factor in our perpetual maladjustment to the advancements made in various phases of life is *Youth.* Youth refuses to accept the old. Youth is confident and finds new fields for venture.
Every year, two million boys and girls grow into men and women—two million sources of new vision, new thinking, new ways. In addition to these young people, we have millions of older persons who stay young and demand new ways of life for themselves and others. Life, youth, change—these cannot be mechanized. (*From an advertisement of the Rodney E. Boone Organization.*)

so on we may improve the rose and perhaps even hasten its growth, but we cannot change its nature or its cycle. We cannot create a bush which has no cycle but goes on forever at the flowering stage.

I would say that governments are much in the position of gardeners. By wise or unwise action they may hasten or retard the fear-confidence-over-confidence cycle, but they cannot change it without changing the human nature which produces it or, possibly, putting that human nature in a complete strait-jacket of governmental control for an indefinite period until it may change. . . .

The action of the British government, for example, in going off gold at a critical juncture helped the nation to climb the upward curve of the cycle, as, to a probably much greater degree, did the later balancing of the budget. . . .

These "shots in the arm," so to say, however, are very different from complete control of the cycle. To accomplish that would involve the complete correlation at all times of supply and demand. This would mean that individuals could not produce or consume as they wished but only as they were told. It would also mean that they would have to learn to live at a uniform emotional level of, let us say, moderate confidence, never dropping below it or rising above it—the line of the "flattened-out" economic curve. That would mean, if my preceding argument is at all correct, a "flattened-out" psychological curve.

If I know my own nation, that is the last thing the citizens want. They would die of boredom. When we are in the midst of depression and have lost our shirts, or jobs, we ask the government to print paper money or do something else to start the wheels going again. "When the devil is sick, the devil a saint would be." But when we scent rising prices and the chance to make money again, we are the last people in the world to want a flattened-out economic curve.[14]

As Adams has stated, the control or flattening out of the business cycle is one of the last things we want. We want to continue as living, changing beings rather than as automatons who are manipulated by a central planner. We want to experiment, grow, improve, and let our emotions have play. We do not want a static form of existence, because stagnation and death are too similar. We want to have the benefits of a dynamic order that results in long-term human benefits. For example, in the early days of our country it took nine out of every ten men to grow our food. A farmer needed six hours of his time to grow a bushel of wheat. Today, on technologically equipped farms a bushel of wheat can be produced in six minutes of working time, or just one sixtieth of the former time. This long-term improvement in our agricultural production released seven out of every ten men from agriculture to build cities, construct roads, improve our health, do our manufacturing, carry on our commerce, and do all the other things which have given us progress.

The philosophy of adapting oneself to the business cycle is not a philosophy of despair. Many forces within the universe must be accepted. And we do accept them happily. Con-

---

[14] James Truslow Adams, "Parties and Panics—What Link? A Historian Holds the Cycle of Depressions Unrolls Unmindful of Who Is in Power," *The New York Times Magazine*, September 20, 1936.

sider the changes of the seasons, the ebb and flow of the tides, and the life cycle of birth, childhood, adulthood, old age, and death. We do not avoid these or try to eliminate them. We enjoy them and, when possible, utilize them as opportunities for further satisfactions. In the case of the business cycle, college students prepare themselves to deal more adequately with the lows in business through their extra training for the jobs available. Furthermore, those of unusual initiative start new enterprises and give employment to others.

This does not mean that most individual citizens will ever decide to depend upon themselves to meet the impacts of business cycles. On the contrary, people will continue to ask government to ease the stresses and strains of our economic ups and downs. Furthermore, when serious dangers are impending, we shall follow the appeals offered by promisers of panaceas and by dictators. The cult of the dictator is a very ancient one and comes about in times of hazard and suffering. When the individual cannot or does not care to solve his economic problems by direct attack adjustments he seeks an "all-powerful father" or dictator.

What can the intelligent person do about the "laws" of the business cycle? Most members of the general population cannot be expected to develop any sustaining economic philosophy that will help them endure the rigors of a depression, but intelligent persons can do so. As previously stated, the strength of any nation is not primarily in its natural resources, climate, material comforts, or political system but in its moral fiber. Individual adjustments, attitudes, and beliefs are basic. How shall we approach their development?

Religious training offers an example for us. It may be defined either as a set of beliefs that are to be accepted or as a number of attitudes of faith and a certain aspiration that are to be achieved. Similarly, the individual's adjustment to different problems of life and the economic cycle may be presented in either of these two ways. That is, we may indoctrinate youth and have him believe in an all-wise planner: socialism, communism, some kind of dictatorship, or in some other economic creed. Or we may stimulate each person to learn, evaluate, and

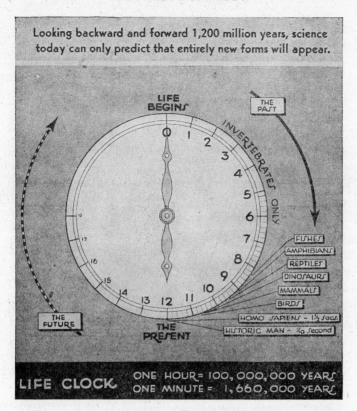

Fig. 84. From James Ritchie, "Life's Distant Unknown Goal," *The New York Times Magazine*, September 29, 1940, p. 12.

When we realize the relatively short time that modern man has been on the earth, we begin to appreciate that, all factors considered, man has achieved a relatively high state of development. In spite of lapses and digressions in his progress, he has done rather well.

adjust to the situation where he finds himself, gaining his satisfactions from living in a world that he enjoys because of its challenges. Happiness cannot be achieved as an end. It is the by-product of activity directed toward the solving of problems and the interpretation of human experience.

American education has not been directed toward the emotional development of individuals who can stand the strains of inevitable changes. Many theorists and educators merely rant at our problems of unemployment, new machines for living, and people as they are. Many demand an economic panacea which, at best, would bring with it new problems, or would be out of tune with life as human beings live it. Certainly no economic or political system will ever remove our problems. Life is a series of changes, and stresses are absolutely certain to arise.

The intelligent person need not wait for a new economic [15] or political system to solve his problems. He can begin at once to develop himself in dealing with the problems within and about himself. Psychologically, the habits of direct attack are the individual's best insurance for meeting the low periods of the business cycle.

Of course, many persons are not capable of doing this and so we shall continue to experiment with economic planning and other alleviative schemes such as unemployment reserves and emergency employment programs.

Industrialists can also work toward a better control of the adverse ups and downs of their industries as these ups and downs affect their own employees. For example, some companies such as the Hormel Packing Co. and Sears, Roebuck & Co. have developed annual wage or constant wage plans. These plans do aid the worker in dealing with some gaps in his employment, but all employers, however anxious to help employees they may be, are still under the control of the many influences that produce business cycles.

The intelligent individual can fortify himself somewhat by anticipating the actions of legislative bodies and the trends in economic forces. He can avoid surprises that throw him off balance. He can subscribe to publications that offer forecasts, such as *The United States News*, the *Washington Letters* of the Kiplinger Washington Agency, the *Business Bulletin* published by the Cleveland Trust Co., and the *Foreign Policy Bulletin* of the Foreign Policy Association, as well as to professional journals that deal with current affairs. But his chief fortification will always be in his personal development, as in training himself to do better work in a job regardless of whether he has a job or not, studying in school or college, analyzing the problems of an industry or profession, and participating in every character-building activity that may be available and appropriate to him.

---

[15] *Business Week,* July 16, 1938, presents a summary of some economic plans.

References

America's Capacity to Produce. Brookings Institution, 1935.

Ayres, Leonard P., *Turning Points in Business Cycles.* The Macmillan Co., 1940.

Clark, John M., *Strategic Factors in Business Cycles.* National Bureau of Economic Research, 1934.

Garver, F. B., and A. H. Hansen, *Principles of Economics,* Chapter XXI. Ginn & Co., 1937.

Hall, O. Milton, "Attitudes and Unemployment," *Archives of Psychology,* No. 165, 1934, Columbia University Press.

Hart, Hornell, *The Technique of Social Progress.* Henry Holt & Co., 1931.

Mackenzie, Findlay (editor), *Planned Society,* Chapters XV-XXV. Prentice-Hall, Inc., 1937.

Mead, J. E., and C. J. Hitch, *An Introduction to Economic Analysis and Policy.* Oxford University Press, 1940.

New York University, Department of Economics, Washington Square College, *Economic Behavior,* Chapters XX-XXIV. Houghton Mifflin Co., 1939.

Rundquist, E. A., and R. F. Sletto, *Personality in the Depression.* University of Minnesota Press, 1936.

Schumpeter, Joseph A., *Business Cycles.* McGraw-Hill Book Co., 1939.

Snyder, Carl, *Capitalism the Creator.* The Macmillan Co., 1940.

Von Haberler, G., *Prosperity and Depression* (rev. ed.). League of Nations, 1938.

Williams, J. M., *Human Aspects of Unemployment and Relief.* University of North Carolina Press, 1933.

Projects

1. Keep a record for a few weeks of predicted trends or events forecast by bulletins offering such service, or similar pages in such magazines as *Newsweek* and the *United States News.* Evaluate the results in terms of their accuracy and their exclusive nature.

2. Make a balance sheet of the advantages and disadvantages of a rigidly controlled economy such as that of Nazi Germany or the Soviet Union. Check the items that would also apply to the United States if we were to embark on such a program, and summarize any conclusions you may have learned.

3. Find some good examples to illustrate secular trends and give the probable influences that caused them.

4. Obtain from a number of friends their opinions on the causes of the last depression. Analyze the causes given as to the part each may have played. Did most persons give a single cause or a number of them?

5. Prepare an inventory of the specific individual differences in people that might play important roles in adjustments to social and economic conditions.

6. Name some of the interest groups in your community. To what extent has each been successful? Which appear to serve the interests of the community as well as their own interest?

7. Study possible changes that might be made in our educational system for a better development of young people to adjust themselves to a changing world.

8. Examine a number of recent proposals for economic planning or control. Give your opinion of the possible consequences if each were to be adopted.

9. Examine the extent to which wars cause us to move from depression into prosperity.

21

Our Social Evolution

If we could first know where we are, and whither we are tending, we could better judge what to do, and how to do it.—Abraham Lincoln.

W E ARE living in a period of rapid social change. Old ways of doing things are changing before our eyes. Systems of human relations in economics and politics are being questioned and new systems are growing up or being advocated. We can see many examples of revolutionary economic doctrines and their effects on human welfare.

Will the future bring more changes? If so, what are they likely to be? Can the intelligent individual direct and manage these changes? Can he improve his chances of making adjustments to them?

These questions refer to the three basic aims of most sciences: description, prediction, and control. The main purposes of the present chapter will be (1) to *describe* in broad outline some aspects of the changing social order, (2) to show the basic pattern of social revolution so that we may try to *predict* some of the changes which may occur in the United States, and (3) to point out any possible ways in which individuals may contribute toward the *control* or direction of these changes. Since great social and economic changes involve the psychological arts, the second part of the chapter will show how the propagandist works; how public opinion, so important today, can be measured; and how public opinion changes can be followed.

The pattern of social revolutions. To decide whether we are passing through a "social revolution" rather than simply a stage in a more orderly "social evolution," we should examine the pattern of social revolutions. Revolutions are of several kinds, as defined by Kenneth M. Gould:[1]

Nationalistic, in which an entire people, conscious of their own racial and cultural unity and spurred by the oppression of a foreign tyranny, rise and throw off their previous sovereignty. Although it is true that many social and economic factors were involved, the American Revolution of 1776 was essentially nationalistic. The life of the average American colonist was not strikingly different in 1790 from his life in 1760. He had merely exchanged the authority of the British King, Ministers, and Parliament for that of the President and Congress.

Political or palace—Simply an internal dispute by which one faction or clique of the same ruling classes plots against and overthrows the one in power, usually through a *coup d'état* without the knowledge or interest of the masses. Intrigues of this kind were frequent in the later Roman Empire where, as with many unstable monarchies, the throne changed hands constantly and bloodily according to who controlled the Praetorian Guard. Similar in origin are the multitudinous overturns which have given Latin America a reputation for petty revolutions.

Genuine social revolutions have been described by Gould as having the following five distinguishing factors:

1. Apparent rapidity of social change, i.e. the compressing of marked changes in the control of the social structure and in the status of large groups of people into a comparatively few years or months. As George Soule and Lyford P. Edwards emphasize, the period after the actual outbreak of revolution is brief, spectacular, and obvious compared to the much longer period of "incubation" which precedes it and which is an essential part of the revolutionary cycle. Soule also insists, perhaps too dogmatically, that this preliminary period of slow loosening of the old sanctions is invariably marked by important technological changes, particularly in methods of production and distribution, occurring spontaneously and without plan, which bring sharp shifts in the numbers and power of social classes.

2. A movement by one class against another. The first class feels itself exploited, repressed, or oppressed in some way and naturally lays the blame on the class in power. Whether or not the conditions of economic hardship which it experiences are directly traceable to the acts of the dominant class makes little difference. There is usually a large psychological element involved. But in any period of hard times the have-nots are inclined to see in the comparative prosperity of the haves the root of their difficulties.

3. The use of methods of direct action or force. That is to say, a revolutionary group abandons as futile the effort to win reform by ballot, by legislation, or by the slow processes of evolutionary change and arms itself, if necessary, to obtain its demands. It may not be necessary to show its hand completely or to use guns and bayonets, but if it is prepared to do so and obtains what it desires through the threat of physical violence it is, philosophically speaking, using force.

---

[1] "Social Factors in Revolution," *The American Scholar,* Winter, 1935.

4. A social revolution must be aimed at some definite, planned goal or program. Many movements of protest against oppression have occurred in a spirit of blind rage or escape; for instance, the slave and peasant revolts, spontaneous mutinies of soldiers and sailors against autocratic officers, or the farm uprisings in the Middle West against high taxes, mortgage payments, and low prices. None of these movements can be said to have a general social program as they are usually unaware of or indifferent to anything but their immediate grievances. In fact, revolutionary movements on the lowest level of protest, where those taking part are usually ignorant, half starved, and poorly organized, cannot hope to succeed although they may furnish a powerful dynamic for more general group movements if canalized by subtle leaders. For this reason middle-class intellectuals, from Marx to Lenin, have usually formed the "brain trusts" of successful revolutions. It is only when a revolutionary party appears, with a well-disciplined organization, a definite plan of reconstruction for the period after seizing power, and the confidence of the exploited masses, that a revolution can succeed.

5. Finally, a revolution must show results of some permanence, that is to say it must succeed in altering the laws, customs, points of view, distribution of wealth, and actual life routine of the entire population, not only those for whom and by whom it has been carried out but even those who must be restrained and controlled under the new order. This essential factor has been well phrased by Edwards as a change "whereby one system of legality is terminated and another originated."

Summarizing these factors, we may define a social revolution as: A comparatively rapid change in the control of the state and the socio-economic system, produced by force or direct action of an exploited or unprivileged class against a dominant class, aiming at a definite social program, and profoundly altering the laws, habits, and attitudes of the entire people. Accepting this definition, the only genuine social revolutions in history have been the French Revolution of 1789 and the Russian Revolution of November 1917.

Gould has briefly summarized the main stages which investigators have observed in practically all revolutionary cycles:

1. A long period of static society.
2. A gradual growth of unrest, usually correlated with spontaneous basic changes in productive processes.
3. A precipitating occasion, bringing on
4. The outbreak of revolution, with seizure of power by the repressed classes.
5. A period of moderate leadership.
6. Counter-revolutionary movements, both from without and within.
7. Rise of radical leaders to power.
8. Period of terror, followed by
9. Either: (a) Triumph of reaction, or
               (b) Exhaustion and voluntary cessation of terror.
10. Slow reconstruction, often punctuated by further interludes of reaction.

This entire cycle, as previously indicated, may cover a very long period of from 30 to 100 years. The active section of it, however, dating from the outbreak of revolution to the complete establishment and general recognition of the new system is comparatively short—say from two to six years—and justifies the designation of rapid social change.[2]

When social revolutions are in process, they often have *preliminary symptoms* that can be recognized as aspects of the revolutionary change. These are an increase in travel, which enables the people to see how others live and to want to enjoy their ways of living; an increase in crime, vice, and frivolity, particularly among the classes which are seeking compensatory outlets for impulsions that lack normal expression; feelings of frustration and defeatism and discontent that spreads from one group to other groups; and freedom of speech with plays and poems as well as other forms of literature and art directed against the existing oppressive forces or persons.

In addition to the preliminary symptoms, Gould, Edwards,[3] and others have stressed the great *advanced symptoms*. These are more significant and reliable as indicators of an impending upheaval. The advanced symptoms are:

1. *The transfer of allegiance of the intellectuals.* In a static society the authors, artists, teachers, scientists, technicians, clergy, and journalists are the beneficiaries of the dominant classes. No matter how important or socially useful their function, they could not exist except upon the largess of the established order. They are supported by the overflow of surplus value. . . .

2. *The emergence of the economic incentive.* The repressed classes, partly through the revelations of the intellectuals but more especially through their own daily experience of hardship, become conscious of the economic pinch and definitely identify its causation with the dominant class. They develop what may be called an *"oppression psychosis"*—an obsession that the whole system is against them, that the only object of life is to fight and destroy it. They look for trouble everywhere, find insults and injustices in every act, and blame them all on the owning class. The previously passive discontent is turned into violent hatred; and hatred of a common enemy is the most powerful unifying motive in any group. . . .

3. Finally, these other great impelling causes must emerge in one overmastering faith, which may be called *"the social myth."* All great revolutions have a certain spiritual or mystical basis, a Utopian belief that revolution can and will bring a millennium of happiness and prosperity. The religious nature of Russian Communism has become a commonplace. Its doctrines supply very clearly a substitute for the theistic dogmas which it denounces and seeks to destroy. In the minds of the masses the social goal is somehow identified with the cosmic purpose.[4]

---

[2] *Ibid.*

[3] Lyford P. Edwards, *The Natural History of Revolution.* University of Chicago Press, 1927.

[4] Gould, *op. cit*

The person unacquainted with the history of revolutions is apt to infer that the oppressed people have suffered a marked decrease in wealth or power, previous to the time of their discontent. Actually, revolutions are likely to be preceded by a general increase in wealth, power, and education among the repressed classes. The apparent increase in misery is due to other factors such as a greater sensitiveness to conditions. For example, the American colonies in 1760 were, at that time, probably the freest and best-governed in the world.

Contrary to popular opinion, revolutions are not typically started and organized by the people who are in the lowest depths of misery. The French Revolution of 1789, for example, was not a revolution primarily of the proletariat. The poor peoples of the city and the peasants of the country were participants in the revolution, but the revolution was really directed by the numerous lawyers, the Third Estate, and certain liberal members of the nobility. The Jacobin Clubs, so important in the French Revolution, were for members of the upper classes who paid high dues for their memberships.

This simply means that extremes of misery and distress such as occur in the depths of a business depression do not cause revolutions. Misery increases docility on the part of the masses. However, clever propagandists who wish to change a form of government or to prevent changes in it often "scare" uninformed people into believing that if the desired policies are not carried out, the "miserable wretches of the depression" will rise up and start a revolution. The unemployed do have outbreaks of rage but they rarely initiate or carry on a revolution. Rather, astute leaders utilize the unfortunates in furthering the ends desired by the clever leaders themselves.

The many common misconceptions as to how social revolutions start and develop into catastrophic disruptions, plus the recognizable preliminary and advanced symptoms, suggest that the intelligent person of our time may well examine some of our recent economic and political changes.

Important contemporary economic and political changes. Certain scholars of our times have suggested that we should now use the term "social revolution" rather than "social evolution." As evidence for the stronger term, they point to our recent eco-

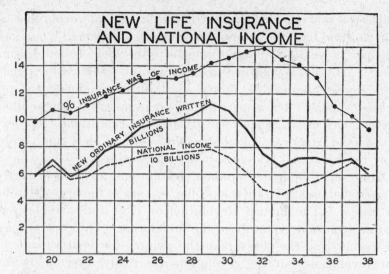

FIG. 85. Life insurance companies find that since 1932 expenditures for ordinary individual life insurance have been rapidly decreasing, both in proportion to the national income and in actual number of dollars. The chart illustrates the trends since 1919.

Representatives of life insurance companies offer two chief explanations of these developments. One is that people have too little faith in the future value of the dollar to be willing to make present sacrifices in return for payments which will be received many years hence. The other explanation is that people consider present thrift unnecessary because they think the government will always take care of everybody through social security and relief payments. (*From the Cleveland Trust Company* Business Bulletin, *March 15, 1939.*)

nomic history. The major business depressions in the United States have typically lasted for five years. On that basis, the secondary post-World War I depression should have ended in 1934-35. At that time an improvement took place, but it collapsed in 1937. Later the very spurious economic prosperity that occurred was obviously the result of "hypodermic" war orders. Hence, the nature of our present unrest, some believe, goes beyond the ordinary processes of social evolution.

Major changes of character in individual citizens have taken place in the last decade or two. The average citizen's attitude toward thrift and provision for his old age has changed, as shown by the sales of new life insurance in relation to national income. See figure 85.

The changing attitude on the part of individuals regarding the extent to which each person should be expected to be responsible for his welfare is indicated not only by life insurance sales but also by the extent to which people have insisted that they become recipients of incomes from the Federal Treasury.

Previous to the Second World War, the size of the monthly payroll and subsidy draft upon the Federal Treasury was evident from the following tabulation from official reports of the Department of Labor, as of January-February 1938:

Branch	Persons on Monthly Roll
Executive Service	787,400
Military Service	333,600
Legislative	5,150
Judicial	2,150
PWA Construction	91,600
RFC Construction	148,300
WPA Projects	1,583,000
CCC	328,000
Farm Security Subsistence	409,000
National Youth Administration	428,000
Direct Relief	4,905,000
Social Security Old-Age Pensions	1,580,000
Blind Assistance	59,000
Dependent Children	560,000
Military Pensions	852,032
Civil Service Pensions	51,206
Total	12,123,438

In addition, the AAA program provided for crop-subsidy payments to approximately 4,000,000 farmers during the following fiscal year. Under this arrangement, the total pay and subsidy rolls of the Federal government extended to some 16,000,000 persons or families.[5]

The idea that government should provide for all people who have no other means of obtaining a living has been indicated by numerous public opinion surveys. Table XXXI is one example.

TABLE XXXI

FORTUNE SURVEY No. XXVIII, MARCH 1940

"Do you think the government should provide for all people who have no other means of obtaining a living?"

	Prosperous	Upper Middle	Lower Middle	Poor	Negroes	Total
Yes	48.2%	55.7%	64.5%	73.9%	82.8%	65.1%
No	45.3	37.7	28.7	18.4	9.1	27.8
Don't Know	6.5	6.6	6.8	7.7	8.1	7.1

[5] Data found in article by Lawrence Sullivan in *Forbes*, May 15, 1938.

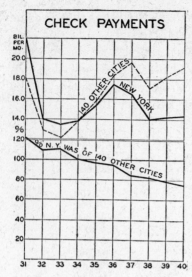

Fig. 86. Releases of census figures have shown that most of our largest cities either had only minor increases in population during the past 10 years, or actually suffered decreases. Our one really booming town of major size has been Washington, which has had a phenomenal increase of population.

The impressive shift of business away from New York is illustrated in the above diagram. The solid line in the upper part shows the annual volume of check payments in New York in billions of dollars per month, while the dashed line shows volume of check payments in the 140 outside cities. The New York payments were larger in 1931, 1932, and 1933. In 1934 the payments in the outside cities were as great as those in New York, and since then they have continued to be greater, and in increasing degree.

The solid line in the lower part of the diagram shows the percentages that the New York payments have been of those of the 140 outside cities in each year. (*From the Cleveland Trust Company* Business Bulletin, *August 15, 1940.*)

Of course, this dependence upon government rather than upon self has forced government to assume many costly responsibilities. As a result of the average voter's wishes and the stimulus of the Second World War, government has had to increase taxes and its regulatory practices regarding business. In 1940 one company prepared an exhibit of its tax reports for the benefit of its employees. The exhibit showed that the company filled in and paid taxes on each of 1,037 tax reports in one year.[6]

A significant change on the part of many people has been their more recent attitude toward businesses and managers. Time was when a successful businessman was an honored citizen of the community. In recent decades success in business has suggested that the successful man should apologize for his success. Some of this changed attitude has come as a reaction against the former worship of big business, failures on the part of individual businessmen, and numerous other influences. The situation lent itself to use by astute politicians who know that an easy way to get votes is to appeal to hatreds toward the fallen idols. Furthermore, initiative and confidence of business enterprisers have often been inhibited because of uncertainties that have arisen as a result of actions by governmental bureaus as exemplified in the following example:

---

[6] "Toledo Scale Co. Displays Its Taxes," *Business Week,* April 20, 1940.

Joseph K. Kidder, a former newspaper man, was making a fair living running the Kidder Oil Company in LaCrosse, Wis. He manufactured and sold a graphite lubricant called Koatsal which, placed in a crankcase along with oil, was said to have various beneficial effects upon an automobile.

The Federal Trade Commission doubted that Koatsal would do the things Mr. Kidder claimed for it. But he refused to sign a stipulation that he was wrong and the Commission right; his business would be ruined.

Whereupon the Commission issued a cease and desist order which Mr. Kidder promptly challenged. After he had fought the case for about five years, the order was made permanent. Meanwhile, the proceedings were steadily publicized; through mimeographed releases the country was informed that Mr. Kidder would not agree with the Commission's finding that his product was of doubtful value.

His money almost gone but his courage still high, Mr. Kidder took the case to the United States Circuit Court of Appeals and a couple of weeks ago won a clean-cut victory.

Koatsal, the court found, was a thoroughly worthy product. The company's claims regarding it were upheld in every particular.

The Commission, properly enough, was discomfited and embarrassed; a break had at last come in its almost endless record of successes.

But how about Mr. Kidder? Was he happy in his triumph? And did he go right ahead dragging in money from all points of the compass now that Koatsal had been legally established and justified?

Let Mr. Kidder answer:

"The Federal Trade Commission was about as successful in putting us out of business as it would have been had we not appealed."

In other words, Mr. Kidder's once flourishing business is pretty sick.[7]

In years to come certain economists may try to explain our economic changes of today as the fifth phase of a logical economic evolutionary process following this suggested sequence:

First phase: Man does everything for himself—fashions his own tools, hunts for food, defends himself.

Second phase: Individuals develop special skills and specialize—the shoemaker, the hunter, the blacksmith.

Third phase: The division of labor develops into the factory system—one man cuts cloth, another sews seams, a third puts on buttons, and so on.

Fourth phase: The Industrial Revolution. Machines supplant manual labor. Great corporations gradually replace individual proprietorships in industries, requiring huge aggregations of capital.

Fifth phase: The state takes over. Instead of many business managers and owners making individual decisions in their own self-interest, the government directs all industrial effort—allots raw materials, determines output, sets hours of labor, and fixes prices.[8]

---

[7] *Printers' Ink*, February 7, 1941.

[8] This fifth phase in our economic evolution has already taken place to some extent in some industries. The student may wish to observe whether the trend increases or decreases.

Have We a "Mature Economy"?

"Industry has been enormously developed, cities have been transformed, distances covered, and a new set of economic tools has been given in profusion to rich countries, and in a more reasonable amount to poorer ones. What is strictly necessary has been done often times to superfluity. This full supply of economic tools to meet the wants of nearly all branches of commerce and industry is the most important factor in the present industrial depression. It is true that the discovery of new processes of manufacture will undoubtedly continue, but it will not leave room for marked extension, such as has been witnessed during the last 50 years, or afford remunerative employment of the vast amount of capital which has been created during that period. . . . The day of large profits is probably past. There may be room for further intensive development of industry in the present area of civilization. . . . Supplying themselves with the full facilities for industry and commerce will give to each of the great nations of Europe and America something to do, but the part of each in this work will be small and far from enough to insure more than temporary activity."

There's a joker in the quotation immediately above, the joker being that we are quoting the lament of the first United States Commissioner of Labor, the Honorable Carroll D. Wright, who wrote the above in his annual report for 1886. Mr. Wright was considered an able economist and was well thought of in his day, but his chief claim to fame today now lies in the above utterance which proved so wrong. (From *Sales Management*, April 20, 1940, p. 11.)

Has economic individualism made contributions to our social improvement? Capitalism, or economic individualism, can be defined as a competitive system where free citizens, by voluntary agreements, produce goods and services for the benefit of customers, having profit as an incentive for giving services. Individual differences, property rights, and private ownership of the materials and equipment of production are additional aspects of capitalism. This system has been so productive as to convince everyone that we could produce far more goods than we have learned how to arrange to distribute under our present financial and employment systems. The fact that people know that it is physically possible to have more goods has caused them to want to experiment with new political systems in the hope that some new way might be found for getting more by doing less. Progress often takes place through such desire and experimentation.

Many people believe that a mere redistribution of wealth would give everyone (except the wealthy) more wealth. Actually, a factual analysis of income statistics will show that if all the individual incomes above $5,000 annually were confiscated and redistributed to the workers, it would result in an increase of less than 10 per cent in the income of those earning less than $5,000. However, all of the income above $5,000 is not available for this redistribution, since a substantial part already is taken for Federal and state income taxes.[9]

The status of American workers can be partially judged by comparisons of real wages for workers of other countries. The shifts in income which occurred as a result of the Second World War make such comparisons difficult for recent years. However, before the war, in 1937, data compiled by the International Labour Office indicated that the cost of foods in minutes of work by steel workers was much lower in the United States than in other countries. See Table XXXII.

TABLE XXXII[10]

COST OF FOODS IN MINUTES OF WORK BY STEEL WORKERS, 1937

	Unit	United States	France	Germany	England	Sweden	Italy	Russia
Bacon	1 lb.	18	30	71	46	48	83	318
Beef	1 lb.	9½	24	52	20	35	105	191
Bread	1 lb.	6	7	23	6½	18	18	34
Butter	1 lb.	22	53	98	52	59	150	378
Eggs	1 doz.	14	70	70	66	75	155	337
Milk	1 qt.	9	11	17	20	12	26	66
Potatoes	1 lb.	1½	2	3	2½	3	6	8
Sugar	1 lb.	4	13	8	7	8	77	76
Total Food Basket		84 min.	210 min.	342 min.	220 min.	258 min.	620 min.	1,408 min.
Average Hourly Earnings of Steel Workers		82¢	39½¢	34½¢	40¢	32¢	20¢	27½¢

Obviously, when we wish to change our own economic system for another, a review of accomplishments under other systems is appropriate. We have heard of many shortcomings of the system of individual enterprise. We should also examine other

---

[9] *Domestic Commerce,* July 30, 1938.

[10] *Steel Facts,* American Iron and Steel Institute, June, 1938.

systems before we completely drop one for another. We should ask ourselves whether people are better off under the systems we seek to imitate before we actually adopt them.[11]

Individual liberty and free enterprise are closely related.[12] Many people, in their desire to improve their status and to progress, are willing to turn to a totalitarian or similar system in order to get more enjoyments for themselves. Many are willing to forego liberty for themselves and others if the denial of liberty promises more material comforts and satisfactions of ease.

Furthermore, certain poorly adjusted individuals have tendencies which are more easily satisfied by a totalitarian form of government than by a democracy. They are so emotionally insecure or lacking in direct attack adjustments that they prefer to let a stronger person "take over" for them. The titles "Fuehrer" and "Duce" both mean "leader."

A democratic form of organization dramatically fails to give to its members what the psychiatrist usually terms "belongingness." A protecting envelopment which absolute monarchies or totalitarian forms provide for the individual is lacking here. In a democracy one speaks of a brother-brother relationship instead of a parent-child relationship. Moreover, the parent gives to the child a certain frame of reference, a certain setting for his life (which we term "belongingness") which is of great value to him quite regardless of the actual acts of that parent (with the exception of the act of rejection).

Democracy replaces the damaging nature of this failure only in the fullest possible development of family life. . . .

This presents the second danger—the individual's fear of change. Perhaps this resentment against growth, this fear of change, is so fundamental a human trait that we cannot hope to alter it. The solution which some 85 out of each 100 adults have for any social problem is to get back to an earlier arrangement or adjustment. So timorous a state of affairs can at least be measurably modified in the upbringing of young children. The search for new objectives and methods just because they are new will lead only to disaster. . . .[13]

However, governments, both totalitarian and democratic, can become as inefficient and as unjust as can corporations. Governments are composed of human beings who seek to retain their

---

[11] Manya Gordon, *Workers Before and After Lenin.* E. P. Dutton, 1941.

[12] The relations between industrial enterprise and democracy are discussed in Philip Cabot, "America's Challenge to Every Man in Business," *Printers' Ink,* May 31, 1940, and in Will Durant, "Self-Discipline or Slavery—'No Great Nation Has Ever Been Overcome Until It Has Destroyed Itself,'" *The Saturday Evening Post,* January 18, 1941.

[13] Plant, James S., "Objectives for Children in a Democratic Society," *The Annals of The American Academy of Political and Social Science,* November, 1940.

special privileges as do other human beings who may be labeled capitalists, workers, professional men, and so on. Governments have a notoriously bad record from the standpoint of stimulating governmental employees to use initiative, do creative work, or be industrious. The human deadwood that accumulates among governmental workers may become so burdensome as to require a war to correct the situation. After Britain had entered the Second World War, an Englishman described certain conditions as follows:

The complaisance, inefficiency, and incompetence which have in many cases characterized the approach to and the conduct of this war on our side are proof enough that a National shakeup was due. The odd thing about it all is that the country is full of practical brains packed with untried efficiency and inventiveness. They are shrieking to be used.

And why, you may ask, are brains and efficiency debarred from functioning to the full in this, the greatest trial in our history? There are several reasons. The chief resistance comes from the existence of a system which has got completely out of hand. That system is bureaucracy. Its flower and fruit never flourished so abundantly. It has no relationship with the natural order of things. It is a negation of progress and a monumental barrier to performance.

I refer to the system which has created a Civil Service[14] which, in its higher reaches, denies the claim of the citizen to his inalienable rights. It has made its own tempo and its movement is adagio. It is for the most part tortuous in its divertings and dictatorial under its thick skin. It is all too powerful and all too aloof from realities.

With some notable exceptions, the hierarchy of the Civil Service has two ends in view—a pension and an honor. With those two things it can retire to its suburban cabbage patch and browse, free of the trammels of buff forms, circumlocution and its overgrowth of smoke-screen phraseology. . . .

I have said that civil servants have two ambitions—a pension and an honor. I have this to add: They must be careful not to make mistakes. Mistakes, quite rightly, are set against possible promotion. The easiest way not to make mistakes is to be noncommittal. In other words, do nothing.

Someone once called the heads of the Civil Service "The Better-Notters." It is better not to do something than to be found out as having done something which it would have been better not to have done.

If the risk of a mistake is taken, in a very ebullient moment, you must be certain, in the Civil Service, to make the mistake in such a way that it will be difficult to trace. If you don't take that precaution you may be put on the carpet three years later—when the subject matter has passed into the limbo of the forgotten.[15]

[14] Civil Service of Great Britain here refers to the permanent employees, ranging in importance from high administrative officers down to typists and clerks. See William Bennett Munro, *The Governments of Europe*, pp. 93-94. The Macmillan Co., 1931.

[15] W. Buchanan-Taylor, *Printers' Ink*, November 29, 1940.

Fig. 87. "Abstract Thinking," a lithograph by Mabel Dwight. (*Reproduced by courtesy of the artist and the Weyhe Galleries, 794 Lexington Avenue, New York.*) Any socio-economic planning must take into consideration the kind of abstract thinking depicted above, as well as that of members of other intellectual strata.

Of course, most decisions regarding individual enterprise, liberty, totalitarianism, and similar momentous questions are voted in a democracy only indirectly. Most people do not know the questions really involved in their voting. Abstractions in these fields are not analyzed very clearly. Voters usually vote for the candidate who appears to be "a good man" or the one who represents the opposite of some hated individual or situation. They think of persons rather than abstract issues and often react in terms of primitive impulsions rather than abstract principles.

Psychologically, one important aspect of totalitarian regimes is the use of propaganda to get people to accept government readings and to have the individual become identified with the national symbols. College students feel elated when "their" eleven wins the big game. Just so do Germans, Italians, and Russians feel elated when their respective governments succeed in some venture. Since government officials control all the avenues of public opinion in those countries having "totalitarianism" ("statism"), there can be no competing propaganda. Young people are not taught to be critical of their governmental officials—quite the contrary. Hence unity and discipline develop strikingly in a dictatorship.

Propaganda. During periods of far-reaching social and political changes, such as the years since 1930, techniques of "social control" are developed and perfected. When old ways of organized life are questioned, when there is uncertainty and lack of agreement among people, attempts are made by individuals and groups to control other people.

For convenience of discussion, social control may be divided into two general types: the *symbolic* and the *non-symbolic*. In the latter class are included attempts to limit or destroy food, shelter, and clothing, in the hope of getting people to behave differently from the way they did formerly. Modern techniques of warfare exemplify the twentieth century's most highly developed non-symbolic social control. Strikes, lockouts, boycotts, and picketing are other examples of means used in this class.

However, modern warfare and modern social strife are always accompanied by the other type of social control, the symbolic forms. The symbolic include attempts by the use of words and symbols to get people to do certain things. Gaining control over men's minds has become a highly developed art if not a specialized science.

The whole field of propaganda is included in this aspect of social control. Modern statesmen know that efficient propaganda is fully as important as effective industrial organization. Hence, during times of crises, the "director of public opinion" or "minister of public enlightenment" may be on a par with the "air marshal" or the "director of transport."

The term *propaganda* has itself become a kind of propaganda. We are apt to pin that label on symbols which anger us, or with which we disagree, or which come from people we dislike. We dismiss a pamphlet or speech or book or paper by saying, "It's only propaganda." We may thus block intelligent analysis of points of view opposed to ours. Before dismissing a statement as "only propaganda," we should try to examine it critically.

It can be predicted with some degree of certainty that propaganda will appear whenever there is a conflict involving large numbers of people. In the United States a century ago there was a conflict between the anti-slavery North and the pro-slavery South. The Civil War was to a large extent the non-symbolic culmination of years of war waged with symbols. *Uncle Tom's Cabin* was as much a part of the symbolic battle as were the pamphlets and meetings of the abolitionists. A century later, after the conflict has been settled, most people do not label as propaganda a book called *Gone With the Wind* which in a way tries to answer *Uncle Tom's Cabin.* Many futile arguments would be avoided if we carefully applied the term "propaganda" only to symbols arising in a conflict situation.

"Propaganda" is an area word. There are about as many definitions of propaganda as the number of people who have written on the subject. These definitions range from moralistic attacks which question the sincerity of the propagandist ("propaganda is lies") to more or less scientific descriptions. One characteristic of definitions, however, is that they do not help very much in deciding whether a particular book or article or speech should be called propaganda.

Since the differing definitions are so little help to the student, no new one will here be added to those already formulated. Propaganda[16] will be considered as an "area word"—a rough guidepost pointing to certain types of publications, speeches, movies, and works of art. At the core of the area are those symbols which almost everyone considers propaganda: publications of the German and Italian libraries of information; Communist pamphlets and magazines; certain appeals of labor organizations as well as those of groups representing manufacturers; the writings of the Anti-Saloon League; certain movies and certain governmental publications; and so on.

The farther we go from this core of agreement, the more we get involved in arguments which start, "But is this *really* propaganda?" and which are seldom satisfactorily resolved. Some people, for instance, feel that publication of consumer commercial rating services are propaganda. Scholars cannot agree

---

[16] The interested student can find a list and classification of definitions in Leonard W. Doob, *Propaganda,* pp. 72-76. Henry Holt & Co., 1935.

on a definition, but most can agree in calling certain publications and speeches propaganda.

An examination of those symbols on which there is common agreement will show that certain elements, or techniques, occur often. They may be classified into one outstanding characteristic and seven commonly-used techniques.

The most outstanding weapon of the propagandist is his constant use of "either-or" terminology: *our* side is "good," "honest," "respectable," "virtuous," "idealistic," and so on; *their* side is "bad," "corrupt," "evil," "sinister." In times of war, *we* are human, just; *they* are inhuman, bestial, and hence must be destroyed.

The propagandist speaks in "polar terms," that is, in opposites. He almost never admits that there is any blemish on his side or a virtue on the other side. This gives him great control, because when people are convinced of the unquestioned rightness of their side and the undoubted wrongness of their opponents, they will enter a conflict willingly.

The tendency to polarize gives propaganda a bad odor. Though statements may be perfectly accurate, they are "slanted" through the omission of all reference to the undesirable aspects of one side or to the desirable aspects of the other side.

The seven other techniques utilized by the propagandist have been discussed by the Institute for Propaganda Analysis. In *The Fine Art of Propaganda* sponsored by the Institute and edited by A. M. Lee and E. B. Lee, the following are listed and illustrated: [17]

Name calling—giving an idea a bad label—is used to make us reject and condemn the idea without examining the evidence.

Glittering generality—associating something with a "virtue word"—is used to make us accept and approve the thing without examining the evidence.

Transfer carries the authority, sanction, and prestige of something respected and revered over to something else in order to make the latter acceptable; or it carries authority, sanction, and disapproval to cause us to reject and disapprove something the propagandist would have us reject and disapprove.

Testimonial consists in having some respected or hated person say that a given idea or program or product or person is good or bad.

Plain folks is the method by which a speaker attempts to convince his audience that he and his ideas are good because they are "of the people," the "plain folks."

[17] Pages 23-24. Harcourt, Brace & Co., 1939.

Card stacking involves the selection and use of facts or falsehoods, illustrations or distractions, and logical or illogical statements in order to give the best or worst possible case for an idea, program, person, or product.

Band wagon has as its theme: "Everybody—at least all of *us*—is doing it"; with it the propagandist attempts to convince us that all members of a group to which we belong are accepting his program and that we *must therefore* follow our crowd and "jump on the bandwagon."

Propaganda versus education and science. Since both the propagandist and the educator try to get people to react in certain ways (social control), how can one distinguish between them? In the first place, education is for the most part concerned with material about which there is little conflict, particularly in the lower grades. No one doubts that it is desirable to teach young people to read, write, and do arithmetic. There is little organized conflict about the content of physics, chemistry, biology, history, and civics courses. Occasionally a teacher tries to make a fundamental change in the attitudes of his students about, say, the American Revolution, the Civil War, the economic system, or the Soviet Union. Then he is apt to enter the realm of conflict, and may become a propagandist.

The second difference between education and propaganda is that the educator does not polarize, does not make one side *all* right; the other *all* wrong. If he is dealing with conflict material, he usually points out arguments on both sides, thus trying to get students to think for themselves. If he forces students to accept one viewpoint as the *only* right one when there are several of more or less equal validity, he ceases to be an educator and becomes a propagandist.

Science can be sharply distinguished from propaganda. The scientist holds his conclusions tentatively and is willing to change if new evidence is presented. Experiment is the final check for a scientist. The propagandist wants no check on his conclusions. He is sure of them and he wants to make others sure of them, so they will do his bidding. Furthermore, the scientist tries to tell the whole truth whenever a complete treatment of a question would change the conclusions. Propaganda need not be a lie; it often succeeds very effectively with part truths.[18]

---

[18] *Science News Letter,* December 2, 1939, p. 367.

Fig. 88.   George Gallup, director of the American Institute of Public Opinion. Readers who are interested in public opinion polls and in analyses of consumers' attitudes may wish to read his book *The Pulse of Democracy* (Simon & Schuster, 1940).

Public opinion and straw polls.   In 1920 the *Literary Digest* sent out several million ballots in an unofficial attempt to predict who would be elected president.   Similar polls were conducted in 1924, 1928, and 1932.   The poll predicted the winner in each of these four presidential years.   In 1936, more than ten million ballots were mailed, but the poll failed to predict the winner.

In the same year, 1936, the American Institute of Public Opinion, under the direction of Dr. George Gallup,[19] made less than one hundred thousand interviews, yet forecast accurately the election of Roosevelt.   How did it happen that several thousand ballots were more accurate than millions?

The answer lies in two fundamental differences between the Institute's polls and the *Digest's:* selection of the sample and timing.   No straw poll regarding a national issue can possibly include all the people who will vote.   The expense would be prohibitive, and not everyone will answer and return an unofficial ballot.   Consequently it is necessary to select a sample of the population which represents the entire group.   The *Digest* se-

[19] G. H. Gallup and S. F. Rae, *The Pulse of Democracy: The Public Opinion Poll and How It Works.*   Simon & Schuster, 1940.

lected the people to whom ballots were sent from two sources: telephone books and car registrations. People with cars and telephones are also apt to have more money than those without. Hence the *Digest*, in most cases, got an *un*representative sample of the entire population, one which was predominantly Republican in sympathy.

The American Institute of Public Opinion uses scientific care in selecting its representative cross-sections. Six "controls" are used to make sure that the sample is like the entire electorate. There must be the same proportion of (1) voters from each state, (2) men and women, (3) urban, small-town, and rural residents, (4) age groups, (5) income groups, including people on relief, and (6) Democrats, Republicans, Socialists, Communists, and so on, as in the population at large. If one third of the voters in a state are farmers, then 33 per cent of the ballots must go to farmers. The same holds for the other controls. Control of the proportions in the sample are usually more easily maintained through personal interviews than through mailed questionnaires.

A second difference between the *Digest* and the Institute polls was in the time the ballots were sent out. Ballots which accurately reflect public opinion in the summer may not reflect it in the fall, since people change their preferences. The *Digest* sent out its ballots in the late spring and summer of 1936; the *Institute* kept sampling opinion up to a week before the election. In some later elections, polls by telegraph have been taken as late as the afternoon before election.

The two factors, representative sample and timing, reflect the difference between the unscientific and the scientific approach to the measurement of public opinion. Sheer numbers, though impressive to the layman, are seldom as accurate in this field as a minimum of numbers carefully selected.

Unfortunately, public opinion polls reveal only what people think in regard to certain very specific questions or persons. They do not reveal the conditions which may bring about major social changes. They seldom indicate basic trends nor how established trends may modify other trends.

The individual should, therefore, study trends and conditions as well as polls in order to become an intelligent participant in

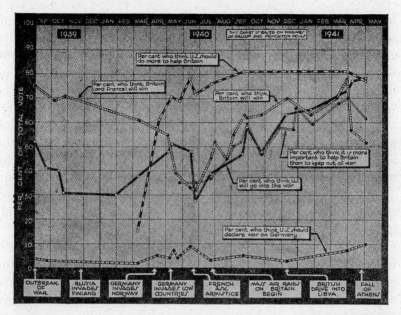

FIG. 89. *American Opinion and The War.* Chart based on findings of Gallup and Princeton polls. (*Courtesy of* The New York Times *and published in the May 11, 1941, issue.*)

his changing world. He cannot hope to steer the world to suit himself, but he can become well adjusted to his part of the world. Sometimes his psychological development, however excellent, may not be sufficient to solve his needs. Oppressive and painful situations may arise and overwhelm the well-adjusted individual, as has occurred in the recent history of the French, Belgian, Norwegian, Dutch, and other nations. Some men among these were undoubtedly of high psychological development, but they, as individuals, could only adapt themselves as well as possible to the existing conditions. Certainly those who had the most intelligent adaptability suffered least. As previously stated, the best insurance for the individual who seeks the resources whereby he may enjoy life is not wealth or power or fame, but adaptability. Adaptability to meet changing conditions is one outstanding requirement for happy living in this age.

No one can hope to turn earth into heaven. Utopia would be boresome if it could be found. Oppressions and injustices have always been a part of life and they will probably continue to be with us. However, being a victim of an oppressive or painful condition is not so oppressive or painful if one can feel himself a worthy participant in the changing order. To lose in a game that one does not understand—in which someone else seems to take all—is far more trying than to take part in a game in which all players know the rules and enjoy the game. The way out for the individual of today is not through a search for abundance by means of a politico-economic system nor through provision by others, but through intelligent participation in the affairs that concern him. That, incidentally, is one reason why many students are in college even though they do not realize it.

To summarize, intelligent participation in our social evolution can be achieved through attention to questions such as the following:

1. If we are now living in a period of social evolution that is following the pattern of former social evolutions, what is the current phase of the cycle? What preliminary symptoms have we experienced? What advanced symptoms, if any, have we experienced?

2. When we hear a threat that the submerged classes will start a revolution unless certain advocated reforms are made, are we frightened?

3. To what extent do increased government services and expenses, because of increased responsibility assumed by government for the welfare of the individual citizen, cause further psychological problems for the individual?

4. To what extent do increased percentages of our citizenry prefer to give up freedom in order to have security?

5. To what extent are the contributions of individual initiative hindered because of red tape, bureaucracy, and centralized authority without compensating effects from the centralization of power?

6. To what extent are the methods of propaganda being used to cover up deficiencies and to keep the established political party in power?

7. To what extent do public opinion polls portray the secular trends in our evolution?

8. To what extent do those persons who want to keep things as they are, or to return to times as they once were, represent

Fig. 90. Charles Bird, University of Minnesota. Readers interested in further study on the problem of incentives and motives should refer to his book *Social Psychology* (D. Appleton-Century Co., 1940).

refusals to adjust to inevitable changes? Do such individuals try to foresee what *will be* as distinct from what they think *ought* to be? To what extent is each motivated by adjustments of regression, projection, parent fixation, or other impulsion?

9. To what extent is our evolution moving toward a strengthening of character and personality of the individuals who belong to important interest groups such as those in the ranks of labor, management, students, government workers, and others. This question of direct attack adjustments on the part of the individual is more or less basic to all others in our evolution.

References

Albig, William, *Public Opinion*. McGraw-Hill Book Co., 1939.

Bernays, E. L., *Crystallizing Public Opinion*. Liveright Publishing Co., 1934.

Cantril, Hadley, *The Psychology of Social Movements*. John Wiley & Sons, 1941.

Childs, Harwood, *Propaganda and Dictatorship*. Princeton University Press, 1936.

Corey, Lewis, *The Decline of American Capitalism*. Covici-Friede, 1934.

Edwards, Lyford P., *The Natural History of Revolution*. University of Chicago Press, 1927.

Gallup, G. H., and Rae, S. F., *The Pulse of Democracy*. Simon & Schuster, 1940.

Lasswell, H. D., *Propaganda and Promotional Activities*. University of Minnesota Press, 1935.

Leighton, Joseph A., *Social Philosophies in Conflict*. D. Appleton-Century Co., 1937.

Nomad, Max, *Apostles of Revolution*. Little, Brown & Company, 1939.

Odegard, Peter, *The American Public Mind*. Columbia University Press, 1930.

Robinson, Claude, *Straw Votes*. Columbia University Press, 1932.

Smith, Charles W., *Public Opinion in a Democracy*. Prentice-Hall, Inc., 1939.

Projects

1. Read the editorials in two or three issues of each of the following and decide whether they tend to favor a free market economy or some form of state planning: *Saturday Evening Post, New Republic, Liberty, The New York Times, Social Justice,* New York *Herald Tribune.* Among those which favor some sort of state control, is there marked agreement as to means?

2. Suppose your college or university were divided on some issue of campus life such as supervision of fraternities, or the extent of student government, or football and its place on the campus. You want to conduct a straw poll to discover what the students think. What variables would you have to control in order to get an adequate representative sample?

3. Bring to class two examples of propaganda, preferably not from newspapers. Spend a period looking at all the propaganda brought.

4. Bring examples of recent public opinion polls to class and discuss the techniques of phrasing the questions.

5. In 1941 the Temporary National Economic Committee, after three years of study and the expenditure of more than one million dollars, made its report and concluded that a system of free private enterprises is the best system. Study recommendations in the report and note the extent to which war affected the carrying out of the recommendation. See *The United States News,* April 4, 1941, and *Business Week,* March 22, 1941, for summaries of the committee's work.

6. Which of the following would you designate as genuine social revolutions?

> The American Civil War.
> The Spanish war between the Loyalists and Franco.
> The Mexican revolution of Francisco Villa.
> The Bolshevist revolution in Russia.
> The Turkish revolution of Kemal Attaturk.
> The Chinese revolution of Sun Yat Sen.
> The Boer War.
> The German revolution of 1918.

Give the reasons for your classification. How would you characterize those which were not genuine social revolutions?

7. Which of the preliminary or advanced symptoms of revolution mentioned by Gould do you find in the United States at present? Suggest reasons for the absence of any you believe not present.

8. Study several paragraphs of a political speech or a propaganda article. Tabulate the number of times each of the seven propaganda techniques mentioned in this chapter are used. Which appear to be used the most effectively? Do you think any of the devices can be used legitimately? If so, give examples.

PART SIX

Influencing the Behavior of the Group

22

Supervising Employees—
Attitudes and Their Measurement

<hr>

Five thousand years ago an ancient Egyptian by the name of
Ptah-Hotep wrote:

"If you are in the position of one to whom petitions are made, be
courteous and listen to the petitioner's story. Do not stop his words
until he has poured out all that is in his heart and has said all that he
came to say. A man with a grievance loves the official who will accept what he states and let him talk out his trouble fully. A kind
word will illuminate his heart, but if an official stops the flow of his
words people will say, 'Why should that fellow have the power to
behave this way?'" [1]

A PROFESSOR who is a student of labor problems described the following experience to illustrate one aspect of
the worker's attitude toward his job. "The other evening I left
my University office after the building had been closed to the
general public and students. As I stepped outside, I met the
night watchman on his rounds. It so happened that two of the
windows in a laboratory had been left open. I suggested to the
watchman that he close the windows to prevent harm to the
building or to possible experiments that might be in process.
His answer was: 'Nope. I don't close no windows. That's the
janitor's job. I ain't supposed to do his work.' Yesterday I
noticed that one of the faucets in the same building was leaking
badly. I happened to pass one of the janitors and mentioned it
to him. His reply was: 'I hain't got nothin' to do with them
faucets. That room belongs to the other janitor. Once I reported a telephone box off in one of the other janitor's rooms and
was told that it was none of my business and that I should tend

---

[1] Quoted from Glenn Gardiner, *How to Handle Grievances*. Elliott Service Co.,
1937.

to my own work. Since then I keep my mouth shut unless it's part of my job.' "

The psychology of the employee. Much has been written about the psychology of the laborer, and incidents of that type are often quoted as evidence of fundamental psychological differences between employers or managers and laborers or employees. However, the mental make-up of the employers is the same as that of employees. Both employees and employers have the same mental traits. Their behavior differs chiefly in that they react to different situations. Some department heads and high-grade executives have been heard to say what the watchman and the janitor said, except that the executives applied the statement to different situations.

Executives, employees, and stockholders have the same psychological characteristics. Most of the conflicts between employers and employees are not the rumblings significant of a history-making class conflict. The points of friction usually boil down to simple individual grievances. Sometimes the grievances have a great deal of accumulated annoyance but their origins and perpetuation are likely to be in the nature of commonplaces. Small commonplaces often become the basis of monstrous misunderstandings.

As Whiting Williams has pointed out, the high-powered economics discussed by the typical dissatisfied but vocal worker is likely to end in statements regarding specific grievances such as:

1. Unfair, dishonest, or hard-boiled foremen (or)
2. No seniority rules to protect the longer-service workers against the foreman's favoritism in discharges or layoffs (or)
3. A wage system too complicated to permit a worker figuring out his day's pay.[2]

Additional grievances that have occurred are giving orders without reasons, ignoring complaints, inadequate instructions, appropriating credit for a workman's idea, uncongenial fellow workers, "high hat" methods of paying employees on pay days, and the same big and little causes of friction that may arise between any two individuals when working together.

The industrial relations interview. The Western Electric Co. developed a systematic plan of interviewing for learning what

---

[2] Whiting Williams, "What the Workers Want," *Scribners*, February 1938, p. 43.

the employees really thought of their jobs, working conditions, fellow employees, supervisors, and their company.

Men were interviewed by men; women were interviewed by women. When the interviewers used prepared questions, the employee often wandered away from the questions and discussed some other matter, seemingly irrelevant but actually very important to the employee. The use of prepared questions was discontinued and the employee was encouraged to talk, not only about grievances toward the management but about any personal matters which bothered him. Gradually, the industrial relations interviewers' techniques were improved, as described by Roethlisberger:

During the period from 1928 to 1930, members of the industrial relations staff of the Hawthorne Plant of the Western Electric Company interviewed some 20,000 employees. In the beginning they hoped to get "facts" in the strict sense. From these data they hoped to improve working conditions and company policy. But what they did get from the interviews was an inextricable mixture of fact and sentiment. This outpouring of human sentiments could not be used in the simple fashion originally conceived. However, it is to the credit of management that they did not throw this material into the rubbish heap. They began to see that sentiments, when properly understood and interpreted, constituted social data of the greatest importance.

Probably one of the most interesting developments of this interviewing program was the experience which the interviewers themselves received and in turn communicated to supervisors. When some of the more enterprising of the interviewers realized the nature of the material they were eliciting from employees, they began to devise rules and techniques for ferreting out and trying to understand the employees' sentiments. Curiously enough, the very rules they devised to improve their interviewing technique, they found were easily translatable into simple rules for the supervisor in handling his personal relations. These rules apply to the first-line supervisor as well as to the higher executive in his relation to individuals with whom he has face-to-face contacts.

The first rule is that the supervisor should listen patiently to what his subordinate has to say before making any comment himself. Probably the quickest way to stop a person from sufficiently expressing himself is to interrupt. Of course, it follows that, besides actively listening and not interrupting, the supervisor should try to understand what his subordinate is saying. Moreover, he should show his interest in what is being said.

The second rule is that the supervisor should refrain from hasty disapprobation of his subordinate's conduct. It is not his business, in the first instance at least, to give advice or moral admonition. If the employee says, "This is a hell of a company to work for," the attitude of the supervisor should not be, "Tut, tut, my good man, you are not displaying the proper spirit." Instead, he should try to get the employee to express himself more fully by asking why he feels as he does. In many instances employees by themselves are not able to state precisely the particular source of their dissatisfaction, but if they are encouraged to talk freely the effect is not merely emotional relief but also the revelation to the critical listener and (sometimes even to the speaker himself) of the locus of the complaint.

The third rule is that the supervisor should not argue with his subordinates. It is futile to try to change sentiments by logic. The best way for the supervisor to avoid arguments is to see that the employees' sentiments do not act on his own. It will be remembered that, when Bill told his employer that his piece rates were too low, he acted upon his employer's sentiments. The employer felt that he had to defend his wage rates.

The fourth rule is that the supervisor should not pay exclusive attention to the manifest content of the conversation. The interviewers had discovered that there is a tendency to rationalize sentiments and that in ordinary social intercourse the participants are likely to become more interested in the truth of the rationalizations than in the sentiments that are being expressed. Bill's employer, it will be remembered, paid attention only to the manifest content of Bill's complaint, with the result that he failed to learn anything about Bill's personal situation.

The fifth rule is that the supervisor should listen not only to what a person wants to say but also to what he does not want to say or cannot say without assistance. A person has difficulty in talking about matters which are associated with unpleasant and painful experiences, and many sentiments tend to remain so much in the background of a person's thinking that he is unaware of them. It is important to listen for what a person regards as so obvious and so common that it never occurs to him to doubt or question it. These implicit assumptions are of the greatest importance in assessing a person's values and significances. . . .

In short, then, as a result of interviewing experience at Hawthorne, a new conception of leadership was developed. This conception began to percolate to the higher ranks of supervision and to the higher executives of the company. They found that one of their functions as supervisors and managers was to listen to, and become better acquainted with, the sentiments of their employees and with the nature of that social structure, or system of sentiments, called the "company." They began to see that each industrial concern had a social structure, that this social structure was related to the wider social structure of the community. They began to see that it was very important for them to understand their own social structure, for this structure defined the limits and degree of collaboration. When they listened to the complaints of their employees, they realized they were listening to the creakings and groanings of their own social structure. When they saw the newly arrived young college man "making an ass of himself," annoyed at the "red tape" which seemed to block his movements at every turn, they began to realize they were watching the painful adaptations of a logically tutored individual to a complicated social structure with which he was unacquainted. They began to understand better the battered and mutilated state in which their own neat plans and policies finally reached the worker, after having been transmitted through an elaborate supervisory hierarchy. Also they began to understand better why the reports they received from their immediate subordinates as to what was happening at the front line, after having been transmitted through an elaborate supervisory hierarchy, did not quite coincide with what they learned from the interviewing program.[3]

The company has developed a permanent personnel-counseling procedure.[4] Approximately 300 employees are assigned to each counselor. The average length of time for the interviews is 80 minutes. All findings are strictly confidential so far as names of employees are concerned in the making of complaints. Only the complaints are given to the management. The few employees who do not care to be interviewed are not interviewed.

The skilled industrial relations interviewer can spot many misunderstandings, grievances, and personal problems which can often be cleared up through frank discussion. When the employee talks himself out and achieves a psychological integration with his working relations, he tends to have fewer frustrations, obsessions, and feelings of fatigue. He feels that he "belongs" and that he is in control of himself in relation to his world.

Attitude scales. Several psychologists have done considerable research work in devising scales and schedules which are designed to reveal the nature and causes of dissatisfaction and satisfaction in the attitudes of employees. See Table XXXIII for excerpts from one carefully developed scale of this kind.

TABLE XXXIII[5]

Attitude Statement	Scale Value (Factor 10)
I am made to feel that I am really a part of this organization.......	9.72
I can feel reasonably sure of holding my job as long as I do good work	8.33
I can usually find out how I stand with my boss..................	7.00
On the whole, the company treats us about as well as we deserve....	6.60
I think training in better ways of doing the job should be given to all employees of the company.....................................	4.72
I have never understood just what the company's personnel policy is	4.06
In my job, I don't get any chance to use my experience...........	3.18
I can never find out how I stand with my boss...................	2.77
A large number of the employees would leave here if they could get as good jobs elsewhere..	1.67
I think the company's policy is to pay employees just as little as it can get away with...	0.80

[3] F. J. Roethlisberger, "Understanding: A Prerequisite of Leadership," appearing in *Business & Modern Society,* by Malcolm P. McNair and Howard T. Lewis. Harvard University Press, 1938. See also *Personnel Journal,* Vol. 14, No. 9. Reprinted by permission of the President and Fellows of Harvard College.

[4] Stuart Chase, "What Makes the Worker Like to Work? A Great Corporation Discovers that the Stop Watch Killeth, but the Spirit Giveth Life," *Readers' Digest,* February 1941.

[5] Harold B. Bergen, "Finding Out What Employees Are Thinking," *The Conference Board Management Record,* April 1939.

FIG. 91.   Erland Nelson, Newberry College. Readers who are interested in further study on the problem of attitudes should refer to his article, "Attitudes: Their Nature and Measurement," *Journal of General Psychology*, 1939, Vol. 21, pp. 367–436.

These examples are taken from an attitude scale consisting of fifty statements arranged in haphazard order in the questionnaire. Instructions were printed, requesting the employee to check only those statements with which he agreed.

The range of values in the attitude scale, while statistically reliable, must be recognized as arbitrary. For the purpose of interpreting results, therefore, it will help to multiply each scale value by 10 and to think of the possible scores as ranging roughly from 0 to 100.

Unfortunately, some of the academic psychologists have become so enthralled by the statistical aspects of developing attitude scales that they have ignored the spirit of their use. An attitude scale can be psychologically worth while only when it is first developed by the co-operative action of management and employees. The nature of the scale or schedule is not so important as having employees or their representatives participate in the construction of the device which is used in the study of their attitudes and grievances. Several studies of this kind have been made.

E. B. Roberts has reported some results of the use of such a co-operatively developed audit of employee morale:

The plant is located in an industrial town of moderate size. There are about 2,500 employees, of whom 2,000 are hourly paid and 500 salary paid. The work is of a range requiring every degree of skill. The salary-paid workers include clerks, draftsmen, engineers, accountants, a sales force and all the usual service departments. It is a well-rounded, self-contained unit that might well be a small company independent of other units. Its product is a capital goods product that is sold in a highly competitive field. The employee group is that of a normal Western Pennsylvania community. The average service is perhaps ten years or even a little longer. At the time the test was made (April 1938) business was good without being either brisk or depressed. There was no labor crisis of any sort. Pay rates and takeout, both salary and hourly, were high—above the level of community average. . . .

Scores for the whole range of questions we call *Morale Scores*. One hundred per cent would be perfect, with a possible range downward to 0. The *Morale Scores* by groups were as follows:

Managerial Groups
    Foremen.. 87.7
    Production..................................... 74.2
    Engineering................................... 71.2
    Sales—Accounting—Order—etc.................. 78
Entire Salary Group 71.1 (Ranging by depts. from 63.8 to 86.3)
Entire Check (hourly) Group 72.6 (Ranging by depts. from 63 to 80)

Much discussion might grow out of these figures considered on a departmental or functional basis. Some illuminating discussion might grow out of the following findings:

The markedly greater range of departmental scores for the salary than for the hourly groups.

The relatively high score of foremen.

The relatively low score of technical departments.

Also there is much for management to consider in the over-all response to some of the specific questions. For instance:

Does the belief on the part of only 29 per cent of the workers that the best qualified people are promoted to better jobs indicate the desirability not only of keeping careful individual qualification records, but a wider dissemination of information about openings and more careful detailing of reasons for promotion where this is practicable?

Does the satisfaction of only 37 per cent of the workers with methods of setting base pay indicate the need of a more extensive job analysis to insure that comparable demands, both physical and mental, are met with comparable pay?

Does the belief of only 39 per cent that pay increases come when deserved, prompt more careful and effective salary and rate reviews and a more thorough dissemination of information about them?

About 41 per cent of the workers thought that no department was favored more than others.

Does the belief on the part of only 30 per cent of the workers that they are judged more by the quality than by the quantity of their work again prompt analysis of jobs and the suitable recognition of the quality aspects of them?

Does the conviction on the part of only 37 per cent of the employees that they never get contradictory nor conflicting orders show the need for attention to the correcting of hazy authority and responsibility lines?

Departmental scores certainly served to reveal not only "sore spots," but "hot subjects." Some of these could be and were cured almost overnight. Merely the attention of "first-aid" was all that was needed. . . .

The report showed that the morale at this plant—the general satisfaction of employees—is above the average of organizations in which parallel studies have been made. It showed that the most important desires of employees are connected with good work. It showed that the strongest influence on general satisfaction is the opportunity for an individual to do the kind of work he would like to do. It showed that the things most injurious to his morale are those which prevent doing good work. The report emphasized the necessity of "fairness" but also the need for agreement on what the elements of "fairness" are by a study of organization and individual jobs—the putting down accurately, in writing, of the nature of the jobs. In addition to these points it showed the desire, though unexpressed, on the part of the individual, to be treated as an individual on the basis of his merits and the worth of what he is able to do.

Summing up results, I should say that a good Management armed with policy of high level found:

1. That it should promote more carefully
2. That it should watch out for favoritism
3. That it has been ineffective in informing employees
4. That it should re-study its work in definition of jobs, positions, and organization lines
5. That it is placing too much emphasis on tangibles and neglecting intangibles—that things alone are not enough—that "wages and hours and working conditions" are not everything—that workers want psychological satisfactions as well as material satisfactions. . . .

An objective audit of employee morale and attitudes can be helpful and stimulating to Management as well. Management may try to give its people every possible consideration and may feel that its policies are fair and liberal. Yet it is extremely difficult to know just how these policies are regarded by the workers. No matter how well intentioned a policy may be, it is only as good as the employees think it is.[6]

The use of an audit of the employee's attitudes and morale is exceedingly helpful in revealing to the management the extent to which its imagined altruism is or is not appreciated. The writer has used with effective results the schedule appearing on pages 758 to 761. The use of this schedule and related lists of questions in one company resulted in Table XXXIV, showing the percentages of employees who were and were not satisfied with their placement within the company. The employees' job

---

[6] From *Office Personnel Administration*, Office Management Series Number 84, published by the American Management Association, 1938.

dissatisfactions were largely the reflection of the lack of any worthwhile personnel program or department. The man who had the title of personnel director was also the comptroller of the company, a former officer of the Marines, and an example of adjustment by means of "closed mind compartments." Eventually another man was appointed to take his place.

Results of surveys of attitudes. Psychologists and others who have made researches of industrial relations by means of attitude scales and similar morale audits often find the following:

1. *Grievances.* Many workers react more intensively in terms of things that annoy them than in terms of what management does for them. Workers express their grievances freely, frequently, and with intensity if they feel that they are free to do so.

Workers react to specific factors in the work situation. The writer made an attitude study of the office employees of one company and found that the most important problem to many of the women employees was the rough corners on the office desks. The women were tearing their stockings on the desk splinters.

TABLE XXXIV

SUMMARY OF EMPLOYEE PREFERENCES REGARDING PLACEMENT AS FOUND IN ONE COMPANY HAVING 323 EMPLOYEES

		Per Cent	
1.	Percentage of employees who are completely *satisfied* regarding the department in which they are employed..................	32	
2.	Percentage of employees who are *satisfied* with the department where they are now, but have also named one other department in which they would be equally satisfied....................	6	
	Total *satisfied*.................................		38%
3.	Percentage of employees who are *dissatisfied* with the department where they are now and have indicated a department where they would be happier.....................................	34	
4.	Percentage of employees who are *dissatisfied* with the department in which they are now but are not certain as to which one of two or more departments they would like to be transferred	12	
	Total *dissatisfied*.............................		46
5.	Percentage of employees who failed to indicate their choices; most of these employees were too old to want a transfer or too recently employed to know what they preferred..............	16	
			100%

Several women had complained about the situation and the supervisor had asked the janitor to correct the situation. The janitor sandpapered the corners of the desks but new splinters always appeared in a few weeks. The girls had grown tired of making the same complaint and having the same ineffective remedy applied. Accordingly, the morale score for the department was low partly because their annoyance over an incidental factor had spread to other aspects of the work situation. When the department head realized how the girls felt and why, he corrected the difficulty by means of a few dollars' worth of rubber over the offending desk corners.

2. *Workers are greatly concerned about what their fellow workers think of them.* Managers often fail to appreciate that a workman's allegiance is bound to be felt more strongly toward his fellow workers and friends than toward the company. T. North Whitehead has reported considerable evidence of this fact as found in the Western Electric Company's Hawthorne plant studies of industrial relations.

One of these studies has been described briefly on pages 420-423 of this book. It related to a group of five women who performed routine assembly work. The girls worked together in a small room for about five years; they were skilled workers; they were paid on a system of group piece-work. Very detailed reports of output, physical conditions, and social relations were made, and among other interesting facts it was found that output began to rise only when the girls began to form friendships within the group. Also, individual weekly fluctuations of output did not correlate with any recorded physical circumstances such as room temperature. Rather, the fluctuations in output synchronized with the extent to which any two girls developed an interest in one another. The interplay of social relations within the group definitely influenced the morale and efficiency of the workers. The girls increased markedly their output in the course of the experiment.

However, the same company conducted an experiment with fifteen young men who did wiring, soldering, and inspecting of electrical apparatus, and obtained quite different results from those found in the experiment with the women workers.

Nine wiremen were organized in three groups of three men.

Each group of three wiremen had one solderman. Two inspectors judged the work of these twelve men, and one supervisor was in charge of the fourteen employees. All fifteen men worked together in a small shop. Payment was on the basis of group piecework. Within the group, the supervisor had the highest official status, the inspectors ranked second, the nine wiremen third, and the three soldermen lowest. However, a more elaborate social organization soon developed. The group split into two cliques. These cliques were not divided according to the social status levels but cut across one of the wiring groups and across the various occupations. Each clique had its own leader.

The customs that developed within the group related mainly to the organization and performance of the work. Output and performance of the work were soon controlled through the customs which developed among the men. Certain levels of output from each individual were decided upon and controlled by the men themselves. They maintained their output at the levels they determined through breakdowns, interruptions, and other behavior that wasted time. If any worker indicated that he was exceeding his allowance of work, he was "disciplined" by the others. The supervisor, too, was more or less forced to accede to the workers' control. The control of output which was exercised by the workers was largely for the purpose of protecting the group from managerial interference. They jealously guarded what they believed to be their rights and privileges as workers. However, the workers were not protecting themselves against economic injustice but against social ignorance on the part of management.

The contrasting results of the experiment with the two groups of workers of the same company, the five girls versus the fifteen men, cannot be attributed to a sex difference but rather to the fact that the girls' group ways and sentiments were integrated to a much greater extent with the economic purposes of the management.

One lesson revealed and emphasized by the experiment with the fifteen men is that the administrator should appear to the members as one who is guarding and developing *their* life and the emotional character of *their* group, rather than representing only the economic policies and wishes of the management. The men resisted outside threats to the character of *their* group. This suggests that an executive should not only promote the efficiency of his employees but should also guard and develop their social sentiments toward each other.[7]

Industrial workers have a group consciousness. They are loyal to their fellow workers. They recognize a gap between themselves and the executives and professional workers. Many of them are descendants of men who were grossly mistreated by executives of a generation or two ago. Some of the old men who recite their tales of abuse were treated cruelly by perhaps but one employer. Yet that one unfair employer becomes a symbol of employers in general. As with all of us, the dramatic instance outweighs an overwhelming array of opposing figures. Horrible accidents to fellow-workers knit the others closer together. Poverty and mistreatment of workers in other parts of the world arouse a sympathetic feeling and accentuate the group consciousness. Need we marvel that the labor union leader is a welcome messenger?

This group allegiance does not mean that an executive should judge employees according to one standard and his associates by another standard. Rather, the executive must treat employees as associates and raise them up to where they can understand some of the problems of management. We do not develop children into strong adults by keeping them only with other children and treating them as children. No, we prepare them for adulthood by gradually treating them as adults and by giving them grown-up problems and situations to meet. A similar policy guides the business leader who merits his position and wishes to meet his responsibilities to society and future business prosperity.

3. *Most workers do not want important jobs.* Responsibility or more important work is surprisingly seldom desired by the lower ranks of workers. The worker does not feel any too certain of his present job. Why should he seek more difficult problems? When he reads about "the heights by great men

---

[7] T. North Whitehead, "Social Motives in Economic Activities," *Occupational Psychology*, Vol. XII, No. 4, Autumn, 1938. See also, F. J. Roethlisberger and W. J. Dickson, *Management and the Worker*, Chapters XXII-XXIII. Harvard University Press, 1941.

reached and kept," as captains of industry are described in the inspirational magazine articles, he does not see any relationship between the efforts of those masters and his own position and opportunities. Like all human beings, he rationalizes and believes that "pull" is what lifts all men above the lower rungs of the ladder. He sees no chance of breaking through. True, he knows that he could attract the attention of the boss by working a little harder or a little longer than his fellows, but that would brand him among his friends as a "bootlicker," a "sucker," or a "tool of the capitalists." Moreover, he may have tried it once and have done the wrong thing and the boss may have given him "hell" for his well-meant efforts. Besides, some of the old men of the shop who have grown gray in the company's service seem to be getting just about the same pay that he is getting.

4. *The immediate supervisor is the most potent representative of management.* He, rather than the major officials of the company, influences attitudes by his personality, mannerisms, ability, and personal leadership.

The corporation and business as a whole are personified in the foremen who are over the employees. The workman has no profound philosophies or attitudes regarding the splendid service that his company and he are rendering society by the work that is done in the shop. The part he plays in the manufacturing of the company's product is so isolated and infinitesimal that he cannot idealize his labor. His job has no halo. He does not work for an abstract principle but for a very ordinary foreman who is just as human as he. To the factory employee, the company is "but the lengthened shadow" of the foreman. Psychologically, the worker is in a state of readiness for a precipitating stimulus that will give an outlet for his dammed-up feelings. The foreman may be an able man, but he is in a difficult position. His simplest criticism of error when handling a workman may release an accumulation of feeling or action that is wholly out of proportion to the seriousness of the foreman's offense. Truly, the foreman needs much training for his job, in order that he may fulfill his function in one of the key positions in industry.

5. *Industrial workers react to problems of management regarding concrete aspects.* Industrial employees are of lower

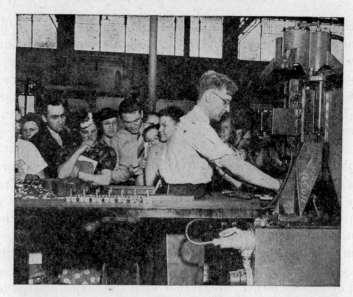

Interesting machine operations were included in Western Electric's Hawthorne Works "Open House" itinerary. This machine welds together cobalt steel magnets and permalloy cores for receiver coils.

Mother and the neighbors get an entirely different opinion of modern shop conditions on an "Open House" tour.

FIG. 92. Western Electric Company held "Open House" for employees, employees' families, friends and the public. Total attendance for the two-week period was 46,013 persons. Along the entire route which was roped off, visitors found at each operation signs with brief

Quality of the product was emphasized by showing visitors the exhaustive tests Western Electric equipment receives to insure that it will stand up in service.

Fun must be part of an "Open House" program and Western Electric provided it by giving members of "the family" a chance to listen to their own voices.

descriptions of the operation. The guide book offered more detailed information to those who wished it. Piece parts produced on the various machines also were displayed to show stock and finished parts.

Fig. 93. Glenn Gardiner, Forstmann Woolen Co., Passaic, N. J. Readers interested in the study of foremanship and related problems are referred to his book *Better Foremanship* (McGraw-Hill Book Co., 1941).

general intelligence than the managers. In the studies of army occupational intelligence levels, as shown in figure 56, it was evident that unskilled laborers, as a group, were of definitely lower intelligence than the skilled workers, the skilled workers were of lower grade than the office workers, and the men of managerial ability were of the highest grade. In intelligence, the corporals in the army were slightly above the privates, the sergeants above the corporals, and the lieutenants above the sergeants. Of course, many privates in the army were more intelligent than some of the colonels, but the masses of each class differed appreciably. These differences in intelligence should be recognized by executives when dealing with factory and office employees. The employees have a limited view of business. They cannot appreciate the problems of management and they develop distorted convictions of the operations and profits of business.

One of the easiest ways of making a satisfied employee dissatisfied is constantly used by the labor agitator. His conversation with the contented employee is of this variety:

"Well, Bill, how much you makin' on this job?"

IT WORKS THIS WAY

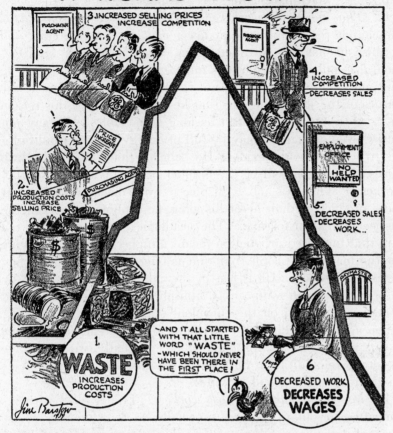

Fig. 94. Cartoon from *General Electric News*, published Friday of each week by the General Electric Company in the interest of the employees of the Schenectady Works. Taken from the June 2, 1939, issue.

"Oh, not so bad. Made nine dollars yesterday."

"That ain't bad for your job, but think of what the company made on that. Them gears you cut yesterday will be sold for $122 to the customer. You see what you get. Look at what they get. Figure it out for yourself. Is it right?"

Most industrial workers are so low in abstract intelligence that they have no appreciation of the costs of producing and selling commodities. They know little or nothing of the expense of selling, advertising, financing, managing, and so on. They estimate costs in the most naïve manner. To them, the purchasing power of the dollar, wages, and politics are the result of the capitalist's machinations or "big business."

6. *The industrial worker "feels" much and reasons little.* He cannot reason, because of lower capacity for reasoning and because he has not the facts from which to reason. His elemental impulses and emotions must govern him. The job is to him most important. He is not so greatly concerned about the nature of the job as the fact that he has a job. For this reason he tries to have the job last as long as possible. He may not hurry, even though he may be full of energy that he would prefer to let loose on the job. He believes that the less he produces, the greater will be the number of jobs available to other workers. When his job is displaced by a machine that is far more productive than he or his gang, he cannot understand the justice of his misfortune. The academic economists may tell him that increased production means a higher standard of living for the masses of people, but that is offering him a stone when he asks for bread. He is lost in the changes being wrought by the new American tempo. To himself, he appears to be tossed about as driftwood on the turbulent sea. Can we blame him? When a war has ended, the government must rehabilitate some of our veterans. It is probable that, eventually, we shall have to set up rehabilitation bureaus to readjust the veterans of industry to the changes of our times.

7. *Life is insecure for most workers.* Life is filled with insecurities for all of us, but especially so for the man whose sweated brow marks his position in the industrial and social scale. His job is insecure in the presence of the "robots" of business, the many mergers, the possibilities of ill health, and the whimsicalities of executives whose word is law. The worker is not blind to these ever-present menaces to his job.

One winter afternoon, the writer called at the office of a personnel manager of a large industrial firm. During our pleasant chat an elderly working man came into the office, with tears in his eyes, and said to the executive: "I know I didn't do what I should 'a' done, but I'm willin' to do the right thing. I'm sorry." He took his discharge slip and left. This workman was a skilled worker who had taken excellent care of the company's many elevators for twelve years. That morning he came to work as usual, but one of the main elevators that transported factory employees happened to be out of order. He worked feverishly to get it repaired. While he was working, various employees kept ringing the bell in spite of the card that hung at the shaft on each floor which stated that the elevator was out of order. In the midst of his labors, some one continued to ring the bell. Exasperated, he yelled several words of profanity up the shaft to the "boob" who kept ringing the bell. The "boob" happened to be one of the company's young executives, and the repairman was immediately discharged. Hundreds of incidents of this type happen every day, and we shall always have them, but the workman who sees or experiences them realizes the insecurity of his job, and he sometimes harbors a bitter feeling of injustice when he notes how his job is lost while the executive is smiled at when he smashes his golf club merely because the ball sliced into the woods. His feelings are most bitter when he believes that he may be spied upon by hired company detectives who are disguised, or when he imagines that a discharge places him on a black list. To such a worker the whole scheme of society and industry is unjust.

Labor information by and to employees. In view of the situation in which laborers find themselves, it is only natural that they should want to present their side of industrial relations questions to the public. As a form of self-expression, they use the lobbyist, the labor union leader, printed matter, and the great eruptive protest—the strike. Employers have their trade associations and their representatives in legislative halls. Laborers use the same social tools. The labor union organizer deals with the workman's most vital interests. He is often a better student of labor psychology than the employer, for the organizer directs his appeals to the worker's problems and interests. And labor has developed a fairly extensive scheme of propaganda. True, it is not so formidable as it might be if it were well organized, but it is worth noting.

According to a directory prepared by the University of Wisconsin and released by the American Council of Public Affairs, 10,000,000 persons regularly read newspapers or magazines published by U. S. labor unions or affiliated groups. All told, there are 676 such publications. Out of that number 327 are official

A. F. of L. branch organs and 110 are published by C. I. O. units. Communists and other left wingers print 29. Unclassified are 131.[8]

It is fair to say that, on the average, each one of the country's unionized workers gets at least one labor paper. This may be either the official organ of the international union to which he belongs, a local labor body publication, or the paper of the state federation. In most cases, union dues entitle the member to a subscription. Distribution is usually through the mail or by hand-out at union meetings. In most cases the paper is taken home, carefully and sometimes laboriously read and reread, for labor editors fill their sheets with information close to the interests of their readers. About half of these publications accept local and national advertising.

The labor press is frankly propagandistic, in fact supplementing the never-ending organizing work which many unions conduct. The function of the labor press is to bring workers information about their trade and industry and to interpret for them their economic interests in such affairs.[9] On the whole, they see their job as counteracting what they consider to be the "anti-labor bias" of the daily press, the radio, and movies, and anchoring the member's loyalty to his union.

Only a handful of labor papers are self-supporting. Most are subsidized by unions whether or not they have official status, and this explains their stereotyped character. Until a few years ago their mortality rate was high. A union falling on lean days, anxious to pare its expenses, and thinking of its paper as a luxury, would fold it early in a campaign of retrenchment.[10]

Legitimate methods of telling the employer's side to labor. Many executives assume that once error has been exposed, truth has been established. Actually, no point in employee education is ever disposed of. It will simply crop up the next day in another form. No criticism is ever really answered; someone did not hear or read the answer. No case ever is proved; rebuttal is eternal.[11] The management of every plant uses some means

---

[8] "Labor Data," *Tide*, October 1, 1940.
[9] *Business Week*, October 5, 1940, p. 58.
[10] *Business Week*, October 5, 1940, p. 58.
[11] "The Trading Post," *Business Week*, August 12, 1939. Editorial by W. T. C.

TABLE XXXV[12]

A CAPITULATION OF REPLIES

	Per Cent Yes	Per Cent No
Do you like your work or would you prefer some other occupation?...........................	65 like	35 dislike
Are you experienced and qualified for some other occupations?...............................	39	61
If married, is your wife or husband satisfied with your present employment? (63% married, 37% not married)...............................	65	35
Do you think your employer can afford to pay better wages to all out of the profits the company makes?	69*	25*
If so, how much MORE per week do you think you should be paid?............................	$4.87**	
Do you KNOW approximately how much money your company made or lost last year?..............	29	71
Have you seen a recent statement of your company's financial situation . . . or has an official talked to groups of employees about it?..............	27	73
Would you be interested in knowing more about the finances of your company and how it is run?....	76	21
Do you ever talk man-to-man with any of the officials of your company other than the foremen?...	34	66
Do you belong to a union?......................	53	47
If so, do you feel that your union is helping you?...	79	21
If you were convinced that your employer had your interest at heart, would you rather negotiate direct with him or through a labor organization?......	61 direct	37 labor
Do you think there is a chance for advancement in the future?.................................	46	51
Would you take another, similar job, not knowing the conditions under which you would work, if you were offered $2.00 more per wk.?...........	36	64
Excepting those advantages that would be costly for your company to install, do you think the management is doing its best to make working conditions pleasant?............................	65	35
If invited by the management, would you join a committee and take an active part in helping your employer find ways to make the business a better one . . . even if it meant sacrificing some of your own free time?...............................	88	12
Would you attend classes, on your own time, to learn more about the business if the instruction was offered free by your employer?.................	78	19

[12] From "Employe-Employer Relations," a survey of employee opinions conducted in Philadelphia by Remsen J. Cole and Associates, 1940.

* Where the aggregate percentage of "Yes" and "No" replies does not reach 100 per cent, the difference is compensated for by those who have no opinion or did not reply to the question.

** The wage increase average is based on the total number of workers surveyed, including those who do not feel that they should receive more money as well as those who do.

of imparting the company's directions, wishes, and reasons why the workers should be kindly disposed toward their employer. Some of these channels of distributing information to employees should be given more careful attention by managements.

The fact that employees welcome information about the business has been proved over and over again. Unfortunately, too many employers fail to realize that their own knowledge must be passed out to employees repeatedly and in a mutually respectful manner. One of the most extensive cross-sectional surveys of employee-employer relations was made of Philadelphia employees by Remsen J. Cole and Associates. A capitulation of their findings is shown in Table XXXV. Their survey revealed a direct relation between having seen a financial statement of the company and a favorable attitude toward the job. A 58 per cent improvement in attitude toward jobs was found among the informed employees. See Table XXXVI.

The following cross-capitulation proves most conclusively that there is a distinct relation between a comprehensive knowledge of company finances and other factors that contribute to or indicate an employee's attitude toward his job, employer, and company.

TABLE XXXVI[13]

The Importance of the Financial Statement

		Of the 27% who have seen financial statement		Of the 73% who have not seen financial statement	
1.	Like their jobs	Yes 81%	No 19%	Yes 59%	No 41%
2.	Think employer can pay more...	44	44	78	18
3.	Would negotiate direct	85	11	52	47
4.	See opportunity for advancement	67	33	39	58
5.	Would quit for $2 more per week	8	92	47	53
6.	Find working conditions pleasant	85	15	58	42
7.	Criticize company policies	52	48	62	38
8.	Average wage increase desired	$3.07		$5.53	

There is an increase of 12 per cent among those who like their jobs when informed of finances in a regular company report rather than depending upon outside, unofficial sources for the information. Similarly, the employee's belief that his employer can pay higher wages decreases proportionally in this group.

Sound financial information apparently eliminates almost completely the

[13] From "Employe-Employer Relations," a survey of employee opinion conducted in Philadelphia by Remsen J. Cole and Associates, 1940.

HOW GENERAL MILLS TELLS EMPLOYES OF ITS ACTIVITIES

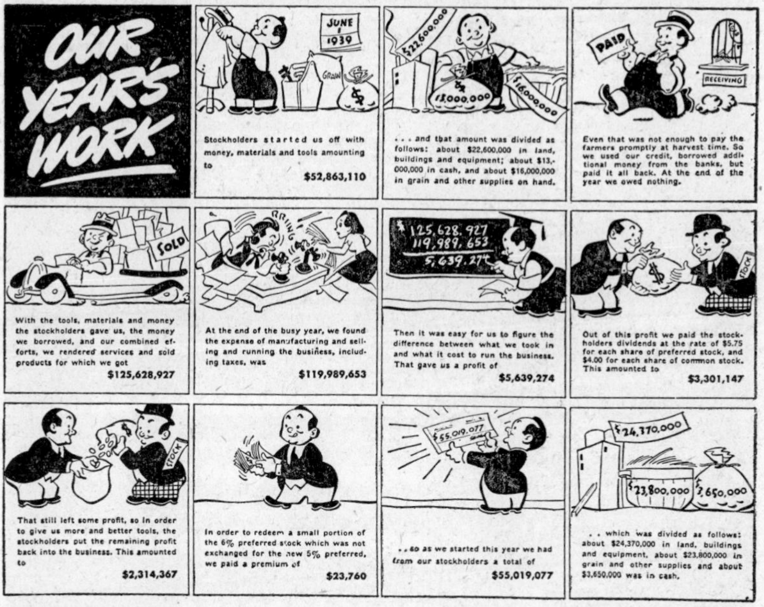

OUR YEAR'S WORK

Stockholders started us off with money, materials and tools amounting to **$52,863,110**

... and that amount was divided as follows: about $22,600,000 in land, buildings and equipment; about $13,000,000 in cash, and about $16,000,000 in grain and other supplies on hand.

Even that was not enough to pay the farmers promptly at harvest time. So we used our credit, borrowed additional money from the banks, but paid it all back. At the end of the year we owed nothing.

With the tools, materials and money the stockholders gave us, the money we borrowed, and our combined efforts, we rendered services and sold products for which we got **$125,628,927**

At the end of the busy year, we found the expense of manufacturing and selling and running the business, including taxes, was **$119,989,653**

Then it was easy for us to figure the difference between what we took in and what it cost to run the business. That gave us a profit of **$5,639,274**

Out of this profit we paid the stockholders dividends at the rate of $5.75 for each share of preferred stock, and $4.00 for each share of common stock. This amounted to **$3,301,147**

That still left some profit, so in order to give us more and better tools, the stockholders put the remaining profit back into the business. This amounted to **$2,314,367**

In order to redeem a small portion of the 6% preferred stock which was not exchanged for the new 5% preferred, we paid a premium of **$23,760**

... so as we started this year we had from our stockholders a total of **$55,019,077**

... which was divided as follows: about $24,370,000 in land, buildings and equipment, about $23,800,000 in grain and other supplies and about $3,650,000 was in cash.

Typical of the manner in which enlightened management is now telling its story to employes in simple, understandable terms is this illustrated story of "Our Year's Work" which appears in the current issue of General Mills' employe house organ.

FIG. 95. From *Advertising Age*, September 16, 1940.

tendency to attach little value to the job. .... All down the line, this one factor seems to contribute heavily to favorable employee attitudes.

Forms of reports to employees. An analysis of the 1938 annual stockholder reports of 145 leading companies indicated that only 7 per cent had financial tables a layman could understand, 25 per cent discussed finances in terms a layman could understand, and 32 per cent discussed their relations with employees.[14]

However, many progressive companies are writing annual reports which the employee of average intelligence can understand. See figure 95 as an example.

Executive salaries. Many employees who hear of the larger salaries of the executives tend to assume that the large salaries have an important influence on the costs of products to consumers and on wages of workers. The only way to dispose of this question is to answer it honestly and frankly. Johns-

[14] *Sales Management*, June 15, 1939.

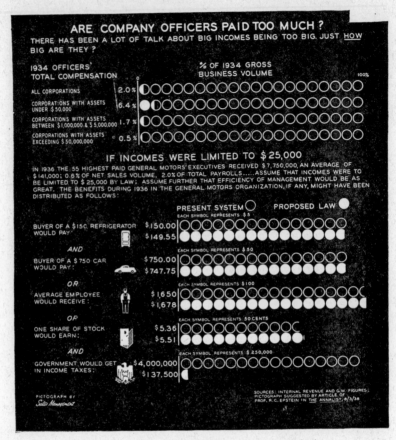

FIG. 96.   (*Courtesy* Sales Management *magazine.*)

Manville Corporation has included a section in its financial report where questions regarding profits of stockholders and salaries of officers have been answered as follows:[15]

Question: "Do our common stockholders get too much profit?"

Answer: "During the last twelve years, our common stockholders have averaged $2.02 a share each year in dividends. Mind you, this is an average per year. In one year they got as high as $4.75 but in 1932, 1933, and 1934 they got nothing and in one other year only 50 cents. The average dividend of $2.02 a share for the past twelve years would have amounted to only 3 per cent."

Question: "If the officers of the corporation weren't paid such big salaries, wouldn't the employees be able to get a lot more?"

[15] *Notes and Quotes.* Connecticut General Life Insurance Company, April 1940.

Answer: "The eighteen officers and directors of Johns-Manville Corporation in 1939 were paid a total of $304,297. This is 1.6 per cent of the total amount paid out during the year in wages and salaries and if the salaries of the officers were cut in half and the balance divided up it would amount to six cents per work day to each job-holder."

The employees' magazine or plant organ should be conducted for the benefit and interest of the employees; only a small part of it should be devoted to a statement of the company's position. At least 70 per cent of the copy should deal with personal items such as athletics, marriages, births, deaths, and promotions. The copy should not talk down to the employees nor make them conscious of being members of the working class. The subject matter should be *we* and not the *company*. The management should inform the employees of some of the company's problems and conditions. New orders, installations of new equipment, certain costs of producing and selling the products, and the allocation of the company's income dollar can be presented. Whenever the manager or the president has an impulse to preach to the employees, he should be big enough to ask the advertising manager and personnel director whether his article is merely a sermon or a worth-while mental food. These executives should also be free to express frank opinions to their superior officers regarding suitable material for the magazine.

In view of the need for a better appreciation of the management's problems, the employees' journal should be educational as well as entertaining. Most employees believe that advertising is a waste of money and that their wages could be raised if those funds were added to the wages. Many think that orders are easy to get, that any business can borrow plenty of money, that the government could operate all businesses more cheaply than private concerns, that there is a fixed amount of money in the world, and that factory workers have all the "grief" and office workers all the "snap" jobs. Such erroneous impressions should be corrected by factual articles with convincing data. All the material in a plant paper can be made as interesting and as attractive as the company's advertising if the periodical has a sound policy and the advertising department collaborates with the personnel department in fulfilling that policy.

The International Harvester Co. publishes thirteen monthlies for the employees of its many plants in various communities. The management wished to find out the employees' reactions to the works' monthlies and included a blank copy of a questionnaire for this purpose with each copy of a certain issue. The total number of questionnaires voluntarily turned in was 2,812. Of these, 26.1 per cent contained written suggestions or comments in addition to check-mark answers on specific questions.

The survey indicated that 78.7 per cent of the employees were taking the magazines home regularly; that 42.9 per cent save it; that when they do take it home 65 per cent find that the women in their families read it; that 32.6 per cent of these like the women's pages; and that 54.4 per cent find that other members of their families read it. Furthermore, 50.9 per cent of the men show the magazine to their friends.[16]

Bulletin boards are necessary to most plants. However, in many firms they are performing the function of wastebaskets. Notices are allowed to accumulate on them for months. Employees decorate them with witty remarks and cartoons. Hence, when an important notice is posted, it is likely to be neglected by the workers.

The bulletin board should be painted, inclosed in glass, and lighted. The inside of the board should have a number of brass nails upon which small colored boards can be hung. Every bulletin should be tacked to one of these colored boards. As the colors are changed, they gain attention for the new notices. Several headline boards should be prepared for special types of notices, such as "Read the bulletin to-day," "The cause of an accident," "See our national advertising," "What our competitors are doing."

The bulletin board should have photographs to illustrate the principles of safety. Broken goggles and old shoes may be displayed if they have played an important part in an accident. Human interest pictures of employees who have caught a big fish while on a camping trip, the bride and groom of a recent plant marriage, and valuable suggestions made by employees are examples of items that can be posted. The bulletin board

---

[16] Herbert E. Fleming, "What Factory Workmen Want in Plant Magazines," *Printers' Ink Monthly,* March 1940.

should never be used for sermonizing by the general manager. It should be kept inviolate for the interest and information of the employees. As a rule, all notices should be changed every three days.

Company picnics, banquets, dances, plays, and other events for the pleasure of the employees should be wholly given over to such pleasure. The management should not attempt to give any talks that boost the company. Few things are so annoying to the employees as being compelled to sit and listen to a hired spellbinder harangue them on the "family spirit of business" while they anxiously wait for the entertainment to begin. Years ago all stories for children had a moral tacked on the end. As parents once did, so many managers still deem it their duty to moralize to the employees in return for the company's entertainment. On these occasions of amicability the aim should be to give the employees so joyful an experience that they will be glad they are working for their particular employer. The associations with the job should be so pleasant that they consider themselves fortunate to be working there. Dances and plays should not be held at regular intervals nor too frequently. They should be spaced far enough apart for the employees to anticipate them rather than to go to them as a part of their obligation to the company. No time should be given to politics or to religious problems at any employees' meetings.

Moving pictures can be made more educational rather than only entertaining. It is seldom well to invite all the personnel of factory and office to see a film. It is better to appeal to definite groups. The invitation should state the nature and purpose of the film or meeting in order that the employees will not come expecting to see a wild west picture and find that they are being given a pictorial description of the sources of the raw materials used in the manufacture of the product.

Displays of the company's products have much educational value if they are displayed in an informative manner. To put some of the products in glass show cases in the lobby has little value, because most of the factory employees never step into the general office lobby. Such displays should be located where employees congregate. They should include placards which show why the product is made in certain ways, its points of superiority,

FIG. 97. "The Musical Steelmakers" are a nationally known organization consisting of Wheeling Steel workers and their sons and daughters. Their work has left them with enough leisure, money, and spirit to produce professionally perfect music that has pleased millions of radio listeners.

the costs, the fluctuations in sales, and the pictures of the men who are responsible for the improvements. Practically all this information is given to the salesmen, but for some reason executives seem afraid to tell the factory employees the same facts that are freely presented to prospective purchasers of the product.

Occasional training courses can be given to selected groups of employees such as foremen, machinists, and salesmen. The chief points that are apt to be overlooked are the systematic organization and aims of the courses. Many executives begin such courses without planning more than the first two or three meetings and then allow the matter to drop without an application or summation of the material. Where it would be burdensome or expensive to have a training course within the plant, it is possible to study the needs of individual employees and to recommend to them suitable correspondence or evening school courses. When college professors or other outsiders are invited to come into the factory and give special courses, it is well to have the instructor outline the course in advance and to state his attitude toward capital and labor. A few of these teachers are snobbish toward workingmen and others are unable to appreciate the problems of management. The fact that they are connected with a well-known institution does not always guarantee the usefulness or objectivity of their instruction. Experience indicates, however, that the employees or the executives within the company are seldom capable or desirous of conducting courses of training for the employees. As a rule, trained teachers are required.

References

Baker, Helen, *The Determination and Administration of Industrial Relations Policies.* Industrial Relations Section, Princeton University, 1939.

Cooke, Morris L., and Philip Murray, *Organized Labor and Production.* Harper & Bros., 1940.

First Yearbook of the Society for the Psychological Study of Social Issues, "Industrial Conflict—A Psychological Interpretation." Edited by George W. Hartmann and Theodore Newcomb. Gordon Company, New York, 1939.

Griffin, John I., *Strikes—A Study in Quantitative Economics.* Columbia University Press, 1939.

Hall, Milton, *Training Your Employees.* Society for Personnel Administration, Washington, D. C.

Laird, Donald A., *How to Use Psychology in Business.* McGraw-Hill Book Co., 1936.

National Association of Manufacturers, *Making the Annual Report Speak for Industry.* McGraw-Hill Book Co., 1938.

Reporting to Employees on Company Operations. Policyholders Service Bureau, Metropolitan Life Insurance Co., undated.

Rosenstein, J. L., *Psychology of Human Relations for Executives.* McGraw-Hill Book Co., 1936.

Shepard, Jean L., *Human Nature at Work.* Harper & Bros., 1938.

Tead, Ordway, *The Art of Leadership.* Whittlesey House, 1935.

Values of Psychology in Industrial Management, Personnel Series No. 43, 1940. American Management Association, New York.

Walton, Albert, *The New Techniques for Supervisors and Foremen.* McGraw-Hill Book Co., 1940.

Watkins, Gordon S., and Paul A. Dodd, *The Management of Labor Relations.* McGraw-Hill Book Co., 1938.

Whitehead, T. N., *Leadership in a Free Society.* Harvard University Press, 1936.

————, *The Industrial Worker* (2 vols.). Harvard University Press, 1938.

Projects

1. Collect and compare data regarding the ages of workers in two or more American industries. For example, the American Iron and Steel Institute in New York published a booklet called *Half a Million Men* (May 1938) which stated that the average age of steel workers is rising. In 1938 the average age was 38, two years more than in 1930. The distribution of ages by percentages of workers in the steel industry was reported as the following for 1938: 25 years and less, 20 per cent; 26 to 40 years, 40 per cent; and 41 years and over, 40 per cent.

2. Employees can be made conscious of costs involved in the use of their equipment. Do you think that college students could be made cost-conscious through the use of the method of Monarch Machine Tool Company?

"Employees operating costly machines rarely have any conception of the amount of the company investment entrusted to their care. Believing that a realization of the value of equipment would result in more care being exercised in its use, the Monarch Machine Tool Company tried the experiment of attaching to each machine in its own plant a plate showing what the machine cost the company when it was purchased. Results have been so gratifying that customers are beginning to request that machines purchased from the company be similarly equipped." [17]

3. Would the morale of the employee be improved by employee meetings at which some of the older men of the company describe their experiences and advancements with the company?

4. In one company the coal bill had increased 30 per cent when the board of directors ordered an investigation. The chief fireman reported that he had been shoveling more slate than coal. He knew that the coal was inferior, but he did not think it was his place to report it. Analyze this situation as to possible causes of such an attitude on the part of the employee. How can such attitudes be prevented?

5. Andrew Carnegie wrote his epitaph for himself:

> *Here lies a man*
> *Who knew how to enlist*
> *In his service*
> *Better men than himself.*

What attitudes are necessary for an executive to pursue such a policy?

6. How can the management convince the employees that "pull" is not essential for promotion?

7. Collect copies of employees' magazines or plant organs and analyze them as to style, selection of material, illustrations, size, and so on.

8. A Canadian Mountie is credited with the statement: "Human beings are only twelve meals away from the dumb animal stage." To what extent do you accept this point of view? How does it affect industrial relations?

---

[17] Quoted from *Management Record,* National Industrial Conference Board, August 1939.

23

Supervising Employees—Formal Methods

Two real comrades know all about each other and are tolerant. Each knows what the other is up against and, understanding each other, wanting to work out the common task which is theirs, they make allowances as one man to another. Then there is fun in the day's work, there is that sense of going places with other men, there is a click in the job. That is great; that is a priceless possession. When it exists among men in industry, so-called "personnel management" is simple. But you cannot define this relationship; you cannot blue-print the course of comradeship. It is a mistake to try. But we can create the physical environment that is conducive to comradeship. We can have good "personnel management" and then give comradeship a chance.[1]

SYSTEMS of personnel management in industry are relatively unimportant. A given company may have the finest industrial-relations mechanisms or formal systems and still have poor industrial relations. Another company may have almost no personnel-management mechanisms and yet have fine industrial relations. If the executives have the indefinable qualities of leadership and management which inspire comradeship and confidence between management and men, the formal methods of supervision are incidental. Many examples of this fine relationship exist in American industry.

One example is the Studebaker Corporation.[2] At the same time that many of the largest corporations in the automotive industry were beset by costly labor controversies, this company had little or no disturbance. In its eighty-eight years of activity, the company has had no serious labor disturbances. Its factory workers have been organized under C. I. O. Investigators who

---

[1] Roderic Olzendam, *The Importance of Personnel Administration to Public Relations*. Weyerhaeuser Timber Company.
[2] Glenn Griswold, *Public Opinion Quarterly*, September 1940.

have studied the reasons for its pleasant industrial-relations history have been unable to find evidence of any plan or system to account for the results. The relationship between management and men is surprisingly informal. The company has no printed statement of labor policy or procedures, no codified rules of conduct, and no commitment on the part of the company or its workers except the intent to comply honestly and fairly with a simple union agreement which has fixed wages and working conditions.

The National Association of Manufacturers has made an intensive study of employee relations and believes that:

. . . there is no specific plan, formula or procedure which can satisfactorily meet the varying conditions and problems of different plants in different industries and communities, but it also believes that satisfactory relations between management and employees will result from application of the following fundamental principles:

1. A mutual respect and consideration by each for the problems and viewpoints of the other.
2. Promotion of the widest understanding that the greatest measure of well-being for both employers and employees and maximum possibility of obtaining the full economic value of their services lies in the development of the common enterprise in which they are engaged.
3. Free interchange of ideas between management and employees in all matters and company policies of mutual interest, such as wages, hours, and conditions of employment.
4. The development by each company of a sound and well-defined employment policy.[3]

In spite of the recognized greater importance of man-to-man relationships in industry, most managements use some personnel plans in order that frictions may be diminished and understandings improved. These schemes or plans are likely to be rated somewhat differently by union and non-union employees, as indicated by Table XXXVII.

The need for personnel systems is obviously greater in the large industrial establishments than in those with few employees. If we assume that an establishment should have more than 500 employees to need an organized personnel department to supply the "human touch" rather than have the owner himself or his man-

---

[3]The complete statement regarding employee relations practices and policies is printed in *Suggested Employment Procedures*. National Association of Manufacturers, 14 West 49th Street, New York. This bulletin may be obtained for a small price per copy.

TABLE XXXVII[4]

ATTITUDE OF EMPLOYEES

	Most Important		Best Carried Out		Least Important		Most Irritating	
	Union	Non-Union	Union	Non-Union	Union	Non-Union	Union	Non-Union
1. Employee stock subscription	5%	2%	15%	12%	100%	93%	49%	44%
2. Voice or share in management	13	6	3	9	78	69	26	65
3. Fair adjustment of grievances	80	24	52	23	6	27	—	29
4. Chance of promotion	28	47	18	18	13	7	19	51
5. Steady employment	65	93	50	55	3	10	4	—
6. Medical and dental service	—	6	3	32	72	17	15	15
7. Safety	57	21	79	53	6	7	37	7
8. Amount of pay	49	51	9	6	—	3	41	36
9. Working conditions	49	45	50	55	3	3	22	7
10. Hours of work	13	23	38	29	3	21	19	15
11. Type of man in charge	18	38	15	6	28	34	90	44
12. Methods of pay	—	2	21	15	25	65	37	44
13. Insurance systems and pensions	18	36	12	89	16	10	26	15
14. Chance to show initiative	5	6	6	—	47	34	15	29

Rexford B. Hersey reported in this table the results of a survey of 250 workers to determine what they would mark as the four most important management policies, the four least important, the four best carried out, and the four most irritating.

"Union workers are more concerned about fair adjustment of grievances than they are about steady employment; most of them think this item and safety and working conditions are among the best carried out by management. (Note that safety irritated many of them.) They are not much interested in stock subscription plans, do not want a voice or share in management or chances to show initiative, and do not appreciate medical or dental services. (In other words they react against so-called paternalistic company policies.) The only factor that irritates them much is the type of man in charge, presumably the foreman.

"Non-union workers are not much concerned about grievances, but are much concerned about steady employment. Most of them think insurance systems and pensions are the best carried out management policies and rate them high in importance. They do not, however, appreciate stock plans. They are more irritated by not being given a share in management, by low chances for promotion. They are not so much stirred up by the foreman but quite a few are irritated because of grievances."[5]

[4] From Rexford B. Hersey, "Psychology of Workers," *Personnel Journal,* January-February 1936, Vol. 14, Nos. 7, 8.
[5] *Ibid.*

FIG. 98. Rexford B. Hersey, Professor of Industry, University of Pennsylvania, and consultant in mental hygiene for the Pennsylvania Railroad. Readers interested in further study of the worker's adjustment and efficiency may refer to his book *Workers' Emotions in Shop and Home* (University of Pennsylvania Press, 1932. Industrial Research Studies XVIII).

ager do so, about 38 per cent of industrial employees should have the benefit of a personnel department. See Table XXXVIII.

Establishments having less than 500 employees usually have several foremen or supervisors who function as liaison officers to the employees. However, many individual employees of both large and small concerns have almost no personal contact with the heads of the concern or its owners. This means that the foreman is a key figure in industry.

The foreman in labor relations. The importance of foremen is suggested by their number in industry. Of the 27,000,000 employees in business and industry, about 25,000,000 may be con-

TABLE XXXVIII[6]

Classes of Establishments by Number of Employees	Percentage of U. S. Industrial Employees in the Class
Employing 1 to 5 persons	3%
Employing 6 to 20 persons	7
Employing 21 to 100 persons	20
Employing 101 to 500 persons	32
Employing 501 to 2,500 persons	27
Employing more than 2,500 persons	11

[6] Adapted from R. L. Duffus, "American Industry: Many-Headed Giant," *The New York Times Magazine*, March 13, 1938, p. 21.

sidered wage-earning workers, 500,000 as salaried executives, and 1,500,000 as foremen. When the National Association of Manufacturers queried 6,000 employees in 1937, the answers indicated that workers believed that the troubles and misunderstandings between themselves and management were largely management's fault. However, the importance of the foreman in the misunderstandings was indicated by the fact that 43 per cent of the workers who blamed management in general also went on to blame the foreman in specific particulars.[7]

The foreman may or may not accentuate friction, depending upon his skill in leadership and tact. The good foreman has the human touch which enables him to build morale because he himself thinks and feels sincerely. Glenn Gardiner offers an excellent example:

Riding on a freight elevator with the superintendent of the U. S. Gypsum Company on Staten Island, I was impressed by this incident. As we stepped on the elevator the superintendent said, "I want to introduce you to Tony who has been running this elevator for more than eight years and has never had a single accident of any kind, which is a record we're proud of."

The way Tony grinned and stuck out his hand made one realize that he appreciated the credit being given him and that he was 100 per cent sold on the idea of running that elevator for many years to come without any accidents.[8]

The good foreman begins his art of handling employees with each new employee. The new employee is introduced to his fellow workers, is given complete instructions, and encouraged to believe that he is becoming an accepted member of the personnel. The good foreman aids the new employee in acquiring the "feeling of belongingness," which psychologists have found to be exceedingly important for happy social adjustment.

Recent legislation, particularly the National Labor Relations Act, has increased the importance of careful hiring, instructions, and other aspects of supervision. Care must be exercised to avoid discrimination against employees because of personality differences. When an employee must be discharged, the foreman must be able to prove that the decision is not whimsicality on his part

---

[7] *Tide,* June 1, 1939, p. 25.

[8] Glenn Gardiner, "Reaching the Individual Worker." Address delivered before the Second Annual Greater Philadelphia Safety Conference May 27, 1935.

Fig. 99. An example of confused unionism. The picket's sign says, "This job is non-union." Signs on the window say work has been done by C. I. O. and A. F. L. (*Photograph courtesy of the Buffalo* Evening News.).

and to prove the fairness of his act, if necessary, before a legally established tribunal or board of review.

Labor unions. Labor unions have so many psychological aspects that any attempt to treat their nature is likely to be a description of human nature itself. Examples of good and bad unionism are as plentiful as the examples of good and bad psychological adjustments by individuals. Some labor union leaders have been indicted and convicted of racketeering;[9] others have

---

[9] See *Business Week,* March 19, 1938, p. 18.

made splendid contributions to human welfare. Certainly many modern trade union practices have had pronounced influence on some industries and arts, as exemplified by a New York producer of shows:

In contemplative and not entirely cheerful mood, a producer looked out of his office window in the Forties the other day and remembered out loud when show business could be referred to with a straight face as a field for investment. But now, he said, it's a curious thing: the man who wants to put something into a show is from the start outnumbered by the people who want to take something out of it. Moreover, the latter are firmly organized, so that you encounter them at every turn under these labels:

. (1) The Actors Equity Association, (2) Chorus Equity, (3) the United Scenic Artists (including costume designers), (4) the International Alliance of Theatrical Stage Employees (stagehands), (5) the Theatrical Managers, Agents and Treasurers Union (this one calls for payoff on three fronts), (6) the Dramatists Guild, (7) the American Federation of Musicians, (8) the International Brotherhood of Teamsters and Chauffeurs (transfer men), (9) the Billposters Union, (10) the Service Employees in Amusement and Cultural Buildings (porters, watchmen, and cleaning staff), (11) the International Brotherhood of Electrical Workers.

To be sure, said the producer, still looking wistfully out of the window, there is a good reason for the existence of each—the abuses that prevailed in the buccaneer days. And they have served another worthy purpose, too; they have largely eliminated the "shoestring" manager. Still, he reflected, it is enough to scare the "angels" away—in fact, it is scaring them away, and there isn't much for a producer to do about it.

About all he can do, indeed, is to get up from his desk and join the League of New York Theatres, if he has the strength. Or wait until Summer and become an impresario on the rustic circuit, where his hand is momentarily freer.[10]

Unions have also contributed toward easing some employers' burdens. For example, unions are likely to call the management's attention to rates of pay and other conditions that hinder production. Workmen are more apt to speak their minds freely when they know they have the union to defend their rights. Foremen of unionized plants must also improve their skills in handling their men. Foremen cannot take out grouches on men who are unionized. Recognition of the union tends to clear the atmosphere for the employees and enable them to express their grievances. On the other hand, many unions also act as a kind of wedge between the management and the men, thus preventing

---

[10] *The New York Times,* May 8, 1938.

management and men from ever understanding each other or co-operating wholeheartedly.

Phillips L. Garman[11] pointed out that "before a union can do any co-operating of any sort there must be unqualified acceptance by management of *bona fide* collective bargaining." He emphasized a point of view stated by Slichter, who was reported as saying that the employer should:

> . . . eliminate the issue of union status, either by encouraging membership in the trade union or by granting the closed shop. To most American employers, the "closed shop" is a symbol for union domination. As a matter of fact, the employer is likely to have more freedom in a closed shop or its equivalent than in one where the union is uncertain of its status.[12]

> In many recently organized plants in the automobile industry, the rubber industry, and other industries, new union leaders are compelled to develop their thinking on seniority, on the length of the work week, on daywork versus payment by results, and many other matters with little help from employers toward understanding these problems. I think that this situation is dangerous for both unions and employers. Unions cannot do a good job of representing the real interest of wage earners unless they have a good understanding of the problems of employers and of the industry, and no one can give them that understanding except the employer. And he cannot do it unless he has a friendly relationship with the union.[13]

Another student of industrial relations, Ordway Tead, tells of a discussion of the hostility of employers that he had with a labor leader:

> "If only they would take us for granted. . . ." "That phrase," he said, "is the key to the situation. Once employees and unions get a clear and perfect confidence in the attitude and intention of the employer and of management that there is no question in the management's mind about the *continuance* of the organized relationship which collective bargaining represents; once that relationship is established *with no reservations* on the part of management to exercise its right to pull out of the contractual arrangement, then many industrial relations issues which seem vital today will become secondary and minor. Notably, such questions as the closed shop, which has assumed in the minds of employers proportions out of any relation to its importance, will be-

---

[11] Phillips L. Garman, *How Organized Labor Can Co-operate with Management*. Personnel Series No. 44, American Management Association, 1940.

[12] Sumner H. Slichter, "The Changing Character of American Industrial Relations," *American Economic Review*, March 1939, Part 2, p. 124.

[13] Sumner H. Slichter, "Employees' Right to Deal Collectively with Management," *Collective Bargaining and Cooperation*, Bureau of Industrial Relations, University of Michigan, Bulletin No. 8, 1938, p. 51.

come insignificant once the employer decides to go ahead with collective bargaining ad infinitum." [14]

In certain unionized industries, the unions have established impressive records of co-operation with managements. Some of the best examples of union-management co-operation have occurred where companies were faced with bankruptcy and unions were faced with loss of jobs. In addition to economic adversity, union recognition with a long history of collective bargaining, strength of the union, integrity of intelligent union officials, and genuine sympathy on the part of management have also been important factors in union-management co-operation. Examples of effective co-operation are the following:

An Ohio steel plant demanded a 10 per cent wage cut because of its bad competitive position in the market. SWOC protested, sent in its research staff. Time studies showed that the labor cost per ton of steel was $1.30—13¢ a ton would be saved by the proposed wage cut. SWOC engineers discovered that 40 gallons of oil at 4¢ a gallon were being used in making each ton of steel. The men at the furnaces were told the story. They devised some short cuts, conserved on fuel, reduced the gallonage of oil per ton to 29 —a saving of 44¢ per ton of steel. There was no wage cut.

In a Canadian steel plant that recently entered into a co-operative agreement with SWOC, a rolling mill was down some 20 hours a week because of the breakage of guides. Time loss on the mill was estimated at $600 an hour —a $12,600 loss weekly for a small mill that was not operating on too profitable a basis. A rolling-mill employee went to the union-management committee and explained that he had been trying to get the superintendent— or someone—to try the guide he had designed. Under union pressure the guide was made and installed. The mill ran 28 days without stoppage! [15]

Some unions and companies have co-operated in developing programs of education for workers. Examples of such programs are the Labor Relations College of The Paraffine Companies, Inc., of San Francisco, and the School for Workers in Industry, University of Wisconsin. Such attempts, when sincerely and objectively conducted, are likely to result in long-term improvements in industrial relations.

---

[14] Ordway Tead, "The Effect of Collective Bargaining on Company Personnel Policies," a paper presented in a conference series conducted by the Bureau of Personnel Administration on *Industrial Democracy in Process: The Call for Industrial Statesmanship,* February 4, 1938.

[15] "Can Unions Increase Profits?" *Modern Industry,* May 15, 1941, Vol. I, No. 4. SWOC refers to Steel Workers Organizing Committee.

These examples, so favorable to the unions, should not cause one to assume that strikes have been eliminated from industries which have had a long experience with unionism. Continuing high levels of strikes have occurred in some highly unionized industries.[16] However, the strike records of individual industries vary so greatly that the results of unionization in specific industries are likely to depend upon factors other than extensive unionism. Unionism may become popular in a specific industry because, for example, employees resent certain policies of a particular management.

Remsen J. Cole and Associates questionnaired employees of a number of Philadelphia companies to find out whether employees are chiefly *for labor organizations* or merely *against management*. The results shown in Table XXXIX indicated that the workers were probably against management rather than for labor organizations. This suggests that managements have a heavy psychological responsibility toward their employees. Some managements are trying to fulfill this responsibility through the use of methods such as multiple management.

Multiple management. In the early 1930's Charles P. McCormick,[17] president of McCormick & Co., Baltimore wholesale grocery and spice manufacturing concern, put into operation the democracy-in-business plan of management which is called "multiple management." Under this system, several groups of employees, who function in the manner of boards of directors, make suggestions to the responsible board of directors at the top. These subordinate or junior boards, usually chosen by the management, may consist of groups of employees who have related functions. Thus one board may be made up of factory employees, another of salesmen, a third of office employees, and so on. The employee boards do not supersede the regular board of directors but supplement that board's judgment, especially with regard to improvements in employee and customer relations.

Employees are taken into complete confidence regarding all the ins and outs of production, sales, finance, and other phases of

---

[16] John I. Griffin, "Conclusions" from "Strikes—A Study in Quantitative Economics," *Studies in History, Economics, and Public Law*, No. 451. Columbia University Press, 1939.

[17] Charles P. McCormick, *Multiple Management*, Harper & Brothers, 1938.

operations. In 1941, more than 200 United States firms had adopted principles of multiple management as pioneered by McCormick & Co. The management of one company, Williamson

TABLE XXXIX[18]

"For" Labor Organizations—or "Against" Management?

This question was based on the purely theoretical supposition that management could and would co-operate with labor to the fullest extent on policies and problems that are the backbone of union philosophy and their only justification for existence, i. e., fair wages and good working conditions. Although a situation such as this exists in only a few cases (Hershey Chocolate Co. and Endicott-Johnson Shoe Co. as examples), here are the comparative attitudes of those who would negotiate directly with management and those who believe the outside union would still be superior as a bargaining agency.

	Of the 61% Who Would Negotiate Direct		Of the 37% Who Would Prefer a Labor Organization	
	YES	NO	YES	NO
1. Like their jobs................	74%	26%	49%	51%
2. Qualified for other work........	43	57	32	68
3. Married.....................	69	31	54	46
4. Spouse satisfied with job.......	74	26	45	55
5. Think employer can pay more...	64	31	81	14
6. Know what company earns.....	33	67	22	78
7. Talk man-to-man with boss.....	46	54	14	81
8. See opportunity for advancement	62	38	16	76
9. Would quit for $2 more per week	20	80	65	35
10. Find working conditions pleasant	74	26	49	51
11. Criticize company policies......	52	48	68	32

Workers are not "for" labor organizations, but "against" management. If those who indicate that they prefer an outside agency had shown percentages running parallel to the general average, it would have established an honest belief that unions can do what management cannot. But because the labor group is negative throughout in all questions pertaining to attitude toward job, employer, and the company, it can only be assumed that they are antagonistic toward management and therefore cannot answer the question impartially. Thus it can be assumed that labor organizations are selected not from preference but because the union can provide more material benefits than management is willing to give. . . .

If it were true that unions could fill a need for workers that is beyond the abilities of management, the problem of improving industrial relations might be seriously complicated. The fact that it is a negativism toward management that must be overcome rather than a positivism toward unions, places the problem and its solution directly in the employer's lap.[19]

---

[18] From "Employee-Employer Relations," a survey of employee opinions conducted in Philadelphia by Remsen J. Cole and Associates, 1940.

[19] *Ibid.*

FIG. 100. "Multiple Management" junior board in session in junior board room at McCormick & Co., Baltimore. "Friendship Court" consists of a board room, tea museum, tea house, model store, spice office, and so on. It was designed to inspire calm deliberation and genuine co-operation. See *Pioneering with Products and People* (McCormick & Co., 1939) and Charles P. McCormick, *Multiple Management* (Harper & Bros., 1938).

Heater Co., which adopted the plan in 1938, summarized certain results in the following published statements, quoted in part:

1. Employees are happier and more secure in their jobs. In a business which for years operated under the handicap of a production schedule that peaked during a 30-weeks' season, employment has been stabilized to the point where labor is guaranteed at least 48 weekly pay checks through the year. Last year there were actually 50 weeks with pay.

2. The younger men in the company who are in executive or semi-executive capacities are developing into first-rate material for bigger jobs. Future capable man-power is assured. These men in turn understand that their own opportunities to progress depend largely upon their ability and willingness to develop capable understudies.

3. More efficient factory methods enabled the company last year to turn out a 25 per cent increase in production without increasing building capacity.

4. By plugging the leaks and finding better ways of doing things, all-around efficiency of operation has been increased. Both sales and profits have increased steadily. In 1939 sales increased 15 per cent over 1938. In 1940 indications are that sales will increase 25 per cent over 1939. Profits have been proportionately greater.

5. The company is keeping out of ruts in its general management thinking, in its product design, in its selling methods, in its conception of service to its customers.[20]

Among the things we learned was that certain matters which might seem inconsequential to us, sitting apart as we do in the executive offices, could loom very big with the people on the floors. Here are a few examples:

1. There was a rough spot on the floor. To us it was just a rough spot. But to the men who had to run many trucks over it in a day, it was an evil. Boxes fell off trucks. They had to stop and reload them. That was lost time. We fixed the spot and ended the trouble.

2. Some of the girls didn't like the soap in the washroom.

3. A group of girls had no way of telling the time while they worked. They wanted a clock, and got it.

4. One machine was not functioning as it should, making extra work and slowing up manufacture. We cleaned that up.

5. One man complained because his lunch hour was irregular.

6. A suggested change in the layout in the shipping room improved working conditions and gave much faster service to customers.[21]

Suggestion systems.

Certain managements do not care to adopt multiple management or a similar scheme for obtaining employees' suggestions. Some companies find it necessary to use a suggestion system. Ideally, of course, a suggestion system should be unnecessary. Management and men should work so closely with each other that each would make his suggestions regarding the work as the work is carried on. Practically, such ideal relations do not exist. A suggestion system may, to some extent, enable alert employees to participate more actively in the operations of the business. The value of such employees' suggestions is indicated by reports such as the following:

During the past eighteen months ending September 17, 1940, the Illinois Central System paid $21,000 to its employees for 2,117 suggestions telling the railroad how to improve operations and services or to make the railroad a better place in which to work. The combined efforts of the 25,120 contributors brought about a gross savings of more than $100,000.

The suggestion system adopted March 6, 1939, was founded on the belief

[20] W. L. McGrath and L. B. Murphy, "Democracy in Management—How Williamson Makes It Work," *Sales Management*, August 1, 1940.

[21] George H. Williamson, "What Happened When We Gave Employees a Voice in Management," *Sales Management*, May 1, 1939.

that the eyes, ears, and minds of all the employees and officers should be directed toward bettering the work of the railroad.

It is the belief of J. L. Beven, president, and other officers that the most important element in the crusade for ideas and suggestions is mass thinking of employees. They are the ones who are most likely to bring to light ideas for the improvement of service along the line. It is also emphasized that all the brains are not in the Chicago offices.[22]

The General Electric Company tabulated its record from 1919 to 1939 and found that more than 300,000 suggestions and ideas for better ways to do their work had been received from employees of the company and that 75,000 had been accepted. In that period, approximately $1,250,000 had been paid to the employees in cash awards for these suggestions, or an average bonus of $17. The awards paid are not fixed in amount but are determined by estimated savings, ingenuity shown by employees, etc. A single award has run as high as $1,500.[23]

Employees will not offer ideas unless they have learned through years of experience that suggestions are welcome. The executive who calls employees into his office and makes a direct request for suggestions is likely to be disappointed for several reasons. One is the fact that most employees are like students; they try to give an answer that they think will agree with the questioner's ideas.

Another reason for the employee's hesitancy in offering suggestions directly to a higher executive is the employee's fear of his own foreman or supervisor. Many employees have such a fear of their department heads and immediate supervisors that their own personalities are submerged and their thinking is hedged in by emotional impediments.

Employees who are paid on a piece-rate basis may be able to make suggestions that would speed up their work, but they have learned that the new method would bring about a retiming of the job and a lower rate of pay. They can make more money by keeping the discovery to themselves and retaining the old rate of pay than if they were to be paid a small reward for the suggestion.

To operate a successful suggestion system, the management must do more than merely hang up a few tin boxes with a sign, "Suggestions Wanted." Considerable managerial thought and effort are essential to operation of a satisfactory suggestion scheme.

---

[22] *American Business,* October 1940.
[23] *Sales Management,* December 15, 1939.

1. Small concerns have found it best to conduct a contest for suggestions. The contest should start and end on definite dates. Announcements should state that rewards are given for each accepted suggestion and also prizes for the best of these suggestions. The disadvantage of this method is that awards cannot be made until all the suggestions have been considered; and many suggestions require considerable time for study and investigation.

2. Large concerns find it better to conduct extended campaigns and to award prizes at definite periods, or simply to pay for suggestions when they are accepted or put into effect.

3. It is well to obtain the co-operation and good will of the foremen and other executives. Many a department head considers an employee's suggestion for improvement as a reflection upon his ability. This really is not true, but foreman lethargy and company politics can be quite effective in throttling employees' suggestions. To overcome employees' fears, some companies request that all suggestions be submitted on a standard three-part form, each bearing the same number. The largest part of the form is reserved for the description of the suggestion; each of the two smaller parts is for the name of the employee and the number of the suggestion blank. When the suggestion form is submitted, it is first sent to one of the higher officials of the company, who tears off the parts which include the name of the employee, files one of these in a private safe, and sends the other to the employee, acknowledging its receipt and expressing appreciation for the suggestion. The employee is also told when the suggestion will be given its first hearing by the committee in charge. By using this plan, the committee does not know the name of any of the suggestors, and therefore it is easier for them to avoid unfair personal influences.

4. The announcements and requests for suggestions should explain to the employees the specific kinds of suggestions that are desired. A mere invitation to employees to *think* does not stimulate them to think. The management that really wants employees to think should list and describe problems that are within the employees' areas of experience.

5. When suggestions are considered by the appointed committee, complete records of proceedings should be kept in order that

Fig. 101. Manning, Maxwell & Moore, Inc., have a special display of their products, arranged by the employees and exhibited for the interests of the employees. (*From* Printers' Ink Monthly, *June 1940.*)

copies of the minutes and other records may be submitted to the management. Each item of business should have an identifying number; thus all activities of the committee can be traced. Monthly and annual reports can be made from the proceedings of the recorded meetings. These reports will be available for guidance in the elimination of duplicate suggestions. The foreman in charge of each department should be informed of all suggestions that are made by employees of his department and he should be congratulated when his employees make good suggestions.

6. When a suggestion is rejected, the reason for the rejection should be explained in writing to the employee. A member of the suggestion committee should discuss the rejection personally with the employee in order that he may understand why the suggestion was not acceptable. Few things will cause a suggestion scheme

to die more quickly than to ignore or to forget the employees who make the suggestions. An important factor in the rejection interview is the personality and the manner of the rejector. His manner may stimulate the employee to submit additional ideas or discourage him permanently.

7. The employee should have the right of appeal when his idea has been rejected. If he cannot be convinced that his idea is valueless, he should have the privilege of preparing new charts, drawings, or evidence of its worth.

8. The members of the awarding committee should include several employees. The employees will then know that they are represented in the determination of awards. If they are not thus represented, some of the employees may suspect the company of stealing some of their brilliant ideas.

9. The awards or rewards should be commensurate with the value of the idea. If the company demands from each employee a waiver of rights for a patentable idea, the flow of suggestions is certain to decrease. If a suggestion has little cash value to the company, the reward may be small, but not less than five dollars. The employee who is given small rewards is likely to be teased by his fellow workers with such statements as "Well, Bill, are you gonna buy a new house and car with that two dollars and a half you got for your bright idea?"

10. The employees who make the best suggestions should receive publicity in the plant paper, on the bulletin board, or at a general meeting. A few firms give no financial reward for accepted ideas, but consider promotion, prestige, and personal pride a sufficient reward. Such a policy is often harmful because it stimulates the sycophants rather than the more balanced personalities.

Suggestion systems, like all other group methods of influencing employees, depend for their success upon the alertness and ability of the management. One of the country's leading manufacturers of a highly technical product receives about forty suggestion letters a day. An expert examines each suggestion to determine if it is of any possible value to the company. This company has found that it pays to examine one thousand ideas in order to find six that are definitely valuable and can be adopted with satisfactory results to the company. The management of this company, however, is "on its toes" in many respects, and its careful consideration of submitted ideas is simply one phase of an aggressive management.

Profit sharing. Profit sharing is not a new idea, as the plan was in operation in agriculture in England during the thirteenth century. Records show that it was used in shops in England in 1870 and in France as early as 1842. The first plan instituted in the United States was that of Albert Gallatin, who introduced it in his glassworks at New Geneva, Pennsylvania, in 1794. In 1889 the United States had thirty-two recorded schemes for profit sharing. Most of these schemes were short-lived, although one St. Louis firm has been operating on a profit-sharing basis since 1886. The Procter & Gamble plan was begun in 1887, but it has been modified several times since then. Few schemes now operating were started before 1900.

A survey in 1935 of 2,452 representative companies of the United States, employing 4,502,608 employees, indicated that 4.7 per cent of the companies reported use of a profit-sharing plan. However, the report also showed that 48.3 per cent of the total number of instituted plans had been discontinued.[24]

Westinghouse Electric & Mfg. Co. is often mentioned as one large company that has a successful profit-sharing plan. The plan has been in operation since May 1936 and 50,000 employees received approximately $33,000,000 in the first five years of its operation. During this time the labor relations, on the whole, have been good. There have been only a few minor section and department stoppages and a one-day plant-wide stoppage.[25] Most Westinghouse factory employees belong to labor unions and the main local union has officially opposed the "adjusted compensation" or profit-sharing plan. Most employees probably like the plan which they erroneously call a bonus.

In most cases, profit sharing should be distinguished from bonuses, which are given as a reward for high production by an individual worker. It is not part of a wage system. True profit

---

[24] *What Employees Are Doing for Employees,* National Industrial Conference Board Studies, No. 221, March 1936, p. 12.

[25] "Profit Sharing—Can It Solve Today's Problems?" *Modern Industry,* February 15, 1941.

sharing is an agreement between the employer and the employees under which the profits allocated to the workers rise or fall in proportion to the increase or the decrease in the profits realized by the employer. Because the method of distributing the profits varies, the difficulties in determining the amount of profits that a given employee should receive have been an important factor in preventing the adoption of profit sharing.

Most of the plans have been started in the hope that efficiency would be increased, costs decreased, and the working force stabilized. Some were begun by wealthy employers who wished to share their success with the employees whose hard work contributed toward the profits of the enterprises. The employers' motives were an attempt to give social justice and to increase their own sense of well-being. Where such an attitude prevailed, and was coupled with reasonable managerial efficiency, some benefits actually accrued from profit sharing and similar plans of employee relations. The plans started by such humanitarians were usually abandoned at their deaths, when inevitable changes in management took place. In a few instances, the owner of the business provided for the perpetuation of the plan after his death.

In general, profit sharing has not been so successful as many of its advocates anticipated. One important reason is that employees prefer to have a definite salary or wage that is known in advance. They declare "a bird in the hand is worth two in the bush." In the years when the company makes unusually large profits, the money distributed is accepted as a gift from a kind, industrial Santa Claus; but when profits are negligible or a deficit must be written on the books, the employees may be sorely disappointed. To say the least, an employee will be shocked if, after he has spent his anticipated profits, he finds that the practice of distributing profits has been suddenly discontinued. When profits are shared for a long time, they are often confused with or considered as a part of the wages.

When the profits of the company do not allow any distribution to the employees, the employees tend to doubt the honesty of the management, particularly if they note that the president or the general manager of the company has purchased a new house or a new limousine. They do not, as a rule, have access to the accounts of the employer; but even if they did, they would not be able to understand the accounts. A negligible number of the employers who have a profit-sharing plan have a disinterested accountant audit their books and prepare a report, which he presents to the employees. However, the great masses of workers cannot understand how profits in modern business are made or computed. It is only natural, therefore, that they should be suspicious of the management when the plan of distribution remains a mystery to them.

The individual employee can seldom see any relationship between his own daily efforts and the profits at the end of the year. In most plans, the profits divided are a small fraction of the annual wages. In one third of the plans studied, it was found that the dividends amounted to less than 6 per cent of the annual wages of the participants. Hence the interested employee who decides to work hard in order to increase the company's profits at the end of the year, a proportionate share of which he will receive, finds that the lazy worker by his side receives a check just as large as his own. As a result of his discovery, during the following year he may decide to work as slowly and as carelessly as the poorest workman in the shop. Thus profit sharing, under some conditions, tends to bring the efficiency of the best workers down to the level of the poorest rather than to raise the efficiency of the poorest workers. The profit-sharing sun shines just as brightly on the undeserving as on the deserving. It is for these and other reasons that profit sharing for workmen has been found deficient as an incentive to work. The only type that appears to have incentive values for modern business is that of managerial profit sharing.

The making of profits in modern business is largely beyond the control of the factory workers. Profits depend upon the managerial ability to purchase economically, to organize the whole scheme of production efficiently, to sell the goods at a satisfactory profit, to finance the operations during the depressions that are bound to occur in business, and to find new markets to take the place of contracting markets. The key executives of a business— the sales manager, the production manager, the comptroller, the purchasing agent, and a few others—can see the direct relations between their own efforts and the profits made. They are the

Fig. 102. Richard S. Uhrbrock. Readers who wish to study further the problem of supervising employees will wish to read his article, "A Psychologist Looks at Wage-Incentive Methods," American Management Association, Institute of Management Series, No. 15, May 24, 1935, pp. 1–32.

men who are responsible for profits and losses, rather than the workers in the factory.

Most of the important executives of a company receive a fixed salary. They know that they are getting the highest salary that the board of directors will give them. From this standpoint, they have no incentive to do their best and they tend, therefore, to lean back and take life more or less easily. They assume this easy attitude unintentionally and even subconsciously; they are working under conditions that do not stimulate them to do their utmost. Thus they constitute the one group to which profit sharing is a direct motive to give the best that is in them. They know that their efforts are a vital factor in causing profits or deficits. The fact that they are allowed to share in the profits stimulates them to do their best and gives them a feeling of partnership and responsibility in the business. The effect of this privilege upon General Motors executives is well known in industrial circles. For wage earners, profit sharing is largely incidental to a humanitarian motive or managerial attitude of fairness toward the employees. As a rule, it does not give the workers a strong sense of participation in the enterprise.

Employee stock purchase plans. It has been argued that stock ownership, rather than profit sharing, is more advantageous to the employee for the following reasons: Under the latter plan, although the employee may gain a little by sharing in the profits, he is not required to expend any extra effort or to take any risks. Thus the profit-sharing plan does not give him any feeling of responsibility in the management of the company.   On the other hand, under the stock purchase plan, the employee, by being allowed to purchase some stock, is made to regard himself as a partner in the business; consequently he naturally takes an active interest in the affairs of the business and acquires a sense of importance as a budding financier!

Advocates of the plan claim that stock ownership would be an incentive to the employee to eliminate waste, to be more industrious, to attend work regularly, not to quit for a better job, to criticize the employer less, and to refuse to harm the company's property in case of a strike.   Some advocates even think that by purchasing enough stock, the employees could have direct representation on the board of directors and in the management of the company.

Actually, the employee stock ownership plans have not worked out as anticipated.   It has been found that employees purchase stock mainly for three reasons: as a speculative investment; in the hope of attracting the good will of management and of gaining promotion; and as a nest egg for old age.   The extent to which these hopes have been dashed in some unfortunate instances is illustrated in the case of the employees of a company that suffered severely in a business depression.   When the company was only a few jumps ahead of the sheriff, the executives had to retrench and, consequently, many of the employees were dismissed.

Certain employers who have sold negotiable stock to employees have found that the employees have become interested more in the market value of the stock than in increasing its real value through extra diligence.   At the very time when the employer has needed employee loyalty—a keen desire on the part of the workers to pitch in and lift a little harder—he has found them busy watching the stock market!   In a few cases, employees have made paper profits that would have given them substantial annual incomes had they sold at the right time; but they held on, hoping to make still more or fearing that the employer would look upon their transactions as disloyalty to the company.   When the paper profits were wiped out, the former "well-to-do" employees lost heart in their work and blamed the company for their misfortune.

The Industrial Relations Section of Princeton University studied a number of employee stock ownership plans after the depression that began in 1929. The findings are partly summarized in the following:

Although reasons for establishment of the plans were various, they were primarily a device to encourage employee thrift. As such they competed with other forms of savings, and their experience must first of all be measured by certain essential standards for any employee-savings plan. Did they assure security of the investment? Were funds available when needed? In most cases, the answer to both questions is "No." The exceptional cases are those in which the company had made generous contributions to the fund or repurchased employee stock on request.

The mortality rate of these plans was high even early in the depression. By 1932, 19 of 50 plans studied by the Industrial Relations Section had already been discontinued and 12 more were suspended. The stock market crash had been a death blow to many. Others which survived to 1932 were ended within the next few years, and the present record is still worse. By 1936, only one fourth of the plans established prior to 1929 were still in existence and many of them were not being actively "pushed." Such a record alone tells the story of employee stock ownership. However, additional information on specific plans verifies the statistical record, and shows the reasons that lie back of the wholesale discontinuance of plans.

It is perhaps unnecessary to say that the chief cause for the discontinuance of stock selling to employees was the decline in security values. Company executives stated this repeatedly, however, and reported the resulting losses to employees. Other reasons were a more roundabout statement of the same fact: Financial loss to the company (especially in permitting the cancellation of subscriptions); difficulties connected with a long-purchase period; and depreciation in investment when employees were least able to bear it. Two other reasons given were lack of employee interest and the passage of the Securities Act of 1933. . . .

The loss in employee morale is even harder to measure than the employees' financial loss. However, it was sufficiently tangible to be felt in many cases. A desire to sustain employee good-will towards management, as well as a feeling of moral responsibility, was at the base of most of the decisions to permit cancellation of employee stock subscriptions.[26]

Some stock purchase plans are open only to selected employees, such as managers, department heads, salesmen, or others whose services are highly respected or who can afford to stand a loss in case of a decline in value. Stock purchase plans can give the em-

---

[26] Helen Baker, *Employee Savings Programs—An Analysis of Recent Trends.* Industrial Relations Section, Princeton University, 1937.

Fig. 103. Bruce V. Moore, of Pennsylvania State College. Readers who are interested in further study on the problem of industrial psychology will appreciate his article, "How Can Psychology Help Industry?" Personnel Series No. 43, American Management Association, 1940.

ployee a sense of participation in the industry only when he has rights in shares in which the public does not participate, or when he is really a partner in the business, as demonstrated by the successful commonwealth organizations.[27]   Otherwise the employees who are encouraged to purchase stock should be of the intelligent class, who are mentally capable of understanding the fluctuations in price, or who diversify their investments.

Summary.   Many formal methods of dealing with employee relations are available to management and employees.   The extent to which various methods or plans are used and factors to consider in their use may be studied from reports published by scores of research organizations.   Among the organizations that report valuable studies of industrial relations are the National Industrial Conference Board, Inc., The Brookings Institution, the Industrial Relations Section of Princeton University, the American Management Association, and the Policyholders Service Bureau of the Metropolitan Life Insurance Company.   Those who

---

[27] Henry C. Metcalf, *Industrial Experimenters.* Bureau of Personnel Administration, February 1933.

deal with employee relations should become acquainted with the publications of these and other sources of information such as the current professional and business journals.

Studies of such publications indicate that industrial relations activities are a mark of alert management rather than a desire to exploit workers. Intelligent managers wish to supply pleasant working conditions, vacations with pay, rest rooms, physical examinations, insurance, and perhaps pensions for some employees. The money spent for such provisions is not necessarily taken out of the employees' pay envelopes.

The National Industrial Conference Board investigated the cost to the employer during one year for each of twelve specified activities—namely, bonuses for length of service; bonuses for attendance or punctuality; bonuses for the quality of the article produced; profit sharing for the wage earners; profit sharing for the office employees, the salaried staff, and the executives; vacations with pay; cafeterias; group life insurance; group sickness and accident insurance; pensions; medical service; and mutual benefit associations.

The average annual cost of the selected activities to these concerns was $26.65 for each employee who shared in one or more of the benefits. Profit-sharing awards for the office employees, the salaried staff, and the executives were not included. In the group including plants employing less than fifty workers, the average expense was $49.17, the cost of wholesale insurance omitted; in the next higher group, those employing from fifty to one hundred wage earners, the cost was $26.31.

It may be said that industrial relations programs offer something of pecuniary value to the employee but that their cost is charged to the employee's pay check. Stated differently, some employers say that they do not believe in setting up these activities and prefer to put into the pay envelope the sums which would thus be spent. In order to determine the validity of this claim, the Conference Board ascertained the annual wage cost per employee in almost 1,300 concerns. In 60 per cent of these plants, which utilized one or more of the specified activities, the average wage cost in 1927 was $1,338, while in the other 40 per cent, which used none of the selected plans, the figure was $1,291. In other words, the companies that engaged in industrial relations activities did not do so at the expense of the payroll, but paid their employees more than did those which did not follow such benefit plans. In addition to paying a yearly wage about $50 higher, the employers in plants which engaged in industrial relations activities spent about $27 per worker for cash or pecuniary benefits.[28]

The above study also indicated that the weak management cannot bolster itself by the use of welfare devices. On the other hand, the strong management tends to be intelligent in its employee relations as well as in its customer and financial relations.

Whenever industrial psychologists have studied methods of management, the usual result has been that the spirit back of the methods has been more important than the method itself. After all, we should expect this to be true. Employees are human beings. When owners and managers prefer to continue to operate their businesses in the old boss-subordinate manner, difficulties tend to develop and owners may wonder whether they should quit entirely. Actually, adaptation to the more modern methods, coupled with genuine expressions of colleagueship, may bring new satisfactions as reported in the following example:

About a year ago one of my friends, a prosperous small manufacturer in a Western city, came to me with his dilemma. He had been in business for a number of years; had always conducted his business in a clean, orderly manner; he owed no money to the banks or anyone else and yet labor troubles were looming. He didn't understand either the theory or the principle of the Government's attitude toward labor. He knew there was a feeling of unrest among his employees, who had never been on strike. He had sort of a paternal relation with them that was almost ideal and his problem was hadn't he better liquidate now, get out of business, save what he had rather than risk the uncertainty of the future. He consulted his local attorney and his local bank. Both of them advised him to tell the agitators to go to blazes; that he would run his business as he wanted to, as he had been doing it, and if they didn't like it he would close the plant.

It was about that time he came to me. I spent practically one whole night in preaching to him the gospel of the marvels of business today; how easy it was to throw up the sponge—but the accomplishments of a successful business and the creation of goods that are needed was about the finest and grandest adventure man could be in today. I pointed out that this was a fast changing world that had changed the sociological aspect of business; that it was no longer a purely private enterprise, it was semi-public and social-political in nature; that these foreign labor agitators that he had never dealt with before were merely a passing phase; that he would have to treat with his employees in a manner that he had never treated before. I asked him to review carefully whether he had conscientiously treated his labor as fairly and carefully as he should have. He had most of his figures at his fingertips and he admitted frankly that in some departments he had not.

---

[28] *Industrial Relations Programs in Small Plants,* pp. 39 ff. National Industrial Conference Board, 1929.

I advised him to go back, re-rate his entire factory to what he thought was a fair, equitable distribution of the returns, and announce to his employees that he was ready to treat with them in any manner that they elected; to have his attorney study the Wagner Labor Act to the last detail and to do nothing in spirit or in letter (more especially in spirit) to violate that Act. I suggested that he look upon it as a great game that he was playing; to put into these new and changed conditions the best that he had and that I would, on my part, give him every bit of advice I could from the broader aspect of New York. But I impressed upon him most emphatically that he could never again view his business as purely a personal thing; he would have to view it from the new aspect of a public trust. True, he owned the machinery of production, but he was part of a new social order and there was a public relation interest in his business that he couldn't overlook.

By dawn he grasped it, and I take great pride in the fact that he went back on the job with renewed vim and vigor and a new point of view; and today he is perhaps happier in business than he has been in many years. He looks upon it entirely as a new game and a new problem. He had his labor troubles later but they are behind him now and his relations with his employees are better and stronger than ever.[29]

Fig. 104. Dale Yoder, of the University of Minnesota. Those interested in the problem of industrial relations may wish to refer to his book *Personnel and Labor Relations* (Prentice-Hall, Inc., 1938).

References

Arnold, Thurman W., "Labor's Hidden Holdup Men," *Reader's Digest,* June 1941.

Balderston, C. C., *Executive Guidance of Industrial Relations.* University of Pennsylvania Press, 1935.

[29] F. E. Moskovics, "Business a Social Force," *Printers' Ink,* March 10, 1938.

Clark, Marjorie R., and S. Fanny Simon, *The Labor Movement in America*. W. W. Norton & Co., 1938.

Gardiner, Glenn, *How to Handle Grievances*. Elliott Service Company, 1937.

Moore, B. V., and G. W. Hartman, editors, *Readings in Industrial Psychology*. D. Appleton-Century Co., 1931.

Moore, Herbert, *Psychology for Business and Industry*, Chapter X. McGraw-Hill Book Co., 1939.

Slichter, Sumner H., *Union Policies and Industrial Management*. The Brookings Institution, 1941.

Strong, Edward K., Jr., *Psychological Aspects of Business*, Chapters XXVIII-XXX. McGraw-Hill Book Co., 1938.

Tead, Ordway, and Henry C. Metcalf, *Personnel Administration*, Chapters VII-X. McGraw-Hill Book Co., 1926.

Projects

1. Discuss the good and bad aspects of the foreman's procedure described in the following example.

I recall a situation where a foreman in charge of an unloading crew went to the superintendent and recommended that inasmuch as certain roller conveyors had been put into use in the unloading of cars, a reduction in the tonnage rate paid to workers for unloading cars should be put into effect. His recommendation was accepted and a reduction in rates was installed.

In announcing this reduction to his workers, the foreman explained to them that the superintendent had called him in and told him that rates would have to be cut.

"In spite of everything I could do and in spite of every argument I could put up against this cut in rates, the superintendent insisted it had to be done anyhow," the foreman explained.[30]

2. Collect newspaper accounts of recent strikes and list the grievances and demands of the strikers. Analyze them. What additional factors of importance did you note?

3. Draw up in outline form a collective-bargaining contract such as might be used in a specific unionized industry. Let a union officer or member examine the contract and discuss its provisions with him.

4. The foreman is a key figure in labor relations. Work out a system for selecting foremen in a large factory. Describe specifically each quality you would want to consider and how you would use it in the selection plan.

5. Compile a list of industrial relations services a company can give its employees at a nominal cost. Ask several workers to check those they like and those they may not care for. Do workers seem to agree as a whole or are individual differences pronounced?

6. Examine the magazines in your library and list those which have regular departments that treat industrial relations problems. Examples of such magazines are *Business Week*, *Modern Industry*, and the *United States News*.

---

[30] Glenn Gardiner, "Reaching the Individual Worker," delivered before the Second Annual Greater Philadelphia Safety Conference, May 27, 1935.

24

Supervising Women Employees

Business has much to contribute to a woman's life, and, through her, to the home. . . . In a democracy our interest must lie in the richest flowering of the individual, not in the deflowering of the individual for the sake of an impersonal concept such as "business." Our national emphasis must be upon what women can take from business to the home, not on what they can bring from the home into business. Business must be a means to an end—the living of the good life—and not an end in itself.[1]

MOST of our opinions of psychological differences between men and women are the result not of scientific observations but of incidental contacts or conversations. Every man has had the unpleasant experience of finding himself in situations where he had to listen to the telephone conversations of women who were talking with each other about trivialities that appeared very important to them but which dealt with such subjects as clothing, "dates," movie heroes, and similar topics. It is for this reason that some executives find it necessary to prohibit social conversations over the telephone during working hours. However, the differences in conversation have been studied systematically. Dr. Carney Landis listened to casual conversations in three cities—London, New York, and Columbus, Ohio. He made notes on the spot and tabulated the subjects under various headings. Money and business led the list of men's conversations. "How's business?" was the subject discussed in 35 per cent of the conversations of the men in London, 48 per cent in New York, and 49 per cent in Columbus. If women were talking, 5 per cent of the conversations in London, 3 per cent in New York, and 12 per cent in Columbus dealt

[1] Elisabeth Cushman, "Office Women and Sex Antagonism," *Harper's Magazine*, March 1940.

with business. When men were talking together, they tended to discuss amusements and sports to the extent of about 15 per cent of the conversations; when women were talking they tended to discuss men. In New York, 44 per cent of the confidential chats of women with each other dealt with men, and 23 per cent of the conversations between New York women concerned clothing and decorations, whereas men gave far less conversation to clothing.

It is probable that men acquire their patterns of behavior toward the opposite sex from early childhood experiences. The boy who is reared by a mother and several older sisters often has an antagonistic attitude toward women, with the result that when he marries he tends to oppose anything that his wife suggests. The individual executive's attitude toward women employees may often be discovered in the study of his childhood environment, as his early contacts with the females of the family and school have definitely conditioned him toward women. Quite often the executive also develops a defense-mechanism toward women employees as the result of some unpleasant experience that he had when girls first became very attractive to him. If, during his youthful courting days, he found that he had a tendency to give way to a strong but abhorrent sex impulse, he may have learned to control himself by a frigid manner toward women in general. This would be apt to happen especially if he had had an unpleasant experience with the opposite sex wherein he was socially disgraced, or if he had been involved in some situation where he might have been disgraced had his conduct become known to his superiors and associates.

Psychological differences. Professor Thorndike has made some studies of sex differences and, in general, has found that the most important characteristic of measurable differences is their small amount. The mental differences between the sexes are very small compared with the differences within one sex. Men and women are psychologically very much alike. Women are able to do work of collegiate grade just as readily as men.

In many of the coeducational colleges the highest average for the men's groups is lower than the lowest average for the women's groups. Of course, men claim that this does not prove that women are mentally superior to men. The women who go

to college are a more highly selected class than the men who go.
Boys go to college more casually than girls. Girls are also apt
to be more conscientious in school work than boys.

When women are given equal opportunity with men in professional and business fields, they often compete successfully
with them. The general conclusion from investigations indicates that this equality of achievement comes from an equality
of natural gifts rather than from an overstraining of the lesser
talents of women. Thorndike [2] has reported studies which
show the probable per cent of men who reach or excel the
median woman in respect to each of the following traits:

TABLE XL

PER CENT OF MEN WHO EQUAL OR EXCEL THE MEDIAN WOMAN

1.	In accurate and orderly retention of what is read	73%
2.	In love of sedentary games of skill	71
3.	In independence	70
4.	In zeal for money making	69
5.	In quickness of recovery from grief	66
6.	In love of sports	62
7.	In humor	61
8.	In talkativeness	40
9.	In gayety	40
10.	In vanity of person	40
11.	In patience	38
12.	In sympathy	38
13.	In excitability	37
14.	In religiousness	36
15.	In dissatisfaction with oneself	36
16.	In activity (of the aimless sort)	36
17.	In impulsiveness	34
18.	In desire for change	32
19.	In emotionality	30
20.	In temperance in the use of alcoholic drinks	30 or less
21.	In adroitness in manual work	28
22.	In industry	28
23.	Interested in persons rather than in things	15

According to this table, men excel women in the first seven
traits and women excel in the remainder. On the basis of past
investigations only, we can conclude that the greatest psychological difference between men and women is that women are more
interested in persons than in things. As a group, they are also
probably more interested in children than are the men, but it

---

[2] Adapted from Edward L. Thorndike, *Educational Psychology*, p. 201, Vol. III.
Teachers College, Columbia University, 1914.

is problematical whether these differences are inherited or acquired. Recent studies indicate that these differences are acquired. It is even doubtful whether girls would play with dolls if they were not trained to do so by their mothers. When little girls are persuaded to play with dolls, the doll is more of an opportunity for manipulating it by dressing and undressing it than a "baby" upon which an early maternal instinct can be directed. Sometimes a doll is a companion, but it is seldom a "baby." When boys are trained to play with dolls, they will play with them just as affectionately as girls. The doll is personified as a companion and not as a child. Little evidence has been found which indicates that women, as a group, inherit more of a parental instinct than men do; nor are men more pugnacious by inheritance than women. Such psychological differences are the result of adjustments rather than inheritance.

Men and women, as members of the two groups, have few differences in character and personality traits such as truthfulness, tolerance, superficiality, stupidity, ability to draw, mimicry, ear for music, patriotism, straightforwardness, trustfulness, kindness to animals, snobbishness, and pleasure seeking.

The fact that history has given us very few great women in comparison with the number of great men might be attributed to greater variability among men even though the average general intelligence is the same. Studies of variability have not yielded any definite evidence to indicate that men do vary more than women with respect to intellectual traits. It is true, of course, that we have more men than women in institutions for the feeble-minded, but this difference may be the result of economic pressure. Men must be economically self-supporting, or they are confined in an institution, whereas women are more apt to be kept in the home and allowed to perform routine tasks for which a feeble-minded person may be trained.

Interests of women are centered in the home. Business and world affairs are of secondary importance to them. Even world-shaking events of historical significance have been found to be less interesting to women than recipes for a pie filling.

The time was a Thursday late in April 1940. The Germans had invaded Norway and, driving the British before them, were once again proving the might of the *Blitzkrieg*.

On this day, a newspaper in an Ohio city carried an eight-column streamer head on its front page, telling the latest war news. On the front page were three war stories, news of the world, history in the making.

The main war story was read by 28 per cent of the women who saw the paper. A second war story was read by 24 per cent of the women, and a third by 19 per cent.

The first-column story, about a harbor tie-up, was read by 30 per cent of the women.

On the same page was another story. Its headline covered only two columns and was dropped toward the center of the page, beneath a picture. It said: "4000 Women Attend First Session of Cooking School."

That story was read by 48 per cent of the women who saw the paper and only one other story on that page, headed, "Girl Hurt by Automobile," had higher feminine readership.

The cooking school story was continued on page 28. Here it was read by 34 per cent of the women who saw that issue of the paper. Compare this with the 28 per cent, 24 per cent and 19 per cent of the women who read the three war stories on the front page. This carry-over had higher feminine readership than any front-page item, except the automobile accident story and the local first-column story. And it was on page 28. Also on page 28 was an advertisement, three columns wide by 7¾ inches deep. It pictured a lemon pineapple pie and in a block two inches by 3¾ inches gave the recipe for that pie.

Some part of this advertisement was read by 31 per cent of the women, and the recipe itself by 27 per cent.

Nine square inches of copy, telling how to make a pie, had higher feminine readership than two front-page war stories, and only 1 per cent less than the main story with its eight-column head.

These figures are taken from data furnished by The Continuing Study of Newspaper Reading conducted by the Bureau of Advertising of the American Newspaper Publishers Association.[3]

The psychological problems of married women compared with those of single women. In Chapter 1 a report was presented of certain psychological problems of 1,000 normal women and men. A tabulation was also made of the problems of married and single persons. The average number of problems reported by each of four groups were:

Groups	Problems
Married men	16.1
Single men	17.5
Married women	16.3
Single women	18.0

The data indicated that the four groups were similar in the number of problems reported. The reader can give his own

---

[3] C. B. Larrabee, "Women Read Service Copy More Eagerly than Hot War News," *Printers' Ink*, August 2, 1940.

interpretation of the causes of the differences reported and presented in the following table:

TABLE XLI

PROBLEMS OF MARRIED WOMEN COMPARED WITH THOSE OF SINGLE WOMEN

	Percentage of married women having the problem	Percentage of single women having the problem
Problems which married women have more than single women:		
Tendency to take life too seriously...............	30	22
Tendency to give up my rights for the sake of others	20	7
Inability to remember important matters.........	17	9
Fear of serious illness............................	15	10
Fear of being poverty-stricken....................	15	9
Fear of being injured in traffic...................	15	6
Inability to get along with relatives..............	15	5
Fear of old age..................................	14	9
Lack of opportunity to succeed in life............	12	5
Tendency to "fish for compliments"..............	9	6
Inability to select the right clothes..............	8	4
Lack of humor...................................	8	3
Problems which single women have more than married women:		
Worrying about what others think of me..........	25	35
Habit of daydreaming............................	13	30
Fear of getting fat..............................	20	29
Inability to save money..........................	15	28
Feeling myself inferior to others.................	13	21
Being too easily led by others...................	12	21
Being more interested in pleasure than work......	2	17
Inability to find the right life mate..............	3	16
Lack of faith in others..........................	8	15
Lack of enthusiasm..............................	8	15
Habit of tardiness...............................	9	14
Lack of popularity..............................	5	14
Habit of biting finger nails......................	4	12
Tendency to be cynical..........................	4	10
Belief that I am very homely.....................	4	10
Tendency to tease others........................	4	10
Belief that I am below average in ability.........	3	10
Blushing too much...............................	5	9
Worry about halitosis............................	4	8
Lack of interest in opposite sex..................	1	8

Sex differences of interest to the executive. Significant shifts are taking place in the occupational life of women.

Women are eager to escape domestic and personal service as a means of livelihood. They no longer wish to be servants in the home, laundresses, or boarding-house keepers. On the other hand, there has been a great increase in women barbers, hairdressers, manicurists, restaurant and lunch room keepers, and waitresses. About one ninth of all women who work away from home are engaged in professional pursuits such as chemistry, teaching, the ministry, drafting, the law, osteopathy, and so on.

1. The chief trait of women that interests the business executive is the fact that, as a rule, they take a job temporarily. Most women expect to marry eventually and have a home rather than a career. Women do not regard a job as a permanent part of their destiny as men do. Consciously or unconsciously, they hope to escape into matrimony. Their employment in industry is merely a casual premarital state which must be ended as soon as possible. It is for this reason that women will leave their jobs or be absent from work in order to do some Christmas shopping or remain at home to take care of home duties. One textile plant which employed 500 women of whom approximately one third were married found that records of absences for one year showed that single women were absent 2.9 per cent and married women 10.8 per cent of the available working time.

Relatively few women in business have definite vocational ambitions for themselves. At one time the writer made a systematic study of the relation between ambitions and the jobs held by 776 men and 769 women in a general office. It was found that the men, as a group, who had a definite vocational ambition and were in the kind of job that was in harmony with the ambition were clearly more efficient than the men, as a group, who had a definite ambition but were in a job not in line with their ambitions. For example: men who wanted to be accountants and were working in the accounting department rated higher in efficiency than men who wanted to be accountants but were in a technical research department. However, no such group differences in efficiency were found among the women. In fact, it was very difficult to locate women in the organization who had a definite ambition. The women worked without any definite vocational objectives.

Inasmuch as many women do not consider their jobs as a permanent part of their lives, it is difficult for labor leaders to organize them. They do not care to join a union, and, once they are members of a labor group, they drop out very quickly. Only a great emotional strain, such as a strike, will stimulate them to join a labor organization.

2. Women measure their like or dislike for a job by the personalities about them in shop or office. Men more often seek a specific job because the job is of intrinsic interest and value to them. Women accept a job in a casual manner and then base their attitude toward the work in accordance with their attitude toward their fellow employees and supervisors. If a woman likes her boss, she tends to like her job. If a man likes his boss, he may or may not like his job. At any rate, he is more apt to consider other factors to be of equal or greater importance than the supervisor. It is for this reason that some successful executives make special efforts to have their women employees like them. They know the importance of a friendly but not too cordial greeting. Every sensible married man knows that his wife will appreciate some little thoughtfulness toward her more than gifts of gold and frankincense. The husband who says, "I never buy my wife any flowers on our wedding anniversary because she has the money and privilege to buy anything she wants," has not learned the fine art of dealing with women.

Women appreciate admiration of their personal selves, but they greatly admire the man who respects them. It is because of their lack of opportunity for professional and other worthwhile training that they have endeavored to gain attention and admiration through sexual charm. The youth who would win the lady of his heart should show by his conduct not only that he admires her, but, more important still, that he respects her for herself. Similarly, the executive who adopts a condescending manner toward women will lose influence over them in comparison with the man who shows that he respects them and values their points of view and special abilities. The man who says that "women are dumb" has missed the valuable contributions they can make to the success of a business. An executive policy of condescension and familiarity will result in meager returns from the weak-willed, whereas a respectful and friendly manner will yield a rich reward from the stronger-minded women.

Fig. 105. Mrs. Hortense M. Odlum whose contacts with business had been limited to keeping tab on a personal checking account, took over the management of Bonwit Teller, a bankrupt New York specialty store, in 1934. In six years she had increased sales from $3,500,-000 to $10,000,000!

"Main secret of Mrs. Odlum's phenomenal success evidently has been an ability to look the word 'consumer' in the eye without flinching. One of her first acts as president was the creation of a consumers' advisory committee, made up of a cross-section of the store's clientele. And by instituting such practices as that of writing thank-you notes to new cash customers, Mrs. Odlum proved that a specialty store could have a heart."—*Business Week*, October 19, 1940.

3. Women are not jealous of the success of men who move up the business ladder, and will help them to climb and ask little in return for their assistance; but they are often jealous of the other woman who capitalizes her personal attractiveness for her own benefit. Most women still expect men to hold the responsible positions and are more willing to follow a domineering, fatherly type of executive than a sisterly type of woman.

A normal male Protestant Republican can work in an office with Jews, Catholics, atheists, and Democrats, even though he himself is a member of organizations wholly opposed to the religious, political, and racial views of those about him. Few women find their work congenial when they disagree with the religious, political, and racial affiliations of their associates. Any advancements of such associates are apt to be interpreted as evidence of favoritism; and, if a woman is promoted, the other women tend to find more fault than if a man with the same prejudices is advanced over them. Conversely, a man objects to a woman who knows more than he does; only the exceptional man cares to marry a woman who is markedly brighter than he. The intelligent women who have married men less intelligent than themselves have had to do so by hiding their brilliance. The woman who wishes to advance in business should not attempt to "show up" a man, even though she is right and he is an ignoramus.

4. Women are more easily discouraged than men. If they find the new job difficult and slightly unpleasant, they will fail to appear for work the next day. Men tend to have more "stick-to-it-iveness" in the face of mild difficulties. Even though a new woman employee does well for a beginner, she is apt to think that she has not been satisfactory. The executive who supervises women soon learns that turnover is reduced if he takes pains to praise the efforts of the new workers.

Companies that employ large numbers of women soon learn that if beginners are introduced to new work, not singly but in groups, they will be more encouraged and remain long enough to learn the work. If a woman finds that some others learn just as slowly as she does, she is greatly encouraged. As previously stated, women are very sensitive to the personalities and opinions of their associates. They cannot analyze the job and their work objectively, but measure their value to their employer by their estimates of the opinions of associates and supervisors. They are also more keenly affected by the criticisms or opinions of men supervisors than of women supervisors. Hence, new women workers should have supervisors who are women.

5. Women are absent from work more than men. Hence, a larger number of women are required on a pay roll to operate the plant than when men are used. Several years ago the writer was in charge of personnel research for one of the rubber companies in Akron, Ohio. The company wished to know whether salaried women office employees should have the same salaries as men when men and women were doing the same kind of work. At the time when the question arose the company was troubled by what appeared to be an excessive amount of absenteeism. Deductions for absence were not made from any salaries. This was during the period of high prices and plenty of jobs following the First World War.

Each office employee, regardless of rank, was required to punch a time clock at the beginning and end of each day's work.

A study of all the time cards, visiting nurses' calls, and dispensary calls for the months of February, March, and April, yielded the following data:

TABLE XLII

ABSENCE REPORT FOR THREE WINTER MONTHS

Causes	Male	Female
Average number of employees............	776	769
Number of absences....................	471	1,627
Total available working hours...........	442,316	442,944
Hours lost, all causes..................	10,724	26,692
Per cent of available time lost...........	2.42	6.02
Visiting nurses' calls..................	263	738
Dispensary calls......................	981	1,552

As shown in this table, the female employees were absent from work, for all causes, two-and-one-half times as much as ·male employees. No material differences in working conditions or nature of work could be noted which would cause one to expect more absenteeism of women. All the employees were in the general office building of the company. Light, heat, ventilation, and so on, were the same for both sexes. The men, on the whole, had more responsible positions than the women.

The company employed visiting nurses who called at the home of the absentee on the same day the absence occurred. The visiting nurse ascertained and reported the real cause of the absence, in so far as possible, and the nurse's statement of cause was accepted rather than the statement of the employee.

From these data it is evident that at least 17 per cent of the absenteeism of the women office employees was caused by ailments peculiar to women only—dysmenorrhea and ovarian congestion.

It was noted that absenteeism for both men and women was less on pay days than on other days. In one case fifty employees were absent the day before pay day and only six were absent on pay day.[4]

Women appear to be absent from work because of sickness more often than men, although infant mortality is higher among boys than among girls. Male natality and male mortality are both greater than female natality and female mortality. In one study made in England, it was found that 104 boys were born for every 100 girls born. But during the first month, 129 boys died to every 100 girls; during the following two months, 132 boys to

---

[4] Harry Walker Hepner, "Absenteeism of Women Office Employees," *Journal of Personnel Research*, April 1925, pp. 454-456.

100 girls; and at the end of the year, 125 boys to 100 girls had died. In Syracuse, New York, in one year, 139 more boys than girls were born, yet only 82 more boys survived the first year.[5] In the United States as a whole, the expectation of life at birth is 60.9 years for white males and 64.4 for white females.[6]

6. Women are adapted to routine tasks. They appear to accept monotony with more comfort than men. They probably do this because of their temporary interest in a job. "A

TABLE XLIII

REASONS FOR ABSENTEEISM OF WOMEN OFFICE EMPLOYEES

Cause of Absence	Number of Absences[7]	Total Hours Lost
Colds	97	1,238
Dysmenorrhea	80	1,198
Illness in family	60	758
Headache	66	505
Biliousness	46	499
Scarlet fever	3	496
Septic throat	15	297
Laryngitis and tonsillitis	13	287
Injuries	7	284
Fatigue	6	276
La grippe	3	256
Toothache	27	245
Mumps	13	192
Miscellaneous	20	162
Nervousness	5	112
Tonsil operation	1	108
Ovarian congestion	1	80
Rheumatism	4	76
Boils	2	76
Dislocated shoulder	1	72
Sore feet	4	60
Dysentery	5	40
Stiff neck	2	30
Eye trouble	9	24
Overslept	3	16
Pain in ear	1	16
Swollen glands	1	16
Pain in side	1	12
Goiter pressure	1	8

[5] Mary V. Dempsey, "Boys Exceed Girls in City," Syracuse *Post-Standard*, December 31, 1928, p. 8.

[6] Harold F. Dorn, "The Increase in Average Length of Life," *Public Health Reports*, Vol. 52, No. 49, December 3, 1937, p. 21.

[7] "Number of absences" is not the same as number of employees absent. For example, one employee may have been absent on two occasions in the month for the same or different causes. "Miscellaneous" included absenteeism for business, recreation, and other reasons.

job is a job," as one woman said when the employment manager asked her whether she objected to a monotonous task. Intelligence is one factor to be considered in relation to monotony; but, as women appear to be as intelligent as men, we cannot attribute the willingness of women to perform routine tasks to low intelligence.

They also make fewer suggestions for the improvement of the work than men do. Initiative should not be expected on the part of the rank and file of women. They appear to be caretakers rather than promoters.

One taxicab company tried out women drivers but found that they lacked initiative and were unsuitable for the work. The vice president and general manager of the company said:

A close investigation and careful analysis of women drivers disclosed the fact that they are not profitable, and neither is it being fair to them, due to the peculiar type of work.

A taxicab driver requires real sales ability. The driving end of the business is not nearly so important as the salesman's ability and initiative and, I might add, plenty of nerve in pushing through congested areas in trying to get a fare. Women are too timid for this type of work, and also, due to the unpleasant parts of this business with which drivers are confronted, especially during the night shifts, it was impractical to have women drive at night. Our investigation showed that the women drivers took in about $3 per shift less than the men.

7. Women expect cleanliness and tidiness in their surroundings. Workrooms should be light and airy. It is the influence of women that has taken the cuspidors out of our hotel lobbies. Men find little difficulty in working in surroundings which are slightly dirty. "Cleanliness is next to godliness" is the motto of more women than men. Lunch rooms and rest rooms where women employees congregate should be kept clean. Clean floors and machinery painted white will attract women to a shop, even though wages are slightly below those of other firms in the community.

8. Women have little mechanical ability. They can operate typewriters successfully but men must repair them. The best book of instructions to women drivers of automobiles consists of but one sentence: "When something goes wrong with the car, take it to or call a garage man." The General Electric Company found that one of the best sales arguments for their re-

frigerator was: "You don't have to be an expert mechanic to run it.   Just leave it alone and it will take care of itself."

Of course, women can be trained to perform many mechanical operations, but their knowledge and skill are usually limited to the job for which they have been trained.

One of the most popular arguments of our day deals with the automobile-driving ability of women in comparison with men. Fortunately, Dr. Harry R. DeSilva, a leading researcher in driving abilities and causes of automobile accidents, has given a summary of his findings:

The mechanized female is less deadly than the male. At least, that is the conclusion to be drawn from a recent study of 3,000 mixed motorists in Connecticut. Dr. Harry R. DeSilva, who conducted the survey as head of the Yale University-Esso Safety Foundation co-operative research, found that women drive about half the mileage of men but get into only one third as many accidents.

"This shows that women are still safer drivers," Dr. DeSilva concluded inexorably, blasting masculine beliefs as he went along, "and that they do not have fewer accidents merely because there are fewer women drivers." This certainly should discourage those people who try to explain away the fact that only 6.6 per cent of the motorists involved in America's 32,600 automobile deaths last year were women.

It may be, however, that Dr. DeSilva just didn't get around among the right female drivers. At any rate, most people don't see eye to eye with him at all. Investigators for the Gallup poll who went around the country last year asking citizens "Would you rather ride in a car driven by a man or a woman?" found that 60 per cent preferred men drivers, 8 per cent felt safer with women, and 32 per cent apparently were fatalists or pedestrians and didn't care. . . .

The questions of sex and driving ability will probably never be settled by statistics; they don't take into account such imponderables as the relative exposure of men and women to tough traffic hazards; the time of day each sex habitually drives; the special case of taxi and truck drivers, who are abroad day after day in all kinds of weather.

The safety people have turned to science for an answer, testing those physical and sensory characteristics of motorists which might affect their driving ability—and the men seem to have the edge. A series of tests given by the American Automobile Association to several thousand men and women in thirty-five American cities showed that men make better scores in reaction time, quickness of action, resistance to glare and recovery therefrom, ability to keep calm, driving proficiency as indicated by a gadget called the drivometer, and, of course, gripping strength. Some of the differences were fairly significant. The average man, for example, required 5.55 seconds to recover from the glare of a bright light; the average woman needed 7.47 seconds. On the road, this would mean the median female would travel a third again as far while blinded by headlights.

On the distaff side, fewer women had a tendency to color-blindness and to have one eye dominant over the other.

Dr. DeSilva has conducted exhaustive driver tests of a similar nature, and the men always come out on top. "On the other hand," he says, "I am coming to believe that women are much safer drivers than men because they are more safety-minded. In other words, men are more skillful, but women have fewer accidents."

So there you are.[8]

9. Women need special supervision and rules in an organization. Female rather than male coaches should direct their recreational play. They require rest rooms and rest periods. Of 66 business concerns in one city, 19 allow women employees to leave the factory several minutes before the men quit. Their hours of work are regulated by the state. Situations of possible embarrassment must be avoided, such as the overtime working of one man and one woman in an office or a shop. Welfare workers must be available to them at all times. Constant standing or other straining postures must be minimized. Repeated lifting of weights of 25 pounds or more must be avoided as well as exposure to temperatures over 80 degrees and under 50 degrees.

10. In spite of the extra bother that women in an organization may cause an executive, they do have a definite superiority in certain fields of work and in specific jobs. Woman is apt to be the superior of man in certain departments of life just as often as his inferior. One good woman will have a refining influence in an organization of men. The head of a department that employs 120 men has found that the language of his men, their manners, and general behavior are better when he has even one woman of the right type working in the department.

One of the baffling psychological problems that confront the management of industrial concerns is the large amount of thinking and conversation of a sex nature on the part of employees. Anyone who has worked in a factory where men only are employed will be able to recall the fact that many workers seem to concentrate as much as 90 per cent of their thinking on lewd aspects of sex. It is an obsession with many otherwise normal workers. The same situation occurs, in a milder degree, in fac-

---

[8] Lewis Bergman, "Less Deadly Than the Male—" *The New York Times Magazine,* July 14, 1940.

tories employing only female help. The question naturally arises, "How can these employees ever develop reasonable efficiency or train themselves for promotion when most of their thinking and talking is directed toward sex?" It is true that they cannot do their best work under such conditions, but the management can substitute better working conditions and supply other subjects for thought and conversation.

One of the best remedies is that of mixing the sexes. Teachers who have taught in a one-sex school, such as a girls' or a boys' academy, know that an unnatural situation exists under such conditions. The reason for it lies in the fact that human beings, in their thousands of years of evolution, did not evolve in an environment where the sexes were segregated. The family life is the normal condition for men and women in school and in business. A factory or office which is deeply colored with shady conversation can be greatly improved by mixing the sexes so that they are more or less equal in number.

Women who work, especially older or married working women, are often criticized for their activities in business. Some companies and boards of education have rules against married women working. Unemployed women as well as men try to have legislation passed to prevent various classes of women from working. Many of the critics fail to appreciate that most of the jobs held by married women are in most cases not really interchangeable with the jobs desired by unemployed men. Miss Mary Anderson has stated some important facts in defense of the women, especially wives who work:

Fixations in jobs decrease efficiency, the younger women argue, and it is only fair that a woman who has had a living from a certain position for a number of years should relinquish it to someone who needs the salary even more. Views of this sort are shared with enthusiasm by men and women on the relief rolls hoping for jobs.

In refutation, Miss Mary Anderson, chief of the Women's Bureau of the Department of Labor, takes up the facts she has compiled. . . . Her office is now the source of the greatest mass of information on the situation and the hub of activity in opposition to the "anti-working-wives" bills.

Of the men reporting themselves unemployed in the 1937 registration, Miss Anderson says, more than one third were laborers, whereas less than one twentieth of the women were so classified; and 18 per cent of the men were skilled artisans, as against less than 1 per cent of the women. The number of jobs interchangeable between the two groups is necessarily small.[9]

---

[9] Kathleen McLaughlin, "Shall Wives Work?" *The New York Times Magazine*, July 23, 1939.

The employed woman not only helps to raise our standard of living through the additional economic goods she helps to produce but she also makes an important psychological contribution to business.

The contribution of woman to business is more than chintz curtains and flowers, more than an insistence upon cleanliness in surroundings and conversation, more than a willingness to perform the detailed monotonous tasks of business. She can present to the executives a point of view that will enable the management to design more beautiful products as well as guide executives in making decisions that affect the success of the business in general. It is exceedingly unfortunate that our system of education trains women to occupy pedestals in life rather than prepares them for a life of economic activity. In spite of traditional methods of education, women are learning how to have careers as well as how to manage homes. Too many middle-class and educated women find an excessive amount of leisure time on their hands which is dissipated in bridge parties and gossip. The sooner they acquire a vocation, the better for them, for men, and for society.

References

Griffith, C. R., *An Introduction to Applied Psychology*, Chapter XIII. The Macmillan Co., 1936.

Hepner, Harry W., *Effective Advertising*, Chapter 7. McGraw-Hill Book Co., 1941.

Hollingworth, H. L., *Vocational Psychology and Character Analysis*, Chapter XX. D. Appleton-Century Co., 1929.

MacGibbon, Elizabeth G., *Manners in Business*, Chapter XI. The Macmillan Co., 1936.

Moss, Fred A., *Applications of Psychology*, Chapter X. Houghton Mifflin Co., 1929.

Poffenberger, A. T., *Applied Psychology*, Chapter VIII. D. Appleton-Century Co., 1927.

Robinson, O. P., *Retail Personnel Relations*, Chapter XVI. Prentice-Hall, Inc., 1940.

Shepard, Jean L., *Human Nature at Work*. Harper & Bros., 1938.

Women's Bureau Bulletins. Government Printing Office, 1918—.

"Women in Industry," *Modern Industry*, June 15, 1941, pp. 14-19.

Projects

1. Prepare several copies of Thorndike's list of traits listed in this chapter and ask several women to check the traits in which they believe women excel men. Ask several men to do the same. On which items was there

general agreement by all the men and women? On which traits was there the least agreement? Did the men or women tend to rate their own sex the higher?

2. Assume that you are about to establish a small manufacturing enterprise employing between 50 and 100 persons. Outline your plans for:

(a) Selecting the women you wish to hire.

(b) Making special provision in the plant and working schedule for the women.

3. Ask a number of women who are employed what they like the most and what they like the least about their jobs. Were the replies concerned chiefly with personal relationships or with methods and things? Assume, in each case, that you are the woman's supervisor, and tell what specific action you would take in the light of the information received.

4. Why is it permissible for men to exchange personal banter with women such as the waitress or the check girl of the cloakroom, but not for women to do so with men of the lower occupational levels?

5. Should the manufacturer of products for women advertise that his products are designed and inspected by women?

6. Should the employer attempt to obtain the good will of the wives of employees? How can he do so? What are the dangers of such an attempt?

7. Write a *Help Wanted* advertisement to obtain women factory employees and a similar advertisement for male employees. How do they differ?

8. Suggest methods of overcoming the tendency of the women customers of clothing stores who take home party frocks on approval, or "spec," and then return them after a party.

9. When women employees are required to wear a shop costume, should it be made of heavy khaki-colored material or of light-weight gingham? Who should select the style of the costume?

25

Appeals in Advertising

A successful merchandiser stated several effective appeals in the following maxims: "Any physical fact, like increasing fatness or the phases of the moon, is much more interesting to any woman than such outside activities as city planning, national politics, or the Bi-Centenary of George Washington; A man customer never grows up, and will spend twice as much time choosing a trout fly as a stair carpet or a refrigerator; People are steadfastly unwilling to skimp on things they buy for their own children. To make sure of a sell-out, at least 25 per cent of the merchandise must be in doubtful taste; and no advertisement, no matter how lavish, will persuade people to buy what they don't want." [1]

RESEARCHERS in advertising who have made studies of the relative importance of various factors such as long copy versus short copy, big pictures or little pictures or no pictures at all, charts and diagrams as an accompaniment of other pictures or used alone, and testimonial versus reason-why copy seem to agree that none of them is so important as the *appeal* or *theme*. The appeal is the dominant idea which is supposed to arouse a dormant desire in the mind of the prospect and stimulate him to purchase the product. The appeal is far more important than type face, illustration, or headline.

One would expect the theme or appeal to be the one great influence in causing us to be affected by the advertisement. Hand a page of closely typewritten material, haphazardly arranged, to a group of people and ask them to look it over. If the names of the readers are among the words on the list, it is easier for them to find their own names than to find the names of strangers. Twenty-

---

[1] Abbott Kimball, Inc., *Advertising and Selling*, August 4, 1932, pp. 42-43.

eight adults were used in such an experiment to find out how long it would take each person to find his name on a page of closely typewritten material. Each person's name appeared five times in the copy. An examiner timed the subject with a stop-watch while the subject looked for and underlined his own name five times. Then the subject or person who had found his own name was asked to find the name of a stranger in the same copy. The stranger's name also appeared in five places in the copy and had to be underlined five times. Accurate records were kept for each name, and it was found that the average length of time required for each of twenty-eight persons to find his own name was 72.6 seconds. For these persons to find the names of strangers required 103.7 seconds, or 43 per cent longer.

A theme or appeal in advertising is any idea used by an advertiser when he seeks to influence people of the particular class who are logical prospects for his product or service. The advertiser does not seek to reach everyone with his message. Even though the advertiser sells a so-called mass product such as soap or food, he has narrowed his choice of appeals to the particular class or classes of people who are apt to buy his soap or food. The advertiser thinks of his advertising appeal as a selective device which is designed to be attractive to his prospects; not to all persons. Prospects are usually analyzed and classified on the basis of two general approaches:

1. The *appeals* effective in stimulating the logical prospects.
2. The *media* that will convey the chosen appeals to the prospects and do so profitably. Examples of advertising media are newspapers, magazines, radio, direct mail, book matches, exhibits, displays, and others.

Studies of consumers for the selection of media can be made more easily than for the selection of appeals because data about the former are more likely to be objective and available in published form. Common classifications for media studies are sex, income, age, geographical location, and occupation. So many volumes of data on these classifications are published each year that we can give only a few examples here.

Classifications of Consumers for Selection of Advertising Media

Relative influence of men and women in buying. Anyone who reads contemporary business literature is likely to find occasional statements to the effect that women do 80 per cent of America's shopping. However, this is an incomplete as well as an incorrect statement. To know who the buyers are is important, but the really significant question for the advertiser and salesman is "Who influences the shopper?" Is the influence of women more important than that of men relative to *price, kind,* or *brand?* Do women consult their husbands and do men consult their wives before they purchase some commodities? These questions, as well as others of a similar kind, were studied in a survey of 1,200 families, and the following data resulted:

TABLE XLIV[2]

PERCENTAGE OF FAMILIES IN WHICH PURCHASING IS INFLUENCED
BY A FEMALE AND BY A MALE

	Price		Kind		Brand	
Commodity	*by a Female*	*by a Male*	*by a Female*	*by a Male*	*by a Female*	*by a Male*
Household Staples:						
Canned goods	88.4%	25.1%	96.2%	73.3%	91.1%	36.1%
Cereals	86.2	25.6	90.5	79.8	89.3	44.1
Coffee and coffee substitutes	81.6	27.3	88.6	48.6	87.4	71.0
Desserts	90.4	18.2	93.5	77.8	94.5	27.2
Toilet soap	87.6	23.6	92.8	46.5	91.8	56.7
Infrequently Purchased Products:						
Automobile	41.6	95.2	79.5	94.8	53.9	96.6
Electrical devices	68.1	75.4	89.2	45.6	70.5	75.6
Electric refrigerator	55.7	88.8	83.2	71.8	74.7	79.0
More expensive rugs	76.4	83.5	95.1	54.0	84.8	43.6
Radio	43.0	90.8	77.4	80.6	58.0	91.3
Personal Products:						
Cosmetics	95.1	23.2	96.5	22.2	97.0	20.5
Toothpaste	86.1	62.5	91.2	63.8	91.3	79.4

The table suggests that the influence of women shoppers varies with the kind of article purchased.

(1) In the purchase of household staples, the women have greater influence than the men regarding *price, kind,* and *brand.*

---

[2] H. W. Hepner, "Relative Influence of Men and Women in the Purchase of 12 Commodities," published by *Redbook* Magazine, 1933.

However, the men have two or three times as much influence for *kind* and *brand* as for the *price* of the staples. Furthermore, the men have some influence in the purchase of all household staples. In the case of coffee and coffee substitutes, men have almost as much influence regarding *brand* as do women. Men have an important influence in the selection of foods and staples, even though women do the shopping. Women buy to please not only themselves but also their husbands and other male members of the family.

(2) In buying the more expensive and infrequently purchased commodities, the men have a very important influence on the *price* to be paid. The men also influence the *kind* of electrical refrigerator, rugs, and other expensive articles purchased. One would expect the men to have almost unanimous influence on the *brand* of automobile purchased, but a considerable percentage of them also influence the *brand* of rugs and of electrical devices.

(3) In the case of personal products such as cosmetics and toothpastes, the women have much the greater influence regarding *price*. However, the survey also revealed that men influence the *kind* and *brand* of cosmetics purchased in one fifth to one fourth of the families studied.

(4) On the whole, the survey suggested that the advertiser could not afford to assume that women do the shopping in America without consulting and trying to please their husbands to a considerable extent. Conversely, too, commodities assumed to be purchased by males, such as automobiles and radios, are purchased by a large percentage of men in order to please their wives or daughters as well as themselves.

Income as a selective influence. Consumer income is one of the advertiser's preliminary criteria in the selection of logical prospects for his article or service. If he has a high-priced article, he knows that some people can afford his product and others cannot. Furthermore, high-income families spend more money for certain staples as well as luxuries. See Tables XLV and XLVI.

Incomes are an important guide to the advertiser in the selection of the media for his advertising message. People of the higher income levels read relatively more magazines as well as more expensive magazines and newspapers, as suggested by Table

TABLE XLV[3]

AVERAGE EXPENDITURE PER FAMILY

All Urban Non-Relief Families—By Income Groups

Income Groups	Food	Personal Care	Tobacco	Clothing	Automobile Purchase & Operation
A ($5,000 & Over)..	$1,258.66	$110.04	$81.12	$731.41	$589.19
B ($3,000-$4,999)...	793.88	62.31	52.86	373.41	327.28
C ($2,000-$2,999)...	641.05	47.00	43.59	227.57	214.57
D ($1,000-$1,999)...	476.84	31.54	31.59	130.38	105.31
E (Under $1,000)...	296.52	16.49	16.56	55.67	23.62

TABLE XLVI[4]

RELATION BETWEEN INCOME AND CONSUMER PURCHASES

(Purchases by $1000-$1499 Income Group = 100)
(Non-Farm, Non-Relief)

Income Group (Dollars)	Expenditure For Food Per Person, Weekly (Dollars)	Fruits Index Number	Meats Index Number	Wheat Products Index Number
Under 500.........	$1.10	38.3	55.6	94.0
500- 999.........	1.62	72.7	83.5	101.0
1000-1499.........	2.18	100.0	100.0	100.0
1500-1999.........	2.67	120.9	111.7	99.0
2000-2999.........	3.17	145.8	125.4	97.0
3000-4999.........	3.71	183.0	148.7	96.0
5000-over.........	6.09	247.7	187.3	91.0

TABLE XLVII[5]

AVERAGE ANNUAL EXPENDITURES FOR MAGAZINES AND NEWSPAPERS

Family Income Bracket	Average Annual Expenditures for Magazines	for Newspapers
$5,000 and over....................	$16.92	$24.16
3,000-4,999.....................	7.25	19.76
2,000-2,999.....................	4.45	16.57
1,500-1,999.....................	2.78	14.19
1,000-1,499.....................	1.54	11.87
Under $1,000.....................	.53	8.07

[3] National Resources Committee, Bureau of Labor Statistics, and Bureau of Home Economics, quoted from Everett R. Smith, "How Five Income Levels Spend Their Money," *Advertising & Selling*, March 1939, p. 37.

[4] Compiled from studies of consumer purchases in 1935-1936 by the Bureau of Labor Statistics and the Bureau of Home Economics with the collaboration of the National Resources Committee. Compilation by the Marketing Section, Agricultural Adjustment Administration. *The Challenge of Under-Consumption,* an address by Milo Perkins, President of the Federal Surplus Commodities Corporation, at the Fourth Annual National Farm Institute, Des Moines, Iowa, Saturday morning, February 24, 1940.

[5] *Magazine and Newspaper Penetration by Income Groups,* Report No. 6, Research Department. Crowell-Collier Publishing Co.

XLVII. According to an analysis of a United States Government study of incomes and purchases of non-relief families living in towns of over 25,000 population, the average annual expenditures for magazines and newspapers by families in each income group were as in Table XLVII.

Incomes alone cannot be used as a guide by the modern advertiser when placing his advertising. He also considers income in relation to location. Families who live in metropolitan centers like New York and Chicago must pay a premium for that privilege as compared with life in a village or on a farm. Certain expenditures such as those for food, housing, and transportation (other than automobiles) are higher in the congested centers. The extra costs are called "costs affected by congestion." A family with an income of $1,500 in New York or Chicago may not have as much money for the purchase of semi-luxuries as a family in Wooster, Ohio, with an income of only $1,000. The costs of congestion often offset the advantage of several hundred dollars' income in a large city. See Table XLVIII for data relative to spendable income in five different types of communities.

TABLE XLVIII[6]

Total Income Versus "Spendable" Income

by Size of Community

	Metropolitan Centers	Large Cities	Middle-Size Cities	Small Cities	Rural Communities
Average income.....	$1,680	$1,558	$1,358	$1,375	$1,141
Costs affected by congestion.......	1,079	812	721	616	517
Remaining "spendable" income.....	601	746	637	759	624

After the modern advertiser has learned the geographical distribution and income classifications of his logical prospects, he is fairly well informed regarding the suitability of different media to

---

[6] Metropolitan centers used in this study were New York and Chicago. The large cities were Providence, R. I.; Columbus, Ohio; Atlanta, Ga.; Omaha, Neb.; Denver, Col.; Portland, Ore. The 257 smaller cities and counties are listed on page 3 in the original report from which this table is quoted. Quoted from *Selective Spending in Rural America*, Commercial Research Division, Curtis Publishing Co., April 1940, p. 17.

Table based upon data obtained from The Consumer Purchase Survey, conducted in 1936 by the Bureau of Labor Statistics and the Bureau of Home Economics.

Fig. 106. Paul F. Lazarsfeld, Columbia University. Those who wish to study the problem of radio research further are referred to his book *Radio and the Printed Page* (Duell, Sloan & Pearce, 1940).

carry his message. He may choose media which are read largely by people of the kind who are his logical buyers, or he may choose a general medium such as radio and adapt his message to his chosen class of prospects. For example, a research study, "Social Stratification of the Radio Audience," analyzed actual program audiences by income groups. In the evening hours class A and B income members listen more to the variety and musical programs, whereas classes C and D listen more to comedy and drama. Symphonic music is relatively more popular in class A, semi-classical in B, quiz programs in C, and crime drama in D. Few programs had a uniform appeal to all income groups.[7]

When typological and other classifications have been discovered, the advertiser's next step is to find the most effective appeals. For example, one company promoted milk as a food for athletically inclined boys after it was indicated from a study of milk consumption in New York City that many boys consider milk-drinking a "sissy" habit. In this study of milk, it was found

---

[7] H. M. Beville, *Social Stratification of the Radio Audience.* Office of Radio Research, 15 Amsterdam Avenue, New York. In this study, incomes were divided into the four groups: A, $5,000 and up; B, $3,000 to $4,999; C, $2,000 to $2,999; and D, under $2,000. The number of families in the D group was, of course, much greater than in the A group; percentages of the total numbers of families were the following: A, 6.7 per cent; B, 13.3 per cent; C, 26.7 per cent; and D, 53.3 per cent.

that 35.5 per cent of the persons studied drank no milk at all and that people between ten and fifteen years of age were most likely to stop drinking milk.[8]

Few if any advertised products have a mass usage. People even differ in their preferences for common staples such as bread, rice, water, butter, and a host of other products. Taste preferences, income, age, reading habits, and other varieties of human characteristics are studied by advertisers in order to select those prospects whom the advertiser may be able to serve. These studies of available objective factors of consumers should be made before specific appeals are considered.

Donald A. Laird has kindly furnished the writer a case history that illustrates how an objective factor such as age may combine with a psychological characteristic to determine an advertiser's logical prospects:

A specialty food had been distributed for many years. It had started as a "health food" and was making steady progress until the health claims were no longer permitted. With the health appeal denied them, the advertising was shifted to a sparkling, gay, country club tempo, and illustrations were of cocktail parties, cafe society, and similar demi-monde scenes—all planned to attract the young sophisticates.

The advertising produced a rush at the grocers the first month. Most of the stores, however, found that their re-orders of the specialty were not selling. The advertising to young sophisticates continued for a couple years, with continually declining sales, until the manufacturer finally decided some outside assistance was needed. He felt that the advertising agency did not put enough words into the copy, and he wanted an outsider's frank judgment.

The history of his product, its nature, and particularly its unavoidable, unusual flavor, all suggested that the natural market for it was among older persons—not among the young people to whom his advertising was being addressed.

A variety of tests were made with consumers concerning the taste-acceptability of the product—age ranges from childhood to senility were covered. It was discovered that there was a general dislike for the taste of the product by people up until they were about fifty years old. After fifty years, the liking for the product's taste increased rapidly.

A change in type of illustration and general tempo of the advertisements was made, with the idea of appealing to the older groups, who were the natural prospects for the product.

One's sense of taste changes greatly through life, and there are a number of foods which have natural markets in rather definite age groups. Advertis-

---

[8] *The Technique of Marketing Research*, pp. 20, 22, 23, prepared by the committee on Marketing Research Technique of the American Marketing Association. McGraw-Hill Book Co., 1937. Also Paul F. Lazarsfeld, "The Use of Detailed Interviews in Market Research," *Journal of Marketing*, July 1937, pp. 3-8.

ing that is directed to other ages in such instances may be wasteful. This age-limitation of natural markets holds, in various ways, for many products, but is perhaps most marked in the case of foods.

Once the advertising man has learned the characteristics of his logical prospects—their sex, age, income, geographical location, or other classification—he can easily select his media accordingly. Almost every modern publisher of a periodical, manager of a radio station or network, and head of an outdoor posting concern can supply printed data that describe the readers or listeners of his particular medium.   By means of such printed data, the advertising man can easily decide which medium or media are most likely to reach the specific classes of prospects whom he wishes to reach.   Once he has collected the data necessary for the intelligent selection of media, he also has much information available for making a choice of effective appeals.

Effective Appeals

Examples of effective appeals.   The experienced advertising man who plans a campaign looks for the dominant idea that will appeal to the consumer classes whom he can reach by means of media available to him.   He wants to find out what can be said that will hook up with the associative linkages of prospects whom he can afford to reach.   When we study the progression of appeals of advertisements and sales talks, we find important changes made to increase their effectiveness.   Let us note some examples.

1. In the past, manufacturers of shoes assumed that readers of their advertising were most interested in style, price, construction of shoe, details about fancy punching, and so on.   However, one shoe manufacturer conducted a survey of 5,000 men and found that when they were asked what they liked about the shoes they were wearing, 42 per cent replied "fit and feel" or some equivalent; 32 per cent said "wear and tear"; 16 per cent said "style and looks"; 9 per cent said "price and value."   The manufacturer changed his advertising accordingly, using themes such as *Walk-Fitted,* and benefited by the change.[9]

2. Advertisements of banks do not try to induce people to save so that they may have more money.   The rainy-day appeal is not

---

[9] Richard Giles, "Bostonian Shoe Advertising Is Revolutionized after Survey Among 5,000 Men," *Printers' Ink,* September 22, 1939.

very strong. But it is possible to persuade people to save money in order to buy something that they want. Thrift is an effective appeal largely as the means to the end of obtaining an automobile, a trip abroad, or a fur coat.

3. One candy manufacturer found that when he advertised the quality of his candy and made references to its excellence he did not sell so much as when he changed his appeal to that of buying his brand as a gift. He discovered that the bulk of his business came from men who buy candy to take home to their wives and daughters and from young men who buy it for girls. Price as an appeal was not so important a consideration as the appropriateness of the article for gift purposes.

4. The maker of a game, well-known to the public, devoted his sales and advertising messages to the story of the pleasure his game would yield to the family circle. His advertisements usually pictured father and mother and the two children playing the game with happy smiles on their faces. His appeal for years was "For Enjoyment." Then, upon consulting a marketing specialist, the appeal was changed: "To Be Popular." With this appeal the players were pictured in a home which was the rendezvous of delighted friends. The response to the advertising doubled in sixty days and the sales of the game tripled.

5. The manufacturer of a liquid to keep men's hair smooth assumed that most men prefer to have "varnished hair" similar to that of actors and male dancers. Another manufacturer of the same kind of liquid directed his appeal to the mothers of small boys having stubborn hair, and his sales soon exceeded those of the first manufacturer.

6. A certain insurance company found that in the advertising of accident insurance the note of protection to loved ones was not nearly so effective as some other appeals, such as the low price of the insurance of this sort. The best-paying advertisement they had was one headed "Three Cents a Day," which explained how many thousands of dollars of protection this small expenditure would bring. The fear motive and the thrift motive were somewhat less effective.

7. One of the most interesting records of appeal effectiveness has occurred in the advertising of "Dr. Eliot's Five-Foot Shelf of Books." Charles W. Eliot, president emeritus of Harvard Uni-

versity, made a famous remark in 1909 to the effect that an individual could acquire the equivalent of a liberal education by devoting 15 minutes every day to the study of great literature. Since that time, the P. F. Collier & Son Corporation has sold 500,000 sets of the Eliot-chosen books at an approximate cost to the consumer of $50,000,000. The price of a set has ranged from $40 to $600, depending upon the binding.

The basic appeal in the advertising has always been to "get ahead"—to grow. The self-improvement theme has been supplemented with appeals to the reader's desires for self-confidence. One insertion, captioned "How to get rid of an inferiority complex," has been used with success for more than 10 years.

Another successful theme, on a slightly different note, was, "Like a conquering army these books have marched triumphant through the centuries," accompanied by an illustration of a medieval army. Introduced in 1925, this insertion was used until some time in 1936. Copy with a bargain appeal, describing the cost per volume of the Harvard Classics as one-third the price of popular fiction, was instituted some time ago and continues in use.

Long reason-why copy, seeking prompt return of a coupon, has always prevailed, and experiments with more emphasis on an artistic layout and less copy have proved that such an approach carries little weight with the reader who seeks to improve himself.

Seriousness is the key. From its inception, advertising of the Five-Foot Shelf represents the efforts of a conservative and serious salesman. Carefully abjuring flippancy, it has employed a wide variety of sales approaches, always characterized by a note of sincerity and earnestness. The man who feels himself inferior to his fellows evidently does not take it lightly, and is deadly serious when he decides to improve himself.

As described by W. W. Beardsley, advertising manager of Collier books for the past 12 years, "People don't go in for education with a fillip. The luxury type of advertising doesn't sell books."

One innovation introduced by Mr. Beardsley is an illustration picturing the 50 books piled on end instead of on a shelf. The illustration borders the copy on one side and has produced good results.[10]

These seven examples from literature in the field of advertising illustrate the reason why advertisers and salesmen seek the one keynote that will touch off the spark of interest in the prospect. The history of advertising reveals many examples of appeals, both ineffective and effective ones. Until recently, psychologists often analyzed instincts as possible effective appeals. Today we no longer study lists of instincts and reflexes in the quest for

[10] Judith Cortada, "The Five-Foot Shelf: Lesson In Merchandising," *Advertising Age,* March 31, 1941.

effective appeals because instincts and reflexes have usually been analyzed by means of armchair or laboratory methods only. The modern marketing analyst does not bother with such obsolete approaches to the choice of appeal. He uses more recent and better research techniques.

Readership surveys as guides in the selection and use of appeals. As previously stated, the appeal is the most important single factor of an advertisement. However, it may be presented in many different forms as with reason-why versus emotionalized copy, positive versus negative, or generalized versus specific application. Furthermore, the appeal in any form may be used in an advertisement that is placed on the back cover of a magazine or buried in the midst of a 64-page edition of a newspaper; it may be in four-color or black and white; and so on. Appeals, therefore, should be studied in terms of their applied form as they are actually used in the chosen media. The readers' reactions rather than those of the armchair psychologists must be studied. Field investigators of readers' reactions to published advertisements are collecting many records concerning the effectiveness of various appeals. One of the most widely used methods was developed by George Gallup when in 1931 he began to study systematically the comparative factors of reader interest in the contents of magazines and newspapers.

The so-called Gallup method has many minor modifications, but it usually means that an interviewer calls at the homes or offices of a representative sampling of persons. The interviewer asks the interviewee whether he has read a certain issue of a periodical. If the answer is "Yes," the interviewer produces an unmarked copy of the periodical, explains the purpose of his investigation, and asks: "Won't you kindly tell me what you have read as I turn these pages?" The interviewer usually marks the advertisements noted or observed, headlines read, and amount of copy read. Sometimes the name of the advertiser or the product is masked (painted out) and then the interviewer inquires whether the interviewee can identify the product or name of the advertiser. Readership reports often present their findings by giving percentages of readers who (a) *noted* or observed the advertisements, (b) read the *headline,* (c) read *most* of the copy, and (d) *identified* the name of the product or advertiser when names were masked.

One particularly extensive readership study by the Gallup Research Bureau included interviews with 29,000 representative readers of 46 issues of 20 different Sunday newspapers located in 16 cities. The effectiveness of the basic advertising themes was tabulated in this study and the themes are ranked in terms of readers per column inch, averaged for men and women. See Table XLIX.

The extreme right-hand column of the table shows the percentages of distribution of the dominant appeals found in a ran-

TABLE XLIX[11]

How Sunday Newspaper Readers React to Basic Advertising Themes

		Readers Per Column-Inch		Distribution of Appeals Found in the Advertisements
	Copy Appeals	*Men*	*Women*	*of One Industry*
1.	News features..................	.653	1.007	4.0%
2.	Sex allure.....................	.377	1.027	1.0 (weak!)
3.	Social advancement............	.476	.837	2.0
4.	Narrative technique (both strip and straight copy)................	.318	.695	10.0
5.	Characters from the product's radio program......................	.388	.541	—
6.	Reason-why copy..............	.316	.563	17.0
7.	Contests.....................	.162	.414	—
8.	Testimonials..................	.200	.356	1.0
9.	Scare appeals.................	.139	.407	1.0
10.	Smartness and newness.........	.271	.251	—
11.	Health appeal.................	.218	.272	—
12.	Product's reaction under test.....	.276	.263	1.0
13.	Price reductions and values.......	.262	.167	2.0
14.	Premiums.....................	.167	.256	—
15.	Service given with a product......	.083	.321	21.0
16.	The product alone with no drama..	.232	.073	40.0
				100.0%

In many of these ads two or more of the above themes have been combined and the classification under which they have been listed is open to challenge. However, when any such conflict has arisen the theme motivating the illustration has been taken as the dominant one.

These advertisements used in this Kimberly-Clark study were national advertisements.

[11] "Let 4,979,875 Newspaper Readers Tell You What They Read on Sunday," made for Kimberly-Clark Corporation by the Gallup Research Bureau, 1935.

dom selection of 100 advertisements of one industry, the figures having been compiled by this writer. Apparently the weakest appeals, those at the bottom of the list, were used by advertisers of the selected industry. Though some differences of opinion would occur in the classification of the appeals used in a large number of advertisements, the table has considerable general significance to the advertiser.

Modern advertisers subscribe to various readership-reporting organizations of which L. M. Clark, Inc., Daniel Starch, and C. E. Hooper, Inc., are examples. The reporting organizations interview consumers and collect vast arrays of data concerning appeals and their effective use. For example, the Advertising Research Foundation conducted a two-year "Continuing Study of Newspaper Reading." This report[12] analyzed the advertising and editorial readership of fifteen evening and nine morning newspapers. The summary included ninety "best-read" advertisements, ten from each of seven classifications and twenty from a miscellaneous group.

Analysis of the data of the report showed that people like news in advertising as exemplified in an announcement of a new model automobile, an unusual price offer, or a timely product. Newsiness and timeliness were important influences in readership. Sometimes the news factor was introduced through pictures and names of people who were in the news.

People are interested in people. They like to see pictures of other people. Human-interest pictures of adults, children, babies, and animals were used in the best-read advertisements. Readers liked especially to see pictures of happy smiling people and characters. Furthermore, the successful copy stressed the *you* approach: for example, "Can You Pick the Lucky Baby?" or "When You Need Adhesive."

Women readers liked advertisements that helped them. All the ten best-read toilet requisite advertisements offered the woman reader help in solving a problem in personal care. Six out of ten of the most successful grocery advertisements had recipes.

---

[12] *Attention for National Advertisers.* Bureau of Advertising, American Newspaper Publishers Association, 1941. See also *Printers' Ink,* April 25, 1941, for a summary of the report.

Many companies conduct special readership studies of their advertising in periodicals. For example, Westinghouse Electric & Manufacturing Co. conducted an observation-identification study of its 1940 institutional advertising and found data such as the following: 7 per cent of the readers misidentified the company's magazine advertisements, 68.7 per cent of those who had observed the copy identified the advertiser correctly, and the remainder were uncertain. The company found that it cost $5.36 per thousand circulation to have its business institutional messages observed; $5.86 per thousand circulation to have them read; and $7.81 per thousand circulation to have them correctly identified.[13]

The readership studies of various kinds show that few fixed rules can be stated for the student of advertising. Each rule has many possible modifications, but certain general principles regarding the use of appeals are offered here as points of reference for the student's consideration.

The Use of Appeals

Reason-why versus emotional appeals. One of the oldest controversies in advertising is whether to use copy that appeals to the intellect or copy that appeals to the emotions. One argument for the emotional appeal is that the human brain, in its genetic development, is largely the "old brain," which functions in the instinctive, emotional, and reflexive reactions rather than in intellectual acts. The "new brain," or those parts which are important in the processes of reasoning and association, is smaller and more recent in organic history. We all know that in an emergency, the old brain takes control and we react as animals rather than as logical beings. We know that tendencies such as sex, food, and care of children are very strong when aroused and that they are easily aroused. Hollingworth[14] has named these two types of appeal the "short-circuit" and the "long-circuit" appeals. The short-circuit are those which are directed to emotions and feelings. He suggested that the short-circuit appeals

[13] " 'Blindfold Test' of Copy Tried by Westinghouse," *Advertising Age,* February 17, 1941, page 14.

[14] H. L. Hollingworth, *Advertising and Selling,* p. 245 ff. D. Appleton-Century Co., 1920.

should be used in the selling of personal and intimate articles—articles of luxury, display, adornment, health, food, and safety. Also articles which are enjoyed for their own sake rather than for the service they render. The long-circuit appeals should be used for articles which are impersonal, utilitarian, or instrumental in their values, such as books, plows, hammers, and trucks.

In addition to the short- and long-circuit appeals we also have the "rationalized" appeal, in which case the article is first desired and then the desire is justified on some logical basis. A large part of the salesman's work consists in arousing desires and then giving the prospect logical reasons for buying. Most people prefer to think of themselves as reasoning beings rather than as impulsive or emotional creatures. They prefer to believe themselves highly civilized and intellectual. Hence they need some logical or logical-sounding ideas to justify their emotionally reached decisions.

Man performs few purely intellectual acts. The book, the plow, the hammer, and the railroad train all take on an emotional aspect under certain conditions. If a mechanic uses a hammer for any length of time he may become quite attached to it, and he may refuse a new hammer of the same or better quality just because he "likes" his present hammer. It may become a personal and intimate belonging that is associated with many pleasant or unpleasant memories.

If we want to see the effectiveness of the emotional appeal versus the intellectual, we need but note the difference in attendance and interest between lectures and moving pictures, between fiction and statistics, between study and play, between saving money and spending it, and between courtship and housekeeping. An important part of the function of advertising has been the injection of emotional life into lifeless and utilitarian commodities. When a need or want is keenly felt, it becomes an emotionally tinted reaction. We do few things merely because we know we should do them. A man may be convinced that he ought to take more exercise; but he seldom takes it until the exercise has an emotional appeal, such as playing golf with pleasant companions or the family physician's warning that it is either exercise or an early death.

Human interest in the copy. There are occasions when people enjoy hearing a lecturer because he uses words and ideas they do not understand, as shown by public interest in the Einstein theories. Many people attend a sermon and say that it was wonderful, because the pastor talked about abstractions which they did not and never will understand. However, the abstractions of Einstein or the intellectual assertions of the spellbinder do not move people to do what we want them to do. Profundity and erudition do not influence us as does the tear of a little child, the assuring grasp of a friend, the kisses of a mother, and the wagging tail of a dog. They move us to forget the magnificent scheme and devote ourselves to the commonplace. Human beings may operate, neurologically, as does the machine; but they respond most quickly to the emotion-gripping commonplaces.

The world of imagination, romance, emotions, and feelings is the *subjective* world, and it is the one in which the individual spends most of his time. In writing copy or presenting a sales talk, the most effective method of approach is the subjective. This type of appeal stimulates the imagination, emotions, and senses of the prospect, so that the sales talk or advertisement becomes a real part of the individual's mind.

Only a few individuals, such as scientists, engineers, and statisticians, really view the world *objectively;* and even they are men and women with imagination and emotions rather than merely structures of flesh and bone. It is probably easier to sell a statistician an electric refrigerator on the basis of its health value to his children than to sell it on the basis of its economy of operation. It is often assumed that utilities should be sold on the objective basis and articles of luxury and personal adornment should be sold with the subjective appeal. However, the objective appeal is very limited in its scope and it can be applied to only a few articles, such as factory equipment. Even an automobile truck which is ordinarily sold for such factors as economy of operation may be given a subjective appeal if the prospect is shown how this big truck will give the pedestrians and other observers the impression that his company is a large concern and does a big business. A piece of silk may be described objectively by its color, number of threads, wearing qualities, and so on, but it will

Psyching the Doodles

Watch the client's doodles during the advertising conference
for clues to what he's thinking—

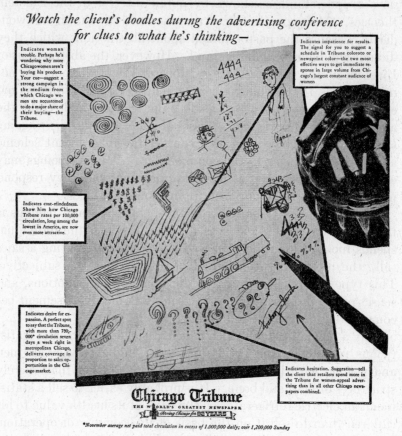

FIG. 107. Some clinical psychologists study the patient's doodles in attempts to obtain clues—not conclusions—regarding influences in the adjustments. The above advertisement which applies analysis of doodles to salesmanship is an attention-getting device.

appeal far more to the woman on the other side of the counter if it is described as something that will cause her to look well and make her distinctive in a group of her acquaintances.

To combine the two methods, it is usually best to use the subjective treatment first and then follow it with the objective or factual treatment. This is the method used in the rationalization appeal, by which the prospect's emotions are stimulated and then objective data are given to bolster up his emotional decision.

The positive versus the negative appeal.   One of the old arguments among veteran advertising men is that of the negative
appeal.   Those in favor of the positive side say that, if a railway
company wishes to persuade the public that the company should
have an increased fare, the company should not advertise to the
patrons its troubles, such as the costs of car operation, bonds outstanding, and the need for new cars.   The patrons are not interested in the company's problems.   The affirmative arguments,
such as the improved service that would result with faster trains,
more comfortable cars, safety devices, and higher wages for the
workers, would be more effective.

In spite of the defects of negative advertising, a few such campaigns have been outstandingly impressive.   Every reader of advertising can recall some advertising campaigns which impressed
him with a negative appeal.   Although some negative advertising seems to have been very successful, certain dangers should be
given emphasis.   A serious danger is the fact that many people
who read the negative advertising accept and believe the negative
side of the copy without going to the end to find the real gist of
the advertisement.   Psychologists have learned that it is dangerous to teach students by first presenting the erroneous arguments
of the subject under discussion.   Many students are more impressed by the errors than by the positive and favorable side, even
though the favorable points far outweigh the negative points.
It is dangerous to say to the child: "You misspelled the word
faverable.   You should spell it *favorable*."   Experiments indicate that it is better to say little or nothing about the errors, but
to proceed at once to the right method.

Most salesmen have learned the importance of ignoring a certain aspect of the negative side of the sales argument, because of
the rule, "We never talk about our competitors."   Such slogans
as "Avoid substitutes" have been discontinued because the reader's attention is called to the substitutes rather than to the commodity that the advertiser has for sale.

The "shock" appeal also tends to lose its force after repetition.
When a person begins work in a noisy office, he notices the noise
and is annoyed by it.   In time he becomes negatively adapted to
it and may be more comfortable in the midst of the noise than
without it.   The mother who constantly scolds her child is unable

---

Glorious Opportunity to Get Rich Quick

Invest in

THE CALIFORNIA RANCHING COMPANY

Now being organized to start a cat ranch in California.

We are starting a cat ranch in California with 100,000 cats. Each cat will average twelve kittens a year. The cat skins will sell for 30 cents apiece. We figure a daily net profit of over $10,000.

NOW WHAT SHALL WE FEED THE CATS?

We will start a rat ranch next door with 1,000,000 rats. The rats will breed twelve times faster than the cats. So, we'll have four rats to feed each day to each cat. Now what shall we feed the rats? We will feed the rats the carcasses of the cats after they have been skinned.

NOW GET THIS

We feed the rats to the cats, and the cats to the rats, and get the cat skins for nothing. Shares are selling at 5 cents each, but the price will go up soon.

Invest While Opportunity Knocks at Your Door
CALIFORNIA RANCHING COMPANY

WARNING

Some gullible people will try to buy this stock. It is a foolish fake, of course, but no more foolish than many "wildcat" schemes being promoted today. Investigate before investing. Don't hand your money over to any unknown glib-tongued salesman.

This poster was placed in the front window of a Cleveland, Ohio, bank as an example of fake schemes which are being offered the public. Unfortunately, many people accepted the negative advertising in the positive manner and wanted to buy some of the stock. When used in another bank, this poster caused sixty-seven people to come into the bank to find out where and upon what terms stock in the cat-and-rat farm might be purchased. Wherever the above poster was used to advise the general public to "investigate before you invest," the result was such great misunderstanding that it had to be removed. See *Printers' Ink,* May 6, 1920, p. 182.

to scare it when the situation justifies a scare.   Similarly, the continued use of the negative appeal loses its shock effect after a few repetitions.

In any discussion of the negative appeal, it is necessary to consider the degree of negativeness.   Some negative appeals are not very shocking, such as "Barking dogs don't bite," "Won't shrink woolens," and "It will not break."   Horrifying negative appeals may be more pronounced in their effects upon those who are psychasthenically inclined.   Showing pictures of wrecked automobiles where several persons are killed, homes without any fire insurance burned down, workmen killed because the company did not provide the right kind of electric switches, and mangled persons lying at the bottom of elevator shafts are examples of negative advertising which tend to scare the reader.

The gruesome is objectionable to many readers and causes them to turn the page quickly to some more happy thought.   Gruesome advertising often injures some innocent industry.   For this reason the electrical industry objects to the advertising of electrical switches by illustrations showing how employees were killed. Describing the thousands and millions of germs that live in most milk and then implying that the milk of the Blank Company has no harmful bacteria often causes some people to use less milk than formerly.

On the other hand, some products have value only or chiefly as preventives of disaster, and the public tends to think of these possibilities of danger as imminent and to be avoided.   For such situations and commodities it may be necessary to use the negative appeal.   But the negative appeal should have the sting removed by showing the positive or desired side of the dangerous situation rather than the catastrophic.   A fence manufacturer can appeal to parents of small children by showing them playing safely in the yard, instead of showing them being hit by passing automobiles.   The escaping of the calamity may be given the chief emphasis, or the calamity may be suggested rather than vividly illustrated.   The correspondence schools could show the American husband as a hopeless failure; but in most of the advertising they show the pleasant side of the good job has attained.

On the whole, one may be justified in generalizing to the extent of saying that, when the product is one which definitely answers a problem of which the consumer thinks mainly as a problem, such as the shrinking of woolens, the sticking of chair varnish, or the skidding of cars, it may be desirable to present the negative side of the situation. However, the appeal may be negative in nature but so mild or so educational in its effects that the readers are informed rather than frightened. The best test of the question is that of the measurement of results. Readership surveys and other tests should answer the question as to whether the appeal should be negative, and to what degree it should be negative.

Appeals are specific rather than general. Many studies have been made as to the relative effectiveness of various appeals, such as health, style, economy, taste, success, prestige, comfort, beauty, and so on. Such studies have little value, because our reactions are made to specific situations rather than to abstract principles. Fear is not a general trait. The amount of fear that one experiences varies in each fear-situation. The fears that one has when the automobile skids, when someone points a pistol, when one sees a banana peel on the sidewalk, and when one must go to the dentist all vary in degree and are attached to specific situations. Likewise, style may be important in the kind of suit one wears but have little importance in the model of car used. One form of economy may be important enough to a woman to cause her to spend two hours and a gallon of gasoline in shopping around to find where she can save five cents on a yard of lace, after which she will spend twenty-five cents for a soda at the most exclusive fountain in town. Economy as an appeal is specific rather than general. Every human trait is specific rather than general.

The advertiser cannot decide which appeal is best until it is applied to a specific situation. Then, too, the appeal varies in effectiveness with the manner of presentation: how the appeal is illustrated, the copy style, the art work, the typography, and so on. To find out the relationship between appeal in the abstract and the appeals in the actual advertised form, an experiment was conducted with 80 advertisements. The 80 advertisements were divided into eight groups of ten each according to general appearance, type, art work, product, and so forth. Then 120 persons were asked to rank the copy when in typewritten form. After the copy had been ranked, the complete advertisements were ranked by the same individuals. The coefficient of correlation of the rankings between appeals in the abstract and appeals when used in actual advertisements was only .40. This is only about 8 per cent better than chance coincidence.

In this experiment one series of ten advertisements of a cigarette was used. All of the ten advertisements were testimonials by actors and actresses. The correlation between the copy in typewritten form and the same copy in the actual advertisements was .86, or 50 per cent better than chance. This was a high correlation. However, where appeals are more varied than those of testimonials of actors, it is well to bear in mind that the effect of an appeal in the abstract is quite different from that of an appeal in actual use in the advertisement or sales talk.

General rules for the appeal.

1. One of the most common errors in the use of appeals on the part of the man who starts a new business is to use generalized abstractions such as *quality, wonderful, helpful, pure,* and *greatest.* If a concern conducts tests of its own products in comparison with competing products and finds that its own actually are best, it is almost useless to attempt to advertise them as *best* to the public. The public is satiated with claims of *best.* Its *bestness* must be presented in some specific situation rather than as an abstract fact. The quality should be applied to some problem that looms large in the minds of the prospects. *Quality* is an abstraction that does not persuade us. The abstractness of quality should be applied to a definite situation, so that it is a concrete, tangible living thing.

2. Very few advertising men attempt to present all the good characteristics of a commodity in a single advertisement. One distinct feature is presented and an attempt is made to impress it on the reader's memory. Many new advertisers are so enthusiastic about their products that they try to tell all the good points in one breath.

3. The beginner in advertising and selling is likely to give undue emphasis to the maker of the product, the size of the company, the length of time that it has been in business, the difficulties encountered in making the article, the number of parts that

are used, and so on. Few of these interest the prospect. The appeal should be directed toward the needs of the prospect rather. than toward the interests of the seller. This is one of the oldest rules in selling and yet few indeed are the advertising men and salesmen who can honestly say that they have never become so interested in the product itself that they talked only about the values of the product to the user. This is one reason why it is well for most business concerns to have an outsider, such as an agency, do their advertising rather than some member of the firm. Heads of small businesses have cited this rule of keeping the "you attitude," and yet when their own advertising was examined it was filled with the interests of the advertiser rather than the interests of the prospects. When we are close to a business or idea, we lose our perspective and need that of the disinterested counselor.

4. The product must be advertised as a means to an end rather than an end in itself. Economy as an appeal is weak for this reason. We do not want to save money just to save it. We may be induced to save money in order to get something else, such as roses, cake, diamonds, travel, or automobiles. The recent advertising of a toothpaste with an economy appeal was used in the right way, because the advertiser showed what the saving would buy. He pictured the articles that might be purchased with the saving.

5. The appeal should be directed toward future or immediate needs rather than past situations. Paying for a past purchase is not nearly so thrilling as the thought of an imminent purchase. Collecting money for deficits of institutions is much harder than collecting money for proposed additions to the institution. "Paying for a dead horse is a burdensome task."

6. *Timeliness* is not an appeal in itself. By timeliness we mean that the mass of prospects have at that moment a set of active neural patterns with which the proposed advertising may be connected. Nor is *humor* an appeal to buy. It is rather an appeal to read and obtain a pleasant feeling. *Curiosity* is not an appeal to buy. It is a means to secure the reading of the message. The advertiser should study his appeal to see whether, after all, it is a reading appeal or a purchase appeal. The appeal should picture to the reader the end or use rather than the means

Fig. 108. Harold E. Burtt, Ohio State University. Readers who are interested in further study of the "Psychology of Advertising" may wish to read his book of that title (Houghton-Mifflin Co., 1938).

to an end. And the end should have intrinsic worth as an end. It should let the reader imagine himself enjoying that commodity.

7. It is probable that we may generalize to the following extent: (a) economy is more important as an appeal in the selling of staples than of specialties; (b) style is stronger than economy; (c) prestige is more important than comfort; (d) taste often outbids health; and (e) social prestige is stronger than personal enjoyment. However, each individual advertiser must find out for himself which appeal is most effective as far as his prospects are concerned. Few rules apply except in a tentative way.

Illusion in advertising is legitimate; delusion is wrong. Within certain limits, human beings dislike humdrum or repetitive acts and ideas. We like to see ourselves in certain situations which lift us out of our actual condition. The movie-goer enjoys the movies because he can project himself into a new world. We attend the theatre not to see life as it is but to see it in a romantic situation. We read fiction not because fiction is written in the same English and style that we use in our daily conversation, but because it is distinctly different. Very few of our best sellers or stories in literature have been written in realistic or conventional style, nor have they painted life as it is lived from day to day. Romance is just as essential in advertising as in the play or the novel. It is the writer's conviction that modern advertising has had some bad effects, but the readers prefer advertising that has the spirit of romance, newness, and exaggerated beauty, even though it is not strictly factual.

Finally, the manufacturer and distributor of merchandise should appreciate the clear-cut distinction between objects as objects and the use of the objects as a means to satisfy some craving or desire. Food is not desired as an object. It is wanted as a means to the pleasant experience of eating. This statement may seem trite, but it emphasizes that we should think in terms of human tendencies or wants and not in terms of machines, cloth, or combinations of metal and wood. The advertiser has the privilege of painting his product in attractive colors. Interest in life is enhanced through the use of products which we have been taught to admire.

References

Burtt, H. E., *Psychology of Advertising*, Chapter IV-VIII. Houghton Mifflin Co., 1938.

Crane, George W., *Psychology Applied*, Chapter VIII. Northwestern University Press, 1940.

Griffith, C. R., *An Introduction to Applied Psychology*, Chapter XXXI. The Macmillan Co., 1936.

Hepner, H. W., *Effective Advertising*, Chapters 8-9, 13-14. McGraw-Hill Book Co., 1941.

Jenkins, John G., *Psychology in Business and Industry*, Chapters XI-XII. John Wiley & Sons, 1935.

Kleppner, Otto, *Advertising Procedure* (Third Ed.). Prentice-Hall, Inc., 1941.

Moore, Herbert, *Psychology for Business and Industry*, Chapter XIV. McGraw-Hill Book Co., 1939.

Nixon, H. K., *Principles of Advertising*, Chapters IV, VI. McGraw-Hill Book Co., 1937.

Poffenberger, A. T., *Psychology in Advertising*. McGraw-Hill Book Co., 1932.

Strong, Edward K., Jr., *Psychological Aspects of Business*, Chapters I-XV. McGraw-Hill Book Co., 1938.

Projects

1. *Match your judgment of popular appeals against their recorded pulling power. True Story* conducted an editorial department entitled "Home Problems Forum." The editors described the forum as follows:[15]

---

[15] "How to Get People Excited," *True Story*, 1937.

Each month a controversial problem involving certain basic human emotions and viewpoints is presented. Every one of these problems stems from actual experience, since they are written from real life by *True Story's* own readers. This is consistent with *True Story's* editorial policy. For the best solution from a reader, a series of prizes is offered. These prizes are kept modest ($15, $10, $5) deliberately so that response may be credited to the problem rather than to the cash!

Some problems bring letters by the thousands—others by the thin hundreds.

The editors admitted that eighteen years of experience in picking the ideas for the forum and predicting response from readers has made the editors loath to offer many dogmatic generalizations. However, two sets of the problems are given below. Rank each of the six problems of Group I and of Group II according to your estimate of its relative pulling power, marking the best as 1, second-best as 2, and so on. After you have made your rankings, turn to the appendix for the correct answers.

Group I

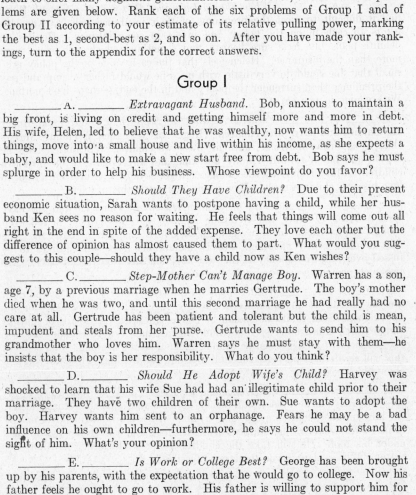

_____ A. _____ *Extravagant Husband.* Bob, anxious to maintain a big front, is living on credit and getting himself more and more in debt. His wife, Helen, led to believe that he was wealthy, now wants him to return things, move into a small house and live within his income, as she expects a baby, and would like to make a new start free from debt. Bob says he must splurge in order to help his business. Whose viewpoint do you favor?

_____ B. _____ *Should They Have Children?* Due to their present economic situation, Sarah wants to postpone having a child, while her husband Ken sees no reason for waiting. He feels that things will come out all right in the end in spite of the added expense. They love each other but the difference of opinion has almost caused them to part. What would you suggest to this couple—should they have a child now as Ken wishes?

_____ C. _____ *Step-Mother Can't Manage Boy.* Warren has a son, age 7, by a previous marriage when he marries Gertrude. The boy's mother died when he was two, and until this second marriage he had really had no care at all. Gertrude has been patient and tolerant but the child is mean, impudent and steals from her purse. Gertrude wants to send him to his grandmother who loves him. Warren says he must stay with them—he insists that the boy is her responsibility. What do you think?

_____ D. _____ *Should He Adopt Wife's Child?* Harvey was shocked to learn that his wife Sue had had an illegitimate child prior to their marriage. They have two children of their own. Sue wants to adopt the boy. Harvey wants him sent to an orphanage. Fears he may be a bad influence on his own children—furthermore, he says he could not stand the sight of him. What's your opinion?

_____ E. _____ *Is Work or College Best?* George has been brought up by his parents, with the expectation that he would go to college. Now his father feels he ought to go to work. His father is willing to support him for two years while he is looking for a job—but thinks college unnecessary. His mother feels it a crime to deprive the boy of his education, in view of the fact that he is a fine student and has won a scholarship. With which parent do you agree?

_____ F. _____ *Sulking Husband.* Before their marriage Helen and Marvin were friends as well as sweethearts. Shortly after, Marvin begins to show traits she never thought he had. At any disagreement he sulks. Will not eat at home for days, or try to come to some agreement. Helen is desperate because of the unhappiness in her home. Marvin says he needs solitude when hurt. Sees no reason why Helen should be distressed but that she should be made to realize the fact when she hurts him. What do you think?

Group II

_____ A. _____ *When Should Insurance Be Cashed?* Joe and Helen find it difficult to meet the premiums of their insurance policy. Now Joe wants to cash in on the policy and invest in some business. He has no definite plans but feels sure he can find something which will bring them more than the insurance. Helen feels that the cash value of the policy is so small that Joe could do very little with it. She would rather scrimp and pay the premiums than surrender the policy and in the end, perhaps have nothing. With whom do you agree?

_____ B. _____ *Father's Attitude to Step-Child.* Mary and Roger are married and have three children. Roger was very fond of Timmy, Mary's child by a former marriage, until his own two children were born. Now he is cold and harsh toward Timmy but kind and affectionate to his own two children. Mary is hurt by the change. Roger says it is natural for a man to love his own children most. How would you settle this problem?

_____ C. _____ *The Unemotional Husband.* Gertrude and Joe have been married 10 years and Gertrude realizes that they are ill mated even though Joe has made money. Though they love each other, she is the type that requires visible affection. Joe is unemotional type who dislikes to be fussed over and says money is the best affection any woman can have. Are two such people wise to marry? Is Joe right?

_____ D. _____ *What Should We Tell Our Children?* Elsie and Stan are the parents of an unusually bright boy of 8. They do not agree on his upbringing. Stan thinks he should be conversant with the details of marital and sex life. Elsie objects. She thinks his attitude can only make the boy sex-conscious at an age when he cannot understand its meaning. She believes this will result in a perverted mental attitude toward life. How do you feel about this problem?

_____ E. _____ *The Dependent In-Laws.* Jack and Ruth are farmers—they have little money but plenty of food and a home. Ruth's sister, her husband and children are in dire straits. Ruth wants them to live on the farm. Jack would rather supply them with food and a little money, but not under his roof. He will take the children for a while until conditions are better. Whose plan do you think most feasible?

_____ F. _____ *Shall Wife Forgive Errant Husband?* Helen goes home to her parents, who live in a town where there is a good hospital, to have her baby. Later she discovers that her husband George has had an affair with another woman while she was away. Unable to stand her husband, she takes baby away to her sister's home where the child dies. She is too dazed to resist George when he comes to take her home, but feels there can be no happiness for them now. George says he loves her and wants another chance. What do you think?

2. One of the country's most successful teachers of dancing says that he does not sell people *dance study.* He sells them what dancing will do for them, such as bring them popularity, health, charm, relaxation, or other benefit. A lawyer, for example, who buys the lessons does not "take lessons"; he relaxes. Apply this principle to the advertising of a canned food, an automobile, a bank account, or a radio.

3. James W. Young has built a business of selling men's ties through the use of split-run tests in *Sunset* magazine. For example, he tried three different headlines: (a) HAND WOVEN by the mountain people of New Mexico, (b) SHABBY HUSBANDS made over—by my hand-woven ties, and (c) HUSBANDS LOVE my hand-woven ties (and you.) The first outpulled the others by a wide margin. Why?

4. A split-run test in *The New York Times Magazine* for the sale of a popular-audience book tried two different appeals in the headline. The headline "How to win friends and influence people" produced twice as many sales as "How to ruin your marriage in the quickest possible way." Why?

5. One advertising man claimed that an advertisement is like a pretty girl —the more she only partly reveals her charms, the more interesting she becomes. Study advertisements which have been written to induce readers to ask for more information. Give examples of the copy that has been written for that purpose.

6. Consider the following goods or services and classify each as to the medium or media that would be most suitable for advertising purposes:

        a. A newly published book on engineering.
        b. Flowers.
        c. Gasoline.
        d. Night-school classes in accounting.
        e. Fresh meat and vegetables.
        f. Farm tractors.
        g. Life insurance.

Give reasons for your classification in each instance.

26

Devices Used in Advertising

One of the easiest ways to answer the consumer who imagines that advertising increases costs to the consumer is to ask him this question: "Assume that you wish to buy a wide variety of commodities, including such items as clothing, cosmetics, canned goods, farm machinery, furniture, radio, sporting goods, plumbing supplies, jewelry, and so on. Where would you go to buy them at reasonable prices, year after year?"

The usual answer to this question is a certain nationally recognized mail-order house. When the consumer is told that the particular mail-order house he chose is one of the world's biggest advertisers, spending more than $10,000,000 a year for newspaper advertising alone, the consumer is likely to realize that advertising does not necessarily increase costs to consumers. Hence, any legitimate devices that measure the effectiveness of advertising or increase its effectiveness are likely to benefit consumers.

Relatively few people pay attention to any one advertisement. One important readership study showed that the average person reads only three of every hundred advertisements exposed to him. This estimate applied to the substantial reading of most of the text.

A further analysis was made to ascertain why the 603 men and women read the particular advertisements which they did. The reasons, or motives, given were as follows: Of each 100 advertisements read, 24 were read because of unusual attention-getting features such as layout, display type, color, white space, and so on; 19 because of the interest appeal of the headline and text; 15 because of the illustration; and 13 for miscellaneous reasons. The other 29 advertisements were read because of factors outside of the advertisements themselves. Of these 29, 21 were read because of special interest on the part of the reader in the product advertised, and 8 were read because the reader was considering the purchase of the product advertised.

This investigation emphasizes the importance of the first requirement of an effective advertisement: namely, that it must be seen to be read. To repeat, again, 24 out of each 100 advertisements were read because of mechanical attention features of the advertisement.[1]

---

[1] Daniel Starch, "What Makes an Advertisement Sell Goods," *Advertising & Selling,* November 27, 1929, p. 57.

The readership reports of national magazine advertising indicate that of every four readers who notice a given advertisement, two glance only at the headline or illustration, one reads part of the text, and one reads all or most of the advertisement. Furthermore, an advertisement may catch attention but fail to catch the mind of the reader or make friends with him. A good advertisement not only (a) catches attention but also (b) develops friends for the advertiser, (c) induces action on the part of the reader, and (d) contributes toward the consumer's satisfactions. Of these four mental processes, attention has been given the most study by psychologists.

Fifteen attention-getting devices in magazine advertising. Hollingworth[2] was one of the first psychologists to classify the devices used to catch attention in advertisements that are published in a periodical. The following incentives to attention are often recognized by advertising experts when they construct an advertisement:

I. Hereditary or mechanical incentives:
    1. Size.
    2. Repetition.
    3. Position.
    4. Line and form.
    5. Isolation.
    6. Color brightness.
    7. Contrast of colors.

II. Interest incentives:
    8. Esthetically pleasing colors.
    9. Novelty.
    10. The comic.
    11. Illustration having:
        a. Interesting human beings, objects, or situations.
        b. Implied action.
        c. Perspective.
        d. Magnification.

When a businessman wishes to write an advertisement, he tends to think first of its *size*. Shall it be a full-page, a half-page, or a one-inch advertisement? Other things being equal.

[2] H. L. Hollingworth. *Advertising and Selling,* D. Appleton-Century Co., 1913.

the larger the advertisement, the more attention it attracts. However, many small advertisements have greater attention value than larger ones. Other factors, such as novelty, may be stronger than size. A skillful advertiser can obtain more attention in a small space than an unskillful one can in a large space.

This has been proved frequently, but especially by "The Continuing Study of Newspaper Reading" mentioned on page 694. This extensive study revealed that of the 90 best-read national advertisements, 13 per cent were large (over 1,000 lines), 57 per cent were medium-size (301-1,000 lines), and 30 per cent were small (70-300 lines).[3] Apparently, getting attention and being read depended on factors other than mere size.

Repetition refers to the number of times an advertisement is published. The oftener the reader sees the product advertised, the more readily will he recall the product. However, increase in attention or in recall value does not increase in the same ratio as the number of repetitions. Repetition can also be used within a single advertisement. An example of this occurs when the same trade name or picture of the product is prominently displayed in several parts of the same advertisement.

Repetition of the same advertisement in the same media, year after year, has been proved quite effective. Advertisers who keep careful records of the returns from their advertising often find that a particular advertisement is especially effective. That advertisement may be used for many years. The well-known Sherwin Cody School of English advertisement which has the headline, "Do You Make These Mistakes in English?" has been used for more than 15 years without a change in copy, except for slipping in a new and better testimonial occasionally. In 10 years' time it has produced $328,860 worth of business[4] at an average cost per inquiry, page space, of 55 cents. Similarly, Postal Life & Casualty Insurance Co. has used the same introductory sales letter for more than 10 years.[5]

---

[3] "Size and Position of Newspaper Ads," *Advertising & Selling,* May 1941. See page 694 for complete reference for "The Continuing Study of Newspaper Reading."

[4] Victor O. Schwab, "An Advertisement That Is Never Changed," *Printers' Ink Monthly,* September 1939.

[5] John Walker, "Significant Lessons We Have Learned About Selling by Mail," *Sales Management,* July 15, 1939.

Fig. 109. Advertisers use trade-mark and copy characters to give continuity of impression to their advertising.

Position refers to the place on the page and in the medium. The upper half of the page usually gains attention better than the lower half. The outside back cover of a magazine is a most preferred position. Other preferred positions are the inside back cover, the inside front cover, the page facing the inside front cover, the page facing the first page of reading matter, the page at the end of the main reading section, the middle spread, and the page facing the end of the most interesting article or story in the magazine. Publishers usually charge extra for certain preferred positions. Position on a right-hand or left-hand page seldom involves an extra charge and research also indicates that neither side is materially better than the other.

Line and form are important attention-getters. The shape of the advertisement, the typography, the borders, and the arrows all influence attention. Quite often they have an element of novelty, and then they become an interest incentive.

Isolation is merely a term applied to the setting off of one part so that the other parts of the advertisement give an added emphasis to the chosen part. For example, if it is desired to have the reader notice the picture of the article to be sold, that picture may have blank space left around it. If the advertisement does not have any copy but merely a picture or a trade name, the near-blank page then attracts attention to the article, because it has no competition from type or other illustrations. Its isolation causes it to be noticed.

Colors are used in advertising to such an extent that the layman does not appreciate the painstaking thoughts that have been applied by the artists. The easiest way to catch the reader's attention by color is to use very bright colors. The advertisement that is just one mass of bright red colors is certain to attract our attention, but it may not hold it. Splashing on brilliant colors has been discarded by most advertisers for the more interesting effects of esthetic colors.

Contrast is closely allied to color brightness. Black on white is one of the oldest combinations of contrasting colors in advertising. Other combinations are used, such as blue on yellow, red on green, and so on. No attempt is made to combine the colors into a pleasing effect, but rather to select colors that clash with each other. When all the parts of a picture, a setting, or a situation are harmoniously arranged, no part tends to attract attention over the other parts. By shifting one part out of the unity of the whole, that part is at once noticeable. So, in contrast, the aim is to attract attention by the sharpness of the differences rather than by a pleasant blending of colors.

The opposite of contrast is obtained by arranging pleasing colors so that an effective blend results. This is the aim of every artist who wants to paint a beautiful picture. He wishes to have the colors blend into a unified whole that expresses an idea. He does not use one color merely to attract attention to itself by its brightness, nor are colors chosen to clash with others just for the sake of attracting attention. Rather, all the colors and other factors are combined into an integrated whole. The use of colors for brightness or contrast values, as such, are mechanical devices that attract but do not hold attention. Beauty of color holds our attention. Some of our present-day advertisements are sufficiently beautiful to merit hanging in our art galleries. One reason why few advertisements have pleasing combinations of color is the added expense of printing the extra eight or more colors that are necessary to obtain truly esthetic effects.

In recent years, colors have been used to an increasing extent because new mechanical methods to reproduce them economically have been invented. Their use is especially important in products which are often purchased because of their physical attractiveness, such as floor coverings and foods. In general, color is more stimulating to women readers than to men, as stated by one man who has supervised thousands of magazine readership surveys:

Color is one of the accessories that may be used to gain a larger proportion of the potential woman audience. It has a far greater effect on women than on men, and usually the brighter and more garish the color the greater the likelihood of an added woman observation.[6]

Novelty is an attempt to gain attention by an appeal to interest. The novelty may have any one of several forms: printing the advertisement upside down, unusual type, peculiar shapes, grotesque faces, remarkable events, stunts, and catchy ideas. Anything that causes the reader to notice the advertisement because it is different from the others of the medium has the element of novelty. Sometimes advertisers confuse distinctiveness of an advertisement with a selling appeal. Novelty does not sell the article; it merely attracts attention.

The *comic* may be a form of novelty, but it is classed as a separate factor. The number of comic-strip advertisements in modern advertising has greatly increased.

We have become so accustomed to reading the "funnies" that some of the best-read advertisements use this technique. Many people read comic strip advertisements from habit because they imagine that they are being entertained. This habit influence means that many readers are not getting the advertiser's message but merely his joke or story.

Only the most skilled advertisers can use the comic successfully. Its main danger is that it may cheapen the product advertised. The great and worth-while things in life are not funny to most people. To use funniness in advertising a product may

---

[6] Henry F. Godfrey, Jr., "What Makes Men and Women Look at Ads," *Printers' Ink Monthly,* April 1939. Data for this article taken from the files of L. M. Clark, Inc.

classify it as inexpensive. It is for this reason that advertisers of commodities such as peanuts and paints have used comedy more often than those who sell pianos or porcelain.

Furthermore, humor is likely to be irrelevant to the main idea in selling the article. It is similar to the lecturer's use of jokes in his speech; the audience laughs heartily but forgets the point or illustrative value of the joke. The reader of humorous advertisements can remember the picture or joke but not the brand or article advertised. Attention is attracted only to the funny situation, and the article and its worthwhileness is often forgotten or ignored. The new advertiser who finds that his advertising is neglected by the readers may become desperate and resort to the use of comedy. By so doing he gets attention, but the attention may have less ultimate value than less spectacular copy and cuts.

The *illustration* is often the essence of the advertisement. Most people are pictorially minded. Picture shows are far more attractive than lectures. Pictures were our first written language. They attract and hold attention more readily than cold words. One of the most common problems of the advertiser who uses an illustration is its relevancy to the product advertised. A picture of a beautiful woman on a calendar attracts attention to the calendar, but it may not attract attention to the product.

One interesting fact which is now known is that in advertisements men look at men, women at women. This is contrary to the beliefs of many advertising men, but, subject to varying product interests, holds as a general rule.

Very few people are fooled into believing that an advertisement is anything but an advertisement, and therefore when their eye is distracted from editorial text an instinctive process of selection or rejection takes place. If a man chances to come upon a picture of a pretty girl, he may glance at it, take in its better points—and forget about it as completely as he forgot the last pretty girl he passed on the street. The advertisement, as a piece of advertising matter, has had little or no effect.

If, on the other hand, the picture is that of a man, selection occurs. The page is a known advertisement and because of the man's picture it is presumably on a subject of some interest to the male reader. Therefore, the attention accorded it is more thorough and contains some degree of advertising impression. Thus, through a quick and visual beginning, advertisements for cosmetics, piston-rings, foods or automobiles are sorted out in the minds of the public. Just as over a period of time men have been conditioned into believing that a man's picture in a known advertisement means that that advertisement is for a man's product, so have women felt that a woman's picture meant a woman's product. The question really then becomes not what men or women see, but what in an advertisement they remember having seen.[7]

The factors within the advertisement that attract attention are the intrinsic interest-value of the person, object, or situation illustrated. Thousands of people are movie fans; hence certain advertisers use pictures of movie stars. Children, famous men, baseball games, airplane trips, prize fights, puppies, and so on, are of interest to many people, and so the advertiser uses them in his illustrations. If possible, he suggests action in the picture. In the physical world, a moving automobile attracts attention more quickly than a parked car.

The *perspective* in the illustration often attracts the reader's attention; it may be a close-up, so that the reader feels himself into the situation illustrated, or he may consider himself as viewing the situation from a distance. When the perspective is well executed, it may be a strong factor in catching as well as holding the attention.

Magnification is an aspect of perspective, but it is used so frequently that it deserves special recognition. We occasionally receive a snapshot from a facetious friend who had his picture taken while sitting on the grass with his feet close to the camera. The feet are given a grotesque effect and are so large as almost to obscure the face. The advertiser often wishes the picture of his product to dominate the illustration; hence the article is magnified or set near the front in so conspicuous a manner that it is out of proportion to the other objects in the picture. For example, tire companies often have a large picture of the tire in the foreground to show the tread. The tire itself is so greatly magnified that it dominates the whole illustration. It may be larger than the pictures of the automobiles, houses, or mountains in the same illustration.

In considering methods of gaining attention, the advertiser should not confuse attention with appeal. The reader's attention must be caught as he scans the magazine, but it must be held by the use of an appeal that is related to the reader's wants.

[7] *Ibid.*

Advertisements may catch attention, hold it, and arouse a desire, but induce no action. Action is brought about through the use of the coupon or similar devices.

A single advertisement may have many of the fifteen attention-getting factors. If we analyze a typical Campbell soup advertisement in *The Saturday Evening Post,* we note that it has size (a full page); repetition (it has elements that have been used in former Campbell soup advertisements); position (it follows the reading matter). It also has borders, color brightness, contrast, esthetic use of color, novelty in the form of poetry, the comic in the form of impish characters for the children, and an illustration. The illustration has an interesting situation with implied action, perspective that places the soup near one's mouth, and the picture of the plate of soup is greatly magnified. The best advertisements have many of the fifteen possible factors mentioned here. Interest factors are far more effective in catching and holding attention than the hereditary incentives. In general, the poorer advertisements depend upon the use of mechanical factors.

Effects of layouts and copy treatments. The advertising expert has many attention-getting devices, media, and layout and copy treatments available to him. His choice of layout and copy treatment is often determined by the way he wishes readers to react to his advertisement. For example, he may want many readers merely to read the headline, or he may wish a select few to read all the copy. His purpose will influence the layout and copy treatment he chooses for his advertisement.

One of the most extensive researches on questions of this kind has been the "Continuing Study of Newspaper Readership."[8] Louis Honig made analyses of the data obtained from representative samplings of readers of 24 newspapers and summarized certain findings in figure 110 (pages 694-695). Six well-known types of layout and copy treatment were analyzed regarding their relation to readership response.

---

[8] This study is sponsored by the Association of National Advertisers and the American Association of Advertising Agencies and conducted by the Advertising Research Foundation.

The data showed that "believe-it-or-not" types were in the lead for "seeing" the advertisement. However, advertisements having the layout and copy treatments characterized by their use of recipes, the comic, a dominant illustration, and conversational balloons also ranked high in being seen. The believe-it-or-not treatment scored 69.8 per line per 100,000 readers for women and 34.9 for men. Copy containing recipes scored 55.2 on attention from women and 9.6 from men—an understandable difference. General advertising was at the foot of the scale for both sexes.

In Chart F, reading the headline, the believe-it-or-not classification was dropped from consideration because no headline was involved. With this omission, copy that featured recipes was far in advance of other types of treatment. Headlines of recipe advertising were read four times as much as those of general advertisements.

Chart G, reading some copy, indicates that the believe-it-or-not treatment made an equally good showing for both sexes. Women are apparently more inclined to read into the copy than are men except where the white space is dominant in the advertisement.

It is worth noting that dominant illustration copy shows up better in the first test of being seen, than in the tests for reading of headlines and "some copy." Evidently the fact that an illustration has attracted attention to an advertisement is no further guarantee that it will aid in getting headline or copy read.

Along with dominant illustration treatment, comic type and strip advertisements show up almost two and three times more effectively than general advertising in visibility—in making the initial visual impression that the advertiser hopes may lead to his message being read and digested.[9]

Words and titles. Words are the "working tools" of the advertiser. The choice of words and their use determines the effect upon hearer or reader. Words are the vehicles of ideas and any idea that we may have can be expressed in words if we but wish to do so.

E. Haldeman-Julius in *The First Hundred Million* tells how

---

[9] Louis Honig, *Sales Management*, January 1, 1941, p. 44.

he sold that number of books at a nickel each. He has had a rich experience in the use of words and gives some interesting examples of how changes in words or phrases, and new ideas, have increased the sale of certain titles. When a book did not

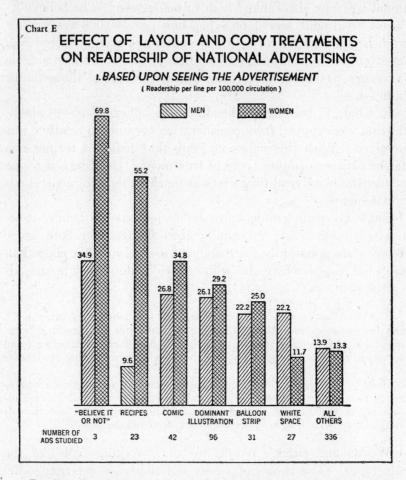

Chart E

EFFECT OF LAYOUT AND COPY TREATMENTS ON READERSHIP OF NATIONAL ADVERTISING

I. BASED UPON SEEING THE ADVERTISEMENT

(Readership per line per 100,000 circulation)

MEN   WOMEN

	"BELIEVE IT OR NOT"	RECIPES	COMIC	DOMINANT ILLUSTRATION	BALLOON STRIP	WHITE SPACE	ALL OTHERS
MEN	34.9	9.6	26.8	26.1	22.2	22.2	13.9
WOMEN	69.8	55.2	34.8	29.2	25.0	11.7	13.3
NUMBER OF ADS STUDIED	3	23	42	96	31	27	336

Fig. 110. Reactions of men and women to six types of layout and copy treatments were analyzed with respect to three degrees of impression made by the advertising: E, seeing the advertisement; F, reading the headline; G, reading some copy. Data were obtained from field readership studies in which people were shown copies of newspapers and asked what they had seen or read; an interviewer marked the advertisements according to each respondent's reactions.

Analysis and charts are by Louis Honig of Erwin, Wasey & Co. and were published in *Sales Management*, January 1, 1941. Findings are taken from "The Continuing Study of Newspaper Reading," by the Advertising Research Foundation, jointly supported by the Association of National Advertisers and the American Association of Advertising Agencies. This study was sponsored by the Bureau of Advertising, American Newspaper Publishers' Association.

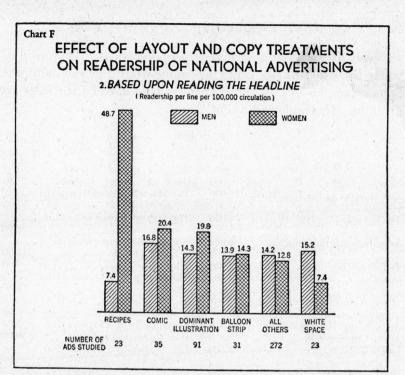

Chart F

EFFECT OF LAYOUT AND COPY TREATMENTS
ON READERSHIP OF NATIONAL ADVERTISING
2. BASED UPON READING THE HEADLINE
(Readership per line per 100,000 circulation)

MEN WOMEN

	RECIPES	COMIC	DOMINANT ILLUSTRATION	BALLOON STRIP	ALL OTHERS	WHITE SPACE
MEN	7.4	16.8	14.3	13.9	14.2	15.2
WOMEN	48.7	20.4	19.8	14.3	12.8	7.4
NUMBER OF ADS STUDIED	23	35	91	31	272	23

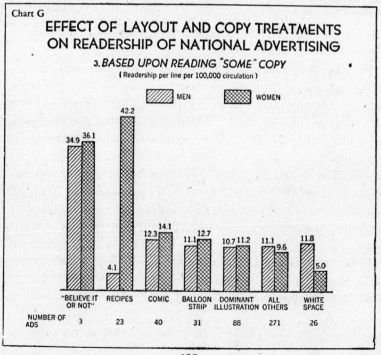

Chart G

EFFECT OF LAYOUT AND COPY TREATMENTS
ON READERSHIP OF NATIONAL ADVERTISING
3. BASED UPON READING "SOME" COPY
(Readership per line per 100,000 circulation)

MEN WOMEN

	"BELIEVE IT OR NOT"	RECIPES	COMIC	BALLOON STRIP	DOMINANT ILLUSTRATION	ALL OTHERS	WHITE SPACE
MEN	34.9	4.1	12.3	11.1	10.7	11.1	11.8
WOMEN	36.1	42.2	14.1	12.7	11.2	9.6	5.0
NUMBER OF ADS	3	23	40	31	88	271	26

sell well, it was sent to a department known as the "hospital" where the title was studied to determine what it lacked in appeal. Some examples of how the changes in title affected the sales are given by Mr. Haldeman-Julius.[10]

TABLE L

Old Title	Yearly Sales	New Title	Yearly Sales
Fleece of Gold..............	6,000	Quest for a Blonde Mistress...	50,000
The Mystery of the Iron Mask	11,000	The Mystery of the Man in the Iron Mask................	30,000
The King Enjoys Himself.....	8,000	The Lustful King Enjoys Himself......................	38,000
None Beneath the King......	6,000	None Beneath the King Shall Enjoy This Woman........	34,000
Ten O'clock................	2,000	What Art Should Mean to You	9,000
Pen, Pencil, and Poison.......	5,000	The Story of a Notorious Criminal......................	15,800
"Patent Medicine" and the Public Health.............	3,000	The Truth about "Patent Medicine"................	10,000
Addison and His Times.......	0	London Life in Addison's Time	7,000
Art of Controversy..........	0	How to Argue Logically......	30,000
Life of Tolstoy..............	2,500	Life of Tolstoy: Russian Novelist......................	6,500
Essay on Shelley.............	2,000	Shelley: Idealistic Dreamer....	8,000
Casanova and His Loves......	8,000	Casanova: History's Greatest Lover....................	22,000
Poems of Evolution..........	2,000	When You Were a Tadpole and I Was a Fish..............	7,000

He also found that when certain titles were put under new classifications the sales increased or decreased. "When You Were a Tadpole and I Was a Fish" was first listed as "Poetry" and then as "Evolution." When it was listed as "Humor," the sales jumped to 21,000. Also, certain titles sold better in different magazines. The results for one year from several magazines of different types gave the following percentages of orders for books that related to sex: *Liberty,* 71; *Smart Set,* 70; *Graphic,* 62; *Nation,* 61; *Time,* 54; *Pathfinder,* 27. He found that the strongest appeals were (1) sex, (2) self-education and improvement, (3) free-thought or skepticism, (4) (a poor fourth on the list) entertainment, fun, and laughter. Words which were especially successful in titles were "true love," "how to," and "facts that you should know." In the advertising that was used to

---

[10] E. Haldeman-Julius, *The First Hundred Million.* Simon & Schuster, 1928. Also reported in Don Gridley, "Advertising and Selling 100,000,000 Books," *Printers' Ink,* November 8, 1928, p. 57 ff.

sell the "Little Blue Books" not one book was favored over another, but each received the same amount of space—one agate
line in each advertisement.

Business words that are changing. Many articles or situations in business are described by words that give them a more
pleasant meaning for the public, such as the word "pool," which
is now called "pocket billiards." A poolroom was classed with
a saloon as a rendezvous for questionable characters; now these
tournaments or games are no longer reported as "pool" but as
"billiard" games. Buying on the "installment plan" has been
changed to the "budget system of purchase." Several meat-
packing companies have started a drive to eliminate the "hot
dog" from the public vocabulary. The term has been changed
to "red hots." Results indicate, however, that "red hots" is less
attractive to customers than "hot dogs." Wrigley had difficulty
in persuading the people of Great Britain to become gum chewers
until he changed the name to "sweet."

A word problem of the clothing dealers has been to find some
term that would not tell fat women that they are fat. Words
such as "heavy," "stout," and "plump" have been used but these
are unsatisfactory. The best term, so far, seems to be "stylish
stout." Unfortunately, laundrymen still "mangle" clothes, and
we all seem to be compelled to use "housewife" for want of a
better word.

When the West Texas Utilities Co. conducted a contest to find
a pleasing substitute for the word "housewife," the first prize was
given to "neolectress"; "neo" meaning new and "lectress" to suggest the modern woman alert to this electric age. Second and
third prizes were given to "domestician" and "homeologist." [11]
Of course none of these has become popular.

Advertisers like to coin new words or adapt old ones to new
meanings as "Skrip" and "Quink" (inks), "Hush" and "Mum"
(deodorants), "4 p.m. letdown" (alkalithia), "Eye-gene" (eye
wash), "Clothespin nose" (Luden's menthol cough drops), and
"liberty steak" for common ordinary Hamburg steak. Incidentally, air lines have found it advantageous to change "safety
belt" to "seat belt."

---

[11] *Tide*, October 1, 1937.

An advertisement for a dentifrice claimed that "tooth was stranger than fiction," and one for a dog soap offered "Shampooch." Glamorous names help to sell goods. Giving shades of hosiery various doggy names such as "Spaniel" and "Collie" has increased sales. Automobile buyers have preferred colors, at times, that had been given Hollywood names.

The use of combinations of words is especially important in retail selling. Goodall Company, manufacturer of Palm Beach suits, operated a retail laboratory and experimented with various sales approaches to customers. The company found that when salesmen addressed customers with a time-honored bromide such as "Can I help you?" 7 per cent bought. When salesmen used the system of letting the customers alone until they asked for help, 12 per cent purchased. But when the salesmen greeted customers with specific comments about the merchandise, such as "This will be this year's most popular tan," 25 per cent purchased.[12]

Headlines. Headlines of advertisements have been studied, and in some cases the headline seems to be a major influence in response to the advertisement. An unusual example occurred with a life insurance company full-page advertisement. A simple switch in headline only from what sounds like a good headline, "Beware of Spiders," to another that appears to be less effective, "Want to Get Ahead?" increased the reader response 4,500 per cent.[13]

Sometimes the use of uncommon words increases reader response to a surprising extent. Examples are "Life's a PUSHOVER when you feel like THIS" and "Why some foods EXPLODE in the stomach." One advertising expert experimented with headlines for a health proposition, using headlines A and B. He used the same amount of space and copy in the same media with the results shown in Table LI.

Headlines are often classified into three general kinds, as aptly stated by "Aesop Glim":[14]

1. *Label* which states the product. For example, "On the subject of pickles."

---

[12] *Business Week*, May 25, 1940.
[13] *Printers' Ink*, December 27, 1940, p. 14.
[14] *Printers' Ink*, April 9, 1931.

2. *Message* which gives information. For example, "Pickles are good for you."

3. *Provocation*, which challenges, arrests, or provokes further reading. For example, "How the pickle got its warts."

Provocative headlines are usually considered most effective. However, a simple label or message headline, "There is only one Waldorf-Astoria," may produce better results than "How tall is a famous hotel?"

TABLE LI[15]

Amount of Money Produced by:

Medium	A. This Is What Doctors Do When They Don't Feel Up to Par.	B. When Doctors "Feel Rotten" This Is What They Do.
Time..........................	$3,032	$5,108
New York Times.............	3,060	4,348
Elks Magazine................	860	1,514

A good headline is selective. The effective headline picks from the millions of readers who see it those few prospects interested in the advertiser's proposition. Most advertisers do not aim to have everyone read their advertising; rather, they want their advertising to be attractive to the logical prospects for their proposition.

The coupon. Advertisers use coupons for several purposes but largely as either a device for measuring the effectiveness of the advertisement or as a means of bringing about a response. An advertiser may make his coupon highly selective in its influence or he may design it to have all kinds of readers respond. If the advertiser wishes to obtain a very wide distribution of his coupons, he may feature it in the copy and place it at the top of the advertisement. Daniel Starch found that the reply ratios for coupon positions were as follows: upper center, 180.0; outside bottom, 100.0; inside bottom, 74.9; across bottom, 66.6; and lower center, 56.1.[16]

Starch also found that the nature of the offer influences the number of returns. See Table LII.

Starch found that copy without a coupon brought, on the average, about one fourth as many replies as a free coupon, and that a charge coupon brought slightly more than one half as many

[15] Victor O. Schwab. "Headline Stoppers," *Printers' Ink*, October 27, 1939.

[16] Daniel Starch, *An Analysis of 5,000,000 Inquiries*, p. 34, 1930.

TABLE LII[17]

Nature of Offer	Reply Ratios
Sample	153.2
Recipe book	137.8
Booklet	100.0
Other novelty	86.4
Name of dealer	69.3
Special service	24.1

as the free coupon. The reply ratios for his data were: free coupons, 100; charge coupons, 55.9; and no coupons, 25.8.[18]

When the coupon is used as a device to measure the effectiveness of advertising, we should bear in mind that an average of less than one fourth of 1 per cent of the paid circulation of a magazine is likely to clip a coupon from a full-page advertisement and send it to the advertiser. Daniel Starch made a study of more than three million inquiries received from 2,339 magazine advertisements and found the relations between size of page and number of replies per 100,000 circulation which are shown in Table LIII.

TABLE LIII[19]

Size of Space	Size Ratios	Number of Replies per 100,000 Circulation	Reply Ratios
One page	100	225.3	100.0
One-half page	50	120.4	53.5
Quarter page	25	71.8	31.9
Sixth page	17	38.9	17.3

When these figures are considered in relation to cost of space, they indicate that many an advertiser who offers to give away samples of his toothpaste or other product often spends $2 of his money to give away each sample. Of course, if an appreciable percentage of the requests for samples results in the development of repeat customers, the cost of giving away the samples may eventually result in profits to the advertiser.

Several advertisers have found that if the advertisement has a designed border and the coupon is separated from this by a diagonal plain rule, the number of replies is consistently less than when the separation is made by a dash rule. Even the dotted rule is less effective than the dash rule. The reason for

[17] *Ibid.*, p. 28.
[18] *Ibid.*, p. 33.
[19] Daniel Starch, *Analysis of Over 3,000,000 Inquiries*, 1927.

Fig. 111. Daniel Starch, Psychologist and Consultant in Commercial Research, New York City.

these results may be the fact that the dash rule suggests actual perforation to the reader.

Here are more rules for the form of the coupon if a large number of returns is desired:

1. The copy in the main part of the advertisement should refer to the coupon and indicate that the reader will be well repaid for his effort if he will send in the coupon. The more the copy boosts the coupon value, the greater will be the returns.

2. The coupon should have a supporting illustration of the booklet or sample that will be sent to the person who mails the coupon. Putting this illustration in colors or having arrows point to it will add to the coupon returns.

3. The coupon should be sufficiently large to be noticeable and should have sufficient space to enable most people to write their names and addresses on the lines. Some coupons are so small that from 5 to 25 per cent of the names and addresses cannot be deciphered correctly.

4. The coupon should contain the name and the address of the advertiser. The reason for this seems to be the fact that many readers clip coupons but do not mail them at once. Later, when they wish to mail the coupon, it is difficult to find the original

advertisement with the address of the firm. One advertiser found that returns fell off 30 per cent when he omitted his name and address.

5. The coupon should refer to a definite person who has had an important part in the offer which is being made through the coupon. Returns are greater if the coupon states, "Emily Harper Stevenson, Expert in Interior Decoration of the Moderne Galleries, has written this book for you."

Effects of big news events on coupon returns. When readers have their attention directed to outstanding news events, they are likely to decrease their response to advertising. This is especially noticeable in periodical advertising, the effects generally decreasing with the length of the interval between publications of the periodical. This means that effects of the news event are most pronounced in daily newspaper advertising, usually somewhat less in newspapers and magazines published weekly, and least pronounced in monthlies. Victor O. Schwab of Schwab & Beatty, Inc., an advertising agency that has done extensive research in inquiry types of advertising, supplied the following illustrative examples of effects of big news events on the number of inquiries received from the same or comparable advertisements that were published before and after great news events:

TABLE LIV

| | | Inquiries Received | |
News Event	Medium for the Paired Advertisements	Before the News Event	After the News Event
Lindbergh kidnapping, occurred March 1, 1932.	a. A daily newspaper Feb. 7, 1932.	554	
	b. Same newspaper, March 27, 1932.		280
	a. A weekly pictorial magazine, Feb. 13, 1932.	125	
	b. Same weekly magazine, March 26, 1932.		37
Germany's Attack on Poland, started September 1, 1939.	a. Monthly magazine A, issue out on Aug. 5, 1939.	470	
	b. Same magazine, issue out Sept. 5, 1939.		322

TABLE LIV (*Continued*)

	a. Monthly magazine *B*, issue out Aug. 1, 1939.	781	
	b. Same magazine, issue out Sept. 1, 1939.		646
	a. Monthly magazine *C*, issue out Aug. 10, 1939.	432	
	b. Same magazine, issue out Sept. 10, 1939.		354
Germany's Invasion of Netherlands and Belgium, May 10, 1940.	*a.* Monthly magazine *A*, issue out April 5, 1940.	964	
	b. Same magazine, issue out May 5, 1940.		619
	a. Monthly magazine *B*, issue out Feb. 15, 1940.	1,172	
	b. Same magazine, issue out May 15, 1940.		340
	a. A Sunday newspaper, issue of April 21, 1940.	112	
	b. Same Sunday newspaper, issue of May 12, 1940.		59

Advertisers who study inquiries and the factors affecting their numbers know that good weather, like a news event, decreases returns. One advertiser who made an 11-year study of weather reports in relation to inquiry response concluded that the response to Sunday newspaper advertisements averaged 19 per cent better for wet-day than for dry-day advertisements.[20]

Seasonal variation. Obviously, people do not respond to bathing-suit and fur-coat advertising to the same extent in the same seasons of the year. The relation between season and response varies with the product and other influences. Daniel Starch studied 3,998,245 returns from 2,500 magazine and newspaper advertisements and found that the reply ratios varied as indicated in Table LV.

His analysis showed that the summer months, when people do less reading, and December, the holiday month, were the lowest in responsiveness to advertising.

Predicting inquiry response by months or weeks. When a couponed advertisement is published in a monthly magazine, returns may continue to come to the advertiser for as long as two

---

[20] Victor O. Schwab, "The Weather and Other Factors Affecting Results from Advertising," *Printers' Ink,* July 14, 1939.

TABLE LV[21]

SEASONAL VARIATION IN THE NUMBER OF REPLIES

Based on 3,998,245 Returns from 2,500 Magazine
and Newspaper Advertisements

Month	Reply Ratios	Month	Reply Ratios
January	120	July	83
February	130	August	92
March	121	September	108
April	99	October	116
May	86	November	99
June	83	December	80

years after publication. The advertiser, however, can predict
the total number of returns at the end of one month. Each
magazine has some influence on the rate of return, but 50 per
cent of the total returns from a monthly are likely to reach the
advertiser within one month after publication.

The same principle operates with the weekly magazines, except for factors such as the geographical area covered by the
magazine and whether the distribution is made by mail or news
stands. However, the advertiser who keeps adequate records
can compute a table of predictions which will not vary more than

TABLE LVI*

TOTAL NUMBER OF INQUIRIES RECEIVED BY:

	Third Day, Per Cent	Sixth Day, Per Cent	Second Week, Per Cent	Third Week, Per Cent	First Month, Per Cent	Second Month, Per Cent	Third Month, Per Cent	Sixth Month, Per Cent
Monthly magazines:								
American	1	4	22	34	48	70	79	90
Cosmopolitan	4	10	24	36	49	71	81	92
Redbook	3	10	25	43	52	70	74	94
Weekly magazines:								
Time	21	40	65	76	85	92	96	98
Liberty	12	40	67	77	85	92	95	98
Collier's	18	44	67	77	83	91	94	98
New York Times Sunday Magazine	43	64	80	86	91	96	98	98½

* Chart furnished through the courtesy of C. T. Stevens of the Phoenix Mutual
Life Insurance Co. Quoted in *Advertising & Selling*, April 28, 1932, p. 30.

5 per cent above or below previous experience. The Phoenix
Mutual Life Insurance Co., for example, developed the predic-

[21] Daniel Starch, *An Analysis of 5,000,000 Inquiries*, p. 19, 1930.

tion charts shown in Table LVI. John Caples explained that the table of rate of response to coupon advertisements

. . . enables you to predict the total number of coupon returns you will receive from an advertisement without waiting six months. For example, suppose you have an advertisement in *Cosmopolitan Magazine* which has brought 100 coupon returns after the magazine has been on sale six days. The chart states that these 100 coupons are 10 per cent of the total you will receive. Therefore you should get approximately 1,000 coupons from the advertisement. This chart is based on an average of seven couponed advertisements in each of the above magazines. An easy rule to remember is that a monthly magazine brings in about half its total in the first month! [22]

Prediction tables like this one, developed for the advertising of one company, do not mean that the advertiser of a different product can use exactly the same chart for making his predictions. Obviously, each advertiser should keep systematic records for returns to his own advertisements and plot his own charts and tables of prediction.

Predicting effectiveness of advertisements previous to extensive use. The marketing expert who believes that he can analyze an advertisement and predict by his subjective analysis the public's response to that advertisement is a dangerous man. His estimate may be worth more than that of the girl at the switchboard in the office, but he is likely to be sadly mistaken if he continues to make predictions based on subjective analyses only.

Consumers' receptiveness to each advertisement of a series can be predicted by means of balanced schedules in daily newspapers or other inexpensive media. For example, some advertisers select six typical cities and run six different advertisements for one week in each city. The advertisements are so arranged that every one of them is run in each of the six orders. For example, the six cities may be designated by letters *A, B, C, D, E,* and *F.* The advertisements may be designated as 1, 2, 3, 4, 5, and 6. A schedule of the test campaign might be arranged as follows:

A	B	C	D	E	F
1	2	3	4	5	6
2	3	4	5	6	1
3	4	5	6	1	2
4	5	6	1	2	3
5	6	1	2	3	4
6	1	2	3	4	5

[22] "Coupon Prediction Chart," *Advertising & Selling,* April 28, 1932, p. 30. See also John Caples, *Tested Advertising Methods.* Harper & Bros., 1932.

Fig. 112. Appeals in modern advertising are no longer chosen from lists of instincts printed in psychology books. Indoor laboratory studies are seldom significant, because not all significant variables in a laboratory experiment can be controlled. Hence, many advertisers make field studies by consumer-panel or similar techniques. These modern field techniques require more training in psychology than was required for the indoor laboratory experiments. The Ross Federal Research Corporation is one of several research organizations which conduct field studies for advertisers.

This kind of test prevents misjudgments because of unusual news events, weather, or the cumulative effects of preceding advertisements. Such a six weeks' method involves a great deal of time and it may be expensive, but it is a fairly safe way to predict the public's reaction to the advertisements proposed for use in an advertising campaign.

Split-run tests. When several advertisements are to be tested in order to predict their relative effectiveness, the conditions under which they are to be tested should be as nearly identical as possible. The split-run test supplies these conditions.

The split-run test means that the publisher of the magazine or newspaper arranges the printing of the copies into two or more divisions. For example, an advertiser may want to know which one of three advertisements, A, B, or C, is the most effective in drawing inquiries. To answer the question, the publisher does the printing so that one third of the copies have advertisement A, the second third have B, and the last third have C. In the printing plant where the three streams of copies meet, a workman or a mechanical device alternates the copies of the several streams. This means that the three advertisements are of the same size, have the same position, appear on the same day, are read by the same classes of readers, and advertise the same product under directly comparable conditions. Any one factor such as the headline may be changed in order to test its several variations.

Scores of newspaper and magazine publishers are now equipped for and willing to help an advertiser make split-run tests. Alert advertisers have used this device to discover the most effective appeals, headlines, copy, illustrations, coupons, and other factors. The procedure is far more accurate in its predictions than the older laboratory method in which people are asked what they like or think they like.

This does not mean that the split-run has displaced all other methods of testing. Certain techniques still have special values. Techniques that are especially useful are the field surveys of readership, spot testing of sales results such as the A. C. Nielsen store audits, and coupon inquiries. Predicting the effects of advertising involves so many influences that almost every technique has its appropriate applications. Even mechanical devices are helpful under certain conditions.

Modern mechanical devices for discovering principles. As pointed out in Chapter 19, advertising men use many techniques to predict the effectiveness of their advertising. Sometimes their researches in making predictions also enable them to discover new principles or to realize the import of known principles. Several mechanical devices have been invented for this purpose. One of these is the Scanacord, an eye camera or special Ophthalmograph which records eye movements of readers of advertisements. The Scanacord was developed and adapted to research in advertising by Herbert A. Thompson and Leonard E. Luce. Drake University has had a similar Visual Research Laboratory under sponsorship of the magazine *Look*. Eye cameras are especially useful in measuring the eye movements of readers over the layout of an advertisement and thereby suggesting helpful principles for planning future advertisements. See page 709 for examples of Scanacord findings.

Automatic recorders have been developed in the field of radio advertising. These recorders are attached to radios and every turn of the tuning dial is recorded on a moving tape. The best-known device of this kind is the "Audimeter" developed by the A. C. Nielsen Company. One study of Audimeter findings indicated that 56 per cent of the time in which radios are turned on people listen no more than 15 minutes without switching to another station; the average of all listening periods is only 28 minutes.[23] These automatic recorders are especially useful in learning the kinds of programs that hold listeners' attention. Much research is being done with such mechanical devices, and further reports will reveal new and unappreciated principles for influencing people through advertising.

Thus far, the following findings regarding 20 well-known network programs indicate the kinds of data obtainable.

1. Certain leading programs have 82 per cent of their audience in cities over 10,000 population, whereas others have only 42 per cent in these cities.

2. Some get 67 per cent of their audience in non-telephone homes, whereas others get only 35 per cent.

---

[23] "Audimeter," *Business Week*, October 21, 1939, p. 34, taken from *The Nielsen Researcher*, house organ of A. C. Nielsen Co., 1939. See also *Advertising Age*, October 16, 1939, p. 16.

What Scanacord Readings Show

Various copy testing methods have revealed wide variations in advertising readership as a result of different headline, layout, and color appeals. Most recent method put to serious use involves mechanical recording of eye movements over the page being studied. The Scanacord (record of scanning) photographs reflections of light on the eye and registers its motion and fixations. Relative concentrations of eye pausings reveal distribution of interest over the page. Typical findings on alternate treatments of the same ads are shown on this spread.

The Scanacord was developed by Herbert A. Thompson and Leonard Luce of Arthur Kudner, Inc.

"If the railroads are so good—why aren't they rich?" attracted 130% higher readership of text than the headline: "There are two sides to the railroad success story."

Value of background is shown in alternate treatments above where inset at left with people using the product led to a 25% better text reading than inset with product only.

Teaser headline: "What breakfast food will be first to benefit from this?" developed 100% higher text readership than fervent claims of Pliofilm's being waterproof (right).

Factual statements in headline at left on research activities—climate, concrete, test cars—brought a 33% better text readership than the puff in headline at right.

Factors of animals, unusual costumes, "something unusual happening" in inset at left (additional to those in inset at right) brought a 38% improvement in readership.

Fig. 113. (*Courtesy of Leonard E. Luce and Herbert A. Thompson of Arthur Kudner, Inc. See also* Advertising & Selling, *December, 1940.*)

3. One of our popular radio stars may be very much surprised when she learns what a large percentage of colored homes listen to her.

4. Some of these leading programs get about 60 per cent of their audience in the upper income groups, whereas others get only 40 per cent.

5. Fifty-four per cent of a certain racial group listen to one of these leading programs, whereas less than 1 per cent of this same group listen to another.

6. One leading hour program, which has a large small town and rural audience, is rated beyond 10th place by the telephone method, whereas by the Audimeter method, with a far more accurate sample, this program ranks second.

Large groups of families listen as much as an average of 5.5 hours per day, whereas others listen only an average of 1.6 hours per day; these averages apply to all days of the week.

An extremely important part of the Nielsen Radio Index is the test which indicates whether a program is selling the sponsor's product or simply drawing listeners. This is secured in combination with the very important and effective Nielsen inventory research technique. In this way the sales effectiveness of each radio program is scientifically determined by income group, city size, and so on. This information is exceedingly vital to the sponsors of a radio program and to the entire broadcasting industry.[24]

References

Burtt, H. E., *Psychology of Advertising*. Houghton-Mifflin Co., 1938.

Griffith, C. R., *An Introduction to Applied Psychology*, Chapter XXXI. The Macmillan Co., 1936.

Hepner, H. W., *Effective Advertising*, Chapters 29-42. McGraw-Hill Book Co., 1941.

Hotchkiss, G. B., *An Outline of Advertising*. The Macmillan Co., 1940.

Jenkins, John G., *Psychology in Business and Industry*, Chapters XI-XII. John Wiley & Sons, 1935.

Moore, Herbert, *Psychology for Business and Industry*, Chapter XIV. McGraw-Hill Book Co., 1939.

Poffenberger, A. T., *Psychology in Advertising*. McGraw-Hill Book Co., 1932.

Sandage, C. H., *Advertising Theory and Practice*. Business Publications, Inc., 1939.

Strong, Edward K., Jr., *Psychological Aspects of Business*, Chapters XIII, XXI, XXII. McGraw-Hill Book Co., 1938.

Weiss, E. G., F. C. Kendall, and C. B. Larrabee, *The Handbook of Advertising*. McGraw-Hill Book Co., 1938.

Projects

1. List some of the ways in which advertising has occasionally been used unethically. Describe how the user of such methods is working against his own self-interest in the long run.

2. Select several advertisements that seem to you to be effective, and

---

[24] *The Nielsen Researcher*. A. C. Nielsen Co., 1939.

several that do not appeal to you. Tally the attention-getting devices used by each group (see page 685). Can you draw some general conclusions from the results you obtained?

3. Study the 15 attention-getting devices listed in this chapter and revise the list so that it might be applied specifically to radio advertising.

4. Advertising is not done in some motion-picture theatres. Suggest reasons for this and outline the advantages the movies would have as an advertising medium. Describe the type of advertising that might be acceptable to movie fans.

5. Look through the advertisements in a recent issue of the *Saturday Evening Post* or some other magazine and list the new names coined by advertisers for familiar products. Check the terms that appeal to you and suggest reasons for their effectiveness.

6. Inspect a large number of coupons in newspaper or magazine advertising and note the methods sometimes used to prevent replies from children and persons who clip coupons merely through curiosity. Discuss with your friends the effectiveness and defects of the methods for which you found examples.

PART SEVEN

Principles of Research
for the Student of Applied Psychology

27

How to Read Reports of Psychological Researches

···

Not the truth in anyone's actual or supposed possession, but the sincere effort he has exerted to master the truth, makes the worth of the man. For not through the possession but through the pursuit of truth comes that widening of a man's powers by which alone is achieved his ever-growing perfection. Possession makes one stagnant, lazy, proud. If God held shut in His right hand the whole of truth, and in His left hand only ever-active striving after truth with the certainty of ever and always erring, and He said to me, "Choose!" I should humbly reach toward His left hand, saying, "Father, give me this! The pure truth is indeed for Thee alone!"
—Lessing, *Eine Duplik*.[1]

THE DIFFERENCE between scientific research as "lived" by the pure scientist and as viewed by the layman may be illustrated by an incident in the life of the great scientist Faraday. He gave a lecture in the Royal Institution in London before a group of celebrities of the day. He brought a magnet close to a coil of wire. An electric current was produced.

After the demonstration a lady asked him, "Professor Faraday, even if the effect you explained is obtained, what is the use of it?"

Faraday replied, "Madam, will you tell me the use of a newborn child?"

The pure scientist conducts his experiments without regard for their practical or commercial value. Eventually some of the experiments may have practical value, but the scientist seeks truth mainly. Louis Agassiz, Lord Kelvin, Oersted, and others made their great discoveries without thought of personal gain. Some of their apparently useless discoveries have led to very valuable results for modern civilization.

The value of research in technical matters is now generally ac-

---

[1] Zechariah Chafee, *The Inquiring Mind*. Harcourt, Brace & Co., 1928.

cepted, and it is probable that research in the human-relations problems of our economic life will make unusual strides in this and the next generation. As Thomas Edison said, the keynote of the twentieth century will be human engineering. Occasionally, political and international disruptions appear to make his prediction incorrect, but such disruptions are only temporary.

The practical man finds himself in many situations where it is difficult for him to utilize scientific research. Lack of time often compels him to make a quick decision. Sometimes business expediency does not permit changes wrought by science. A company may have established a reputation for a certain product or service and it would be difficult to make a change, even though scientific studies indicate that a change to a better product might be made. Moreover, the present "laws" of commerce are not nearly so exact and fixed as the laws of physics and chemistry.

In spite of the many difficulties in the way of predicting and controlling human behavior in business, psychological research has become a recognized phase of modern economic life. The student who becomes a businessman learns that if he wishes to market a new product, he must do more than try it out in his wife's kitchen, ask the opinions of his friends, or consult his salesmen. He finds that his own company's records and past statistics of monthly reports do not enable him to predict the public's reception of a new idea or invention. Snap judgments and empirical rules may lead him astray. But even the best feasible research study is none too reliable.

Professional research organizations. In one issue of a trade journal, ten professional research organizations were advertised. Some of them have been in existence for years. Others seem to advertise once or twice and then disappear. The ability and reliability of these research organizations must be rated in the same manner that we rate individuals. A few individuals are competent for a specific task, but there are many who are not. The executive who hires a professional research worker or research organization should be acquainted with research principles if he wishes to secure competent service. Otherwise he may be handed a voluminous report that looks impressive but is filled with fallacious conclusions. Statistics are often helpful, but they are also very dangerous. The reader should at least know the essential terms and methods which are common to research reports in the field of analyzing and controlling human behavior.

Starting important researches. When an executive or a group of executives decides that a research shall be made of some problem or problems, certain questions should be asked and answered in advance. These are:

1. *Just what is the problem?* What is it that is to be learned? How shall the problem be stated, in order that the persons making the research may keep it clearly in mind? Shall the research be limited to a single specific problem or shall the investigation have a broad and generalized scope?

2. *Who shall perform the research?* In many cases the executives decide that some accountant or statistician now in the company can do the work. Such an attempt to save money is conjectural. The findings of a single research may be used to modify a company's production schedule for a year and may involve thousands of dollars. It does not pay to take chances. Only a few large concerns have a staff of researchers who are qualified to conduct a psychological investigation. The fact that an engineer knows calculus and can plot nice curves does not mean that he is qualified to make a market investigation or standardize psychological tests for employment. Trained and experienced workers are just as important in psychological research as in other branches of industry.

3. *What shall be the method of securing the data?* Shall the company start a research department with laboratories of its own; shall field investigators be used; shall the data be secured by questionnaire; shall a test campaign be conducted; etc.? Can the necessary data be secured? Are the facts now available in the company's records? Is it possible to obtain the facts?

4. *Do the executives have a fair attitude toward the research?* Are they seeking to obtain data to prove a present theory, or are facts wanted regardless of their pleasantness or unpleasantness? Are the executives future-minded or past-minded? Is the research for the purpose of finding out "why the horse was stolen" or to prevent the stealing of horses in the future?

5. *How much time shall be allowed for the investigation?* Does the company expect the researchers to achieve functions of

the administrative executive, or is the research to present facts for the guidance of the executives?   One sales manager hired a research man to make a consumer analysis.   He agreed to expect his report at the end of three months.   However, at the end of two weeks he began to write letters to the researcher, asking him why the sales had not increased in the territory where the analysis was being made.   When a company starts a business research department of its own, definite results of proved commercial value should not be expected for one or two years.   Furthermore, some of the executives of companies having sales researchers are inclined to expect the sales research department to act as a sales promotion department.   If research is to fulfill its function of making discoveries of value to the business, it must be allowed sufficient time and remain advisory and independent of immediate problems of showing a profit on the balance sheet.

Points to look for when analyzing a research report.   When any statistical report is analyzed, it is necessary to look for fallacies regardless of the ability or reputation of the author.   Administrators must operate on the plan of delegating functions and responsibilities to others.   When an executive selects the most competent researcher he can find and gives him a research problem, he tends to assume that whatever the statistician says must be true.   However, the reader of the statistics must be alert to detect and question discrepancies.   It is impossible for the executive or the student to know all or most of the errors in statistics or logic that may occur, but some of the more common ones can be pointed out.

1.   *Is the unit of measurement sound?*   In statistics, the units of measurement are the bricks from which the whole statistical structure is built.   The units of measurement may be individuals, foot-pounds, wages, accidents, or businessmen, but the unit must be sound in its entity.   One sales manager asked his salesmen to predict the condition of business for the next month. Each salesman was to state whether he expected to have an increase in sales over the preceding month.   Approximately 80 per cent of the weekly reports of the sales force were optimistic. They were of the type: "Conditions here look very good for next month.   I expect to sell more than I did this month."   At the end of the month for which the sales had been predicted, less

than 10 per cent of the salesmen had had an increase in sales, and the total volume of business for the sales force was 15 per cent below that of the preceding month. The reason for the unreliability of the investigation was that the salesmen knew that the sales manager usually expected optimistic reports and they sent in the expected viewpoint lest they appear to be alibi-artists and expecters of failure. The prediction could not be reliable because the units of measurement, statements by individual salesmen, were unreliable.

2. *Are the data in the report authentic?* Occasionally statistics are quoted by bankers, salesmen, publishers, and others, and it is impossible to find anyone to substantiate the figures. A notable example is the oft-quoted figures regarding the incomes of men who begin their vocational life at the age of 20. At the age of 45, 16 per cent are supposed to be dead; 65 per cent self-supporting; 15 per cent dependent, wholly or in part; and only 4 per cent are supposed to have accumulated anything and kept it. When they are 65 years of age, 85 per cent of the men stil! living are quoted as dependent on children, relatives, or charity.

An attempt has been made to find the original source of these figures but has met with no success. The life insurance companies that were consulted said that they had seen the figures and their salesmen had used them, but the originator was not known. So far as they know, no one really knows what the correct figures are.

3. *Are single causes interpreted to give rise to single effects or events?* In human relationships, effects are seldom brought about by single events or causes. The "new American tempo" is not the effect of one cause, such as the development of the physical sciences. Increases in crime cannot be attributed solely to a change in religious devotion or divorce. Labor unrest is not caused alone by universal education. Psychological abnormalities cannot be attributed solely to a thwarting of the sex impulse or to heredity. Increases and decreases in sales cannot be attributed to the lone influence of the new sales manager. Decreased labor turnover cannot be interpreted as wholly the result of a newly organized personnel department or of profit sharing.

The veteran advertising manager of an ice-cream company "showed" how his advertising efforts had increased the per capita

consumption of ice cream in his territory.   He should also have
mentioned as factors of influence: improved quality of the product, pure food laws, greater number of retail outlets, lower cost
of production, and greater competence of company management.

4. *Are graphic curves of increase and decrease compared with
basic curves of increase and decrease?*   Frequently they are not.
This kind of error is common in reports of individual executives
to the management.   The sales manager may show that sales
have increased 20 per cent each year over the preceding year for
the past five years.   He should also show how much the industry as a whole has increased during that period.   The employment manager may show that labor turnover has decreased
each year for the past three years.   He should also compare his
curve of decrease with the employment situation of the community.

5. *Are the graphs in the report properly constructed?*   The
person who wishes to understand statistical reports needs an understanding of some of the more common principles of graphic
charting.

If the statistician wishes to construct a simple line curve to
show the amount of building construction in a certain city over
a given period of years, it is possible to construct the graph so
that a small or a great increase or decrease may appear to have
taken place.   This may be done regardless of the actual facts in
the situation.   The curve can be made to appear unstable and
to have fluctuated violently, or to have fluctuated little and to
have great stability.   The construction and type of graph is
often determined by the impression that the statistician wishes
to make on his readers.   One of the best statistical devices for
comparative data is the index number.

Table LVII illustrates three possible sets of index numbers, or
series of simple relatives, which might be constructed from the
actual sales data in the first column.

The method is simply to divide each year's sales by the sales
in the base period which one may think best.   The base periods
here used are (1) the year 1923, (2) the year 1936, and (3) the
yearly average for the five years 1932-1936, inclusive.

What practical purpose is accomplished by the use of these

TABLE LVII[2]

SHOWING ACTUAL SALES BY YEARS AND INDEX NUMBERS THEREOF

| Year | Actual Sales (thousands of tons) | | Index Numbers | | | | | |
| | | | On 1923 Base as 100 | | On 1936 Base as 100 | | On 1932-1936 Base as 100 | |
	XYZ Co.	Entire Industry	XYZ Co.	Entire Industry	XYZ Co.	Entire Industry	XYZ Co.	Entire Industry
1923.....	5.2	31,300	100.0	100.0	36.4	70.8	50.3	73.8
1924.....	4.0	23,513	76.9	75.1	28.0	53.2	38.7	55.4
1925.....	6.3	32,151	120.2	102.7	43.7	72.7	44.4	75.8
1926.....	7.9	42,773	151.9	136.7	55.2	96.8	76.4	100.8
1927.....	8.5	45,060	163.5	144.0	59.4	101.9	82.2	106.2
1928.....	8.0	44,462	153.8	142.1	55.9	100.6	77.4	104.8
1929.....	7.0	34,671	134.6	110.8	49.0	78.4	67.7	81.7
1930.....	8.4	42,132	161.5	134.6	58.7	95.3	81.2	99.3
1931.....	3.6	19,783	69.2	63.2	25.2	44.7	34.8	46.6
1932.....	9.0	44,943	173.1	143.6	62.9	101.7	87.0	105.9
1933.....	7.3	37,932	140.4	121.2	51.0	85.8	70.6	89.4
1934.....	11.5	45,394	221.2	145.0	80.4	102.7	111.7	107.0
1935.....	15.8	48,294	303.8	154.3	110.5	109.2	152.8	113.8
1936.....	14.3	44,214	275.0	141.3	100.0	100.0	138.3	104.2

index numbers?   Examination of the data for the two variables —sales of the company and of the whole industry—is much easier when the data are in the form of index numbers.   The two columns headed "Actual Sales" are much harder to compare than the three index-number arrangements for the same data.

When a base period has been chosen suitable to whatever purpose the analyst may have in mind, the curves are readily brought into each other's neighborhood by the index-number method.   Then it is easy to answer such questions as: How does the long-time growth of our company show up in comparison with our industry as a whole?   How much more, or less, did a boom or depression affect us than it did the industry generally?   How does our recent position compare with that of the industry?

The index number is not the only method of analysis which can be used on occasions to answer such questions as these; but it is one of the most effective, and, when properly understood and applied, one of the easiest.   Some statisticians prefer to use the semi-logarithmic charts.

Graphs are the quickest, clearest, and most condensed method of conveying valuable information to the reader, but he should

---

[2] Table is hypothetical and adapted from *The Executives' Service Bulletin*, Metropolitan Life Insurance Co., December 1928.

realize their potency for misinformation as well as for administrative guidance.

6. *Is the number of units studied sufficiently large to represent the group fairly?*   It is obvious that if we wish to study any single human trait, such as the general intelligence of salesmen, it is necessary to test the intelligence of a large typical group of salesmen.   If we were to draw conclusions from the measurements of only ten salesmen, we would be very liable to fall into error.   Psychometrists have developed several formulas which show the required size of the group, or, in some cases, the unreliability of the conclusions drawn from a group of a given size. We shall leave these more complicated formulas to the statisticians, but the layman can approximate a decision from two simple questions:

Do the measures extend over the entire *range* for the group in question?   An example is that of the study of intelligence of college students.   If we were to measure the intelligence of only those students who fail in college or those who graduate with honors, we should not be testing a representative sampling of the factor under study.   Tests would have to be made of those who fail, those who do passing work, those who do average work, those who are slightly above the average, and those who are the best—all in their proper proportions.

The next question is: How *many* students must we have on each part of the entire scale?   We can answer this by noting whether the number of cases measured distribute themselves according to the normal frequency (normal probability) curve. When the base line of the theoretical probability curve has been divided into five equal parts and vertical lines have been erected at the dividing points, five areas result, which include the following percentages, reading from left to right: 3, 22, 50, 22, 3.   This bell-shaped curve seems to apply to many living characteristics. It has even been found that when the number of hairs on the left hind legs of a large number of bees are counted, the frequency curve has this bell-shape.   Because of this universality of distribution of human traits, many schools and colleges grade their students in conformity with this curve.

When an insufficient number of cases have been studied, the

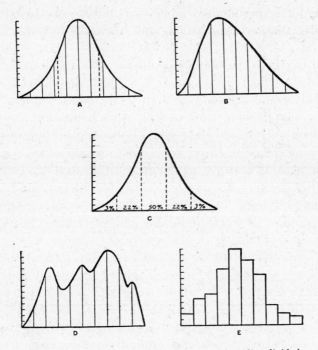

FIG. 114.   (A) Curve of normal frequency; base line divided into three equal parts.   (B) Skewed curve.   (C) Base line divided into five equal parts.   (D) Multimodal curve.   (E) Rectangles representing groups of grades.

frequency curve may be skewed or multi-modal in form. This discussion applies only to human traits or reactions found in a representative number of nonselected persons. That is, if we wish to test the intelligence of only the best 10 per cent of salesmen in one company, the normal frequency curve would not result. But if we were to test the best 10 per cent of all salesmen in a thousand companies, the plotted results would probably follow the normal curve.

7. *Have the data for a group been checked by control groups?* When a group of persons are experimented upon in the laboratory to determine the effects of smoking, caffeine, scolding, praise, music, lighting, or a system of wage payment, it is also necessary to measure the same or similar reactions of another group of persons who are not affected by the same stimuli. One

investigator experimented upon the effects of periodicity of women in the performing of certain mental functions. A control group of men was used because obviously they could not be affected by the same organic condition. It was found that the men had more fluctuations which could be looked upon as cyclical for twenty-eight-day periods than the women! If the control group of men had not been used, it is probable that the data of the women only would have given quite another impression.

Sometimes experimenters try a new method of sales management or lighting or wage payment and find that the production figures go up the next month. These stimuli do cause changes in production, but it is well to check the new plan by allowing certain groups to work under the old system so that the one factor which is blamed or praised for the change may really be known beyond any chance factors that may be bringing about the change. In the experiments on the effects of drugs, it is absolutely essential to have control groups because of the effect of suggestion. It is also essential in proving the effects of new methods of motivating or training employees.

8. *Do the conclusions and suggestions harmonize with general experience and the judgment of persons experienced in the field studied?* Because of the opportunities for misinterpretation of statistics, it is well to compare the findings with empirical conclusions. The man who has had years of experience in any field is likely to know many facts and principles that cannot be revealed by laboratory experiments.

It should be kept in mind at all times that laboratory experiments in human reactions usually deal with one factor or one set of factors only. An experiment may be sound so far as it goes, but *psychological laboratory conditions seldom approximate actual conditions.* Some important human reactions cannot be subjected to experiment. Several psychologists have attempted to measure the reactions of persons when in love, angry, fearful, or sexually excited; but it has been very difficult to achieve genuine mental states in the laboratory. All psychological laboratory experiments should be looked upon as laboratory experiments which may or may not carry over into actual life and business.

If the investigation does not agree with the past experience of those who are conversant with the empirical facts, then it may be necessary to repeat parts of the research.   On the other hand, if the study does indicate that it would be advisable, all things considered, to make certain changes, the research will have been a waste of time and money unless the changes are made.

The measurement of relationship between two series rather than differences within one series.   Psychologists have conducted thousands of investigations in which they have attempted to find how two or more series of measures correlate.   This kind of computation received an impetus from the attempts to find how tests of general intelligence correlated with other tests or measurements.   Problems such as the correlation between grades in high school and grades in college, grades in one subject compared with grades in another, height and its relation to intelligence, the "pulling power" of ads when evaluated in the laboratory and when judged on the basis of the number of inquiries, number of years in school and sales of life insurance are only a few examples of the many attempts to measure relationship between two series.   To enable scientists to compare the results of their researches and to increase the accuracy of their own studies, psychologists have resorted to mathematical formulas, such as the Pearson Product-Moment (r) formula and the Spearman Rank-Difference (ρ) method of computing the coefficient of correlation.   The computations of these formulas give to the scientists, in terms of one figure, the relationship between two variables.   We shall illustrate the use of the latter formula with an example which shows the method of computation rather than indicate all the facts that would have to be considered when using the formula.

Let us assume that ten students in a class take a mid-semester quiz.   Would it be possible to predict the final grades of the students on the basis of what they did in the quiz?   Most persons would expect to find some definite relation between quiz grades and final grades.   It would vary with certain factors, such as the instructors, the courses, and the teaching methods.   Let us assume that the names of the students, their grades in the quiz, and their final grades are as follows:

Names	Quiz Grade	Final Grade
Brown, John S.............	71	71
Bundit, William F..........	91	85
Devern, Samuel P..........	85	90
Everson, Paul T...........	88	80
Fullerton, Newton.........	60	72
Graff, Marion.............	77	70
Hunter, Lewis.............	60	50
Jutterton, Isaac...........	75	75
Lewisorn, Beatrice.........	72	65
Turner, B. Houghton.......	78	80

By inspection of the grades of the two examinations, we recognize that the students who did well on the quiz also *tended* to do well on the final examination. There are some differences, as in the case of the two students who made 60 on the quiz. One of them did better and the other did worse on the final examination. It is necessary, therefore, to have a simple device for the expression of the correlation. The Spearman Rank-Difference formula is:

$$\rho = 1 - \frac{6\Sigma D^2}{n(n^2 - 1)}$$

ρ (rho) stands for the degree of correlation, or the measurement of correspondence, and is usually called the coefficient of correlation. D stands for the differences in rank of the two series of measurements. The number of items in the series is indicated by n, which is 10 in this problem. Σ is the symbol for "sum of."

The correlation for the above two series is found by the method illustrated here:

Names	Quiz Grade	Final Grade	Rank in Quiz	Rank in Final	D	D²
Brown, John S.............	71	71	8	7	1	1
Bundit, William F.........	91	85	1	2	1	1
Devern, Samuel P..........	85	90	3	1	2	4
Everson, Paul T...........	88	80	2	3.5	1.5	2.25
Fullerton, Newton.........	60	72	9.5	6	3.5	12.25
Graff, Marion.............	77	70	5	8	3	9
Hunter, Lewis.............	60	50	9.5	10	.5	.25
Jutterton, Isaac...........	75	75	6	5	1	1
Lewisorn, Beatrice........	72	65	7	9	2	4
Turner, B. Houghton.......	78	80	4	3.5	.5	.25
						35.00

The sum of $D^2 = 35$

$n = 10$

$n(n^2 - 1) = 990$

Hence $1 - \dfrac{6 \times 35}{990} = 1 - \dfrac{210}{990} = 1.00 - .21 = +.79$

By use of the formula, we now know that the relationship between quiz grade and final grade in that course was +.79. The relation was positive.   That is, those who did well in the quiz tended to do well in the final examination.   If the answer had been —.79, then the relation would have been in inverse order; that is, those who did well in the quiz tended to do poorly in the final examination and those who did poorly in the quiz tended to do well in the final examination.

This question naturally arises in the above problem: "Does the coefficient of correlation of +.79 mean that 79 per cent of the students who did well on the quiz also did well on the final examination?"   It does not.   The coefficient of correlation, as stated above and as it is usually given in research reports, is not on a percentage basis.   To put it on a percentage basis, we must compute its "per cent of better than chance coincidence":

$$\text{Per cent of better than chance coincidence} = 1 - \sqrt{1 - \rho^2}$$

By use of this formula we see that the above correlation of +.79 means that there was a per cent of better than chance coincidence in this case of about 0.39.   To assist the reader in judging the values of coefficients of correlation, it is well for him to keep in mind the following general and rough evaluations from the predictive standpoint:

Coefficients	Their Predictive Value
0.00 to 0.20...........	No correlation or chance.
0.20 to 0.40...........	Slight correlation.
0.40 to 0.70...........	Definite correlation, but little predictive value.
0.70 to 1.00...........	Correlation of definite predictive value.

To use the coefficient of correlation it is necessary to be a trained statistician, because of the many possibilities for erroneous conclusions.   In the above example of ten students, we could not say that the class of next year would do the same and that we could therefore omit the final examination entirely. It might not be safe to omit the final examination the following year even if the coefficient of correlation had been +.95.   The number of students studied was small.   In such cases the statisticians use the formula for finding the Probable Error (P. E.):[3]

$$\text{Probable error of the correlation} = .6745 \frac{1 - \rho^2}{\sqrt{n}}$$

_____

[3] A similar measure which is coming into greater use is the Standard Error (σ). For a discussion of the relative merits of the Probable Error and the Standard

In this example of correlation, where the coefficient of correlation is +.79 and the number of cases is 10, the P. E. is ±.08. *When the coefficient of correlation is less than four times its probable error, the coefficient indicates no predictive value, regardless of how near to 1.00 it may be.* In this case the coefficient is almost ten times its probable error and we are safe in saying, assuming all other factors to be equivalent, that the coefficient of correlation of .79 indicates a better than chance correspondence. In the long run, if estimates of students' final grades are based upon their quiz grades, predictions would be right more often than wrong. It would, however, be dangerous to try to predict any single student's grade on the basis of the quiz grade only. The predictions usually apply to groups only.

TABLE LVIII[4]

PREDICTIVE VALUES (CHANCES IN 100) FOR
CORRELATION COEFFICIENTS (r)

r	Chances in 100	r	Chances in 100
.00	50	.55	58
.05	50	.60	60
.10	50	.65	63
.15	50	.70	66
.20	51	.75	69
.25	51	.80	74
.30	52	.85	80
.35	53	.866	82
.40	54	.90	89
.45	55	.95	97
.50	56	1.00	100

A high coefficient of correlation really means that, when one variable is given, the other can be predicted within a certain range. The range is determined by the amount of the coefficient of correlation, the probable error, the soundness of the units of measurement, and other factors which are recognized by psychological researchers. This discussion of a very technical field has been presented not to train the reader in the use of these methods but to indicate how he should interpret statistics quoted by psychologists. It is also hoped that the reader who handles data of this sort will recognize the pitfalls and consult with statisticians of the biometrical fields when he attempts to carry

Error, refer to R. A. Fisher's *Statistical Methods for Research Workers,* p. 46. Oliver & Boyd, Edinburgh, 1932.

[4] Douglas Fryer and Lyle H. Lanier, "Prediction in Terms of Chances in 100 from the Correlation Coefficient," *Industrial Psychology,* May 1927, p. 261.

on investigations in relationships between human reactions.

Measures of central tendency. Statisticians use the *mean* and the *median* to note the central tendency of the series of measures. The mean is synonymous with the *arithmetic average*. In a series where the measures are distributed in a perfect normal frequency curve, the mean and the median are the same.

We determine the arithmetic mean or average in the usual manner. Let us compute the average wealth for the following members of a summer camp:

Occupation	No. in the Occupation	Wealth of Each Man	Total for the Occupation
Lawyer................	1	$ 10,000	$ 10,000
Teacher..............	2	{4,000} {5,000}	9,000
Bank clerk...........	3	2,000	6,000
Salesman............	2	15,000	30,000
Undertaker..........	1	20,000	20,000
Financier............	1	1,000,000	1,000,000

Total number of people.. 10
Total wealth for the camp...................... $1,075,000
Average wealth............................... 107,500

In this case, the members of the summer camp can truthfully say that the average wealth for each member of their little community is over $100,000. However, only one member of the community can afford the standard of living which $100,000 would permit. Per capita figures frequently give a wrong impression, because the average always takes into consideration all the measures of the series. To overcome the effect of extremes in the series, the median is used.

The *median* is that measure of a series, arranged in order of magnitude, above which and below which one-half of the measures fall. Sometimes it is the middlemost measure.

When the members of the above summer camp are arranged in order of wealth, the series is:

Bank clerk................... $	2,000
Bank clerk...................	2,000
Bank clerk...................	2,000
Teacher.....................	4,000
Teacher.....................	5,000
Lawyer.....................	10,000
Salesman...................	15,000
Salesman...................	15,000
Undertaker.................	20,000
Financier...................	1,000,000

In this example, what is the median wealth? We cannot take the middlemost measure, because we have an even number of cases. If we had eleven members of the camp, we could take the wealth of the sixth member of the series as the median wealth of the community. In the present case of ten members we can find the median wealth of the community by calculating the arithmetic average of the two middle members of the series. The median wealth in this camp is $7,500. This more truly represents the per capita wealth of the community than the average wealth. At any rate, a salesman would be more justified in approaching the members of the community with a product that could be afforded only by people whose incomes are $7,500 than would the salesman whose product could be afforded only by persons whose incomes are over $100,000.

In this example, the mean and the median are not the same in value, because the curve of distribution is skewed toward one end of the scale. In general, when a series of measures is truly representative of human nature, the mean and the median are approximately the same.

In some situations neither the mean nor the median is of value as a measure of central tendency. The *mode* may have to be used. The *mode* is the measure that occurs most frequently. Let us assume that the general manager of a concern manufacturing window shades sends an investigator out to measure the sizes of the windows in a community. The investigator returns with the data and then computes the mean and the median sizes of windows. These sizes would have no value for determining the sizes of shades to be manufactured. Theoretically, not one window might fit the mean size and perhaps one might fit the median size. The modal size would be better, as the mode is that measure which occurs most frequently in the series. In the case of the members of the summer camp, the modal wealth of the community is $2,000, because that is the amount of income which occurs most often.

Correcting for guessing. Teachers of psychology and other subjects have been giving objective questions of the true-false type for a number of years. Students are often given true-false statements and told to put a circle around T if the statement is true and around F if it is false. If the answer is not known, the student may omit the question. Statistically, a student might not study the assigned material at all and yet be able to have the answers correct for one-half the questions. To overcome the factor of chance, the answers are usually scored so that the student is doubly penalized for each question incorrectly answered. This is done on the theory that he will guess right about as often as he guesses wrong. The score for an examination of this type is:

$$\text{Score} = \frac{\text{Total number}}{\text{of questions}} - [\text{No. unanswered} + (2 \times \text{No. wrong})]$$

In the case of 20 questions a student who has not read the material might answer 16 and have 4 blanks as doubtful and unanswered by him. By chance, 8 should be right, and 8 wrong. His score for the questions would then be:

$$\text{Score} = 20 - [4 + (2 \times 8)]$$
$$= 0$$

By experiment, we find that some students can answer some true-false questions even though they have not studied the lesson for which they are quizzed. From contacts with other subjects or materials related to the course, their guesses will be more often right than wrong. Hence the correct method of scoring for these questions would be:

$$\text{Score} = \frac{\text{Total number}}{\text{of questions}} - \left[\begin{array}{c} \text{No. unanswered} + \\ (2 \times \text{No. wrong}) \end{array} \right] - \frac{\text{Average No. known}}{\text{from other sources}}$$

If a correction is made for overlapping information acquired from sources other than the course itself, it is necessary to standardize the questions on a group having intelligence and experience similar to that of the students who are supposed to have studied the material before taking the examination.

Conclusion

In the first chapter of this book, the reader was given a list of the psychological problems of normal individuals with special tabulations of the problems of people in business. In the second chapter the claim was made that the basic attitude of the leader should be that of adjustment to a changing rate in the rate of change. Succeeding chapters dealt with certain aspects of psychology applied to modern life and work and with methods of predicting and influencing behavior in social and business situations. The research "tools" presented in this chapter are not comprehensive, but the discussion is an attempt to stimulate certain types of students to go on and acquire further skills in measuring human reactions. At any rate, exact methods are coming to play a vital part in our adjustments to the new American tempo.

References

Arkin, H., and R. R. Colton, *An Outline of Statistical Methods.* Barnes & Noble, 1938.

Burtt, H. E., *Principles of Employment Psychology,* Appendices I-III. Houghton-Mifflin Co., 1926.

Davies, G. R., and Dale Yoder, *Business Statistics.* John Wiley & Sons, 1937.

Jenkins, John G., *Psychology in Business and Industry,* Chapters XIV-XVI. John Wiley & Sons, 1935.

Nixon, H. K., *Principles of Advertising,* Chapter V. McGraw-Hill Book Co., 1937.

Sutcliffe, W. G., *Statistics for the Business Man.* Harper & Bros., 1930.

Wheeler, F. C., *et al., The Technique of Marketing Research,* Chapters XV-XIX. McGraw-Hill Book Co., 1937.

Yoder, Dale, *Personnel and Labor Relations,* Chapter IV. Prentice-Hall, Inc., 1938.

Projects

1. Suggest titles and headings for advertising a booklet on child training which is to be sent to young mothers. Assume that the headings are to set forth the main appeal in a direct-mail booklet. As a suggestion, consider the results of a questionnaire answered by mothers who gave their votes for first choice of these six terms as follows:

	Votes
Scientific child training	3
Psychological study of the child	3
Happy childhood	39
Better parenthood	17
Character education	30
Preparing the child for life	40

2. A doctor made the following statement: "I had all the nicotine removed from a cigarette, making a solution out of it. I injected half the quantity into a frog with the effect that the frog died almost instantly. The rest was administered to another frog with like effect. Both frogs were grown and of average size. The conclusion is evident that a single cigarette contains enough poison to kill two frogs."

Is this a valid argument to prove the harmfulness of cigarette smoking? What would be the effect of taking the white of an egg and injecting a part of it into the human bloodstream? (For guidance in obtaining the answer, look up the chemical nature of rattlesnake venom.)

3. In reading a research report, how can one detect whether the writer tried to prove a point or merely to present the facts that he happened to find? What are the distinguishing characteristics of reports that *defend a position* compared with those that *try to promote an idea?*

4. In a discussion group of thirty industrial executives, the leader of the group was opposed to a bonus for the foreman of a gang of seven workers. Three of the members of the group had had experience with bonuses for the foreman of small units of production. These three men were heartily in favor of a bonus for the foreman as well as the workers. The leader of the discussion group then asked the members of the group to vote for or against a foreman's bonus. The three who had had experience with such a situation voted in favor of the bonus; the remaining members of the group who had had no such experience opposed it.

How can the voting of these executives be explained?

5. Statistically, is the difference between two and three the same as the difference between ten and eleven? If 10 men can build a house in 100 days, can 1,000 men build the house in one day?

6. Discuss statistical data of business which are often compared but which really are not comparable, such as bond prices during the Civil War and World War II or wages in London and in Chicago. Is homogeneity in comparisons of psychological data possible?

7. Distinguish between immediate or superficial causes and remote or fundamental causes. How does this apply to retail costs? To unemployment? To sales records?

8. Examine a standard book on the construction and interpretation of graphs and charts and list some of the common errors and fallacies in this field. Find a graph or chart that misrepresents the data on which it is based and reconstruct it so that it presents a true picture.

Appendix

Social-Knowledge Test*

I. KNOWLEDGE OF THE LOWER SOCIAL STRATA

Each question has several possible answers. Underline the one answer that is correct or the most nearly correct, and put its number in the parentheses at the end of the dotted line. Do not omit any question even if you must guess.

1. "Ball and chain" refers to a:
   (1)Watch ornament (2)Wife (3)Surveying device (4) Sculptor's tool ....( )
2. To "beef" means to:
   (1)Diet (2)Promise action (3)Complain (4)Substitute ....( )
3. "Grunt" is a name applied to:
   (1)Dwarfs (2)Marines (3)Inexperienced workers (4)Bell-hops ....( )
4. To "give the bird" is to:
   (1)Heckle (2)Give a dinner party (3)Double-cross (4) Pay tuition ....( )
5. "On the blink" means:
   (1)On a spree (2)Out of repair (3)Flirting (4)On probation.( )
6. A "Gapper" is:
   (1)An addict in need of dope (2)Ditch digger (3)Consumptive (4)Fishing rod ....( )
7. "Broad" is a slang term for a:
   (1)Negro (2)Woman (3)Religious fanatic (4)Southerner ..( )
8. "Bull" is a common expression for:
   (1)Bunk (2)Violent threat (3)Deceit (4)Great energy ....( )
9. To "burn" is to:
   (1)Sin (2)Warn (3)Betray (4)Electrocute ....( )
10. "Caboodle" signifies a:
    (1)Railway car (2)Jail (3)The whole lot (4)Dance ......( )
11. A "Cartwheel" is a:
    (1)Canadian dime (2)Square dance (3)Roulette (4)Dollar..( )
12. "Cheaters" are:
    (1)Overshoes (2)Spectacles (3)Football spies (4)Blue-points ....( )
13. A "Dip" is an:
    (1)Old horse (2)Amusement park (3)Pickpocket (4)Red-head ....( )
14. "In the dog house" means:
    (1)In disfavor (2)Jealous (3)Ill (4)On a sucker list ......( )
15. "Dominie" is a term referring to a:
    (1)Game (2)Priest (3)Sugar (4)Profanity ....( )
16. The term "to fade" is used in:
    (1)Dice (2)Golf (3)Billiards (4)Horse racing ....( )
17. A "Fink" refers to a:
    (1)Strike-breaker (2)Instructor (3)Razor (4)Carnation ...( )

*Copyright 1941 by Harry W. Hepner.

18. To be "flush" means to be:
    (1)Drunk   (2)Well supplied with money   (3)On probation
    (4)Angry ....( )
19. A "Floozey" is a:
    (1)Bad defeat   (2)Phonograph   (3)Cocktail   (4)Girl ....( )
20. The term "Shiv" refers to a:
    (1)Bad cold   (2)Deliriums   (3)Chaplain   (4)Knife ....( )
21. To "fork over" means to:
    (1)Relinquish   (2)Pass the buck   (3)Examine hastily   (4)
    Betray ....( )
22. A "Frog" is a:
    (1)Railroad worker   (2)Prostitute   (3)Thief   (4)Frenchman   ( )
23. A "Goon" refers to a:
    (1)Strong-arm man   (2)Cuspidor   (3)Large fish   (4)Ballet
    dancer ....( )
24. How many dollars is a "Grand"?
    (1)A million   (2)A thousand   (3)A hundred   (4)Ten ......( )
25. "Hant" is a name referring to a:
    (1)Stolen car   (2)Gangster's girl   (3)Ghost   (4)Insect ......( )
26. To be "leery" means to be:
    (1)One-sided   (2)Vulgar   (3)Suspicious   (4)Weak ....( )
27. A "Harp" is a:
    (1)Bowling device   (2)Irishman   (3)Shyster   (4)Old woman..( )
28. "Heft" signifies:
    (1)Weight   (2)Speed   (3)Accuracy   (4)Persistence ....( )
29. "On the lam" means to:
    (1)Submit   (2)Escape hastily   (3)Suffer   (4)Feign death ....( )
30. To be "hep" means to be:
    (1)Vigorous   (2)Well informed   (3)Successful   (4)Lazy .....( )
31. "Java" is a common term for:
    (1)Negroes   (2)Fruit   (3)Coffee   (4)Enamel ....( )
32. To "highball" is to:
    (1)Stagger   (2)Tip-toe   (3)Dance   (4)Go at top speed ......( )
33. A "Plug" is a:
    (1)Horse   (2)Cigar   (3)Union leader   (4)Coach ....( )
34. "Pins" refer to one's:
    (1)Legs   (2)Fingers   (3)Arms   (4)Feet ....( )
35. To "hit the ceiling" means to:
    (1)Blow up emotionally   (2)Be inspired   (3)Faint   (4)Be-
    come rich ....( )
36. To "hit the hay" means to:
    (1)Eat breakfast   (2)Reform   (3)Go to bed   (4)Shadow-box..( )
37. The term "Jack" refers to a:
    (1)Counterfeiter   (2)Dope fiend   (3)Money   (4)Sworn rival..( )
38. A "Jag" is a:
    (1) Spree   (2)Stool-pigeon   (3)Night club   (4)Trap ....( )
39. To "jibe" means to:
    (1)Dance   (2)Fit   (3)Diminish   (4)Speed up ....( )
40. To "knock down" means to:
    (1)Complicate   (2)Apologize   (3)Embezzle   (4)Resign ......( )

41. "Murphy" is a term applied to:
    (1)Eggs (2)Steaks (3)Melons (4)Potatoes ....( )
42. To "lamp" is to:
    (1)Look at (2)Expose (3)Understand (4)Suspect ....( )
43. "The Long Green" refers to:
    (1)Bowling alleys (2)Indian summer (3)Paper money (4)
    Spinach ....( )
44. A "Lunger" is a:
    (1)Consumptive (2)Track star (3)Barker (4)Vain person..( )
45. Something that is "the McCoy" is:
    (1)Profound (2)Deceptive (3)Prejudiced (4)Genuine .....( )
46. A "Mick" is a:
    (1)Musician (2)Irishman (3)Jockey (4)Minstrel ....( )
47. A "Moocher" is a:
    (1)Glutton (2)Sleep-walker (3)Beggar (4)Silent partner ..( )
48. "Panty-waist" refers to an:
    (1)Effeminate man (2)Gambler (3)Dishwasher (4) Mas-
    culine woman ....( )
49. "P.D.Q." means:
    (1)Secretly (2)Quietly (3)Quickly (4)Please reply ....( )
50. "Pineapple" is a slang term for a:
    (1)Bowling ball (2)Bomb (3)Stolen car (4)Free pass .....( )
51. To "puke" means to:
    (1)Act snobbish (2)Faint (3)Surrender (4)Vomit ....( )
52. A "Puss" is a:
    (1)Fur neck-piece (2)Face (3)Smile (4)Sneer ....( )
53. A "Rag" refers to a:
    (1)Newspaper (2)Retired gangster (3)Finger-print expert
    (4)Trusty ....( )
54. A "Rake-off" is a:
    (1)Prison term (2)Suicide (3)Bonus (4)Cut or share ....( )
55. "Red-eye" is a term for:
    (1)Strong cigars (2)Betting experts (3)Chinese (4)Cheap
    whisky ....( )
56. To "renig" means to:
    (1)Rest up (2)Laugh scornfully (3)Repeat (4)Back out ..( )
57. A "Scab" is a:
    (1)Sailor (2)Camp-follower (3)Nurse (4)Strike-breaker ...( )
58. "Shafts" refer to:
    (1)Spectacles (2)Lunch rooms (3)Legs (4)Contagious dis-
    ease ....( )
59. A "Sinker" is a:
    (1)Degenerate man (2)Coal mine (3)Ambulance (4)
    Doughnut ....( )
60. To "skunk" means to:
    (1)Defeat badly (2)Exile (3)Ask for mercy (4)Bootleg
    liquor ....( )
61. "Smacker" is a term meaning a:
    (1)Cyclone (2)Notice of dismissal (3)Dollar (4)Unpaid
    bill ....( )

62. A "Stiff" is an:
    (1)Escaped convict (2)Corpse (3)Generous host (4)
    Woman ....( )
63. A "Sucker" is a:
    (1)Dupe (2)Cheater (3)Dope addict (4)Hockey device ..( )
64. People "talk turkey" when they:
    (1)Lie (2)Evade the point (3)Write in code (4)Speak
    frankly ....( )
65. "Tripe" is a term meaning:
    (1)Lectures (2)Advice (3)Nonsense (4)Swindles ....( )
66. A "Twist" is a:
    (1)Woman (2)Tennis racket (3)Prison trusty (4)In-
    formal dance ....( )
67. "The works" means:
    (1)Everything (2)Bad habits (3)Pool rooms (4)Crime
    record ....( )
68. The term "Yegg" applies to a:
    (1)Black-Jack card (2)Omelette (3)Social worker (4)
    Safe-cracker ....( )
69. "Flying tackle" is a term used in:
    (1)Aviation (2)Kite flying (3)Football (4)Baseball ....( )
70. A "Puck" is something used in:
    (1)Golf (2)Lacrosse (3)Hockey (4)Soccer ....( )
71. A "Chippy" is a:
    (1)Billiard ball (2)Girl (3)Small ship (4)Score of three in
    dice ....( )
72. A "Bridge" is a device used in:
    (1)Tennis (2)Hockey (3)Boxing (4)Billiards ....( )
73. A "Leatherneck" belongs to which of the following?
    (1)Marines (2)Artillery (3)Infantry (4)Cavalry ....( )
74. A slang term for Spaniards is:
    (1)Frogs (2)Spics (3)Wops (4)Dagos .....·.............( )
75. A "Bull" is a:
    (1)Crook (2)Stoker (3)Drug addict (4)Policeman ....( )
76. A "Cokey" is a:
    (1)Horse (2)Bad mistake (3)Drug fiend (4)Imbecile .....( )
77. "Welterweight" boxers must not be heavier than:
    (1)175 lbs. (2)145 lbs. (3)190 lbs. (4)165 lbs. ....( )
78. A "Palooka" is a:
    (1)Man from Poland (2)Ball player (3)Cheap prize-fighter
    (4)Forger ....( )
79. "Black Maria" is a term referring to a:
    (1)Colored comedian (2)Woman thief (3)Patrol wagon
    (4)Mulatto ....( )
80. A "Daisy cutter" is a:
    (1)Farm implement (2)Milliner (3)Low ball (4)Rustic ..( )
81. The highest possible bowling score for one game is:
    (1)45 (2) 250 (3)300 (4)500 ....( )
82. "Flying mare" is a term associated with:
    (1)Recreation parks (2)Racing (3)Wrestling (4)Avia-
    tion ....( )

83. A "Night line" is a:
    (1)Policeman's beat   (2)Sheik's conversation   (3)Fishing device   (4)Rendezvous .... ( )
84. "Palming" is used in:
    (1)Vice   (2)Gambling   (3)Children's games   (4)Dive bombing .... ( )
85. The term "to show" is associated with:
    (1)Dice   (2)Boxing   (3)Racing   (4)Football .... ( )
86. Earle Sande was a famous:
    (1)Bowery preacher   (2)Explorer   (3)Jockey   (4)Politician   ( )
87. A "Snow-bird" is a:
    (1)Dope fiend   (2)Nude painting   (3)Race horse   (4)Night club .... ( )
88. A "Sawbuck" is:
    (1)$1   (2)$5   (3)$10   (4)$100 .... ( )
89. A "Pan-handler" is a:
    (1)Miner   (2)Dishwasher   (3)Beggar   (4)Peddler .... ( )
90. "Mugging" has reference to:
    (1) Making faces   (2)Nervous maladies   (3)Beer drinking   (4)Blundering .... ( )
91. The figures on the opposite sides of a "dice" always add up to:
    (1)4   (2)6   (3)7   (4)11 .... ( )
92. A "Bindle-stiff" is a:
    (1)Flower   (2)College professor   (3)Tramp   (4)Dead crook   ( )
93. The term "Soup" is slang for:
    (1)Nitroglycerine   (2)Jail   (3)Freighter   (4)Poison gas ..... ( )
94. In dice games, "Snake eyes" means:
    (1)One and one   (2)Two and three   (3)Two and two   (4) Four and three .... ( )
95. The term "Slap-happy" is associated with:
    (1)Boxers   (2)Dope addicts   (3)Lunatics   (4)Negroes ...... ( )
96. "Little Phoebe" is a:
    (1)Stolen purse   (2)Dice term   (3)Famous horse   (4) Deputy sheriff .... ( )
97. An "Uncle" is a:
    (1)Jockey   (2)Hockey goalie   (3)Gambler   (4)Pawnbroker ..( )
98. "Hit me" is a term used in:
    (1)Wrestling   (2)Baseball   (3)Card playing   (4)Polo .... ( )
99. "Close hauled" is an expression used in connection with:
    (1)Trucking   (2)Boxing   (3)Debating   (4)Sailing .... ( )
100. "Whiffing the reefer" refers to:
    (1)Hay fever   (2)Sailing   (3)Winning a bet   (4)Using marijuana .... ( )
101. The term "Natural" is used in:
    (1)Baseball   (2)Fishing   (3)Dice games   (4)Billiards .... ( )
102. "Ice" is an expression meaning:
    (1)Pearls   (2)Diamonds   (3)Opium   (4)Cocaine .... ( )
103. A "Violin" is a:
    (1)Minister   (2)Machine gun   (3)Chorus girl   (4)Musician ..( )
104. The object of "Black-Jack" is:
    (1)37   (2)21   (3)50   (4)44 .... ( )

105. To "catch a crab" means to:
(1)Hunt for bait (2)Splash water with an oar (3)Tease a grouch (4)Catch an elusive criminal ....( )

106. A "Prat-digger" is a:
(1)Potato farmer (2)Blackmailer (3)Ballistics expert (4)Pickpocket ....( )

107. "To scratch" is an expression used in:
(1)Water polo (2)Baseball (3)Horse racing (4)Touch-football ....( )

108. "Little Joe" is a term used in:
(1)Golf (2)Cards (3)Dice (4)Horse racing ....( )

109. A "Fin" is a:
(1)Swordfish (2)Inhabitant of Finland (3)Five dollar bill (4)Detective ....( )

110. A "Mickey Finn" is a:
(1)Knock-out drink (2)Irish boxer (3)Cocktail (4)Hockey player ....( )

111. "Annie Oakley" refers to a:
(1)Free pass (2)English actress (3)Tom Oakley's wife (4)Machine gun ....( )

112. A "Tommy gun" is a:
(1)Sub-machine gun (2)Englishman's revolver (3)Police billy (4)Cannon ....( )

113. A "Beezer" refers to an:
(1)African dagger (2)Stiff test (3)Nose (4)Magazine ....( )

114. The term "Cinnamon head" applies to:
(1)Colored boxers (2)Candy bars (3)Wrestlers (4)Feeble-minded ....( )

115. A person who has "dropped his candy" has:
(1)Gone broke (2)Lost prestige (3)Ended an alliance (4)Reformed ....( )

116. "Travelers" are:
(1)Nervous twitches (2)Head lice (3)Crutches (4)Tears in stockings ....( )

117. "Bones" is a term associated with:
(1)Cards (2)Wrestling (3)Dice (4)Colored pencils ....( )

118. A "Harpoon" is a:
(1)Large ape (2)Tropical storm (3)Hypodermic needle (4)Band instrument ....( )

119. A "Buzzard" is a:
(1)Warden's wife (2)Prison cook (3)Ambulance (4)Village constable ....( )

120. The expression "Croaker" refers to:
(1)Morticians (2)Bootleggers (3)Doctors (4)Preachers ...( )

121. A "Finger" is a:
(1)Stolen purse (2)Officer of the law (3)Embezzler (4)Cripple ....( )

122. A "Singer" is a:
(1)Drunken play-boy (2)Stool-pigeon (3)Cocktail (4)Machine gun ....( )

123. A "Frail" is a slang term for an:
    (1)Athlete   (2)Pair of crooked dice   (3)Girl   (4)Salesman ..( )
124. "Slum" has reference to:
    (1)Boarding houses   (2)Meat stew   (3)Prison clothes   (4)
    Beer ....( )
125. A "Round-heel" is a:
    (1)Politician   (2)Poor prize-fighter   (3)Alcoholic   (4)Sales-
    man ....( )

II. KNOWLEDGE OF THE UPPER SOCIAL STRATA

Encircle "T" if the statement is true; "F" if it is false.

T F   **1.** When one is introducing a friend to another friend, the younger person is presented to the older person.

T F   **2.** When casual acquaintances meet, the man should be the first to speak to the woman.

T F   **3.** The man should offer to shake hands when introduced to a woman.

T F   **4.** Women should always remove their gloves before shaking hands.

T F   **5.** It is correct to say, "Mrs. Jones, this is Mr. Smith."

T F   **6.** A proper reply to an introduction is, "Charmed, I'm sure."

T F   **7.** When a newcomer is introduced to a group, his name must be repeated for each person.

T F   **8.** When one is introduced to a famous person, it is proper to say, "I've heard so much about you."

T F   **9.** It is correct form for a man to shake hands without removing his gloves if they cannot be removed quickly.

T F **10.** In introducing one's self say, "I'm Henry Brown," rather than, "I'm Mr. Henry Brown."

T F **11.** Children should remain seated when being introduced.

T F **12.** It is correct to blow on very hot soup if very little noise is made.

T F **13.** In eating soup, dip the spoon "away" from you.

T F **14.** When served with soup, crackers may be broken into the cup.

T F **15.** It is permissible to drink bouillon by lifting the cup, as one would drink tea.

T F **16.** Blue-point cocktails should be eaten with a spoon.

T F **17.** Asparagus should be eaten with a fork.

T F **18.** When a hot dish is served at a formal dinner of twenty guests, one may begin eating after four guests have been served.

T F **19.** When declining a dish at dinner, one should explain why the dish was declined.

T F **20.** After one has finished eating, the fork should be laid on the plate with the tines upward.

T F **21.** When serving a meal, all drinks should be served on the right.

T F **22.** The entire portion of meat on one's plate should be cut to pieces before one begins to eat any of it.

T F **23.** The mouth should be wiped before one drinks water.

T F **24.** One should moisten his napkin in the finger bowl and gently wipe the lips.

T F **25.** At a formal dinner a man should sit to the left of his partner.

T F 26. A distinguished guest should be seated at the right of the hostess.

T F 27. When the waitress sets down your dishes, you should thank her.

T F 28. It is necessary to wait for the hostess to begin before starting to eat.

T F 29. Candle light is acceptable for formal dinners.

T F 30. Hors d'oeuvres are appetizers or relishes served before dinner begins.

T F 31. Red wine is preferable to white wine with fish courses.

T F 32. A man escorting a woman on the street should always walk at her left.

T F 33. A man who is escorting two women on the street should walk between them.

T F 34. A man raises his hat when giving directions to a strange woman on the street.

T F 35. Men should remove their hats when in private offices.

T F 36. In most cases a man need only touch his hat instead of lifting it when he meets a woman on the street.

T F 37. If no usher is present, the man should always precede the woman when approaching their seats in a theater.

T F 38. A man sitting next to a strange woman in a theater should assist when she wishes to take off her coat.

T F 39. A woman should keep her hat on in the theater unless asked by the usher to remove it.

T F 40. At the theater, one should wait until the final curtain has gone down before rising to put on one's coat or to leave.

T F 41. In a church, a woman's contribution should be placed in the collection box by her escort.

T F 42. A man precedes his woman companion in alighting from a bus or street car.

T F 43. A woman precedes her escort in going through a revolving door.

T F 44. The term "My dear" in correspondence is more formal than "Dear."

T F 45. It is never necessary to answer informal invitations.

T F 46. A bachelor who gives a formal dinner should send engraved invitations.

T F 47. In sending out invitations to a wedding, the added inquiry of R.S.V.P. is permissible.

T F 48. Engraved engagement announcements are correct.

T F 49. Letters of condolence should be written on black-edged paper.

T F 50. One should acknowledge only the invitations he expects to accept.

T F 51. The typewriter may be used to answer formal social letters.

T F 52. Formal invitations are written in the third person.

T F 53. The use of initials on visiting cards should be avoided if possible.

T F 54. The calling-card of a married woman is smaller than that of her husband.

T F 55. An unmarried woman signs her name "Alice Burt" rather than "Miss Alice Burt."

T F 56. When signing a letter to a stranger, a married woman should sign her married name, as, "Mrs. John Smith."

T F 57. One should congratulate a woman on her engagement.

T F 58. When an engagement is broken, gifts, letters, etc. are returned.

T F 59. A fur coat is an appropriate gift from a man to his fiancee on the occasion of their engagement.

T F 60. Wedding announcements are invitations to attend the ceremony.

T F 61. The wedding reception may be given at the home of the groom.

T F 62. The bride should always carry flowers if the wedding is a formal one.

T F 63. The bridegroom should pay the expenses of the wedding.

T F 64. It is correct to pay a condolence call.

T F 65. The children of the deceased are not expected to wear mourning clothes.

T F 66. A man's shirt cuffs should show when he is wearing a coat.

T F 67. The vest may be left off when a double-breasted sport suit is worn.

T F 68. It is permissible to wear a derby with a tuxedo.

T F 69. The bridegroom should wear a tuxedo.

T F 70. A black tie should be worn with a tuxedo.

T F 71. Tuxedos may be worn to any strictly formal occasion.

T F 72. Men's formal evening clothes should not be worn before about 6 p.m.

T F 73. A freshly pressed gray felt hat is appropriate for men on formal occasion.

T F 74. A woman entertaining a party of friends informally at a club or restaurant should wear a hat.

T F 75. The proper way for a bachelor to entertain a debutante is to ask her to tea or to the theatre.

T F 76. At a formal dinner-dance, the guests should wait for the hostess to dance before they dance.

T F 77. At an informal dinner, the men should give the women their arms when going into the dining room.

T F 78. Any guest who is older than the guest of honor may leave before the honored guest does.

T F 79. When a couple leaves the supper-table to go onto the dance floor, the other men at the table should always rise.

T F 80. A woman should take her escort's arm when leaving the dance floor.

T F 81. In a public restaurant, the man rises whenever a woman leaves or returns to the table.

T F 82. When a man approaches a table at which a man and a woman, whom he knows, are eating, the man who is seated at the table should rise.

T F 83. In a restaurant, a woman waits until she is seated before removing her coat.

T F 84. When dining, a woman should place her purse or gloves on the table near her escort.

T F 85. When the proprietor of a restaurant waits on one, it is proper to tip him.

T F 86. When one is invited for the week-end, a personal gift for the hostess, such as a piece of jewelry, is most acceptable.

T F 87. If the door to her home is locked, the woman should always give the key to her escort and allow him to open the door.

T F 88. When registering at a hotel, it is proper to sign, "Mr. John Doe and wife."

T F 89. The time limit for occupancy of a hotel room is usually around 5 or 6 p.m. of the following day.

T F 90. In hotels, "European plan" means that meals are included in the rate charged.

T F 91. In a Pullman car, a woman may dress either in her own berth or in the dressing room.

T F 92. The bowl in a wash-room of a Pullman should be wiped after one uses it.

T F 93. On entering a taxi, a lady should sit on the right in order to let the man cross in front of her and sit at her left side.

T F 94. A toot on the horn is an appropriate way of replying to a courtesy by a pedestrian.

T F 95. When speaking to servants or trades-people, the wife should refer to her husband as "Mr. Johnson" rather than "My husband" or "Alfred."

T F 96. When shopping, it is poor etiquette to thank the salesman.

T F 97. It is better to say "Pardon me" than "I beg your pardon."

T F 98. A walking-stick or an umbrella should be carried horizontally.

T F 99. "What are you doing tonight?" is bad taste when phoning for a date.

T F 100. It is fashionable to be a little late at a dinner party.

KEY TO (I) KNOWLEDGE OF THE LOWER SOCIAL STRATA

 1. (2) Wife.
 2. (3) Complain.
 3. (3) Inexperienced workers.
 4. (1) Heckle.
 5. (2) Out of repair.
 6. (1) An addict in need of dope.
 7. (2) Woman.
 8. (1) Bunk.
 9. (4) Electrocute.
10. (3) The whole lot.
11. (4) Dollar.
12. (2) Spectacles.
13. (3) Pickpocket.
14. (1) In disfavor.
15. (2) Priest.
16. (1) Dice.
17. (1) Strike-breaker.
18. (2) Well supplied with money.
19. (4) Girl.
20. (4) Knife.
21. (1) Relinquish.
22. (4) Frenchman.
23. (1) Strong-arm man.

24. (2) A thousand.
25. (3) Ghost.
26. (3) Suspicious.
27. (2) Irishman.
28. (1) Weight.
29. (2) Escape hastily.
30. (2) Well informed.
31. (3) Coffee.
32. (4) Go at top speed.
33. (1) Horse.
34. (1) Legs.
35. (1) Blow up emotionally.
36. (3) Go to bed.
37. (3) Money.
38. (1) Spree.
39. (2) Fit.
40. (3) Embezzle.
41. (4) Potatoes.
42. (1) Look at.
43. (3) Paper money.
44. (1) Consumptive.
45. (4) Genuine.
46. (2) Irishman.

47. (3) Beggar.
48. (1) Effeminate man.
49. (3) Quickly.
50. (2) Bomb.
51. (4) Vomit.
52. (2) Face.
53. (1) Newspaper.
54. (4) Cut or share.
55. (4) Cheap whisky.
56. (4) Back out.
57. (4) Strike-breaker.
58. (3) Legs.
59. (4) Doughnut.
60. (1) Defeat badly.
61. (3) Dollar.
62. (2) Corpse.
63. (1) Dupe.
64. (4) Speak frankly.
65. (3) Nonsense.
66. (1) Woman.
67. (1) Everything.
68. (4) Safe-cracker.
69. (3) Football.
70. (3) Hockey.
71. (2) Girl.
72. (4) Billiards.
73. (1) Marines.
74. (2) Spics.
75. (4) Policeman.
76. (3) Drug fiend.
77. (2) 145 lbs.
78. (3) Cheap prize-fighter.
79. (3) Patrol wagon.
80. (3) Low ball.
81. (3) 300.
82. (3) Wrestling.
83. (3) Fishing device.
84. (2) Gambling.
85. (3) Racing.
86. (3) Jockey

87. (1) Dope fiend.
88. (3) $10.
89. (3) Beggar.
90. (1) Making faces.
91. (3) 7.
92. (3) Tramp.
93. (1) Nitroglycerine.
94. (1) One and one.
95. (1) Boxers.
96. (2) Dice term.
97. (4) Pawnbroker.
98. (3) Card playing.
99. (4) Sailing.
100. (4) Using marijuana.
101. (3) Dice games.
102. (2) Diamonds.
103. (2) Machine gun.
104. (2) 21.
105. (2) Splash water with an oar.
106. (4) Pickpocket.
107. (3) Horse racing.
108. (3) Dice.
109. (3) Five-dollar bill.
110. (1) Knock-out drink.
111. (1) Free pass.
112. (1) Sub-machine gun.
113. (3) Nose.
114. (4) Feebleminded.
115. (2) Lost prestige.
116. (2) Head lice.
117. (3) Dice.
118. (3) Hypodermic needle.
119. (4) Village constable.
120. (3) Doctors.
121. (2) Officer of the law.
122. (2) Stool-pigeon.
123. (3) Girl.
124. (2) Meat stew.
125. (2) Poor prize-fighter.

NORMS FOR KNOWLEDGE OF THE LOWER SOCIAL STRATA

Rank for College Students	Raw Score or Number Right	
	Men	Women
Highest fifth............	106–125	101–125
Second fifth.............	102–105	96–100
Middle fifth............	97–101	91– 95
Fourth fifth.............	90– 96	83– 90
Lowest fifth............	0– 89	0– 82

Key to Knowledge of the Upper Social Strata

1. True.	26. True.	51. False.	76. True.
2. False.	27. False.	52. True.	77. False.
3. False.	28. True.	53. True.	78. False.
4. False.	29. True.	54. False.	79. True.
5. True.	30. True.	55. True.	80. False.
6. False.	31. False.	56. False.	81. True.
7. False.	32. False.	57. False.	82. True.
8. False.	33. False.	58. True.	83. True.
9. True.	34. True.	59. False.	84. False.
10. True.	35. True.	60. False.	85. False.
11. False.	36. False.	61. False.	86. False.
12. False.	37. True.	62. False.	87. True.
13. True.	38. False.	63. False.	88. False.
14. False.	39. False.	64. True.	89. True.
15. True.	40. True.	65. True.	90. False.
16. False.	41. False.	66. True.	91. True.
17. True.	42. True.	67. True.	92. True.
18. False.	43. True.	68. False	93. True.
19. False.	44. True.	69. False.	94. False.
20. True.	45. False.	70. True.	95. True.
21. True.	46. False.	71. False.	96. False.
22. False.	47. True.	72. True.	97. False.
23. True.	48. False.	73. False.	98. False.
24. False.	49. False.	74. True.	99. True.
25. True.	50. False.	75. True.	100. False.

Norms for Knowledge of the Upper Social Strata

Rank for College Students	Raw Score or Number Right Men	Women
Highest fifth............	79–100	85–100
Second fifth.............	76– 78	81– 84
Middle fifth.............	72– 75	78– 80
Fourth fifth.............	69– 71	74– 77
Lowest fifth.............	0– 68	0– 73

Executive Reaction Pattern

Underline the term or degree which most adequately describes your likes, beliefs, record, etc. Do not try to think of what you would or should do, but answer according to what you have done.

1. Number of meetings of a technical nature or of trade associations attended—local organizations as well as national or state:

      a. Ten or more per year.
      b. From 5 to 10.
      c. From 1 to 5.
      d. Few or none.
      e. None.

2. Activity in trade or technical association meetings:
- a. Took very active part as a leader.
- b. Frequently took part in discussions.
- c. Occasionally asked questions.
- d. Rarely took part.
- e. Never took part.

3. Time devoted to personal appearance:
- a. Large amount.
- b. Considerable amount.
- c. Moderate amount.
- d. Few minutes a day.
- e. Neglect it.

4. Amount of study given to subjects related to my business since leaving school:
- a. Spent all available time on such subjects.
- b. Studied business subjects frequently.
- c. Occasionally spent time in study of my business.
- d. Seldom gave any.
- e. Never gave any.

5. When I have read the daily papers, I have read items relating to business:
- a. Almost exclusively.
- b. Much of the time.
- c. Frequently.
- d. Occasionally.
- e. Never, except by accident.

6. My record of leadership in my youth:
- a. Frequently organized games, teams, or clubs.
- b. A leader in activities.
- c. Little marked leadership.
- d. Willing to follow other leaders.
- e. Disregarded playmates.

7. I actually associated with men whose ability was:
- a. Much greater than mine.
- b. Somewhat greater.
- c. About the same.
- d. Slightly less than my own.
- e. Considerably less.

8. When I was not busy taking recreation or taking care of routine matters and had some time for thinking along any line, I devised new methods, plans, or systems. The percentage of such available time devoted to improvements was from:
- a. 75–100 per cent
- b. 50–75 " "
- c. 25–50 " "
- d. 5–25 " "
- e. 2–5 " "
- f. 0–2 " "

9. My thinking of improvements dealt with problems relating to (underline as many as apply):

>   a. Organization of company as a whole.
>   b. Organization of work within one department.
>   c. Organization of work between departments.
>   d. Stimulating employees.
>   e. Cutting costs.
>   f. Increasing sales.
>   g. Better service to customers.
>   h. New mechanical inventions.
>   i. Better financing.
>   j. Helping society in general.

10. My family influence has:

>   a. Greatly stimulated me to do my best.
>   b. Stimulated me slightly.
>   c. Had no effect—good or bad.
>   d. Had slightly negative effect.
>   e. Had pronouncedly negative effect.

11. A rival or rivals:

>   a. Stimulated me strongly and I tried to beat them.
>   b. Stimulated me slightly.
>   c. Did not affect me at all.
>   d. Discouraged me slightly.
>   e. Discouraged me greatly.

12. I met my financial obligations:

>   a. Always promptly.
>   b. Fairly promptly.
>   c. As best I could.
>   d. Sometimes with failure.
>   e. Sometimes with neglect.

13. In times of failure or discouragement:

>   a. I persisted.
>   b. I persisted to a limited extent.
>   c. I thought of ways out of the difficulties and applied them to the problems.
>   d. I thought of remedies but did not apply them.
>   e. I just quit and regretted that I was not trained to solve them.

14. My energy supply:

>   a. Compels me to keep busy at all times.
>   b. Is plentiful.
>   c. Is enough to meet my needs.
>   d. Is small and I force myself to keep going.
>   e. Prevents my attaining many possibilities.

15. My attitude toward risks:

>   a. I took many serious business risks.
>   b. I took a few serious business risks.
>   c. I took no serious risks.
>   d. I took a few minor chances.
>   e. I took no serious or minor chances.

16. The extent to which I tried to make a favorable impression on important persons:

    a. I made definite plans and devoted much time to impressing the right persons.

    b. I devoted a slight amount of time to making a good impression.

    c. I seldom planned to do so in advance, but, if opportunity arose, I tried to make a good impression.

    d. I never noticed such opportunities.

    e. I disliked the practice in others and never indulged myself.

17. Problems or difficulties around me:

    a. Stimulated me greatly.

    b. Stimulated me mildly.

    c. Had no effect.

    d. Caused slight discouragement.

    e. Caused pronounced discouragement.

18. Criticisms from others regarding my work have:

    a. Greatly stimulated me to do better.

    b. Slightly stimulated me to do better.

    c. Had no effect.

    d. Worried me.

    e. Caused resentment.

19. Anticipating problems before they arose:

    a. Gave them much thought.

    b. Gave them some thought.

    c. Planned to meet present problems only.

    d. Let all problems take care of themselves.

    e. Passed them on to experts.

20. When conversing with superiors:

    a. I felt at ease and talked freely.

    b. I talked freely, but was not at perfect ease.

    c. I talked fairly freely, but was ill at ease.

    d. I talked little, because I was ill at ease.

    e. I felt inferior and said nothing.

21. When conversing with inferiors:

    a. I tried to make them feel at ease.

    b. I let them talk.

    c. I talked more than they.

    d. I monopolized the conversation.

    e. I tried to make them feel inferior.

    f. I did not think of any differences between us.

22. In group discussions:

    a. I said nothing.

    b. I spoke occasionally.

    c. I spoke when I had something worth saying.

    d. I dominated the conversation.

23. The amount of time I devoted to work has been:

    a. Far too much to enjoy life fully.

    b. About the right amount.

        c. Too much.
        d. Too little.
        e. Decidedly too little.

24. Ability to influence others:
        a. I could influence large numbers of persons.
        b. I could influence small numbers of persons.
        c. I could influence some individuals.
        d. I could influence those who were under obligations to me.
        e. Had difficulty in influencing anyone.
        f. Don't know—I never tried.

25. The number of technical or trade journals I read fairly regularly:
        a. 5 or more.
        b. 3 to 5.
        c. 2 or 3.
        d. 1 or 2.
        e. None.

26. My interest in my past work has been:
        a. Very great and enjoyable.
        b. Usually enjoyable.
        c. Slightly enjoyable.
        d. Little or none.
        e. Mostly negative.

27. The number of my friends who would help me in putting across a really good idea:
        a. A great many—50 or more.
        b. Many—10 to 50.
        c. Few—5 to 10.
        d. Very few—1 to 5.
        e. None.

28. The extent to which I have gone out of my way to help others:
        a. Often inconvenienced myself.
        b. Occasionally inconvenienced myself.
        c. Seldom inconvenienced myself.
        d. Never inconvenienced myself.
        e. Believed in taking care of myself and in letting others do the same.

KEY TO THE EXECUTIVE REACTION PATTERN TEST

1.	a.	+10	3.	a.	0	5.	a.	+ 6
	b.	+ 2		b.	+ 2		b.	+ 2
	c.	− 3		c.	− 5		c.	0
	d.	− 5		d.	− 2		d.	− 6
	e.	− 5		e.	− 3		e.	− 8
2.	a.	+ 6	4.	a.	+ 3	6.	a.	0
	b.	+ 4		b.	0		b.	+ 3
	c.	− 6		c.	− 1		c.	0
	d.	− 2		d.	− 8		d.	− 5
	e.	− 6		e.	− 8		e.	0

7.	a.	+ 1
	b.	+ 3
	c.	− 5
	d.	0
	e.	0

8.	a.	+ 6
	b.	+ 5
	c.	0
	d.	− 1
	e.	− 5
	f.	− 5

*9.	a.	+ 2
	b.	0
	c.	+ 2
	d.	+ 2
	e.	0
	f.	0
	g.	0
	h.	+ 2
	i.	+ 2
	j.	+ 2

10.	a.	+ 2
	b.	− 5
	c.	− 3
	d.	+ 3
	e.	− 3

11.	a.	+ 3
	b.	− 1
	c.	− 2
	d.	0
	e.	− 5

12.	a.	+ 4
	b.	− 4
	c.	− 5
	d.	− 5
	e.	− 5

13.	a.	+ 4
	b.	− 3
	c.	− 3
	d.	0
	e.	0

14.	a.	+ 5
	b.	+ 2
	c.	− 2
	d.	0
	e.	0

15.	a.	+ 5
	b.	0
	c.	− 2
	d.	− 3
	e.	− 5

16.	a.	− 6
	b.	+ 2
	c.	+ 1
	d.	0
	e.	0

17.	a.	+ 4
	b.	− 2
	c.	− 5
	d.	− 5
	e.	− 5

18.	a.	+ 2
	b.	− 2
	c.	0
	d.	− 4
	e.	+ 4

19.	a.	+ 4
	b.	0
	c.	− 3
	d.	− 4
	e.	+ 5

20.	a.	+ 4
	b.	− 2
	c.	− 4
	d.	− 4
	e.	− 4

21.	a.	+ 3
	b.	+ 6
	c.	− 3
	d.	− 3
	e.	− 3
	f.	− 3

22.	a.	− 5
	b.	− 5
	c.	+ 5
	d.	+ 5

23.	a.	− 2
	b.	+ 6
	c.	0
	d.	− 2
	e.	− 2

24.	a.	+ 4
	b.	+ 2
	c.	− 1
	d.	− 4
	e.	− 4
	f.	− 4

25.	a.	+10
	b.	+ 5
	c.	0
	d.	− 4
	e.	+ 2

26.	a.	+ 5
	b.	− 3
	c.	0
	d.	− 6
	e.	− 6

27.	a.	+10
	b.	0
	c.	− 4
	d.	0
	e.	0

28.	a.	+ 4
	b.	− 4
	c.	− 4
	d.	− 4
	e.	− 4

* Number 9 should also be scored on the total number of items underlined. If only one or two items are underlined, give no extra credit. If three or more items are underlined, give a plus score equal to the total number of items underlined. Example: if the five items c, d, h, i, j are underlined, each item having a +2 score, the total score for question No. 9 would be 10 + 5, or 15.

Assign plus and minus values to your own answers according to the above key. Add all the values having a plus sign. Add all those having a minus sign. Then add the two sums algebraically. Find the position of your final score in one of the six grades in the extreme left-hand column of the probability table. Read to the right and the per cent figures will indicate, statistically, the percentage of businessmen who made the same score in the test.

Example: of the businessmen who made a score of minus 40 to minus 120, 100 per cent made less than $2,500 per year; of those who made a score of plus 81 and above, 14 per cent made a salary of from $5,000 to $10,000 per year; 29 per cent, from $10,000 to $20,000 per year; and 57 per cent, $20,000 or more per year.

PROBABILITY TABLE SHOWING THE RELATION BETWEEN SCORES IN
EXECUTIVE REACTION PATTERN TEST AND SALARIES

Score in Test	0 to $2,500 per yr.	$2,500 to $5,000 per yr.	$5,000 to $10,000 per yr.	$10,000 to $20,000 per yr.	$20,000 per yr. and up
+81 and up	......	....	....	14%	29%	57%
+51 to +80	......	....	13%	22%	22%	43%
+21 to +50	......	7%	30%	33%	21%	9%
−9 to +20	......	15%	39%	34%	9%	3%
−10 to −39	......	59%	18%	18%	5%	....
−40 to −121	......	100%	....	....	....	....
Mean	−23.1	+14.8	+23.0	+40.5	+62.9
Median	−25.	+13.5	+26.0	+41.0	+66.0

Key to Ranking of 14 Students in Character Analysis Experiment (Figure 39)

Student's Letter of Designation	Rank in Scholastic Record	Rank in Amount of Time Spent in Study	Rank in Studiousness by the 88 Businessmen
A	8	4	11
B	12	11	6.5
C	13.5	1	5
D	10	14	—
E	3	9	1
F	6	8	3.5
G	5	2	2
H	9	10	11
I	7	13	—
J	13.5	5	11
K	11	12	3.5
L	4	7	8.5
M	1	6	8.5
N	2	3	6.5

The least talkative two are B and G.
The boys are G, K, L, and N.

Typical Rating Scale for Office Workers

Name .... dept. ....
Position .... date ....
Rated by ....

I. QUALITIES SHOWN IN JOB

1. *Accuracy:* Consider care and exactness of performance of work in relation to volume handled.
   a. Exceptionally accurate.
   b. Very accurate and careful.
   c. Moderately accurate.
   d. Inexact, somewhat careless.
   e. Many errors, slovenly.

2. *Speed:* Consider rapidity of performance and promptness of completing work.
   a. Very rapid, exceptional production.
   b. Rapid, better than average production.
   c. Average.
   d. Slow.
   e. Unsatisfactory output.

3. *Neatness of work:* Consider neatness and appearance of completed job.
   a. Exceptionally neat.
   b. Good.
   c. Satisfactory.
   d. Fair.
   e. Inclined to be careless.

4. *Knowledge of job:* Consider knowledge of own and related work.
   a. Knowledge completely adequate for own job and related work.
   b. Satisfactory specialized knowledge.
   c. Moderately qualified.
   d. Incomplete training.
   e. Deficient.

II. CHARACTERISTICS SHOWN ON JOB

5. *Punctuality:* Consider promptness of reporting for work.
   a. Frequently on the job ahead of time.
   b. Rarely tardy.
   c. Satisfactory.
   d. Fair.
   e. Frequently tardy.

6. *Dependability:* Consider ability to accept responsibility without continuous supervision.
   a. Finishes work, keeps busy, good performance.
   b. Finishes work but next job must be suggested.
   c. Good workman but needs supervision.
   d. Fairly industrious but occasionally fails to do good job.
   e. Shiftless and tends to loaf whenever possible.

7. *Co-operation:* **Consider** ability to get along with others and promote a "team" spirit by lending a helping hand.

    a. Exceptionally willing and helpful, co-operation to fullest degree.
    b. Co-operates, willing and helpful.
    c. Passively interested.
    d. Somewhat negative attitude.
    e. Individualistic—interested in own work only.

8. Manner in contacting public or other departments.

    a. Pleasing manner, very diplomatic.
    b. Courteous, meets strangers readily.
    c. Average disposition, meets strangers satisfactorily.
    d. Not friendly, makes poor impression.
    e. Antagonistic.

9. *Attitude toward work:* Consider interest in work and effort to learn job.

    a. Excellent.
    b. Interested.
    c. Good.
    d. Fair.
    e. Unsatisfactory.

10. *Ability to learn:* Consider case of learning new methods and following directions, adaptability to new circumstances.

    a. Learns quickly; exceptional capacity and versatility.
    b. Learns easily, fairly adept at meeting changing conditions.
    c. Slow in grasping ideas; has difficulty in adaptation to new situations.
    d. Needs repeated instruction.
    e. Forgets quickly; usefulness limited.

11. *Initiative:* Consider ability to grasp situation and act without direction, make suggestions, originality.

    a. Creative, aggressive, original construction, resourceful.
    b. Fairly resourceful and aggressive; moderate ability to act without supervision.
    c. Routine worker, lacks originality, aggressiveness, and planning ability.
    d. Might be able to make suggestions if he were given training in making them.
    e. Devoid of originality and aggressiveness.

12. *Potential Executive Ability:* Consider judgment and ability to lead rather than drive, to plan and apportion work.

    a. Exceptional leadership qualities and ability to inspire co-operation.
    b. Fairly successful in leading others.
    c. Leadership qualities limited to only a very few persons.
    d. Leadership qualities may be present but are not evident.
    e. Could not be developed into a leader.

13. *Special Aptitude:* Consider ability and interest for any particular type of work. Enumerate any unusual abilities for special types of work.

....

....

III. General Characteristics

14. *Appearance:* Consider personal neatness, taste in dress, carriage.
    a. Very pleasing.
    b. Neat.
    c. Average.
    d. Passable.
    e. Careless.

15. *Self-confidence:* Consider his opinion of his own ability.
    a. Completely confident but not egotistic.
    b. Confident but not outspoken.
    c. Average.
    d. Reserved.
    e. Self-conscious and retiring.

16. *Ability to meet people:* Consider poise and effect of his personality on customers.
    a. Meets people easily, customers have mentioned his pleasing personality.
    b. Likes people; average in ability to deal with them.
    c. Comfortable with people.
    d. Prefers own friends or solitude.
    e. Tends to antagonize some people.

17. *Judgment:* Consider logic of reasoning and soundness of decisions.
    a. Good foresight, quick decisions, and usually right.
    b. Makes good decisions but sometimes rather slow.
    c. Fairly satisfactory.
    d. Not always good but honest.
    e. Cannot make up his own mind.

18. *Health:* Consider general physical conditions rather than sickness with contagious diseases.
    a. Excellent.
    b. Good.
    c. Average.
    d. Fair.
    e. Poor.

    List any physical handicaps not previously reported:
....

19. *Studiousness:* Consider effort to improve knowledge of own job and of the business.

    a. Studies job and reads all available literature.

    b. Studies job and does much outside reading of basic theories of business.

    c. Studies company's routine operations but not basic theories of business.

    d. Makes little effort to increase knowledge.

    e. Does not study; works from day to day.

20. *Membership in company or other educational courses:* Consider record of class attendance and participation in organized programs.

    a. Takes classes and active in work.

    b. Makes good class grades.

    c. Attends a few classes.

    d. Member only occasionally of classes.

    e. Not a member of any classes nor student of his work.

List courses taken during past year or now being taken:

. . . .

21. *Qualifications for other job:* Consider suitability for promotion and ability to do other work.

List jobs for which qualified and indicate recommendation regarding promotion:

. . . .

. . . .

22. Note any habits of importance: liquor, gambling, etc.

. . . .

. . . .

23. *General trend of his growth.*

    a. Improving rapidly.

    b. Improving.

    c. Stationary.

    d. Has reached his limit of growth.

    e. Definitely going backward.

Remarks by rater:

Example of Form and Items Used in a Study of Employee Morale

Confidentially,
Let's See How Well We Agree—or Differ

The purpose of this blank is constructive. Mere faultfinding does little good for anyone. However, an occasional inventory of ourselves, our attitudes, and our problems is valuable if it leads to a friendly consideration of the findings.

You are not to sign your name or reveal your identity on this form. You are asked to be frank, but fair. Please fill in the form at a place where your answers will not be observed by anyone. When these blanks have been filled in, the blanks will be taken out of the building and no executive of the company will see any one employee's form or answers. We are interested only in the responses of groups of employees. Later, we shall discuss those problems or situations which can be improved or clarified by discussion.

Most of the items on this list apply to every employee. In the case of the few items that do not apply to you or you cannot answer, make no check mark. Bear in mind that this inventory will be valuable to the employees and the management to the extent to which you and others are reasonably honest and frank.

	YES, I Strongly Agree	Yes, I Agree	Yes and No, or I Don't Know	No, I Dis-agree	NO, I Strongly Dis-agree
1. I feel that I have been properly instructed regarding the methods of work desired by my superiors....					
2. I know that my duties are completely defined—I am not at a loss as to what is expected of me....					
3. When changes are ordered in methods of doing my work, adequate reasons are given me, so that I can help carry out the orders because I understand the reasons for the changes					
4. The chief way in which I know whether my work is satisfactory is through criticisms—if I do something wrong, I hear about it............					
5. I feel that I am free to make the decisions that are necessary to doing my own work well..........					
6. I feel insecure in my job. I do not know when I may be dismissed without sufficient notice to enable me to adjust myself to another position					
7. I feel that I am under a constant pressure to do my utmost. I am being forced too hard..........					
8. When things go wrong in my work or I feel out of sorts, I know to whom I can go to "talk things out" and regain a satisfying, efficient mental state........................					
9. I feel that my work is hampered in certain respects by my supervisor's personal habits such as his methods of giving instructions......					
10. I am given sufficient help to get the kind of results that the management expects.................					

	YES, I Strongly Agree	Yes, I Agree	Yes and No, or I Don't Know	No, I Dis-agree	NO, I Strongly Dis-agree
11. In most cases, the best-qualified person is given any promotions that occur......	___	___	___	___	___
12. I know that when and if it is possible for the management to do so, I will receive advancement and remuneration as I deserve them......	___	___	___	___	___
13. I feel that, in comparison with the other employees of this organization, my present remuneration is reasonably in line with the value of my services to the organization........	___	___	___	___	___
14. I wish the management would explain to me how I can earn promotion to a *job of a different kind*......	___	___	___	___	___
15. I wish the management would explain to me how I can develop myself and earn promotion *in or through my present job*....................	___	___	___	___	___
16. My working efficiency and comfort would be improved if I had:					
(a) More space for working.....	___	___	___	___	___
(b) Better lighting.............	___	___	___	___	___
(c) Better ventilation in summer	___	___	___	___	___
(d) Better ventilation in winter..	___	___	___	___	___
17. When my supervisor finds some cause to reprimand or criticise me, he embarrasses me by doing it:					
(a) In the presence of fellow-employees..............	___	___	___	___	___
(b) In the presence of customers	___	___	___	___	___
18. I know that I have opportunity for fair treatment and a square deal in any and all cases of irritating grievances that arise in my mind...	___	___	___	___	___
19. I have opportunities for offering suggestions regarding my work and the suggestions receive intelligent and fair consideration.............	___	___	___	___	___
20. Our social program and activities are satisfactory to me.........	___	___	___	___	___

21. When employees are rated periodically by officers and supervisors, I would like to be given a friendly

	YES, I Strongly Agree	Yes, I Agree	Yes and No, or I Don't Know	No, I Dis- agree	NO, I Strongly Dis- agree
constructive explanation of how I was rated and why. Also, I would like to be given suggestions on how I might improve my ratings.............					
22. I usually receive information about plans and results which concern my work; I feel that I am kept acquainted with those plans of management that affect me..............					
23. In general, the management here is impartial. Partiality is not shown to certain members of the organization. In other words, there are no special "favorites" here.........					
24. I feel that my work would be of more value to the organization if I were in another department or in some other job in this organization..					
25. I feel that my work is monotonous and has very little significance					
26. I feel that I receive too many conflicting orders................					
27. I feel that I have too many superiors—I am not always certain as to whom I should ask for further instructions.......................					
28. I feel that there is unnecessary irregularity in the amount of work that I am expected to do..........					

Answer to Five-Circle Character Test
(Figure 48)

If you have a plus score on any one trial, the probabilities are very great that you "peeped."

Page 529

Answer to Project 1 is *d.*

Answers for True Story "Home Problems Forum"
(Chapter 25)

Group I	Group II
A — 3	A — 5
B — 2	B — 6
C — 1	C — 2
D — 4	D — 1
E — 5	E — 4
F — 6	F — 3

Index